# Multimedia and Animation

# Multimedia and Animation

**ER. V.K. JAIN**

BE, M.Tech, FIE, FIETE, MISHRAE

Charted Engineer, Author, Visiting/Guest Faculty and

MEP Consultant Engineer, Intelligent Services Consultants (MEP)



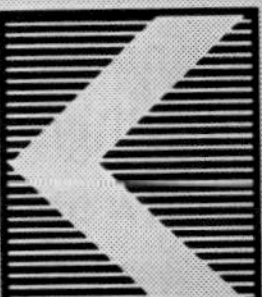

**KHANNA BOOK PUBLISHING CO. (P) LTD.**

Publisher of Engineering and Computer Books

4C/4344, Ansari Road, Darya Ganj, New Delhi-110002

**Phone** : 011-23244447-48 **Mobile:** +91-9910909320

**E-mail** : contact@khannabooks.com

**Website** : www.khannabooks.com

Dear Readers,

To prevent the piracy, this book is secured with HIGH SECURITY HOLOGRAM on the front title cover. In case you don't find the hologram on the front cover title, please write us to at contact@khannabooks.com or whatsapp us at +91-99109 09320 and avail special gift voucher for yourself.

Specimen of Hologram on front Cover title:

Moreover, there is a SPECIAL DISCOUNT COUPON for you with EVERY HOLOGRAM.

How to avail this SPECIAL DISCOUNT:

Step 1: Scratch the hologram
Step 2: Under the scratch area, your "coupon code" is available
Step 3: Logon to www.khannabooks.com
Step 4: Use your "coupon code" in the shopping cart and get your copy at a special discount
Step 5: Enjoy your reading!

**ISBN:** 978-93-86173-12-6

**Multimedia and Animation**
*by* V.K. Jain

**Edition: 2025**
**Reprint: 2026**

To view complete list of books, Please scan the QR Code:

*Published by:*
**Khanna Book Publishing Co. (P) Ltd.**
*CIN: U22110DL1998PTC095547*

Visit us at: **www.khannabooks.com**
Write us at: **contact@khannabooks.com**

*Printed in Bharat.*

# Preface

Popularly Definition of Multimedia Applications Development is the creation of exciting and innovative multimedia systems that communicate information customised to the user in a non-linear interactive format using a combination of digital media types, such as text, images, audio, video and animations.

The overall goal of the book is to provide a broad understanding of multimedia systems and applications in an integrated manner. A user enjoys a multimedia application only if all pieces of the end-to-end solution fit together. This means that a multimedia application and its user interface must be developed in an integrated fashion with underlying multimedia middleware, operating systems, networks, security, and multimedia devices. The book explains the fundamental concepts of storage, compression and decompression, and display technologies used for multimedia systems.

While composing this book my intention was not to introduce a collection of new techniques and protocols, but rather to selectively present techniques from those currently available in the public domain.

Computer science has the greatest drawback of non- standardization of the stuff, not only of its software but in courseware also. A vast amount of curriculum exists at different levels of various Universities. As such I have tried to include all desired courseware from the syllabi for different levels.

The various facades of computer science are changing its attributes with such a fast speed that its very difficult to keep track of latest development and its a great task to get aware with the latest happenings in the field. Therefore in presenting the state-of-the art text ware, immense help had been sought by the author from various literature forms who in turn expresses his gratitude to the authors of the works from where information has been derived.

I am to acknowledge with great sense of gratitude to Mrs. Heera Jain and Naveena Bajaj M.Sc., Anurag Jain Director NICT (Vikas Marg Branch) and Jyotsna Agarwal for the great help provided in Manu scripting and in preparation of the figures etc.

**Er. V.K.Jain**

# Contents

# Introduction to Multimedia and Animation

CHAPTER 1

**Leaning Objectives**

In this chapter we shall learn about:

1. Different Types of Multimedia tips
2. Characteristics and Desirable features of a Multimedia media System
3. Components of a Multimedia media System
4. Application Areas of different Multimedia media systems

## 1.1 INTRODUCTION TO MULTIMEDIA

Multimedia information systems make use of many different ways of communication (or media). These can include **text, record-based data, numeric data, graphics, image, audio** and **video**. Many applications are multimedia in the sense that they use more than one of these forms. A desktop publishing package, for example, supports both text and graphics.

The term multimedia-alias "interactive media" or "hypermedia" - is difficult to define, which accounts for much of the general confusion. At the simplest level, in today's use of the term, it simply means adding sound to your applications. At the most advanced level, it is the amalgamation of text, graphics video, digitally recorded sounds and animation, - with all of these presentation media controlled by a single PC.

The term 'multimedia' is generally used, however, to describe more sophisticates systems - particularly those that support **moving images** and **audio**. The common factor in that each of these new forms of communication is mostly generated outside the computer. Speech and music, photographs and video have to be converted from analogue to digital forms before they can be used in computer applications. In contrast text, graphics and even animations are created on the computer and thus do not extend its use. Some people refer to audio and video, together with animation, as time-sensitive, dynamic or continuous media. However, these terms have not achieved the widespread popularity of multimedia.

**A good general definition is:**

***Multimedia*** is the field concerned with the computer-controlled integration of text, graphics, drawings, stills and moving images (video), animation, audio, and any other media where every type of information can be represented, stored, transmitted and processed digitally.

A ***Multimedia Application*** is an application which uses a collection of multiple media sources *e.g.* text, graphics, images, sound/audio, animation and/or video. Multimedia can be recorded and played, displayed, dynamic, interacted with or accessed by information content processing devices, such as computerized and electronic devices, but can also be part of a live performance. Multimedia devices are electronic media devices used to store and experience multimedia content. Multimedia is distinguished from mixed media in fine art; by including audio, for example, it has a broader scope. The term "rich media" is synonymous for interactive multimedia. Hypermedia scales up the amount of media content in multimedia application.

## 1.2 TYPES OF MULTIMEDIA

### 1.2.1 Linear and Non-linear

Multimedia may be broadly divided into **linear and non-linear** categories. Linear active content progresses often without any navigational control for the viewer such as a cinema presentation. Non-linear uses interactivity to control progress as with a video game or self-paced computer based training. Hypermedia is an example of non-linear content.

Multimedia presentations can be live or recorded. A recorded presentation may allow interactivity via a navigation system. A live multimedia presentation may allow interactivity via an interaction with the presenter or performer.

### 1.2.2 Analog and Digital

Analog (Continuous) media saves sounds, pictures, and text in non-electronic forms. This can include more traditional types of media, such as cassette tapes, records, and videocassettes, which use waves to transmit information. Analog equipment is generally more specialized than digital. Analog devices rely on tape recorders, video cameras, and older playback equipment to edit their contents.

Continuous (time based) media refers to time-based media (*e.g.* Sound, moving images, and animation). Continuous media is also referred to as dynamic media or time-based media or temporal media.

Digital (Discrete) media transmits the information recorded in the waves into a more flexible format, namely, digitized code that can be transferred across a variety of devices, such as computers, internet systems, digital cameras, and more. Scanners, sound cards, and video compression are all used to record these types of media.

Discrete media refers to media involving space dimension only (*e.g.* Still images, text and graphics). Discrete media is also referred to as static media or non-time-based media or non-temporal media or space-based media.

### 1.2.3 Captured Versus Synthesized Media

Captured media refers to information types captured from the real world (*e.g.* Still pictures, moving pictures, and sound). Synthesized media refers to information types synthesized by the computers (*e.g.* Text, graphics and computer animation).

### 1.2.4 HyperMedia

*Hypertext* is a text which contains links to other texts. The term was invented by Ted Nelson around 1965. Hypertext is therefore usually non-linear (as indicated below).

*HyperMedia* is not constrained to be text-based. It can include other media, *e.g.*, graphics, images, and especially the continuous media - sound and video. Apparently, Ted Nelson was also the first to use this term.

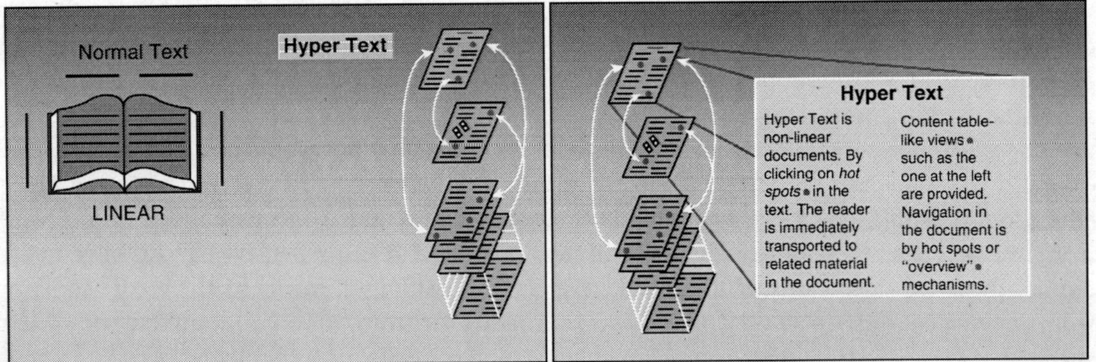


## 1.2.5 Web Hypermedia

The first multimedia works to be considered seriously in humanities computing circles were hypertexts like The Dickens Web by George P. Landow, a work created to explore the possibilities for hypertext and multimedia in education. It was an exemplary educational hypertext that illustrated and informed Landow's theoretical work around hypertext theory. With the evolution of the World Wide Web as a common means for distributing and accessing hypertextual information, we now have thousands of educational and research Web hypertexts, some of which combine multiple media and can be called hypermedia works. The early technologies of the Web, like HTML, have been extended with technologies like XML and the Macromedia Flash file format (SWF for Shockwave-Flash) that make sophisticated interactive graphics and animation possible.

## 1.2.6 Computer Games

By far the most commercially successful multimedia works are computer games, whose short but rich history is interwoven with the development of multimedia technologies. Games like Myst (Cyan) introduced consumers of all ages to the effective use of images, animations, and environmental sound to create a fictional world characterized by navigation and puzzle-solving. More recently, advancements in hardware and software technologies for graphics, audio, animation, and video, and sophisticated artificial intelligence and physics models are making game worlds look and act more convincing. Games are normally distributed on CD-ROM or DVD, but the Web is frequently used for distributing software updates and game demos.

## 1.2.7 Digital Art

Artists have been using multimedia to create interactive installations that are controlled by computers and use multiple media. An example would be David Rokeby's Very Nervous System (1986–90), an interactive sound installation where the user or a performer generates sound and music through body movement. These playful works are exhibited in galleries and museums as works of art that bring multimedia into the traditions of art exhibition. Other digital artists have created Web works that are submitted to online exhibitions like those mounted by the San Francisco Museum of Modern Art in their E•SPACE, which collects and commissions Web art objects.

## 1.2.8 Multimedia Encyclopedia

Multimedia has been used widely in education and for the presentation of research. A common form of educational and reference multimedia is the multimedia encyclopedia, like the Encyclopedia Britannica Online and Microsoft's Encarta (on CD-ROM). Multimedia encyclopedias are the logical extension of the print genre, taking advantage of the computer's capability to play time-dependent media like audio, animation, and video to enhance the accessibility of information.

These are but examples of types of multimedia. A proper topology would be based on criteria. For example, we could classify multimedia works in terms of their perceived use, from entertainment to education. We could look at the means of distribution and the context of consumption of such works, from free websites that require a high-speed Internet connection, to expensive CD-ROM games that require the latest video cards to be playable. We could classify multimedia by the media combined, from remediated works that take a musical work and add synchronized textual commentary, to virtual spaces that are navigated. Other criteria for classification could be the technologies of production, the sensory modalities engaged, the type of organization that created the work, or the type of interactivity.

**Businesses currently use digital media most often in their multimedia applications, such as:**

1. Accounting and employee records management
2. CDs for catalogs, records, and presentations
3. Interactive training sessions for employees
4. Internet tools such as company Web sites
5. Product refinement and development using various computer-assisted design programs
6. Sales presentations, and other communication to a wide audience.
7. Self-running media presentations that can be used for commercial purposes

## 1.3 VARIOUS ELEMENTS OF MULTIMEDIA

Multimedia items generally fall into one of five main categories and use varied techniques for digital formatting:

1. **Text:** It may be an easy content type to forget when considering multimedia systems, but text content is by far the most common media type in computing applications.
2. **Images:** Digital image files appear in many multimedia applications. Digital photographs can display application content or can alternatively form part of a user interface. Interactive elements, such as buttons, often use custom images created by the designers and developers involved in an application.
3. **Audio:** Audio files and streams play a major role in some multimedia systems. Audio files appear as part of application content and also to aid interaction.
4. **Video:** Digital video appears in many multimedia applications, particularly on the web. As with audio, websites can stream digital video to increase the speed and availability of playback.
5. **Animation:** Animated components are common within both web and desktop multimedia applications. Animations can also include interactive effects, allowing users to engage with the animation action using their mouse and keyboard.

## 1.4 CHARACTERISTICS OF A MULTIMEDIA SYSTEM

A Multimedia system has four basic characteristics:

1. Multimedia systems must be ***computer controlled***.
2. Multimedia systems are ***integrated*** and can be played on all sorts of micro-processor based devices
3. The information they handle must be represented ***digitally***.

4. The interface to the final presentation of media is usually ***interactive***.
5. Multimedia presentations may be viewed in person on stage, projected, transmitted, or played locally with a media player.
6. A broadcast may be a live or recorded multimedia presentation. Broadcasts and recordings can be either analog or digital electronic media technology. Digital online multimedia may be downloaded or streamed. Streaming multimedia may be live or on-demand.
7. Multimedia games and simulations may be used in a physical environment with special effects, with multiple users in an online platform.

### 1.4.1 Desirable Features for a Multimedia System

The following features are desirable (if not a prerequisite) for a Multimedia System:

1. **Very High Processing Power is** needed to deal with large data processing and real time delivery of media in special hardware common place.
2. **Multimedia Capable File System is** needed to deliver real-time media — *e.g.* Video/Audio Streaming. Special Hardware/Software needed e.g RAID technology.
3. **Data Representations/File Formats that support multimedia** — Data representations/file formats should be easy to handle yet allow for compression/decompression in real-time.
4. **Efficient and High I/O** — input and output to the file subsystem needs to be efficient and fast. Needs to allow for real-time recording as well as playback of data. *e.g.* Direct to Disk recording systems.
5. **Special Operating System** — to allow access to file system and process data efficiently and quickly, needs to support direct transfers to disk, real-time scheduling, fast interrupt processing, I/O streaming etc.
6. **Storage and Memory** — large storage units (of the order of 50 -100 GB or more) and large memory (50 -100 Mb or more). Large Caches also required and frequently of Level 2 and 3 hierarchy for efficient management.
7. **Network Support** — Client-server systems common as distributed systems common.
8. **Software Tools** — user friendly tools needed to handle media, design and develop applications, deliver media.

## 1.5 COMPONENTS OF A MULTIMEDIA SYSTEM

Now let us consider the Components (Hardware and Software) required for a multimedia system:

1. **Capture devices** — Video Camera, Video Recorder, Audio Microphone, Keyboards, mice, graphics tablets, 3D input devices, tactile sensors, VR devices. Digitising/Sampling Hardware
2. **Storage Devices** — Hard disks, CD-ROMs, Jaz/Zip drives, DVD, etc
3. **Communication Networks** — Ethernet, Token Ring, FDDI, ATM, Intranets, Internets.
4. **Computer Systems** — Multimedia Desktop machines, Workstations, MPEG/VIDEO/DSP Hardware
5. **Display Devices** — CD-quality speakers, HDTV, SVGA, Hi-Res monitors, Colour printers etc.
6. **User-interfaces**
7. **Databases**

## 1.6 USES OF MULTIMEDIA APPLICATIONS

Examples of uses of Multimedia Applications include:

- World Wide Web
- Video-on-demand
- Home shopping
- Hypermedia courseware
- Interactive TV
- Games
- Video conferencing
- Groupware
- Virtual reality
- Digital video editing and production systems
- Multimedia Database systems

## 1.7 MULTIMEDIA SYSTEMS DESIGN

Multimedia systems design is the process of building a system with the technologies and the architecture able to support multimedia applications.

### 1.7.1 Operations Required for Multimedia

Each multimedia application handles one or more media type of information.

**There are two levels of description for an application:**

1. **Functional level** — what the application does and source and display data formats. *E.g.* An application may deal with the retrieval and display of movies. It retrieves movies and displays them in a window.
2. **System Level** — The entities that the application deals with and how it deals with them. In the above example we deal with video frames and voice samples and need to process these accordingly.

**The following functionality should be provided by a multimedia system:**

1. Digital Representation of Media — many standardised formats for many media
2. Capture: Digitisation of Media — special Hardware/Software
3. Creation and editing — assemble media and alter it
4. Storage Requirements — significant for multimedia
5. Compression — related to above and below, *i.e.* can save on storage but can hinder retrieval
6. Structuring and retrieval methods of media — simple to advanced DataBase Storage
7. Display or Playback methods — effect of retrieval must view data
8. Media Synchronisation — display multimedia as it is intended

**Typical Range of operations required for common media include:**

**(1) Text**

1. Editing
2. Formatting
3. Sorting
4. Indexing
5. Searching
6. Encrypting

**The above operations involve basic processing such as:**

a. Character Manipulation
b. String Manipulation

**(2) Image**

1. Pixel operations
2. Geometric Operations
3. Filtering
4. Conversion
5. Indexing
6. Compression
7. Searching

**The above operations involve basic processing such as:**

*Pixel Manipulation*

Area Manipulation, copy image areas, delete area, process areas of interest

### (3) Graphics

1. Graphic Primitive Editing
2. Shading
3. Mapping
4. Lighting
5. Viewing
6. Rendering
7. Searching
8. Indexing

**The above operations involve basic processing such as:**

1. Primitive Manipulation
2. Structural/Group Manipulation

### (4) Audio

1. Audio Editing
2. Synchronisation
3. Conversion/Translation
4. Filtering/ Sound Enhancing Operators
5. Compression
6. Searching
7. Indexing

**The above operations involve basic processing such as:**

1. Sample Manipulation
2. Waveform Manipulation

### (5) Animation

1. Primitive/Group Editing
2. Structural Editing
3. Image Overlaying
4. Rendering
5. Synchronisation
6. Searching
7. Indexing

**The above operations involve basic processing such as:**

(a) Pixel Manipulation

(b) Area Manipulation, copy image areas, delete area, process areas of interest

(c) Frame Manipulation, Copy frame(s) to frame(s), Process frame(s)

### (6) Video

1. Pixel Operations

2. Frame Operations
3. Editing
4. Synchronisation
5. Conversion
6. Mixing
7. Indexing
8. Searching
9. Video Effects/Filtering

**The above operations involve basic processing such as:**

(a) Pixel Manipulation
(b) Area Manipulation, copy image areas, delete area, process areas of interest
(c) Frame Manipulation, Copy frame(s) to frame(s), Process frame(s)

### 1.7.2 Distributed Networking Systems

The development of large networked of distributed has had a major impact (indeed it has also been influenced by) the requirements of multimedia systems. There is clearly a huge need in the requirements for performance and application.

Many of the issues that concern distributed computing research is complimentary to multimedia systems, **For Examples:**

1. Network design and choice of network, or
2. Delivery of data, Scheduling and bandwidth, or
3. Load balancing and load sharing.

Multimedia systems are concerned with real-time delivery and scheduling which is a challenge for any distributed systems.

**Many Multimedia applications would not be possible without a distributed system architecture, for example:**

1. Video conferencing
2. Video on Demand
3. Hypermedia based application (WWW etc.)
4. Multimedia Databases
5. Interactive TV
6. Many many more

## 1.8 APPLICATIONS

Examples of Multimedia Applications include:

1. World Wide Web
2. Hypermedia courseware
3. Video conferencing
4. Video-on-demand
5. Interactive TV
6. Groupware
7. Home shopping

8. Games
9. Virtual reality (VRML)
10. Digital video editing and production systems
11. E-commerce

Finding facts and information in encyclopedias on CD-ROM

Learning new concepts and skills in mathematic, science, art, and languages from home- based and school- based computers

**TABLE 1.1:** Provides SWOT analysis of different types of multimedia

| Characteristics | Strengths | Weaknesses | Transfer Speed |
|---|---|---|---|
| Text Sentences and notes Standard, | Easy to print | Limited dimension | Very fast |
| Images Visual, Graphical | Visually descriptive, Great for graphs | File size | Moderate |
| Video | Engaging Lifelike, Testimonial, | File size, quality | Usually slow |
| Animation Representative, | Fun Professional, Eye candy | File size | Slow |
| Slides Presentations | Powerful for presentations | Requires overhead | Contents may load slowly |

**We shall discuss the application of multimedia in different fields:**

## 1. Education

Schools and other educational institutions such as Libraries are extremely fertile areas for multimedia development, and many production companies can rightfully call them bread-and-butter clients. These kinds of projects can range from community outreach program to courseware for students. The market is a lucrative but by no means a simple one, from either a technical or marketing perspective. Many schools are now wiring the classrooms with either PC stations or PC "laboratories" in which students perform their own research on CD-ROMs or Web sites. In fact, many schools now allow and even encourage their students to actually develop their own multimedia productions. The possibilities here for the professional multimedia developer are numerous: CD-ROMs, Web sites, hypertext-based courseware, and interactive learning games for young students.

This market is in a constant state of expansion. New course material are developed every year, and older materials must be updated, often by the producers who developed the original materials. A project successfully sold to one school district might easily mushroom into numerous districts, thereby making one project many times more profitable to the producer.

Materials for schools, however are usually held to rigorous sets of technical, financial, and content requirements. School districts are public institutions bound by local and federal statues. These institutions rigorously control the content for these multimedia presentations, and they expect the content to live up to established standards. Further, they have tightly controlled budgets. In most cases, the producer will have no flexibility with the assigned budget and schedule. In other words, this is a market with great possibility, but the work is exacting and often subject to many different opinions, sometimes by people who don't know a thing about multimedia. Still, much work and money is available to the multimedia producer in the educational sector. Don't ignore this market.

Distance Education/Learning - instructions that takes place when the student and instructor are separated by physical space and/or time. Correspondence courses provide one type of «distance learning". Networked computers, especially those linked into the Internet, provide many remote education opportunities. In fact, you can now obtain a degree from a «virtual university" - Athena University. In North Carolina, through NCIH (North Carolina Information Highway) the entire statewide 2-way interactive network has been setup.

NC-REN (NC Research and Education Network) is the portion of NCIH connecting the state's 19 teaching hospital research centers and public universities. UNCG is one of the universities participating in NC-REN.

Graphics are heavily used in education in textbooks for subjects such as geography, science and math to illustrate theories and concepts. Diagrams are also used to label photographs and pictures. A common example of graphics in use to educate is diagrams of human anatomy.

Educational animation is an important emerging field of graphics. Animated graphics can have advantages over static graphics for explaining subject matter that changes over time.

## 2. Electronic Encyclopedia

The important exception is encyclopedias. The development of the electronic, multimedia encyclopedia, and dramatic changes in the pricing of encyclopedic content, has transformed the market and the world in which encyclopedia companies conduct business. Printed encyclopedias, no matter the publisher, have declined greatly in popularity for a variety of reasons:

- For one thing, electronic encyclopedias give the appearance of being more interactive, accessible, and interesting than their printed counterparts: Electronic encyclopedia don't just provide pictures, but also animations, video, and music, offer advanced searching capabilities, and links to the Internet.
- Another set of reasons is economic. Encyclopedias have gone from being expensive, one-time purchases costing \$ 67500, to mass-market items costing between \$ 1350 and \$ 67500 in year 2009. They're even available by subscription over the Internet, or sold to computer manufacturers, who bundle them with new computers. (One expert claims that more compact disc encyclopedias have been given away in the last ten years than print sets were sold in the previous 20. The price difference between the printed and electronic versions of magazines and newspapers is generally minimal: for most people, even the difference between spending fifty cents for a newspaper and spending nothing is not quite worth changing their spending habits. The difference between \$1500 and nothing is something else entirely.

Further, the money that people used to spend on encyclopedias now gets spent on personal computers - which often come bundled with a multimedia encyclopedia. The markets for electronic media have also segmented somewhat. In the past, our principal consumers - the people who actually paid for encyclopedias - were individuals. Today, the Britannica publishes a printed encyclopedia, a compact disc (Britannica CD, or BCD), and a Web site Britannica Online, or BOL. The three versions have gradually diverged, like a super continent breaking apart into three similar but separate continents. The electronic encyclopedias have more articles than the printed version; audio, video and animations, which are impossible to include in a print encyclopedia; and a search engine and hyperlinks that change the experience of accessing and reading the encyclopedia. The electronic versions, in turn, differ slightly from one another: BCD and BOL have slightly different interfaces, and BCD has several features not available in BOL (timelines, a statistical program called Analyst, and multimedia spotlights).

The Oxford's online Illustrated Dictionary, and the worlds largest Wikipedia encyclopedia uses graphics and technical illustrations to make reading material more interesting and easier to understand. In an encyclopedia graphics are used to illustrate concepts and show examples of a particular topic being discussed. In order for a graphic to function effectively as an educational aid, the learner must be able to interpret it successfully. This interpretative capacity is one aspect of graphicacy.

### 3. Multimedia Design Training

Multimedia presentations are a great way to introduce new concepts or explain a new technology. In companies, this reduces the indigenous Design and Training time of multimedia. Individuals find it easy to understand and use.

Although multimedia systems were initially very expensive to develop, early users of training systems reported overall economic benefits from the use of the technology. Successful organisations need to maintain high levels of staff training and development. Through reductions in the expenses associated with holding conventional training courses, the costs of developing a multimedia training system can be recouped within a few years. These savings in training costs are achieved because:

- each course can be used by many more people;
- time spent away from the office, including travel time, can be reduced;
- employees can work at their own pace so the average training time per employee is reduced.
- full-time classroom instructors are no longer required;
- expensive demonstrations can be used without jeopardising safety.

As the best instructors prepare and take part in each course, the quality of courses may also be improved. Both the content the quality of courses will be consistent across the whole organisation. Furthermore it is likely that student retain more from interactive multimedia training than from traditional classroom courses. A study for the British Audiovisual Association showed that people retain 10 per cent of what they see, 20 per cent of what they hear and 50 per cent of what they see and hear.

Distance learning projects can also benefit from interactivity. In the past these courses were supported by materials such as audio cassettes and videotapes, distributed to students by post, and by terrestrial broadcasts of television and radio programmes. Feedback from students was by means of post, telephone or meetings with tutors. In future satellite broadcasts of studio discussions will be supported by live feedback from students over audio or videoconferencing links.

### 4. Interactive Multimedia in Entertainment

Multimedia is heavily used in the entertainment industry, especially to develop special effects in games, movies and animation for cartoon characters. One of the earliest applications of multimedia was for games. Multimedia made possible innovative and interactive games that greatly enhanced the learning experience.

Games could come alive with sounds and animated graphics. Multimedia video games are a popular pastime and are software programs available either as CD-ROMs or online.

Multimedia applications that allow users to actively participate instead of just sitting by as passive recipients of information are called Interactive Multimedia.

Two gloring examples are interactive multimedia games and social sites. For instance, users can play a simulated multimedia soccer match without actually being on the field. The simulation is just an illusion, but it makes the users think that they are playing a real match. The environment is created by using controls like joysticks and sensors and by using media output devices like headsets and goggles. The various multimedia components are coordinated with a technique Multimedia and Applications called virtual reality. They provide an environment which is experienced by users as similar to reality. This technique is used in some arcade games and also in flight simulators, to impart training to pilots, without having to go for a real flight.

**5. Multimedia Business**

Even basic office applications like a word processing package or a spreadsheet tool becomes a powerful tool with the aid of multimedia business. Pictures, animation and sound can be added to these applications, emphasizing important points in the documents.

One can change the face of their company image through multimedia technologies.

The world of advertising and media is very dynamic in terms of changes it undergoes to capture the target market. This tool proves to be an effective medium to accomplish this task. Web multimedia outsourcing companies can accomplish various development services, including web testing, multimedia designing, planning, media production, and more.

The use of multimedia features in a website gives an impression that the website is tech-savvy and follows the latest designing trends. However it should be well merged with web content. Never make a website with only multimedia presentations. Product presentations, online tutorials, online games, corporate presentations, etc. can be successfully presented with the aid of multimedia technology. Kiosks in trade shows utilize multimedia to keep the audience occupied, motivated, and inspired, and can greatly influence the buying decision.

More and more educational institutions are turning to interactive learning through multimedia. This has helped in international education and training of masses. A DVD or CD-ROM can be shipped for enhanced flexibility.

Sales and marketing have experienced a newer approach to the target customers through multimedia usage. Apart from imparting education and entertainment through kiosks, they can be programmed with apt databases to organize customer information.

Online presentations give deeper insight into your business for the user. Sometimes these multimedia presentations serve as an eye candy for the onlooker. It keeps your audience alert and interested, thus leading to better chances for sales.

Some websites require extensive use of multimedia, whereas some need minimal use. This can be decided accurately by a multimedia professional after going through your business requirements. Outsourcing is gaining momentum each day as it provides high quality services within your budget restrictions.

**6. Multimedia Communications**

Multimedia communication (broadband) applications are typical examples of the growing qualitative and quantitative requirements placed on telecom networks and services. Started 1990, "multimedia technology" has grown to include **data, text, graphics, image, video,** and **audio** communication. Its applications are gaining in importance with increasing demand and with the advent of more powerful PCs and workstations, high-performance central computer systems, high capacity storage devices, and high speed networks.

The main reason for this integration is to have fewer and fewer applications using only one single information (like video telephony). Instead, applications with mixes of different information types, service components, and services will play a growing role. "Multimedia best suits human beings" complex perceptions, communication behaviors and ways of acting. It not only provide communication capabilities and information sharing among people irrespective of location and time but also easy and immediate access to widely distributed information banks and information processing centres.

The essential features of multimedia communication are 'variety' and integration'.

This includes dynamic control of multimedia application sessions with regard to connections, interactions, information types, bit rates,and quality on demand, which is supported by session management, knowledge robots (know bots), and intuitive and transparent user interfaces. Role of Multi-media in Effective Communication.

Effective communication means understanding what is being delivered whether it is through the television, the internet, through radio, or in a newspaper. To understand the message being delivered requires understanding of the medium (the computer, the television, the radio), and familiarity with the media content (digital media, the weather, songs and announcements) being delivered. For most people, a thunderstorm warning on the television or radio is effective communication through media. The media informs you of a possible chance of thunderstorms, the message beeps on the screen or radio, and because you have heard it before, understand how a television operates, you understand the message.

Talking about the impact of digital images, the colors used to make the images, and describing examples all through the use of text would be a very ineffective use of media communication. The internet could display pages of text files about images but the message would never be really clear.

Use PowerPoint to create a slide about an example of effective media communication.

Create the use of first slide using a title with your name, and three bullet points describing the three areas of media you find most interesting on the web. Examples include text, images, imagemaps, animation, video, and vrml. Make three more slides describing two or three advantages and disadvantages in the use of these mediums to communicate information.

**In office:** Multimedia workplace, Interconnection of workplace, Office archives & workflow

**In Telemedicine:** Multimedia inside hospitals and between physicians, Medical workplace, Electronic patient record.

**In Telepublishing:** Transmission of printdata, Distributed editorial, Individual electronic newspaper.

**Teleeducation:** Computer aided learning at school, Interactive education at home, Teletraining at the workplace Telecomputing Production Workplace: City planning, 3D weathercast "on demand", Simultaneous engineering, Multimedia error diagnosis

**Infosystems tourism:** City Hotel information, Interactive teleshopping, Tourism info and booking systems

**Infotainment:** Video on demand, Movie on demand, Music on demand, Electronic selling of movies and music

**Telecommerce:** Electronic marketplace, Multimedia product information, Telebanking

## 7. Video Conferencing

Another multimedia application is videoconferencing. Videoconferencing is conducting a conference between two or more participants at different sites by using computer networks to transmit audio and video data. Video conferencing actually encompasses a range of technologies used in a wide range of situations, often it is not just video and audio that is transmitted, but also data, allowing collaborative working though shared applications. Video conferencing may be:

(a) One-to-one meetings, also known as point to point communications, usually involving full two-way audio and video.

(b) One-to-many involving full audio and video broadcast from the main site, where other sites may be able to send audio. For example in a lecture situation, students could ask questions.

(c) Many-to-many, known as multi-point communication, provides audio and video between more than two sites. With most multi-point systems only one site in a conference can be seen at time, with switching between sites either controlled manually or voice activated (i.e., the loudest site is on screen).

**Physically, the most common scenarios of video conferencing are:**

Desktop video conferencing - usually a small camera is located on top of the PC or workstation monitor. The actual video is usually displayed in a small window, and shared applications, such as a shared whiteboard are often used.

Studio-based systems - a studio is specially equipped for video conferencing. This will normally include one or more cameras, microphones, one or more large monitors, and possibly other equipment such as an overhead camera for document viewing. Usually used for more formal meetings in practice a 'studio' may not be a dedicated room, but a standard seminar room with portable equipment that can be set up when required.

Multimedia, such as mobile marketing, livecasting and podcasting, photo, video and file sharing, can spread the word about your company and help build brand awareness in a very unique and powerful way.

**Uses of Video Conferencing**

Video conferencing is used for a variety of purposes, including:

1. Personal communication. Informal communication would normally use desk top systems. More formal meetings with several participants at each site would probably use dedicated studio settings.
2. Collaborative work between researchers using shared applications
3. Presentations
4. Education. Teaching usually involves one to many connections. The student sites may receive audio and video but only send audio.

**Video Conferencing is very useful whenever there is a clear communication need, and the benefits described by those using video conferencing systems include:**

1. reduced travel costs
2. face to face rather than telephone meetings
3. better quality teaching
4. easier collaborative working

**Examples**

Desktop video conferencing using Apple Macintosh computers and the CUSeeMe program is being used at the University of Derby. The computers are mainly connected over a LAN with a 64K Internet connection. The system is used to link students with tutors, small group meetings between different sites, and informal contact between dispersed colleagues. Livenet at the University of London provides videoconferencing to several of its colleges over three ISDN 2 lines. A range of equipment allows the system to be used for one to one meetings through to lectures.

Staff at the Council for the Central Laboratory of the Research Councils hold regular meetings between two remote sites at Daresbury Laboratory in Cheshire and Rutherford Appleton Laboratory in Oxfordshire, using SuperJANET. Since staff from the two sites need to meet regularly this arrangement saves a great deal in travel time and costs.

### Implications

It is likely that the use of video conferencing will continue to increase over the next few years. PCs and workstations often have many of the components of a video conferencing system built in, and networks, particularly internal ones, will be better able to cope with the increased traffic. These factors, and others such as increased travel problems and financial restraints will encourage the uptake of video conferencing to provide remote lecturers, remote seminars and courses, distance learning and telecommuting.

Apart from technological aspects, there are a number of other factors that affect the success of a video conference. It is necessary to be aware of the conventions used in a conference, how to ask questions or interrupt, how to switch site and so on. Although many of the conventions may be those used in traditional face to face meetings, the environment is slightly different, and some training will be required. In particular teaching staff will need to learn an additional set of skills to use video conferencing facilities. Different strategies for presenting material and encouraging student interaction will be required.

Without training the video conferencing systems will be under used. Therefore there will be an increasing need for courses on using the basic video conferencing hardware and software, and on presentation skills.

### Teleconferencing

Behavioral research suggests that for most effective conferencing no more than six participants at any one time should be involved. Many multimedia conferencing systems today are designed with this limit in mind. On the other hand, several virtual conferences can be taking place simultaneously within an interactive enterprise that may also be involved in multiple virtual corporate projects. As a result, multimedia transmission facilities above the workgroup level should have the capacity to handle numerous simultaneous multimedia transmissions.

The capacity of such links is not readily predictable because it depends on the specifies of each virtual corporate effort, which vary in time and scope. This presents an opportunity for individual multimedia services that may develop to provide such facilities on a temporary basis to groups of interactive enterprises combining into virtual corporate organizations.

### 8. Collaborative Multimedia Computing

The interactive enterprise must streamline its operations to eliminate redundant and inefficient activities and provide facilities for collaboration of any corporate worker with anyone, anywhere in the world, regardless of time, location, computer hardware and software deployed, or actual differences. This means the use of local area networks (LANs), metropolitan area networks (MANs), wide are networks (WANs), and internet working facilities that can handle massive multiuser, real-time, and interactive multimedia data traffic with relatively low latency. This also means multimedia data handling capabilities within databases, client-servers, bridges, routers, gateways, and on LANs and backbone networks with real-time video transmission capabilities in all the interconnections.

In addition to the economic benefits of videoconferencing, social benefits may arise through the conservation of natural resources and reduction in pollution levels as unnecessary travel is eliminated, improving the quality of life. A pilot project in California shows that telecommuting by state employees has led to an average reduction in the total distance travelled of about 40 miles for each day travel with consequent implications for the need for new road building programmes.

### 9. Marketing and Sales

Marketing can be boosted by internet marketing, online advertising and website promotion that will skyrocket anybodies small, medium or home based business profits through the roof.

**Trading on computer can be through:**

- Web page promulgation and design
- Other on-line services (Compuserve, AOL, Prodigy, Genie)
- Online classified ads
- Newsgroup promotions
- Promotions through discussion lists and newlsetters
- Bulk e-mail autoresponders
- Bulletin boards
- Electronic malls
- Ranking at the top of search engines

One point is worth mentioning here is that while it is true that millions of computer owners are now online, it simply isn't true they are just sitting there eagerly waiting to send your money the moment you contact them.

In the retail field multimedia is changing the traditional methods and concepts of marketing. Both consumers and retailers benefit from the consistency of information that results from the introduction of point-of-sale systems. The benefits to the retailers are savings on space, inventory and distribution, estimated at up to 50 per cent of retail profit. Retailers can afford to bring more products to market and to explore alternative sales channels. Some see the introduction of shopping kiosks as a way of regenerating the high street, attracting customers back from out-of-town shopping malls. Benefits to the retailer be matched by problems for the rest of society. For example, the introduction of remote consultations using video communications on personal computers, coupled with the drive for banking over the phone, will radically transform the banking industry. It may well lead to the closure of many high-street branches, with the consequent loss of thousands of jobs.

**10. Interactive Multimedia Advertising**

The interactive multimedia advertising came into existence some years ago with the introduction of the so-called electronic brochure. These are diskettes targeted at PC users that promote specific products such as automobiles or services of a company using graphics, animation and images as well as sound. Now interactive messages can be made available on CD-ROM disks for those with multimedia PCs and CD-ROM players.

A more sophisticated concept involves networked multimedia advertising. In some cases it takes the form of public information kiosks or displays that are networked to present information about an area or event intermixed with advertising messages for associated products and local services. Others are simply multimedia displays without interactivity features, but in all cases these are centrally controlled systems for updating information and advertising messages as rapidly as necessary with the least amount of effort. The most sophisticated systems consists of a WAN that provides multimedia advertising messages to a professional target audience such as physicians.

**Learning Outcomes**

In this chapter we have learnt about:

1. Various elements of Multimedia media system such as Text, Graphics, Audio Video and Animation.
2. Difference between Various types of Multimedia media systems like linear and non linear, captured and synthesized Analog and digital, Hyper media
3. Components of Multimedia media
4. Possible Applications of Multimedia media

# Multimedia Hardware and Software Tools

CHAPTER 2

**Leaning Objectives**

In this chapter we shall learn about:

1. Details of various hardware components of Multimedia media
2. System units and motherboard cards and peripherals
3. Various Types of Memories
4. Components of CPU and CPU of different Brands
5. Various types of Drives
6. Output Devices like Printers, plotters
7. Network cards, routers and firewalls
8. Mutimedia Development Platforms and their Levels

## 2.1 THE MULTIMEDIA WORKSTATION'S HARDWARE

Your computer is made up of several hardware components. The hardware consists of the physical devices that you can touch and see. All of the following are hardware devices:

- The system unit
- The disk and CD-ROM drives
- The keyboard
- The monitor screen
- The printer
- The mouse
- Speaker
- Scanner

Fig. 2.1 contains a diagram that illustrates each of these hardware components. The disk and CD-ROM drives, keyboard, monitor, printer, and mouse often called peripheral devices because they plug into the system unit and support the computer's operation.

Peripheral devices are either input devices, output devices, or input/output devices (sometimes called I/O devices), depending on the data flow direction between the device and the system unit. If data flows out from the system unit to a device such as the printer, that device is an output device. The keyboard is an input device because data goes from the keyboard into the system unit. Disk drives are I/O devices because data flows in both directions between the system unit and the disk drives.

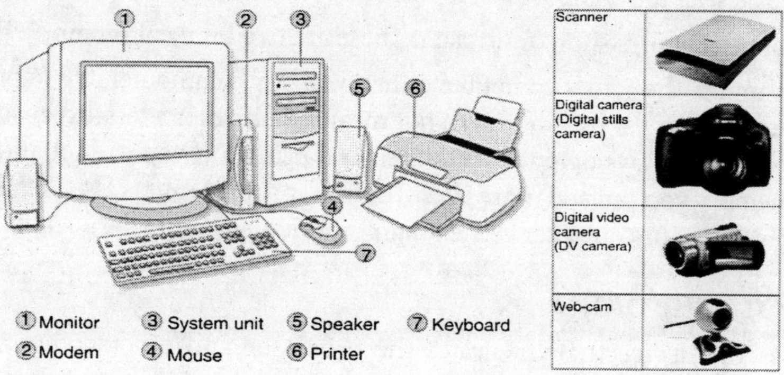


**Fig. 2.1:** Your computer is made up of many hardware devices.

**A breakdown of the major components in a computer system as shown in Fig.2.2:**

1. Monitor, 2. Motherboard, 3. CPU (or microprocessor), 4. Memory (or RAM), 5. Expansion cards (graphics and sound cards are the most common examples), 6. Power supply, 7. Optical disk drive (CD or DVD), 8. Hard disk drive, 9. Keyboard, 10. Mouse

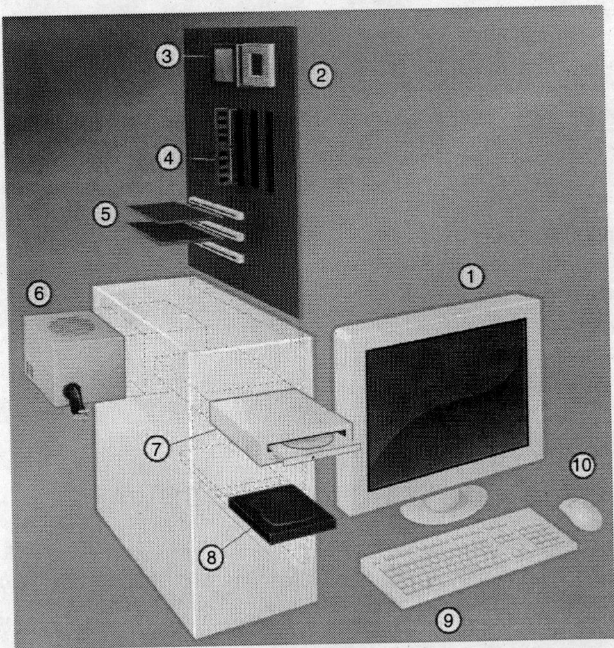


**Fig. 2.2:** A breakdown of the major components in a computer system

## 2.2 THE SYSTEM UNIT

The system unit is the primary controlling unit of your computer. Often the system unit is a large box that sits on the floor or on your desktop. Many people put their video screens on top of their system units. The system unit holds the following elements:

1. The CPU, which stands for the Central Processing Unit. The CPU controls the rest of your computer and processes all the data that goes through the machine. The CPU resides on a wafer-like integrated circuit chip that is small enough to fit in the palm of your hand The small size of the CPU makes laptop computers and pocket calculators possible. It is also known as processor.
2. The memory that stores short-term data. These are two kinds of memory: RAM and ROM.

The system unit is the actual computer. When you buy a computer, try to buy the latest system unit and as much memory as possible, even if it means settling for a less-expensive video screen and printer. Later, you can always upgrade the screen and printer. If you cannot afford more than eight megabytes of memory you can add more later. The power supply unit is also located inside the system unit and ensures that your computer gets enough continual power to perform its computing tasks.

## 2.3 THE MOTHERBOARD

Motherboard is the device that integrates the processor and other components including the memory, disk drives, keyboard, and displays. It includes the central processor chip, BIOS (Basic Input Output System) chip, and the data bus interface that allows disk drives, video, memory, and processor to communicate with the central processor. Typically, devices that connect to the motherboard directly , that is, directly into the data bus, are platform specific, which means they can only be used for the specific equipment they were created for.

Remember that there are a number of other micro-processors are needed in a computer for specific purposes like math co-processor and graphic accelerator. The basic architecture of a modern motherboard is discussed in section 2.9.2.

## 2.4 THE MICRO-PROCESSOR (CHIP): THE CPU

The Processor (precisely microprocessor) is the heart of the computer. At the most basic level, it is a very fast and very powerful arithmetic machine capable of millions of calculations per second. The processor is based on the computing, adding, and subtracting of ones and zeroes. Beyond arithmetic, basic processor functions include:

1. Processing control instructions that tell the computer what to do
2. Managing input and output operations that connect the computer to the world
3. Managing the storage of data in memory

It executes instructions of different programs like games, word processors, and Internet browsers and gets other devices to perform tasks like printing and copying. All other components work under the microprocessor, helping it to do its job.

Processors are usually measured by their speed in terms of millions of cycles per second (megahertz). Each cycle is the period of time required for the processing of partial or complete instructions.

To understand what should be the configuration of multimedia workstation, a complete list of micro chips and their following characteristics is given in Table 2.1.

1. Type/Generation
2. Year
3. Data/Address Bus Width
4. Level 1 Cache (Kb)
5. Memory Bus Speed (Mhz)
6. Internal clock Speed (Mhz)

Clock speed is a measure of how quickly a computer completes basic computations and operations. It is measured as a frequency in hertz (Hz), and most commonly refers to the speed of the computer's Central Processing Unit (CPU). While computer developers and users can refer to this term regarding CPU performance, this has fallen out of favour as CPUs have become more complex.

### 2.4.1 Comparing CPUs

When comparing one Intel® chip to another, for example, the clock speed is a fairly good indicator of differences between them. All other components being equal, an 800Mhz Pentium® computer performs most processor-based tasks roughly twice as quickly as a 400MHz Pentium® computer. When comparing a Pentium® chip and an AMD® chip, however, the AMD® tends to perform most tasks faster than a comparable Pentium®.

Each class of CPU comes in various flavours including: single core, dual core and quad core. A single core CPU is only able to perform one stream of operations at a time. A dual core CPU is able to perform two simultaneous streams of operations at the same time. Say, for example, that you

**TABLE 2.1:** Various Generations of Microprocessors and their Characteristics

| 1. Type | 2. Year | 3. Data/Address Bus Width | 4. Level 1 Cache (Kb) | 5. Memory Bus Speed (Mhz) | 6. Internal clock Speed (Mhz) |
|---|---|---|---|---|---|
| **First Generation** | | | | | |
| 8088 | 1979 | 8/20 bit | None | 4.77-8 | 4.77-8 |
| 8086 | 1978 | 16/20 bit | None | 4.77-8 | 4.77-8 |
| **Second Generation** | | | | | |
| 80286 | 1982 | 16/24 bit | None | 6-20 | 6-20 |
| **Third Generation** | | | | | |
| 80386DX | 1985 | 32/32 bit | None | 16-33 | 16-33 |
| 80386SX | 1988 | 16/32 bit | 8 | 16-33 | 16-33 |
| **Fourth Generation** | | | | | |
| 80486DX | 1989 | 32/32 bit | 8 | 25-50 | 25-50 |
| 80486SX | 1989 | 32/32 bit | 8 | 25-50 | 25-50 |
| 80486DX2 | 1992 | 32/32 bit | 8 | 25-40 | 50-80 |
| 80486DX4 | 1994 | 32/32 bit | 8+8 | 25-40 | 75-120 |
| **Fifth Generation** | | | | | |
| Pentium | 1993 | 64/32 bit | 8+8 | 60-66 | 60-200 |
| MMX | 1997 | 64/32 bit | 16+16 | 66 | 166-233 |
| **Sixth Generation** | | | | | |
| Pentium Pro | 1995 | 64/32 bit | 8+8 | 66 | 150-200 |
| Pentium II | 1997 | 64/32 bit | 16+16 | 66 | 233-300 |
| Pentium II | 1998 | 64/32 bit | 16+16 | 66/100 | 300-450 |
| Pentium III | 1999 | 64/32 bit | 16+16 | 100 450 | 1.2GHz |
| **Seventh Generation** | | | | | |
| AMD Athlon | 1999 | 64/32 bit | 64+64 | 266 500 | -2.2GHz |
| Pentium 4 | 2000 | 64/32 bit | 12+8 | 400 | 1.4GHz-3.6GHz |
| **Eighth Generation** | | | | | |
| AMD Athlon 64 | 2003 | 64/64 bit | 64+64 | 400 | 2GHz-2.4GHz |
| Intel Core 2 Duo | Conroe | 64/64 bit | — | — | 1.86 GHz -2.67 GHz |

open two programs on your computer at the same time. If each program independently takes 10 seconds to open, then on a single core computer you would need to wait for 20 seconds whereas on a dual core computer you would only need to wait for 10 seconds. A quad core CPU would be able to open four similar programs in 10 seconds whereas it would take a single core CPU 40 seconds and a dual core CPU 20 seconds. Typical consumer workloads do not exceed two fully busy cores so there is normally little benefit in having more than a dual core desktop processor.

Multi core floating point speed is a server orientated CPU benchmark. It measures the ability of a processor to perform 32 floating point operations simultaneously. Typical tasks that would utilise this type of processing include multimedia encoding, numerical analysis, graphics design and CAD.

## 2.4.2 Clock Speed and Throughput of Processor

There is a huge variety of modern processors designed for specific purposes. Some have more than one processor on the chip (dual core, quad core etc), meaning computer systems can work on more than one task at a time. Some are designed to run in low-power, mobile devices and will usually have a 'reduced instruction set' - meaning the processor will be less complex and will require more operations to complete a task, but will work with less electrical power compared to a large desktop processor.

The processor has a clock that sends out a signal to keep all the instructions it deals with synchronised. The clock speed is measured in Hertz (Hz) and is a good indication of how quickly the processor can complete tasks.

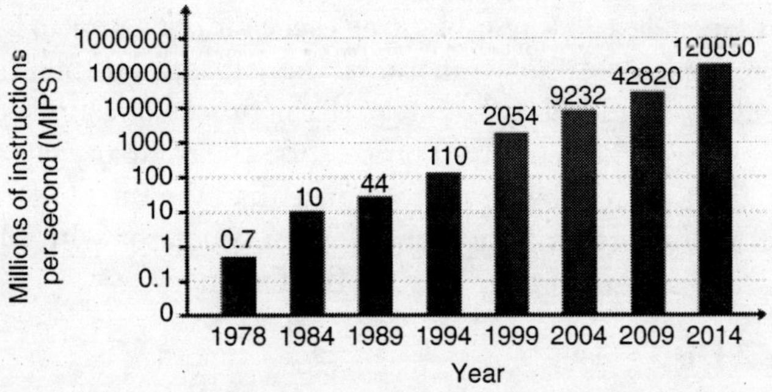


**Fig. 2.3:** Increase in clock speed of the various processors over years

## 2.4.3 PassMark CPU score

It is a multi-threaded, server orientated, processor benchmark test.

The PassMark CPU benchmark, like all processor benchmarks attempts to estimate how quickly a processor is able to perform a wide variety of calculations. The test issues as series of complex instructions to the processor and times how long the processor takes to complete the tasks. The faster the processor is able to complete the tasks, the higher the benchmark score. The PassMark CPU test is a multi-threaded test which means that it will run as many simultaneous tests as the processor is able to handle in parallel (number of cores), this characteristic makes Passmark a good measure of server orientated performance, where multiple cores are often simultaneously loaded.

At the lowest level (or 'entry-level' as they say is computer jargon), a typical user would be looking at a computer system which has at least a Pentium 200 MMX or an equivalent alternative microprocessor. If you are a software developer, or someone using a lot of graphics applications and you are looking for a more powerful computer system, then the Pentium II class of microprocessors would be the starting point.

### 2.4.4 Intel Pentium with MMX Technology

In January, 1997 Intel released its newest, and presumably last, fifth generation processor, the Intel Pentium with MMX Technology. It is an evolutionary design, adding some enhancements for graphic purposes and new capabilities to the "classic" Pentium.

The chief difference between the Pentium with MMX and the Pentium Classic is the inclusion of the MMX instruction set extensions. Running software that is designed for MMX on a Pentium MMX will result in a significant increase in performance over the regular Pentium; some claim up to 70%. Even running non-MMX software on the MMX chip results in an improvement of about 20% over a regular Pentium of the same clock speed, due to the following other improvements over the older chip:

The Pentium with MMX has 16 KB for each of the level 1 data and instruction caches, as opposed to 8 KB each for the regular Pentium.

### 2.4.5 Intel Celeron: A cheaper alternative to Pentiums

Intel introduced its P6-architecture-based Celeron processors in 1998. Targeted at home and business users, the 266 MHz and 300 MHz Celeron processors provide a base-level of functionality which is apt for entry-level computing environments, according to the Intel product release.

The Celeron processor offers MMX and Dynamic Execution technology and provides increased processor core frequencies and reduced power consumption with Intel's 0.25 micron manufacturing process. Other features include a 32 K non-blocking cache for fast access to heavily used data.

The processor core has 7.5 Million transistors and is based on Intel's advanced 0.25 micron CMOS process technology. In addition, the Intel Celeron processor claims to benefit from the same P6 micro-architecture core as the Pentium II processors. The company says that Celeron processor 300 MHz delivers up to 11 percent better performance than the Intel Celeron processor 266 MHz and up to 35 percent more performance than Pentium processor with MMX technology-based systems. The 440 EX AGP set supports up to 256 MB of memory.

### 2.4.6 Intel Core 2 Duo

8th-generation processor is Core 2 Duo that was launched in July 2007. This processor uses the x86 microprocessor architecture. Architecture is by Intel called the Intel Core micro-architecture, where the architecture is replacing the old architecture from Intel, called the NetBurst since the year 2000. Use of Core 2 also marks a new era of Intel processors, where Intel's Pentium brand that has been used since 1993 was changed to Intel Core.

NetBurst, was applied on the Pentium 4 to put forward a very high clock speed.

Processor Intel Core 2 has features such as EM64T, Virtualization Technology, Execute Disable Bit, and SSE4.

### 2.4.7 AMD Athlon 64

The Athlon 64 is an eighth-generation, AMD64-architecture microprocessor produced by AMD, released on September 23, 2003. It is the third processor to bear the name Athlon, and the immediate successor to the Athlon XP. The second processor (after the Opteron) to implement AMD64 architecture and the first 64-bit processor targeted at the average consumer, it was AMD's primary consumer microprocessor, and competes primarily with Intel's Pentium 4, especially the "Prescott" and "Cedar Mill" core revisions.

The Athlon 64 X2 is the first dual-core desktop CPU manufactured by AMD. In 2007, AMD released two final Athlon 64 X2 versions: the AMD Athlon 64 X2 6400+ and 5000+ Black Editions. Both processors feature an unlocked multiplier, which allows for a large range of over-clocked settings. The 6400+ is based on a 90 nm Windsor core (3.2 GHz, 2x1MB L2, 125W TDP) while the 5000+ is based on a 65 nm Brisbane core (2.6 GHz, 2x512KB L2, 65W TDP). These Black Edition processors are available at retail, but AMD does not include heat sinks in the retail package.

While the processor is working on any instruction, it needs some space to keep track of all the calculations it has to do.

## 2.5 RANDOM ACCESS MEMORY (RAM) AND ROM

The most important is RAM, which stands for Random Access Memory. Before your CPU can process data and run programs, that data and those programs must be in RAM. As a secretary creates a document using a word processor, that document live in RAM memory and is saved permanently, only if the secretary, saves the document to a disk drive. When you purchase a computer, you should buy as much RAM as you can afford because the more RAM that your computer has the faster the computer typically runs. Windows 95 requires eight megabytes of memory to run well.

In multimedia computing, memory refers to the computer hardware devices used to store information for immediate use in a computer; it is synonymous with the term "primary storage". Computer memory operates at a high speed, for example random-access memory (RAM), as a distinction from storage that provides slow-to-access program and data storage but offers higher capacities. If needed, contents of the computer memory can be transferred to secondary storage, through a memory management technique called "virtual memory". An archaic synonym for memory is store.

The term "***memory***", meaning "***primary storage" or "main memory***", is often associated with addressable semiconductor memory, i.e. integrated circuits consisting of silicon-based transistors, used for example as primary storage but also other purposes in computers and other digital electronic devices. There are two main kinds of semiconductor memory, volatile and non-volatile. Examples of non-volatile memory are flash memory (used as secondary memory) and ROM, PROM, EPROM and EEPROM memory (used for storing firmware such as BIOS). Examples of volatile memory are primary storage, which is typically dynamic random-access memory (DRAM), and fast CPU cache memory, which is typically static random-access memory (SRAM) that is fast but energy-consuming, offering lower memory areal density than DRAM.

The two widely used forms of modern RAM are static RAM (SRAM) and dynamic RAM (DRAM). In SRAM, a bit of data is stored using the state of a six transistor memory cell. This form of RAM is more expensive to produce, but is generally faster and requires less dynamic power than DRAM. In modern computers, SRAM is often used as cache memory for the CPU. DRAM stores a bit of data using a transistor and capacitor pair, which together comprise a DRAM memory cell. The capacitor holds a high or low charge (1 or 0, respectively), and the transistor acts as a switch that lets the control circuitry on the chip read the capacitor's state of charge or change it. As this form of memory is less expensive to produce than static RAM, it is the predominant form of computer memory used in modern computers.

DRAM is widely used in digital electronics where low-cost and high-capacity memory is required. One of the largest applications for DRAM is the main memory (colloquially called the "RAM") in modern computers; and as the main memories of components used in these computers such as graphics cards (where the "main memory" is called the graphics memory). In contrast, SRAM, which is faster and more expensive than DRAM, is typically used where speed is of greater concern than cost, such as the cache memories in processors.

Double data rate type three SDRAM (DDR3 SDRAM) is a type of synchronous dynamic random-access memory (SDRAM) with a high bandwidth ("double data rate") interface, and has been in use since 2007. It is the higher-speed successor to DDR and DDR2 and predecessor to DDR4 synchronous dynamic random-access memory (SDRAM) chips. DDR3 SDRAM is neither forward nor backward compatible with any earlier type of random-access memory (RAM) because of different signaling voltages, timings, and other factors.

DDR3 is a DRAM interface specification. The actual DRAM arrays that store the data are similar to earlier types, with similar performance.

The primary benefit of DDR3 SDRAM over its immediate predecessor, DDR2 SDRAM, is its ability to transfer data at twice the rate (eight times the speed of its internal memory arrays), enabling higher bandwidth or peak data rates. With two transfers per cycle of a quadrupled clock signal, a 64-bit wide DDR3 module may achieve a transfer rate of up to 64 times the memory clock speed megahertz (MHz) in megabytes per second (MB/s). With data being transferred 64 bits at a time per memory module, DDR3 SDRAM gives a transfer rate of (memory clock rate) × 4 (for bus clock multiplier) × 2 (for data rate) × 64 (number of bits transferred) / 8 (number of bits/byte). Thus with a memory clock frequency of 100 MHz, DDR3 SDRAM gives a maximum transfer rate of 6400 MB/s.

The DDR3 standard permits DRAM chip capacities of up to 8 gibibits, and up to 4 ranks of 64 bits each for a total maximum of 16 GiB per DDR3 DIMM.DDR4 is fourth generation of DDRs. While DDR3 maxed out at 8GB, DDR4 now maxes out at 16GB per module. The DDR3 standard was announced in 2007, and while the specs have slowly improved over the last seven years, the standard's being pushed to its limit. DDR4 breaks through that limit, with dramatically faster clock speeds and double the bandwidth and it uses less power, too. If you play high-resolution games or you run data-intensive applications like video editing, you need the significantly better performance that DDR4 offers. The primary advantages of DDR4 over its predecessor, DDR3, include higher module density and lower voltage requirements, coupled with higher data rate transfer speeds. The DDR4 standard theoretically allows for DIMMs of up to 512 GiB in capacity, compared to the DDR3's theoretical maximum of 128 GiB per DIMM.

DDR4 provides up to a 50% increased performance and bandwidth capabilities while decreasing voltage and power efficiency of your overall computing system.

Starting at lower end model DDR4-2133 the throughput is 20.4GB/s and with the highest model it is 35.4 20.4GB/s.

### 2.5.1 Multi-Media Card (MMC)

A Multi-Media Card (MMC) is a tiny memory card that uses flash memory to make storage portable among various devices, such as car navigation systems, cellular phones, eBooks, PDAs, smartphones, and digital cameras, music players, and video camcorders, and personal computers. MMC was jointly developed by SanDisk and Siemens AG/Infineon Technologies AG, who introduced the product in 1997. About the size of a postage stamp, MMC weighs approximately two grams. This is similar to the Secure Digital (SD card), and smaller than older memory card formats, such as the SmartMedia card and CompactFlash (CF card). By October 2002, the MultiMediaCard offered a range of storage capacities up to 128 MB.

## 2.6 COMPUTER PERIPHERALS

A peripheral is a device that is used to put information into or get information out of the computer. A peripheral is a piece of computer hardware that is added to a computer in order to expand its abilities. The term peripheral is used to describe those devices that are optional in nature, as opposed to hardware that is either demanded or always required in principle. There are all different kinds of peripherals you can add your computer. The main distinction among peripherals is the way they are connected to your computer. They can be connected internally or externally.

Fig. 2.4 shows all popular peripherals of a multimedia computer along with its major internal parts.

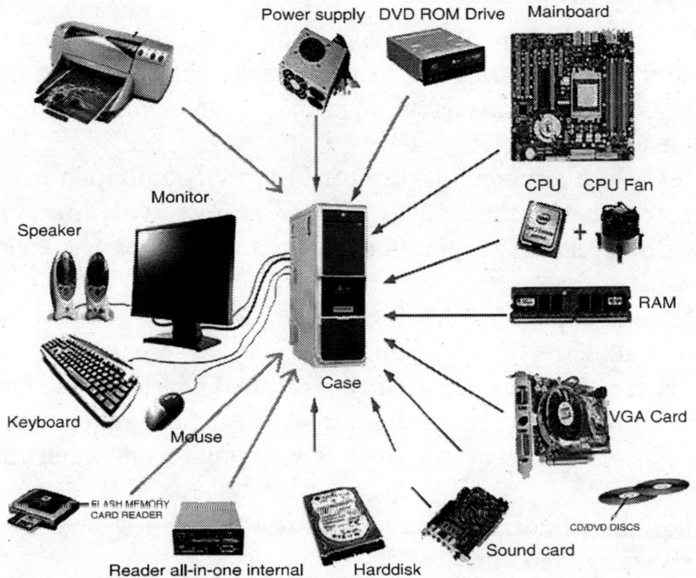


**Fig. 2.4:** Multimedia Computer with its internals and peripherals

There are three different types of peripherals: input devices, which interact with or send data from the user to the computer (mouse, keyboards, etc.), output devices, which provide output to the user from the computer (monitors, printers, etc.), and input/output devices that perform both functions. Touch screens are an example that combines different devices into a single hardware component that can be used both as an input and output device.

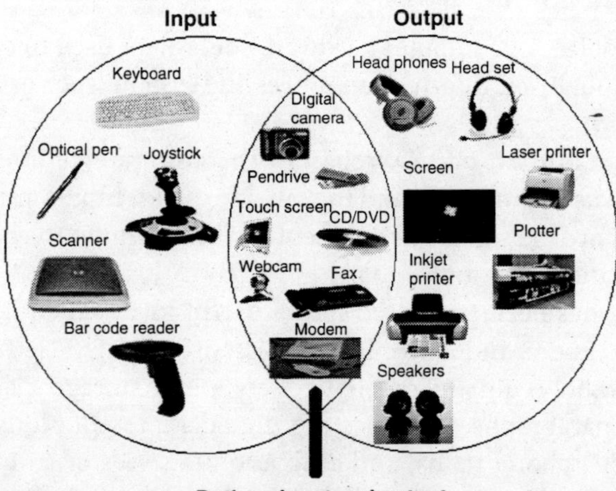


**Fig. 2.5:** Input and Output Devices of a Multimedia Computer

## 2.7 INPUT DEVICES

An input device is any peripheral (piece of computer hardware equipment) used to provide data and control signals to an information processing system such as a computer or other information appliance. Input and output devices make up the hardware interface between a computer and a **scanner**. Many input devices can be classified according to: Modality of input (*e.g.* mechanical motion, audio, visual, etc.)

The input is discrete (*e.g.* key presses) or continuous (*e.g.* a mouse's position, though digitized into a discrete quantity, is fast enough to be considered continuous) the number of degrees of freedom involved (*e.g.* two-dimensional traditional mice, or three-dimensional navigators designed for CAD applications)

Pointing devices, which are input devices used to specify a position in space, can further be classified according to: Whether the input is direct or indirect. With direct input, the input space coincides with the display space, i.e. pointing is done in the space where visual feedback or the cursor appears.

Touch screens and light pens involve direct input. Examples involving indirect input include the mouse and trackball. Direct input is almost necessarily absolute, but indirect input may be either absolute or relative. For example, digitizing graphics tablets that do not have an embedded screen involve indirect input and sense absolute positions and are often run in an absolute input mode, but they may also be set up to simulate a relative input mode where the stylus or puck can be lifted and repositioned.

Whether the positional information is absolute (*e.g.* on a touch screen) or relative (*e.g.* with a mouse that can be lifted and repositioned)

### 2.7.1 Composite Devices

Input devices, such as buttons and joysticks, can be combined on a single physical device that could be thought of as a composite device. Many gaming devices have controllers like this. Technically mouse are composite devices, as they both track movement and provide buttons for clicking, but composite devices are generally considered to have more than two different forms of input.

## 2.8 OUTPUT DEVICES

An output device is any piece of computer hardware equipment used to communicate the results of data processing carried out by an information processing system (such as a computer) to the outside world.

In computing, input/output, or I/O, refers to the communication between an information processing system (such as a computer), and the outside world. Inputs are the signals or data sent to the system, and outputs are the signals or data sent by the system to the outside. We will read about them in details in subsequent sections.

Output is data that has been processed into a useful form called information. Four types of output are text, graphics, audio, and video. Text consists of characters (letters, numbers, punctuation marks, or any other symbol requiring one byte of computer storage space) that are used to create words, sentences, and paragraphs. Graphics are digital representations of non-text information such as drawings, charts, photographs, and animation (a series of still images in rapid sequence that gives the illusion of motion). Audio is music, speech, or any other sound. Video consists of images played back at speeds to provide the appearance of full motion. An output device is any computer component capable of conveying information to a user.

## 2.9 COMPUTER INTERNAL HARDWARE AND PERIPHERALS

### 2.9.1 Buses

A bus is a subsystem that transfers data between computer components inside a computer or between computers. Unlike a point-to-point connection, a bus can logically connect several peripherals over the same set of wires. Each bus defines its set of connectors to physically plug devices, cards or cables together. There are two types of buses: internal and external. Internal buses are connections to various internal components. External buses are connections to various external components. There are different kinds of slots that internal and external devices can connect to.

There are many different kinds of internal buses but only handful are popular ones, different computers come with different kinds and number of slots. It is important to know what kind and number of slots you have on your computer before you go out and by a card that matches up to a slot you don't have.

### 2.9.2 The Data Flow on the Motherboard

On the motherboard, you will find the CPU, which is the "brain" of the PC and the buses. The buses are the nerve system of the motherboard. They connect the CPU to all the other components. There are at least three buses, which you can see below. You can read more about those on the following pages.

The buses are the PC's expressways. They are "wires" on the circuit board, which transmit data between different components.

One "wire" can move one bit at a time. In the following text, we start from a typical Pentium board.

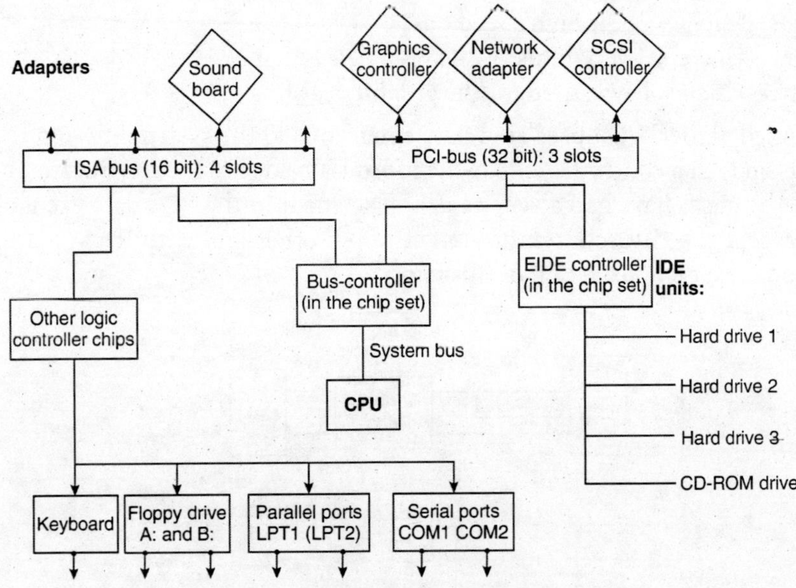


**Fig. 2.6:** Data flow in the motherboard

The PC receives and sends its data from and to buses. They can be divided into:

1. The system bus, which connects the CPU with RAM
2. I/O buses, which connect the CPU with other components.

The point is, that the system bus is the central bus. Actually, it connects to the I/O buses, as you can see in this illustration. It is not completely correct, since the architecture is much more complex, but it shows the important point, that the I/O-buses usually derive from the system bus:

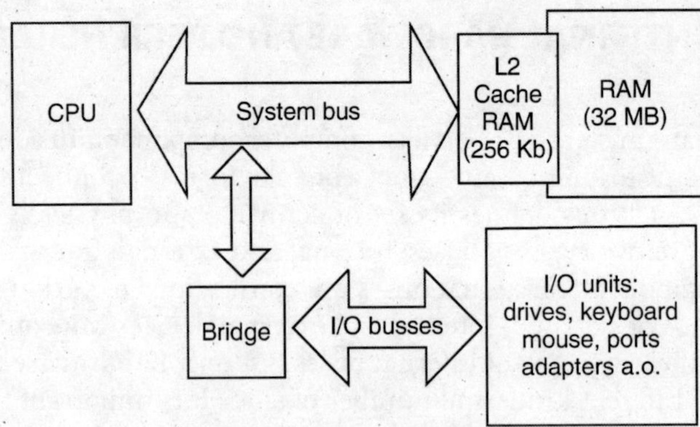


**Fig. 2.7:** Types of Buses

### 2.9.3 Types of Buses

I/O buses connect the CPU to all other components, except RAM. Data are moved on the buses from one component to another, and data from other components to the CPU and RAM. The I/O buses differ from the system bus in speed. Their speed will always be lower than the system bus speed. Over the years, different I/O buses have been developed. On modern PCs, you will usually find four buses:

1. The ISA bus, which is an old low speed bus, soon to be excluded from the PC design.
2. The PCI bus, which is a new high speed bus.
3. The USB bus (Universal Serial Bus), which is a new low speed bus.
4. The AGP bus which solely is used for the graphics card.

As mentioned earlier, I/O buses are really extensions to the system bus. On the motherboard, the system bus ends in a controller chip, which forms a bridge to the I/O buses.

All in all, the buses have had a very central placement in the PC's data exchange. Actually, all components except the CPU communicate with each other and with RAM via the different I/O buses. Here you see a demonstration of this logic:

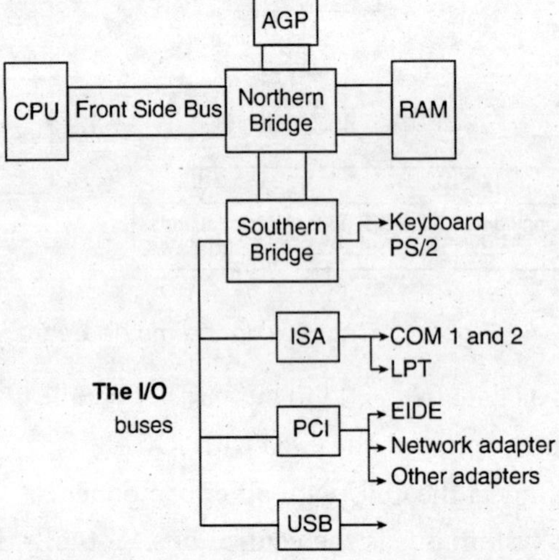


**Fig. 2.8:** Types of Buses in a motherboard

In modern PCs you only find the PCI and ISA buses and USB. But, over the years, there have been other buses. Here is a diagram of the various I/O buses. A more detailed description of each of the buses is given in Table 2.2:

**TABLE 2.2:** Technical and historical background for the I/O uses

| Bus | Year | Bus width | Bus speed | Max. Throughput (theoretical) |
|---|---|---|---|---|
| PC and XT | 1980-82 | 8 bit | Synchronous with CPU: 4.77 - 6 MHz | 4-6 MBps |
| ISA (AT) Simple bus. | 1984 | 16 bit | Synchronous: 8-10 MHz | 8 MBps |
| MCA. Advanced, intelligent bus by IBM. | 1987 | 32 bit | Asynchronous: 10.33 MHz | 40 MBps |
| EISA. Bus for servers. | 1988 | 32 bit | Synchronous: max. 8 MHz | 32 MBps |
| VL. High speed bus, used in 486s. | 1993 | 32 bit | Synchronous: 33-50 MHz | 100-160 MBps |
| PCI. Intelligent, advanced high speed bus. | 1993 | 32 bit | Asynchronous: 33 MHz | 132 MBps |
| USB. Modern, simple, and intelligent bus. | 1996 | Serial | | 1.2 MBps |
| FireWire (IEEE1394). High-speed I/O bus for storage, video etc. | 1999 | Serial | Full Duplex | 80 MBps |
| USB 2.0 | 2001 | Serial | Half Duplex, 500 w buspower | 12-40 MBps |
| USB 2.0 (High Speed) | 2001 | Serial | Half Duplex | 480 MBps |
| Firewire 400 and 800 | | | Full Duplex | 400/800 MBps |
| USB 3.1 | 2015 | Serial | 900 mw bus power | 5 GBps |
| USB 3.2 | 2001 | Serial | | 10 GBps |
| Thunderbolt ports First Generation | | | Data over one PCI Express lane | 10 GBps |
| Thunderbolt ports Second Generation | | | Data over two PCI Express lane | 20 GBps |

## 2.9.4 Accelerated Graphics Port (AGP)

To combat the eventual saturation of the PCI bus with video information, a new interface has been pioneered by Intel, designed specifically for the video subsystem. It is called the Accelerated Graphics Port or AGP.

The need for increased bandwidth between the main processor and the video subsystem originally lead to the development of the local I/O bus on the PCs, starting with the VESA local bus and eventually leading to the popular PCI bus. This trend continues, with the need for video bandwidth now starting to push up against the limits of even the PCI bus.

Much as was the case with the ISA bus before it, traffic on the PCI bus is starting to become heavy on high-end PCs, with video, hard disk and peripheral data all competing for the same I/O bandwidth.

AGP was developed in response to the trend towards greater and greater performance requirements for video. As software evolves and computer use continues into previously unexplored areas such as 3D acceleration and full-motion video playback, both the processor and the video chipset need to process more and more information. The PCI bus is reaching its performance limits in these applications, especially with hard disks and other peripherals also in there fighting for the same bandwidth.

Another issue has been the increasing demands for video memory. As 3D computing becomes more mainstream, much larger amounts of memory is required, not just for the screen image but also for doing the 3D calculations. This traditionally has meant putting more memory on the video card for doing this work. There are two problems with this:

1. **Cost:** Video card memory is very expensive compared to regular system RAM.
2. **Limited Size:** The amount of memory on the video card is limited: if you decide to put 6 MB on the card and you need 4 MB for the frame buffer, you have 2 MB left over for processing work and that's it (unless you do a hardware upgrade). It's not easy to expand this memory, and you can't use it for anything else if you don't need it for video processing.

AGP gets around these problems by allowing the video processor to access the main system memory for doing its calculations. This is more efficient because this memory can be shared dynamically between the system processor and the video processor, depending on the needs of the system.

The idea behind AGP is simple: create a faster, dedicated interface between the video chipset and the system processor. The interface is only between these two devices; this has three major advantages: it makes it easier to implement the port, makes it easier to increase AGP in speed, and makes it possible to put enhancements into the design that are specific to video.

AGP is considered a port, and not a bus, because it only involves two devices (the processor and video card) and is not expandable. One of the great advantages of AGP is that it isolates the video subsystem from the rest of the PC so there isn't nearly as much contention over I/O bandwidth as there is with PCI. With the video card removed from the PCI bus, other PCI devices will also benefit from improved bandwidth.

AGP is a new technology and was just introduced to the market in the third quarter of 1997. The first support for this new technology will be from Intel's 440LX Pentium II chipset. More information on AGP will be forthcoming as it becomes more mainstream and is seen more in the general computing market.

AGP (Accelerated Graphics Port) is a high-speed point-to-point channel for attaching a graphics card to a computer's motherboard, primarily to assist in the acceleration of 3D computer graphics. AGP has been replaced over the past couple years by PCI Express. AGP cards and motherboards are still available to buy, but they are becoming less common.

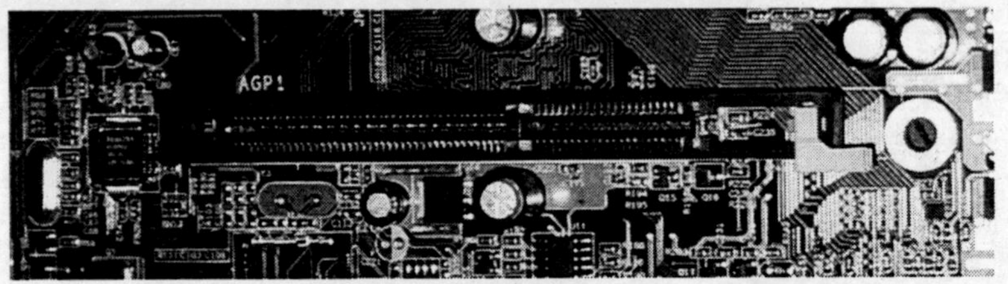


**Fig. 2.9:** AGP Slot

### 2.9.5 Peripheral Component Interconnect (PCI)

The PCI is the high speed bus of the 1990s. PCI stands for Peripheral Component Interconnect. This bus is made by Intel. It is used today in all PCs and other computers for connecting adapters, such as network-controllers, graphics cards, sound cards etc. This kind of bus had been succeeded by PCI Express. Typical PCI cards used in PCs include: network cards, sound cards, modems, extra ports such as USB or serial, TV tuner cards and disk controllers. Video cards have outgrown the capabilities of PCI because of their higher bandwidth requirements. He PCI is actually 32 bit wide, but in practice it functions like a 64 bit bus. Running at 33 MHz, it has a maximum transmission capacity of 132 MBps.

According to the specifications - not in practice, it can have up to 8 units with a speed up to 200 MHz. The bus is processor independent. Therefore, it can be used with all 32 or 64 bit processors, and it is also found in other computers than PCs.

The PCI bus is compatible with the ISA bus in that it can react on ISA bus signals, create the same IRQs, etc.

#### (a) PCI with two faces

On modern system boards, the PCI bus (like ISA) has two "faces:"

- Internal PCI bus, which connects to EIDE channels on the motherboard.
- The PCI expansion bus, which typically has 3-4 slots for PCI adapters.

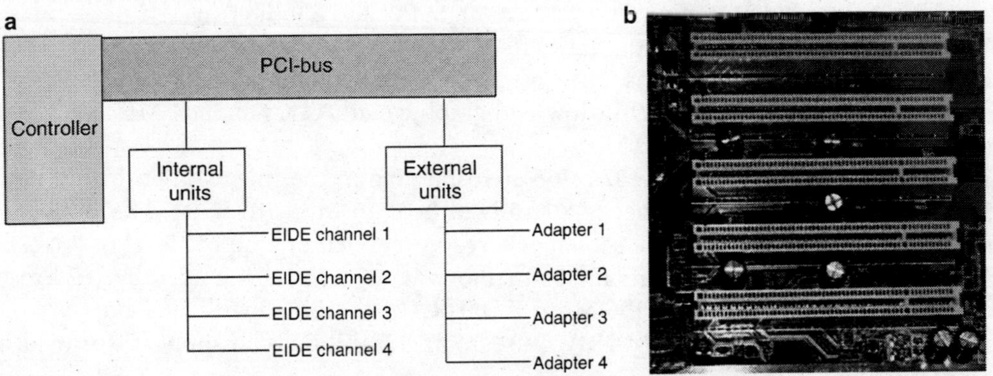


**Fig. 2.10:** (a) PCI Schematic diagram (b) PCI Slots

#### (b) PCI Express

PCI Express was introduced by Intel in 2004. It was designed to replace the general-purpose PCI expansion bus and the AGP graphics card interface. PCI express is not a bus but instead a point-to-point connection of serial links called lanes. PCI Express cards have faster bandwidth then PCI cards which make them more ideal for high-end video cards.

#### PCMCIA

PCMCIA (also referred to as PC Card) is the type of bus used for laptop computers. The name PCMCIA comes from the group who developed the standard: Personal Computer Memory Card International Association. PCMCIA was originally designed for computer memory expansion, but the existence of a usable general standard for notebook peripherals led to many kinds of devices being made available in this form. Typical devices include network cards, modems, and hard disks.

## 2.10 THE 3D GRAPHIC CARDS

3D graphics cards are video cards that, apart from providing basic video display functions, carry additional hardware for handling 3D-graphics intensive tasks. The common features of 3D graphics cards are:

1. Graphic cards
2. Video RAM
3. Memory Controller

### 2.10.1 Graphic Processor

These cards carry processors that support the necessary 3D functions like alpha blending, fogging, flat and Goraud shading, perspective correction, and Z-buffering (See glossary).

In addition, some graphics processors support X and Y video interpolation and colour space conversion in hardware for video playback. It also incorporated a geometry engine for handling scaling, rotation, lighting and clipping. It transforms the 3D-world description and prepares it for rasterisation (display). A dedicated geometry processor offloads these tasks from the computer processor.

### 2.10.2 Video RAM

Most lower-end 3D cards today use EDO, WRAM, SDRAM and the higher-end cards use MultiBand DRAM and SGRAM. Part of this RAM is used in 3D acceleration while the rest of the memory is utilised for implementing functions like texture-mapping and Z-buffering.

The X,Y and Z co-ordinates of the entity in 3D space are stored here and are used to determine the relative distance of the polygons that have been constructed in memory and resolve the order in which they are finally drawn. While low-end graphic cards carry about 4 MB to 8 MB of RAM higher-end cards have 16 MB of RAM.

To accommodate a moderate 1024x768 at 16-bit colour, the image buffer has to hold about 1.6 MB of data. Thus, the CPU needs a bandwidth of 16 Mbps to write data to the graphics board. To get the image out to the screen ar a recommended ergonomic level of refresh rate of 75 Hz the board must read from its image memory at 120 Mbps. For 1280 by 1024 resolution, you need a sustained throughout 196 Mbps. FDO-RAM combined with a 64-bit bus can deliver a throughout of 240 Mbps while MDRAM used on a 128-bit bus can support bandwidths of up to 1000 Mbps.

### 2.10.3 Memory Controller

This chip on the 3D card manages the video RAM requirements. Depending upon the 3D architecture, it co-ordinates different memory strategies like allocating a shared memory pool among the z-buffer, gesture and frame buffers.

## 2.11 TYPES OF MULTIMEDIA CARDS

The following are essential cards that are used in Multimedia PC.

1. Video Card
2. Accelerated Graphics Ports (AGPs) or PCI Card
3. Sound Cards
4. TV Tuner and Capture Cards
5. Input/Output (USB) Cards
6. Network Card (NIC)

### 2.11.1 Video Cards

The first, and arguably one of the most important, types of adapter cards are video cards. Also known as *graphics accelerators, graphics processors, display cards, or graphics cards;* video cards do the heavy lifting in allowing you see and interface with what you are doing in your computer. Video cards generate the graphics to be shown and send the finished signal out to your monitor, screen or projector.

**Fig. 2.11:** Example of a Video Card.

A video card is an expansion card whose function is to generate and output images to a display. Some video cards offer added functions, such as video capture, TV tuner adapter, ability to connect multiple monitors, and others. Most video cards all share similar components. They include a graphics processing unit (GPU) which is a dedicated microprocessor optimized for 3D graphics rendering. It also includes a video BIOS that contains the basic program that governs the video card's operations and provides the instructions that allow the computer and software to interface with the card. If the video card is integrated in the motherboard, it may use the computer RAM memory. If it is not it will have its own video memory called Video RAM. This kind of memory can range from 128MB to 2GB. A video card also has a RAMDAC (Random Access Memory Digital-to-Analog Converter) which takes responsibility for turning the digital signals produced by the computer processor into an analog signal which can be understood by the computer display. Lastly, they all have outputs such as an HD-15 connector (standard monitor cable), DVI connector, S-Video, composite video or component video.

The first connector type listed on the exam is a PCI connector type. While PCI type video cards weren't the first type out, there were definitely a standard and milestone in connections. PCI video cards replaced the EISA, ISA, MCA and VESA buses from 1993 onwards. PCI made it easier to use video cards as there were no manual adjustments, such as jumpers, that needed to be made. PCI slots allowed the video card to connect dynamically between devices. A PCI slot is a 32 to 64-bit bus set at 33MHz to 100MHz. PCI buses can handle up to 800MB/s of bandwidth.

### 2.11.2 Accelerated Graphics Ports (AGPs)

Accelerated Graphics Ports (AGPs) were first used in 1997 and are arguably the most popular and long running graphics port up until about 2006 when PCI Express reached double the data-transfer rate of AGP. AGP Graphics cards come in four flavors. 1x, 2x, 4x, and 8x. While all are 32-bits and rated at 66MHz, they are separated by their bandwidth ability. Starting at 264MB/s for 1x and going up to 528MB/s for 2x, 1000MB/s for 4x and 2000MB/s for 8x.

### 2.11.3 PCI Express

PCI Express (PCIe 1.0) cards have been standard since about 2006 and offer tremendous amounts of bandwidth and a much higher rate of speed. As of 2009, they have completely replaced AGP cards, as proved by the fact that the world's two largest video card companies, ATI and nVidia, now create PCIe cards exclusively. While the highest clock rate seen before was up to 100MHz with PCI, PCIe is rated at 2,500-5,000MHz. PCIe video cards are the first to separate themselves from the standard Parallel interface, moving on to the Serial interface. PCIe also comes in four flavors differentiated by their bandwidth; PCIe x1 can support up to

500MB/s, PCIe x4 can support up to 1,000MB/s, PCIe x8 can support up to 4,000MB/s, and PCIe x16 can support up to 8,000MB/s.

While PCIe x16 2.0 is not on the 2009 A+ Bridge Exam, I feel it is important to cover as it is the latest technology set to replace PCI Express 1.0. PCI Express 3.0 is still in the works. PCIe x16 2.0 runs at up to 10,000MHz and supports up to 16,000MB/s of bandwidth. These specifications, which double todays high-end standard, set it apart from the rest in terms of high end computing, especially in terms of gaming, HD, and 3D development video cards.

**Fig. 2.12:** Eight Channel PCI Sound Card.

## 2.11.4 Sound Cards

One of the most common cards would have to be the sound card. Sound cards do exactly what you would expect; they generate sound signals to be sent to your speakers and sound systems. In most cases, they are also usually where you would find a microphone or input jack for recording. Sound cards are increasing in importance as new technologies like HD audio discs and Blu-Ray discs allow for high definition and multi-channel audio.

Most of your music collection is probably in digital format, either on CDs or as files on your computer. In order to be able to listen to your music, a sound card converts digital data to analog sound waves you can hear. The output signal is then connected to a headphone or set of speakers. You can also use a sound card to record audio with a microphone.

### Sound Card Features and Functions

The motherboard on most computer systems has an integrated sound card, which is often sufficient for many users. However, to get higher quality sound you can upgrade to a separate sound card, which uses better and more expensive components.

Audio files on a computer consist of digital data just like any other file on a computer. Sounds we can hear consist of waves that travel through the air - sounds are analog. The primary function of a sound card is to translate between digital and analog information, just like a video card. Sound cards typically have four major components:

The digital-to-analog converter (DAC), which makes it possible to convert digital data to analog sound

The analog-to-digital converter (ADC), which makes it possible to make digital recordings from analog sound inputs

An interface to connect to the motherboard, typically using Peripheral Component Interconnect (PCI)

Input and output connectors so you can plug in headphones, speakers or a microphone - many computer systems have speakers and microphone built-in, but connectors allow you to use higher quality external devices to play or record sound

On some sound cards, the two types of converters are integrated into CODEC a single coder/decoder chip. Some sound cards also have a digital signal processor (DSP), a built-in processing unit. The DSP takes some of the load of the central processing unit (CPU) to convert between digital and analog. Similarly, some sound cards have their own memory. Sound cards without a DSP or memory will use the motherboard's CPU and memory.

Computer systems typically have built-in speakers, which are reasonably good if you don't turn up the volume too high. If you want to use your computer for some serious music for a party, you probably want to connect a set of external speakers. Relatively small external speakers can be powered using a USB connection, while larger ones need their own power supply. Similarly, most computer systems have a built-in microphone, but you can also connect an external microphone.

Serious audiophiles who use their computer as their sound system will typically upgrade to a high-end sound card, a set of good external speakers, and a good external microphone (if they want to make their own recordings). A high-end computer system can rival dedicated music equipment. In general, with the improvements in sound and video, computer systems have turned into multimedia systems rather than simply computing devices to run software.

Standard or built in sound cards are usually not powerful enough to process the high end sound files, cannot send audio to more than two channels, and produce lower quality results. In the past, high end sound cards were generally only used in studio recording environments. Today, upgrading your sound card allows the average consumer to listen to high quality audio in music, games, and movies, and allows your computer system to be connected to surround sound systems taking advantage of all available sound channels.

### 2.11.5 TV tuner and Capture Cards

TV tuner cards are another type of multimedia adapter card. TV tuners are used to process coaxial and other types of video inputs to display on your computer system. TV tuners are able to differentiate different channels much like your TV does, essentially turning your computer system into a television and digital video recorder. Many TV tuners also function as AM/FM radio tuners, allowing you to listen to your favorite local radio stations right on your computer system.

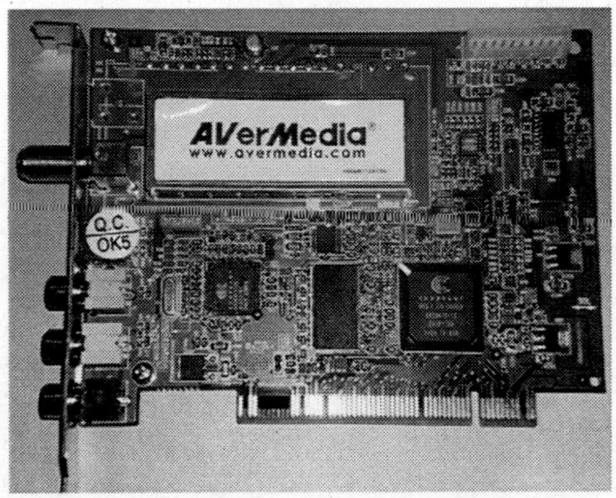

**Fig. 2.13:** Example of a Capture Card

Capture cards are much like TV tuners, except rather than focusing on its ability to tune into different channels of video, capture cards focus on pulling one stream of high quality video from an external source, such as a video camera. Capture cards are generally used to capture video inputs from digital sources like Firewire, and analog inputs like RCA and S-Video. While some capture cards do allow you to capture coaxial TV inputs as well, they are generally only used for single video input sources.

### 2.11.6 I/O Cards

Input/Output cards, also known as expansion cards, are simply cards that add extra functionality to your current motherboard. For example, if your motherboard does not have any USB 2.0 slots, you can connect a USB 2.0 I/O card into your PCI slot to add a few USB 2.0 slots to the back of your computer. There are four types of I/O cards that are mentioned in the 2009 A+ Bridge Exam, but they all essentially do the same thing.

The first is a SCSI (commonly pronounced Scuzzy) expansion card. A SCSI expansion card allows you to connect internal and external SCSI hard drives to your computer system. Serial cards are also covered, since serial ports have been removed from most newer computer systems, serial expansion cards (usually connected through PCI) are an alternative way to connect serial devices to your computer system.

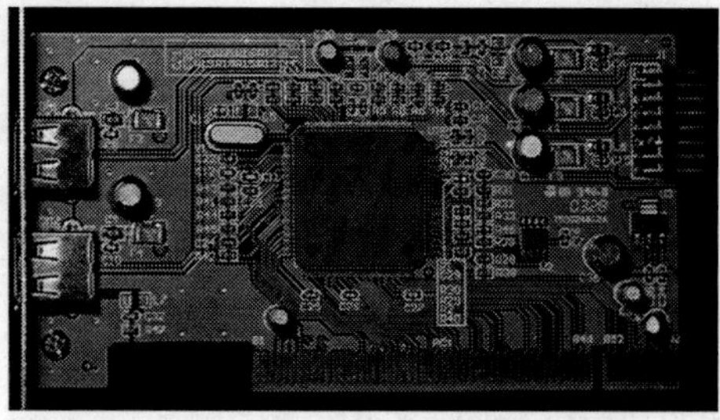

Fig. 2.14: Example of a USB Card.

As noted above, USB expansion cards either add USB functionality, or add extra ports to your computer. Finally, parallel expansion cards add parallel ports to your computer system. Parallel ports were commonly used as printer ports, however, with USB and Ethernet replacing the printing interface, parallel ports are now mostly used for custom-made peripherals due to it's architectural simplicity.

## 2.11.7 Communications Cards

There are two types of communications cards used in computer systems today: Network Interface Cards (NIC) and Modem Cards. NIC cards are generally used to give you access to wired Ethernet networks between 10Mbit and 1Gbit connection speeds. Some NIC cards also include wireless networking as well. Modems are used for dial-up access to the internet, phone systems, and can also function as a FAX machine would.

### Network Interface Card

A computer uses a network interface card (NIC) to become part of a network. The NIC contains the electronic circuitry required to communicate using a wired connection (*e.g.*, Ethernet) or a wireless connection (*e.g.*, WiFi). A network interface card is also known as a network interface controller, network adapter, or Local Area Network (LAN) adapter.

Early NICs typically consisted of an expansion card connected to a computer's motherboard. This separate card contained the electronic circuitry and the physical connectors. Here's an example of a typical NIC:

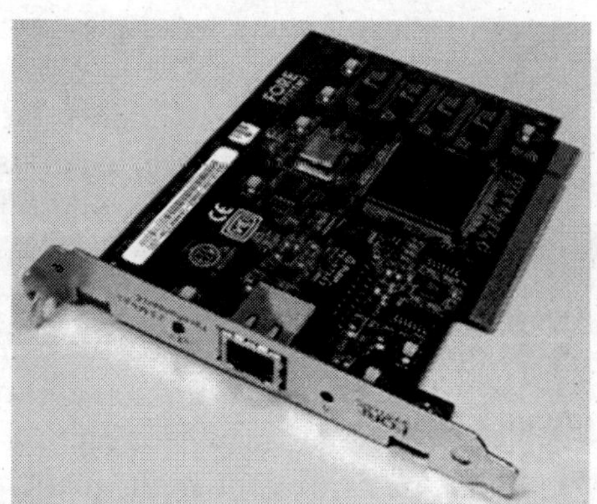

Fig. 2.15: Network Card

### Ethernet Connection

The most widely used network connection for personal computers is an Ethernet connection. Ethernet is really a standard for computer network technologies that describes both hardware and communication protocols. Ethernet was commercially introduced in 1980 and has largely replaced other wired network technologies.

Since Ethernet is so widely used, most modern computers have a NIC built into the motherboard.

A network card is an expansion card that allows computers to communicate over a computer network. It allows users to connect to each other either by using cables or wirelessly. Although other network technologies exist, Ethernet has achieved near-ubiquity for a while now. Every Ethernet network card has a unique 48-bit serial number called a MAC address, which is stored in ROM carried on the card. You can learn more about networking in the introduction to networking lesson.

## 2.12 EXTERNAL TYPES OF CONNECTIONS: USB, FIREWIRE AND THUNDERBOLT

USB (Universal Serial Bus) is a serial bus standard to interface devices. USB was designed to allow many peripherals to be connected using a single standardized interface socket and to improve the plug-and-play capabilities by allowing devices to be connected and disconnected without rebooting the computer. Other convenient features include providing power to low-consumption devices without the need for an external power supply and allowing many devices to be used without requiring manufacturer specific, individual device drivers to be installed. USB is by far the dominating bus for connecting external devices to your computer.

Over the years, the USB connection has taken on many forms. The rectangular port you're most familiar is called USB Type-A. The blocky, almost square port used in many large peripherals like printers is USB Type-B. Add micro and mini versions of each of these into the fold and suddenly you've got a half dozen connection type and a recipe for confusion.

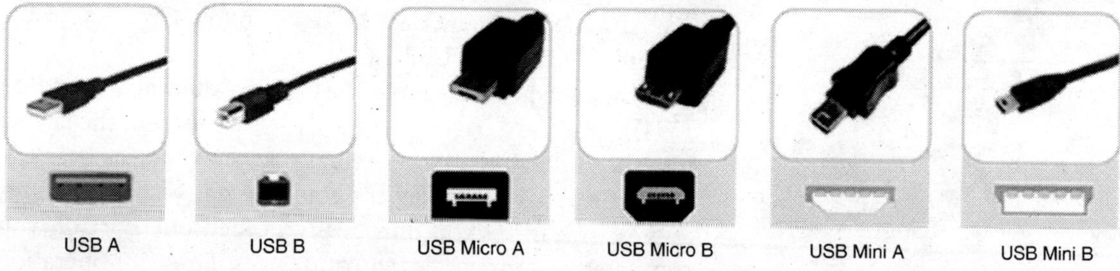


**Fig. 2.16:** A and B Forms of Type 2 USBs

USB Type-C is a description of the port connection itself. It's small, compact, and replaces the standard USB Type-A and B connections as well as the myriad of micro and mini USB ports. Basically, it's one USB connection type to rule them all. And best of all, it's reversible, so the days of flipping your USB cable three times before inserting it correctly may finally be numbered. Over the next few years, look for USB Type-C to begin becoming the universal port for all devices including desktop, laptop, and mobile.

One thing to note, because announcements of Type-C connections have come hand in hand with USB 3.1, many people assume they're the same, or at the very least that all Type-C runs on the 3.1 spec. This is not the case. Remember, Type-C is the connection type and may actually run on a lesser spec – USB 2.0 even – so don't assume you'll be getting all that 3.1 goodness just because you see that tiny reversible port.

### What is USB 3.1?

USB 3.1 (aka USB 3.1/gen 2) is the successor to USB 3.0. Identifiable by its bright turquoise port, USB 3.1 doubles the transfer speed of 3.0 to a whopping 10 Gbps. USB Power Delivery 2.0 makes a big step forward as well with upto 100W of power. And like previous versions of USB, it is fully backwards compatible with its predecessors.

**Fig. 2.17:** USB Type-C and USB Type-A side-by-side in harmony

When used with the Type-C connection, things get really interesting for 3.1. The 100W of PD v2.0 is enough to power and charge full sized notebooks, which means the proprietary AC port may soon be replaced by this universal alternative. With 4 data lanes, USB 3.1 Type-C can even carry DisplayPort and HDMI video signals, further adding to its ubiquity. Again, one port to rule them all.

The familiar USB 2.0 and FireWire 800 formats offer convenient plug and play interfaces with 480 and 800 Mbps (megabits per second) transfer rates.

### 2.12.1 Firewire

Firewire (technically known as IEEE 1394 and also known as i.LINK for Sony) is a serial bus interface standard for high-speed communications and isochronous real-time data transfer, frequently used in a personal computer. Firewire has replaced Parallel ports in many applications. It has been adopted as the High Definition Audio-Video Network Alliance (HANA) standard connection interface for A/V (audio/visual) component communication and control. Almost all modern digital camcorders have included this connection.

Fig. 2.18: Firewire Cable

eSATA brings the internal SATA interface out of the box to offer another step in improvement, up to 3 Gbps for SATA 3G. And then the new USB 3.0 steps up to 5 Gbps, or around ten times faster than USB 2.0.

One such port was **FireWire** (known alternatively as IEEE 1394), a standard backed primarily by Apple from the late 90s into the early 2010s. FireWire has a few advantages over USB at the time. FireWire devices could be daisy-chained to one another, meaning you only really needed one port on your computer to connect dozens of devices; FireWire operations didn't require as much work from the host system's CPU; and FireWire could transfer data in both directions simultaneously ("full-duplex") where USB 1.1 and 2.0 could only transfer things in one direction at a time ("half-duplex"). FireWire was also typically faster than contemporaneous USB ports. FireWire 400 supported speeds of up to 400Mbps, compared to 12Mbps for USB 1.1 devices, and FireWire 800 went up to 800Mbps while USB 2.0 operated at 480Mbps.

### 2.12.2 ThunderBolt 3

Thunderbolt 3 is an entirely different specification that is defined and owned by Intel. Its maximum (theoretical) data rate is 40Gbps and it has adopted the USB Type-C connector as a part of its specification. Additionally it contains support for other components of the USB 3.1 specification, allowing Thunderbolt 3 ports to operate in what's called "alt mode" when a USB 3.1 device with Type-C connectors is plugged into the Thunderbolt 3 port.

**Where does Thunderbolt 3 fit?**

And now there's Thunderbolt, a new interface championed by Intel and released on new Apple products which provides 10 Gbps rates. Thunderbolt is based on PCI Express technology for data transfer and DisplayPort for displays, so it can be used to daisy-chain multiple high-speed devices without using a hub or switch, including external RAID arrays, video capture devices, and high-resolution displays. You also can connect legacy devices to Thunderbolt using adapters, including DisplayPort, DVI, HDMI, and VGA displays, USB and FireWire peripherals, and Gigabit Ethernet and Fibre Channel networks.

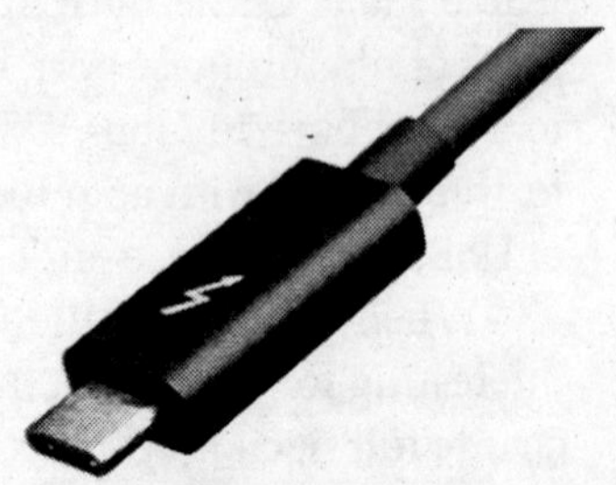

Fig. 2.19: Thunderbolt 3

## 2.13 MULTIMEDIA HARDWARE

A wide variety of hardware is in vogue and is to be adopted as per requirement of content. Six Categories of Multimedia Devices are required:

1. General Purpose Devices
2. Interaction Devices
3. Digital Media Devices
4. Analog Media Devices
5. Synchronization Devices
6. True Multimedia Platforms

### 2.13.1 General Purpose Devices

These devices known as secondary storage devices include storage devices of two types:

1. Fixed Internal
2. Portable Outside

Both may be in form of Disk and Disk drive. Most devices are digital.

## 2.14 FIXED TYPE SECONDARY STORAGE DEVICES

Your computer has one or more disk drives—devices that store information on a metal or plastic disk. The disk preserves the information even when your computer is turned off. There are three popular secondary storage drives:

1. Hard Disk Drive
2. Solid State Drives (SSD)
3. Solid-State Hybrid Drive

### 2.14.1 Hard Disk Drive

Your computer's **hard disk drive** stores information on a **hard disk**—a rigid platter or stack of platters with a magnetic surface. Because hard disks can hold massive amounts of information, they usually serve as your computer's primary means of storage, holding almost all of your programs and files. The hard disk drive is normally located inside the system unit.

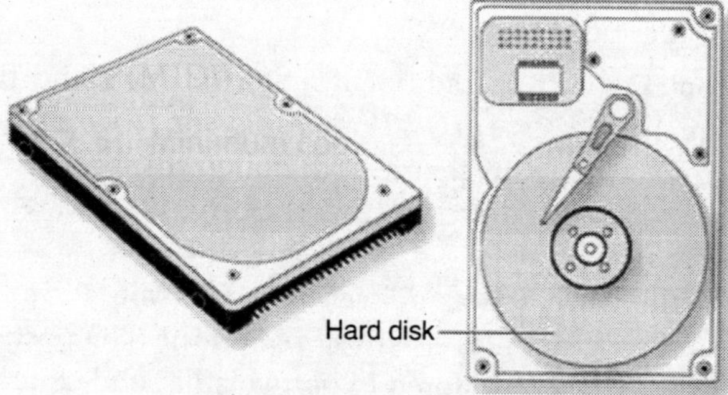


**Fig. 2.20:** Hard disk drive

### 2.14.2 Solid State Drives (SSD)

While processor, memory, and GPU all help accelerate local video processing, working efficiently with multiple files and higher resolutions also requires efficiently moving the video frames from and to files on disk. Especially if you tend to composite many layers in your timeliness, your hard drive not only needs to have the capacity to store all of your original, edited, and intermediate clips, but also requires the bandwidth to simultaneously deliver the frames from all the files for real-time playback. And again film resolutions will further push the hard drive requirements.

SSD stands for solid-state drive. It's basically the same as a USB flash drive, but on a bigger, much faster scale. Unlike a traditional mechanical hard disk, an SSD has no moving parts. Storage is provided by memory chips instead of spinning magnetic platters.

One developing answer for fast mass storage is the SSD (Solid State Drive), basically memory packaged as a hard drive, and often a good option for the main disk on a laptop system. But good old spinning magnetic disks still provide a much more cost-effective option for very large storage devices, as even portable drives pass 1 TB in capacity. The limitation in accessing these drives has been the interface, particularly the external cabling to attach mass storage to your computer.

### 2.14.3 Solid-State Hybrid Drive (SSHD) or HSSD

It's a traditional hard disk with a small amount of solid-state storage built in, typically 8GB. The drive appears as a single device to Windows (or any other operating system), and a controller chip decides which data is stored on the SSD and what's left on the HDD. SSDs are still much more limited on storage capacity than traditional hard drives, and even though you can buy a 1TB SSD, it will set you back around £350.(Year 2015) An equivalent HDD is about £50. A 1TB SSHD costs around £70, and is the best compromise if you want a balance of storage space and performance.

To get the advantages of both, many power users and PC gamers use both a solid-state drive and mechanical drive in their systems. The solid-state drive is used for system files, programs, application data, and anything else that really benefits from the speed. The larger mechanical drive can be used for long-term storage of files that don't need to be accessed as quickly — a media or photo collection, for example. This requires installing both drives in the computer and choosing which files and programs to place on each drive. If you want to move a file to a different drive, you'll have to move it yourself. If you want to move a program to a different drive, you may have to uninstall it and reinstall it at a different location.

#### (1) Benefits of SSHD Technology

A hybrid hard drive contains both a traditional magnetic drive and the amount of solid-state storage you'd find in a small solid-state drive. Importantly, this hard drive appears as a single drive to your operating system. You're not in charge of deciding which files go on the mechanical drive and which files go on the solid-state drive. Instead, the drive's firmware manages what is and isn't on the solid-state drive.

The SSD portion of the drive acts as a "cache" — files you access frequently, such as your operating system files and program files — are stored on the SSD portion of your drive by your firmware. Although this is a cache, it's stored in non-volatile solid-state memory — that means it persists across reboots, so it speeds up your startup process.

The goal is to have the drive access system and program files with the speed of a solid-state drive, and provide the storage capacity of a magnetic drive for other files. The drive handles this on its own — you don't have to shuffle files around or decide what goes where.

Hybrid drives can be cheaper than solid-state drives because they contain a smaller amount of solid-state memory. A 2 TB hybrid drive with 8 GB of solid-state cache memory will be more expensive than a simple 2 TB mechanical drive, but likely less expensive than a 256 GB solid-state drive with even less total space. Computer manufacturers include these drives in their computers to offer solid-state speeds at a lower price with more storage.

A hybrid drive is also a single physical drive, which can be a big advantage.

### Hybrids Don't Have Much SSD Storage

Importantly, most hybrid drives have a fairly small amount of SSD storage. The top hybrid hard drives on Amazon have 1 TB of mechanical space and only 8 GB of solid-state memory. 8 GB is a decent amount of storage space for holding system files and programs, but it doesn't compare to 128 GB or 256 GB that can hold all your system and program files.

Apple's "Fusion Drive" is also a hybrid drive, offering 1 TB or 3 TB of mechanical drive space alongside 128 GB of solid-state flash storage.

Whether you want to extend the mileage of your old desktop or get increased performance from a newer system, you might be ready for a change. A simple storage upgrade can bring a performance boost to your current desktop computer without the cost and complexity of adding a separate solid state drive (SSD). SSHD technology is a simpler, more effective solution to achieve your desired levels of high-capacity storage and performance.

SSHD is a relatively new hybrid storage category that integrates a small amount of solid state storage onto the core architecture of a traditional hard drive. This combination of storage technologies delivers an ideal blend of speedy performance and high capacity, at just a slight price premium to a typical hard drive. SSHDs give you fast access to your data without compromising on storage space. This means that your desktop system can smoothly and reliably handle all of your data — whether in the workplace or at home.

Solid State Hybrid Drives deliver speed and capacity for gaming and high-performance desktop applications.

For a richer gaming experience, Seagate SSHDs deliver faster map load speed for non-stop performance and play.

Get the kick of an integrated solid state drive (SSD) with the massive 4TB capacity of a hard drive – all at a surprisingly low price!

1. Boots Windows® 8 in less than 10 seconds
2. Performs up to 5× faster than 7200 RPM desktop hard drives
3. Improves overall system responsiveness by 30% or more
4. Backed by a five-year limited warranty

There are a number of important factors to consider, and none of the available solutions always provides the best performance in each category. As with most important decisions, you have to choose the option that can best meet your unique needs.

## (2) Selecting among HDD, SSD and HSSD

Let's break down the key criteria to help you decide which option is right for you.

**1. Form factor**

Without any moving parts, SSD products are the thinnest of the available storage options. They're especially good for thin and light PCs and complex, industrial designs. For standard notebooks, SSDs are available in 5mm and 7mm heights. By comparison, HDDs are available in standard 7mm and 9.5mm designs. SSHDs debuted at 9mm, will be available at 7mm soon, and 5mm designs have been announced for shipment in 2013.

**2. Capacity**

HDDs are the workhorses when it comes to sheer capacity and how much data can be stored. SSHD technology also offers maximum capacity points at affordable price points while SSDs are only affordable at lower capacities. High-capacity SSDs are extremely expensive.

**3. Speed**

SSDs provide peak performance for booting and high read/write performance to supporting computing that requires enhanced multitasking capabilities. On the other hand, a SSHD can provide near SSD performance for booting, launching, and loading data. HDDs usually provide ample performance for the majority of PC platforms available today.

**4. Cost**

At a system level, low-capacity SSDs can be affordable in the 32GB to 64GB range. But high-capacity SSDs are very expensive, especially when measured by cost per gigabyte. HDDs provide the lowest cost per gigabyte. SSHDs provide a cost per gigabyte that's just slightly higher than HDDs.

**5. Battery Life**

In general, storage will not impact battery life in a laptop computer by more than about 10%. Processor power and LCD really run down the battery. However, SSD is the most power-efficient, and SSHD is a close second because it can spin down more frequently than an HDD.

**6. Reliability**

Failure rates on SSD, HDD and SSHD technologies have very similar ratings. SSHD has benefits because it uses both the SSD and HDD portions more efficiently than if they were separate.

**7. Durability**

SSDs are viewed as more durable simply because of their solid state design. Without moving parts, they can withstand higher extremes of shock, drop and temperature.

High-end systems offer top-of-the-line components, like the latest CPUs that will give you all the power you need for multimedia projects, loads of storage (a 512GB SSD or at least 1TB hard drive, but typically 2TB or more), 3D graphics capability for gaming, or a combination of all three. These high-performance machines typically start at $1,500, and can go up to $5,000 and beyond for workstations or gaming rigs with customized paint jobs and multiple GPUs.

## 2.15 OPTICAL DISCS

An optical disc is designed to support one of three recording types: read-only (*e.g.*: CD and CD-ROM), recordable (write-once, *e.g.* CD-R), or re-recordable (rewritable, *e.g.* CD-RW). Write-once optical discs commonly have an organic dye recording layer between the substrate and the reflective layer.

Optical discs are most commonly used for data and programs for personal computers (PC), for storing music (*e.g.* for use in a CD player), and video (*e.g.* for use in a Blu-ray player). For computer data backup and physical data transfer, optical discs such as CDs and DVDs are gradually being replaced with faster, smaller solid-state devices, especially the USB flash drive. This trend is expected to continue as USB flash drives continue to increase in capacity and drop in price.

Six types of optical disc media are available:

1. Laser,
2. Compact disc,

3. Mini Disc,
4. DVD,
5. HDDVD and
6. Blu-ray.

**TABLE 2.3:** shows the various types of optical discs along with their first availability date (Year)

| Name | Capacity | Year |
|---|---|---|
| Laserdisc (LD) | 0.3GB | 1971-2001 |
| Compact Disc (CD) | 0.7-0.9GB | 1981-today |
| MiniDisc (MD) | 0.14GB | 1989-today |
| Digital Versatile Disc (DVD) | 4.7-17GB | 1995-today |
| HD DVD | 15-51GB | 2002-2008 |
| Blu-ray Disc (BD) | 25GB<br>50GB<br>100GB (BDXL)<br>128GB (BDXL) | 2002-today |

## 2.15.1 CD-ROM

A single CD ROM can hold the entire text of an encyclopedia and video clips, enhanced with sound to illustrate many of the items in the encyclopedia. As discussed earlier, a CD-ROM is a compact disk that can hold 660 MB of digital data. CD is used to store clip art collections, games, entertainment titles, reference works, how to disks, and whatever else might be successful subject material for a CD-ROM production.

The CD-ROM is essential because of all the great clip art and other software you can get these days-literally thousands of discs full of stock photos, fonts, buttons, backgrounds, sounds, movies, and so on. They're a powerful resource for multimedia producers.

Compact Disc (CD) is a digital optical disc data storage format. The format was originally developed to store and play only sound recordings but was later adapted for storage of data (CD-ROM). Standard CDs have a diameter of 120 millimeters (4.7 in) and can hold up to about 80 minutes of uncompressed audio or about 700 MB of data. The Mini CD has various diameters ranging from 60 to 80 millimeters (2.4 to 3.1 in); they are sometimes used for CD singles, storing up to 24 minutes of audio, or delivering device drivers.

The Compact Disc is an evolution of LaserDisc technology, where a focused laser beam is used that enables the high information density required for high-quality digital audio signals.

Prototypes were developed by Phillips and Sony independently in the late 1970s. In 1979, Sony and Phillips set up a joint task force of engineers to design a new digital audio disc. After a year of experimentation and discussion, the Red Book CD-DA standard was published in 1980.

In June 1985, the computer-readable CD-ROM (read-only memory) and, in 1990, CD-Recordable were introduced, also developed by both Sony and Phillips. Recordable CDs were a new alternative to tape for recording music and copying music albums without defects introduced in compression used in other digital recording methods. Other newer video formats such as DVD and Blu-ray use the same physical geometry as CD, and most DVD and Blu-ray players are backward compatible with audio CD.

CD-ROM drives were standard issue on virtually all new PCs but later on superseded by DVD (Digital Video Disks), which offered video, audio, and graphic performance many times more capable than today's limited media.

For the first few years of its existence, the CD was a medium used purely for audio. However, in 1988, the *Yellow Book* CD-ROM standard was established by Sony and Phillips, which defined a non-volatile optical data computer data storage medium using the same physical format as audio compact discs, readable by a computer with a CD-ROM drive.

There is so much digitized art already available that it may not be necessary for you to get a scanner. Even if you have original photography that needs to be digitized, you can avoid the cost of a scanner by having the film converted to Photo CD format and reading the images into your computer directly.

Video CD (VCD, View CD, and Compact Disc digital video) is a standard digital format for storing video media on a CD. VCDs are playable in dedicated VCD players, most modern DVD-Video players, personal computers, and some video game consoles.

The VCD standard was created in 1993 by Sony, Phillips, Matsushita, and JVC and is referred to as the White Book standard.

### 2.15.2 Digital Video Discs (DVD)

DVD ( "digital versatile disc" or "digital video disc" is a digital optical disc storage format invented and developed by Phillips, Sony, Toshiba, and Panasonic in 1995. The medium can store any kind of digital data and is widely used for software and other computer files as well as video programs watched using DVD players. DVDs offer higher storage capacity than compact discs while having the same dimensions.

**Fig. 2.21:** Digital Video Disc

Pre-recorded DVDs are mass-produced using molding machines that physically stamp data onto the DVD. Such discs are a form of DVD-ROMs, because data can only be read and not written or erased. Blank recordable DVD discs (DVD-R and DVD+R) can be recorded once using a DVD recorder and then function as a DVD-ROM. Rewritable DVDs (DVD-RW, DVD+RW, and DVD-RAM) can be recorded and erased many times.

The 12 cm type is a standard DVD, and the 8 cm variety is known as a MiniDVD. These are the same sizes as a standard CD and a mini-CD, respectively. Ordinary DVDs are available upto 16 GB and rewritable upto 4 GB.

#### DVD Drives and Players

DVD drives are devices that can read DVD discs on a computer. DVD players are a particular type of devices that do not require a computer to work, and can read DVD-Video and DVD-Audio discs.

### 2.15.3 Laser Optical Discs

All four common optical disc media (Compact disc, DVD, HDDVD and Blu-ray) use light from laser diodes, for its spectral purity and ability to be focused precisely. DVD uses light of 650 nm wavelength (red), as opposed to 780 nm (far-red, commonly called infrared) for CD. This shorter wavelength allows a smaller pit on the media surface compared to CDs (0.74 μm for DVD versus 1.6 μm for CD), accounting in part for DVD's increased storage capacity.

In comparison, Blu-ray Disc, the successor to the DVD format, uses a wavelength of 405 nm (violet), and one dual-layer disc has a 50 GB storage capacity.

### 2.15.4 HD DVD

HD DVD was one of two formats for high definition DVDs. The other format was Blu-ray. HD DVD specifications were put in place in 2002. Negotiations among consumer electronics companies to have only one product for playing high definition discs ended when there was no consensus about royalties.

HD DVD (short for High Definition/Density Digital Versatile/Video Disc)[1] is a discontinued high-density optical disc format for storing data and playback of high-definition video.[2] Supported principally by Toshiba, HD DVD was envisioned to be the successor to the standard DVD format.

On 19 February 2008, after a protracted format war with rival Blu-ray, Toshiba abandoned the format, announcing it would no longer develop or manufacture HD DVD players and drives.

### 2.15.5 Blu-Ray (BR) Disc (BRD)

*Blu-ray* or *Blu-ray Disc (BD, BRD)* is a digital optical disc data storage format. It was designed to supersede the DVD format, in that it is capable of storing high-definition & ultra high-definition video resolution (2160p). The plastic disc is 120 mm in diameter and 1.2 mm thick, the same size as DVDs and CDs.

The main application of Blu-ray is as a medium for video material such as feature films and physical distribution of video games for the PlayStation 3, PlayStation 4, and Xbox One.

Blu-ray faces competition from video on demand[64] and from new technologies that allow access to movies on any format or device, such as Digital Entertainment Content Ecosystem or Disney's Keychest.

## 2.16 INTERACTION DEVICES

Multimedia application means ability to interact within the application itself. Interaction devices enable user direct control over the multimedia application behavior.

- Examples: keyboard, mouse, joystick, electronic pen

### 2.16.1 The Mouse

A computer mouse is a pointing device (hand control) that detects two-dimensional motion relative to a surface. This motion is typically translated into the motion of a pointer on a display, which allows a smooth control of the graphical user interface.

Although you can enter several kinds of information using the keyboard, the mouse is the fundamental controlling input device for Windows. Due to the graphical nature of Windows except touch screen computers, you need the mouse for pointing and moving graphics around the screen.

Almost all of laptop computers contain *mice or trackballs* that are built into the keyboards or attached to the side of the computer.

Graphical interfaces (GUIs) are designed to be used with pointing devices, but key commands may be substituted. However, graphics applications, such as CAD and image editing, demand a mouse-like device. On a PC, the mouse generally connects to a serial port via a 9-pin DB or PS/2 connector or USB.

Mouse movement is *relative*. The screen cursor moves from its existing location. The mouse could be moved across your arm, and the screen cursor would move as well. The mouse-like object on a graphics tablet, which is correctly called the tablet cursor or puck is not relative. It contacts the tablet with absolute reference. Placing it on the upper left part of the tablet moves the screen cursor to the corresponding location.

After years of use by millions of users, it is now widely known that mice can be hazardous to your health. Many applications require endless clicking and dragging to accomplish tasks. Continuous use puts enormous stress on the wrist, and constant double clicking can be the most strenuous function.

## 2.17 DIGITAL MEDIA DEVICES

These devices deal with digital signal and can be divided into 3 sub categories:

1. Capturing Devices
2. Processing Devices
3. Presentation Devices
4. Capturing Devices (Input)
5. Keyboard
6. Image Scanner
7. OCR Device

### 2.17.1 Wireless Keyboard

A wireless keyboard is a computer keyboard that allows the user to communicate with computers, tablets, or laptops with the help of radio frequency (RF), infrared (IR) or Bluetooth technology. It is common for wireless keyboards available these days to be accompanied by a wireless mouse.

Wireless keyboards based on infrared technology use light waves to transmit signals to other infrared-enabled devices. But, in case of radio frequency technology, a wireless keyboard communicates using signals which range from 27 MHz to up to 2.4 GHz. Most wireless keyboards today work on 2.4 GHz radio frequency. Bluetooth is another technology that is being widely used by wireless keyboards. These devices connect and communicate to their parent device via the bluetooth protocol.

A wireless keyboard can be connected using RF technology with the help of two parts, a transmitter and a receiver. The radio transmitter is inside the wireless keyboard. The radio receiver plugs into a keyboard port or USB port. Once the receiver and transmitter are plugged in, the computer recognizes the keyboard and mouse as if they were connected via a cable.

### 2.17.2 Multifunctional Keyboards

Multifunctional keyboards may feature customised keypads, fully programmable function or soft keys for macros/presets, biometric or smart card readers, trackballs, etc. New generation multifunctional keyboards feature a touchscreen display to stream video, control audio visual media and alarms, execute application inputs, configure individual desktop environments, etc. Multifunctional keyboards may also permit users to share access to PCs and other information sources. Multiple interfaces (serial, USB, audio, Ethernet, etc.) are used to integrate external devices. Some multifunctional keyboards are also used to directly and intuitively control video walls.

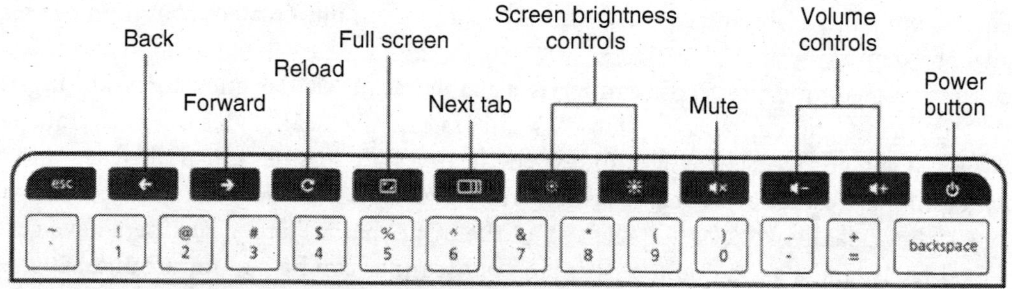

Fig. 2.22: Special Keys on Multimedia Keyboard

### 2.17.3 Scanner

Scanning a piece of artwork (a photo, say) requires controlling the scanner from your computer with some kind of software, which also handles transferring the digital data from the scanner to your hard drive. Some scanners have their own proprietary applications; these may range from very simple one-button programs to the full-featured (and expensive) custom applications required to run high-end scanners. Many manufacturers, however, just write a simple Adobe Photoshop plug-into interface their hardware and the computer, and bundle Photoshop with the hardware. The scanner can then be controlled from with Photoshop, with the scans opening directly into the program ready for editing. This is one of the best solutions, as no standalone scanning program has all the features and power of Photoshop (or an equivalent image-manipulation program). This kind of plug-in is called an acquire module, and needs to be installed in Photoshop's plug-ins folder before launching Photoshop to be accessible.

Most scanners accommodate a wide range of resolutions: from 72 ppi (or lower) up to as high as 2400 ppi or more for slide scanners. As a rule, you shouldn't scan at much higher resolution than you need for your final output, as it just wastes disk space. For example, final-processed images to be viewed on the World Wide Web should never be higher than screen resolution (72 or 80 ppi), as they can only be viewed at this resolution, and higher resolutions require much longer download times, which tends to turn off your potential surfers. Sometimes in order to yield a better quality scan, it's worthwhile to scan your artwork at a higher resolution-say, double the screen resolution-and then reduce the ppi to screen resolution. You should yield final artwork only at higher-than screen resolution if you need to zoom into the image in an animation, for instance.

On the other hand, you should always scan at the highest possible bitdepth, 24-bit if at all possible, even if your final output will be 8-bit. This is so that when you create optimized palettes, you always have the largest and most realistic range of colors to sample. An optimized palette created from a full 24-bit image will be more accurate than one created from in image scanned at a lower bit depth.

The most common type of scanner is a flatbed scanner, designed for scanning relatively large, flat prints and pages. Some flatbed scanners can also scan slides or other transparencies; however, if you need to scan a lot of slides, a dedicated slide scanner is usually faster and provides cleaner, higher-resolution scans. Scanners are usually SCSI devices, and tend to be somewhat finicky; they usually work best at the end of the SCSI chain. Flatbed scanners have gotten a lot cheaper lately, and a good quality, 24-bit, 6--ppi scanner can be had for around $500. Scanners create bitmapped images; look for one that interfaces directly with an image-editing program such as Adobe Photoshop. This lets you scan directly into Photoshop and have its superb image-editing tools available immediately.

Besides being useful for acquiring photographs and textures for backgrounds and 3-D models, scanners can also be sued for optical character recognition, or OCR. Many scanners come bundled with OCR software, which lets you scan a printed page of text and turn it into digital text, ready for word processing. This is particularly useful for multimedia producers who need to input large amounts of printed historical text and turn it into searchable data. Even the best OCR programs have an accuracy of no more than 98 percent, so you'll still have to go back into the text to proof and correct it all. This definitely beats having to type all that text yourself, though.

## 2.17.4 OPTICAL CHARACTER READER (OCR)

OCR, is the mechanical or electronic conversion of scanned images of handwritten, typewritten or printed text into machine-encoded text. — It is widely used as a form of data entry from some sort of original paper data source, whether documents, sales receipts, mail, or any number of printed records. — It is a common method of digitizing printed texts so that they can be electronically searched, stored more compactly, displayed on-line, and used in machine processes such as machine translation, text-to-speech. OCR is a field of research in pattern recognition and artificial intelligence.

## 2.17.5 Digital Cameras

Some manufacturers use dots per inch to represent a digital camera's resolution, or the sharpness and clarity of the image it produces. Dots per inch (DPI) is the number of pixels in an inch of screen display. A pixel is a single point in an electronic image. Digital cameras for the consumer range from 640 x 480 dpi to 1,792 to 1,200 dpi. The actual photographed resolution is called the optical resolution. Some manufacturers also state enhanced resolution, which uses a special formula to add pixels between those generated by the optical resolution. With the price of digital cameras decreasing, will the era of film-based cameras soon come to an end?

### Webcam

A webcam can give you an excellent introduction to working with digital video. Image size is rather limited with a webcam. A webcam is a little and cheap camera. It is also very easy to install.

The camera itself is a little box, into which both an objective and a microphone are built into. The software in the computer operates the camera.

The word webcam refers to the fact than the camera is designed for use in connection with the Internet. This means that the camera has to be permanently connected to the net and that you have to have the right software.

The camera is (in the vast majority of cases) connected to the computer via a USB cable, which is convenient for everyday use. Only a little thin cable is needed.

The USB cable transmits data (audio and image) from camera to computer. It also sends instructions from the camera's software to the camera:

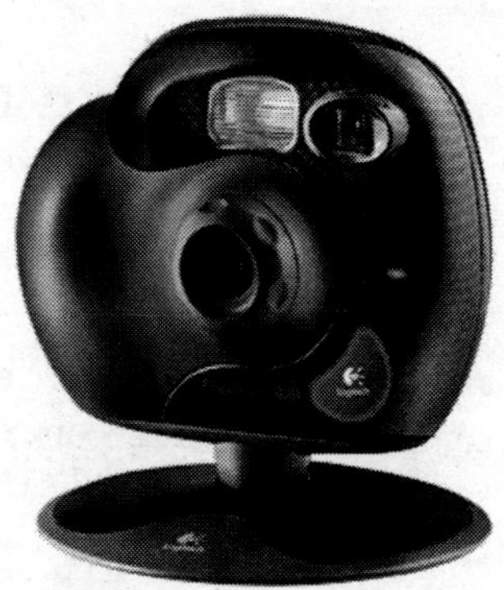

Fig. 2.23: Webcam

### What can a webcam do?

Don't expect high quality recordings from a webcam, this hasn't been intended. But you can produce small video sequences, which are both quick to produce and easy to distribute. And on top of this, mini videos from both webcam and digital cameras can be burnt onto a video CD in a surprising good quality so that they can be watched on the television screen.

Webcams are often supplied with software, which gives the camera a number of additional functions:

Video surveillance (can be, for example, activated by a movement in the image).

Automatic distribution to the Internet (requires constant access to a webserver).

Net meetings or similar séances and Internet telephony.

Finally, all webcams can take single images (stills), but the quality isn't very convincing. You can take stills with a certain interval between them (*e.g.* every 10 minutes), after which they are sent out automatically to a wondering audience all over the world. Or you can keep pace with what is happening in your driveway or whatever else you have chosen for us all to participate in.

You can also make a live broadcast, which means that you, in principle, create your own television station on the net.

All of these things are, in fact, possible with Logitechs webcams, which are supplied with programs for one thing and another.

## 2.17.6 Graphic Tablet

A pressure-sensitive graphics tablet is also a useful tool for multimedia production.

Most consist of a thin tablet or pad connected to your computer's serial port, ranging in size from 4 by 5 inches up to 24 inches square or more, and an electronic pen, which may be cabled or cordless. The cordless models are generally easier to use. If you're a traditional artist, a pressure-sensitive pen is essential.

This, coupled with software that supports pressure, such as Adobe Photoshop or Fractal Design Painter, lets you create amazingly realistic natural-media artwork completely digitally. Even if you can't draw or paint, a graphics tablet is still useful for modifying photos by smudging or cloning and for creating original textures for backgrounds and 3-D elements. Wacom's series of tablets and cordless pens, including new pens with digital erasers, are among the most popular and flexible models.

In addition to devices that are normally used in a multimedia PC following items are also required for interactive graphics system. These devices may be used to either create, point to, or move objects.

### 2.17.7 Light pen

The lightpen is one of the most common manual input device on graphic displays (and even on some alphanumeric ones), for use in identifying ("picking") information displayed on the screen for subsequent computer processing. For example, in text editing pointing at a certain character on certain line with the lightpen might indicate to the program that a string of characters about to be typed by the user should be inserted after the identified character. Pointing the lightpen at a particular resistor in an electronic schematic on the screen might mean that the user wants that particular resistor moved, scaled up, deleted, or manipulated in some other specified way.

Physically, the lightpen is a photosensitive transducer that converts light emanating form the screen to an electric signal, which is typically used to interput the processor servicing the displays. Associated with the interput is some sense data, usually either the x-y coordinates of the lightpenned display element (point, line, or character) on the screen,and the address in the display buffer of the display command which caused display of the element that the lightpen detected.

In either case, the program has the problem of relating such coordinate or address sense data to the particular text character or logical picture entity which the user selected for processing by the program. This process is known as correlation of the physical sense data to the logical subpicture items that the user wanted to indicate, and usually involves some amount of table searching.

Some lightpens aid the user in accurate positioning by projecting "finder beams" of light on th spot on the screen where the lightpen photodetector is focused. Nevertheless,most lightpens are not easily used for fast, accurate picking, and have the additional disadvantage that they are not natural for freehand input. A data table with its stylus allows such input without special programming aids, while a lightpen must be provided with special "tracking" algorithms. In such in algorithm, the program displays a tracking cursor, or cross, and makes it follow the lightpen.

## 2.18 GRAPHIC OUTPUT DEVICES

(1) Processing Devices
   1) Video Encoder/Decoder
   2) Audio Encoder/Decoder
   3) Digital Video Effects Device
   4) Digital Audio Effect Device

(2) Presentation Devices (Output)
   1) Printer
   2) Monitor
   3) Projector

A variety of different types of computer output equipment are used to provide hard copy of the graphics information created on a display. This information may be output when it is created or when it is retrieved from storage. The output may be generated directly from the user's terminal or workstation while it is on-line, or it may be generated off-line from a remote terminal.

There are three basic classes of graphics output equipment, each of which includes several different types. The selection of a particular type of output equipment depends on user requirements, such as speed, quality, size, and cost.

## 2.19 THE PRINTER

Many kinds of printers are available. Windows 95 supports over 1,600 printer makes and models. Although many printers exist, almost every printer connected to a PC today falls into one of these three categories.

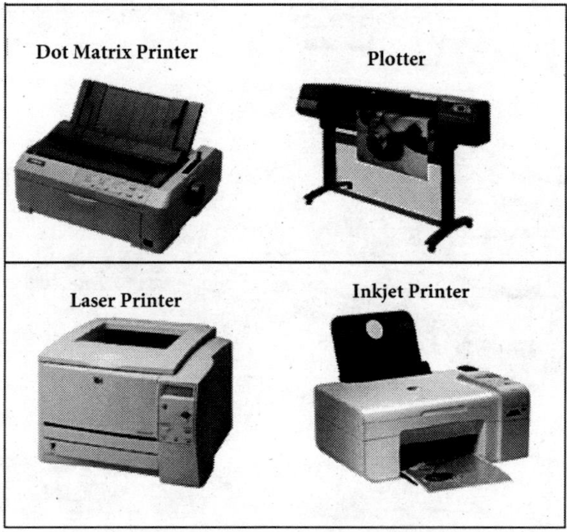


**Fig. 2.24:** Types of Printers

### 2.19.1 Dot-Matrix

A printer that produces graphics and text by printing dots onto the page much like the way your screen displays output by combining small dots together. Dot-matrix printers are inexpensive and often support a letter-quality mode that helps smooth curved lines and make the printer's output look more like typeset letters.

### 2.19.2 Ink-Jet

This printer prints text and graphics on the page by shooting ink onto the paper. Ink-jet printers are fairly inexpensive and produce high-quality output. Many of today's ink-jet printers also print in color. The low cost and high quality of ink-jet printers has lessened the demand for dot-matrix printers.

- These are used to produce high quality hard copies (on paper).
- Although the quality of Inkjet printouts is not as good as Laser printers, it is far better than Dot Matrix printers.
- Ink is stored in and delivered to the paper via an ink cartridge.
- Inkjet's can print in both black and white and colour.
- Inkjet printers have small amounts of internal memory (RAM) to store print jobs so printing is done a bit at a time. The whole document cannot be stored in printer's RAM so there is often a pause while the computer sends the rest of the data
- Inkjet printers work by spraying ink onto a page of paper.
- The link is held in 'ink cartridges' and there are **4 different colours – black**, cyan, magenta and yellow. These mix to form a vast amount of other colours.

- **Motors** are used to position the ink cartridges over the correct position of the page and to drag the paper through the printer.

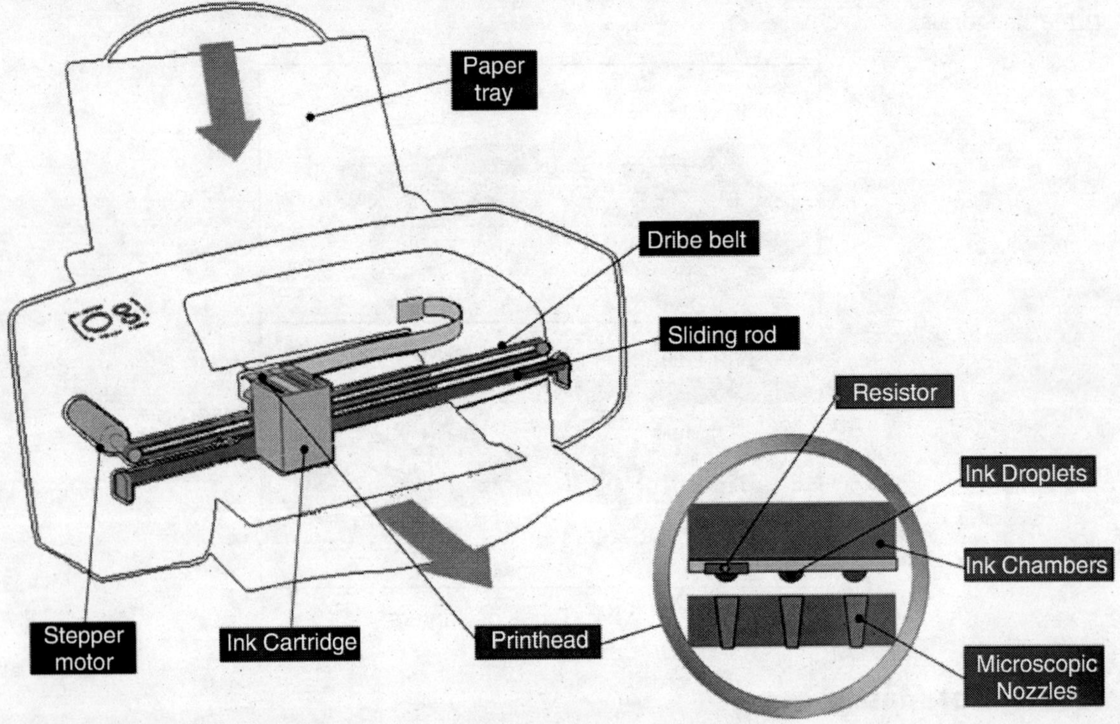


- These produce high quality hard copy outputs (on paper).
- Laser printers use Toner pressed on a page to produce printed documents.
- They can print large amounts of pages at a very quick rate.
- You can buy both black and white and colour laser printers.
- They use a buffer memory which stores the information for the whole document before the pages can be printed out.

  **For example:** Once you press print, the document is sent to the printers memory **(RAM)** and stored there. The printer will then output whatever is in the memory when it is ready to do so. Think of the Buffer Memory as a **kind of waiting room**
- Laser printers work by using a **laser beam** to **'draw'** onto a drum. The laser leaves a **positive electric charge** on the drum in the places where it drew.

A special power know as **'toner'** is sprayed onto the drum and it sticks to the parts that contain the positive electric charge.

The drum is then **pressed** onto a sheet of paper and the paper is heated **(fused)** so that the toner is bound to the paper.

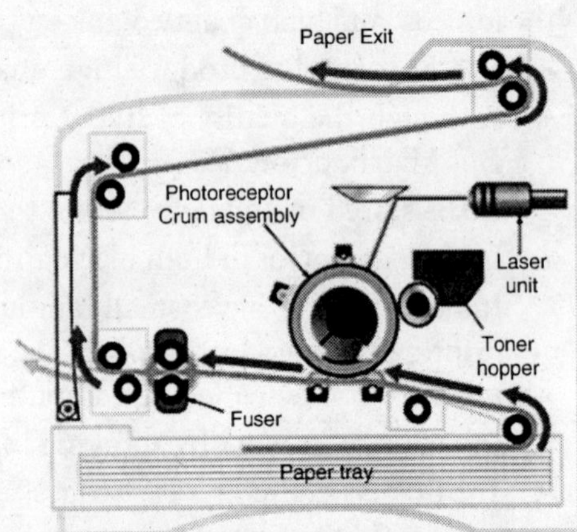


**Fig. 2.26:** Working of Laser Printer

**Fig. 2.25:** Inkjet Printer and its cartridges

### 2.19.3 Laser printer

The printer draws graphics and text on the page using a laser beam to burn ink into the page. The output quality of laser printers is extremely good, and laser printers are fast. Laser printers are often more expensive than dot-matrix and ink-jet printers, but their prices are coming closer to the lower-end printer prices every day.

Characteristics of Laser Printer

You also can find color versions of ink-jet and laser printers. Color ink-jet printers produce fairly good quality output. Color laser printers produce high-quality output, but fairly expensive.

### 2.19.4 Comparison of qualities of various printers

A dot matrix is example of an impact printer, while lasers and ink-jets are non impact printers.

The speed of dot matrix printers can vary form 50 to 500 cps. They are capable of producing NLQ. However, they are notorious for the noise generated while printing. Inkjet printers produce near laser quality and are generally capable of printing between 1 and 3 pages per minute (PPM). Laser printer produce near laser quality and are generally capable of printing between 1 and 3 pages per minute (PPM). Laser printers produce the best quality output at speeds of between 4 and 20 pages of text per minute.

The monitor is the component that displays the visual output from your computer as generated by the video card. It is different from most of the other components of the PC due to its passive nature; it isn't responsible for doing any real computing, but rather for showing the results of computing. In this way, the monitor is in many respects more similar to your printer than to anything else in the PC, although of course most people don't think in these terms.

## 2.20 MONITOR

Monitor (also called screen or Visual Display Unit) are important not because of their impact on performance, but rather their impact on the usability of the PC. A poor quality monitor can hamper the use of an otherwise very good PC, because a monitor that is hard to look at can make the PC hard to use. Despite the fact that they don't have a direct impact on performance, many people spend almost as much on their monitor when buying a new PC as they do on the PC system itself.

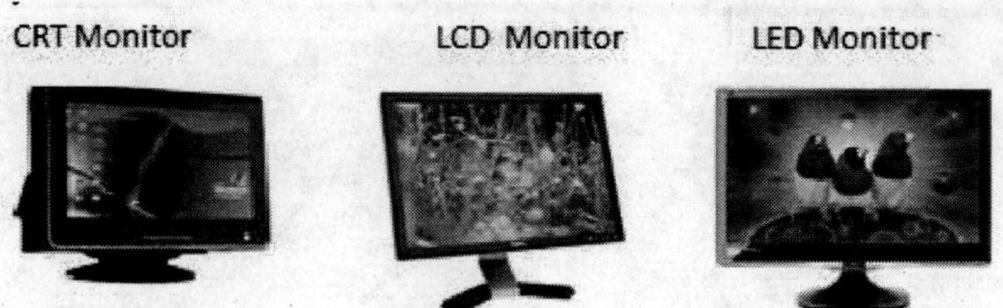


Fig. 2.27: Three Types of Monitor

## 2.20.1 Cathode-Ray Tube (CRT) Monitors

Cathode-Ray Tube (CRT), the technology used in most televisions and computer display screens.

The cathode ray tube (CRT) is a vacuum tube containing one or more electron guns, and a phosphorescent screen used to view images.

A CRT works by moving an electron beam back and forth across the back of the screen. Each time the beam makes a pass across the screen, it lights up phosphor dots on the inside of the glass tube, thereby illuminating the active portions of the screen. By drawing many such lines from the top to the bottom of the screen, it creates an entire screen full of images.

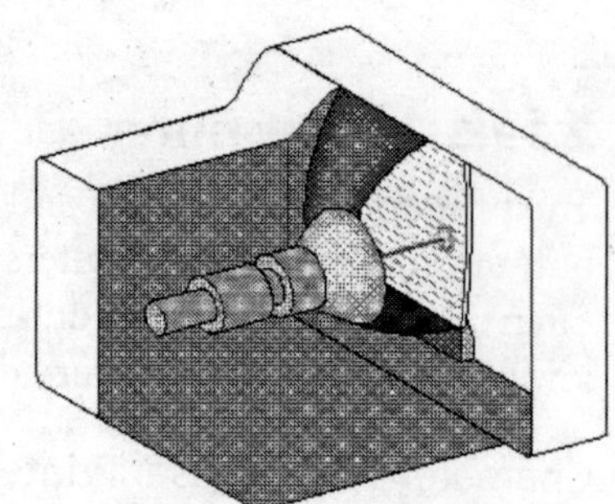

Fig. 2.28: CRT Screen

Since the late 2000s, CRTs have largely been superseded by newer display technologies such as LCD, plasma display, and OLED, which have lower manufacturing costs, power consumption, weight and bulk.

## 2.20.2 Liquid Crystal Display (LCD) Monitors

The LCD screens can today be equipped with the technology TFT (Thin Film Transistor). The screens of laptops were the first to employ this technology that, since, has spread and reached the area of tv screens. This technology is still a relatively recent has many advantages, but is not all rosy of disadvantages.

The TFT screens use a complex technology. The aim is to achieve a homogeneous illumination on the set of the slab (of the screen in sum), the light emitted by the inner tube will be managed by a set of reflectors that will standardize the radiation. The slab itself is made up of two types of cells independent juxtaposed covered by a filter that can be red, blue or green. Each set of three colors will be assigned to a dedicated transistor.

TFT stand for 'thin film resistor'. These are thin flat screened monitors that are commonly seen today. As they become cheaper, these have taken over from CRT monitors as the most popular computer screens. TFT's are used with the newer desktop PC's, laptops and mobile phones.

TFT screens are made up of thousands of tiny pixels. Each pixel has 3 transistors - red, green and blue and each transistor can produce different intensities. This allows huge amounts of colours to be produced (16.7 million). A back light is used to shine light onto these pixels in order

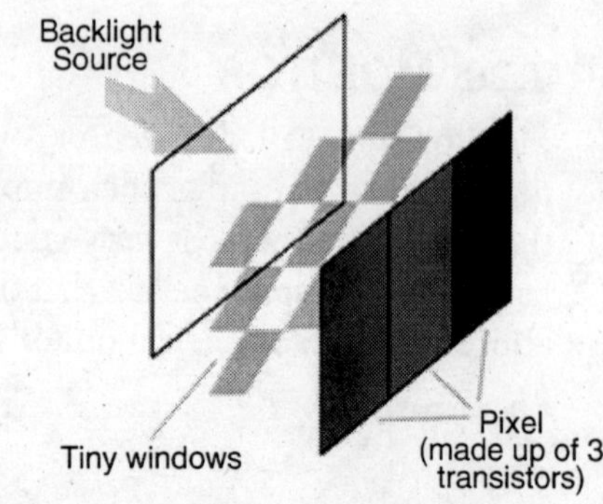


Fig. 2.29: TFT Screen Technology

for the colours to be produced. In order to light a single pixel, tiny windows can be opened and closed to allow the light to pass through and onto the pixel.

Based on the information which they are transmitted, the crystals will change their inclination and thus divert the light which will then pass through a filter of the desired color.

Three families of TFT screens

1. Twited Nematic (TN) + Film which employ a technology to both economic and swift, but which do not produce deep blacks. The angle of vision on this type of screen is 90°, useful if it is many to look at the screen and that we should be able to see through.
2. The Super TFT screens (or IPS for In-Plane Switching) allow a higher angle of vision of 170 °. In addition, the blacks are deep and made perfect. However, the response time is more important.
3. The screens MVA (for Multi-Domain Vertical Alignment) have a reduced response time, a wide angle and a deep black. They combine the advantages of the two previous systems.

**TABLE 2.4:** Advantages/Disadvantages of TFT Monitors:

| Advantages | Disadvantages |
|---|---|
| Lightweight so they are perfect for portable laptops and wall mounting. | Images can appear unclear when viewed from an angle.<br>(you need to look straight at the screen for the best image) |
| They are very thin and do not take up as much desk space as a CRT monitor. | |
| They produce much less glare than CRT's and so are friendly to the eye. | Lower picture quality (definition) compared to a CRT monitor. |
| They use less power than CRT monitors (cheaper to run). | Cannot be used with Light Pens yet.<br>(Computer Aided Drawings are not yet possible on TFT monitors) |
| They emit less radiation than CRT monitors. | |
| They produce less heat than CRT's. | |

## 2.20.3 Basics of Selecting Monitors

Regardless of the kind of monitor, there are some general factors to consider:

**(1) Size:** Desktop monitors generally fall between 15 inches and 34 inches. The size of the panel is measured diagonally. While it is always nice to have a big viewing area, it may not be practical, given desktop space constraints. Plus, the bigger the screen, the more you can expect to pay. A 24-inch monitor is a good choice for users who wish to view multipage documents or watch movies, but have limited desk space. However, there›s nothing like watching a movie or playing a game on a large screen, so if you have room on your desktop, a 27-inch display delivers a big-screen experience for a reasonable price. Viewing distance should be at least six times of the size of screen.Or, if space is not an issue, consider a massive 34-inch, curved-screen model to bring a true movie-theater experience to your desktop. If you're looking to replace a dual-monitor setup with a single display, check out one of the ultra-wide, big-screen models. They are available in sizes ranging from 29 to 35 inches with curved and non-curved panels, have a 21:9 aspect ratio, and come in a variety of resolutions, including Wide Quad High-Definition (WQHD) and Ultra High-Definition (UHD).

**(2) Resolution:** The display resolution or display modes of a digital television, computer monitor or display device is the number of distinct pixels in each dimension that can be displayed. It can be an ambiguous term especially as the displayed resolution is controlled by different factors in cathode ray tube (CRT) displays, flat-panel displays (including liquid-crystal displays) and projection displays using fixed picture-element (pixel) arrays.

It is usually quoted as width × height, with the units in pixels: for example, "1024 × 768" means the width is 1024 pixels and the height is 768 pixels. This example would normally be spoken as "ten twenty-four by seven sixty-eight" or "ten twenty-four by seven six eight".

One use of the term "display resolution" applies to fixed-pixel-array displays such as plasma display panels (PDP), liquid-crystal displays (LCD), Digital Light Processing (DLP) projectors, OLED displays, and similar technologies, and is simply the physical number of columns and rows of pixels creating the display (*e.g.* 1920 × 1080). A consequence of having a fixed-grid display is that, for multi-format video inputs, all displays need a "scaling engine" (a digital video processor that includes a memory array) to match the incoming picture format to the display.

Common resolutions for multimedia projectors are SVGA (800 × 600), XGA (1024 × 768), WXGA (1280 × 800), and WUXGA (1920 × 1200), though 4K is just over the horizon. The most popular resolution is XGA, and is generally suitable for PowerPoint presentations—but, because it is a 4:3 format, may not be ideal if you plan to screen high definition. This is the number of pixels a monitor can display, both horizontally and vertically. For example, a monitor with a 1,920-by-1,080 resolution can display 1,920 pixels across the width of the screen, and 1,080 pixels from top to bottom. The higher the resolution, the more information can be displayed on the screen. These days, most monitors in the 22- to 27-inch range have a resolution of 1,920 by 1,080 and are referred to as Full HD monitors. There are also plenty of 24- to 27-inch displays that offer a WQHD (2,560-by-1,440) native resolution. Stepping up to a UHD (3,840-by-2,160) or 4K monitor usually means you'll need a 28-inch or larger screen, although we have seen a few 24-inch UHD models. UHD monitors are ideal for viewing highly detailed images or viewing multiple pages in a tiled or side-by-side format.

| Standard | Aspect ratio | Width (px) | Height (px) | Standard | Aspect ratio | Width (px) | Height (px) |
|---|---|---|---|---|---|---|---|
| SVGA | 4:3 | 800 | 600 | WXGA+ | 16:10 | 1440 | 900 |
| WSVGA | ~17:10 | 1024 | 600 | | | | |
| XGA | 4:3 | 1024 | 768 | HD+ | 16:9 | 1600 | 900 |
| XGA+ | 4:3 | 1152 | 864 | UXGA | 4:3 | 1600 | 1200 |
| | | | | WSXGA+ | 16:10 | 1680 | 1050 |
| WXGA | 16:9 | 1280 | 720 | FHD | 16:9 | 1920 | 1080 |
| WXGA | 5:3 | 1280 | 768 | WUXGA | 16:10 | 1920 | 1200 |
| WXGA | 16:10 | 1280 | 800 | WQHD | 16:9 | 2560 | 1440 |
| SXGA | 5:4 | 1280 | 1024 | | | | |
| HD | ~16:9 | 1360 | 768 | WQXGA | 16:10 | 2560 | 1600 |
| HD | ~16:9 | 1366 | 768 | 4K UHD | 16:9 | 3840 | 2160 |

**(3) Pixel Response Rate:** Measured in milliseconds, this is the time it takes for a pixel to change from black to white (black-to-white) or to transition from one shade of gray to another shade of gray (gray-to-gray). The faster the pixel response rate, the better the monitor is at displaying video without displaying artifacts, such as ghosting or blurring of moving images. Monitors with a fast 1-millisecond (gray-to-gray) pixel response are very good for gaming, but even monitors with a higher 6 millisecond (gray-to-gray) pixel response can display games without much blurring or ghosting. The fact is, most users won't notice lag, which is the time it takes for the display to react to a command, but hardcore gamers consider this a key factor when choosing a monitor and typically seek out the fastest models available. The fastest monitor we've seen has a lag time of 9.5 milliseconds, but you can get by with up to around 25 milliseconds before lag becomes a problem.

**(4) Price(2016):** Monitor prices depend on the type, size, and features of the display. For around $160 to $200, you can pick up a 22-inch, no-frills model, but don't expect niceties such as USB ports and a height-adjustable stand at this price. However, these panels do use LED backlighting, require very little power, and are very bright. Performance is adequate for most entertainment purposes or for viewing business and productivity apps, but not well-suited to tasks where color and gray-scale accuracy are key. At the other end of the spectrum are your high-end models that are geared toward graphic design professionals and photographers. These are 30- to 34-inch high-end panels that can display four times the resolution of a typical Full HD (1,920-by-1,080) monitor. Moreover, they offer such features as a highly adjustable stand, USB ports, and a wealth of advanced image settings, including calibration hardware and software. Expect to pay $2,000 and up for a fully loaded, high-performance 4K or Ultra-High-Definition (UHD) monitor. Bottom line: Be prepared to pay for extras, but don't overspend on features you will never use.

**(5) Extra Features:** If you have to share a monitor with a co-worker or family members, consider a model with an ergonomic stand that lets you position the screen for your most comfortable viewing angle. A fully adjustable stand offers tilt, swivel, and height adjustments, and you can rotate the panel for Portrait-mode viewing. If you transfer lots of data back and forth between USB devices, look for a monitor with built-in USB ports. Ideally, at least two of these ports will be mounted on the side of the cabinet, making it easy to plug in thumb drives and other USB peripherals. Embedded webcams are ideal for Web conferencing, but don't expect stellar image quality, as they are typically low-resolution cameras.

Most monitors come with built-in speakers that are adequate for everyday use, but usually lack the volume and bass response that music aficionados and gamers crave. If audio output is important, look for speakers with a minimum rating of 2 watts per speaker. As a general rule, the higher the power rating, the more volume you can expect, so if you want a monitor with a little extra audio pop, check the specs. A display with a built-in card reader makes it easy to view photos and play music without having to reach under your desk to plug in a media card. Finally, glossy screens can provide very bright, crisp colors, but may also be too reflective for some users. If possible, compare a glossy screen to a matte screen before you buy to decide which works best for you.

**(6) Display Trends:** In the not too distant past, most LCD monitors used Cold-Cathode Florescent Lamp (CCFL) technology for backlighting, but nowadays LED-backlit monitors are ubiquitous, and with good reason. LEDs offer a brighter image than CCFLs, they are smaller and require less power, and they allow for extremely thin cabinet designs. CCFL displays are generally less expensive than their LED counterparts, but they are few and far between these days. The next wave of monitors will feature Organic Light Emitting Diode (OLED) technology that promises ultra-high contrast ratios, true blacks, and a super-fast pixel response. Expect these displays to carry a hefty price when they first hit the market. Monitors that utilize Quantum Dot Technology are also slated to hit the market this year. Quantum Dot displays are supposed to offer superior color accuracy, increased color gamut, and a higher peak brightness than what you get with current panel technologies.

Popular panel types used in desktop displays are Twisted Nematic (TN), Vertical Alignment (VA), Patterned Vertical Alignment (PVA), Super PVA (S-PVA), Multi-Domain Vertical Alignment (MVA), and In-Plane Switching (IPS).

Up until recently, the majority of displays used TN technology, as it is the least expensive panel to manufacture, and offers superior motion-handling performance. However, affordable IPS monitors are out in force; there are plenty of 27-inch IPS models that cost around $250 and offer very good color quality and wide viewing angles. VA monitors also offer robust colors, but viewing-angle performance, while better than a typical TN panel, is not quite as sharp as what you get from an IPS panel.

To deliver full HD imagery, the panel must have a native resolution of at least 1,920 by 1,080, and it must have a 16:9 aspect ratio to do it without stretching or cropping the picture. **Graphic design professionals** who require a high degree of image detail should be looking for a WQHD or a UHD monitor.

What was once a novelty aimed at the gaming crowd, 3D technology has taken the desktop monitor market by storm, thanks to the proliferation of 3D movie and gaming content, as well as 3D-ready Blu-ray players and 3D cameras. The two major technologies used today are passive 3D, which uses inexpensive polarized glasses to create depth, and active-shutter 3D, which uses battery-operated glasses with lenses that turn on and off in sync with a 120Hz panel to deliver 3D imagery.

Each type of 3D technology has its benefits and drawbacks. Passive 3D doesn't require a 120Hz panel, and the image remains bright, but it is prone to motion artifacts and doesn't always look good from a side angle. Active 3D typically offers good side viewing and does a good job of displaying jag-free images, but it produces more crosstalk than passive technology, and the glasses are usually uncomfortable and require charging. Either way, expect to pay a bit more for a 3D-enabled monitor if you want to watch 3D movies or bring your gaming experience to the next level.

## 2.20.4 Popular Monitors

We've broken this guide down into five categories, all of which target different audiences:

1. Budget,
2. Business/Professional,
3. Multimedia,
4. Touch-Screen, and
5. Gaming.

We will discuss second and third out of above.

### (a) Business/Professional

This category includes a wide variety of monitor types, from small screen energy-conscious "green" models for everyday office use, to high-end, high-priced, 32-inch-andup professional-grade models that uses Indium Gallium Zinc Oxide (IGZO) or Advanced Hi-performance In-Plane Switching (AH-IPS) panel technology and cater to graphics professionals who require a high degree of color and gray-scale accuracy. Business monitors usually offer ergonomic stands that can be adjusted for maximum comfort. Very often, they will offer pivot adjustability, which lets you rotate the screen

90 degrees for viewing in Portrait mode. Look for a monitor that has an auto-rotate feature that flips the image automatically when you change the orientation. Other business-centric features include a generous (three-year) warranty with an overnight exchange service, built-in USB ports, and an aggressive recycling program.

A fully loaded model with a high-end panel is going to cost plenty, but for photographers and other graphics pros, it is money well spent. At the other end of the price spectrum are the no-frills, energy-efficient monitors; they don't offer much in the way of features, but their low power characteristics can help businesses save money through reduced energy costs.

**Multimedia:** Multimedia displays are popular because they typically offer a nice selection of features to help you create home photo and video projects, offer decent performance, and in some cases, include digital TV tuners. A good multimedia panel will usually provide a variety of connectivity options, such as HDMI, DVI, and VGA inputs, while the more robust entertainment-class models will also include component video and audio connections and a DisplayPort connection. At least two USB ports should be available, preferably mounted on the side or front of the cabinet for easy access, and the speakers should be a cut above the typical low-powered versions found on most monitors. If audio output is a deciding factor, look for displays with speakers rated at 2 watts or better. Other multimedia bells and whistles include a built-in multicard reader, which makes it easy to view photos and video directly from your camera's media, and a webcam for video chats and for taking quick stills and videos that are easy to email. (If you're a serious photographer, check out our picks for **photography-friendly displays**.)

Hybrid displays are multifunction devices that pull double-duty as a desktop monitor and a TV set. You'll pay a bit more for the TV tuner, but these displays are ideal for dorm rooms, studio apartments, RVs, and other environment where space is an issue. Again, expect to pay a premium for a 3D-capable multimedia model.

### 2.20.5 Top Screens Manufacturers

Below is the list of some top most screen manufacturers worldwide.

1. Acer
2. Asus
3. Dell
4. BenQ
5. ViewSonic
6. Phillips
7. AOC
8. Samsung

## 2.21 MULTIMEDIA PROJECTORS

Ideal for delivering lectures and presentations to large groups, as well as watching movies and other videos, projectors can be found in a variety of environments. Projectors are commonly used in classrooms, corporate meetings, houses of worship, concerts, movie and home theaters. It is helpful to have an understanding of the different types of projectors, their intended uses and the type of lens needed to determine what type of projector is best for a given situation.

**Fig. 2.30:** DLP projector

Today's projectors are based on one of four imaging technologies:

1. DLP,
2. LED Based DLP
3. LCD,
4. LCOS, and
5. Laser Raster.

Laser Raster projectors, actually draw the images using lasers, with models that simply use lasers as a light source for another imaging technology, like a DLP or LCOS chip.)

The technology used in projectors can generally be broken down into two types: transmissive or reflective. Because LCD projectors pass light through the LCD panels rather than bouncing it away, they are considered a transmissive medium. A DLP projector uses mirrors to direct the light in an image, so it is considered to be "reflective." The third typé of projector discussed, an LED projector, is named for the light source, not the type of projection technology.

Most inexpensive DLP projector and some LCOS-based pico projectors, including both data and video models, project their primary colours sequentially, rather than all at once. This can lead to a rainbow effect, with light areas on screen breaking up into little rainbows for some people when they shift their gaze or something moves on screen. Those who are sensitive to this effect can find it annoying, particularly for long sessions.

LCD projectors don't have this problem, but tend to be bigger and heavier. The general consensus is that standard-size LCOS projectors offer the best-quality images, but they tend to be bigger and heavier than DLP or LCD projectors, and far more expensive. There aren't yet many laser raster projectors, so it's hard to make general statements about them. However, the one clear advantage of using a laser is that the image doesn't require focusing.

## 2.21.1 Digital Light Processing (DLP)

DLP is a display device based on optical micro-electro-mechanical technology that uses a digital micromirror device. It was originally developed in 1987 by Dr. Larry Hornbeck of Texas Instruments. While the DLP imaging device was invented by Texas Instruments, the first DLP-based projector was introduced by Digital Projection Ltd in 1997.

DLP is used in a variety of display applications from traditional static displays to interactive displays and also non-traditional embedded applications including medical, security, and industrial uses.

DLP technology is used in DLP front projectors (standalone projection units for classrooms and business primarily), DLP rear projection television sets, and digital signs. It is also used in about 85% of digital cinema projection, and in additive manufacturing as a power source in some printers to cure resins into solid 3D objects.

Smaller "pico" chipsets are used in mobile devices including cell phone accessories and projection display functions embedded directly into phones.

### Advantages and Disadvantages to DLP Projectors

DLP projectors require less maintenance than LCD projectors because they have a filter-free and sealed chip design, which means dust can't settle on the chip and cause an image spot. They are effectively immune to color decay. Furthermore, they are not subject to the misalignments that can occur in LCD projectors with a three-panel design, which require each panel to be in perfect position to combine the image at the proper angle. However, DLP projectors with slower color wheels may give off a rainbow effect; flashes of color that appear on the screen, like rainbows.

Furthermore, while the chip is sealed, other components are not, so dust can settle on the color wheel and affect image quality. Another disadvantage may be the poor viewing range. Most DLP projectors are not readily compatible with zoom lenses or lens shift functions, which means they are best suited to smaller environments.

### 2.21.2 LED Projectors

As previously stated, LED projectors are defined not by the display technology used, but the lighting. In fact, some DLP projectors with "solid-state illumination" technology are actually LED projectors. Another type of projector, the pico projector, commonly uses LED technology as well. Pico projectors are essentially handheld devices that use LCoS (Liquid Crystal on Silicon, which is similar to an LCD panel but reflective rather than transmissive) or DLP technology. In these cases, the projector replaces the traditional lamp with longer-lasting and more efficient LEDs, colored in red, green, and blue. In DLP projectors, this also replaces the color wheel technology, instead letting the red, blue, and green LEDs shine directly on the DMD chip.

**The Advantages and Disadvantages to LED Projectors**

The LEDs in an LED projector have a much longer life than traditional projector lamps, rated at 10,000 or even 20,000 hours as opposed to 1,000 hours to 5,000 hours. As such, the LED light source is meant to last the entire life of the projector without ever needing to be replaced. This is a big advantage because replacing traditional lamps can be a major expense in projector maintenance. There is no warm-up or cool-down time needed because the LEDs are much more energy efficient than traditional light sources, and they are also much quieter. This reduces maintenance and operating costs.

### 2.21.3 LED-based DLPs

The first commercially available LED-based DLP HDTV was the Samsung HL-S5679W in 2006, which also eliminated the use of a color wheel. Besides long lifetime eliminating the need for lamp replacement and elimination of the color wheel, other advantages of LED illumination include instant-on operation and improved color, with increased color saturation and improved color gamut to over 140% of the NTSC color gamut. Samsung expanded the LED model line-up in 2007 with products available in 50-, 56- and 61-inch screen sizes. In 2008, the third generation of Samsung LED DLP products were available in 61" and 67" screen sizes.

Ordinary LED technology does not produce the intensity and high lumen output characteristics required to replace arc lamps. The special patented LEDs used in all of the Samsung DLP TVs are PhlatLight LEDs, designed and manufactured by US-based Luminus Devices.

### 2.21.4 LCoS

LCoS (Liquid Crystal on Silicone) is also called SXRD (Silicon X-tal Reflective Display) on Sony products and D-ILA (Digital Direct Drive Image Light Amplifier) on JVC projection TVs. It is a reflective technology like three-chip DLP, but in this case, the light is reflected from three silicone-backed LCD panels rather than micro-mirror arrays. This system currently claims to produce the least screen-door effect and, because it is LCD, is free from the "rainbow effect" and other colour-wheel-related artifacts associated with single-chip DLP. It is used in multimedia projectors targeting critical viewing applications and some high-end home theatre projectors.

### 2.21.5 Factors to Consider when Buying LED, LCD, and DLP Projectors

When buying a projector, consumers should weigh the advantages of each type of device. The differences between the projectors can be summarized in the following chart:

| Projector Type | | Technology Type | Light Source |
|---|---|---|---|
| 1. | DLP | Reflective | LED or standard lamp |
| 2. | LCD | Transmissive | Standard lamp |
| 3. | LED | Transmissive or reflective | LED |

Beyond the technology used, however, there are other significant differences. LCD projectors are typically less expensive for smaller venues, such as home theaters. They also give the user the advantage of a longer throw distance and greater zoom capability, both of which are lacking in many DLP projectors. This makes LCD projectors ideal for larger environments. However, DLP projectors do not suffer the color decay that LCD projectors do and they are easier to maintain because of their filter-free design.

DLP projectors with LED technology are even simpler because the lamp will not need to be replaced, saving time and money for users. Pico projectors that use LED technology have the same long life, but are designed to be ultra-portable, connecting to smart phones, tablets, and other mobile devices. As such, they do not offer the same high levels of brightness found in larger projectors. They typically have a brightness of less than 200 ANSI lumens, whereas larger projectors can have a brightness of 1000 ANSI lumens, up to 4500 ANSI lumens or more.

Data projectors will most likely do well with data images, like PowerPoint presentations, spreadsheets, and PDF files, while home theatre projectors are best at handling full-motion video well. Any projector that handles video well should also do a good job with photos, since photos have a lot in common with video, but without the added complication of movement, which opens the door to additional image artifacts.

### 2.21.6 Application type Multimedia Projectors

Technically, multimedia projectors range from the smallest pico projectors to the heftiest 100 lbs.+ large venue projectors. Therefore, to put it simply, basically every projector is a multimedia projector nowadays.

Home theatre projectors,

1. Business projectors,
2. Education projectors,
3. Portable projectors,
4. D projectors and
5. Pico projectors

Multimedia projectors are general purpose, and are used for everything from giving PowerPoint presentations to screening video clips and slideshows at weddings. They are typically considered portable, weighing from 3 pounds for the ultra-slim models and going up from there, and their brightness ranges from 2,500 to 4,500 lumens or so. Apart from the special sub-category of short-throw, they virtually always have zoom lenses. However, the zoom range is usually shorter than that of their home theater counterparts: 1.2x to 1.5x (compared to 2x in the home-theater realm). This means special care needs to be taken when choosing, to make sure the screen size is compatible with the projector's throw ratio. Multimedia projectors virtually always have VGA and composite video inputs, and most models now feature HDMI as well. In some cases, a DVI-D port will be provided instead of HDMI, but an HDMI device can still be connected using an inexpensive adapter. Similarly, DVI devices can be connected to a projector with only HDMI using a DVI to HDMI cable or adapter.

### 2.21.7 Throw Ratio

Projectors have a very important specification called "throw ratio". Throw ratio is a specification that is determined by the first two pieces of information in the equation:

1. How far the projector is from the screen (throw distance)
2. How wide the screen is

For example, if your screen is 3 meters (10 feet) wide and the projector is 4.5 meters (15 feet) away, you will need a lens that covers a throw ratio of 1.5:1.

The first step in choosing a projector, therefore, is pinning down how wide the screen is and how far it can be placed from the screen—once you've done this, your choices will narrow considerably. Of course, you may have flexibility. Maybe your space allows you to mount the projector anywhere you want on the ceiling. In this case, while you might technically be able to choose any projector you want, you should consider mounting the projector as close to the screen as you comfortably can. Light is subject to the Inverse Square Law, meaning brightness drops logarithmically with increased distance, so the closer you can mount it, the fewer lumens you will need. At the other extreme is a case where you have an existing mount installed on the ceiling that you want to reuse. In this case, you will need to find a projector that features the exact throw ratio dictated by the position of the mount relative to the width of the screen.

### 2.21.8 Resolution

Ideally, you should match the projector's native resolution (the number of physical pixels in the projector's display) to the resolution you expect to use most often, whether you're planning on connecting to a computer, video equipment, game box, or some combination of the three. Projectors can scale images up or down to their native resolutions, but they lose image quality in the process.

If you plan to show data images, you should also consider how detailed the images will be. For a typical PowerPoint presentation, SVGA (800 by 600) is easily good enough, and getting an SVGA projector will save money compared with getting one with a higher resolution. The more detailed the images, however, the higher resolution you'll want.

For video, 1080p resolution is the best choice, assuming you have a Blu-ray player, upscaling DVD player, or other 1080p device. If there's any chance you'll be watching video at lower resolutions, check out how well the projector handles those resolutions too. We are starting to see 4K projectors, with horizontal resolutions on the order of 4,000 pixels, but they're still very expensive, and as yet little content is available that can take advantage of their ultra-high resolution.

### 2.21.9 Brightness of the Projector

Brightness of the projector is rated in lumens. The higher the lumen value, the higher the potential brightness of the image. Projector usage and surroundings determine the type and brightness of projector needed. When used in a small room projecting on a small screen, an LCD or one-chip DLP projector with a lumen rating of 1,500 to 3,000 may be used with appealing results. In large venues using larger screens or when ambient light may affect the image, a three-chip DLP projector with a lumen rating of 10,000 to 28,000 should be used.

There is no single best level for brightness, and brighter isn't always better. For a home-theater projector you plan to use in a dark room, for example, 1,000 to 1,200 lumens can easily give you a large, bright image, while2,000 lumens may be so bright that it's hard on the eyes. On the other hand, for a portable data projector you expect to use in well-lit locations, 2,000 to 3,000 lumens is the right range. For large rooms, you may want something even brighter.

The best level of brightness depends on the amount of ambient light, the size of the image, and even the material in the screen you're using. If you're setting up a projector for permanent installation, whether at home or in your office, your best bet is to buy from a knowledgeable source that can help you match brightness to the lighting conditions and screen in the room.

If you're trying to choose between two models, keep in mind that small percentage difference in lumens—2,000 versus 2,200 for example—isn't terribly significant. Perception of brightness is nonlinear, which means you need far more than twice as many lumens for a projector to appear twice as bright. Also, a projector's true brightness tends to be a little less than its rated brightness.

### 2.21.10 VGA or HDMI Port

Multimedia projectors often have one or more USB ports, though figuring out what the USB port does isn't always easy. Possible USB functions include:

1. A video interface—as an alternative to using VGA or HDMI
2. Plugging in a presentation mouse
3. A port for a USB flash drive for giving "PC-less" presentations
4. Connector, for an optional Wi-Fi dongle
5. Remote controlling the projector from a computer
6. Multimedia Projector Brands: Sony, Panasonic, Epson, Sharp, Canon, Optoma, Mitsubishi, and InFocus.

Most projectors offer at a minimum a VGA (analog) connector for a computer and a composite video connector for video equipment. If your computer has a digital, you may also want a digital connection on the projector, because it will eliminate any chance of problems, such as jittering pixels caused by poor signal synchronization. For video sources, the preferred connection choice is HDMI (assuming your video equipment has HDMI connectors), with component video a close second. Some projectors are now adding Mobile High-Definition Link (MHL)-enabled HDMI ports, which let you project from Android devices, and in some cases, charge them as well. Many models offer Wi-Fi connectivity through a (usually optional) wireless dongle that fits in a USB port that also supports projecting from a thumb drive.

## 2.22 PLOTTERS

This is the most common class of output equipment used for graphics applications, particularly for drafting systems. There are two basic types of plotters.

**(a) Pen plotters**

The pen plotter an outgrowth of NC technology uses stepping motors to control the motion of the pen relative to the drawing board, it traces the image as an outline drawing stored in the computer. Because of this, pen plotter cannot handle a lot of intricate detail or solid-color areas efficiently. Although they are also relatively slow, they can be inexpensive and can be equipped to use multiple pens for color plotting. Pen plotters are most often used in a "flatbed" form to plot horizontally on single sheets for paper (or another drawing material),just like a drafting board. The drum or "beltbed"-type plotter can also handle continuous feeding of paper.

**(b) Electrostatic plotters**

These are faster and can handle more intricate designs. An electrostatic charge is used to produce an image on paper, and then a tonger is applied to th paper to create the printed image. This is accomplished either by using a matrix of needles to "write" the electrostatic image or by using a photo-conductor which is written on by a light from a CRT or laser, asin copying machines.

## 2.23 ANALOG MEDIA DEVICES

These devices deal with analog media, but may be under computer control finally. Divided into 3 sub categories:

1. Sources
2. Filters
3. Sinks
4. Interaction Devices

This category includes a variety of devices that can be used to measure, point to, or code coordinate positions by converting analog signals (*e.g.*, speed, direction, distance, rotation) to digital signals. They are often used to trace drawings so that the designs can be entered into th graphics systems. There are two basic approaches to analog input device.

**Flat-surface devices**

There are digitizer tablets that trace drawings. They can use a number a difference techniques, such as electromagnetic, touch sensitive, sonic,incremental, and light detector techniques. Each differs is speed, accuracy, and cost. The electromagnetic digitizer is the most common and precise.

**Positioning tools**

These are devices that the operator can move, which in turn signal the cursor on the screen to move in the same direction and speed. They include the mouse, joystick, trackball. Their principal advantages are ease of use and speed.

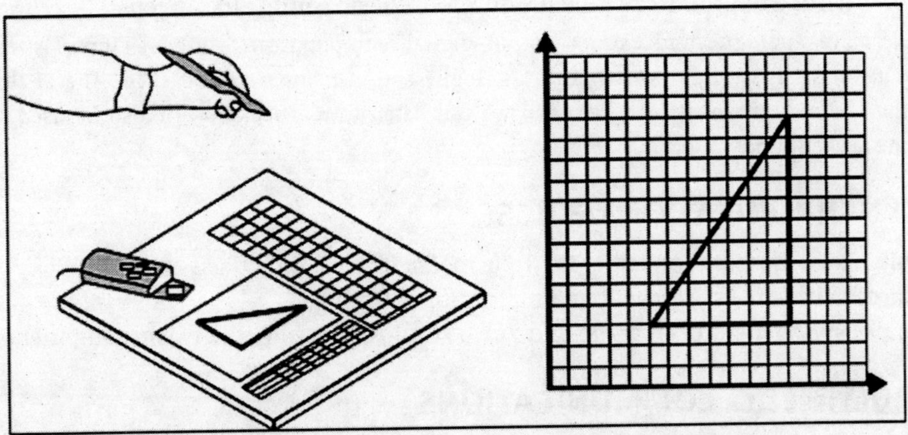

**Fig. 2.31:** Graphics System with Positioning Input Devices

(1) Sources (Analog Input)

1. Microphone
2. Video Camera
3. Photographic Camera

Multimedia application means ability to interact within the application itself

- Interaction devices enable user direct control over the multimedia application behavior
- Examples: keyboard, mouse, joystick, electronic pen

(2) Filters (Analog Processing)

1. Analog Video Effects Device
2. Analog Audio Effects Device
3. Audio Mixer

(3) Sinks (Analog Output/Storing)

1. Multimedia Speaker
2. Video Display
3. Video Tape Recorder
4. Audio Tape Recorder

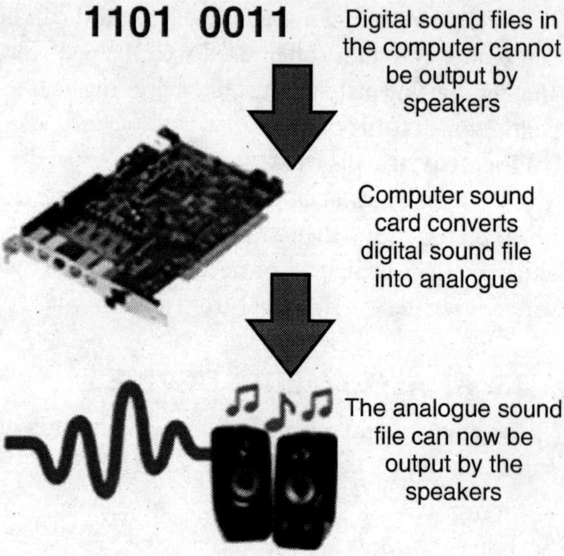

1101 0011

Digital sound files in the computer cannot be output by speakers

Computer sound card converts digital sound file into analogue

The analogue sound file can now be output by the speakers

**Fig. 2.32:** Multimedia Speaker System

- Many everyday uses of a computer require the user to listen to different types of sounds. For example:
  - Listening to a music album
  - Watching a movie.
  - Browsing videos on YouTube
  - Multimedia encyclopedias.

In order for the computer to output these sounds it requires some sort of **speaker system**! Speakers can be connected directly to a computer or are built into the monitor or casting.

**Note:** Most computers have small **built in speakers** to alert users when they do something wrong but these can only produce very **basic sounds** like **'beeps'**.

- Speakers are **analogue** and cannot output digital 'computerised' sounds. **Digital data** from the computer must first be **converted into analogue** sound using a **sound card**. The analogue sound can then be output via the speakers and we can listen to it. Speakers can also be used to **alter the volume** of the sounds.

## 2.24 SYNCHRONIZATION DEVICES

- Simultaneous presentation using multiple media (text, audio, video etc).
- Requires hardware assistance to maintain proper timing.
- Example: sync generator in audio and video studios, Macromedia Flash, computer games etc.

## 2.25 MULTIMEDIA COMMUNICATIONS

The key issue for multimedia communications is bandwidth; that is the amount of information that can be transmitted across a network of computers within a fixed period of time. Bandwidth is often measured in kilobits per second (Kbps) or megabits per second (Mbps) that can be carried by a network. Multimedia data file sizes, especially for graphics, audio, and video, can be quite large. Communication speeds for real-time presentation of audio and video in a computer network must be as fast as that for direct disk access within a single computer. Primary communications devices and functions include:

1. **Modems:** Analog modems to 28,800 bits per second (bps), digital modems (ISDN-Integrated Services Digital Network ) to 64,000 bps.
2. **Networks**: up to 10 megabits per second (mbps) including shared bandwidth systems (multiple users share total bandwidth to 10mbps).
3. **Digital Audio**: Audio files are downloaded or streaming audio systems for real-time communications; quality good for voice with insufficient bandwidth for higher quality music.
4. **Digital Video**: Similar to audio; video files are downloaded or steaming video for near real-time presentation; quality limited to very low frame rates.

Remote application sharing: multiple users sharing a single application across a network.

Communications systems have created two classes of multimedia products: ***synchronous*** or ***real time*** and ***asynchronous***. Synchronous applications are able to transmit and receive data in real-time allowing the end user to view or hear data as it is being captured or created Asynchronous applications use a store and forward method in which data is transmitted and stored for future presentation.

Let us consider two user scenario for connectivity based on communication services:

1. Office-based with network up to 100 mbps, typically1 to 10 mbps
2. Home users with modem 14,400 to 28,800 bps

The communications bandwidth for each scenario depends on Network - configuration of the network, number of machines on the network, and amount of activity

## 2.26 NETWORKED MULTIMEDIA

Networked multimedia applications are rapidly being deployed in campus LAN and WAN environments. From the corporate perspective, network multimedia applications, such as network TV or videoconferencing, hold tremendous promise as the next generation of productivity tools. The use of digital audio and video across corporate network infrastructures has tremendous potential for internal and external applications. The World Wide Web is a good example of network multimedia and its manifold capabilities.

It is not uncommon for computers to run video editing or image processing applications (such as Adobe Premiere and Photoshop) in addition to basic "productivity" applications (word processing, spreadsheet, and database applications).

The proliferation of multimedia-enabled desktop machines has spawned a new class of multimedia applications that operate in network environments. These network multimedia applications leverage the existing network infrastructure to deliver video and audio applications to end users, such as videoconferencing and video server applications. With these application types, video and audio streams are transferred over the network between peers or between clients and servers.

To successfully deliver multimedia over a network, it is important to understand both multimedia and networking. Three components must be considered when deploying network multimedia applications in campus LAN and WAN environments:

Bandwidth-How much bandwidth do the network multimedia applications demand and how much bandwidth can the network infrastructure provide?

Quality of service-What level of service does the network multimedia application require and how can this be satisfied through the network?

Multicasting-Does the network multimedia application utilize bandwidth-saving multicasting techniques and how can multicasting be supported across the network?

## 2.27 MODEMS

It's a device that can be plugged into your computer to let you communicate with other computers over telephone lines. With a modem, you and your computer can connect with all the cool stuff happening on the Internet today. There are modems all around you -in shops, in petrol stations, and banks.

A modem (modulator-demodulator) is a network hardware device that modulates one or more carrier wave signals to encode digital information for transmission and demodulates signals to decode the transmitted information. The goal is to produce a signal that can be transmitted easily and decoded to reproduce the original digital data. Modems can be used with any means of transmitting analog signals, from light emitting diodes to radio. A common type of modem is one that turns the digital data of a computer into modulated electrical signal for transmission over telephone lines and demodulated by another modem at the receiver side to recover the digital data.

A modem takes the digital information that your computer generates and turns it into analog information (up and down, constantly varying sound waves) that can travel along the telephone network to another computer somewhere else and Vice versa. At that other location, there is another modem that converts the incoming analog information back into digital data that the other computer can understand. Two computers can have a lengthy conversation over the phone, just like two people chatting away, providing there is a modem at each end of the line to translate the digital information they generate into analog signals that can travel back and forth along the telephone line. (Incidentally, if you're uncertain about the difference between analog and digital, we have a simple article about analog versus digital technology.)

Most modems can also send and receive faxes directly from your computer to a fax machine or another computer. With the right software and modem, your computer can act as a telephone answering machine.

There are two types of modems.

1. An internal modem installs like a sound card or video card, inside your PC.
2. An external modem plugs in like a mouse or keyboard, into a "serial port".

To access the Internet through a cable Internet connection, you must obtain or purchase a cable modem. The modem facilitates the transferring of all data, including streaming video and audio, from the Internet. Internet service providers are typically the source from which most Internet subscribers obtain a modem, but you can also purchase your own from most electronics retailers. In addition to a cable modem, you must also have an Internet-ready computing or electronics device, such as a computer or Internet-ready TV, to watch and listen to streaming content.

Modems are also generally classified by the amount of data they can send in a given unit of time, usually expressed in bits per second (symbol bit/s, sometimes abbreviated "bps"), or bytes per second (symbol B/s).

Modems can also be classified by their symbol rate, measured in baud. The baud unit denotes symbols per second, or the number of times per second the modem sends a new signal. For example, the ITU V.21 standard used audio frequency shift keying with two possible frequencies, corresponding to two distinct symbols (or one bit per symbol), to carry 300 bits per second using 300 baud.

**Fig. 2.33:** Information flow through telephone lines upto computer via Ethernet connection or through wireless router

## 2.28 WIRELESS ROUTER

A wireless router is a device that performs the functions of a router and also includes the functions of a wireless access point. It is used to provide access to the Internet or a private computer network. It can function in a wired LAN (local area network), in a wireless-only LAN (WLAN), or in a mixed wired/wireless network, depending on the manufacturer and model.

**Fig. 2.34:** 802.11ac Router

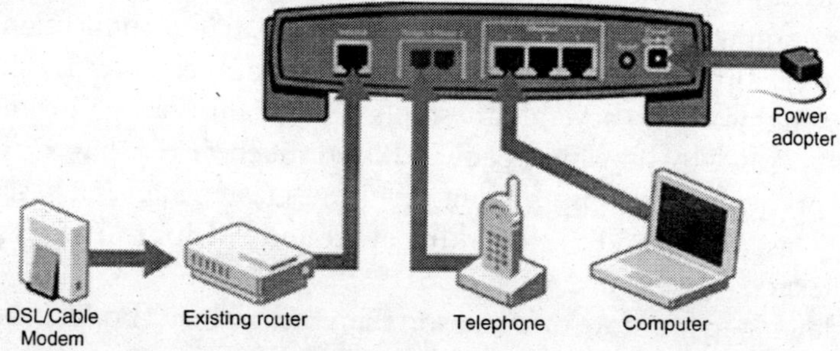


**Fig. 2.35:** Quick installation with existing router or combination of modem and Router

### 2.28.1 Speed of the Modem and Line Noise

In all cases bandwidth is also dependent on point-to-point connectivity. Generally:

The slowest communications links in the network will bring overall speed down. High number of users will slow down access.

Amount of traffic (file sizes) can slow down network.

Table 2.4 provides sample content sizes and associated transmission. Note that the speeds listed here are under ideal conditions (actual performance may be 2 to 5 times less).

**TABLE 2.5:** Sample content sizes and associated transmission

| Type | Typical Sample | Assumes ideal conditions |
|---|---|---|
| Data | At 28,800 bits per second (3600 bytes/second) | |
| Text | Page of text (100 characters/line, 30 lines) | <1 second =3000 bytes |
| Pictures | Full screen (640 *480 pixels), 256 color bitmap | 91 seconds |
| | Compressed graphic format =75,000 to 20,000 | Compressed file, |
| | bytes (depends on type, detail, colors) | 20 to 55 seconds |
| Audio | Voice, one minute = 600,000 bytes (at 11 Khz sampling, monaural ) | Voice, 166 seconds (nearly 3 minutes) |
| | Music, one minute = 10.5 gigabytes (at 44 Khz sampling, stereo) | Music, #000 seconds (50 minutes) |
| Video | One minute, uncompressed = 414 megabytes (image size of 320 x 240 pixels, 24-bit colour, 30 frames per second) | Uncompressed, 115,000 seconds (1.9 hours) |
| | One minute, compressed = 10-15 megabytes (image size of 320 * 240 pixels, 24-bit color, 30 frames per second and depending on compression scheme) | Compressed, 2777 seconds (46 minutes) |

## 2.29 BROADBAND CONNECTION

Broadband works a completely different way. Instead of treating your phone line as a single, narrow pipe between your computer and the ISP's computer, like a dialup connection, it divides the line into many different channels. Information can travel in parallel streams down these channels. It's like dividing a highway into several lanes: lots more traffic can go down it in parallel than down a single-lane road. This is why broadband is so much faster than dialup. Even a slowish broadband line, working at 512Kbps, is about nine times faster than the best dialup connection, while a moderately fast broadband line, working at around 8MBps (megabits per second), can be over 100 times quicker!

Most people download far more information than they upload (browsing web pages is almost exclusively downloading—because most of the data is flowing into your computer from the Net), so broadband allocates more channels to downloading than to uploading. This is why broadband computers download several times faster than they upload. In other words, downloading and uploading are not equivalent or "symmetrical" processes: they are asymmetric. That's why the technical name for this type of broadband is Asymmetric Digital Subscriber Line or **ADSL**. Another type of broadband called **DSL** allows uploading and downloading at the same speed.

If most people are just downloading, why doesn't broadband Internet scrap the uploading channels altogether and make browsing even faster? Any type of web browsing involves a certain amount of two-way traffic between your computer (which is called a client) and the remote computers (servers) that host the pages you're looking at. Even though most of the data is flowing *into* your computer, a certain amount still has to flow in the opposite direction each time your computer requests a new page. In other words, even when all you're apparently doing is downloading, there's some uploading going on in the background to make that happen.

### 2.29.1 Types of Broadband Connections

Broadband includes several high-speed transmission technologies such as:

1. Digital Subscriber Line (DSL)
2. Cable Modem
3. Fiber
4. Wireless
5. Satellite
6. Broadband over Powerlines (BPL)

The broadband technology you choose will depend on a number of factors. These may include whether you are located in an urban or rural area, how broadband Internet access is packaged with other services (such as voice telephone and home entertainment), price, and availability.

**(1) Digital Subscriber Line (DSL)**

DSL is a wireline transmission technology that transmits data faster over traditional copper telephone lines already installed to homes and businesses. DSL-based broadband provides transmission speeds ranging from several hundred Kbps to millions of bits per second (Mbps). The availability and speed of your DSL service may depend on the distance from your home or business to the closest telephone company facility.

The following are types of DSL transmission technologies:

1. **Asymmetrical Digital Subscriber Line (ADSL)** – Used primarily by residential customers, such as Internet surfers, who receive a lot of data but do not send much. ADSL typically provides faster speed in the downstream direction than the upstream direction. ADSL allows faster downstream data transmission over the same line used to provide voice service, without disrupting regular telephone calls on that line.
2. **Symmetrical Digital Subscriber Line (SDSL)** – Used typically by businesses for services such as video conferencing, which need significant bandwidth both upstream and downstream.

   Faster forms of DSL typically available to businesses include:

   a) High data rate Digital Subscriber Line (HDSL); and

   b) Very High data rate Digital Subscriber Line (VDSL).

**(2) Wireless**

Wireless Local Area Networks (WLANs) provide wireless broadband access over shorter distances and are often used to extend the reach of a "last-mile" wireline or fixed wireless broadband connection within a home, building, or campus environment. Wi-Fi networks use unlicensed devices and can be designed for private access within a home or business, or be used for public Internet access at "hot spots" such as restaurants, coffee shops, hotels, airports, convention centers, and city parks.

Mobile wireless broadband services are also becoming available from mobile telephone service providers and others. These services are generally appropriate for highly-mobile customers and require a special PC card with a built in antenna that plugs into a user's laptop computer. Generally, they provide lower speeds, in the range of several hundred Kbps.

Wireless broadband connects a home or business to the Internet using a radio link between the customer's location and the service provider's facility. Wireless broadband can be mobile or fixed.

Wireless technologies using longer-range directional equipment provide broadband service in remote or sparsely populated areas where DSL or cable modem service would be costly to provide. Speeds are generally comparable to DSL and cable modem. An external antenna is usually required.

Wireless broadband Internet access services offered over fixed networks allow consumers to access the Internet from a fixed point while stationary and often require a direct line-of-sight between the wireless transmitter and receiver. These services have been offered using both licensed spectrum and unlicensed devices. For example, thousands of small Wireless Internet Services Providers (WISPs) provide such wireless broadband at speeds of around one Mbps using unlicensed devices, often in rural areas not served by cable or wireline broadband networks.

**(3) Difference Between Modem and Router**

From a physical perspective, a modem, router, and switch all look very similar. However, there are key differences between them internally, and each are used for different purposes on a network.

**(4) Modem**

A modem is provided by the Internet Service Provider (ISP) and provides a network access to the internet. Some ISPs, such as Verizon's FIOS service instead use an ONT which provides many of the same capabilities. In order to use more than one device with a modem or ONT, a router is generally required in addition to the modem.

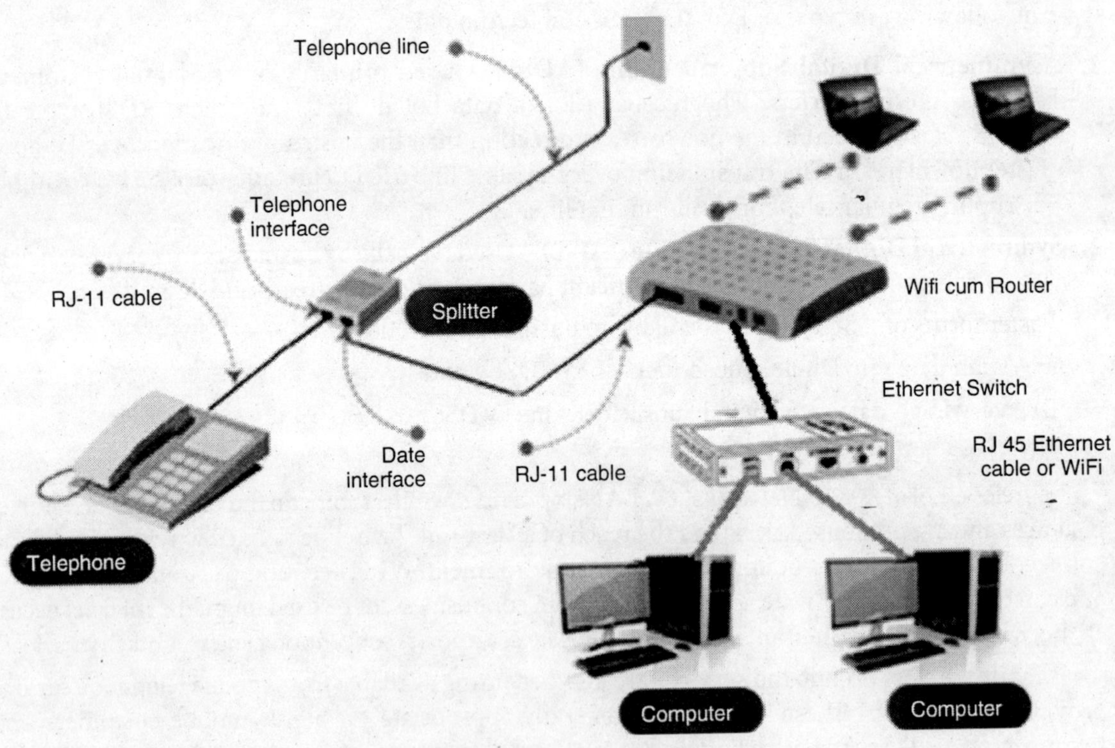


A. Connect phone line from the socket to ADSL Splitter line port
B. Connect the phone cord of your phone instrument to splitter at phone-interface.
C. Connect ADSL modem/router to splitter at date/moden interface with RJ-11 cord supplied.
D. Connect PC to ADSL modem/router with Ethernet cable
E. Power-up modem through power adsptor connectivity to power point.

**Fig. 2.36:** Functions of Router

Note: In some rare cases ISPs provide "hybrid" modem/routers to their customers. It is recommended to request a standalone modem whenever possible to increase the available resources on the network. Please verify with your ISP that this can be done on your network prior to purchasing a standalone router.

**(5) Router**

A router (such as the My Net N900) is the "traffic director" of a network. It takes information provided by the modem or ONT and routes it to the various devices that are connected, and creates internal IP address for the devices so they can be accessed (this is done using a built in DHCP Server). Devices (such as computers, WD TVs, game consoles, digital picture frames, etc.) can be connected to a router in one of two ways- wired directly to the router (or an attached switch) or wirelessly. A second router can also be connected in order to be used as a Access Point, similar to how a switch would be used. Routers also provide advanced functionality including (in most cases) a built in firewall to help protect the network from unwanted traffic (hackers, some viruses, etc.).

**(6) Switch**

A switch is used to provide additional ports, expanding the capability of the router. A switch will not provide routing capability and should not be connected directly to the modem. In slow speed connections hub can be used but it is not as intelligent.

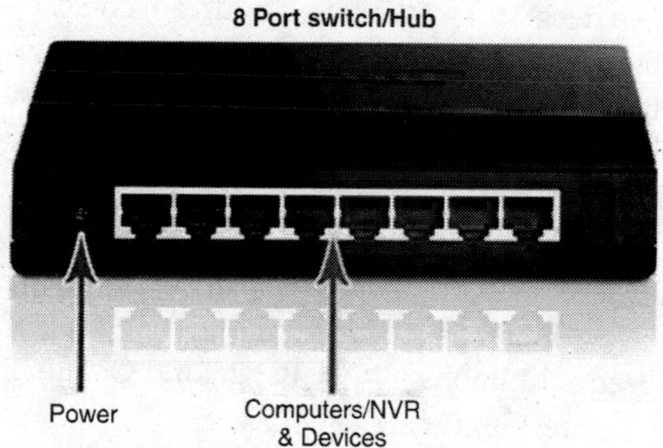


**Fig. 2.37:** 8 Port switch

## 2.30 BROADCAST STANDARDS

The principal standards for analog broadcast transmission are as follows:

1. **National Television Standards Committee (NTSC)**-The broadcast standard in Canada, Japan, the United States, and Central America. NTSC defines 525 vertical scan lines per frame and yields 30 frames per second. The scan lines refer to the number of lines from top to bottom on the television screen. The frames per second refer to the number of complete images that are displayed per second.
2. **Phase Alternation Line (PAL)**-The broadcast standard in Europe and in the Middle East, Africa, and South America. PAL defines 625 vertical scan lines and refreshes the screen 25 times per second.
3. **Système Electronique pour Couleur Avec Mémoire (SECAM)**-The broadcast standard in France, Russia, and regions of Africa. SECAM is a variant of PAL but it delivers the same number of vertical scan lines as PAL and uses the same refresh rate.

To produce an image on a television screen, an electron gun scans across the television screen from left to right moving from top to bottom, as shown in Figure 2.37. Television scan gun operation.

Mbps, the metric used to measure bandwidth, stands for Megabits per second, not megabytes per second (MBps). When it comes to data rates, 1byte = 8bit.

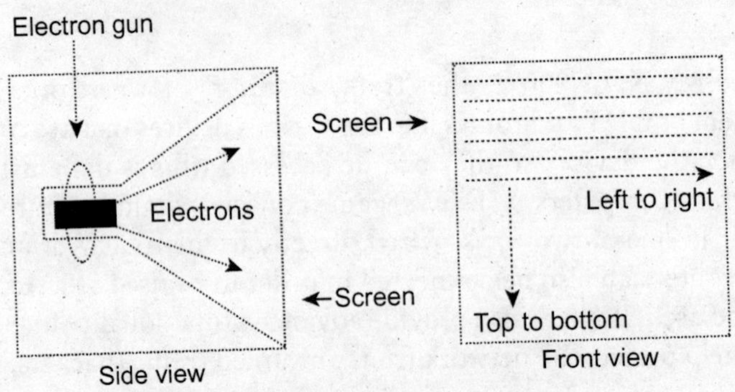


Fig 2.38: Television scan gun operation.

## 2.31 NETWORK SPEED REQUIREMENTS

Streaming with a cable modem refers to a method used to stream content -- usually in the form of video and audio content — from the Internet to a computing or electronics device. Cable modems are used in conjunction with cable Internet connections, which offer faster rates than those offered by DSL connections.

The following is the in exhaustive list of Broadband Suppliers in India showing the broadband speed and area covered.

1. Hayai Top Speeds: 1Gbps Cities: Mumbai
2. Hathway, Top Speeds: 50mbps Cities: Mumbai, Delhi, Hyderabad, Bengaluru, Surat, Pune, Goa, Vishakapatnam, Navi Mumbai
3. ACT Fibernet Top Speeds: 125mbps Cities: Bangalore, Chennai, Vijaywada, Nellore, Eluru, Vishakapatnam, Coimbatore, Guntur
4. YOU Broadband, Top Speeds: 100mbps, Cities: Ahmedabad, Bengaluru, Chennai, Gurgaon, Hyderabad, Kakinada, Mumbai, Navi Mumbai, Navsari, Powai, Pune, Surat, Thane, Vadodara, Vishakapatnam.
5. Den Boomband, Top Speeds: 100mbps, Cities: New Delhi, Kanpur, Jodhpur, Gurgaon
6. Spectranet, Top Speeds: 100mbps, Cities: Bengaluru, Chennai, Delhi, Ghaziabad, Gurgaon, Mumbai, Noida, Pune
7. Asianet, Top Speeds: 100mbps, Cities: Trivandrum, Salem, Coimbatore, Kottayam, Palakkad, Cochin, Calicut, Thrissur, Alleppey, and more.
8. Jetspot Fiber, Top Speeds: 60mbps, Cities: Bhubhaneshwar
9. Airtel, Top Speeds: 100mbps, Cities: Mumbai, Delhi NCR, Bengaluru
10. Tikona Broadband Plans
11. Reliance Broadband
12. BSNL Broadband

The table below shows the amount to be paid (in May 2016) for some service providers.

**WHAT YOU'RE REALLY PAYING**

| INTERNET PROVIDER | CONNECTION SPEED | POST-FUP SPEED | BROADBAND CHARGES | NETFLIX CHARGES (HD) | WHAT YOU PAY | HOW LONG IT LASTS* |
|---|---|---|---|---|---|---|
| Airtel | 40MBPS (upto 100GB) | 512KBPS | ₹2,199 | ₹650 | ₹2,849 | Seamless for 16 days. Then, painfully slow. |
| MTNL | 2MBPS (upto 250GB) | 1MBPS | ₹3,550 | ₹650 | ₹4,200 | Initial 30 sec buffering, but lasts the month. |
| Hathway | 50MBPS (upto 50GB) | 1MBPS | ₹4,499 (for 3 months) | ₹650 | ₹2,149 (monthly) | Seamless for 8 days; then frequent buffering. |
| Tikona | 4MBPS (upto 50GB) | 512KBPS | ₹950 | ₹650 | ₹1,600 | Seamless for 8 days; nearly unusable post that |
| Tata Docomo | 5MBPS (limitless) | NA | ₹2,999 | ₹650 | ₹3,649 | Seamless; lasts the month. |

*Calculated for Netflix HD, at an average usage of 2 hours per day, at 3GB per hour (as per Netflix USA's estimate of HD usage). Only high-end internet packages evaluated.

**WHAT IS FUP:** Fair Usage Policy is a bandwidth cap on data available at your subscribed speed (even if your connection in 'unlimited'). Post that, data rates drop to post-FUP speed. Network providers implement it to prevent network congestion. When asked about FUP caps in India, Netflix USA refused to comment on it.

Varying video sites require varying speeds. While YouTube's bandwidth system requirement is just 0.5Mbps, Hulu recommends three times that, with 1.5Mbps. Roku's support site suggests 3Mbps. Netflix also suggests 3Mbps for DVD-quality video. Three Mbps should be enough for standard-definition video and audio streaming. Higher quality requires higher bandwidth. For example, Netflix suggests a 5Mbps connection for high-definition video and a whopping 12Mbps for 3-D content.

## 2.31.1 Netflix

Netflix is a global provider of streaming films and television series. Netflix started as an American DVD-by-mail service in 1998, and began streaming in 2007. Netflix expanded with streaming to Canada in 2010 and now serves over 190 countries. Netflix's first widely advertised original series was *House of Cards*, which debuted in 2013, and Netflix now produces hundreds of hours of original programming around the world. As of April 2016, Netflix reported over 81 million subscribers worldwide, including more than 46 million in the U.S.

### Internet video streaming

In addition to its disc-rental service, Netflix separately offers an Internet video-streaming service which gives Internet-connected devices access to Netflix's library of online content, and allows numerous individuals to take advantage of one individual's subscription by insuring they login to their subscribing profile while on the non-subscriber's computer. The two libraries differ markedly, with the disc library having more film titles available, while the streaming library has more Netflix original content. According to a 2013 report by Sandvine, Netflix is the biggest source of North American downstream web-traffic, at 32.3%.

Netflix and others say your Internet service needs to run atleast 5Mbps for streaming HD shows and movies—streaming 4K videos requires much greater speed—but 5Mbps is sufficient for only one user at a time.5 Mbps of bandwidth for an HD stream and 25 Mbps for those lucky ones streaming in Ultra HD .

TV shows originally encoded in HD will play in 720p resolution or better provided that 5.0 Mbps bandwidth threshold is met. Remember that all the other devices (and people) in all the unit connected either by wi-fi or lan unitedly use up your bandwidth. Every smart-phone, computer, smart TV, smart Blu-ray player, cable box, satellite box, Roku or Apple TV connected to your network may be sending and receiving data at any given moment. After you account for every person watching at the same time, you have to remember every Internet-connected device in your house is sucking bandwidth: phones, tablets and computers are all frequently checking for email and software updates. Many apps on your phone check in for status updates, alerts and other reasons. Even light bulbs are now connected to the network. All those tiny vamps add up.

HD availability is subject to your Internet service and device capabilities. Not all content is available in HD. An Internet speed of at least 5.0 megabits per second is recommended to receive HD content (defined as 720p or better),

Each streaming service encodes and serves the video slightly differently, which means that the recommended bandwidth for each varies.

1. Netflix: 5.0 Mbps for HD
2. Amazon Prime Instant video: 3.5 Mbps for HD
3. HBO Now: 3 Mbps for HD

For example: In typical household, a 50 Mbps plan serves three simultaneous Netflix HD streams (and all the other Internet activity) fairly reliably. Just because you're paying for 50 Mbps doesn't mean that's what you'll get all the time. Your neighbours probably like to stream content around the same times you do, and if you're all sharing the same neighbourhood Internet pipe, it may clog up from time to time. For example, you may get really close to the promised speed at 3 a.m. when overall traffic is down, but probably not at 8 p.m., when residential usage is likely at its peak.

The company claims that one hour of its HD programming eats up about 3GB of data — Ultra HD content bumps that up to about 7 GB per hour.

## 2.32 WI-FI DEVICES

Devices on which streaming video and audio are accessed need to connect to the modem through a wireless or wired connection as part of a local area network. Wireless connections are typically provided by the modem or a connected wireless router. You can use these devices to access streaming content once they have established a wired or wireless connection through internal components that facilitate data transferring, such as Wi-Fi standards. Some intermediary devices, such as video game consoles, may also be needed to provide TVs that are not Internet-ready with access to streaming content.

### 2.32.1 Wi-Fi Stream Network Considerations

Just because your cable Internet connection and modem are capable of transferring streaming content at a high rate of speed doesn't mean the device on which you view and listen to streaming content will be able to keep up. For instance, if your computer is equipped with the Wi-Fi 802.11a, 802.11b or 802.11g standards, it will only be able to transfer data at up to 54 Mbps. This rate is also sufficient for streaming video and audio content, but when you factor in variables such as network traffic and available bandwidth, your computer might encounter buffering issues. The Wi-Fi 802.11n standard transfers data at up to 600 Mbps and is ideal for accessing streaming content through a cable modem and Internet connection.

If you still use an 802.11G wireless router, you're missing out on the better range and capacity of an 802.11N or newer router. 802.11ac was finalised in 2013 and you will find it in every major smartphone, laptop and desktop computer and smart television. It succeeds the equally-badly named '802.11n' which has been around since 2007 and brings some major benefits.802.11ac works exclusively in the 5GHz band, uses a ton of bandwidth (80 or 160MHz).

Each Wi-Fi standard is rated according to its maximum theoretical network bandwidth:

1. 802.11a offered up to max. 54 Mbps, 5GHz band adopted in Sept. 1997,
2. 802.11b offered up to Max. 11Mbps, 2.4 GHz band, adopted in Sept. 1997,
3. 802.11g offered up to 54 Mbps, 2.4 GHz band adopted in June 2003.
4. 802.11n offered up to 300 Mbps, both 2.4 and 5GHz band, adopted in 2007
5. 802.11ac offers up to 1 Gbps and 5GHz band adopted in 2013

The performance of Wi-Fi networks practically never approach these theoretical maximums. 802.11b networks, for example, generally operate no faster than about 50% of theoretical peak, around 5.5 Mbps. Likewise, 802.11a and 802.11g networks generally run no faster than 20 Mbps.

### 2.32.2 WiMax Overview

WiMAX is a unique technology being deployed by BSNL for the first time in India. This technology provides fixed as well as fully mobile high speed broadband connectivity alongwith roaming feature. It provides users a thrilling Internet browsing experience.

BSNL offers large variety of Customer Premises Equipments (CPE) including Outdoor, Indoor and USB dongles from which customers can choose as per their application requirements.

**Indoor**: Best suited for Home/Office users. Can be used in moving vehicle also

**Dongle:** Small Dongle can be connected directly to PC / Laptop via USB port.

**Outdoor:** Suitable for remote and rural areas. Can be used upto 15 Km distance (Line of sight) from BTS site.

**WiMAX Services**

1. High speed broadband connectivity upto 7Mbps
2. Leased Lines
3. VPN Services
4. Web based Video Conferencing

## 2.33 MULTIMEDIA SOFTWARE

Components of multimedia presentations are combined using authoring software. These are discussed in chapter 10 in detail. There are many authoring programs; some good ones include HyperCard for the Macintosh, Hyperscreen and Linkway for MS.DOS computers, Toolbox for Windows and Hyperstudio for the Apple IIGS. Authoring software allowes individuals to blend audio files, video, and animation with text and traditional graphics.

The Windows Media Control Interface, or MCI, provides a common interface to a variety of multimedia devices, including Audio Video Interface (AVI) playback, animation players, video disk players, CD players, and the Wave audio and synthesizer systems on our sound cards.

Musicians use the MIDI standard to create music for movies and television and sound for multimedia presentations. Truly professional interactive multimedia presentations can be fairly expensive, running about $500 per minute of presentation time.

Even if you aren't a great artist, collections of clip media can make your presentation look professional. Clip media include photos, drawings, movies,sound, and ready-to-use backgrounds Be certain to read the licensing agreements for any clip media that you use. Some can used freely; others can not be used for any project that will generate income.

## 2.34 SOFTWARE DRIVERS

Software drivers for multimedia are used to control specific hardware functions. The drivers must be able to interface the operating system, and ultimately the application program, to the specific hardware. Drivers are usually specific to hardware devices although some de facto industry standards have emerged that make drivers much more universal. Software drivers for multimedia devices include:

- Video display drivers
- Video capture
- Sound capture and playback
- Scanners
- Mouse, joysticks, and track balls

In each of these cases, the application accessed specific functions of the device(or is controlled by the device) via calls to the operating system. Functions such as "record audio, record video and play audio" are standardized by the operating system making it easier for application developers to take advantage of many devices without worrying about specific control operations or characteristics for any one device. An additional benefit is that and users can also switch devices such as sound boards without having to worry whether or not the application software will still work.

## 2.35 BASIC SOFTWARE TOOLS

The basic tool set for building a multimedia project can be divided into five categories: –

1. Painting and Drawing Tools
2. 3-D Modeling tools
3. Image editing tools
4. Sound editing tools
5. Animation, Video and digital movies editing tools

**(1) Painting and Drawing Tools**: Painting and drawing tools generally come with a graphical user interface with pull down menus for quick selection.

- You can create almost all kinds of possible shapes and resize them.
- Drawing file can be imported or exported in many image formats like .gif, .tif, .jpg, .bmp, tec.
- A good drawing software – **"CorelDraw".**

**(2) 3D Modeling Tools**: Realism means that you depict things in the way they actually are. Any modeling tool, tools the objects that appear in perception in your project can look realistic. These tools offer features like multiple windows to view your design in each dimension. Tools provide drag and drop menu. A good ***3D modeling tool is "3D Studio Max".***

**(3) Image Editing Tools**: These tools are used to edit existing bitmap images and pictures.

- They are similar to painting and drawing tools as they can also create images from scratch.
- It is also capable of converting the image data type file format.
- They are used usually for reinventing and recreating the image.
- Image process software – *Adobe Photoshop & Paint Shop pro.*

**(4) Sound Editing Tools**: Sound editing tools let you hear sound as well as visualize it.

- You can cut/copy and paste sound edit it with great accuracy.
- You can integrate sound into your multimedia project very easily by using sound editing tools.
- A good sound editing software is "Cool Edit" and "Sound Forge".

**(5) Animation, Video and digital movies editing tools**: Animations are graphic scenes played back sequentially and rapidly.

- These tools enable you to edit and assemble video clips captured from camera, animations and other sources.
- The completed clip with added transition and visual effects could be played back.
- ***Adobe Premiere and Media Shop Pro*** are two good example of these tools.

**(6) Engineering Drawing and Graphic Software**

Graphic software for drafting includes facilities for drawing lines, arcs, circles, creating 3 dimensional designs using wire-frame or solid modeling techniques. Various text fonts and text editing software is also desirable.

Computer-aided drafting (CAD) is the use of computer systems to aid in the creation, modification, analysis, or optimization of a design. CAD software is used to increase the productivity of the designer, improve the quality of design, improve communications through documentation, and to create a database for manufacturing. CAD output is often in the form of electronic files for print, machining, or other manufacturing operations. The term CADD, (for Computer Aided Design and Drafting) is also used.

Computer-aided design is used in many fields. Its use in designing electronic systems is known as electronic design automation, or EDA. In mechanical design it is known as mechanical design automation (MDA) or computer-aided drafting (CAD), which includes the process of creating a technical drawing with the use of computer software.

CAD software for mechanical design uses either vector-based graphics to depict the objects of traditional drafting, or may also produce raster graphics showing the overall appearance of designed objects. However, it involves more than just shapes. As in the manual drafting of technical and engineering drawings, the output of CAD must convey information, such as materials, processes, dimensions, and tolerances, according to application-specific conventions. CAD may be used to design curves and figures in two-dimensional (2D) space; or curves, surfaces, and solids in three-dimensional (3D) space.

CAD is an important industrial art extensively used in many applications, including automotive, shipbuilding, and aerospace industries, industrial and architectural design, prosthetics, and many more. CAD is also widely used to produce computer animation for special effects in movies, advertising and technical manuals, often called DCC digital content creation.

The benefit of CAD systems over manual drafting are the capabilities one often takes for granted from computer systems today; automated generation of Bill of Material, auto layout in integrated circuits, interference checking, and many others. Eventually CAD provided the designer with the ability to perform engineering calculations.

CAD is one part of the whole Digital Product Development (DPD) activity within the Product Lifecycle Management (PLM) processes, and as such is used together with other tools, which are either integrated modules or stand-alone products, such as:

Computer-aided engineering (CAE) and Finite element analysis (FEA)

Computer-aided manufacturing (CAM) including instructions to Computer Numerical Control (CNC) machines

Photo realistic rendering and Motion Simulation.

Document management and revision control using Product Data Management (PDM).

**Commercial (market leaders)**

1. Autodesk AutoCAD
2. Autodesk Inventor
3. Dassault CATIA
4. Dassault SolidWorks
5. Siemens NX
6. Siemens Solid Edge
7. PTC Pro/ENGINEER (now renamed Creo)

**Top rated in 2016**

1. TurboCAD Deluxe
2. DesignCAD 3D Max
3. SketchUp Pro
4. TurboCAD LTE Pro
5. CADopia
6. progeCAD
7. formZ pro
8. ₹66965.07
9. Review
10. Visit Site
11. ZWCAD+
12. BricsCAD Classic

## 2.36 OTHER IMPORTANT SOFTWARE TOOLS

**(1) 3Dstudio Max**

The successor to 3DStudio 2.0. 3DStudio Max runs under Windows NT. It is entirely object oriented, featuring new improvements, such as volumetric lighting, spacewarps, and all new redesigned interface.

**(2) LightWave3D**

Light Wave 3D is another high end PC 3D computer software package. Originally developed for the Amiga platform, it's considered the best 3D product for the PC. This software has been used for quite a few television productions such as Babylon 5 and SeaQuest.

**(3) Adobe Premiere**

Adobe Premiere is a tool that is used to composite Digitized video, stills, and apply a variety of transitions and special effects. Adobe Premiere runs both on Macintosh and PC Windows.

**(4) Alias/Wavefront**

Alias is one of the topmost animation packages in the market. Produced by two companies, Alias and Wavefront who work in collaboration, it runs on the SGI's. Alias is well known for it's great modeler which is capable of modeling some of the most complicated objects. Also, this software package is very flexible allowing programmers that will allow the programmers to create software that will run in tandem.

**(5) Animator Studio**

Animator Studio is a cell animation program from AutoDesk. Animator runs on Windows. It has a multitude of features that minimize the animation creation time.

**(6) Elastic Reality**

This is one of the top of the line programs used for morphing. Elastic Reality runs on Mac's and SGI's. One of the distinctive features of Elastic Reality is that it uses splines as opposed to points to define the morphing area. Elastic Reality allows to morph video as well as still images.

**(7) SoftImage**

SoftImage is one of the three top most computer animation software packages. SoftImage is used in many top production studios around the country and around the world.

**(8) Strata Studio Pro**

Strata Studio Pro is probably known the most known 3D graphics application on the Mac. Created by Strata Inc. Strata Studio Pro is mainly a still graphic rendering application, but it does have animation capabilities.

**(9) Director**

Director Born in the world of CD-Rom creation and developed in-house by Macromedia, Director is treated as one of the grandfathers of multimedia. Director was originally VideoWorks Interactive, the first in a new breed of multimedia authoring applications designed for the Apple Macintosh back in the 1980s. It was later released for DOS/Windows in 1994. Since 1995, the Director with its Shockwave Player has become all-platform. With its flexible programming language, Lingo, Director continues to be the flagship product of Multimedia.

**(10) Micromedia Flash**

Flash on the other hand was purpose built for the Web and was purchased by Macromedia in the mid-90s from a company called FutureSplash. The product earlier known as the Animator was rechristened as Flash. Flash is based on scalable vector graphics instead of fixed size bitmapped images, and a growing number of Web builders have adopted Flash as a somewhat replacement for HTML. The Shockwave Player, in contrast, doesn't lend itself well to full window presentations because of the bitmapped Director graphics. Flash graphics can bend and stretch and still look gorgeous, but bitmapped graphics end up distorted when manipulated. Director content is usually developed for a fixed size and the included as a supplement to standard HTML text. Streaming differences In the beginning streaming was a big advantage of Flash over Director. However the playing field has been leveled recently. Director now has streaming capabilities. From the user's point of view there is not a big difference between the streaming performance of Flash and Director content. The quality of playback in both the tool is about the same.

**(11) Director Vs Flash**

Two of the currently popular and widely used tools are; Director and Flash. Both are products of the same company but interestingly enough have developed unique audiences often working in separate even opposing campuses.

(a) Animation Styles and Asset Management: As mentioned earlier Flash artwork can be used as symbols but Director automatically turns everything into a cast member. Because it functions as an illustration and an animation program, Flash can afford more flexibility. The lines and shapes of animation sequence in Flash are easily editable without too many obstructions. On the other hand, using bitmaps and having limited drawing tools Director cannot support free-form animation. Thus Flash provides a more interactive animation platform.

(b) The Interfaces: Flash and Director have interfaces similar in function but quite different in appearance and implementation. Director has a very strictly defined authoring metaphor of Cast, Score and Stage. All objects-including pictures, sounds and behaviors--used in a movie are called Cast Members and are centrally organized in the window. Time based activity is laid out and edited using the Score window, which allows only one object per layer. On the other hand Flash has a slightly fuzzy authoring metaphor. Artwork may or may not be designated as symbols. The Timeline places no restrictions on the number of object combinations that can occupy a single layer, and scripting can be organized according to the developer's whim Extensibility and networking Director promises more extensibility than Flash. Director can take on more responsibilities by dynamically loading Xtras. Flash movies can take advantage of prepackaged scripts and symbols but the non-modular nature of the Flash Player rules out the possibility of Director-styled additions.

**(12) Cost and availability**: According to Macromedia's sales reports, Flash has more buyers lined up for it than Director. And this could be a function of the disparity in the tag prices of Flash and Director at $399 and $999 respectively. Though the extras offered by Director could make it less expensive in the long run.

## 2.37 CHOOSING SOFTWARE

Following factor are to be taken care of while selecting any multimedia software:

1. **Usability** – Should have a capability to deal with a variety of text, images video and sound formats with precision and ease.
2. **Animations** – Should have wide ranging capabilities in terms of interactive simulations, media support, animated buttons, illustrations,maps,etc.
3. **Smoothness** – Should have anti-aliasing feature, meaning that all letter and image edges are smooth.
4. **Integration** – Should have integration capabilities with a wide range of software used for different jobs like Real, ActiveX, Shockwave, Flash, QuickTime, Photoshop and other applications .
5. **Delivery** – Should be able to develop one piece of content for delivery on different media types.
6. **User friendliness** – Should be the easiest, most versatile, and have the most pre-built models
7. **Clientele** – Should have applications for instructional designers, subject matter experts, training developers and others.

Some of the popular software packages used by the companies, schools and individuals all around the globe include some of the following;

## 2.38 MULTIMEDIA DEVELOPMENT PLATFORMS

Multimedia Development platforms can be broadly divided in three classes:

1. Entry level Desktop/Laptop Based system more commonly known as MPC
2. Home Theatre type Middle Level Systems
3. Professional Development High End Systems

Multimedia computers need to have a strong processors, large hard drives or other storage options, and good networking capabilities. They can be either desktop-size or compact PCs and the main difference between the two designs is the space they have to fit components. Some people prefer desktops, since they can house components like high-performance hard drives and processors. Others want compact computers they can easily fit in to home theatre setups.

Midrange desktops will stay functional longer, thanks to more CPU power and speed, memory for multitasking, storage, or a larger built-in screen. You will be making some tradeoffs compared with high-end systems, but even demanding users will be able to find a midrange system that will last them for at least five or six years. Look for a capable AMD A8 or A10 processor, or an Intel Core i5 CPU in this category, along with 8GB to 16GB of memory, and a 1TB hard drive or at least 256GB solid-state-drive (SSD) storage.

High-end systems offer top-of-the-line components, like the latest CPUs that will give you all the power you need for multimedia projects, loads of storage (a 512GB SSD or at least 1TB hard drive, but typically 2TB or more), 3D graphics capability for gaming, or a combination of all three. These high-performance machines typically start at $1,500, and can go up to $5,000 and beyond for workstations or gaming rigs with customized paint jobs and multiple GPUs.

## 2.39 ENTRY LEVEL DESKTOP/LAPTOP BASED SYSTEMS (MORE COMMONLY KNOWN AS MPC)

### 2.39.1 Evolution of Multimedia PC

The basic IBM-PC-compatible machine was weak on processing power and had no integral support for audio and video; use adapter boards for Audio Visual. Extensions to the operating system were also required to control various external equipments like microphones, audiotapes, VCRs and video cameras. (Now we have System software like Microsoft Multimedia Extension for windows. Probably the weakest feature of PC in context of Multimedia is the bus architecture.

- Data bus: internal communication line carries data between components within / different PCs.

The legacy bus architecture (ISA bus) handled small packets of data, in bursts with error checking. Now, PC have Peripheral Component Interconnect (PCI); using 3 basic types of buses in one board for increasing speed.

1. Control,
2. Address, and
3. Transfer.

Networking to transmit multimedia information requires multiplexing / demultiplexing software; requires extra processing in computers and possible extensions to the OS.

Big industry of adapter boards and related equipment for multimedia applications grew up around IBM PC and its clones. In order to standardize the developments relating to multimedia PC (MPC), the software publishers association (SPA) set up its subsidiary called MPC marketing council in the early 1990s. A certification procedure has also been developed allowing members to attach a special logo to their products provided compatibility conditions are met. Recently a software and information industry association (SIIA) has also been formed .

### 2.39.2 Hardware Compatibility

For hardware products, compatibility means compliance with the MPC hardware requirements and for the software products this means the ability to run on an MPC platform.

**MPC level 1**

The first specification (MPC Level 1) was intended to encourage the adoption of a standard computing platform as an extension of the personal computer. Systems that conform to it may carry the MPC trademark. Upgrade kits must meet the CD-ROM, audio subsystem and input. output (I/O) requirements of the specification. The Council licenses the systems and upgrade kits that pass its certification test suites. Because it charges fees for the use of its trademark, not all products that meet the specification carry the MPC mark.

Most of the early MPC products sold were upgrades for existing computers with Intel 386 or 486 processors. However, computer manufacturers such as Compaq are starting to ship machines with integrated CD-ROM drives. Recent market research indicates that about 13 million such drives had been installed by the end of 1993 (EMB 1994). As CD-ROM becomes popular as a medium for distributing software, such machines are likely to become commonplace.

MPC level 1 specifications were meant to energize the adoption of a standard multimedia computing platform. The characteristic features were:

1. Adopting standard computing platform as an extension of personal computer.
2. Includes CD-ROM, audio subsystem and I/O requirements.
3. Most MPC level-1 were sold as upgrade for existing Computers. (Intel 386 / 486)
4. MPC-1 cost too high with too little capabilities

### MPC Level 2

The original MPC specification was criticised as being too limited, costing too much money for too little capability. A revised version (MPC Level2) was introduced in May 1993 to establish a performance standard for enhanced multimedia computing. It was designed for software-based video and new applications such as Photo CD, a form of compact disk for the storage of photographic images developed by Kodak that requires data to be recorded in more than one session.

1. Design includes software based Video and new applications (Photo CD).
2. Backward compatibility with MPC-1

As Table 2.5 shows, this new specification is backwardly compatible with MPC Levell. Both specifications are intended to define minimum functionality rather than to act as a recommendation for a particular system configuration. An existing IBM PC-compatible machine can be upgraded by adding features such as a CD-ROM drive and support for audio input and output for as little as $300, through a full MPC Level 2 upgrade currently costs twice this amount. The MPC is just the first step towards the fully fledged multimedia platform. From the point of view of the business user who in interested in multimedia, the MPC specification is unsatisfactory because of its concentration on audio. Within the audio specification, the emphasis is on music rather than business requirements for audio - a point emphasised by the need to conform to the Musical Instrument Digital Interface (MIDI) standard.

**TABLE 2.6:** Minimum configuration for MPCs

| | Level 1 | Level 2 |
|---|---|---|
| Processor | 16MHz 386SX | 25MHz 486SX |
| Memory | 2 MB | 4 MB |
| Hard disk | 30 MB | 160 MB |
| Floppy disk | 2.5inch high density | |
| Video display | 640x480,16 colours | 640x480,65,536 colours |
| Sound | 8-bit digital sound | 16-bit digital sound |
| | 8 note synthesiser | 8 note synthesiser |
| | MIDI playback | MIDI playback |

| CD-ROM drive | 150KB/s sustained transfer rate max average seek time 1 second | 300KB/s sustained transfer rate max average seek time 400 milliseconds CD-ROM |
|---|---|---|
| I/O devices | 101 key keyboard two | button mouse |
| Ports | MIDI I/O joystick | MIDI I/O joystick |
| Operating system | Windows 2.0 with multimedia extensions or Windows 2.1 | Windows 2.0 with multimedia extensions or Windows 2.1 |

### MPC Level 3 specifications

In 1995 the MPC level 3 specifications were announced once again raising the standard for multimedia PCs with following characteristics:

1. 75 MHz Pentium CPU
2. 8 MB RAM
3. 540 MB hard disk
4. Video system that can show 352×240 at 30 frames per second, 16-bit color
5. MPEG-1 hardware or software video playback
6. 4× CD-ROM drive using no more than 40% of CPU to read, with < 250 ms seek time
7. Sound card outputting 44 kHz, 16-bit CD quality sound
8. Windows 3.11 or Windows 95

Both MPC2 and MPC3 maintain backward compatibility.

## 2.40 MIDDLE LEVEL SYSTEMS: HOME THEATRE ENVIRONMENT

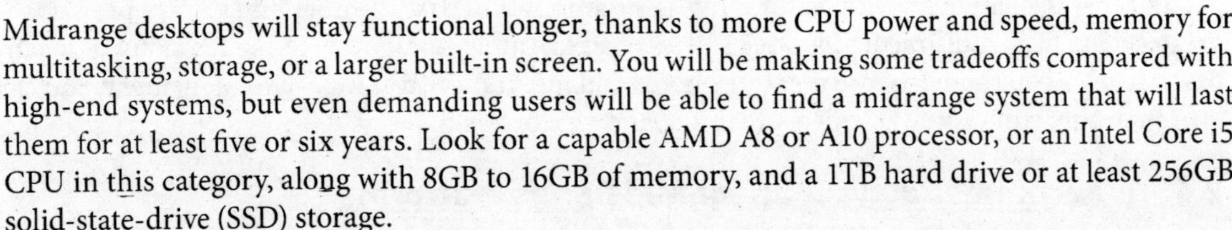

Midrange desktops will stay functional longer, thanks to more CPU power and speed, memory for multitasking, storage, or a larger built-in screen. You will be making some tradeoffs compared with high-end systems, but even demanding users will be able to find a midrange system that will last them for at least five or six years. Look for a capable AMD A8 or A10 processor, or an Intel Core i5 CPU in this category, along with 8GB to 16GB of memory, and a 1TB hard drive or at least 256GB solid-state-drive (SSD) storage.

For computers to be effective in a home theatre environment, issues besides storage and processing horsepower are important. Unlike standard desktops or laptops, home theatre PCs require a unique set of features, including these secondary factors:

**(1) Connectivity: Hooking Up Your Devices**

Especially in a home theater environment, an effective multimedia computer needs to be a Swiss army knife with loads of entertainment options, including photo viewing and video streaming. Features like Bluetooth and internal Wi-Fi allow your computer to cover functionality that typically requires a separate dedicated device.

**(2) Gaming: Turning Your Computer into a Console**

Dedicated graphics cards are typically exclusive to full-size desktops, but for more upscale home-theater-size computers, gaming is an option. Dedicated graphics cards have the processing overhead needed to play games like "BioShock Infinite" or "Crysis 3." While these options are typically not included in the basic configuration of mainstream multimedia computers, they are often offered as upgrades for those who find them desirable.

**(3) Must-Have Features for the Best Multimedia Computer**

The best specifications for your multimedia computer vary depending on your exact multimedia needs. For instance, a multimedia PC that acts as a local media server needs specifications like ample memory and a fast quad-core processor. By comparison, small form factor multimedia PCs can get by with less powerful components when they're supplemented with features like storage options and connectivity support. One way to start thinking about configuring your video editing computer is to build up from the minimum requirements of your particular editing software. Products like Adobe Premiere Pro CS5.5, Apple Final Cut Pro X, and Sony Vegas Pro 10 typically recommend at least a 2 GHz multi-core processor (*e.g.*, Intel Core 2 Duo), 2 to 4 GB of RAM, a GPU-accelerated graphics card like the NVIDIA GeForce with at least 256 MB of internal memory, and a 7200 RPM hard drive for editing compressed video formats or RAID 0 for uncompressed.

The traditional answer for serious video editing is still a dedicated workstation system. These are engineered for performance, often with Xeon processors offering high-performance speed and cores, video acceleration from a professional-grade GPU, integrated high-performance hard drives, and more attention to system integration issues like heat dissipation.

If you're doing more intensive editing, you can step up to a mid-range system for improved rendering speeds and real-time playback on the timeline. This might include a next-generation processor like the Core i5, quad cores for better multi-processing, redoubled memory at 4 to 8 GB, a more professional-grade GPU like the NVIDIA Quadro or AMD Radeon HD with more internal memory (512 MB to 1 GB), and higher-performance hard drives at 10,000 RPM /3 Gbps.

These dedicated editing workstation systems are particularly appropriate for higher-end work such as compositing, effects, and 3D, as well as for working with higher resolutions such as from the RED camera.

In general, computers with features like large amounts of base memory and storage provide the greatest benefit as multimedia PCs, regardless of size. Ample storage – whether it's cloud or locally based – gives you room to store files like photos and movies. With at least 4GB of memory, you can also smoothly run tasks like video streaming and web browsing.

## 2.40.1 Recommended set up for Mid Range Platform

(1) Processor

The following is a list of top ten Central Processing Unit (CPU):

1. Intel Core i5-4460
2. Intel Pentium G3258
3. Intel Core i5-4260U
4. AMD Sempron 2650
5. Intel Celeron 1017U
6. Intel Celeron 2957U
7. Intel Celeron 2955U
8. Intel Celeron 2957U
9. Intel Celeron 2955U
10. Intel Atom D2550

(2) CPU Generation: 2nd to 7th

(3) CPU Speed (GHz): 3.2GHz down to 1.86GHz

(4) Passmark CPU Score: 6672 down to 1488

(5) List of Recommended Graphics Card:

1. NVIDIA GeForce GT 730
2. NVIDIA GeForce GTX 960
3. NVIDIA GeForce 610M
4. Intel HD Graphics
5. AMD Radeon HD 8240

(6) Memory & Storage

Primary Hard-Disk Drive: 1TB
Primary Solid-State Drive: 60GB
Memory (GB): 8 DDR4
Memory Card Reader

(7) Connectivity

1. USB 3.0: 4 down to 2 numbers
2. USB 2.0
3. HDMI
4. Wi-Fi
5. IR Remote Support
6. Bluetooth
7. Optical Drive

## 2.41 PROFESSIONAL HIGH END MULTIMEDIA SYSTEM FOR PROJECT/PRODUCTION

### 2.41.1 Multimedia Project Studio

The Multimedia Project Studio is a computer lab specializing in tools for the production of multimedia and graphic content.

Fig. 2.39: Multimedia Project Studio

The lab features high-end, integrated hardware and software that encourages imaginative creation and editing of graphics, web pages, audio and video. Production tools include industry standard software.

1. Apple's Final Cut Pro, Motion, and Compressor for video editing
2. Adobe Creative Suite (Photoshop, Illustrator, Indesign, Flash, Dreamweaver, AfterEffects, etc.)

The top-of-the-line 5K workstations in each lab are equipped with specialized peripherals, such as drawing tablets, scanners, video digitizers, and DVD burners.

## 2.41.2 Studio Workstation Computer Setup

**iMac Retina 5K, 27", Late 2014**

4 GHz Intel Core i7 or The Core i7-6700K is Intel's latest "Skylake" flagship processor. It replaces the hugely successful i7-4790K and takes the crown as the fastest mainstream consumer

1. 16 GB 1600 MHz DDR3 RAM
2. AMD Radeon R9 M290X 2048 MB Graphics Card
3. 500GB Apple SSD SM512G Hard Drive
4. Mac OS X 10.10.5*
5. MediaNET Storage System

**Peripherals**

1. 1 Epson Perfection V700 Photo Scanner
2. 1 Epson Perfection 2450 Photo Scanner
3. 1 Nikon COOLSCAN IV ED 35mm/IX240 film scanner with Nikon SA-21 Strip Film Adapter

**Video Importing Stations** with support for DV, VHS, and DVD

1. Gefen Personal Video Recorder
2. Samson C01U
3. VHS and DVD decks for lab use
4. Wacom Bamboo
5. Headphone Amp on each workstation

**Audio Booth @MPS West**

1. 2 Samson C01U Microphones
2. 2 Microphone Shock Absorber
3. 1 Microphone Pop Filter
4. 1 Samsung 550 37" Full 1080p HD LCD TV
5. 27" iMac

MPS Studio @West (Now Available)
Updated for the 2015-2016 Academic Year
Simplified use system no longer requires Crestron or advanced control
High Quality Panasonic Robotic camera with built in streaming and control
SoundStructure automated audio control and echo cancellation

Apple system with full MPS software load-out
55" 3D HDTV
Wacom Cintiq 22HD Touch Screen (new)
Whiteboard
Black Cyc

### 2.41.3 Selected Software

(List is not exhaustive)

1. Adobe Creative Suite 6
2. llustrator
3. InDesign
4. Photoshop
5. Dreamweaver
6. Flash
7. AfterEffects
8. Encore
9. Fireworks
10. Premiere
11. Soundbooth
12. Apple
13. iLife Suite
14. GarageBand
15. iMovie HD
16. iPhoto
17. iWeb
18. Apple Final Cut Pro X
19. Apple Compressor 4.1
20. Apple Logic Pro***
21. Apple Motion 5
22. Audacity
23. SketchUp 14 with STL Exporter
24. Microsoft Office
25. Amadeus Pro
26. MakerWare Desktop
27. PreForm
28. Handbrake

MPS utilizes an advanced network storage solution. For most of our users, this transition will be completely seamless. The contents of users' Documents, Movies and Photos folders will now be stored in the cloud and accessible instantly from any MPS workstation.

### 2.41.4 MPS Video Suite

**Fig. 2.40:** Multimedia MPS Video Suite

The MPS Video Suite provides a place for recording video using tools such as Camtasia and QuickTime. A green screen and black curtain are available for use as backdrops.

### 2.41.5 MPS Audio Suite

The MPS Audio Suite provides professional quality microphones to allow up to two people to record audio in a sound controlled environment using Garage-band, Audacity, or Logic.

**Learning Outcomes**

In this chapter we have learnt about :

1. Use of various components input/output and CPU units of a Multimedia media workstation
2. Working of CPU unit and its peripherals
3. Requirement of different software and tools for running Multimedia media workstation
4. Different Levels of development platforms

# Multimedia Colour and Design

CHAPTER

3

**Leaning Objectives**

In this chapter we shall learn about:

1. Different types of colours and colour theory
2. Primary and secondary colours
3. Additive and subtractive colours–RGB and CMYK
4. Colour wheels, Maps and Models
5. Basic colour Display styles
6. Colour palettes in different Multimedia media Graphics software
7. Multimedia designs and Authoring software
8. Making a story Board

## 3.1 COLOUR THEORY

Colour can be one of the key ingredients to graphic design. It can be used to enhance and emphasise information. Colour must be used with an understanding of the other fundamentals of graphic design otherwise it can spoil an otherwise good composition. If too much strong and vivid colours are used at the expense of everything else, a presentation can look overdressed. Colour must be used cautiously. While it can add charm to your work, it can also destroy the harmony and balance of a composition.

Colour appreciation is universal and plays an important role in our daily lives. Colour can excite or sooth, or create a variety of other emotions. Red is a dominant colour and is used to signify danger. It is a colour that immediately catches the eye and creates alertness. Strong and vivid colours fill us with excitement, while quiet and gentle ones suggest tranquility and calm. Colours are highly expressive and go beyond just recording the realism of a picture. In theatre, a stage designer can create a variety of moods by careful choice of coloured lighting, without even altering the makeup scene.

As a multimedia designer, you can create atmosphere through the careful use of colour. Colour choice must suit your client. Bright reds, blues and greens in cartoon style graphics may not be suitable for a conservative, formal business client. Colours should be chosen to suit pictures you are displaying. A picture of a classical work of architecture, may not work with bright colours.

When developing a colour scheme for your multimedia work, it is often a good idea to limit yourself to three colours for your interface and design elements. By limiting colours, you can avoid the difficulties in maintaining balance and harmony in a composition. This rule can be broken once you have gained a greater understanding of colour. Trial and error will help you discover what works and what does not. The artist Matisse, used a range of vivid colours, patterns and textures in his paintings, while maintaining balance and harmony. We are not all Matisse artists, but we can try.

## 3.2 COLOUR BASICS

Colour is the perceptual characteristic of light described by a colour name. Specifically, colour is light, and light is composed of many colours—those we see are the colours of the visual spectrum: red, orange, yellow, green, blue, and violet (read as VIBGYOR inversely). Objects absorb certain wavelengths and reflect others back to the viewer. We perceive these wavelengths as colour.

### 3.2.1 Describing Colours

A colour is described in three ways: by its name, how pure or desaturated it is, and its value or lightness. Although pink, crimson, and brick are all variations of the colour red, each hue is distinct and differentiated by its chroma, saturation, intensity, and value.

- **Chroma, intensity, saturation and luminance/value** are inter-related terms and have to do with the description of a colour.

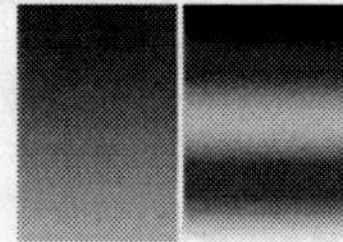

- **Chroma:** How pure a hue is in relation to gray
- **Saturation:** The degree of purity of a hue.
- **Intensity:** The brightness or dullness of a hue. One may lower the intensity by adding white or black.
- **Luminance / Value:** A measure of the amount of light reflected from a hue. Those hues with a high content of white have a higher luminance or value.
- **Shade and tint** are terms that refer to a variation of a hue.

- **Shade:** A hue produced by the addition of black.
- **Tint:** A hue produced by the addition of white.

### 3.2.2 Working With Systems

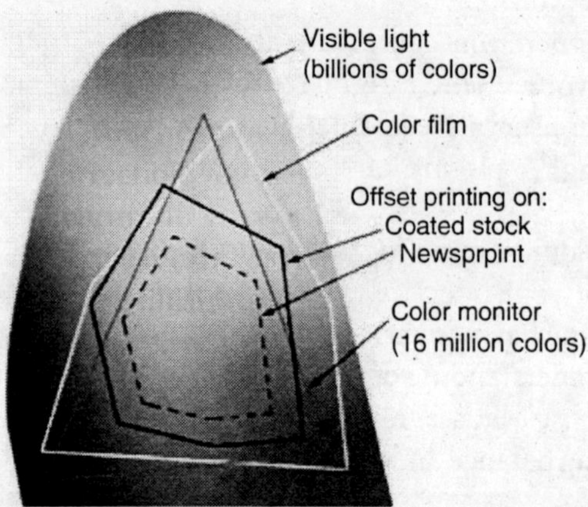


**Fig. 3.1:** Colour Spectrum on Various Utilities

The Visible spectrum consists of billions of colours, a monitor can display millions, a high quality printer is only capable of producing thousands, and older computer systems may be limited to 216 cross-platform colours.

Reproducing colour can be problematic with regard to printed, digital media, because what we see is not what is possible to get. Although a monitor may be able to display 'true colour' (16,000,000 colours), millions of these colours are outside of the spectrum available to printers. Since digital designs are generated using the RGB colour system, colours used in those designs must be part of the CMYK spectrum or they will not be reproduced with proper colour rendering. Working within the CMYK colour system, or choosing colours from Pantone© palettes insures proper colour rendering.

### 3.2.3 The Colour Wheel

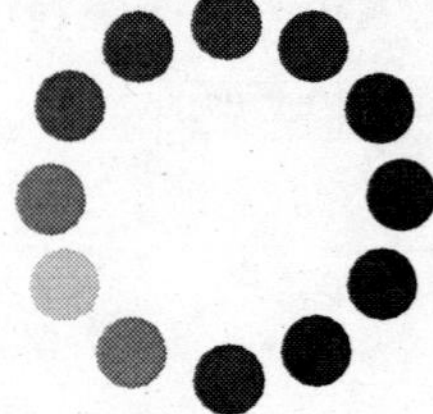

**Fig. 3.2:** Concept of colour wheel

A colour wheel (also referred to as a colour circle) is a visual representation of colours arranged according to their chromatic relationship. Begin a colour wheel by positioning primary hues equidistant from one another, then create a bridge between primaries using secondary and tertiary colours.

A colour circle, based on red, yellow and blue (RYB), is traditional in the field of arts. Sir Isaac Newton developed the first circular diagram of colours in 1666. Since then, scientists and artists have studied and designed numerous variations of this concept. Differences of opinion about the validity of one format over another continue to provoke debate. In reality, any colour circle or colour wheel which presents a logically arranged sequence of pure hues has merit. Fig. 3.3 shows three popular colour wheels.

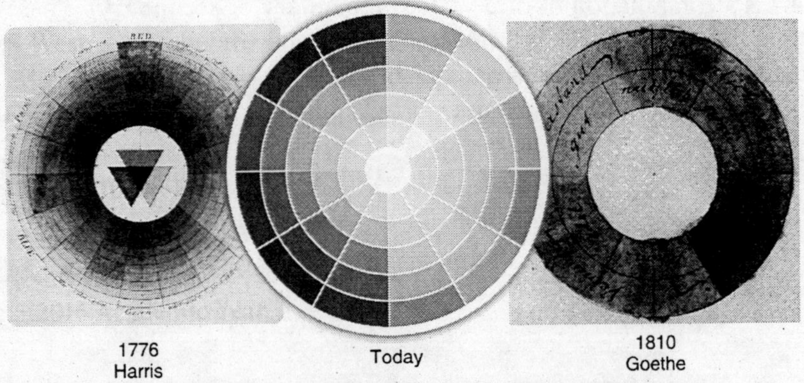


**Fig. 3.3:** Three Popular Colour Wheels

There are also definitions (or categories) of colours based on the colour wheel. We begin with a 3-part colour wheel.

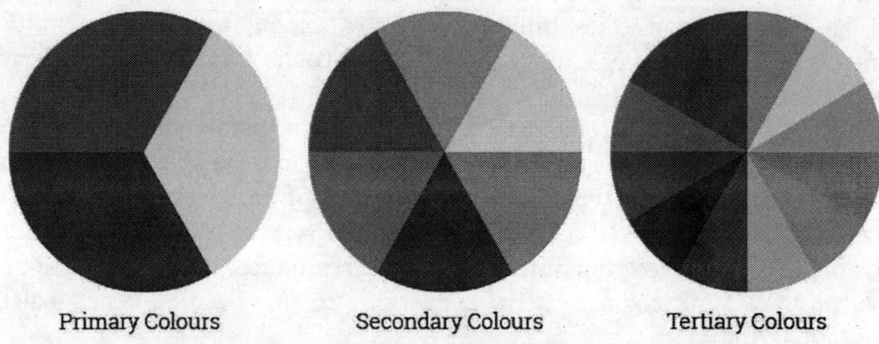


**Fig. 3.4:** The concept of three original and derived Colours

## 3.3 THE CONCEPT OF THREE ORIGINAL AND DERIVED COLOURS

**Colours had been developed in three categories:**

a. Primary Colours System
b. Secondary Colours System
c. Tertiary Colours System

### 3.3.1 Primary Colours: Red, Yellow and Blue (RYB)

A *primary* colour is a colour that cannot be made from a combination of any other colours.

In traditional colour theory (used in paint and pigments), primary colours are the 3 pigment colours that can not be mixed or formed by any combination of other colours. All other colours are derived from these 3 hues.

### 3.3.2 Secondary Colours: Green, Orange and Purple

A *secondary* colour is a colour created from a combination of two primary colours.

These are the colours formed by mixing the primary colours.

### 3.3.3 Tertiary Colours: Yellow-Orange, Red-Orange, Red-Purple, Blue-Purple, Blue-Green & Yellow-Green

*Tertiary* colour is a combination of three colours (**primary** or **secondary**). These are the colours formed by mixing a primary and a secondary colour. That's why the hue is a two word name, such as blue-green, red-violet, and yellow-orange.

**Complementary Colours:** The colours located opposite to each other on a colour wheel.

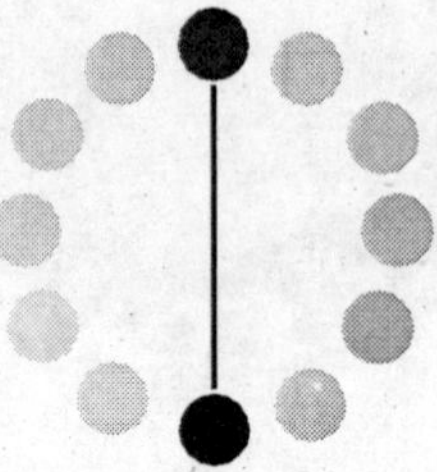

**Analogous Colours:** The colours located close together on a colour wheel.

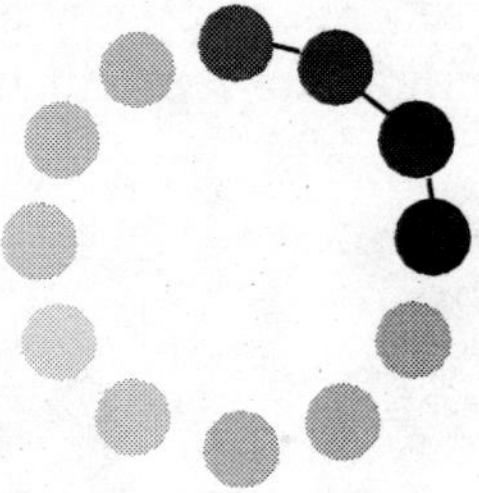

### 3.3.4 Colour Harmony

Harmony can be defined as a pleasing arrangement of parts, whether it be music, poetry, colour, or even an ice cream sundae.

In visual experiences, harmony is something that is pleasing to the eye. It engages the viewer and it creates an inner sense of order, a balance in the visual experience. When something is not harmonious, it's either boring or chaotic. At one extreme is a visual experience that is so bland that the viewer is not engaged. The human brain will reject under-stimulating information. At the other extreme is a visual experience that is so overdone, so chaotic that the viewer can't stand to look at it. The human brain rejects what it can not organize, what it can not understand. The visual task requires that we present a logical structure. Colour harmony delivers visual interest and a sense of order.

In summary, extreme unity leads to under-stimulation, extreme complexity leads to over-stimulation. Harmony is a dynamic equilibrium.

### 3.3.5 Colour Context

How colour behaves in relation to other colours and shapes is a complex area of colour theory. Compare the contrast effects of different colour backgrounds for the same red square.

Red appears more brilliant against a black background and somewhat duller against the white background. In contrast with orange, the red appears lifeless; in contrast with blue-green, it exhibits brilliance. Notice that the red square appears larger on black than on other background colours.

#### Different readings of the same colour

If your computer has sufficient colour stability and gamma correction you will see that the small purple rectangle on the left appears to have a red-purple tinge when compared to the small purple rectangle on the right. They are both the same colour as seen in the illustration below. This demonstrates how three colours can be perceived as four colours.

### 3.3.6 Types of Primary Colours: Additive and Subtractive

Artists and Scientists (computers) have different definitions for primary colours. The *traditional* primary colours that artists and painters have used are red, yellow, and blue (RYB). Television and Computer videos use Red, Green and Blue (RGB). These two primary colour systems obviously do not agree. Modern printing press use secondary colours are magenta, yellow, and cyan. *Additive* and *subtractive* are the two *modern* methods for reproducing a range of colour.

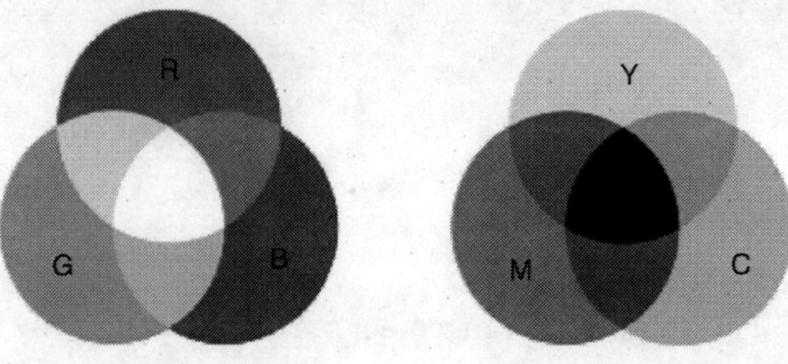


**Additive Colour**
**(Red+Green+Blue = White)**

**Subtractive Colours**
**(Cyan+Magenta+Yellow = Black)**

## 1. Additive colours

Additive colours synthesis (**Red + Green + Blue = White**) is the creation of colour by mixing colours of *light*. Human vision relies on light sensitive cells in the retina of the eye. There are two basic kinds of sensors. These are rods and cones. Rods are cells which can work at very low intensity, but cannot resolve sharp images or colour. Cones are cells that can resolve sharp images and colour, but require much higher light levels to work. The combined information from these sensors is sent to the brain and enables us to see.

There are three types of cones in our eye's retina. Red cones are sensitive to red light, green cones are sensitive to green light, and blue cones are sensitive to blue light. The perception of colour depends on an imbalance between the stimulation level of the different cell types.

Additive colour processes, such as television and computer monitors, work by having the capability to generate an image composed of red, green, and blue light (RGB). Since the intensity information for each of the three colours is preserved, the image colour is preserved as well. The spectral distribution of the image will probably be wrong, but if the degree of intensity for each of the primary colours is correct, the image will appear to be the right colour.

Example 1 shows how the light from red, green and blue flashlights would appear if shone on a dark wall.

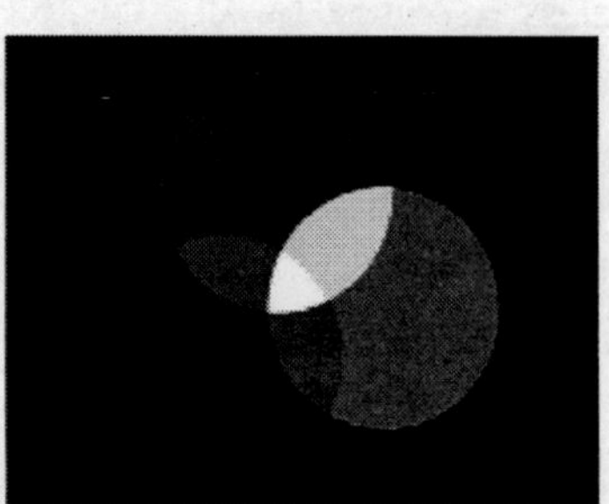

**Example 1:** Additive principle of color combining (light)

Derivation of Additive Secdonaries from Additive Primary Colors

Red + Green = Yellow
Red + Blue = Magenta
Green + Blue = Cyan

Printers' primaries yellow, cyan, and magenta are typically used by professional designers and printing presses .

When all of the colours of the spectrum are combined, they add up to white light.

2 parts Red + 1 part Green = Orange

2 parts Green + 1 part Red = Lime

4 parts Red + 1 part Blue + 1 part Green = Brown

## 2. Subtractive Colour (CMYK)

Subtractive colour synthesis is the creation of colour by mixing colours of *pigment,* such as paint or ink in your computer's printer. This type of colour is what is used in the art and design world. When learning basic colour theory, art students typically use familiar colours like red, yellow, and blue.

Subtractive colour processes work by blocking out parts of the spectrum. The idea of subtractive colour is to reduce the amount of undesired colour reaching the eye. If, for example, you had a yellow image, you would want to have a dye that would let red and green reach the eye, and block out blue. The additive secondaries become the printers' subtractive primaries, because each of the additive secondaries will reflect two of the additive primaries, and absorb one of the additive primaries.

The three primaries on the artists' colour wheel are *red, blue,* and *yellow.* Example 2 illustrates subtractive colour by showing how primary colours mix on a piece of white paper.

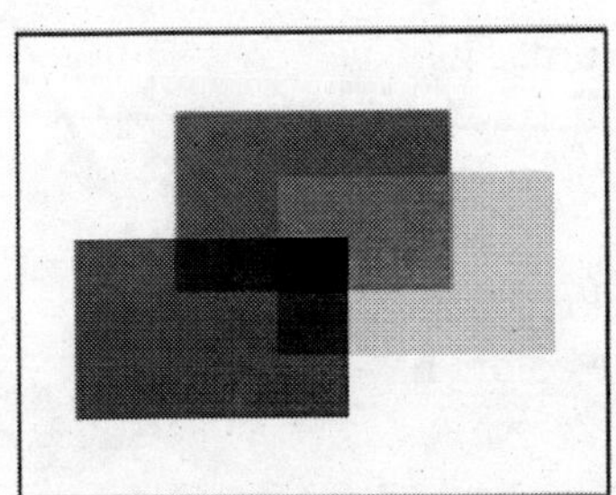

**Example 2:** Subtractive principle of color combining (pigment)

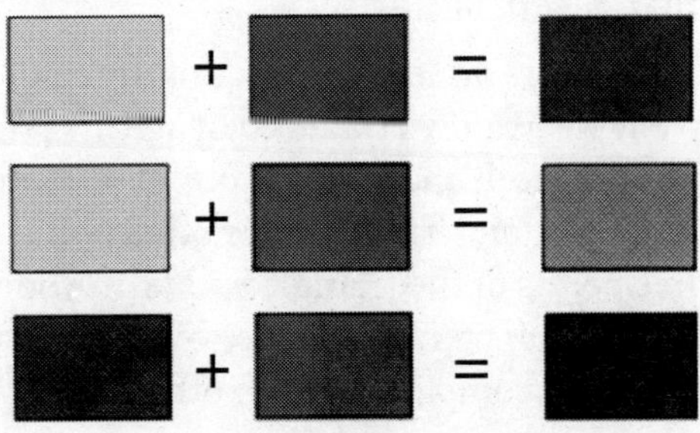

Painting Primaries Mixing chart

Yellow + Blue = Green

Yellow + Red = Orange

Blue + Red = Violet

When all of the colours are combined, they create black pigment.

| Colour | Reflects | Absorbs |
|---|---|---|
| Yellow | Red and Green | Blue |
| Magenta | Red and Blue | Green |
| Cyan | Green and Blue | Red |

### Additive Primaries/Secondaries Absorption Chart

With this information, if we wanted red, we would mix magenta and yellow. Magenta would absorb green, and yellow would absorb blue, leaving only red to be reflected back to the eye. For black, a combination of all three would be used, which should block out all light in theory. Printers use black as well, since the dyes used in printing are not perfect, and some light from other parts of the spectrum gets through.

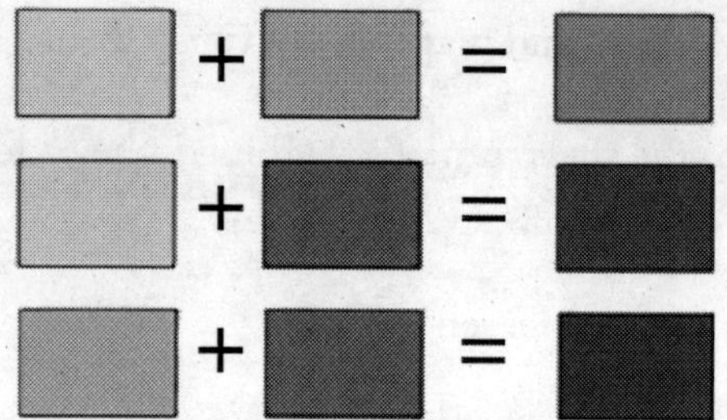

Subtractive primaries mixing chart

For printers mixing:
Yellow + Cyan = Green
Yellow + Magenta = Red
Cyan + Magenta = Blue

### 3.3.7 Effective Color Scheme

Here are 3 of the commonly accepted structures for a good colour scheme: triadic, compound, and analogous:

1. Triadic Colour Scheme

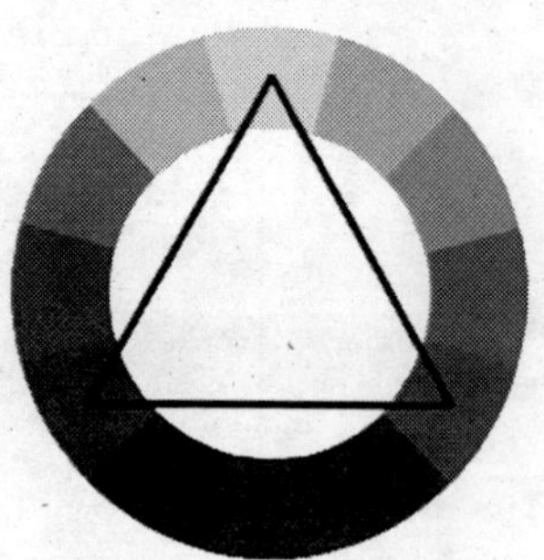

Composed of 3 colors on separate ends of the color spectrum. There is a very easy way to create a Triadic color scheme:

Take a color wheel, and choose your base color.

Draw an Equilateral Triangle from this point.

The three points of the triangle will form your tri-color scheme.

By using an Equilateral Triangle, you can ensure the colors have equal vibrancy and compliment each other properly.

2. Compound Colour Scheme (aka Split Complimentary)

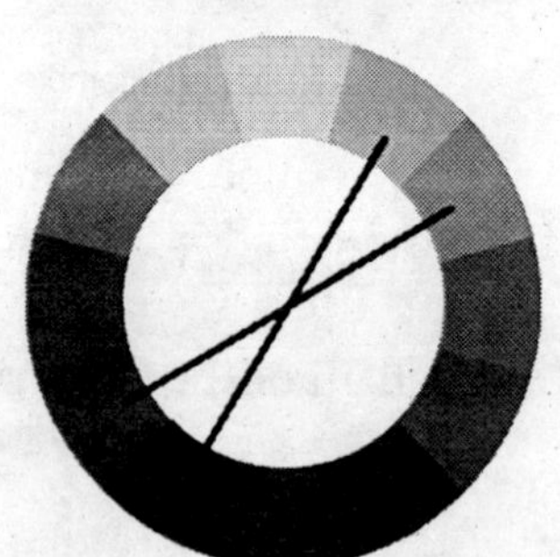

The Compound color scheme is based on providing a range of Complementary Colors: two colors are chosen from opposite ends of the color spectrum. By doing so, the designer is allowed more freedom in their design while also benefiting from the visual appeal of complementary colors.

3. Analogous

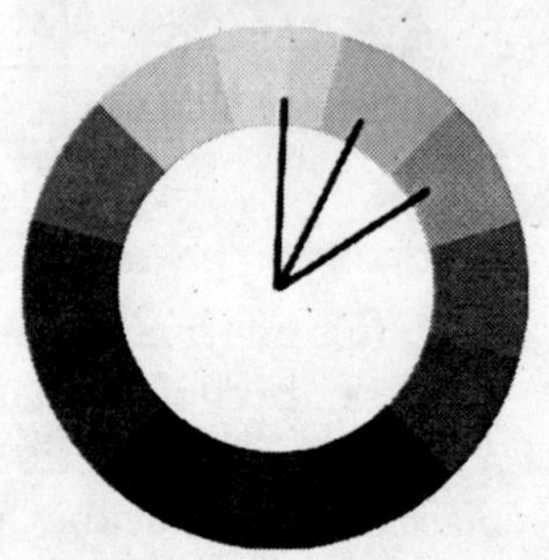

An Analogous color scheme is based on a careful selection of colors in the same area of the color spectrum. Usually the colors are differentiated by their vibrancy, and their contrast when compared to each other.

Two examples of an Analogous color scheme are:

Shades Yellow and Orange

A Monochromatic Selection **(Shades of a base color).**

### 3.3.8 Description of Colour

***Hue***: Is the name of the colour itself, the dominant wavelength of light or the choice of pigment.
***Lightness (brightness)***: Is the lightness or darkness of the colour, the among of light reflected or transmitted.
***Saturation:*** Is the level of white, black or grey, ranges from neutral to brilliant (pastel to full colour).
***Tint***: Base colour plus white.
***Tone***: Base colour plus grey.
***Shade***: Base colour plus black.
***Value***: How light or dark a colour is.
***Aggressive***: AKA 'Warm'. The yellows, oranges, and reds. These come towards the eye more (spatially) and are generally 'louder' than passive colours.

***Passive***: AKA 'Cool'. The greens, blues, and violets. These recede from the eye more (spatially) and are generally 'quieter' than the aggressive colours.

### 3.3.9 Images and Colour

Computer image colour ranges from simple black and white to millions of colours. Line art illustrations are an effective use of a black and white image while a photographic image of a flower garden is ideally presented by systems that support the display of over 16 million colour. The use of colour in multimedia depends on two factors:

1. The subject or content of the image
2. The technical capability of the computer hardware and software

The key to using colour in the computer is to understand what colour is. Colour is based on the perception of light, which is part of the electromagnetic spectrum offer colours including red, orange, yellow, green, blue, indigo, and violet. Interestingly, computer-generated white and black are a function of the presence of all colours or none at all. White is created by combining all colours and black is created by the absence of colour. Computer colour is based on adjusting combinations of additive primary colours: red, green, and blue (RGB). Printed colours, based on reflective light, use subtractive colours: **Cyan**, **Magenta**, **Yellow**, and **Black**.

The perception of colour is the function of the eye's receptors, called cones, in the cornea of the eye are sensitive to red, green and blue frequencies of the electromagnetic spectrum.

## 3.4 COMPUTER DISPLAY

Computer display resolution is the number of pixels that make up the height and width of the display presented by the computer monitor. Early monochrome display-based computer relied on two-colour displays that ware measured in lines and characters, typically 25 lines by 80 characters. Early (Intel-based graphic ) systems used pixel width/height measurements and colour ranges from 2 to 16 colours while Apple-based systems commonly used 640 by 480 pixels and 16 colours.

Multimedia-based computer systems since the early 1990 have established minimum capabilities when it comes to presenting graphics ; 640 by 480 pixels and 256 colours. Depending on the capability the graphics display hardware including both the monitor and the graphics adapter (the computer video board that processes the image ), graphics capability includes:

| Image size of | Colour depth of |
|---|---|
| 640 × 480 pixels | 256 colours |
| 800 × 600 pixels | 32,768 colours |
| 1024 × 768 pixels | 65 ,536 colours |
| 1280 × 1024 pixel | 16,777,216 colours |

The ability to display large numbers of pixels and colours is dependent on the amount of video memory to handle storing the image display as well as refresh image. Refresh images are important because they enable computer display systems to create responsive and lifelike presentations cycling the images.

## 3.5 DISPLAY MONITOR'S COLOUR CHARACTERISTICS

Computer monitors display colour shining an electron beam off phosphorescent colour dots (red, green, and, blue) at very high speeds. The creation of visible colour is a function of three characteristics: hue, saturation, and brightness (HSB). Saturation, brightness and lightness are defined x percentages-lightness of 100 percent is white while 50 percent is a pure colour. Hue, saturation, and brightness are further defined as follows:

Hue is based on a vector value moving from 0 to 360 degrees on a colour wheel.

Saturation is the intensity of the colour in a percentage scale: 100 percent is a pure colour,0 percent is black, white, or gray.

Brightness and lightness are a function of how much black or white is mixed with the colour. A pure colour has 50 percent lightness ( or brightness ) with 100 percent being white and 0 percent being black.

## 3.6 COLOUR PALETTES AND COLOUR LOOK-UP TABLES

Computers manage colour via palettes or colour look-up tables (CLUT), which are mathematical tables that define the colour of any particular pixel displayed and the total number of colours that can be displayed on a system. Most multimedia systems are based on ranges can never distinguish 16 million separate colours, the richness of the palette ensures that any hue is possible for any type of image.

Colour palates are defined indexing values correlated to red, blue, and green colours. The value range for multimedia computers is 0 to 255, for 256 possible hues for each of red, blue , and green for a total of 16,777,216 colour combinations. Using the indexed values, Table 3.1 show some of the colours that can be created.

**TABLE 3.1:** Hue Values in a colour palate

| Red Value | Green Value | Blue Value | Resulting Colour |
|---|---|---|---|
| 0 | 0 | 0 | White |
| 255 | 255 | 255 | Black |
| 255 | 0 | 0 | Red |
| 0 | 255 | 0 | Red |
| 0 | 0 | 255 | Green |
| 255 | 255 | 0 | Yellow |
| 128 | 0 | 128 | Purple |

Computer images store colours in a palette with each image having a unique palette. The palette keeps track of the indexed colour values used in the image. Computer graphic systems depend on the ability to display pixels within a specific number of colours (ranging from 2 to 16 million colours). The computer display has a "system palette" that manages the display & its palate is mapped into the system palette. The system palette is limited to the number of colours that the system is capable of displaying depending on its hardware and software configuration. Palettes are defined the number of bits required to generate colours:

1 bit: two colours
4 bit: 16 colours
8 bit: 256 colours
15 and 16 bit: 32,768 and 65,536 colours
24 bit: 16, 777,216 colours

Kilobytes of video RAM occupied by various colour depths and resolutions

| Colour depth | Resolution (pixels) | | | | |
|---|---|---|---|---|---|
| | 640x480 | 800x600 | 1024x768 | 1280x1024 | 1600x1200 |
| 16 | 150 | 234 | 384 | 640 | 938 |
| 256 | 300 | 469 | 786 | 1280 | 1875 |
| 65536 | 600 | 938 | 1536 | 2560 | 3750 |
| 16.7 million | 900 | 1406 | 2304 | 3840 | 5625 |
| 4.29 billion | 1200 | 1875 | 3072 | 5120 | 7500 |

**Note**: Figure are in kilobytes of video RAM. 1024 kilobytes = Megabytes

## 3.7 MODIFYING COLOUR VALUES (HUES, SATURATION AND LUMINANCE *i.e.* BRIGHTNESS) WITH FAMOUS COLOUR PALATES

Hexadecimal values are similar to RGB values. Increasing or decreasing the individual digits of the hue's hexadecimal number will provide a variation in your selected colour. The first two digits designate the red value, the next two the green, and the last are blue values. The lowest value that can be given to one of the light sources is 0 (hex #00). The highest value is 255 (hex #FF). Lowest to highest: 0 1 2 3 4 5 6 7 8 9 A B C D E F

You can copy & paste these values into the input areas to view variations of red: #330000, #660000, #AA0000, #DD0000, #FF0000, #FF7777, & #FF3333.

**(1) Paint Brush Colour Edit**

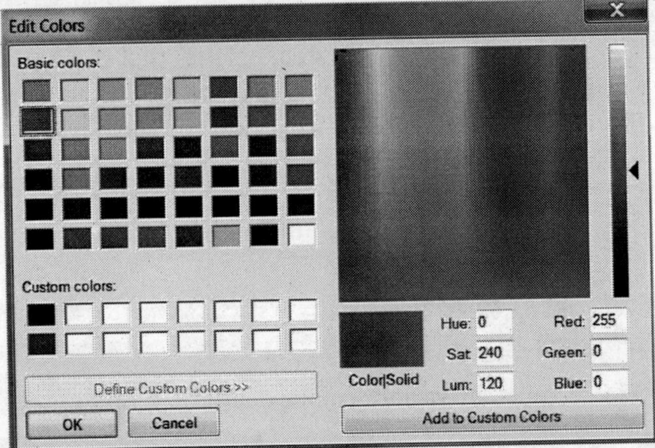


**(2) Kuler**

A tool developed Adobe, Kuler is aimed at providing an intuitive way to create a color palette. Every color on the palette can be individually modified, or chosen as the base color, with a few simple clicks. Palettes can be saved and published, and there are a number of great community entries available on their site. Under each color, the export codes are provided (including hexadecimal). However, the interface can be cumbersome at times, adjusting the vibrancy of a specific color can alter the entire palette (I wish they had a "lock" feature which prevented other colors from shifting). Overall, I would recommend this tool for those with a decent grasp of the concepts and patience for when things don't run as smoothly as they would hope.

Adobe Kulers' user-friendly, versatile, cloud-based interface creates a slick experience. It's built around three core principals: Users can browse, build and share color schemes through the site, desktop (Adobe Air) app or (Mac OS X) Dashboard widget. It's also available inside the Adobe CS4 Creative Suite applications.

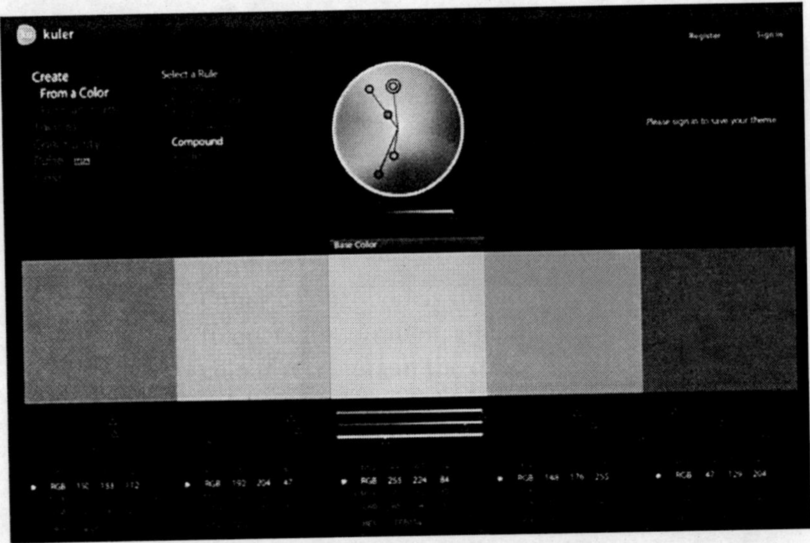


Bottom of Form

You can search color schemes color, concept, hex values, tags and more. The ability to create a scheme based on the colors of an image you upload is also an incredibly useful feature. Once you've settled on your color combination, download it as an Adobe Swatch Exchange file or simply accessing the color table values.

### (3) COLORlovers

COLORlovers is much more than a color scheme designer; it's an active, creative community of people passionate about color, a place to discuss color-related topics and create and share colors, palettes, patterns and the latest trends. At present, it boasts 6.2 million colors in 3.6 million color palettes created and shared its users.

Of special note is Copaso, an advanced color palette tool that lets you create beautiful color schemes and custom themes. Pick colors from a color wheel or upload an image and optionally pixelate it to isolate particular colors. Furthermore, the impressive community has generated a useful search facility to find colors and palettes.

### (4) ColoRotate

With ColoRotate, explore colors and select color combinations generating color palettes in real time 3D, just as the human brain perceives color. It's available free online or as an iPad app, and can connect to Adobe Photoshop CS5 or CS6 to update foreground and background colors and send palettes to your desktop.

The interactive 3D color pyramid is fun and intuitive to use and enables you to vary the color hues or tints, as well as blend two colors simultaneously. You can check how your chosen palette works with typography, browse through a selection of palettes and export your own color palette in various formats.

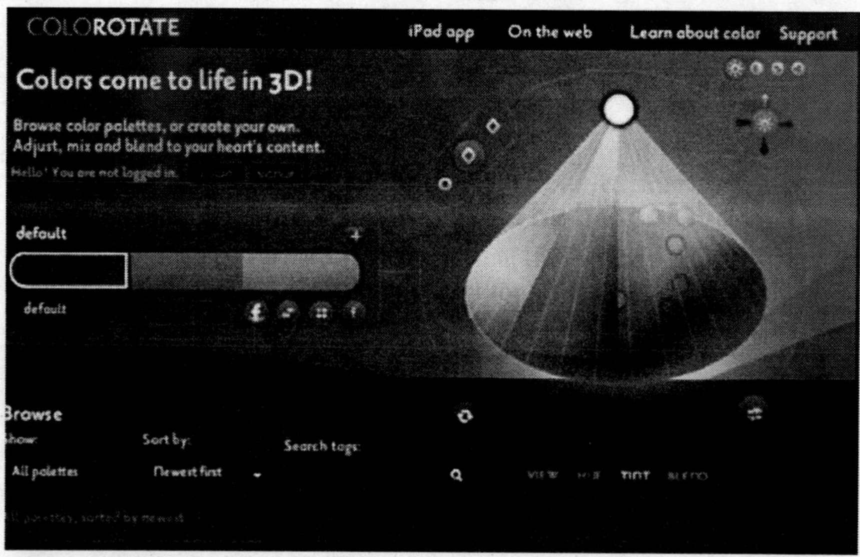


### (5) Colors On The Web

Colors on the Web is a dedicated resource to color theory and the importance of colors within web design. Of particular note is Color Wizard, which lets you start with a base color and returns a matching color palette. What started as an ASP application back in 2000 is now a full flash app with enough features and variations to create a complete palette.

Along with generating a matching five-color palette from your base color, the application returns a set of hue, saturation and tint and shade variations. You can also generate a random color palette if you are having trouble creating your own. Colors are outputted as hex code values.

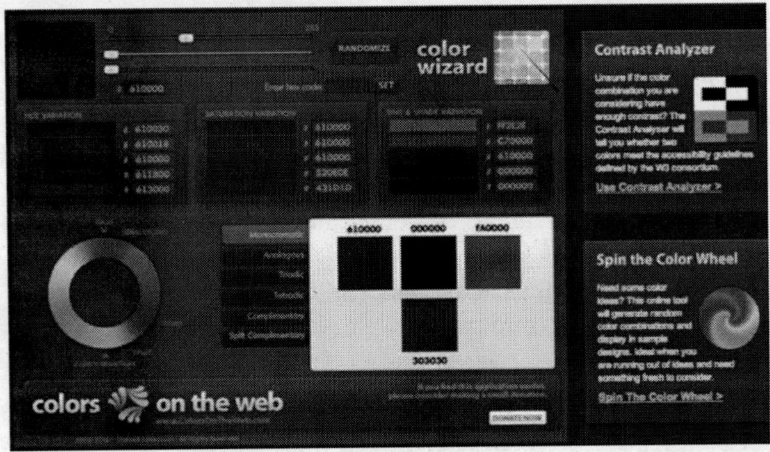


**(6) Color Munki**

ColorMunki offers solutions to color control for both photographers and designers. Usually this is as hardware; however, it also offers a Palette Creation Area free on its website. It provides introductory functionality to get you started creating your own color scheme.

You can generate palettes from either the Munsell or PANTONE Goe coated color systems. Once you select a color, clicking on it will give you a list of options, including "Add Patch," which adds that color to your palette. From there, you can view similar and harmonious colors, save it for reference or download it (as a CSV file). It also gives you the ability to search user-submitted palettes using keywords.

Albert Munsell, a professor at an art school in Boston developed a color system which offered a means to name colors. With a published system, people could be specific about which red they were referring. Munsell's system has been reworked for today's use with the Pantone color system, TRUEMATCH, CIE systems and others.

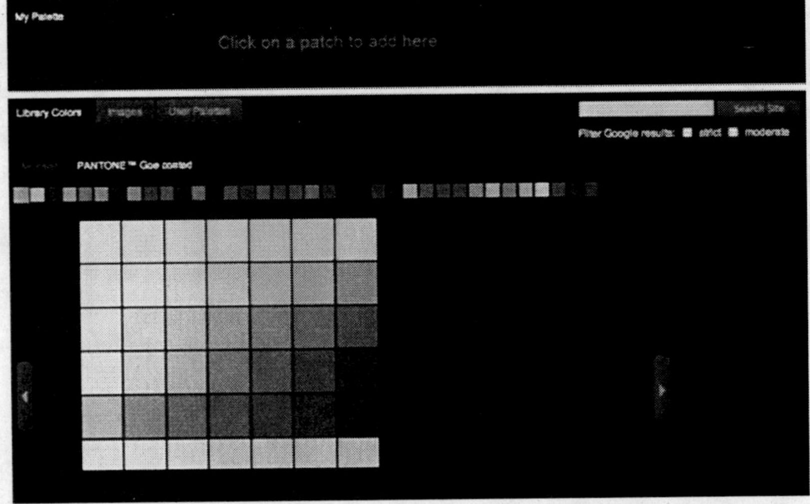

**(7) Color Scheme Designer**

The interface of Color Scheme Designer is incredibly simple to use, which means you can start creating a color palette in seconds. There are a wealth of options in the type of scheme you require, from monochromatic to accented analog. These affect the number of colors used in the palette and also how the colors interact with one another. If you're not familiar with these terms, go to Help and click Tool-tips to display an explanation of each part of the interface.

Along with the ubiquitous color picker, there are several other options to fine tune your palette, or if you choose Adjust Variants, you can edit colors individually. The color-blind preview is particularly useful to simulate how people with common color vision deficiencies will see your color scheme. You can export your palette in a variety of formats, with the text option offering the greatest flexibility.

**(8) Color Blender**

ColorBlender's main feature is to generate a six-color "blend" from your chosen base color, making it easy and efficient to create a complementary color scheme. To start, select a preferred color using the color picker, then a six-color matching palette is automatically calculated.

If you would like to take more control over your palette, you can choose to edit colors individually switching to "Direct Edit." In this mode, you can select any of the six color swatches and edit the color using the RGB sliders. There are several options to export your palette, either as a Photoshop Color Table (.ACT), via email or you can bookmark the palette in your web browser for future reference.

**(9) Color Explorer**

Color Explorer is packed full of useful tools for designing and working with color palettes. It has a well-organized set of features, which can be used individually or together. You can jump straight into the Color Picker, try the color matching tool using the traditional RGB mix or take the hue, saturation and lightness approach. There are eight color-matching algorithms to experiment with, which use scientific and theoretical models, or you can explore the color libraries and analysis and conversion tools.

The color import extracts a palette from an uploaded image or from HTML, CSS or text files to evaluate and work with colors. Native Adobe Swatch Exchange (.ASE) allows for export to Adobe Photoshop, Illustrator and InDesign. Export is also available as plain text or a PNG overlaid, with RGB values and HTML color codes.

**(10) 0 to 255**

Perhaps the simplest tool listed here, that doesn't mean 0 to 255 is any less useful. Instead of spending an age manually finding lighter or darker shades of your chosen color, 0to255 allows you to find colors in the same spectrum as one another, within seconds. Ideal for finding that perfect hover, border or gradient color.

Start picking a color, enter its hex value, and you will be presented with a range of colors from your chosen color through to black and white, using an interval optimized for web design. Once you've found a color you like, simply click on it, and the hex code is copied to your clipboard.

## 3.8 COLOUR MAPS

Different PCs have different resolutions, but in general you can assume that most people who view your pages will have a screen capable of 256 colours at a time. Of this, Netscape Navigator takes about ten colours for its windows. If you can manage it, make sure that your images look OK viewed in this many colours. A surprising number of people have PCs with a VGA adapter, which can only handle 16 colours at once-a challenge, but worth bearing in mind.

A useful tip when working with GIF files is to try and keep the number of colours to a power of two. A sixteen-colour GIF can be saved as a four-bit GIF which is half the size of a 32-colour GIF (which needs to be saved in 5-bit format). In effect, this means that a 17 colours GIF is twice the size of a 16-colour one. The same effect applies with 2-colour, 4-colour, 64-colour and 128-colour images, if you can limit your icons to four or eight colours, you can benefit generating very small files.

You can ignore how colour works and let Windows and VC++ do their own thing if you don't need to create interesting visual effects. But what good is a multimedia application if it's not visually interesting? To create the animation and other imaging effects that help users what they're learning, you'll need to understand how Windows and your computer manage colour. The capabilities of your display system determine what Windows can do with colour images. The systems supported today come in three classes: VGA, super VGA(SVGA), and true colour. (The MPC standard specifies VGA as the minimum display capabilities of I'll ignore the older CGA and EGA system). The standard VGA system can display 16 colours simultaneously with a resolution, of 640x 480 pixels. Super VGA provides more colours and/or greater resolution, and true colour provides sufficient colours and resolution to display images that look like colour photographs. (That's the theory, anyway). As you'll see, the waters start to get a little muddy when we look at SVGA and true colour systems. SVGA systems can draw from a dazzling array of 16,777,216 colours. However, only 256 colours out of that vast selection can appear on the screen simultaneously. Some so-called SVGA systems display only 64 simultaneous colours, though these are usually found in colour notebook computers. SVGA resolution start at 640x480 and go up from there. Some SVGA systems even reach resolutions exceeding 1200x1000pixels.

Systems that display the full 16 million colour range are often called true colour displays. What does "true colour" mean? It is derived from the idea that if a colour display shows an extensive range of colours, the images will look natural or "true". True colour displays use 24 bits to determine the colour of each pixel. The 24 bits are divided into three 8-bit colour components that indicate the intensity of the red, green, and blue colour components. For this reason, 24-bit colours are referred to as RGB colours. Each primary colour may vary in intensity according to an integer scale of 0 through 255. When all three RGB components are set to 0, the pixel appears black; when all are set to 255, the pixel is white. The total number of RGB combinations equals 256 cubed, or 16,777,216 colours.

Since older technology like photographs and analog television can display a virtually infinite variety of colours, it may seem presumptuous to call this digital version "true colour" but right now, this is the state-of-the-art in desk-top0 computer colour technology. In fact, most hardware capable of digitizing colour images provides a maximum colour resolution of 24 bits, which means that a true colour displays the maximum colour resolution found in current image data.

Unfortunately, SVGA systems can't display all of their colours at once because of their memory limitations. These systems display at least 307,200 pixels (640x480) and to produce full 24-bit colour requires three bytes for each pixels, a total of 921,600 bytes. Until recently, having this much dedicated display memory was considered an extravagance. Many SVGA cards come configured with only 512 kilobytes of memory, enough to support 8 bits per pixel at resolutions of 800x600. Some of the latest display interfaces support resolutions up to 1280x1024, which at 24 bits of colour resolution would require almost 4 Mb of display RAM! As memory prices continue to fall, more systems will include 24-bit colour displays but right now, most of the PCs sold as Windows system come equipped with 8-bit colour displays. So this is the standard we should accommodate in our programs.

## 3.9 COLOUR MODELS

Models or methodologies used to specify colours in computer terms are RGB, HSB, HSL, CMYK, CIE, and others. Using the RGB (red, green, blue) model, you specify a colour setting the amount of red, green and blue, in the range 0 to 65535. Colour Plate 2 illustrates the RGB colour cube, where the three dimensional represent the values of the three colour channels that specify a colour.

| Red | Green | Blue | Colour |
|---|---|---|---|
| 65535 | 65535 | 65535 | White |
| 65535 | 65535 | 00000 | Yellow |
| 65536 | 00000 | 65535 | Magenta |
| 00000 | 65536 | 65535 | Cyan |
| 65536 | 00000 | 00000 | Red |
| 00000 | 65535 | 00000 | Green |
| 00000 | 00000 | 65535 | Blue |
| 00000 | 00000 | 00000 | Black |

In the HSB (hue, saturation, brightness) and HSL (hue, saturation, lightness) models, you specify hue or colour as an angle from 0 to 360 degrees on a colour wheel, and saturation, brightness, and lightness as percentages. Lightness or brightness is the percentage of black or white that is mixed with a colour. A lightness of 100 percent will yield a white colour; 0 percent is black; the pure colour has a 50 percent lightness. Saturation is the intensity of the colour. At 100 percent saturation, the colour is pure; at 0 percent saturation, the colour is white, black or grey. Colour Plate 3 shows the location of colours on a colour wheel, as defined in the following:

| Colour | Degrees |
|---|---|
| Red | 0 |
| Yellow | 60 |
| Green | 120 |
| Cyan | 180 |
| Blue | 240 |
| Magenta | 300 |

The CMYK colour model is less applicable to multimedia production. It is used primarily in the printing trade where cyan, magenta, yellow and black are used to print process colour separations. Other colour models include CIE, YIQ, YUV, and YCC, CIE describes colour value in terms of frequency, saturation, and illuminance (blue/yellow or red/green, which in turn corresponds to the colour receptors in the cones of the eye). CIE more closely resembles how human beings perceive colour, but certain devices such as scanners are unable to replicate the process. YIQ and YUV were developed for broadcast TV. They are based on luminance and chrominance expressed as the amplitude of a wave and the phase of the wave relative to some reference. Detail is carried byluminance (black and white), so reduction in colour does not result in the loss of image definition detail.

## 3.10 WORKING WITH COLOUR IN CORELDRAW

CorelDRAW offers an impressive array of tools that give you full control over the colours that appear in your image, as well as the means to select and edit new colours. Millions of colours are available at every stroke of your brush or click of your mouse but as the range of available colour options becomes broader, it also becomes more difficult to get colours just right. Greater capabilities also mean more variables, more potential pitfalls, and a greater need for tools to help you deal with the sometimes baffling world of colour.

### 3.10.1 Calibrating your colour devices

Make sure that you calibrate your system using Corel Colour Manager before you begin creating and editing drawings. Corel Colour Manager looks after colour production, conversion, and selection of colours on your system to reduce the potential for surprises at printing time. Corel Colour Manager ensures that your hardware devices - scanners, monitors, and printers - are synchronized with your Corel software to produce the colours your want. It is important to calibrate your system even if your system does not include all devices mentioned.

### 3.10.2 Colour Models

Colour models are essentially colours that have been arranged into charts. You can use these charts to choose or identify colours for your image. Colour models use mathematical representations of a colour space to provide a standard against which we can measure colour. There are nine available colour models in CorelDRAW.

### 3.10.3 Colour Palettes and colour-matching systems

A Colour Palette is a collection of colours. Use the Colour Palettes displayed in the Colour Roll-Up, the Uniform Fill dialog box, the on-screen Colour Palette, and others to pick colours for your drawing.

Most of the other palettes available in CorelDRAW are from colour- matching systems. Colour-matching systems are collections of colours created and maintained companies that specialize in colour reproduction. They allow you to define colour clearly using an internationally accepted standard. For example, if you want a specific shade of blue to appear in your final printed output, you can choose the exact colour using a swatch book from a universally accepted colour-matching system like PANTONE Process Colours (*e.g.*, PANTONE S184-6).

### 3.10.4 Corel Colour Manager

Corel Colour Manager works with CorelDRAW to manage the production of colour all the devices in your system. Devices include scanners, monitors, and printers. The user interface allows you to select profiles for your devices from Colour Manager's extensive lists, or to create your own device profiles using sophisticated calibration tools. For more information, see "Using Corel Colour Manager".

**(1) Colour Correction Command**

The Colour Correction command, found in the View menu, activates the settings you've selected in the Colour Manager, ensuring that the colours you see on your monitor match the capabilities of the other devices in your system. For more information, see "Applying colour correction to your on-screen image".

**(2) Gamut Alarm**

The gamut alarm alerts you to the colours in your drawing that cannot be reproduced your printer.

It does this displaying a single colour in place of the out-of-gamut colours. For more information, see "Setting the gamut alarm".

**(3) Using Colour Models**

CorelDRAW provides a number of colour models from which you can choose colours. These include RGB, CMY, CMYK, CMYK255, HSB, HLS, Lab, and YIQ. If you are printing your work, the CMYK model is recommended. If your work will be displayed solely on screen, use whichever model is most intuitive to you.

The term "colour model" is used in two ways in CorelDRAW: first, you can select colours from a variety of different colour models (*e.g.*, HSB, CMYK, etc.). Second, once a colour model has been selected, you can edit this colour using a "visual selector" in the Uniform Fill dialog box (*e.g.*, HSB - Wheel Based, CMYK - 3D Subtractive, etc.). This visual selector is also sometimes referred to as a colour model.

CorelDRAW allows you to select and apply colours from a variety of different colour models. Each model contains slightly different colours, giving you hundreds of colours to choose from. In addition, you can modify these colours adjusting their component values. For example, if you want to use a colour that appears in the CMYK colour model (*e.g.*, red), but the colour is not quite dark enough, you can adjust the colour manually using the controls found in the Uniform Fill dialog box.

## 3.11 NEED OF USING COLOUR STYLES

Colour styles are especially useful if your drawing contains multiple shades of a particular colour. You can use colour styles to create a series of parent and child colours automatically. This, in turn, provides a valuable resource for creating any drawing that requires multiple shades of a particular colour. You can also open a CorelDRAW drawing, or a piece of Clipart, and use the Auto-Create feature to convert all of your drawing colours into colour styles. Once this is done, you can experiment with changing the hues of the parent colour styles. It is important to note that the Auto-Create feature will change the fill and outline colours in your document. This allows you to control all of your red objects, for example, with one parent colour, or to have a number of different parent colours, each representing a different hue of red.

Like graphic and text styles, colour styles are saved with the drawing and can be copied to other drawings and documents.

## 3.12 DIGITAL MEDIA DESIGN

Today, digital is synonymous with computer. According to Wikipedia digital media (as opposed to analog media) are usually electronic media that work on digital codes. Today, computing is primarily based on the binary numeral system. In this case digital refers to the discrete states of "0" and "1" for representing arbitrary data. Computers are machines that (usually) interpret binary digital data as information and thus represent the predominating class of digital information processing machines. Digital media like digital audio, digital video and other digital content can be created, referred to and distributed via digital information processing machines. Digital media represents a profound change from previous (analog) media.

The ability to access, interpret and create digital information has increased its level of importance in the continuum of literacy in recent years. The use of computers, the Internet and the World Wide Web has become integral to many forms of information access, communication, and knowledge generally. When information, music, voice and video are turned into binary digital form, they can be electronically manipulated, preserved and regenerated perfectly at high speed. The millionth copy of a computer file is exactly the same as the original. While this continually drives the software industry crazy protecting its copyrights, it is nevertheless a major advantage of digital processing.

### 3.12.1 Multimedia Systems Design

Multimedia Systems Design is the process of building a system with the technologies and the architecture able to support multimedia applications.

Each multimedia application handles one or more media type of information.

There are two levels of description for an application:

1. **Functional level**: What the application does and source and display data formats. *E.g.* An application may deal with the retrieval and display of movies. It retrieves movies and displays them in a window.
2. **System Level**: The entities that the application deals with and how it deals with them. In the above example we deal with video frames and voice samples and need to process these accordingly.

The following functionality should be provided by a multimedia system:

Digital Representation of Media – Many standardised formats for many media.

Capture: Digitisation of Media – Special Hardware/Software.

Creation and Editing – assemble media and alter it.

Storage Requirements – significant for multimedia.

Compression – related to above and below, *i.e.* can save on storage but can hinder retrieval.

Structuring and retrieval methods of media – simple to advanced Database Storage.

Display or Playback methods – effect of retrieval must view data.

Media Synchronisation – display multimedia as it is intended.

## 3.13 AUTHORING SOFTWARE

Authoring is a significant part of multimedia design and production. The function of authoring software is to incorporate the various components of multimedia. It provides tools, templates, and techniques to construct the application with interactive links. Most authoring software use a high-level facility which allows authoring without the need for programming skills. But, as with any other type of software, the various multimedia software packages have their weak points. Some software may only do an adequate job for certain tasks. Because of this, most people who develop multimedia rely on additional software packages to create or modify specific types of files before incorporating them in the multimedia programme. This supporting software may be a charting tool, a graphic or animation software.

There are several authoring packages for the PC applications under DOS, Windows and Macintosh. The cost of these multimedia development tools range from about US$300 to $8,000 or more. Authoring tools costing around US$500 or less include Multimedia Toolbook, Microsoft Multimedia Development Kit, HyperWriter, HyperCASE, LinkWay, HSC Interactive, AskMe 2000 and AuthorWare Star. Higher-end software includes IconAuthor (about US$5,000) and AuthorWare Professional (about US$8,000). The more expensive authoring tools generally provide a richer programming environment and support better animation and sound effects. Software changes so rapidly that any detailed information of specific packages can easily become obsolete. Recent computer magazines and periodicals are good sources for up-to-date software comparisons and reviews.

Another critical consideration is the license arrangement that will be needed to allow the application to be delivered. This is especially true in higher level software in which the authoring package creates presentations that are run on delivery systems with a smaller programme called 'Runtime'. The runtime programme determines how the media is packaged and delivered to the training sites.

## 3.14 DESIGN ELEMENTS OF 2D

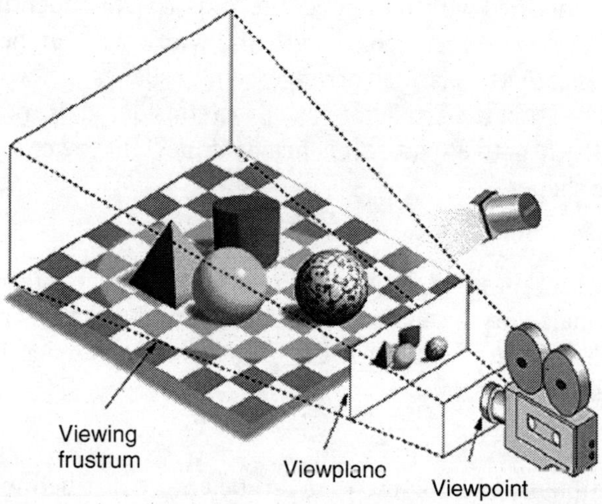


'2D' stands for 2-dimensional. A 2D shape is any shape that has two dimensions. Think about what it means to have two dimensions for a moment. If we had only one dimension to work with, we could only move backwards or forwards in a line. When we look a three D shape from a camera, whatever we see on a plane perpendicular to viewing angle (say its projection) will be a two dimensional drawing.

The elements are components or parts which can be isolated and defined in any visual design or work of art. They are the structure of the work, and can carry a wide variety of messages. The details may be differentiated by researchers, but I included 'point or mark', 'line', 'shape', 'forms', 'space', 'colour', and 'texture' .

2D animation focuses on creating characters, storyboards, and backgrounds in two-dimensional environments. Often thought of as traditional animation, the figures can move up and down, left, and right. They do not appear to move toward or away from the viewer, as they would in 3D animation.

### (1) Point or Mark

A point or mark is the smallest and most basic element. Often it is the personal 'handwriting' of the artist that can be natural or learned. These can vary in size, value, regularity or irregularity, and can be used alone or as a unit in a group which forms a line or shape in the image. Marks can be used to form a value or pattern (placed close together forms a darker value, further apart forms a lighter value), or to delineate space (larger means closer, etc.).

Even though there is only one point or mark on a white blank page, it can catch our sight. If there are two points, we will make a connection and see a line. If there are three points, it is unavoidable to interpret them as a triangle; the mind supplies the connections. These are called as grouping, or gestalt. Gestalt is the fundamental tool the designer or artist uses to build a coherent composition.

**(2) Line**

A line is a form with width and length, but no depth. Artists use lines to create edges, the outlines of objects. A line is created by the movement of the artist's pen. The direction of a line can convey mood. Horizontal lines are calm and quiet, vertical lines suggest more of a potential for movement, while diagonal lines strongly suggest movement and give more of a feeling of vitality to a picture.

**(3) Shape**

Shape is an area that is contained within implied line, or is seen and identified because of colour or value changes. Shapes have two dimensions, length and width, and can be geometric or free-form. Design in painting is basically the planned arrangement of shapes in a work of art.

In a picture, the shapes that the artist has placed are considered the positive shapes. The spaces around the shapes are the negative spaces. It is just as important to consider the negative space in a picture as the positive shapes.

**(4) Forms**

Form describes volume and mass, or the three dimensional aspects of objects that take up space. (Shape is two-dimensional) Forms can and should be viewed from any angles. When you hold a baseball, shoe, or small sculpture, you are aware of their curves, angles, indentations, extensions, and edges—their forms.

**(5) Space**

Actual space is three-dimensional volume that can be empty or filled with objects. It has width, height, and depth. Space that appears three-dimensional in a two-dimensional painting is an illusion that creates a feeling of actual depth. Various techniques can be used to show such visual depth or space.

**(6) Colour**

Colour has three properties. The first is hue, which is the name of the colours. The primary hues are yellow, red, and blue. Secondary colours are made by mixing two primaries. Intermediate colours are mixtures of a primary and adjacent secondary colour. The second property of colour is value, which refers to the lightness or darkness of hue. The third property of colour is intensity, which refers to the purity of the hue (also called "chroma").

**(7) Texture**

Texture refers to the surface quality, both simulated and actual, of artwork. Techniques used in painting serve to show texture, *i.e.* the dry brush technique produces a rough simulated quality and heavy application of pigment with brush or other implement produces a rough actual quality.

## 3.15 DESIGN PRINCIPLES OF 2D

### 3.15.1 Balance

Balance is a psychological sense of equilibrium. As a design principle, balance places the parts of a visual in an aesthetically pleasing arrangement. In visual images, balance is formal when both sides are symmetrical in terms of arrangement. Balance is informal when sides are not exactly symmetrical, but the resulting image is still balanced. Informal balance is more dynamic

than formal balance and normally keeps the learner's attention focused on the visual message. There are three main types of balance, horizontal balance, vertical balance, radial balance.

There are two systems for achieving balance: **symmetry and asymmetry.**

Symmetry means a mirror image – one side is the mirror image of the other. Symmetry can occur in any orientation as long as the image is the same on either side of the central axis.

This type of image has great appeal – it makes for "good" shape relationship. Many people automatically gravitate to symmetry. We are symmetrical after all – two eyes, two ears, etc. Look around at consumer products and graphics (printed materials) to see how many use symmetry. You will find that it is the dominant organizational concept. Symmetrical balance is formal balance.

## 3.15.2 Symmetrical Balance

A vertical axis is required to achieve balance with symmetry. Part of the reason is that we have struggled throughout our lives to perfect our balance in order to stand, walk, ride a bike, etc. To do this we must have exactly the same weight on both sides of our bodies. Our axis of symmetry is vertical and this makes a good model for symmetry in visual information.

Symmetrical balance is also called formal balance because a form (formula) is used — a mirror image about a vertical axis. The results look formal, organized and orderly.

There is a strong emphasis on the center axis in symmetry since all of the information is reflected from there. This should be taken into consideration when designing with symmetry. It is easy to over emphasize the center.

Symmetrical balance guarantees left to right balance, which is the most important aspect of balance. But there is more to balance than that. Top to bottom balance is also important. Most images seem more stable if the bottom seems slightly heavier. If the top seems too heavy the composition can look precarious.

Balance between the center and the outsides of the image must also be considered. Fortunately our own sense of balance is usually good enough to feel when the balance in a composition is wrong. Pay attention to your own sense of balance and you will do well. Your sense of balance, like anything else, can be improved with practice and experience.

## 3.15.3 Types of Symmetry

Symmetry means that the sides are exact mirror images of each other. This limits symmetry's application to abstract images since objects in the real world are not truly symmetrical. Try folding a leaf down the center and notice that the opposite sides do not exactly correspond with one another. Fine artists rarely use pure symmetry for this reason. It is more applicable to commercial designs.

### (1) Near Symmetry

Near symmetry is based on symmetry but the two halves are not exactly the same. Slight variations will probably not change the balance but there is more potential for variety and hence more interest. When the sides become too different, symmetry ceases to exist and balance must depend on other concepts (asymmetry).

Near symmetry is more versatile than pure symmetry. It is used in many graphic images since type throws off the symmetry but the balance is still achieved. It is also occasionally used for formal fine art images, especially early Christian religious paintings.

**(2) Inverted Symmetry**

Inverted Symmetry uses symmetry with one half inverted like playing cards. This is an interesting variation on symmetry but can make for an awkward balance.

**(3) Biaxial Symmetry**

A symmetrical composition can have more than one axis of symmetry. Biaxial symmetry uses two axes of symmetry – vertical and horizontal. These guarantee balance: top and bottom as well as left and right. The top and bottom can be the same as the left and right, or they can be different. The most regular and repetitive image occurs when they are the same.

More than two axes are possible. Snow flakes and kaleidoscopes have three axes of symmetry.

Radial symmetry is a related concept and can use any number of axes since the image seems to radiate out from the center, like a star.

## 3.15.4 Unity and Variety

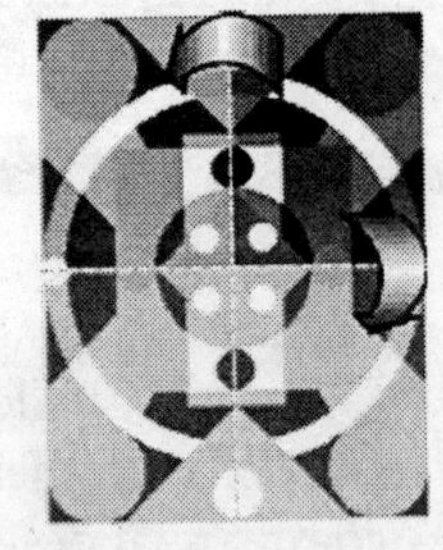

Symmetrical images have a strong sense of unity because at least half of the image is repeated. At the same time they lack variety because only half is unique. A biaxial image is only unique in one fourth of its format since that fourth is repeated in all the corners.

When the top/bottom and left/right are the same, only one eighth is unique. As the repetition increases, so does the unity. In other words, symmetrical images are usually well balanced and formal with good unity, but can lack excitement since they are so repetitive.

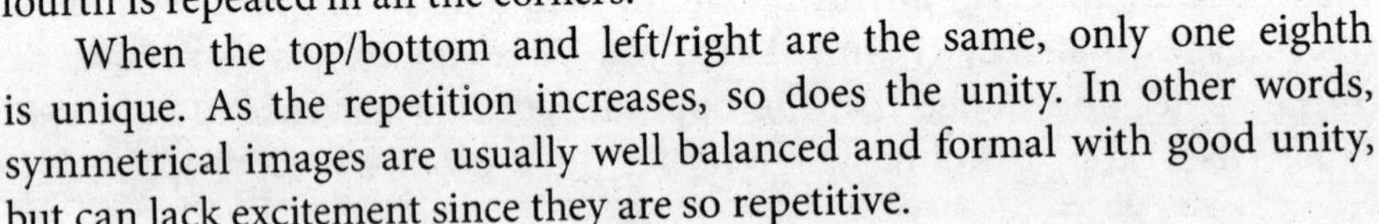

The strong sense of order and repetition make symmetrical images more acceptable to many people. That is why they are used so often in the applied arts. It is for the same reason that symmetry is rarely used in the fine artist. It is not that order is not wanted, but rather that variety is wanted to generate interest and to give the artist more freedom.

## 3.15.5 Asymmetry

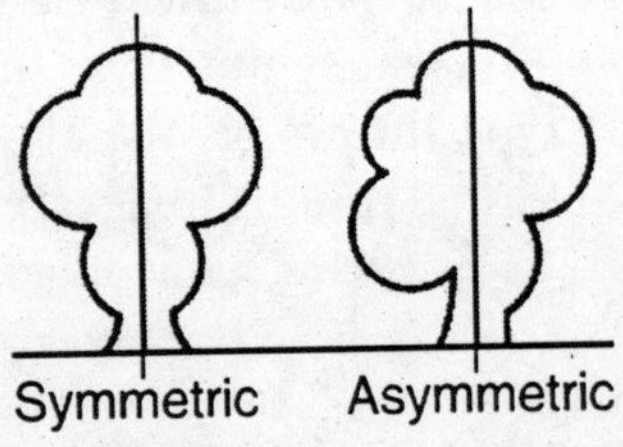


Asymmetry, also known as informal balance, means without symmetry. Have you ever seen a room design that included objects of differing sizes, shapes, and colours, yet it all worked together? This is an example of asymmetrical balance which is achieved by the careful juxtaposition of different elements. For example, a large area of dull colour can be balanced out by a much smaller area of bright colour. And a small, very complex shape can be balanced by a large, simple shape.

There are two types of balance: *symmetrical* and *asymmetrical.* In symmetrical balance, if an imaginary line is drawn through the center of the work, both sides are exactly the same, and balanced in that way. In asymmetrical balance, the two sides are not identical, but differ from one another. However, the elements are arranged so that there is a sense of balance.

In the illustration below, both examples use the exact same objects. The one on the left, however, is symmetrical, identical on each side. The one on the right uses the same shapes in the same colours, and balances them asymmetrically. Both sides are different, yet arranged in such a way that they feel balanced.

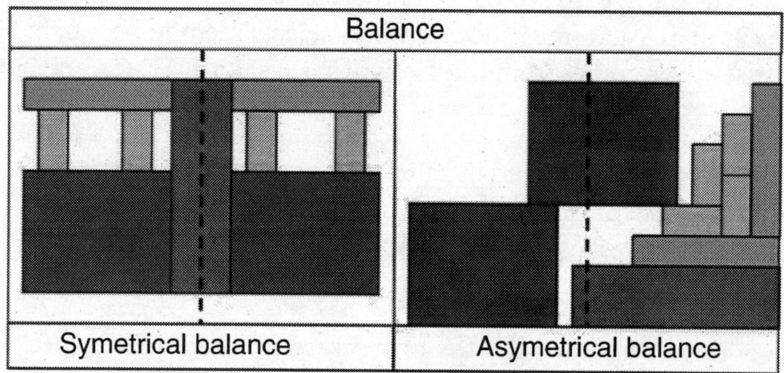


Symmetrical balance often has more variety, visual interest, and liveliness.

Asymmetrical balance can be achieved by using some of the following principles: Visually–

1. a large form is heavier than a smaller form.
2. dark values are heavier than light values.
3. a textured form is heavier than a smooth form.
4. a complex form is heavier than a simple form.
5. two or more smaller forms balance one large form.
6. a smaller darker form balances a larger lighter form.
7. objects toward the edge or corner of the composition appear heavier.
8. intense colours are heavier than muted colours.

### 3.15.6 Other Properties

**(1) Proportion**

Proportion refers to the relative size and scale of the various elements in a design. The issue is the relationship between objects, or parts, of a whole. This means that it is necessary to discuss proportion in terms of the context or standard used to determine proportions.

**(2) Perspective**

Perspective is created through the arrangement of objects in two-dimensional space to look like they appear in real life. Perspective is a learned meaning of the relationship between different objects seen in space.

Is the dark rectangle in front of a circle, or beside a semi-circle? Perspective adds realism to a visual image. The size of a rectangle means little until another object gives it the size of a desk, or the size of a building. Perspective can be used to draw the audience into a visual. Perception can be achieved through the use of relative sizes of objects, overlapping objects, and blurring or sharpening objects.

### (3) Emphasis

Emphasis is used by artists to create dominance and focus in their work. Artists can emphasize colour, value, shapes, or other art elements to achieve dominance. Various kinds of contrast can be used to emphasize a center of interest.

### (4) Movement

The way the artist leads the eye in, around, and through a composition. The path the eye follows. Motion or movement in a visual image occurs when objects seem to be moving in a visual image. Movement in a visual image comes from the kinds of shapes, forms, lines, and curves that are used.

### (5) Pattern

Pattern uses the art elements in planned or random repetition to enhance surfaces or paintings or sculptures. Patterns often occur in nature, and artists use similar repeated motifs to create pattern in their work. Pattern increases visual excitement enriching surface interest.

### (6) Repetition

Repetition works with pattern to make the artwork seem active. The repetition of elements of design creates unity within the artwork.

### (7) Rhythm

Rhythm is the repetition of visual movement of the elements-colours, shapes, lines, values, forms, spaces, and textures. Variety is essential to keep rhythms exciting and active, and to avoid monotony. Movement and rhythm work together to create the visual equivalent of a musical beat.

### (8) Variety

Variety provides contrast to harmony and unity. Variety consists of the differences in objects that add interest to a visual image. Variety can be achieved using opposites or strong contrasts. Changing the size, point of view, and angle of a single object can add variety and interest to a visual image. Breaking a repeating pattern can enliven a visual image.

### (9) Harmony

Harmony in visual design means all parts of the visual image relate to and complement each other. Harmony pulls the pieces of a visual image together. Harmony can be achieved through repetition and rhythm. Repetition reemphasizes visual units, connecting parts and creating an area of attention. Rhythm is the flow depicted in a visual. Rhythm helps direct eye movement. Patterns or shapes can help achieve harmony.

Repeating patterns in an interesting arrangement, the overall visual image comes together.

### (10) Unity

Unity means the harmony of the whole composition. The parts of a composition made to work together as a total visual theme.

Unity is the relationship among the elements of a visual that helps all the elements function together. Unity gives a sense of oneness to a visual image. In other words, the words and the images work together to create meaning.

## 3.16 DESIRABLE QUALITIES OF MULTIMEDIA DESIGN

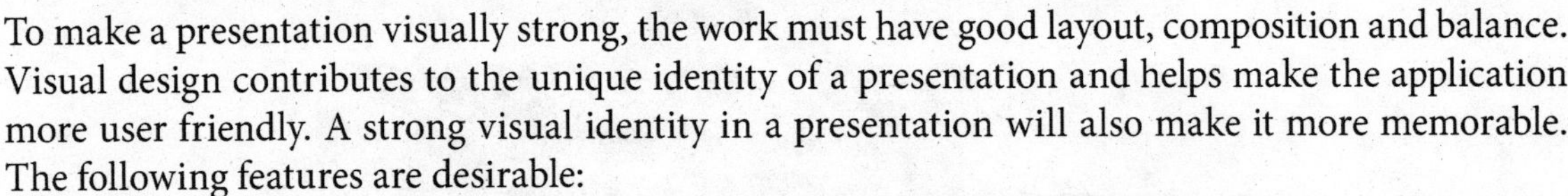

To make a presentation visually strong, the work must have good layout, composition and balance. Visual design contributes to the unique identity of a presentation and helps make the application more user friendly. A strong visual identity in a presentation will also make it more memorable. The following features are desirable:

### (1) Originality and Creativity

This overlaps with many of the other issues that will follow but it is worth the extra emphasis. To make a presentation effective, it is essential to be creative and develop a unique identity for the work. Good graphic design employ techniques and skills in new and innovative ways.

### (2) Layout and Composition

Effective use of space can significantly enhance a page design. It is important to think about the space you create around the visual content you place on screen. While it is OK to have empty space around your visual content, it should be carefully organised. This negative space should never be thought of as 'left-over' space otherwise it will appear as random, arbitrary and insignificant. The negative space provides a visual connection and balance to your scene.

When integrating various elements for a scene, only necessary design items should be included. Work cluttered with irrelevant clip art, background colours or free animated gifs, can make a scene appear tacky and unprofessional. There are many sites that provide such free 'artwork'. Remember, they are free for a reason. You don't want your work to look like a cliché with tired and overused graphics.

A good scene in a presentation has a focal point that draws and captures your attention. A lack of focal point or too many focal points makes the scene difficult to understand. The focal point should not be the navigational bar. While the interface is an important part of the scene, your content should not overwhelm the interface.

Direction is an important part of composition. You can angle text or include images that lead your eye across the screen giving direction to a page, the audience can understand how to read the composition. Direction can create a sense of movement and make a page dynamic without any animation.

Related items on a page should be grouped together to provide organisation and cohesion. Similar items grouped together will reflect a relationship between the elements and help make the scene more readable to your audience. You should not create relationships with elements that don't belong together. Items that are not directly related to each other should be separated in space. Varying the amount of space between elements indicates closeness or the importance of the relationship.

### (3) Hierarchy

To 'read' a scene effectively, it is important to be able to distinguish different levels of importance of elements in the composition. Hierarchy of elements contributes to understanding of a scene. Hierarchy can be displayed use of a dominant size, location, shape or colour.

**(4) Layering and Depth**

A presentation can be easier to read and understand if the scenes have different layers. There are three basic layers, foreground, midground and background.

Foreground describes the part of a composition that appears closest to the viewer. The foreground is one of the three zones of recession in linear perspective—foreground, middle ground, and background. Middle ground describes the part of a composition between the foreground and background. Background describes the part of a composition that appears to be farthest from the viewer.

**Fig. 3.5:** Various layers in a Sketch

**Fig. 3.6:** Various layers in a scenery

Having these three layers give sense depth and visual interest. The background can be a colour or image that provides the backdrop for visual information placed on top. A graphical interface placed in its own layer is much easier to identify and understand.

**(5) Repetition (Consistency)**

When you repeat visual elements across a presentation, you create a unified look and strong consistency throughout the work. Repetition can be in colour, graphical interfaces, spatial arrangements, and typefaces of text. Unity and continuity through the presentation are vital features of good design. Maintaining similar placement of navigational elements from scene to scene makes it easier for users to understand how to navigate through the work. Repeating visual elements gives the work order. Design should be consistent in placement of elements, size and colour. A website with consistency in design will allow the user to feel comfortable browsing from page to page. If each section is very different and feels like you have moved into a different site, instead of feeling comfortable, the user will feel disconcerted and confused, resulting in an ineffective communication of your site's message.

**(6) Balance**

The human body has a finely tuned sense of balance as evidenced when you walk, run or simply stand. Our sense of balance carries over into our visual perception. Balance in composition involves creating a layout of graphics so the result achieves a sense of evenness. Balance can be achieved through symmetry, where there is an exact proportion of parts across an axis, or through or asymmetrical composition.

**(7) Alignment**

Alignment is important whether you are designing a poster, business card or multimedia presentation. You should not place visual elements together in an arbitrarily manner. Every element should have a visual connection to each other. The lack of alignment causes major design problems. Strong, sharp edges create a strong, sharp impression. A lack of alignment of visual elements can give a sloppy, disorganised and weak impression.

When using alignment, make sure it is strong. If the alignment is slightly out, it looks like a mistake. Breaking alignment can be used for emphasis in certain situations, such as to illustrate a button has been pressed down.

**(8) Contrast**

The use of contrast within your menus or scenes provides visual interest. Contrast can also show the hierarchy of information in your scene, allowing the audience to easily find the most important information and understand what it is about. Contrast can appear in text or images, in colour, size, shape or spatial relationships. Contrast is only effective if it is strong, otherwise it can look accidental.

**(9) Multimedia Design Styles**

Whether designing a website, interactive multimedia CD-ROM or kiosk application, you will need to choose a design approach or style for your application. This style will need to consider the audience type, their needs and the objectives of the application. These design styles fit into 5 broad categories as illustrated in the diagram below.

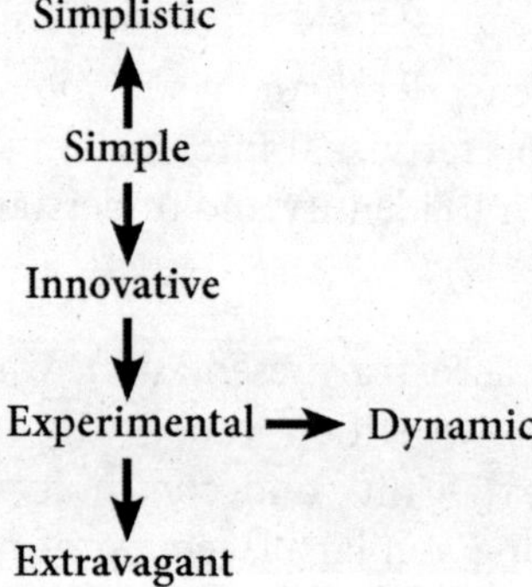


At the top of the tree, is simplistic design. At the other end is extravagant work, which is the design opposite to the simplistic approach. Simplistic work results from under use of elements while extravagance is the over use or over design of work. Extravagance can result from an experimental approach gone wrong or a lack of innovation and understanding of the relevant issues relating to the project. Between simplistic and extravagant design are design approaches of varying degrees of innovation.

## 3.17 INTERNATIONAL TELEVISION STANDARDS

Not all the world TV receivers work in the same way. Different countries use different types of broadcast TV system, most of which are to varying extents incompatible with each other.

### 3.17.1 Why Did This Happen?

In order to work TV receivers require a source of *field timing reference signals*. These are signals that tell the TV receiver to be ready to receive the next picture in the stream of images. Early set designers decided to use the Mains power supply frequency as this source for two good reasons. The first was that with the older types of power supply, you would get rolling hum bars on the TV picture if the mains supply and power source were not at exactly the same frequency. The second was that the TV studios would have had enormous problems with flicker on their cameras when making programs.

There are two Mains power frequencies widely used around the World, 50Hz and 60Hz. This immediately divided the worlds TV systems into two distinct camps, the 25 frames per second camp (50Hz) and the 30 frames per second camp (60Hz).

Later the 60Hz camp made a small adjustment and changed the field rate to 59.94Hz when they added color to the signals. The issue of field frequency remained sufficiently deep rooted in both TV standards that the vested interest remained long after the original technical justification had gone.

The biggest compatibility problems between TV standards remain related to the field rate; these are also the hardest problems to solve.

### 3.17.2 Compounding The Problem

Beyond the initial divide between 50 and 60Hz based systems, further sub-divisions have appeared within both camps since the inception of Color broadcasting. The majority of 60Hz based countries use a technique known as **NTSC** originally developed in the United States a committee called the National Television Standards Committee. NTSC works perfectly in a video or closed circuit environment but can exhibit problems of varying hue when used in a broadcast environment.

This hue change problem is caused by shifts in the color sub-carrier phase of the signal. A modified version of NTSC soon appeared which differed mainly in that the sub-carrier phase was reversed on each second line; this is known as **PAL**, standing for Phase Alternate Lines. PAL has been adopted by a few 60Hz countries, most notably Brazil.

Among the countries based on 50Hz systems, PAL has been the most widely adopted. PAL is not the only color system in widespread use with 50Hz; the French designed a system of their own - primarily for political reasons to protect their domestic manufacturing companies - which is known as **SECAM**, standing for Sequential Couleur Avec Memoire. SECAM was widely adopted in Eastern Block countries to encourage incompatibility with Western transmissions - again a political motive.

In general, since the field and scan rates are identical, you can expect to get a monochrome picture from a PAL video recording replayed on SECAM equipment, and vice versa.

**The Main Video Signal Standards**

| Name | Frame/Field rate<br>TV standard | Aspect Ratio<br>Color System | Scan Lines<br>Subcarrier Freq |
|---|---|---|---|
| NTSC | 29.97/59.94<br>EIA | 4:3<br>NTSC | 525<br>3.58MHz |
| PAL-M | 29.97/59.94<br>EIA | 4:3<br>PAL | 525<br>3.58MHz |
| ME-SECAM | 29.97/59.94<br>EIA | 4:3<br>SECAM | 525<br>?.??MHz |
| PAL | 25/50<br>CCIR | 4:3<br>PAL | 625<br>4.43MHz |
| SECAM | 25/50<br>CCIR | 4:3<br>SECAM | 625<br>4.25/4.40MHz |

The frame rate is standards-dependent, and for conventional broadcasting appears in 50 progressive frames per second in former PAL/SECAM countries (Europe, Australia and others), and 59.94 frames per second in former NTSC countries (North America, Japan, Brazil and others).]

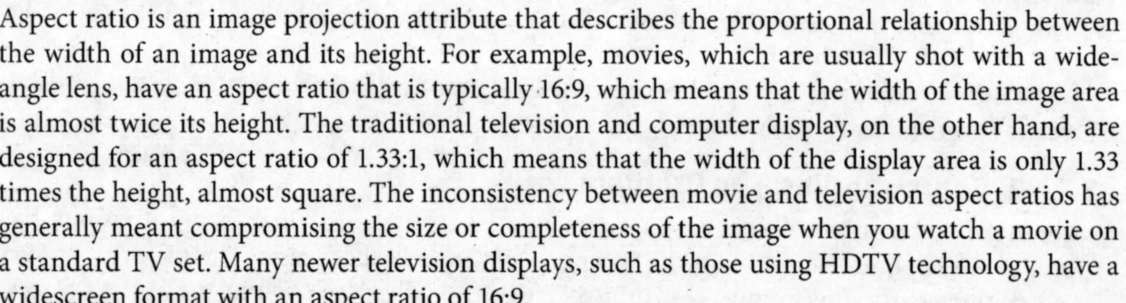

## 3.18 ASPECT RATIO

Aspect ratio is an image projection attribute that describes the proportional relationship between the width of an image and its height. For example, movies, which are usually shot with a wide-angle lens, have an aspect ratio that is typically 16:9, which means that the width of the image area is almost twice its height. The traditional television and computer display, on the other hand, are designed for an aspect ratio of 1.33:1, which means that the width of the display area is only 1.33 times the height, almost square. The inconsistency between movie and television aspect ratios has generally meant compromising the size or completeness of the image when you watch a movie on a standard TV set. Many newer television displays, such as those using HDTV technology, have a widescreen format with an aspect ratio of 16:9.

### (1) 4:3 and 16:10

Until about 2003, most computer monitors had a 4:3 aspect ratio and some had 5:4. Between 2003 and 2006, monitors with 16:10 aspect ratio became commonly available, first in laptops and later also in standalone computer monitors. Reasons for this transition was productive uses for such monitors, i.e. besides widescreen movie viewing and computer game play, are the word processor display of two standard letter pages side, as well as CAD displays of large-size drawings and CAD application menus at the same time. 16:10 became the most common sold aspect ratio for widescreen computer monitors until 2008.

### (2) 16:9

In 2008, the computer industry started to move from 4:3 and 16:10 to 16:9 as the standard aspect ratio for monitors and laptops. A 2008 report Display Search cited a number of reasons for this shift, including the ability for PC and monitor manufacturers to expand their product ranges offering products with wider screens and higher resolutions, helping consumers to more easily adopt such products and "stimulating the growth of the notebook PC and LCD monitor market".

## 3.19 ANIMATION

Animation can be defined as a sequence of images which are designed to appear at about 16 fps to create the perception of movement. This frame rate is just above the threshold of jerky motion and creates a satisfactory simulation. However, animation sequences can be developed with any specific frame rate at which objects will move across the screen for creating special effects.

Most animation objects are graphics considerably smaller than the screen although some animation sequences can be very complex. Designers exercise considerable control over animation sequences which can be arranged to reduce bandwidth requirements without affecting the quality of the presentation. With actual video this option is not available because the image itself is beyond the control of the designer and is a reflection of reality captured by a camera.

Complex high-quality animation sequences require about 20 Mbps, bandwidth and compression is normally used to reduce that requirement. Some animation forms such as those used in complex visualizations, product simulations, and virtual-reality applications require considerably more bandwidth for storage and transmission.

## 3.20 DRAWING AND ILLUSTRATION

Drawing, often referred to as illustration, is a form of visual expression and is one of the major forms within the visual arts. Drawing shares some of the materials, techniques, and qualities of painting, but there are important differences. Most notably, painting typically focuses on the application of pigments to a prepared surface using a brush or other supplies, while drawing involves the marking of lines on paper. Drawing can often be an exploratory experience, heavily influenced observation and composition. Drawing and illustration are commonly included in the process of painting—Often, painting is used as a means to finish a piece of art once the drawing has been completed.

Probably the most common tools used for drawing and illustration are pencils, pens, and brushes. It's possible, though, to use all sorts of materials to draw, each with its own unique artistic qualities.

The idea of someone noticing me drawing him/her makes me extremely uncomfortable. That's when I find blind sketching helpful. Blind sketching is a very simple technique that helps me loosen my drawing line and gives me an interesting starting point for character design. It forces me to go out of my "comfort zone" and improve my style.

The principle is very simple. The idea is to not look (or at least, look less) at the drawing paper while sketching quickly an object that's being observed. Very often it gives nothing, just a pile of gibberish lines. But sometimes it can catch the essence of a posture or a movement in a very unique way. The unpredictable distortion that's created as a result of the process can be a good start for designing or illustrating characters.

## 3.21 SKETCH

A sketch is a rough or brief outline of something. If you hand in a sketch, instead of your full paper, don't expect to get a very high grade!

The word sketch can be used when talking about something visual, particularly a drawing. An artist might sketch a friend in an hour, and then go home and take weeks to complete the portrait. A sketch can also refer to a short verbal or narrative account. You might want to give your friend a brief sketch of what happened to you today, instead of boring her with every last detail, including the hours you spent washing and then folding your laundry.

## 3.22 STORYBOARD

A storyboard is a graphic organizer in the form of illustrations or images displayed in sequence for the purpose of pre-visualizing a motion picture, animation, motion graphic or interactive media sequence. The storyboarding process, in the form it is known today, was developed at Walt Disney Productions during the early 1930s, after several years of similar processes being in use at Walt Disney and other animation studios.

Once a concept or script is written for a film or animation, the next step is to make a storyboard. A storyboard visually tells the story of an animation panel, kind of like a comic book.

Your storyboard will should convey some of the following information:

- What characters are in the frame, and how are they moving?
- What are the characters saying to each other, if anything?
- How much time has passed between the last frame of the storyboard and the current one?
- Where the "camera" is in the scene? Close or far away? Is the camera moving?

**A storyboard** is a low fidelity prototype consisting of a series of screen sketches. Storyboards are a tool for turning your story into a visual and they use the same techniques as comics or movie storyboards. They are used designers to illustrate and organize their ideas and obtain feedback. They are particularly useful for multi-media presentations. Making even just a short film or video without a storyboard is like writing an essay without an outline. "Story-Boarding is a popular management tool to facilitate the creative-thinking process and can be likened to taking your thoughts and the thoughts of others and spreading them out on a wall as you work on a project or solve a problem." Your storyboard should show your users' experiences of using your services over time. These experiences may be shared in several different scenarios for using the service depending on who is involved and what activities they are doing (*e.g.*, nurse or patient, routine check-up or medical emergency). Use captions in the images to describe what is happening. Creating a storyboard will help you plan your animation out shot. You can make changes to your storyboard before you start animating, instead of changing your mind later. You will also be able to talk about your animation and show your storyboard to other people to get feedback on your ideas.

### 3.22.1 Making a Storyboard

Most commonly, storyboards are drawn in pen or pencil. If you don't like to draw you can also take photos, cut out pictures from magazines, or use a computer to make your storyboards. Keep in mind that your drawings don't have to be fancy! In fact, you want to spend just a few minutes drawing each frame. Use basic shapes, stick figures, and simple backgrounds. If you draw your storyboard frames on index cards, you can rearrange them to move parts of the story around.

You can sketch stick figures, shoot photos, use stock photography or use creative commons licensed images for the visuals. You may also be interested in using the Toy Comics Toolkit released by Bryce Johnson, or the Design Comics Library of free images made available by Martin Hardee.

### 3.22.2 Benefits of adopting Storyboarding

1. Provides an overview of the system
2. Demonstrates the functionality of the storyboard elements
3. Demonstrates the navigation scheme
4. Can check whether the presentation is accurate and complete
5. Can be evaluated by users.

### 3.22.3 Use in Business

Storyboards are used today in industry for planning advertising campaigns, commercials, a proposal or other business presentations intended to convince or compel to action. Consulting firms teach the technique to their staff to use during the development of client presentations, frequently employing the "brown paper technique" of taping mock-up presentation slides to a large piece of kraft paper which can be rolled up for easy transport. The initial storyboard may be as simple as slide titles on Post-It notes, which are then replaced with draft presentation slides as they are created. Storyboards also exist in accounting in the ABC System (Activity Based Costing System) to develop a detailed process flowchart which visually shows all activities and the relationships among activities. They are used in this way to measure the cost of resources consumed, identify and eliminate non-value-added costs, determine the efficiency and effectiveness of all major activities, and identity and evaluate new activities that can improve future performance.

"**Design comics**" are a type of storyboard used to include a customer or other characters into a narrative. Design comics are most often used in designing web sites or illustrating product usage scenarios during design.

### 3.22.4 Methods of Storyboarding

**Use context of use and scenarios as input.**

Brainstorm ideas, this may include lists, charts, doodles, and quick notes

Select the best ideas: re-consider the project requirements, time and resource constraints, and the target audience and end users. Select the top ideas and try to get feedback from others involved.

Sketch each screen, and describe any pictures, images, animations, sound, music, video or text.

## Variations

Storyboards can be used as a way of describing the user's everyday activities as well as the potential designs and impact they will have.

Storyboards are most flexible when they are hand-drawn, but more realism and some animation and interaction can be created using a package like PowerPoint.[5]

Newer technologies such as Prezi can make your presentations of ideas more dynamic and interactive.

Importantly for entrepreneurship, storyboards can be very useful for pitching - like your pitch, your storyboard must pull readers into your narrative or offer up the meatiest content you can offer or your audience will move on to something else.

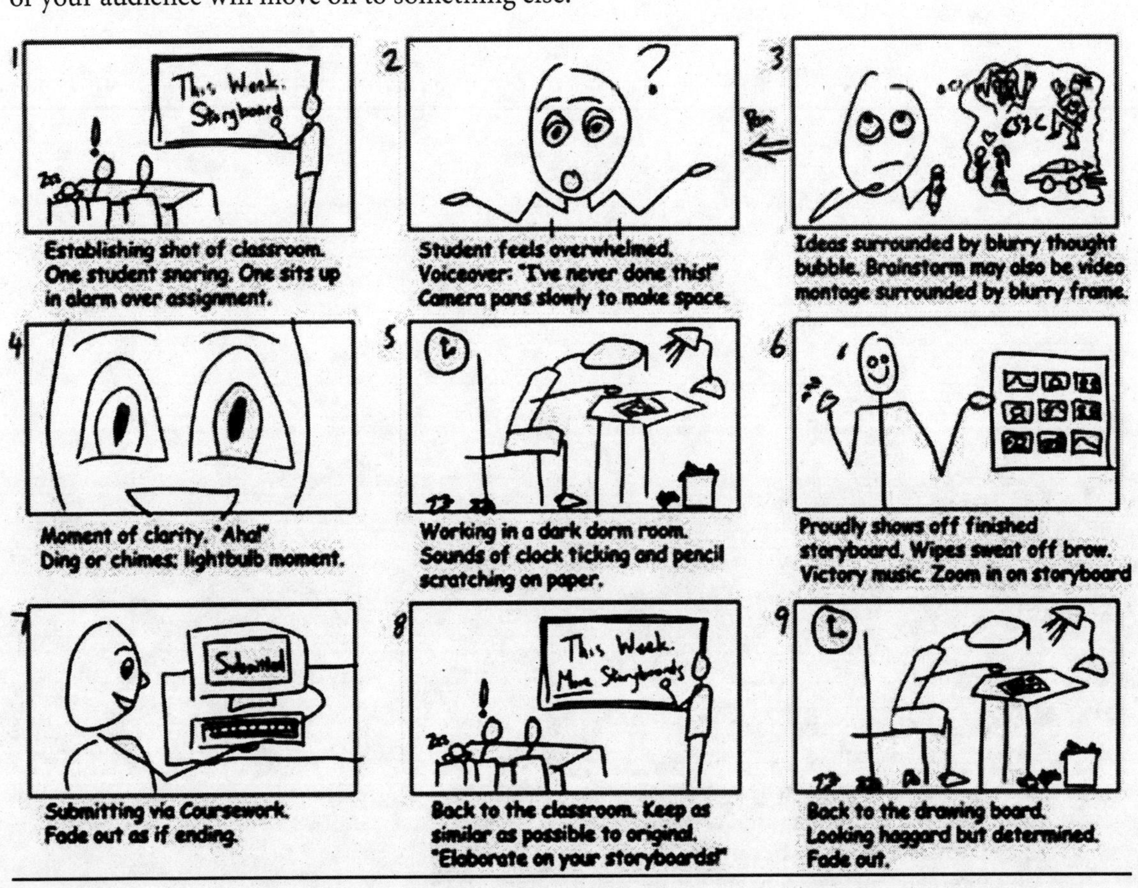

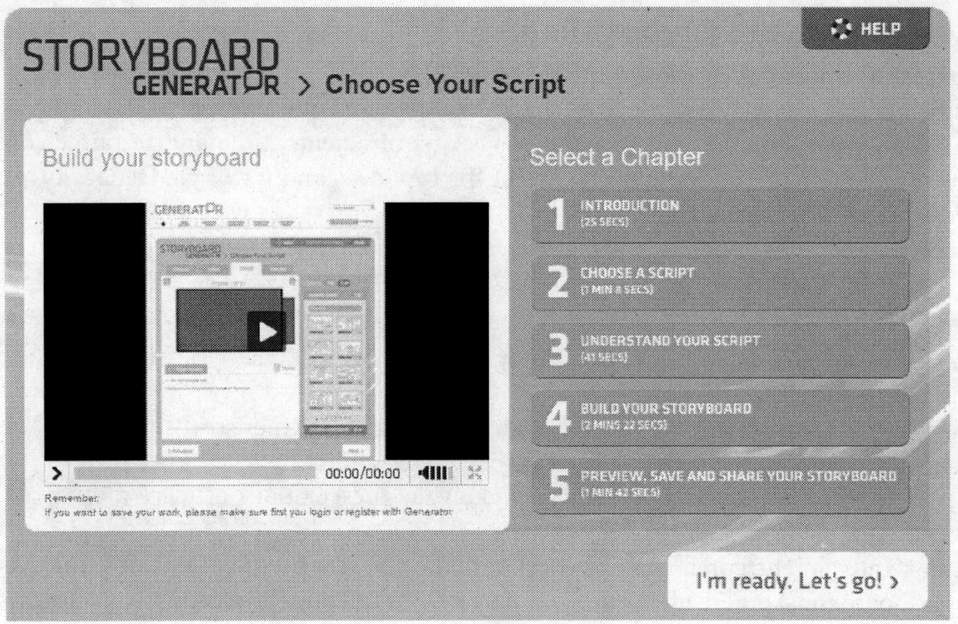


**Learning Outcomes**

In this chapter we have learnt about:

1. How to set colours schemes in computer Display
2. Working with colours in Coreldraw
3. Digital Multimedia Design principle
4. International Television Standards
5. Animation and Making Storyboard

# Multimedia Text and Hypertext

CHAPTER 4

**Leaning Objectives**

In this chapter we shall learn about:

1. Different types of Multimedia text styles and Fonts
2. Codes for Information Exchange on Internet/Web Design
3. Character sets and Designing Fonts of different types
4. Use of Rich and Hypertext

## 4.1 USAGE OF TEXT IN MULTIMEDIA

Text technology forms the basis for many multimedia systems. How text is created and edited, how it is stored, and how is it used are all critical to the development and successful delivery of multimedia products and systems. This chapter describes the features of text, how it is stored, and how to use it in a multimedia product.

### Elements of textual matter

Multimedia applications depend on text for many things and for a variety of proposes, some of which includes:

- Page titles
- Instructions for operating the application
- Providing identification of objects such as pictures or program labels
- Delivering information in the form of captions and bulk text
- Assisting the user in navigating around the application

## 4.2 FAMILIES AND FACES OF FONTS

A font is a collection of characters of a single size and style belonging to a particular typeface family. A typeface is a family of graphic characters that usually includes many type sizes and styles. Fonts come in many varieties when used in computers graphic environments. It is common for personal computers to be able to access and use dozens of fonts in a variety of applications. Typical font styles are boldface and italic. Other style attributes, such as underlining and outlining of characters, may be added by your computer software. Type sizes are usually expressed in points; one point is .0138 inches or 1/72 of an inch. The font's size is the distance from the top of the capital letters to the bottom of the descenders in letters such as *g* and *y*. Helvetica, Times, and Courier are typefaces; Times 12- point italic is a font.

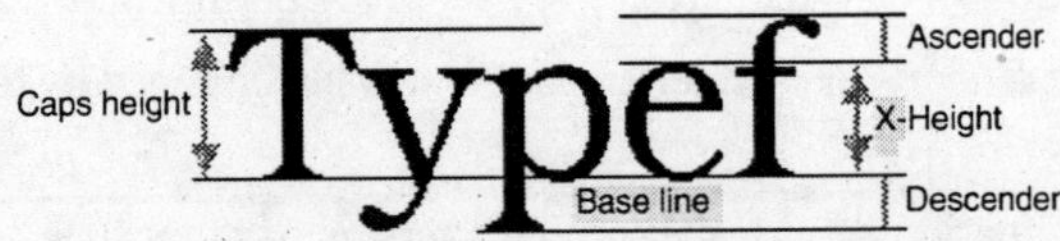


**Fig. 4.1:** Various Characteristics of Typeface.

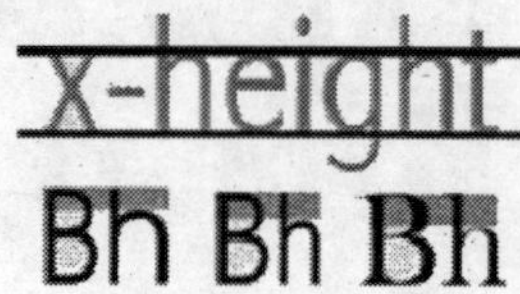

Typefaces of the same point size but differing x-heights.

**Fig. 4.2:** The Measurement of Type.

In the computer world, the term "font" is commonly used when describe or face would be more correct. A font's size does not exactly describe the height or width of its characters. This is because the x-height (the height of the lowercase letter x) of two fonts may vary, while the height of the capital letters of those may be the same (See Figure 4.2).

Computer fonts automatically add space below the descender (and sometimes above) to provide appropriate line spacing, or leading (pronounced "ledding"). There can be significant variation among fonts. Leading can be adjusted in most programs on both the Macintosh and in Windows. Typically you will find this fine-tuning adjustment in the Paragraph menu, though this is not an official standard. No matter where your application has placed the controls for leading, you will need to experiment with them to achieve the best result for your font.

In addition to typeface and size, Figure 4.3 describes a number of characteristics that are used to physically describe text:

- Ascender is an upstroke on a character and can be found in the letters h, b, and d.
- Descender is the downstroke below the baseline of a character; for example p,q, and y all have descenders.
- Leading (pronounced ledding) is the spacing above and below a font: that is the line spacing.
- Tracking is the spacing between characters.
- Kerning is the space between pairs of characters, usually as an overlap for improved appearance.
- Serif is the flag or decoration at the end of a character stroke.

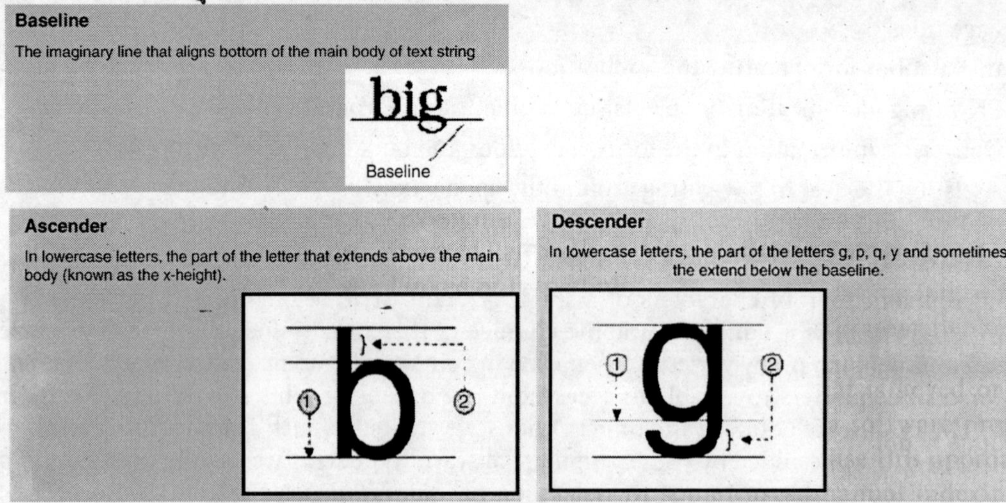


**Fig. 4.3:** Different Characteristics of fonts.

Fonts also take on a number of effects that are useful for bringing the viewer's attention to content:

- **Case :** Upper and lower versions of each letter; case is usually changed by the shift or caps lock function of the keyboard.
- **Regular :** used in most situations: this is the standard version of a font such as Times New Roman or Arial.
- **Bold :** provides standout emphasis for highlighting and titles.

- **Italic :** slightly slanted, used to derive attention of viewer.
- **Condensed and expanded :** narrowing or expanding the overall width of text characters.
- **Underline :** used for highlighting.
- **Usually indicates text has been removed :** for example, She went to the 87 o'clock show.

Font effects as are usually selected within a word processing program by accessing a dialog that allows the user to select the desired effects.

Figures 4.4 (a) and (b) show different examples of serif and sans serif fonts. Serif fonts include:

Times New Roman
Bell MT
Bodoni
Courier New
Garamond
Georgia
Goudy Old Style

**Fig. 4.4(a):** Fonts with Serif

Famous Sans serif fonts include:

Arial
Century Gothic
Franklin Gothic
Gill Sans
Lucida Sans
Tahoma
Trebuchet
Verdana

**Fig. 4.4(b):** Fonts without Serif (San Serif)

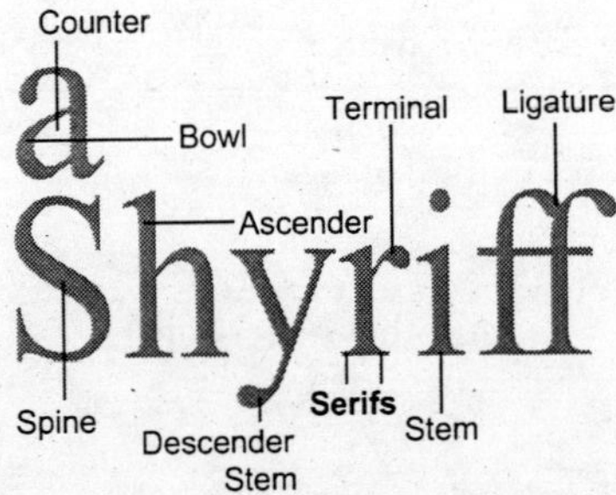


**Fig. 4.4(c):** Definition of Terms in Serif Type Fonts

## 4.3 RASTERIZATION AND ANTI-ALIASING

Graphical systems are able to create and use fonts due to a process called rasterization. Rasterization occurs when the computer draws the font into the display one pixel at a time. Fonts depending on the side and the number of pixels used to draw them, can appear jagged making them more difficult to read and follow. A technique called anti-aliasing is used to blend the background by transitioning the color from the font color to the background color. This technique minimizes the jagged edge is commonly used in paint and drawing software packages where it is desirable to make the transition between the image background and text elements look smooth and seamless.

### 4.3.1 Rich Text Format

Rich Text Format (RTF) has gained significant acceptance as a means to store and manipulate text. It is a proprietary format owned and controlled by Microsoft Corporation for use with word processors. RTF provides a number of font formatting features including font typing, sizing, and bolding as well as paragraph formatting functions such as alignment. Many multimedia development applications have incorporated features to import and export RTF data to maintain formatting established in other documents.

## 4.4 HYPERTEXT / HYPERMEDIA

Hyperlink is the colored and underlined text or a graphic that you click to go to a file, a location in a file, an HTML page on the World Wide Web, or an HTML page on an internet. Hyperlinks can also go to newsgroups and to Gopher, Telnet, and FTP sites.

Hypertext systems use text that is indexed or "marked-up" to navigate through large volumes of information. Hypertext, as shown is a navigational device that is very popular in multimedia and World Wide Web applications because it allows the interface to combine information and user control.

**Summary**

- NCS Departments
- NCS Organization
- Number of Employees 2005
- NCS Services
- BamaMail Account Quotas
- NCS's Major Goal

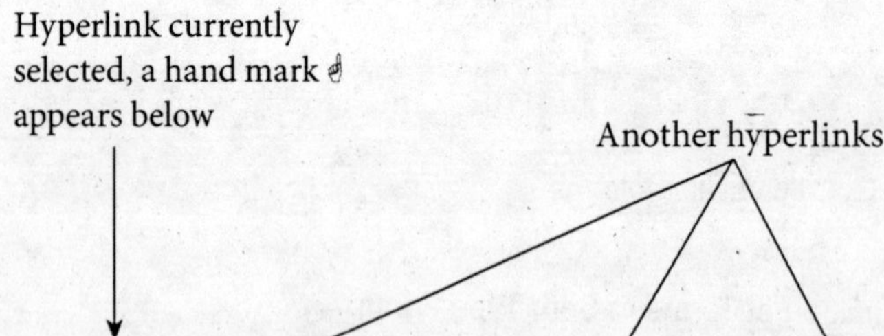


In computing, a **hyperlink** (or *link*) is a reference to a document that the reader can directly follow, or that is followed automatically. The reference points to a whole document or to a specific element within a document. Hypertext is text with hyperlinks. Such text is usually viewed with a computer. A software system for viewing and creating hypertext is a *hypertext* system. To *hyperlink* (or simply to *link*) is to create a hyperlink. A user following hyperlinks is said to *navigate* or *browse* the hypertext.

**Fig. 4.5:** Hypertext example: By clicking on a Marked-up (highlighted or underlined) word or phrase, the user is provided with another layer of information.

In Windows folders, hyperlinks are text links that appear in the folder's left pane. You can click these links to perform tasks, such as moving or copying a file, or to go to other places on your computer, such as the My Documents folder or Control Panel.

In simple terms, hypertext consists of nodes or chunks of information and links between them. Stated in this way, it might seem easy to find examples of hypertext.

- any text which references another can be seen as two nodes of information with the reference forming the link;
- any text which uses footnotes can be seen as containing nodes of information the text and the footnote with the footnote marker providing the link or pointer from one node to the other.

As we shall see later, the idea of a node is very general, and there are no rules about how big a node should be or what it should contain. Similarly, there are no rules governing what gets linked to what. The term "hypertext" is often used where the term hypermedia would be more appropriate.

It is generally accepted that the idea of hypertext was first described and published in 1945, when Bush (1945) proposed a system called Memex in his article. In 1965, the term "hypertext" was coined by Nelson who had a visionary idea of a system called Xanadu (Nelson, 1981). Other early hypertext systems developed by computer specialists include Hypertext Editing System (1967) from Brown University, ZOG (1972) from Carnegie-Mellon University, NoteCards (1985) from Xerox PARC, and Intermedia (1985) from Brown University. Guide (1986), developed at the University of Kent in the UK and introduced by Office Workstations Limited, was the first commercial product to run on microcomputers. In 1987, **HyperCard**, the most widely known hypertext authoring system, was announced by Apple Computer. Because of its ease of use and the widespread use of Macintosh computers, HyperCard gained popularity and many instructional designers have found it very useful for developing computer-based training materials. More recently, the concepts of hypertext have had considerable adaptation and reshaping with the advent of multimedia PC and the rapid growth of the Internet, particularly the World Wide Web utilizing hyperlinks for the presentation of non-linear information. Hypertext system can be used to navigate through large amounts of information. There are two general strategies for hypertext systems:

- Indexed Retrieval
- Linked or Hyperlink

### 4.4.1 Indexed Retrieval Systems

Indexed retrieval systems consist of text that is keyed or indexed to other words. In most cases, these systems are automated so that a software program is used to build the indexes from the raw text resource. Help programs use this approach to create list of terms to make finding help topics easier. In some cases, manual indexing may be used to identify special words or phrases or to eliminate trivial indexes; for example, the words "and," "or," and "the." As previously stated, indexed retrieval systems may be fully or partially indexed. In partially indexed systems:

- Text is usually highlighted indicating a link to an other word or another part of the document containing related material.
- Sets of words (keywords) are identified and automatically linked to other keywords or terms.

In fully indexed systems, text is fully categorized; in other words, all words are indexed for fast retrieval. This is usually very processor intensive and may require significant storage space to track all links.

Search mechanisms may be applied to either type of indexing system:

➢ Searches mechanisms can be used to search all words or indexed words.

➢ Searches can also be made using complex Boolean constructs (AND, OR, NOT, and BOTH). For example, a search construct could be : "auto AND car" or "engine OR transmission OR chassis."

When referring to systems that include a variety of non-textual node types such as graphics, sound, and moving images, people frequently use the term "hypermedia" instead of hypertext. Hypermedia can be defined as the combination of hypertext and multimedia. In hypermedia applications, we can access and link together a rich collection of multimedia resources (Ashworth, 1996; Barker, 1993; Nielsen, 1990; Picher, Berk, Devlin & Pugh, 1991; Seyer, 1991). Hypermedia implies managing and retrieving information from multimedia databases and allows users to choose their own non-linear paths through text, graphics, audio and video. Empowered by hypermedia, we can create and explore flexible information structures using interactive selection strategies in electronic networks.

The most distinctive feature of hypertext is the users' freedom to explore banks of information (McAleese, 1989). Users can take control of a set of dynamic links in obtaining non-linear information of the hypertext system. They are allowed to browse and navigate by means of the links set up by the author of the system. This reflects the fact that the author of hypertext can determine the numbers of the possible links. At this point, Gilster (1997) argues that the author of hypertext should think critically about the routes users will be allowed to select. In the creation of hypertext, therefore, the author's critical judgments need to be applied as well as his/her technical knowledge.

On the other hand, one of the possible problems of hypertext is that users may become disoriented and lost in the network of nodes (Conklin, 1987; Edwards & Hardman, 1989; Seyer, 1991). Due to the complexity of hypertext structures, the users might have difficulties in understanding where they are and in deciding where to go next. The hypertext system, therefore, needs to provide a clear access structure and means for recovery to help the users through interactive information-seeking activities. In other words, hypertext should offer a supportive environment in which the users can access and retrieve information, find their own paths while browsing and navigating, and expand webs of information without getting lost in working through it.

A document can be static (prepared and stored in advance) or dynamically generated (in response to user input). Therefore, a well-constructed hypertext system can encompass, incorporate or supersede many other user interface paradigms like menus and command lines, and can be used to access both static collections of cross-referenced documents and interactive applications. The documents and applications can be local or can come from anywhere with the assistance of a computer network like the Internet. The most famous implementation of hypertext is the World Wide Web.

### 4.4.2 Difference between Hyper and Normal Text

What makes hypertext different, what sets it apart from the most conceptually inter-linked paper document, is that in hypertext the links are active, they are hot spots that, when touched, cause something to happen. When the reader selects a hypertext link, the movement between the two nodes takes place automatically.

Conceptually at least, hypermedia is no different from hypertext. The term hypermedia is a more general term than hypertext and suggests that links exist to information held on different media, *e.g.*, video, CD, and so forth. Both terms refer to a system of linked information. We will therefore use the term hypertext to refer to any document with such properties irrespective of the media which contain it. In the same way that the general term a text refers to documents which may also contain graphics, so we shall use a hypertext as a generic term to denote a document which may in fact be distributed across several media.

### The authoring of original hypertexts

Hypertext certainly places new burdens on the author. No matter how badly it is written, every part of a book is accessible to the reader simply by turning the pages. A badly authored hypertext is far more restrictive when the reader can only follow the links provided by the author. Even if readers are given facilities to add new links, they must still be able to access all parts otherwise how are they to know that they want to add a link? With the lack of existing authoring tools, it is still relatively easy for the author to leave sections completely unlinked (information islands) or to leave links dangling. Nor is it sufficient to link everything to everything else. The resultant spaghetti does not help the reader in any way.

## 4.5 CODES FOR INFORMATION EXCHANGE

In the United States, there are two common character codes:

- American Standard Code for Information Interchange (ASCII)
- Extended Binary Coded Decimal Interchange Code (EBCDIC)

These two are competing coding standards. Most supercomputers and mainframe computers use EBCDIC. EBCDIC was defined by IBM for use on large computers. The simplest form of data encoding for text is ASCII (American Standard Code for Information Interchange). It is a 7-bit coding scheme for text yielding128 characters that includes lower and uppercase characters, punctuation, numbers, math symbols, and 32 control characters. Figure 4.6 list the 128 characters found in the ASCII character set.

ASCII code compromises 94 printable characters and 34 non-printing control characters. There are standard two and three-letter abbreviations for the names of control of control characters. Almost all smaller computers, including minicomputers and personal computers, use the ASCII. As shown in Table 4.1, the character representations differ. ANSI, a superset of ASCII, is the basis of the code used in Microsoft Windows.

In the ASCII code, the control character abbreviated as SP is used to print a space. The other control character are based on signal for teletypewriter machines. A few are used to control printing and displays, particularly CR or carriage return (move to start of line), LF or line feed (move to next line), HT or horizontal tab (move to next tab stop), BS or backspace (move one character width toward the left), and FF or from feed (move to next page or screen). Program statement of the C language use 91 printable characters (all the printable character in ASCII except those for values 36, 64, and 96).

| Dec | Hex | Oct | Chr | Dec | Hex | Oct | HTML | Chr | Dec | Hex | Oct | HTML | Chr | Dec | Hex | Oct | HTML | Chr |
|---|---|---|---|---|---|---|---|---|---|---|---|---|---|---|---|---|---|---|
| 0 | 0 | 000 | NULL | 32 | 20 | 040 |   | Space | 64 | 40 | 100 | @ | @ | 96 | 60 | 140 | ` | ` |
| 1 | 1 | 001 | SoH | 33 | 21 | 041 | ! | ! | 65 | 41 | 101 | A | A | 97 | 61 | 141 | a | a |
| 2 | 2 | 002 | SoTxt | 34 | 22 | 042 | " | " | 66 | 42 | 102 | B | B | 98 | 62 | 142 | b | b |
| 3 | 3 | 003 | EoTxt | 35 | 23 | 043 | # | # | 67 | 43 | 103 | C | C | 99 | 63 | 143 | c | c |
| 4 | 4 | 004 | EoT | 36 | 24 | 044 | $ | $ | 68 | 44 | 104 | D | D | 100 | 64 | 144 | d | d |
| 5 | 5 | 005 | Enq | 37 | 25 | 045 | % | % | 69 | 45 | 105 | E | E | 101 | 65 | 145 | e | e |
| 6 | 6 | 006 | Ack | 38 | 26 | 046 | & | & | 70 | 46 | 106 | F | F | 102 | 66 | 146 | f | f |
| 7 | 7 | 007 | Bell | 39 | 27 | 047 | ' | ' | 71 | 47 | 107 | G | G | 103 | 67 | 147 | g | g |
| 8 | 8 | 010 | Bsp | 40 | 28 | 050 | ( | ( | 72 | 48 | 110 | H | H | 104 | 68 | 150 | h | h |
| 9 | 9 | 011 | HTab | 41 | 29 | 051 | ) | ) | 73 | 49 | 111 | I | I | 105 | 69 | 151 | i | i |
| 10 | A | 012 | LFeed | 42 | 2A | 052 | * | * | 74 | 4A | 112 | J | J | 106 | 6A | 152 | j | j |
| 11 | B | 013 | VTab | 43 | 2B | 053 | + | + | 75 | 4B | 113 | K | K | 107 | 6B | 153 | k | k |
| 12 | C | 014 | FFeed | 44 | 2C | 054 | , | , | 76 | 4C | 114 | L | L | 108 | 6C | 154 | l | l |
| 13 | D | 015 | CR | 45 | 2D | 055 | - | - | 77 | 4D | 115 | M | M | 109 | 6D | 155 | m | m |
| 14 | E | 016 | SOut | 46 | 2E | 056 | . | . | 78 | 4E | 116 | N | N | 110 | 6E | 156 | n | n |
| 15 | F | 017 | SIn | 47 | 2F | 057 | / | / | 79 | 4F | 117 | O | O | 111 | 6F | 157 | o | o |
| 16 | 10 | 020 | DLE | 48 | 30 | 060 | 0 | 0 | 80 | 50 | 120 | P | P | 112 | 70 | 160 | p | p |
| 17 | 11 | 021 | DC1 | 49 | 31 | 061 | 1 | 1 | 81 | 51 | 121 | Q | Q | 113 | 71 | 161 | q | q |
| 18 | 12 | 022 | DC2 | 50 | 32 | 062 | 2 | 2 | 82 | 52 | 122 | R | R | 114 | 72 | 162 | r | r |
| 19 | 13 | 023 | DC3 | 51 | 33 | 063 | 3 | 3 | 83 | 53 | 123 | S | S | 115 | 73 | 163 | s | s |
| 20 | 14 | 024 | DC4 | 52 | 34 | 064 | 4 | 4 | 84 | 54 | 124 | T | T | 116 | 74 | 164 | t | t |
| 21 | 15 | 025 | NAck | 53 | 35 | 065 | 5 | 5 | 85 | 55 | 125 | U | U | 117 | 75 | 165 | u | u |
| 22 | 16 | 026 | Syn | 54 | 36 | 066 | 6 | 6 | 86 | 56 | 126 | V | V | 118 | 76 | 166 | v | v |
| 23 | 17 | 027 | EoTB | 55 | 37 | 067 | 7 | 7 | 87 | 57 | 127 | W | W | 119 | 77 | 167 | w | w |
| 24 | 18 | 030 | Can | 56 | 38 | 070 | 8 | 8 | 88 | 58 | 130 | X | X | 120 | 78 | 170 | x | x |
| 25 | 19 | 031 | EoM | 57 | 39 | 071 | 9 | 9 | 89 | 59 | 131 | Y | Y | 121 | 79 | 171 | y | y |
| 26 | 1A | 032 | Sub | 58 | 3A | 072 | : | : | 90 | 5A | 132 | Z | Z | 122 | 7A | 172 | z | z |
| 27 | 1B | 033 | Esc | 59 | 3B | 073 | ; | ; | 91 | 5B | 133 | [ | [ | 123 | 7B | 173 | { | { |
| 28 | 1C | 034 | FSep | 60 | 3C | 074 | < | < | 92 | 5C | 134 | \ | \ | 124 | 7C | 174 | | | \| |
| 29 | 1D | 035 | GSep | 61 | 3D | 075 | = | = | 93 | 5D | 135 | ] | ] | 125 | 7D | 175 | } | } |
| 30 | 1E | 036 | RSep | 62 | 3E | 076 | > | > | 94 | 5E | 136 | ^ | ^ | 126 | 7E | 176 | ~ | ~ |
| 31 | 1F | 037 | USep | 63 | 3F | 077 | ? | ? | 95 | 5F | 137 | _ | _ | 127 | 7F | 177 |  | Delete |

**Fig. 4.6 :** The ASCII Character Representation

**Table 4.1:** ANSI Character set (only first upto 151 are shown here.)

The **ANSI** character set includes the standard **ASCII** character set (values 0 to 127), plus an extended character set (values 128 to 255).

| Dec | Hex | Unicode | Char | Name |
|---|---|---|---|---|
| 128 | 80 | U+20AC | € | Euro Sign |
| 129 | 81 | | | Undefined |
| 130 | 82 | U+201A | ‚ | Single Low-9 Quotation Mark |
| 131 | 83 | U+0192 | ƒ | Latin Small Letter F With Hook |
| 132 | 84 | U+201E | „ | Double Low-9 Quotation Mark |
| 133 | 85 | U+2026 | … | Horizontal Ellipsis |
| 134 | 86 | U+2020 | † | Dagger |
| 135 | 87 | U+2021 | ‡ | Double Dagger |
| 136 | 88 | U+02C6 | ˆ | Modifier Letter Circumflex Accent |
| 137 | 89 | U+2030 | ‰ | Per Mille Sign |
| 138 | 8A | U+0160 | Š | Latin Capital Letter S With Caron |
| 139 | 8B | U+2039 | ‹ | Single Left-pointing Angle Quotation Mark |
| 140 | 8C | U+0152 | Œ | Latin Capital Ligature Oe |
| 141 | 8D | | | Undefined |
| 142 | 8E | U+017D | Ž | Latin Capital Letter Z With Caron |
| 143 | 8F | | | Undefined |
| 144 | 90 | | | Undefined |
| 145 | 91 | U+2018 | ‘ | Left Single Quotation Mark |
| 146 | 92 | U+2019 | ’ | Right Single Quotation Mark |
| 147 | 93 | U+201C | “ | Left Double Quotation Mark |
| 148 | 94 | U+201D | ” | Right Double Quotation Mark |
| 149 | 95 | U+2022 | • | Bullet |
| 150 | 96 | U+2013 | – | En Dash |
| 151 | 97 | U+2014 | — | Em Dash |

## 4.5.1 International Character sets

As the computer market has become more international in the past ten years, one of the resulting problems has been handling the various international language alphabets. It was at best difficult, and at times impossible, to translate the text portions of programs from one script to another. For example, the differences between the Roman Script used by western European writers and the Kanji script used by Japanese writers made it particularly challenging to transfer innovative programs from one market to another.

Since 1989, a concerned effort on the part of linguistics engineers, and information professional from many well-known computer companies has been focused on a 16-bit architecture for multilingual text and character encoding. Called Unicode, this new standard can accommodate up to about 65,000 characters and will ultimately include the characters from all known languages and alphabets in the world. In version 1.0, the Unicode standard contains 34,168 distinct coded characters covering the principal written languages of the Americas, Europe the Middle East, Africa, India, Asia and Pacific.

Where several languages share a set of symbols that have a historically related derivation, the shared symbols of each language are unified into collections of symbols (called scripts). A single script can work for tens or even hundreds of languages (for example, the Latin script used for English and most European languages). Sometimes, however, only one script will work for a language (such as the Korean Hangul). Here are the primary scripts supported by Unicode version 1.0:

| | | |
|---|---|---|
| Arabic | Gujarati | Latin |
| Armenian | Gurmukhi | Lao |
| Bengali | Han | Malyalam |
| Bopomofo | Hangul | Oriya |
| Cyrillic | Hebrew | Phonetic |
| Devanagara | Hiragana | Tamil |
| Georgian | Kannada | Telugu |
| Greek | Katakana | Thai |

The Unicode standard includes more than 18,000 Han characters (ideographs for Japanese, Chinese, and Korean), and future releases will include obsolete alphabets such as cuneiform, hieroglyphs, and ancient Han characters. In addition, character space will be reserved for users and publishers to create their own scripts, designed especially for their own applications. For example, a carpenter, might develop a script that included a character meaning "half- inch Sheetrock," another character meaning "three-quarter-inch plywood," and so forth.

## 4.6 DIGITAL FONT TECHNIQUES

### Font Editing and Design Tools

Special font editing tools can be used to make your own type, so you can communicate exactly an idea or graphic feeling. With these tools, professional typographers create distinct text and display faces. Graphic designers, publishers, and ad agencies can design instant variations of existing typefaces.

#### (1) Fontographer

Fontographer, supplied by Macromedia, is specialized graphics editor for both Macintosh and Windows platforms. Now it is integrated into the Font lab line of digital typography tools. You can use it to develop PostScript language fonts for Macintosh, IBM-compatible PCs, and NeXT Workstations, as well as TrueType fonts for the Macintosh and PC. Designers can also modify existing typefaces, incorporate PostScript artwork, automatically trace scanned images, and create designs from scratch.

You can easily expand existing fonts to include fractions, symbols, foreign characters, and logos in Type 1, Type 3, and TrueType fonts, or create an entire typeface from scratch. Fonts created with Fontographer can be used in any program with a font menu on Windows and Macintosh platforms.

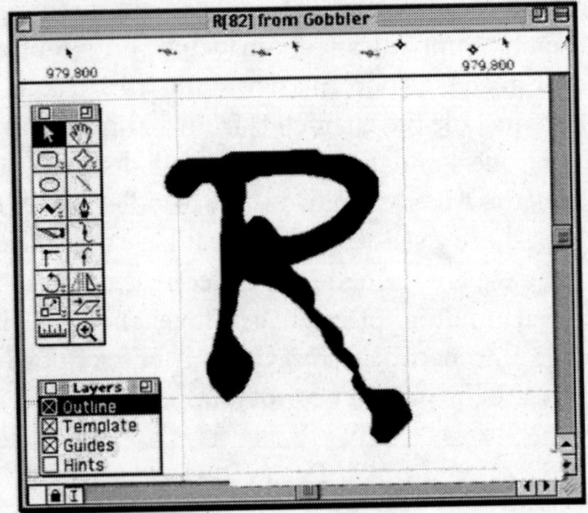


**Fig. 4.7:** Fontographer is a powerful font editor for Macintosh and Windows

A sample Fontographer screen is shown in Figure 4.6, and a working version is included on the Macromedia Showcase CD-ROM included with this book.

Fontographer's features include a freehand drawing tool to create professional and precise inline and outline drawings of calligrahpic and script characters, using either the mouse or alternative input methods (such as Wacom pressure-sensitive pen systems, Kurta digitizing tables, and Cal Comp DrawingBoardII). Fontographer for Windows opens any PostScript Type 1 or TrueType font for the PC, and lets you create condensed, expanded, and oblique versions of the same font or modify any of those fonts to suit your design needs. One character, several characters, or entire fonts can be scaled, rotated, and skewed to create new and unique typefaces. A metric window provides complete control over character width, spacing, offset, and kerning. The current Windows version of Fontographer does not make Multiple Master fonts (PostScript fonts that allow you to adjust a range of certain characteristics for a set of characters, for example, serif to sans serif or condensed to extended) to be generated with Type 3 PostScript fonts, and it does not have an Option-Copy, Paste feature for bringing drawings through the Clipboard from FreeHand or Illustrator. Nor can the current version read a Macintosh Fontographer database; font transfer is accomplished through Type 1 PostScript.

### (2) Type-Designer

Type-Designer for Windows from DS Design is a font editor that lets you create, convert and manipulate PostScript Type 1 and True Type fonts as well as EPS file format illustrations. An extensive palette of editing tools allows you to make changes to a font's outline. Type-Designer allows you to open up to eight typefaces simultaneously and cut-and-paste characters between them.

## Adobe Type Manager

Adobe Type Manager (ATM) is required to display Type 1 PostScript fonts at all sizes without jaggies. This software is available for both the Macintosh and Windows. Once it's installed, ATM works automatically with work processing, page layout, spreadsheet, and graphics applications, including multimedia authoring systems.

In Windows, the ATM software requires about 450K of disk space, and each Type 1 PostScript outline font will take up another 40K. Using the ATM Control Panel (see Figure 4.6), you can add to and take away from your list of installed fonts. PostScript fonts typically reside in a directory called PSFONTS in the root of your hard disk.

On the Macintosh, you need to install the proper ATM driver into your System Extensions folder and the ATM desk accessory into your Control Panels folder. You also must place the outline fonts, sometimes called printer fonts, into your System folder.

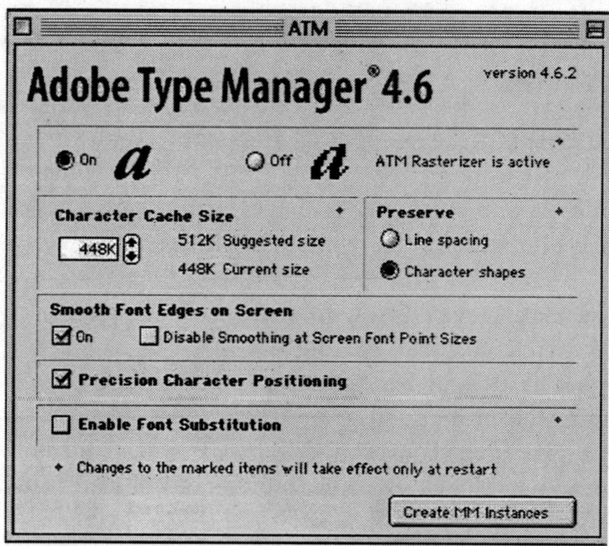


**Fig. 4.8:** Adobe Type Manager (ATM) Control Panel

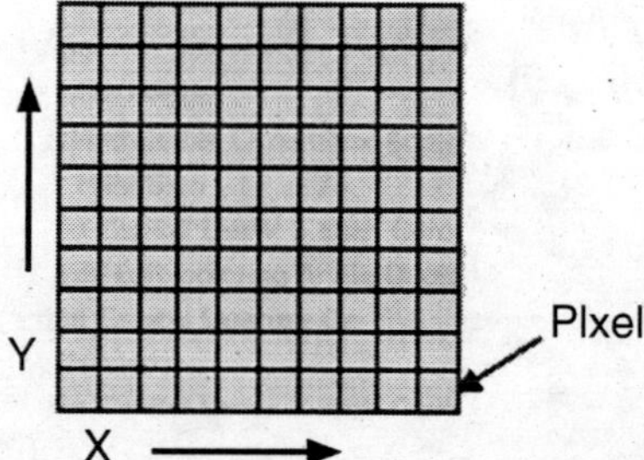


## 4.7 IMAGE FORMATS PIXELS

There is a delicate balance between the crispness of a picture and the number of pixels needed to display it. Let's say you have two images, each is 5 inches across and 3 inches down. One uses 300 pixels to span that five inches, the other uses 1500. Obviously, the one with 1500 uses smaller pixels. It is also the one that offers a more crisp, detailed look. The more pixels, the more detailed the image will be. Of course, the more pixels the more bytes the image will take up.

So, how much is enough? That depends on whom you are speaking to, and right now you're speaking to me. I always go with 100 pixels per inch. That creates a ten-thousand pixel square inch.

I've found that allows for a pretty crisp image without going overboard on the bytes. It also allows some leeway to increase or decrease the size of the image and not mess it up too much.

The lowest I'd go is 72 pixels per inch, the agreed upon low end of the image scale. In terms of pixels per square inch, it's a whale of a drop to 5184. Try that. See if you like it, but I think you'll find that lower definition monitors really play havoc with the image.

## Graphics

Computer graphics are anything that can be displayed on the screen except the text and sometimes even text falls into the graphics category if it is save in a graphics format.

There are basically two types of computer graphic.

- Raster (bitmapped)
- Vector/structured.

Raster (Bitmapped) graphics are images that are mapped to the monitor or screen. The screen is made up of tiny dots called pixels. These dots can display various colours depending on the type of computer hardware and software you have. Using shades of red, green and blue (RGB) an image can be displayed on the screen by mapping different colours to the screen in different sequences.

Vector graphics use objects created from mathematical formulas to represent things like lines, curves, fills, line thickness, etc. to create the image.

Each type of graphic has it's own advantages and disadvantages. Older versions of HTML were only able to recognize bitmapped graphics so most graphics created for the Internet, using standard HTML, are created or converted to a bitmap format. The newest version of HTML or XHTML is able to display vector graphics but not all browsers are able to display these graphics.

Within each of the two main types there are dozens of different formats.

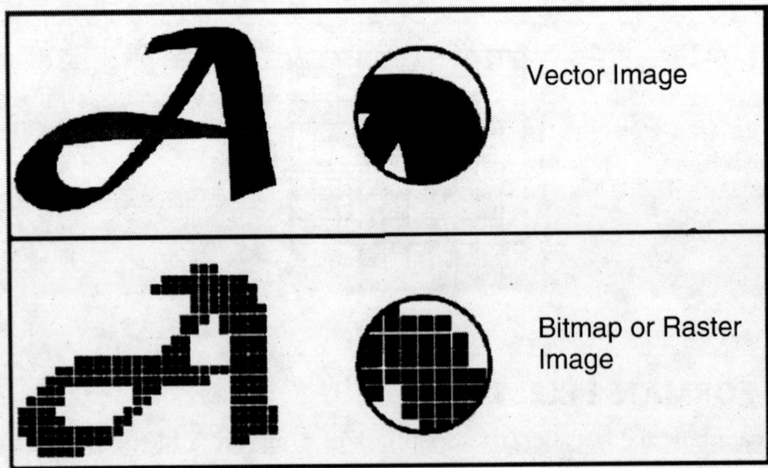


## 4.8 VECTOR GRAPHICS

Vector graphics (also known as Object-Oriented Graphics), maintains the image as a series of points, lines, arcs and other geometric shapes. Vector graphics are made up of lines and curves defined by mathematical objects called vectors.

Vectors describe an image according to its geometric characteristics. For example, a bicycle tire in a vector graphic is made up of a mathematical definition of a circle drawn with a certain radius, set at a specific location, and filled with a specific color. You can move, resize, or change the color of the tire without losing the quality of the graphic.

Vector graphics are resolution-independent—that is, they can be scaled to any size and printed at any resolution without losing detail or clarity. As a result, vector graphics are the best choice for representing bold graphics that must retain crisp lines when scaled to various sizes—for example, logos.

Vector graphics are good for reproducing crisp outlines, as in logos or illustrations. They can be printed or displayed at any resolution without losing detail.

Because computer monitors represent images by displaying them on a grid, both vector and bitmap images are displayed as pixels on-screen.

**Learning Outcomes**

In this chapter we have learnt about :

1. Types of Fonts used in Multimedia design for visual display
2. Image types used on Internet/Web design
3. Different Code for digital Information Exchange
4. Designing Rich and Hypertext

# Multimedia Images and Graphics

CHAPTER 5

**Leaning Objectives**

In this chapter we shall learn about:

1. Rastor and Vector Images
2. Different Types of Image Formats
3. Image Resolution and display size
4. Methods of data compressions
5. Compressed file formats
6. Applications of computer based Graphics

## 5.1 LEARNING OBJECTIVES

In this chapter we shall learn about:

(1) 2D Graphics,
(2) Image Compression and File Formats : GIF, JPEG, JPEG 2000, PNG, TIFF, EXIF, PS, PDF,
(3) Colour Science, Colour, Colour Models, Colour palettes,
(4) Dithering

Called computer graphics, it is the creation and manipulation of picture images in the computer. It is defined here as graphics to keep it next to the other entries that begin with "graphics."

Computer graphics technology evolved from the basic hardware and software capabilities of computers to perform design and engineering tasks. Interactive graphics systems permit the user to work with the hardware and software to create, analyze, and change graphics systems can significantly increase the productivity of engineers and speed up the process of designing a product. A graphics computer system requires a graphics display screen, a graphics input device (tablet, mouse, scanner, camera), a graphics output device (ink jet printer, laser printer, plotter) and a graphics software package; for example, a CAD, drawing or paint program.

A wide variety of graphics systems are available, in terms of the functions and performance capabilities that can be tailored to the needs of the application in which they will be used. This can range from relatively simple drafting systems to compels, high-performance design and engineering systems. There are also many type of graphics hardware to choose from, each with its own advantages and disadvantages. Input, output, and display devices are available with features to satisfy any graphics application (*e.g.*, speed, accuracy, and color). Graphics such as bar charts, line graphs, and pie charts can help business people see core material in an attractive form that is easy to read and understand. These graphics can be created quickly and neatly with the assistance of computer software developed especially for the purpose.

Graphics software provides an interface that enables the user to construct a geometric model and display and manipulate images of it. This software structures the data, transforms it, performs mathematical computation on it, and issues commands for generating graphics images. The user interacts with the system by using high-level commands and special input function devices to construct the model and display the images. Standards have been developed by industry to simplify the programming job and make graphics software more portable between systems.

Graphics applications involve a lot of computations and data handling. This requires more computer power than just the actual generation of graphics displays. Creating a geometric model of an object permits computers to analyze its structure and behavior as well as create and manipulate images. A number of different techniques are used to represent object with geometric model. Only solid models are a true representation of an object. They are complete and unambiguous, and they provide details on internal as well as external structure. A variety of techniques can be used to enhance the images generated by models to improve their realism (*e.g.*, hidden line removal, shading, depth perspective).

Computer graphics is used in many industrial application to improve productivity in the office, in the laboratory, and on the factory floor. As the technology continues to advance, these applications will expand even further. It is one of the key tools which makes computer-automated manufacturing (CAM) possible.

The main advantage of Computer Graphics is that it provides ease in comparative study of two or more systems by simple visual comparison without going into much of statistical details of the system or process. A picture is said to be worth thousands of words, thus graphics representation substantially increases productivity. This may be seen from the various applications for which it is used, some of which are listed below:-

Graphics also can be used to analyze the motion of dancers and athletes to help improve performance. The term bio-mechanics describes the combination of computer graphics biological systems for this type of analysis.

## Two-D Graphics

2D (Length x Breadth but not depth) computer graphics is the computer-based generation of digital images—mostly from two-dimensional models (such as 2D geometric models, text, and digital images) and by techniques specific to them. The word may stand for the branch of computer science that comprises such techniques, or for the models themselves.

2D computer graphics are mainly used in applications that were originally developed upon traditional printing and drawing technologies, such as typography, cartography, technical drafting, advertising, etc.. In those applications, the two-dimensional image is not just a representation of a real-world object, but an independent artifact with added semantic value; two-dimensional models are therefore preferred, because they give more direct control of the image than 3D computer graphics (whose approach is more akin to photography than to typography).

Pictures are prepared on a variety of media ranging from paper and canvas to camera film. For use in the computer, the picture must be translated into a digital format. As we have read in chapter 2, image are two basic strategies applied when pictures in the computer:

1. Raster or bitmap images
2. Vector or metafile images

### 5.1.1 Raster or Bitmap images

The most common and comprehensive form of storage for images on a computer is as a raster or bitmap image. The terms raster and bitmap can be used interchangeably as they refer to images that are created as two-dimensional sets of points on a computer display. Bitmap images use a grid (the bitmap or raster) of small squares known as pixels to represent images. Each pixel is assigned a specific location and color value.

Raster graphics is the TV-like method that uses dots to display an image on screen. Raster graphics images are created by scanners and cameras and are also generated by paint packages. A picture frame is divided into hundreds of horizontal rows, with each row containing hundreds of dots, called pixels.

Unlike TV, which uses one standard (NTSC) for the country, there are dozens of raster graphics standards. Also, unlike TV, which records and displays the dots as infinitely variable shades and colors (analog), computer graphics have a finite number of shades and colors (digital). When you scan an image or paint an object into the computer, the image is created in a reserved area of memory called a bitmap, with some number of bits corresponding to each dot (pixel).

Photoshop and other paint and image-editing programs generate bitmap images. When working with bitmap images, you edit pixels rather than objects or shapes. Depending on the hardware capabilities, each point can display from two to millions of colors. The use of the word comprehensive means that an image looks as much as possibly like the real-world or the original product. This means that the proportion, size, color, and texture must be as accurate as possible.

Bitmap images are the most common electronic medium for continuous-tone images, such as photographs or digital paintings, because they can represent subtle gradations of shades and color. Bitmap images are resolution-dependent— that is, they contain a fixed number of pixels. As a result, they can lose detail and appear jagged if they are scaled on-screen or if they are printed at a lower resolution than they were created for.

A bitmap corresponds bit for bit with an image displayed on a screen, probably in the same format as it would be stored in the display's video memory or maybe as a device independent bitmap. A bitmap is characterized by the width and height of the image in pixels and the number of bits per pixel, which determines the number of colors it can represent.

A colored raster image (a "pixmap") will usually have pixels with between one and eight bits for each of the red, green, and blue components, though other color encodings are also used, such as four- or eight-bit indexed representations that use vector quantization on the (R, G, B) vectors. The green component sometimes has more bits than the other two to cater for the human eye's greater discrimination in this component.

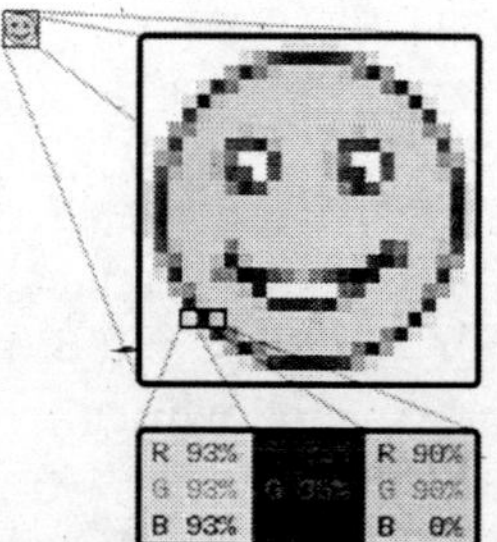


**Fig. 5.1:** Coloured Raster Image

Suppose the smiley face in the top left corner is an RGB bitmap image. Fig 5.1 when zoomed in, it might look like the big smiley face shown at the top. Every square represents a pixel. Zoomed in further we see three pixels whose colors are constructed by adding the values for red, green and blue.

A raster graphics image, digital image, or bitmap, is a data file or structure representing a generally rectangular grid of pixels, or points of color, on a computer monitor, paper, or other display device. The color of each pixel is individually defined; images in the RGB color space, for instance, often consist of colored pixels defined by three bytes—one byte each for red, green and blue. Less colorful images require less information per pixel; an image with only black and white pixels only requires a single bit for each pixel. Raster graphics are distinguished from vector graphics in that vector graphics represent an image through the use of geometric objects such as curves and polygons.

The quality of a raster image is determined by the total number of pixels (resolution), and the amount of information in each pixel (often called color depth). For example, an image that stores 24 bits of color information per pixel (the standard for most high-quality displays in 2004) can represent smoother degrees of shading than one that only stores 15 bits per pixel, but not as smooth as one that stores 48 bits. Likewise, an image sampled at 640 x 480 pixels (therefore containing 307,200 pixels) will look rough and blocky compared to one sampled at 1280 x 1024 (1,310,720 pixels). Because it takes a large amount of data to store a high-quality image, data compression techniques are often used to reduce this size for images stored on disk. Some techniques sacrifice information, and therefore image quality, in order to achieve a smaller file size. Compression techniques that lose information are referred to as "lossy" compression.

Bitmap images are good for reproducing subtle gradations of color, as in photographs. They can have jagged edges when printed at too large a size or displayed at too high a magnification.

A bitmap image is resolution-dependent that is, it contains a fixed number of pixels to represent its image data. As a result, a bitmap image can lose detail and appear jagged if viewed at a high magnification on-screen or printed at too low a resolution. Bitmap images are the best choice for representing subtle gradations of shades and color—for example, in photographs or painted images.

You have three different ways to make a bitmap:

- Make a bitmap from scratch with a paint program MS Paint,Adobe Photoshop.
- Grab a bitmap from an active computer screen with a screen capture program, and then paste it into a paint program or your application.
- Capture a bitmap from a photo, artwork, or a television image using a scanner or video capture device that digitizes the image.

## 5.1.2 Bitmap Formats

Common bitmapped file formats include PICT, BMP, GIF, TIFF, Quick Time movies, AVI movies, and JPEG, with PICT and QuickTime being the standards for cross-platform development. Programs that work with bitmapped images are often called paint programs.

The three main Internet formats, GIF, JPEG, and Bitmap (BMP), are all Raster formats.

Some other Raster formats include the following:

1. CLP Windows Clipart
2. DCX ZOFT Paintbrush
3. DIB OS/2 Warp format
4. FPX Kodak's FlashPic
5. IMG GEM Paint format
6. JIF JPEG Related Image format
7. MAC MacPaint
8. MSP MacPaint New Version
9. PCT Macintosh PICT format
10. PCX ZSoft Paintbrush

11. PNG Portable Network Graphics
12. PPM Portable Pixel Map (UNIX)
13. PSP Paint Shop Pro format
14. RAW Unencoded image format
15. RLE Run-Length Encoding
16. (Used to lower image bit rates)
17. TIFF Aldus Corporation format
18. WPG WordPerfect image format

GIF and JPEG are the two most popular graphics formats that have become standards for graphical use particularly on the Web, and are universally read by most browsers without plug-ins. Both are bitmap formats, images consisting of individual pixels. As a general rule, bitmaps are fixed in their size and resolution. So as you manipulate and scale them, they begin to lose their original quality. PNG is a relatively new bitmap graphics format. It combines the best of GIF and JPG into one file format. These are free from copy right obligations.

Graphics and bandwidth are constantly at odds on the Web, and the designer must mediate in this struggle, always trying to strike the balance between high-impact visual appeal and low-impact delivery. To do this successfully, you need to know the difference between formats used on the Web, and how and when they are best used.

### 5.1.3 GIF: Better For Designed Graphics

GIF stands for Graphics Interchange Format, a bitmap graphics format defined in 1987 by CompuServe, using a lossless compression system that employs the Unisys LZW algorithm. GIF images are 8-bit, 256 colors, can be indexed to a fixed palette, and provide support for transparency. CompuServe originally defined the GIF format for its online graphic images. It's an 8-bit format, which supports a maximum of 256 colors. A Raster format breaks the image into a series of colored dots called pixels. The number of ones and zeros (bits) used to create each pixel denotes the depth of color you can put into your images.

If your pixel is denoted with only one bit-per-pixel then that pixel must be black or white. Why? Because that pixel can only be a one or a zero, on or off, black or white.

Bump that up to 4 bits-per-pixel and you're able to set that colored dot to one of 16 colors. If you go even higher to 8 bits-per-pixel, you can save that colored dot at up to $2 \times 2 \times 2 \times 2 \times 2 \times 2 \times 2 = 256$ different colors.

Raster image formats can also save at 16, 24, and 32 bits-per-pixel. At the two highest levels, the pixels themselves can carry up to 16,777,216 (= 2^24 = 16 million) different colors. The image looks great! Bitmaps saved at 24 bits-per-pixel are great quality images, but of course they also run about a megabyte per picture. There's always a trade-off, isn't there?

One of the GIF big advantages is images can be indexed to a set palette, whereas JPEG images can't. This is important to Web designers who can use indexing to more easily optimize images for browser-safe palettes (browser-safe palettes display 216 colors, which includes all the colors in the Windows and Macintosh system palette). Designing for a browser-safe palette ensures consistent, cross-platform, device-independent display.

GIF images use a lossless compression scheme, meaning no data is lost in the compression or decompression process.

The GIF format was invented (and is owned) by CompuServe, the on-line service providers. Like the windows .BMP format, it stores the image as a rectangular grid of pixels, specifying the colour of each pixel in the image. A GIF file is much smaller than the equivalent BMP file because it uses special compression to group together patches of continuous colour. GIF files are good for drawn graphics and text, because they produce a small file and bold, clear lines. They can only have a maximum of 256 colours so photographs don't come out as well. You can produce a GIF file with a transparent background,which looks nice if your page has a background image.

If you find that your GIF files are too large, consider using the new PNG format. GIF files perform compression by analysing horizontal bands of the same colour: PNG files, on the other hand, can analyse both horizontal and vertical areas. Consequently, they can achieve compression levels up to 30% better than GIFs.

### 5.1.4 GIF Files

There are a number of different versions of the GIF format, describing when the version was defined. Software which can handle a particular version of the format can always handle older versions of the format.

The oldest version of the format is called GIF 87a. This is the "basic"version of the format. The more advanced version is called GIF89a. This extension allows you to specify one colour in the GIF to be transparent, to attach comments to a file, to produce multi-image ("animated") files, and to produce an image in what's referred to as "interlaced" format.

#### (1) Interlaced GIF files

A normal GIF file specifies the image one line at a time, starting at the top of the image and working downwards. An interlaced GIF also specifies one line at a time, but puts the lines in a different order in the file, so that the whole image has at least some information from the beginning.

The effect of this becomes clear when you are downloading the image over the Internet. A non-interlaced GIF files from the top down, as you would expect. An interlaced GIF appears initially out of focus-a bit like those bits on Crime watch where they're disguising someone's face-and the image then gradually comes into focus. This means that someone looking at your page will get the general idea of what the images are before they've been completely downloaded.

#### (2) Transparent GIF Images

It is possible to specify one colour of a GIF89a image to be "transparent". Navigator will allow the background colour or pattern to show through. This allows you to put images on your page which are not just rectangular. Note that the transparent background is still part of the image, so you can't overlap images and if the image is a HyperText anchor, then the corners of the image are still a link.

#### (3) Multiple-Image GIFs

The GIF89a standard allows for a single file to contain more than one image. For years nothing was done with this feature, but Netscape (folowed by the others) used this format to produce animated images. It is possible to specify the amount of time between displaying successive frames, and also whether the animation loops when it gets to the end.

Animated GIFs can be very effective, but when they first appeared animated logos started popping up all over the place. The fashion may begin to get stale very soon, so you should only use an animated GIF if it's absolutely necessary.

At the worst, a ten-frame animated GIF will be ten times the size of a one-frame image. However, the format is clever enough to only encode the differences between successive frames, so if you're crafty you can get an effective animation in not much more space than the plain image.

## 5.1.5 When To Use GIF

Because of its built-in color limitations, GIFs are most useful for images that have fewer colors, such as black and white images, and images with large areas of solid color, such as cartoons and line art. The advantage is you can use GIF's lossless compression, and lose no date for displaying these images. That means solid areas of color remain solid, and hard-edged adjacent colors maintain their distinction. This is different from JPEG, where, depending on the level of compression, solid areas of color get broken down and hard edges between adjacent areas get choppy or fuzzy.

*Here's a good rule of thumb:* If you made the image in a graphics program, such as Photoshop, and it has large areas of flat color, then use the GIF format. For example, if you are setting text in Photoshop to use on your Web page, save it as a GIF. For photographs or other images with wide gradients of tone or color, use the JPEG format.

It's important to remember if you tried to save continuous-tone images, which are better-suited to JPEG as a GIF, you may have to discard so much information in the conversion process, you'd be better off using JPEG's lossy compression method.

Another advantage of GIF is its support for transparency, which makes it easier to silhouette non-rectangular images against patterned backgrounds. This is important on the Web when creating buttons and icons. JPEGs don't offer support for transparency.

Finally, GIF is the best choice to reach the lowest common denominator in terms of machinery and software. Because you can index an 8-bit GIF image down to 216 colors for the browser-safe palette, your images will display consistently on a wide variety of browsers and platforms.

## 5.1.6 JPEG: Better For Photographs

The JPEG format is so named because it originated from the Joint Photographic Experts Group committee, which created the standard in the late '80s and early '90s.JPEG images are 24-bit, 16 million colors, provide the ability to specify the degree of compression, and can be displayed in stages, called a "progressive JPEG." The JPEG format is based on a lossy compression algorithm, which means your image will lose some quality when it's compressed. However, depending on the quality of your original and the amount of compression you apply to the image, the data loss is often imperceptible to the human eye.

The JPEG format was designed to render photographs, and other images intended to look realistic to humans. It uses various psychological tricks to suggest detail which is not actually there the savings from this process can result in very small images indeed. JPEG images use special psychological methods in their encoding. Fine detail is lost, but for photographs it produces a better-looking image than a GIF file will. When you produce a JPEG image you can specify how faithfully you want the image to be replaced: with a low accuracy level you can get amazing compression levels-it's possible to produce quite acceptable images which are under IK in length. JPEG images don't work well if there is text or solid patches of colour in the image-the boundary comes out fuzzy.

When you convert a file to JPEG format, most applications will ask for an "accuracy" value (some describe this as a "compression ratio"). If you choose a high accuracy, then you will retain all the detail in your image, but the resulting file will be very big-were you to choose 100% accuracy the image would be identical to an equivalent TIFF file, and would be just as big. If you are willing to go for a low accuracy, you can get a very small image size (images less than 100 bytes in size are possible), but you lose detail until eventually the image is almost unrecognisable. Losing detail from an image doesn't sound like a very good idea, but for photographs it often doesn't matter-some people even say that a photo or a painting looks nicer on a lower accuracy setting since you are less aware of the pixels of the screen.

JPEG has another advantage over GIF as a format, which is appropriate to its purpose as a format for displaying photographs. A GIF file can only have a maximum of 256 colours, which is fine for line art, but can make a photo look like a painting-by-numbers picture. All JPEG files are saved off in 24-bit format, allowing 16 million colours. Of course, unless you have a 24-bit graphics card, your PC can't display all of them at once, but reducing the number of colours at the graphics-card stage will produce a more realistic image. And, of course those of your readers who do have 24-bit colours will see your pictures in all their glory. There is a recent development on JPEG, called "progressive JPEG". In practice this has the same effect as interleaved GIF files. There are not many graphics packages which will encounter on the Internet-there are a number of proprietary systems as well. The relevant thing here is that in an MPEG video, each frame is stored as a JPEG image.

### 5.1.7 When To Use JPEG

Because JPEGs are 24-bit, they inherently provide significantly more image information than a GIF. The format is better-suited for continuous-tone images such as photographs, scanned artwork, and rendered 3-D graphics.

Another advantage to JPEG is unlike GIF, you can specify the degree of compression applied to the image, letting you strike a balance between size and quality. Compression ratios vary for JPEG, but depending on the image-editing program you're using, you can typically compress an image by 10-to-1 or 20-to-1, and can conceivably compress an image to the extreme of 100-to-1 (with a significant loss of quality).

For instance, when you're working with a JPEG photograph, it's a 24-bit image that can display 16 million colors. So, despite the loss of quality because of lossy compression, compared with the 256-color limitations of GIF, JPEG is still a much better option for more closely matching the quality of the original image. Again, how much loss of quality depends on the size, quality, and type of the source image.

JPEG can also save website visitors time on downloading with the option to save JPEG images as a "progressive JPEG." This means you can specify whether or not you want the image to download in stages rather than all at once. That way, users can get a quick initial idea of what an image looks like and judge for themselves whether they want to wait for the full download. The only problem with progressive JPEGs is they're not supported by older browsers.

### 5.1.8 Portable Network Graphics (PNG): Using The best of the two others

PNG (Portable Network Graphics) is a bitmap graphics format that has been approved as a standard by the W3C. PNG offers up to 256 indexed colors, support for 24- and 48-bit truecolor, full alpha-channel support for transparency, and typically 10 percent to 30 percent better lossless compression than GIF.

In year 1997 it was much trumpeted as the replacement to GIF and JPEG that would soon make both of these standards obsolete. With PNG format, there's flexibility for palette control, transparency, and compression. However, despite PNG's improvements, it has yet to be actually embraced by website designers and producers. It's difficult to find PNG images anywhere on the Web, despite its recent inclusion as a native format for both the Netscape and Internet Explorer browsers. Moreover PNG images are royalty free.

One possible reason for PNG's lack of momentum could be the advantage GIF offers, reaching the lowest common denominator. Because PNG has only recently been included with Netscape version 4.04 and later, and with partial support in IE version 4.0b1 and later, it can't yet be accessed by the majority of Web users.

### 5.1.9 TIFF

Tagged-Image File Format (TIFF) is used to exchange files between applications and computer platforms. TIFF is a flexible bitmap image format supported by virtually all paint, image-editing, and page-layout applications. Also, virtually all desktop scanners can produce TIFF images.

TIFF format supports CMYK, RGB, Lab, indexed-color, and grayscale images with alpha channels and Bitmap-mode images without alpha channels. Photoshop can save layers in a TIFF file; however, if you open the file in another application, only the flattened image is visible. Photoshop can also save annotations, transparency, and multi resolution pyramid data in TIFF format.

### 5.1.10 PDF

Portable Document Format (PDF) is a flexible, cross-platform, cross-application file format. Based on the PostScript imaging model, PDF files accurately display and preserve fonts, page layouts, and both vector and bitmap graphics. In addition, PDF files can contain electronic document search and navigation features such as electronic links.

Generic PDF files are created using applications other than Photoshop, such as Adobe Acrobat and Adobe Illustrator, and can contain multiple pages and images. When you open a Generic PDF file, Photoshop rasterises the image. Photoshop and ImageReady recognize two types of PDF files: Photoshop PDF files and Generic PDF files. You can open both types of PDF files; however, you can only save images to

Photoshop PDF format.

Photoshop PDF files are created using the Photoshop Save As command. Photoshop PDF files can contain only a single image.

Photoshop PDF format supports all of the color modes and features that are supported in standard Photoshop format. Photoshop PDF also supports JPEG and ZIP compression, except for Bitmap-mode images, which use CCITT Group 4 compression.

### 5.1.11 PSD Photoshop Format

Photoshop format (PSD) is the default file format for newly created images—and the only format supporting all available image modes (Bitmap, Grayscale, Duotone, Indexed Color, RGB, CMYK, Lab, and Multichannel), guides, alpha channels, spot channels, and layers (including adjustment layers, type layers, and layer effects).

Vector graphics (also known as object-oriented graphics), maintains the image as a series of points, lines, arcs and other geometric shapes.

A vector graphic is resolution-independent that is, it can be scaled to any size and printed on any output device at any resolution without losing its detail or clarity. As a result, vector graphics are the best choice for type (especially small type) and bold graphics that must retain crisp lines when scaled to various sizes—for example, logos.

Because computer monitors represent images by displaying them on a grid, both vector and bitmap images are displayed as pixels on-screen.

Vector graphics images are typically produced by programs such as Abode Illustrator or Corel's CorelDraw, are created with curves and other mathematical shapes instead of pixels. Because a mathematical curve always stays smooth no matter how closely you look at it, vector graphics always print at the highest smoothness level, and the graphics the size remains small. For print, the most common type of vector graphic language is PostScript, which is a cross-platform standard for manipulating, storing, and printing vector graphics, including fonts. Programs that work with vector graphics are usually referred to as illustration or draw programs. Drawing programs such as Adobe Illustrator® create vector graphics, made of lines and curves defined by mathematical objects called vectors. Vectors describe graphics according to their geometric characteristics. For example, a bicycle tire in a vector graphic is made up of a mathematical definition of a circle drawn with a certain radius, set at a specific location, and filled with a specific color. You can move, resize, or change the color of the tire without losing the quality of the graphic.

Vector graphics don't reproduce photographic detail well, however, and most authoring programs can't handle them anyway. Most multimedia authoring systems provide for use of vector-drawn objects such as lines, rectangles, ovals, polygons, and text.

- Computer-aided design (CAD) programs have traditionally used vector-drawn object systems for creating the highly complex and geometric renderings needed by architects and engineers (CAD tools are discussed in Chapter 6).
- Graphic artists designing for print media use vector-drawn objects because the same mathematics that put a rectangle on your screen can also place that rectangle (or the fancy Bezier curves of a good line-art illustration) on paper without jaggies. This requires the highest resolution of the printer,using a page description languages such as PostScript.
- Programs for three-dimensional (3-D) animation also use vector-drawn graphics.

### 5.1.12 Vector Formats: PGML, VML, SWF

PGML, SWF, and VML are all vector formats, which describe graphics in terms of mathematical formulas rather than pixels. Vectors are typically much smaller than bitmap images, and provide the ability to scale and zoom in on images without any loss in resolution or clarity. Both PGML and VML have been submitted for consideration by the W3C. Both standards are based on XML (Extensible Markup Language (XML).

An up-and-coming standard for Web images, vectors are already familiar to designers working in print. Unlike bitmap images, vectors are based on mathematical data and geometry. Vectors offer several advantages for the Web, primarily their small size compared with bitmap graphics, and their scalability.

In the past few months, several vector standards for the Web have been proposed. Under consideration by the World Wide Web Consortium (W3C) , the main standards body for the Web, are the vying formats of PGML and VML. Macromedia, which backs the VML proposal, has recently opened up its vector Flash format to other developers.

Although general consumer wisdom holds that new usually means improved, in the case of Web graphics, it's not always necessarily better . What's the best format for graphics on your website depends in large part on the source of your original image — for example, whether it's a photograph, line art, information graphic, or scanned artwork.

The right format also depends on your intended use — what kind of images are appropriate to communicate to your targeted audience. Use the following guide to sort out GIF, JPEG, and the new vector formats of PGML, VML, and SWF, and to determine the perfect format for your differing Web-graphics needs.

Both PGML and VML have been submitted for consideration by the W3C. Both standards are based on XML (Extensible Markup Language (XML).

### (1) PGML

PGML (Precision Graphics Markup Language) is a vector format that has been submitted to the World Wide Web Consortium (W3C), the main standards body for the Web, by Adobe Systems, IBM, Netscape, and Sun Microsystems.

### (2) Flash file format (.swf)

SWF (Shockwave Flash) is the vector format for Macromedia's Flash. Simultaneous to the PGML and VML proposals, Macromedia recently published the Flash file format (.swf) as an open Internet standard. Flash is a vector-based multimedia authoring environment for the web that lets developers incorporate vector animation and graphics, and sound and interactivity into Flash titles. Flash's previous disadvantage was that it required a plug-in for users to play back Flash titles. However, in early June, Netscape announced it would incorporate the Flash format into its Navigator browser, and would release a maintenance version of the browser this summer that incorporates native Flash playback capabilities.

### (3) VML (Vector Markup Language)

VML is a vector format that has been submitted to the WC3 by Microsoft, Hewlett-Packard, Autodesk, Macromedia, and Vision.

## 5.1.13 Advantages of Vector formats

Both JPEG and GIF are bitmap formats, based on pixels. On the other hand, vector images are based on mathematical formulas. Vectors provide some distinct advantages over bitmap images, especially for use on the Web. The primary advantage is vector images are much smaller than bitmap images because there is no need to describe each individual pixel. The mathematical formulas that describe vectors take up much less space, and can be read much faster than individual pixels.

Vectors also provide another distinct advantage — the ability to scale and zoom in on images without any loss in resolution or clarity — which is one of the biggest disadvantages to the bitmap format. This is key to being able to easily edit and manipulate images. Therefore, vectors don't require the hassle of juggling between compression schemes and final-display quality.

Although vectors offer distinct advantages over bitmap, because images such as photographs or scanned artwork are made up of pixels, they can't be converted to vectors. Any image created with a drawing program, such as line art, icons, illustrations, maps, information graphics, etc., are native vector images.

The problem with vector graphics on the Web in the past has been there was no way to display them in a browser without a plug-in. To bring vector graphics to the Web without any need for plug-ins, two new vector standards are being proposed to the W3C: the Precision Graphics Markup Language and the Vector Markup Language. PGML is backed by Adobe Systems, IBM, Netscape, and Sun Microsystems. VML is supported by Microsoft, Hewlett-Packard, Autodesk, Macromedia, and Visio. Both standards are based on Extensible Markup Language (XML), the up-and-coming new markup language for the Web that has been much touted as the next successor to HTML (XML has been recommended by the W3C).

So who will win these vector format wars, and how should you plan for future use of vector graphics on the Web? According to Rita Knox, vice president and research director at Stamford, Conn.-based Gartner Group, the ultimate Web vector format will probably be a compromise.

"The W3C is not going to simultaneously work on both standard proposals," Knox says. "Most likely, what we'll see is a working group that will end up combining and using the best features of all the competing standards."

However, according to Joe Butt, analyst at Cambridge, Mass.-based Forrester Research, Flash does have one distinct advantage over the other formats. "Both PGML and VML are paper right now," Butt says. "Flash has been very smart to be the first out there with a large installed base, making it the current de facto standard. And now that it's been incorporated as native in the Netscape browser, that will make it available to the large percentage of users running Netscape." Graphics Pictures are "drawn" into vector graphics images using a digitizer tablet or mouse. Pictures are photographed into raster graphics images with scanners and digital cameras.

Vector graphics is the method employed by computer-aided design (CAD) and drawing packages. As you draw, each line of the image is stored as a vector, which is two end points on an x-y matrix. For example, a square becomes four vectors, one for each side. A circle is turned into dozens or hundreds of tiny straight lines, the number of which is determined by the resolution of the drawing. The entire image is commonly stored in the computer as a list of vectors. A vector graphics image is a collection of graphic elements, such as lines, squares, rectangles and circles. Although grouped together, each element maintains its own integrity and identity and can always be selected and erased or resized independent of all the others. Vector graphics can be transmitted directly to x-y plotters that "draw" the images from the list of vectors.

Older CAD systems used vector screens that also drew the vectors. Today, all monitors are raster graphics displays made up of dots, and the vectors are "rasterized" into the required dot patterns by hardware or software. Table 5.1 compares the various characteristics of Common File Formats.

**TABLE 5.1:** Characteristics of Common File Formats

| Format Colour depth File size | Colours | Comp. | Exchange format |
|---|---|---|---|
| BMP 1, 4, 8, 16, 24<br>format 1.1 MB | 2, 16, 256, 65536, 15.7 m | no | Win's exchange |
| GIF 1, 4, 8<br>228 KB | 2, 16, 256 | yes | Internet |
| JPEG 8 (grey shades),<br>24 internet 228 KB | 256, 15.7 mn | yes | Archiving format |
| PCX 1, 2, 6, 16<br>format 956 KB | 2, 16, 256, 65, 536 | yes | DOS exchange |
| TIFF 4, 6, 8, 16, 24<br>920 KB | 2, 16, 256, 65536, 15.7mn | yes | Retouching pictures |
| Image file used: 800 × 600 pixel resolution at 300 dots per inch | | | |

## Graphics Format Comparison

### GIF

- Lowest common denominator factor
- Readable by the widest audience

- Support for one level of transparency
- Ability to create indexed palettes
- Lossless compression -Suitable for images that have fewer colors, such as black and white images, and images with large areas of solid color, such as cartoons and line art.
- Only supports 256 colors
- Can't control the rate of compression
- Because of color limitations, not suitable for continuous tone images

**JPG**

- Variable compression ratios
- Capable of very high compression
- Offer 24-bit, 16 million colors
- Best suited for continuous tone images such as photographs, scanned artwork, and rendered 3-D graphics.
- Can load as "progressive JPEGs," downloading the image in stages
- Can't index colors to set palettes
- Doesn't support transparency
- Lossy compression
- 24-bit color doesn't display consistently across all hardware

**PNG**

- Offers up to 256 indexed colors
- Support for 24 and 48-bit truecolor
- Full alpha channel support for transparency
- Typically 10% to 30% better lossless compression than GIF -Not a standard (not being readily adapted by Web community)
- Only recently available as a native format in Netscape and IE, meaning it can only be read by a small audience

**VECTORS (INCLUDING PGML, SWF AND VML)**

- Typically smaller size than bitmaps
- Can be scaled and zoomed in on
- Suitable for line art, icons, illustrations, maps, info graphics, etc.
- Up-and-coming standards promising for widespread deployment on the Web - Not standardized for use on the Web
- Requires a plug-in in most cases to display (except for SWF format)

The number of pixels along the height and width of a bitmap image. The display size of an image on-screen is determined by the pixel dimensions of the image plus the size and setting of the monitor. The file size of an image is proportional to its pixel dimensions.

A typical 13-inch monitor displays 640 pixels horizontally and 480 vertically. An image with pixel dimensions of 640 by 480 would fill this small screen. On a larger monitor with a 640 by 480 setting, the same image (with pixel dimensions of 640 by 480) would still fill the screen, but each pixel would appear larger. Changing the setting of this larger monitor to 1152 pixels by 870 pixels would display the image at a smaller size, occupying only part of the screen.

When preparing an image for online display (for example, a Web page that will be viewed on a variety of monitors), pixel dimensions become especially important. Because your image may be viewed on a 13-inch monitor, you'll probably want to limit the size of your image to a maximum of 640 pixels by 480 pixels.

## 5.2 ON-SCREEN DISPLAY SIZE

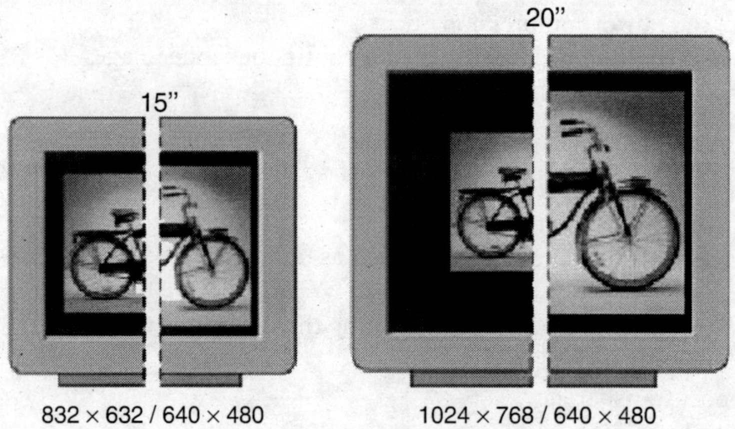


**Fig. 5.2:** On screen display size

How large an image appears on-screen depends on a combination of factors--the pixel dimensions of the image, the monitor size, and the monitor resolution setting. The Figure 5.2 shows a 620 x 400 pixel image displayed with two different monitor sizes and monitor resolutions.

## 5.3 IMAGE RESOLUTION

Image Resolution is the number of pixels displayed per unit of printed length in an image, usually measured in pixels per inch (ppi).

An image's resolution determines the degree of detail it contains, and is measured by the number of pixels, or dots, it contains per inch (dpi). Because the number of pixels in a bitmap is fixed, the resolution of the image is tied in to the size of the printed image. If you print the image at a small size, the pixels are tiny, and the resolution high. Print the image large, and the pixels become enlarged and look coarse, resulting in a lower resolution.

A higher resolution allows for more detail and smoother color transitions than a lower resolution, but also results in a much larger file. Setting the resolution is a balancing act between achieving the level of detail you need and keeping the file size down to a level your system can handle.

An image with a high resolution contains more, and therefore smaller, pixels than an image of the same printed dimensions with a low resolution. For example, a 1-inch-by-1-inch image with a resolution of 72 ppi contains a total of 5184 pixels (72 pixels wide x 72 pixels high = 5184). The same 1-inch-by-1-inch image with a resolution of 300 ppi would contain a total of 90,000 pixels. (See Figure 5.3)

Because they use more pixels to represent each unit of area, higher-resolution images usually reproduce more detail and subtle color transitions than lower-resolution images when printed. However, increasing the resolution of an image scanned or created at a lower resolution only spreads the original pixel information across a greater number of pixels and rarely improves image quality.

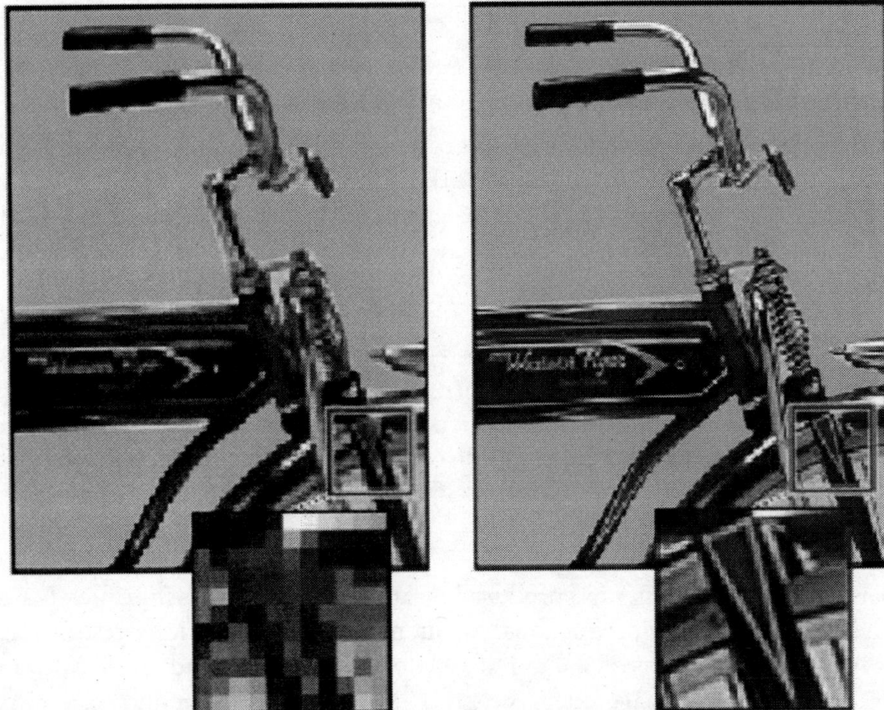

Fig. 5.3: Example of an image : 72-ppi and 300-ppi images; inset zoom 200%

To determine the image resolution to use, consider the medium of final distribution for the image. Base your image resolution on what your output will be. If you are going to print your image, keep the resolution lower than that of the final output device: if you create a 1200 dpi image to print on a 600 dpi printer, you are going to end up with a 600 dpi printed image and a file that is much larger than you need.

If you are going to display your image on screen, you can generally get away with a lower resolution. Again, keep in mind the memory restrictions of your particular setup, and try to set the resolution to correspond with that of the monitor you plan to use.

If you're producing an image for online display, the image resolution only needs to match the typical monitor resolution (72 or 96 ppi). However, using too low a resolution for a printed image results in pixelation—output with large, coarse-looking pixels. Using too high a resolution (pixels smaller than what the output device can produce) increases the file size and slows the printing of the image; furthermore, the device will be unable to print the image at the high resolution.

**About image size and resolution**

When you acquire you images, it's worth paying attention to the resolution in which they will eventually be displayed. Computer screens carry, but most of them have a resolution of about 72 dots per inch (dpi). Most scanners acquire images at 300-1200 dpi. If you put a 300 dpi image in a web page it will come out about four times its original size, which may not be what you were after.

If you change an image's resolution, always make sure you change it by an exact multiple-halve it or quarter it. If the factor by which you change the resolution is an odd amount the image will almost always come out looking awful. For an image scanned to 300 dpi, rescale it to be 75 dpi and accept that it will display a bit big-if you create it to 72 dpi the image will look awful.

### 5.3.1 Monitor Resolution

The number of pixels or dots displayed per unit of length on the monitor, usually measured in dots per inch (dpi). Monitor resolution depends on the size of the monitor plus its pixel setting. The typical resolution of a PC monitor is about 96 dpi, of a Mac OS monitor 72 dpi. Understanding monitor resolution helps explain why the display size of an image on-screen often differs from its printed size.

In Photoshop, image pixels are translated directly into monitor pixels. This means that when the image resolution is higher than the monitor resolution, the image appears larger on-screen than its specified print dimensions. For example, when you display a 1-inch-by-1-inch, 144-ppi image on a 72-dpi monitor, it appears in a 2-inch-by-2-inch area on-screen. Because the monitor can display only 72 pixels per inch, it needs 2 inches to display the 144 pixels that make up one edge of the image.

### 5.3.2 Printer Resolution

The number of ink dots per inch (dpi) produced by an imagesetter or laser printer. For best results, use an image resolution that is proportional to, but not the same as, printer resolution. Most laser printers have output resolutions of 300 dpi to 600 dpi and produce good results with images from 72 ppi to 150 ppi. High-end imagesetters can print at 1200 dpi or higher and produce good results with images from 200 ppi to 300 ppi.

The digital size of an image, measured in kilobytes (K), megabytes (MB), or gigabytes (GB). File size is proportional to the pixel dimensions of the image. Images with more pixels may produce more detail at a given printed size, but they require more disk space to store and may be slower to edit and print. For instance, a 1-inch-by-1-inch 200-ppi image contains four times as many pixels as a 1-inch-by-1-inch 100-ppi image and so has four times the file size. Image resolution thus becomes a compromise between image quality (capturing all the data you need) and file size.

Photoshop supports a maximum file size of 2 GB and maximum pixel dimensions of 30,000 by 30,000 pixels per image. This restriction places limits on the print size and resolution available to an image. For example, an image 100 by 100 inches can have a resolution of at most 300 ppi (30,000 pixels / 100 inches = 300 ppi).

### 5.3.3. Resolution, file size, and output

The file size of an image refers to the total amount of pixel information in the image. For example, a 1-inch-by-2-inch high-resolution image (Fig. 5.4(a)) has more pixels, and thus a larger file size, than a 1-inch-by-2-inch (vide Fig. 5.4(b)) low-resolution image. In print, a high-resolution image has more detail than the same image at low resolution. On-screen, a high-resolution image appears larger. The enlarged on-screen display does not affect the dimensions of the printed image.

a. 1 in. × 2 in. @ 72 ppi; file size 323K. 100% view on-screen
b. 1 in. × 2 in. @ 300 ppi; file size 5.47MB. 100% view on-screen

**Fig. 5.4:** Effect of resolution on file size of an image

## 5.4 METHODS OF FILE COMPRESSION

### 5.4.1 LZW Compression

The Lemple-Ziv-Welch (LZW) procedure uses this to reduces the graphic file size. It stores colour data and identical pixel-information only once thus avoiding storage of repetitive data. Thus, higher the dominance of a colour in a picture, higher the compression. In other words the picture of a red sunset can be condensed to a smaller file than a colorful meadow of flowers. Most formats like PCX, Gif and TIFF use either LZW or its variants to reduce file size.

### 5.4.2 Lossy Compression

If you want a smaller file size then you should use the jpeg format which uses lossy compression method to offer superior compression. Lossy compression makes use of the inability of the human eye to perceive different levels of brightness and combines the neighbouring pixels. The number of pixels that can be combined depends on the compression factor. In case of a compression where you compress the file size by about 15 percent of the original the loss of picture quality is hardly evident even after opening the JPEG file. The thumb rule: Larger the output file, lower the perceivable loss. The only disadvantage is that as pixels have to be combined together, the time taken to save a file in the JPEG format is more than that of any other compressed format. The time taken to open a file however, is comparable with other formats. This makes this format very popular for data transfer through the Internet or CD-ROM.

However, there are some formats like BMP that do not utilise any compression at all. When compared to the pixel format vector format files take lesser space as they archive only information on curves in the picture and thus can be without the compression.

## 5.5 COMPRESSED FILE FORMATS

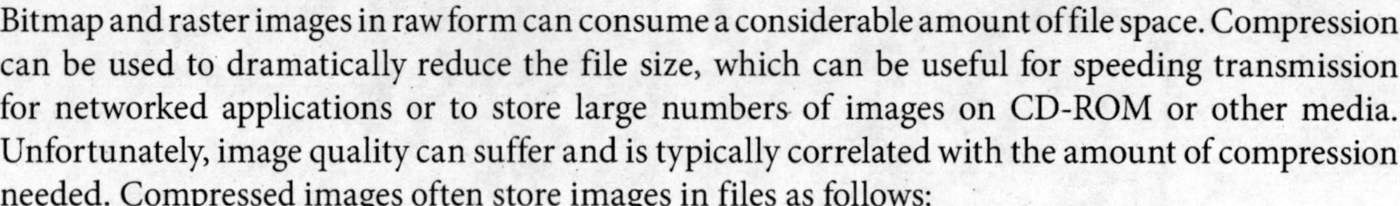

Bitmap and raster images in raw form can consume a considerable amount of file space. Compression can be used to dramatically reduce the file size, which can be useful for speeding transmission for networked applications or to store large numbers of images on CD-ROM or other media. Unfortunately, image quality can suffer and is typically correlated with the amount of compression needed. Compressed images often store images in files as follows:

- File header-stores various information about the type of compression, file size color depth and amount of data.
- Image data-image information that has undergone some type of algormation that has reduced the amount of data while retaining some level of image quality. Many compression schemes can be controlled to increase quality and sacrifice file size or vice versa.

Although there are a number of common compressed file formats, the following are popular formats with widespread acceptance and use:

### (1) Graphics Interchange Format (GIF)

Developed by Compuserve for moving images in dial-up situations; it has become a popular format for use in World Wide Web pages. GIF files use LZW compression, which is a Unisys-owned algorithm that requires royaltich by program developers who use software that creates or reads GIF -formatted files. GIF files are limited up to 256 colors. The file data includes information about the file format, layout of the data, image characteristics (height, width ), color depth, color table (palette), and the image data. GIF files can also contain multiple images which can be extracted and contained in sequence by special software to create simple animation presentations.

### (2) Tagged Image File Format (TIFF)

Very high compression capability, good for black and white images. Used extensively in publishing and fax applications.

### (3) Joint Photographic Experts Group (JPEG and JPG)

Packs a 24-bit color image into a relatively small file size. Microsoft has published the standard, which gained popularity for its use in world wide web applications. The JPEG file includes specific in-formation about the image in the file header (including image size, bits per pixel, and number of colors used), the color palette, and compressed image data.

### (4) Proprietary Formats

Many commercial software paint and drawing packages use proprietary formats for storing graphic images. The same software packings often support other file formats for importing and exporting images.

### 5.5.1 Format Conversions

Pixel format conversion: In order to convert a graphic file from one format to another the graphic has to be loaded in programs that supports both the source and target format. In case of colour depth, a photo, which is saved as a 24-bit TIFF, can be saved as a 24-bit BMP without any loss in quality whenever a 24-bit image is saved as an 8-bit graphic file. If colour correction is not applied the reduction in the number of colours will lead to the appearance of colour rings.

On the flip side, converting a lower bit format to a higher bit format does not carry any benefit in terms of quality. The benefit can only be achieved if you mount a picture within a picture which uses a different spectrum of colours.

Successful conversion can also be hampered by special characteristics of a format. An example is the transparency feature of the GIF format that makes an image seem transparent (except for painted areas) and makes the background visible. This feature is lost when you convert a GIF file to PCX, JPG or BMB and may result in distorted pictures.

### 5.5.2 Vector Format Conversion

Unlike pixel formats vector formats get damaged when converting them from one vector format to another. Although the result might seem very similar at the first glance are often damaged during conversion. The converted format also does not store individual elements were combined with or to which groups the individual elements were combined with or at what levels they were arranged. These affect reprocessing since only unorganised set of objects remains.

Conversion between vector and pixel formats: While vector-to-pixel format conversion is a simple affair the reverse is not. In the case of vector-to-pixel, since areas in the picture which are defined have to be filled with pixels that for displaying on the monitor or for printing they can display saved as pixel-to-vector conversions require special programs called tracers.

A tracer analyses the picture and determines areas with similar colours. Around such areas, it places a such areas it places a curve, which defines the area along with the colour information. This information is then used by the vector program for representing an object, which is very similar in form and colour to the original area in the format. Conversion of the pixel to a vector graphic is useful only if the image shows very few shades. Pictures with 1-4- and 9-bit colour depth thus give the best results in this type of format conversion.

Although more painting tools are added to drawing programs and more drawing tools are added to paint programs, their inherent structure is entirely different. Drawing programs (vector graphics) allow for the creation of objects that can be manipulated independently. Paint programs (raster graphics) provide a canvas that can be covered with electronic paint.

A program known as Canvas specializes in both methods. Canvas combines extensive drawing and imaging tools in one program. The PC internals drawing on top is a vector graphics rendering and the "first mouse" below is a raster graphics image. The open menus show image editing tools that are not normally found in a vector graphics drawing program.

Color is a vital component of multimedia. This section explains from where color comes from and how colors are displayed on a computer monitor. Management of color is both a subjective and a technical exercise. Picking the right colors and combinations of colors for your project can involve many tries until you feel the result is right. But the technical description of a color may be expressed in known physical values (humans, for example, perceive colors with wavelengths ranging from 400 to 600 nanometers on the electromagnetic spectrum), and there are several methods and models to describe color space using mathematics and values.

The cornea of the eye acts as a lens to focus light rays onto the retina. The light rays stimulate many thousands of specialized nerves called rods and cones that cover the surface of the retina. Receptors in the cones are sensitive to red, green, and blue light, and all the nerves together transmit the pattern of color information to the brain. The eye can differentiate among millions or colors, or hues, consisting of combinations of red, green and blue.

Green, blue, yellow, orange, purple, pink, brown, black, grey, and white are the ten most common color-describing words used in all human languages and cultures.

### 5.5.3 Computerized Color

Because the eye's receptors are sensitive to red, green, and blue light, bu adjusting combinations of these three additive primary colors, in between. This is the psychology, not the physics of color: What you perceive as orange on a computer monitor is a combination of two frequencies of green and red light, not the actual spectral frequency you see when you look at that namesake fruit, an orange, in sunlight. All these factors make computerized color pretty tricky to manage.

The reflected light that reaches your eye from a printed page is made up of tiny halftone dots of a few primary colors (printers use the subtractive primary colors, cyan, magenta, and yellow, with black). In contrast, computer monitor screens are, like the sun, sources of light. On the back of the glass face of a monitor are thousands of phosphores chemical color dots (red, green, and blue) that are bombarded by electrons that paint the screen at very high speeds. These dots are each about .30mm or less in diameter (the dot pitch) and are positioned very carefully and very close together.

The red, green, and blue dots light up when hit by the electron beam, and the eye sees the combination of red, green, and blue (RGB) light and interpolates it. When one of the primary colors is subtracted from this RGB mix, the subtractive primary color is perceived, as follows:

As mentioned earlier, a raster or bitmap image is composed of a matrix of elements called pixels. Each pixel consists of two or more colors. The color depth is determined of colors; for example:

- 1 bit yields 2 colors.
- 4 bits yields 16 colors.
- 8 bits (1byte ) yields 256 colors.
- 16 bits (2 bytes ) yields 65,536 colors.
- 24 bits (3 bytes) yields 16,777,216 colors

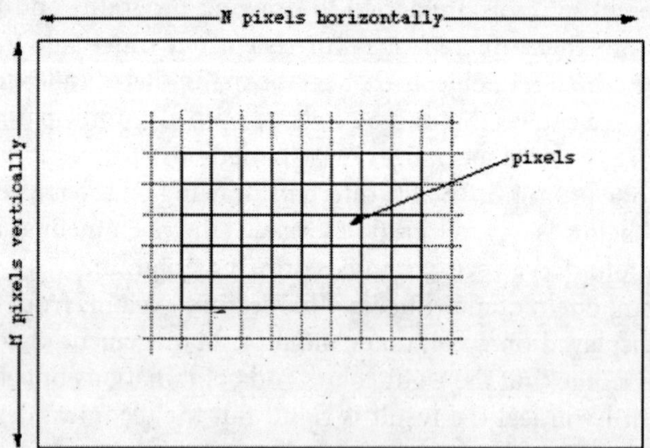


Above figure illustrates how image is created on a pixel by pixel basis. The number of pixels is related to the size of file that is required to store an image. To determine the size of a raster image, multiply the number of pixels in the horizontal plane (X) by the number of pixels in the vertical-plane (Y), then take this value and multiply it by the number of bytes per pixels (divide the number of bits used for color by 8,the number of bits in a byte). The equation is as follows:

$$\text{Image size (in bytes)} = X \times Y \text{ (bits per pixel / 8)}$$

X = width of image in pixels

Y = height of image in pixels

A standard computer VGA display is 640 by 480 pixels for a total of 307,200 pixels. A two-color or monochrome display image consists of 38,400 bytes, while a 256 color display image consists of 307, 200 bytes. Finally, a fullscreen VGA display image using 24 bit colour would require 921,600 bytes. As you can see the more colors used the more bytes are required to encode the image and the more bytes required for an image, the larger the file to store the image.

### 5.5.4 Vector Images

Vector images are based on drawing elements or objects such as lines, rectangles, circles, and so forth to create an image. Vector images are actually stored as a series of commands that define the individual objects. For example the following commands are used to define various objects:

- Line: line $x_1$, $y_1$, $x_2$, $y_2$, color
- Rectangle: rectangle top, left, width, color
- Circle: circle top, left, radius, color

Figure 5.5 provides an example of an image created by a vector image. Each element of the image is built by using commands to draw lines, circles, rectangles, and so forth to create the image.

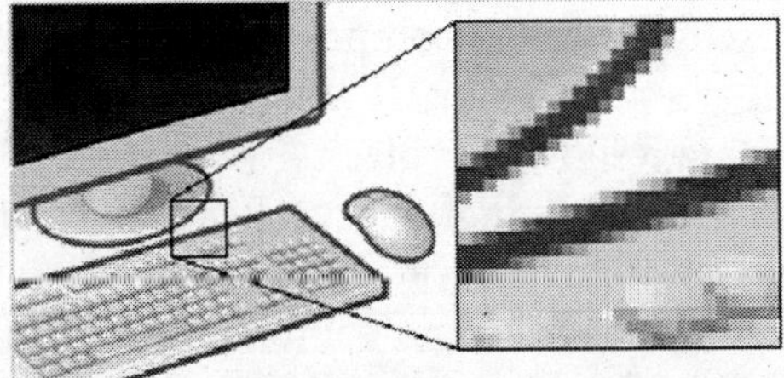

**Fig. 5.5:** One element of a vector format image stores in disk is expanded

Bitmap images can be resized by stretching the image in the x and/or y axis, but the image is often distorted due to the replication of pixel elements. Vector images are created by larger objects (squares, circles, polygons ) that can be proportionately resized without losing the integrity of the original image. By applying a scaling factor an image can be easily resized.

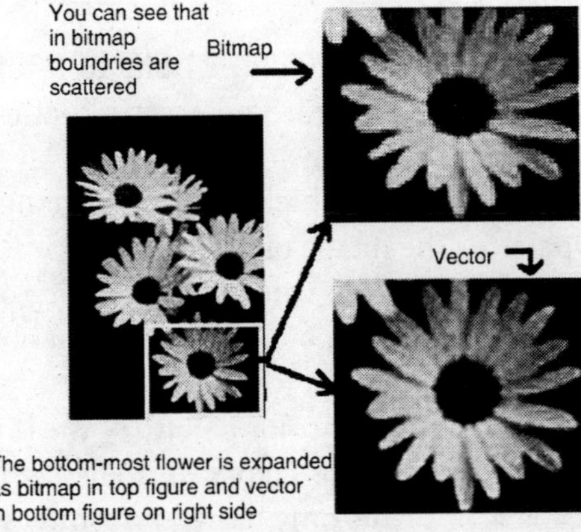


**Fig. 5.6:** Vector image retains more quality if an image than raster bitmap in which image is distorted.

The advantage of a vector image is the relatively small amount of data required to represent the image and therefore it does not require a lot of memory to store. The image consists of set of commands that are drawn when needed. While a bitmap image requires the number of pixels to produce the appropriate height, width and color depth the vector image is based on a relatively limited number of the limited level of detail that can be presented in an image. Simple vector photographs, unsell raster images are stored as component objects that are part of the vector image.

### 5.5.5 Images and Color

Computer image color ranges from simple black and white to millions of colors. Line art illustrations are an effective use of a black and white image while a photographic image of a flower garden is ideally presented by systems that support the display of over 16 million color. The use of color in multimedia depends on two factors:

1. The subject or content of the image
2. The technical capability of the computer hardware and software

The key to using color in the computer is to understand what color is. Color is based on the perception of light, which is part of the electromagnetic spectrum offer colors including red, orange, yellow, green, blue, indigo, and violet. Interestingly, computer-generated white and black are a function of the presence of all colors or none at all. White is created by combining all colors and black is created by the absence of color. Computer color is based on adjusting combinations of additive primary colors : red, green, and blue (RGB). Printed colors, based on reflective light, use subtractive colors: cyan, magenta, yellow, and black.

The perception of color is the function of the eye. Receptors, called cones, in the cornea of the eye are sensitive to red, green and blue frequencies of the electromagnetic spectrum. The eye is sensitive to millions of colors or hues based on combinations of the three colors; red, green, and blue. Combining these colours yields a basic set of working colors;

- Red + Green + Blue = White
- Green + red = Yellow
- Blue + Red = Magenta
- Blue + Green = Cyan
- No color = Black

### 5.5.6 Color Dithering

Scanned or digitized images are often captured at 24 bit, 16 million color depth. If the image is subsequently displayed on a computer monitor and system that is limited to less than 16 million colors, say 256 colors, the image must be transformed for display in the lesser color environment (palette). Dithering is the process through which colors are changed to meet the closest available color based on the available palette. The image plate is mapped into the new plate dimensions with colors substituted with the closest available values. The quality of the dithering will depend on the algorithm used but most systems provide close approximations of the original. An example of dithering is seen in some plate of colors typically 256 or less. Images with formats that include millions of colors are dithered to the limited color palette of the browser application.

Thus it is a process of simulating more colors and shades in a palette or vice-versa. In a monochrome system that displays or prints only black and white, shades of grays can be simulated by creating varying patterns of black dots. This is how halftones are created in a monochrome printer.

In color systems, additional colors can be simulated by varying patterns of dots of existing colors. Dithering cannot produce the exact same results as having the necessary color depth (levels of gray or colors), but it can make shaded drawings and photographs appear much more realistic. Dithering is also used to create a wide variety of patterns for use as backgrounds, fills and shading, as well as for creating anti-aliasing effects.

When there aren't enough colors in a display system to render an image properly, an infinite palette can be created by dithering. Quite often, a 24-bit color image is dithered to 256 colors.

## Algorithms

There are several algorithms designed to perform dithering. One of the earliest, and still one of the most popular, is the Floyd–Steinberg dithering algorithm, developed in 1975. One of the strengths of this algorithm is that it minimizes visual artifacts through an error-diffusion process; error-diffusion algorithms typically produce images that more closely represent the original than simpler dithering algorithms.

### Dithering methods include:

Thresholding (also average dithering): each pixel value is compared against a fixed threshold. This may be the simplest dithering algorithm there is, but it results in immense loss of detail and contouring.

Random dithering was the first attempt (at least as early as 1951) to remedy the drawbacks of thresholding. Each pixel value is compared against a random threshold, resulting in a statistic image. Although this method doesn't generate patterned artifacts, the noise tends to swamp the detail of the image. It is analogous to the practice of mezzo-tinting.

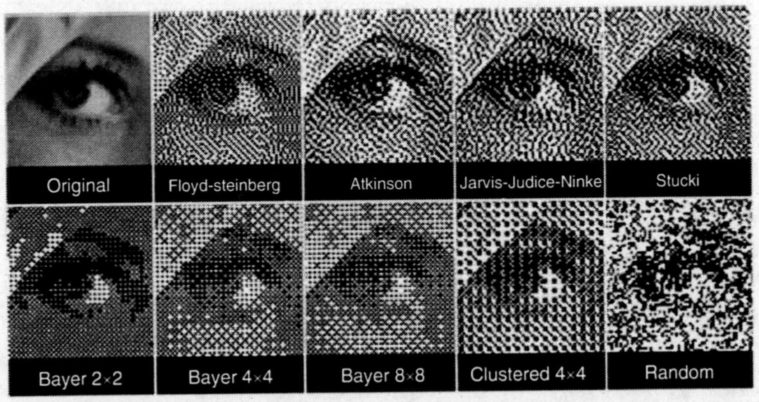


Fig. 5.7: Different dithering techniques.

Patterning dithers using a fixed pattern. For every pixel in the image the value of the pattern at the corresponding location is used as a threshold. Different patterns can generate completely different dithering effects.

Halftone dithering looks similar to halftone screening in newspapers. This is a form of clustered dithering, in that dots tend to cluster together. This can help hide the adverse effects of blurry pixels found on some older output devices.

Ordered dithering produces a cross-hatch pattern. This is a form of dispersed dithering. Because the dots don't cluster, the result looks much less grainy.

## 5.5.7 Dithering Text

Text is also dithered. Notice how much softer the word DATABASE is at the top of this example, compared with the undithered word below it. The magnified view shows where lighter blue pixels filled in for the curves. When dithering is performed against the edges of an image, it is called anti-aliasing.

## 5.6 ADVANTAGES OF COMPUTER GRAPHICS

The traditional approach for designing is to use physical drawings. A computer graphics system offers the designer many advantages:

1. It can increase the productivity of the designer
2. It is more efficient than using paper
3. Designs can be made faster
4. Designs are easier to change
5. The results have better quality
6. It can provide different views
7. It offers added dimensions such as color and depth
8. It makes drawings easier to store and retrieve

A graphics systems takes advantage of the characteristics and strength of the computer to enhance the capabilities of the user. Its speed and accuracy relieves the user of routine, repetitive, and complex tasks. The computational power of a computer increases the logical and analytical ability of the user. Is large storage capacity serves as an extension of the user's memory.

Computer graphics systems are particularly well suited to help us respond to the dynamic nature of the manufacturing environment. A graphics systems can give us easy access to a large amount of information stored in a central database. That information can be complex and can change continually. Most manufacturing operations are geared for fast turnaround, which requires efficient communication and rapid feedback for control.

In addition to the needs and benefits for the manufacturing user, we have computer graphics systems because the technology has progressed to the point where it can provide the functions and features required. The performance of data processing systems in general has increased substantially in terms of speed and capacity. At the same time, the cost of computation and storage has been reduced significantly. Advances in computer hardware have made small, powerful workstation feasible. Complex software has also been developed to permit the efficient generation of high-resolution pictures. It is the result of all these factors that has made computer graphics systems a useful and practical tool in today's manufacturing environment.

Despite the limitations of any particular graphics system, most offer a substantial number of advantages to the user, including:

1. Reducing errors and improving accuracy in drafting and analysis activities.
2. Increasing the rate at which data can be communicated and comprehended (since images are more efficient than text)
3. Increasing analytical capability (i.e., engineering computations and analyses)
4. Increasing the productivity of engineers and designers
5. Increasing the creativity of designers
6. Providing the ability to respond to change easily and rapidly
7. Avoiding the necessity of fabricating and testing prototypes of new designs

8. Creating a database for manufacturing
9. Reducing the cost and time for developing and manufacturing a new product
10. Improving the quality, availability, and cost of providing management information (*e.g.*, business graphics)

## 5.7 APPLICATION OF COMPUTER GRAPHICS

Computer graphics technology has been found to be a tool for improving productivity in a wide variety of applications throughout industry. Some are obviously more demanding than other which may not use all the capabilities of the technology that exist. However, in each case, most of the basic functions of the hardware and software addressed in this chapter are used.

### 1. Information Displays

Since graphics displays can communicate information more efficiently than hard text. So, graphics are being used more frequently in industry for a variety of information display tasks. These include information retrieval systems, telecommunication, management information systems, and manufacturing control system. For example, graphics displays are being used on the factory floor for process monitoring and control . They can be very easy for process operators to use, and at the same time they can communicate important in the form of graphics and text.

### 2. Computer Animation

These are used to produce various animation advertisements, and science fiction movies, like "Star Wars'. Computers have greatly reduced the artists work who earlier had to draw thousands of pictures, each a little different from the previous, to give the effect of motion for a single scene sequence.

### 3. Fashion Designing

Fashion designers use graphics to generate dress-pattern layout. Effects of various colour combinations may be seen by changing the colours of the various portions of the dress on the VDU. Optimum consumption of fabric is also estimated through the computers.

### 4. Engineering Applications

**Architects**

To make drawings of buildings, townships, etc. Any changes if needed can be easily done and fresh plan can be immediately taken out without having to redraft the plan. Estimates of requirements of steel, concrete, bricks, etc. can also be calculated through the computer.

**Civil Engineers**

In designing bridges, dams, factory layouts etc. Effect of various stresses against the materials used in construction can be checked to ensure safety of construction and estimate optimum requirement of materials.

**Machine Designing**

Designing of machines can be drawn of the computer. Library of components may be used to display a specific drawing on the screen and fit into any place in the machine. Effects of changes in the shapes of parts can also be seen on the VDU in seconds without going through the time consuming process of drawing it on paper.

**Electronic Circuit Design**

Revolution in electronic circuitry, specially in the legendary 'chip' have been only possible because of computers. If the whole circuit of a chip were to be drawn on paper, it would perhaps need a drawing board of the size of a football field. Even the effective working of circuit can be checked theoretically on the computer without actually producing the circuit board.

**Automated Drafting**

Automated drafting is one of the earliest and least demanding of the application areas, but it is still very widely used. Automated drafting systems have been developed for electrical, mechanical, and architectural drawings. They provide for the creation of views, scaling, dimensioning, and transformation (*e.g.*, rotation and isometrics). Automated drafting systems are faster and more accurate than manual drafting, and productivity improvement of anywhere from 5:1 to 15:1 have been reported.

**Design**

Computer-aided design systems have been developed for electrical, electronic, mechanical, and architectural application. The design process in all of these areas can be very data-intensive and time-consuming. Some modern, complex products, would be extremely difficult, it not impossible, to design manually. Automated design systems not only speed up the design process; they also provide for design reviews and checking.

**Engineering Analysis**

A number of engineering activities are involved between the initial design of a product and its ultimate manufacture. Computer graphics techniques have been developed which use the database established by an automated design system to perform these engineering analyses more efficiently and accurately than was ever possible before. These activities includes the analysis of stresses, motion, and physical properties; simulation of operation; process planning; and NC programming.

## 5. Business Graphics

The power of computer graphics is also finding many applications in administrative and management offices, where they help run the business. Since graphics is more efficient than text in communicating information, graphics can be used to summarize complex data and focus on the most important information. A business graphics system can make information more visible and accessible to managers. It can also provide lower-cost and higher quality charts than the traditional manual techniques.

**Learning Outcomes**

In this chapter we have learnt about :

1. Differentiate between Rastor and Vector Images and Different Types of Image Formats
2. Work with different Image resolutions and display size
3. Design Computer Graphics
4. Compress the matter by different compression schemes

# Audio Fundamentals And Representations

CHAPTER 6

**Leaning Objectives**

In this chapter we shall learn about:

1. Characteristics of Sound
2. Sound types and synthesis
3. Digitization of Sound
4. Digital Audio Formats
5. Basics of Digital Sound Processing
6. Compression of recorded sound Streaming audio
7. Sound Effects and Multimedia Sound Processing
8. Equipment and software needed for Sound Processing

## 6.1 DIGITIZATION OF SOUND

The great scientist Thomas Edison surprised his audience in 1876 by turning a cylinder out of which his distinctive voice was heard. He successfully created a mechanism that transmitted electrical impulses into an oscillating needle that in turn inscribed groves on a wax cylinder. These electrical impulses were generated by a thin membrane, activated by sound waves. He named this piece of invention as phonograph.

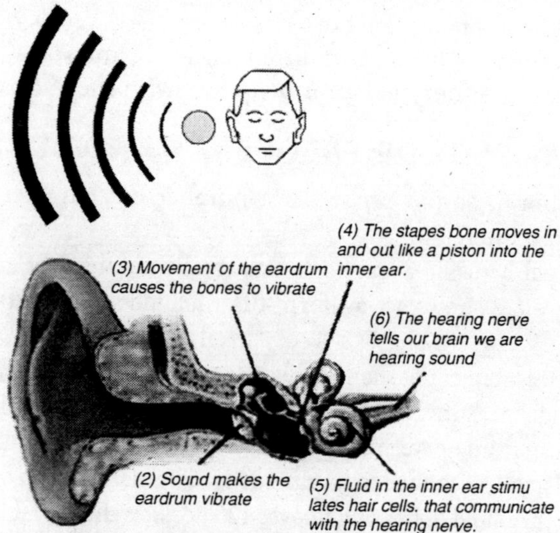


**Fig. 6.1:** The Process of Hearing

Sound is only the brain's interpretation of certain impulses being sent by the inner ear. Human ear cannot perceive some sounds those of very high or low frequency. Sound is basically a vibration.

An object moves back and forth (vibrates) and in doing so, pushes the air immediately next to it a bit to one side and then, when coming back creates a slight vacuum. This process is known as an oscillation. A series of oscillations creates a wave similar to the ripples you create when you throw a stone into still water. A schematic graphic of this process is shown in Figure 6.1.

An oscillating object creates a compression in the air next to it then a vacuum. The continuous oscillation produces sound waves.

The air particles that move in waves make your eardrum oscillate. This movement is registered by a series of small bones, the hammer the inner ear nerve endings, which in turn send impulses to your brain. Your brain perceives them as sounds.

Sound in business multimedia applications enables a user to describe products, give instructions, enhance a presentation, or provide cues for some action by the viewer. Hardware for capturing and processing sounds includes a card attached to the main "motherboard" of the computer system. A sound card contains connections for input and output devices. Usually software is included with the card that allows the user to control volume and devices and to create and edit sound files.

Sound cards capture analog audio signals from microphones, music CDs, musical instrument digital interface (MIDI) devices— electronic keyboards similar to piano keyboards—and other sound sources through a line-in jack on the card. Computer users can plug in record turntables, cassette tape players, or any other device from an audio-out jack on those devices and record sounds. Sound cards also have output jacks for speakers, or the audio-out can be plugged into other sound-recording devices. The card contains two computer chips called the analog-to-digital (AD) and digital-to-analog (DA) chips. These chips convert sound waves to digits and digits to sound waves.

Sound-application software is used to mix different sound sources. Users can add effects, such as fade in and fade out or an echo effect, to the digital sound track. Several competing standards exist for computer sound files. These standards depend on the manufacturer of the hardware or developers of the software. The more users of a given standard there are, the more portable the file is to other users and to Internet applications. MIDI files and wave files found on the Internet are common examples.

Voice-pattern-recognition software allows the user to speak through a microphone directly to a word-processing software package. The analog voice of the user is converted to a digital sound file through a sound card on the computer, and the user's voice pattern is converted into text. Whether the text is entered by keyboard, scanner, or voice-recognition hardware and software, the text can be used for presentations, Web pages, or other media forms to talk with the audience.

## 6.2 WAVEFORM, AMPLITUDE, FREQUENCY, AND DURATION

As interpreted by the brain, sound possesses a number of characteristics described briefly by Amplitude, frequency and pitch.

We can represent sound by using a waveform that recalls the shape of air particles movement while conducting sound. Figure 6.2 shows a waveform that includes some of the characteristics associated with a particular sound.

A waveform gives a measurement of the speed of the air particles and the distance that they travel for a given sound. The amplitude measures the relative loudness of the sound which is the distance between a valley and a crest. The amplitude determines the sound volume. The volume of sound is measured in decibels. A decibel is the smallest change in loudness that a human ear can detect. Human hearing ranges from 1 decibel, called the threshold of hearing to over 120 decibels the threshold of pain.

The distance between two crests is termed the period which usually is measured in seconds. So the number of peaks that occur in one second is the frequency. Another term associated with frequency is pitch. As an object oscillates more rapidly, it creates a high-pitch sound, which is registered as a high-frequency sound.

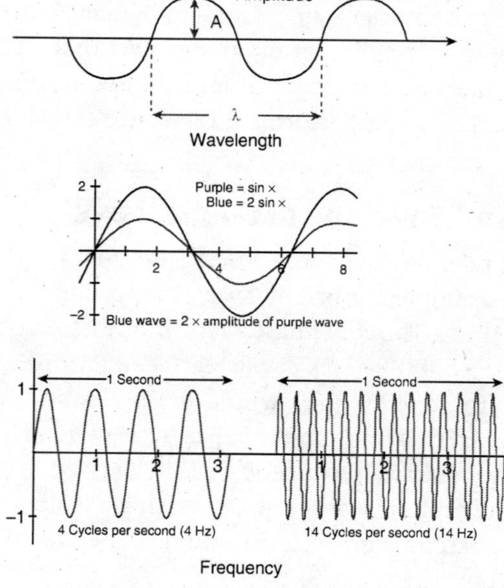


**Fig. 6.2:** Characteristics of a wave

A low frequency sound is produced by a slowly vibrating object, such as the thicker strings on a piano. To measure frequency, in cycles (vibrations) per second, we use the unit HERTZ. The human ear can perceive a range of frequencies from 20 Hz (hertz) to 20,000 Hz (also expressed as 20 KHz). The K stands for "Kilo" or thousand.

Few objects produce sounds at a single frequency. Most musical instruments generate multiple frequencies for every note. This is how you can tell the difference between a violin and a flute, or between a piano and a bass, although they produce notes of precisely the same pitch. The combination of frequencies in an instrument is known as the timbre. There is always a fundamental or main frequency and minor ones referred to as overtones (see Figure 6.3) or harmonics.

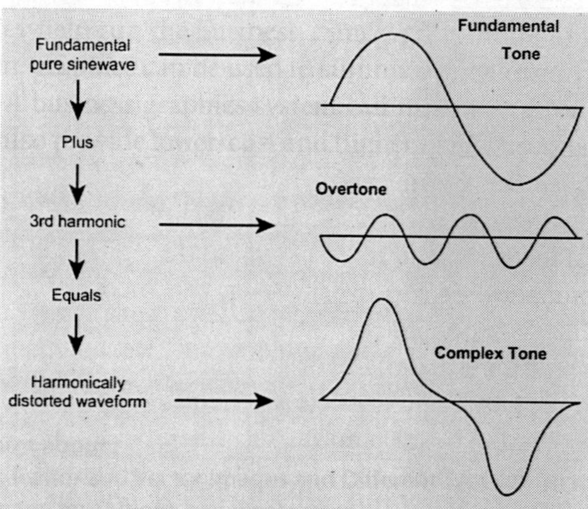


**Fig 6.3:** Harmonics in a Wave Form : A complex sound wave showing a main frequency and minor overtones.

Harmonics in a Wave Form: A complex sound wave showing a main frequency and minor overtones.

Duration measures frequency, amplitude, and timbre over time. It could measure just the simple length of a note or it could measure the length of minor variations in volume and pitch within a particular note. This can occur when performers introduce subtle variations in their singing or playing.

### 6.2.1 Phase, Shape and Envelope of Sound Wave

The Phase of a sound wave refers to a phenomenon that occurs when identical waveforms start at slightly different times. For example, the original wave may produce the same sound at a fraction of a second in delay in one of them. Think of phase as the information our ears use to tell from where a sound originated, because sound arrives at our ear at slight different time. Phase is measured in degrees from 1 to 360. This is how the ear and brain reconcile the idea of sound spreading in circular sound waves and representation on paper by a waveform. The Shape of a sound wave indicates its tonal quality. A sine wave (see the top wave in Figure 6.3) indicates a gentle and smooth, sweet sound. A square wave, (middle wave) reflects a rich and full, harsh sound. A sawtooth wave (bottom wave), indicates a piercing and colorful sound. Generally, the smoother the sound wave, the cleaner and sweeter it sounds.

The Envelope is an imaginary curve that wraps the entire waveform, as if following each crest of the amplitude. You can alter and manipulate sound relatively easily in computer after you will be able by changing a sound's amplitude envelope, to make it appear louder or softer, and in certain software packages, you can envelope to alter the phase of a sound by sending it to the right or left speaker to create stereo effect. The fun just is just beginning, so make an effort to absorb all this techno babble; it pays off later.

Bandwidth width requirements the channel bandwidths needed to transmit various types of signals, using various processing schemes. Every signal observed in practice can be expressed as a sum (discrete or over a frequency continuum) of sinusoidal components of various frequencies. The plot of the amplitude versus frequency constitutes one feature of the frequency spectrum (the other being the phase versus frequency). The difference between the highest and the lowest frequencies of the frequency components of significant amplitudes in the spectrum is called the bandwidth of the signal, expressed in the unit of frequency, hertz. Every communication medium (also called channel) is capable of transmitting a frequency band (spectrum of frequencies) with reasonable fidelity. Qualitatively speaking, the difference between the highest and the lowest frequencies of components in the band over which the channel gain remains reasonably constant (or within a specified variation) is called the channel bandwidth.

Clearly, to transmit a signal with reasonable fidelity over a communication channel, the channel bandwidth must match and be at least equal to the signal bandwidth. Proper conditioning of a signal, such as modulation or coding, however, can increase or decrease the bandwidth of the processed signal. Thus, it is possible to transmit the information of a signal over a channel of bandwidth larger or smaller than that of the original signal.

Amplitude modulation (AM) with double sidebands (DSB), for example, doubles the signal bandwidth. If the audio signal to be transmitted has a bandwidth of 5 Hz, the resulting AM signal bandwidth using DSB is 10 Hz. Amplitude modulation with a single sideband (SSB), on the other hand, requires exactly the same bandwidth as that of the original signal. In broadcast frequency modulation (FM), on the other hand, audio signal bandwidth is 15 Hz (for high fidelity), but the corresponding frequency-modulated signal bandwidth is 200 Hz.

C. E. Shannon proved that over a channel of bandwidth B the rate of information transmission, C, in bits/s (binary digits per second) is given by the equation below, where SNR is the signal-to-noise power ratio. This result assumes a white gaussian noise, which is the worst kind of noise from the point of view of interference.

$$C = B\ log_2(1 + SNR)\ bits/s$$

It follows from Shannon's equation that a given information transmission rate C can be achieved by various combinations of B and SNR. It is thus possible to trade B for SNR, and vice versa.

## 6.3 DECIBEL SYSTEM

Acoustics is the science of sound. Sound pressure levels (loudness or volume) are measured in decibels (dB); a decibel measurement is actually the ratio between a chosen reference point on a logarithmic scale and the level that is actually experienced. When you quadruple the sound output power, there is only a 6 dB increase; when you make the sound 100 times more intense, the increase in dB is not hundredfold, but only 20 dB.

The volume of sound is measured in decibels. As decibel is the smallest change in loudness that a human ear can detect. Human hearing ranges from 1 decibel, called the threshold of hearing, to over 120 decibel, the threshold of pain. This scale make sense because humans perceive sound pressure levels over an extraordinarily broad dynamic range. The decibel scale, with some examples, is shown in Table 6.1; notice the relationship between power (measured in watts) and dB.

**TABLE 6.1:** Typical Sound Levels in Decibels (dB) and Watts.

| dB | Watts | Example |
|---|---|---|
| 195 | 25-40 million | Saturn rocket |
| 170 | 100,000 | Jet engine with after-burner |
| 160 | 10,000 | Turbo-jet engine at 7,000-pounds thrust |
| 150 | 1,000 | |
| 140 | 100 | |
| 130 | 10 | 75-piece orchestra, at fortissimo |
| 120 | 1 | Large chipping hammer |
| 110 | 0.1 | Riveting machine |
| 100 | 0.01 | Automobile on highway |
| 90 | 0.001 | Subway train; a shouting voice |
| 80 | 0.0001 | Inside a 1952 Corvette at 60 mph |
| 70 | 0.00001 | Voice conversation; freight train 100 feet away |
| 60 | 0.000001 | Large department store |
| 50 | 0.0000001 | Average residence or small business office |
| 40 | 0.00000001 | Residential areas of Chicago at night |
| 30 | 0.000000001 | Very soft whisper |
| 20 | 0.0000000001 | Sound studio |

Sound is energy, like the waves breaking on a sandy beach, and too much volume can permanently damage the delicate receiving mechanisms behind the ear-drums. In terms of volume, what you hear subjectively is not what you hear objectively. The perception of loudness is dependent upon the frequency or pitch of the sound: at low frequencies, more power is required to deliver the same perceived loudness as for a sound at the middle or higher frequency ranges. You may feel the sound more than hear it. For instance, when thè ambient noise level is above 90 dB in the workplace, people are likely to make increased numbers of errors in susceptible tasks-especially when there is a high-frequency components to the noise. When the level is above 80 dB, it is quite impossible to use a telephone. Experiments by researchers in residential area have shown that a sound generator at 45 dB produces no reaction from neighbours; at 45 to 55dB, sporadic complaints; at 50 to 60 dB, widespread complaints; at 55 to 65 dB, threats of community action; and at more than 65 dB, vigorous community action. This research from the 1950s continues to provide helpful criteria for multimedia developers today.

## 6.4 SOUND SYNTHESIS

Synthesizers also employ envelopes to alter sound. Each note is processed through envelope generators to give it a specific tonal quality. With a bit of experimentation, you can even customize a particular voice to sound totally different from the original by altering its envelope. In synthesizers, the envelope generators deal with four segments: Attack, Decay, Sustain, and Release, figure 6.4 show an ADSR (Attack, Decay, Sustain, Release) envelope. Attack refers to the beginning of a note, in which the amplitude rise rapidly. The decay, which occurs just after the attack, is a slight decrease In amplitude. The sustain , as the name implies, is the main part of a note, when it plays for its longest duration, the last part is the release (when lifting a finger from a key) in which the amplitude fades out.

### 6.4.1 Octave

The Octave is a musical term that refers to sound that have proportional frequencies measured by half. In other words, the interval between a note that plays at a given frequency and another note that plays at double this frequency is an octave. Remember that lower frequencies refer to notes produced by slower vibrating objects (such as strings). Higher frequencies are produced by rapidly vibrating objects. When you play a low C note, the next C on a keyboard, and so on , you double the frequency (pitch) at every octave. Figure 6.4 shows a superimposition of a note's sound wave and its octave's, whereas Figure 6.5 shows these two notes on a keyboard.

**Fig 6.4:** An octave shown as two sound waves which the same amplitude but with different pitches. The red wave has a frequency double the one behind it.

**Fig 6.5:** An octave interval on the keyboard in this example, the note C is indicated.

This is as far as we go in music theory. You have to provide the test. Those hard piano lessons might pay off now, or, instead, you'll have to pay a talented individual to translate your ideas into music for you.

Registering sound is a complex process. Humans have a binaural hearing ability (hearing from two ears). Because of the angular difference of the source of sound from the two ears, the intensity and the time of arrival of sound to each ear is different (See diagram). The brain measures this difference and determines the possible angular location of the sound source. This process of locating the origin of sound by measuring time difference between the sound heared by two 'hearing' sources is called inter-aural time delay or ITD.

This is further enhanced by the brain's ability to detect the minute difference in 'reflected' sounds or the sounds that have traversed an indirect path to the ears. Called Head Related Transfer Function of HRTF, this helps to identify the relative height of the sound source as compared to the listener.

Finally, there is the Direct to Reverberant Ratio (DRR) which gives the impression of how far the sound source is. This is done by measuring the amount of direct sound against reflected sound.

These three factors help the brain to create a 3-Dimensional map of your surroundings, pin-pointing the approximate location of the sound source. A PC sound system that meets all the above requirements will be able to produce life-like sound.

### 6.4.2 Stereo or Mono

Sound systems can be classified into three broad categories:

- mono
- stereo and
- 3-Dimensional or surround sound.

When you hear a flat, single 'channel' of sound you are hearing mono sound. If the sound perceived by both the ears is identical, as if emanating from a single point-the brain-you cannot get an idea about the source and the depth of the sound.

To overcome this flat audio sound techniques came up with 'stereo' sound. Stereo works by splitting sound into two channels: left and right. Stereo sound is recorded using two microphones that are placed far apart in order to have better appreciation of the sound effects. To understand how stereo sound works, use a set of stereo headphones connected to a music system or a Walkman. Notice how you get different sounds through each ear; some beats come from the left ear-phone while the others come from the right. This creates the illusion that the sound is coming from different locations. Most sound cards these days have stereo capabilities.

Three dimensional or surround sound expands on stereo concept of sound recording. Instead of two channels, the sound is recorded on four or more channels. These channels are then played from multiple speakers which surround the listener creating an environment or an illusion of the listener being in the focus of sound or say in the middle of an incident such as a space-ship directly passing overhead. Presently, this surround sound environments limited to movie theaters using Dolby Digital Surround Sound technology. This is usually delivered through four or more speakers. These speakers are placed in a rectangular, pentagonal or a hexagonal pattern to provide uniform sound effects.

The advantage surround or 3-Dimensional systems is that unlike stereo or mono, it can simulate DRR which contributes in creating life-like sounds.

### 6.4.3 Treble of bass

Sound is broadly classified into three types:

- bass,
- treble and
- midrange.

Heavy booming sounds such as drumbeats are classified as bass. High pitch sounds, screams of an actress in a horror movie, are treble sounds. Sounds falling in between these extremes are classified as midrange sound. The bass part of sound is best reproduced by larger speakers called woofers. In case of woofers the size (measured in inches) does matter. The bigger the better! On the other hand, the treble part of sound is best reproduced by tiny speakers called tweeters. The mid-range sounds are best produced by the mid-range sized speakers.

A combination of these three kinds of speakers ensures that the sound you hear is rich and accurate. Audiophiles will, of course, tell you that many other things go towards making sound more realistic. Housing, or the material which you enclose the speakers in (wood is the best), the wires you use to connect the speakers and of course the actual location of the speakers in the room are some of them.

### 6.4.4 Multi-dimensional Sound

Alternatively, you could go in for the dedicated 3-Dimensional sound systems for computers. You will, of course, require a sound card that supports 3 Dimensional sound. Views conflier here. One view holds that for producing spatial effect of sound the listener has to be surrounded with multiple speakers while the other holds that you don't necessarily need multiple speakers to create the illusion of surround or 3-Dimensional. The latter reiterate that if we can hear three dimensional sounds with two ears, it is possible to produce the same effect with just two speakers-or a two regular speakers stereo system can be used to create an illusion of five speakers placed around the listener.

This technology is called virtual surround sound technology. An example would be the A3D Surround from Aureal.

There is however, a disadvantage in producing three dimensional sounds using just two speakers. In virtual surround sound, two sound sources are used to located at a certain area known as the 'sweet spot'. If the listener changes his position or rotates his head say to the left, the brain expects the various sources (which are virtually created) to change accordingly in terms of intensity and timing. Because the sound sources are virtual (created using two sound source), this does not happen and the illusion of sound coming from five speakers surrounding the listener is shattered.

On the other hand, Creative Labs, the creators of Sound Blaster, believes in creating 3-Dimensional sound using multiple sound. The company has, under its new Environmental Audio technology introduced a new card, Sound Blaster Live! Which can use up to right speakers to create 3-Dimensional sound.

## 6.5 DIGITIZATION OF SOUND (SOUND SAMPLING)

Natural or Analog sound is a continuous stream as the waveforms. Acoustic instruments produce analog sounds. In order to handle sound, a computer or a synthesizer needs to transfer the wound a computer or a synthesizer needs to transfer the sound wave into numbers. This process is analogous to a film for motion pictures. You perceive as movement on the screen only a rapid succession of individual photographic frames. Sound sampling is also known as digitizing, a process that transforms a continuous wave into finite numerical combinations (that employ digits).

A microphone translates are processed through an ADC (analog-to-digital converter). After these numbers are stored in a computer chip the information can be retrieved and edited with a high degree of precision. The stream of data then can be sent to the speakers via a DAC (digital-to-analog converter), which reproduces the analog soundwave that you hear.

When sampling a sound, snapshots of the waveform are processed by the computer. The frequency of these snapshots determine the accuracy of the sound being recorded. See figure 6.6

for a representation of two sampling rates and the resulting quantification of the sound wave. This is called rate. A typical rate can range from 5,000 to 100,000 samples per second. The higher the rate the better fidelity photographic film, one with an 50 ISO rating, which will show the sharpest focus, versus a rating of 1,600 ISO that will return a "grainy" version of the subject.

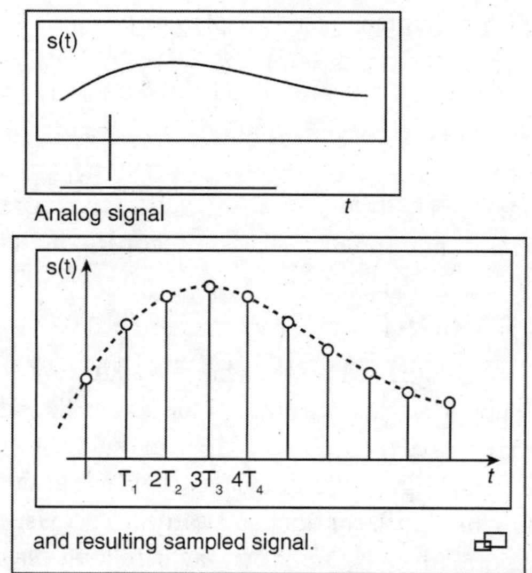


**Fig. 6.6:** A soundwave quantified at small intervals

| Resolution | Sampling rate | Stereo or mono | Bytes needed for one minute | Comments |
|---|---|---|---|---|
| 16-bit | 46.1 KHz | Stereo | 10.5 MB | CD-quality sound. |
| 16-bit | 46.1 KHz | Mono | 5.25 MB | Good Quality for voice-overs. |
| 8-bit | 46.1 KHz | Stereo | 5.25 MB | Good quality for playback on low-end sound boards. |
| 8-bit | 46.1 KHz | Mono | 2.6 MB | Good quality for recording a mono audio source. |
| 16-bit | 22.05 KHz | Stereo | 5.25 MB | Good quality for reproduction due to stereo sampling, but not CD-quality. |
| 16-bit | 22.05 KHz | Mono | 2.5 MB | O.K. for narration. |
| 8-bit | 22.5 KHz | Stereo | 2.6 MB | Good for stereo recording when playback equipment quality is low. |
| 8-bit | 22.05 KHz | Mono | 6.3 MB | Sounds like good AM radio quality. |
| 8-bit | 11 KHz | Stereo | 6.3 MB | No advantage in using stereo. |
| 8-bit | 11 KHz | Mono | 650 MB | Sounds muffled; the lowest standard you should use. |
| 8-bit | 5.5 KHz | Stereo | 650 MB | Stereo is not effective. |
| 8-bit | 5.5 KHz | Mono | 325 MB | About as good as a bad telephone connection. |

The sampling rate, sample rate, or sampling frequency defines the number of samples per second (or per other unit) taken from a continuous signal to make a discrete signal. For time-domain signals, the unit for sampling rate is 1/s. The inverse of the sampling frequency is the sampling period or sampling interval, which is the time between samples.

The concept of sampling frequency can only be applied to samplers in which samples are taken periodically. Some samplers may sample at a non-periodic rate. The common notation for sampling frequency is of which stands for frequency (subscript) sampled.

The other important term in sound sampling is resolution. If you take pictures with an Instamatic camera, through a lens the size of your pinki's fingernail, you certainly cannot expect the same quality as with a professional 35mm single-lens reflex camera, much less the large-format studio cameras. There is simply more "room" on a larger negative to store more information. Because computers use binary bits (1,0) to store information the more digits than can be processed for each measurement the smoother and cleaner your recording will be.

## 6.6 DIGITAL AUDIO FORMAT

Traditional audio devices are analog, because they handle sound waves in an analogous form. Radios maintain the audio signal as rippling waves from antenna to speaker. Sound waves are "carved" into plastic phonograph records, and audio tape records sound as magnetic waves. Audio is processed in a computer by converting the analog signal into a digital code using various techniques, such as PCM.

You can digitize sound from a microphone, a synthesizer, existing tape recordings, live radio and television broadcasts, popular CDs, and your favorite long-playing records. In fact, you can digitize sounds from any source, natural or prerecorded. Digitized sound is sampled sound. Every nth fraction of a second, a sample of sound is taken and stored as digital information in bits and bytes. How often the samples are taken is the sampling rate, and the amount of information stored about each sample is the sample size. The more often you take a sample and the more data you store about that sample, the finer the resolution and quality of the captured sound when it is played back.

The three sampling frequencies most often used in multimedia are CD-quality 46.1 KHz (kilohertz), 22.05 KHz, and 11.025 KHz. Sample sizes are either 8 bits or 16 bits. The larger the sample size, the better the data describes the recorded sound. An 8-bit sample size provides 256 equal units to describe the dynamic range or amplitude-the level of sound at that time-of the slice of sound captured. A 16-bit sample size, on the other hand, provides a staggering 65,536 equal units to describe the dynamic range. As you can see in Figure 6.7, slices of analog waveforms are sampled at various frequencies, and each discrete sample is then stored either as 8 or 16 bits of data.

Figure 6.7. It is impossible to reconstruct the original waveform if the sampling frequency is too low.

The value of each sample is rounded off to the nearest integer (quantization), and if the amplitude is greater than the intervals available, clipping of the top and bottom of the wave occurs. See Figure 6.8. Quantization can produce an unwanted background hissing noise, and clipping may severely distort the sound.

Digital audio comes in many different formats, and multiple formats will be a fact of life for the foreseeable future. Groups like MPEG have created open standards, but even formats based on the same MPEG standard may not be compatible with each other because of proprietary components.

Fortunately for consumers, many hardware and software players are able to support multiple formats-so if you purchase digital music in any of the major formats (MP3, WMA, etc.) you will be in a good shape. If a format does become obsolete, plenty of tools are available for converting digital audio to different formats.

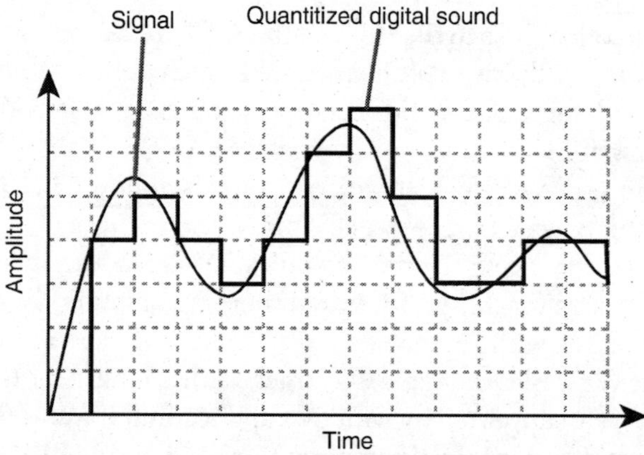

**Fig. 6.7:** Converting Analog signal into Digital

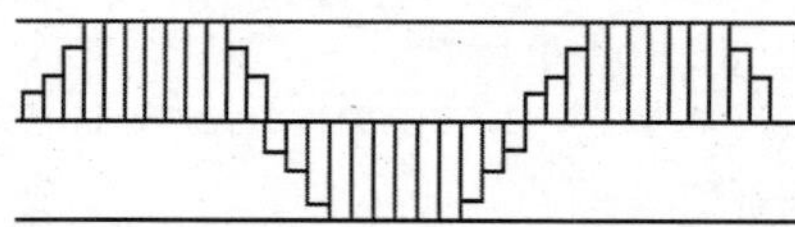
**Fig. 6.8:** Examples of quantizing and clipping

### 6.6.1 Digital Audio Files

An audio file has two main parts: a header and the audio data. The header is used to store information about the file, including the resolution, sampling rate and type of compression. Often a "wrapper" is used to add features, such as license management information or streaming capability, to a digital audio file.

The format of a digital audio file refers to the type of audio data within the file. The file type refers to the structure of the data within the file. It is common for the same format to be used by more than one file type. For example, the PCM format is found in both WAV and AIFF files.

**TABLE 6.2:** Common Digital Audio Formats

| Type | Extensions | Codec |
|---|---|---|
| AIFF (Mac) | .aif, .aiff | *PCM |
| AU (Sun/Next) | .au *u-law | |
| CD audio (CDDA) | N/A | PCM |
| MP3 | .mp3, MPEG | Audio Layer-III |
| Windows Media Audio | .wma | Proprietary (Microsoft) |
| QuickTime | .qt | Proprietary (Apple Computer) |
| RealAudio | .ra, ram | Proprietary (Real Networks) |
| WAV | .wav | *PCM |
| * Can be used with other codecs. | | |

### 6.6.2 WAV

WAV (or WAVE), short for WAVE form audio format, is a Microsoft and IBM audio file format standard for storing audio on PCs. It is a variant of the RIFF bitstream format method for storing data in "chunks", and thus also close to the IFF and the AIFF format used on Macintosh computers. It takes into account some peculiarities of the Intel CPU such as little-endian byte order. The RIFF format acts as a "wrapper" for various audio compression codecs. It is the main format used on Windows systems for raw audio.

The Microsoft Windows WAV format is used in the Windows 3.1, 95, 98 and NT operating systems for recording and playback of recorded sound. The advantage of placing a "WAV" file on your computer is the ease of making the file on your part - a recorder/player for this type of file is already located on your users machine (if it is a Windows computer). The disadvantages are that many people on the Internet will be unable to play the file if they are using another operating system and the fact that WAV files are typically larger, taking longer for the end user to download.

This file format is widely supported by windows application. It was developed by Microsoft as a subset of the RIFF format. It is capable of sampling rates of 8 and 16 bits (mono and stereo).

Though a WAV file can hold audio compressed with any codec, by far the most common format is pulse-code modulation audio data. Since PCM uses an uncompressed, lossless storage method which keeps all the samples of an audio track, professional users or audio experts may use the WAV format for maximum audio quality. WAV audio can also be edited and manipulated with relative ease using software.

WAV files can be used as an intermediary storage type for ripping songs from cassette tapes. People using Windows's Sound Recorder can redirect the output from their old Walkman-type cassette players's ear phone jacks to the PC audio input jacks via an audio cable. Although Sound Recorder can only record for 60 seconds, there are easy ways to lengthen the file for long songs or even the entire tape (record something, choose decrease speed from the effects menu, repeat until file is sufficiently long, and then record over it from the beginning). The WAV file is then converted via freeware packages to other, more compact formats.

As file sharing over the Internet has become popular, the WAV format has declined in popularity, primarily because uncompressed WAV files are quite large. More frequently, compressed but lossy formats such as MP3, Ogg Vorbis and Advanced Audio Coding are used to store and transfer audio, since their smaller file sizes allow for faster transfers over the Internet, and large collections of files consume only a conservative amount of disk space. There are also more efficient, lossless codecs available, such as Monkey's Audio, TTA, WavPack, FLAC, Shorten, Apple Lossless and WMA Lossless.

The WAV format is limited to files that are less than 2 GB in size, due to the way its 32-bit file size header is read by most programs. Although this is equivalent to more than 3 hours of CD-quality audio (46.1 Hz, 16-bit stereo), it is sometimes necessary to go over this limit. The W64 format was created for use in Sound Forge. This format can be converted using the LGPL lib file library.

Contrary to the popular misconception, audio CDs do not use WAV as their storage format. The commonality is that both audio CDs and WAV files have the audio data encoded in PCM, but WAV is a data file format for computer use; if you rip an audio CD to WAV files and burn them onto a CD-R as a data disc (ISO) and insert it into a player that can handle only audio CDs, the CD will not play.

### 6.6.3 Musical Instrument (MIDI Digital Interface)

MIDI is a communications protocol—which is a standard set of rules—for communication between two or more musical instruments or musical instruments and computers. You can hook instruments to computers (more on this in a minute). MIDI is a software program, or sequencer, enables you to make the recording and then view and edit the score of the performance on your computer. The beauty of a MIDI recording is that you can use it to correct individual notes, change the sound, or even transpose the piece. These editing capabilities alleviate the tedium of recording and rerecording until you hit a perfect performance.

MIDI represents a protocol that sends musical data from one MIDI component (such as a keyboard) to another, or to a computer that records the performance. MIDI information only consists of performance data, which includes the instructions for creating music. It communicates things such as turning "on" and "off" notes, a note's velocity, program changes, damper pedal use, and event timing.

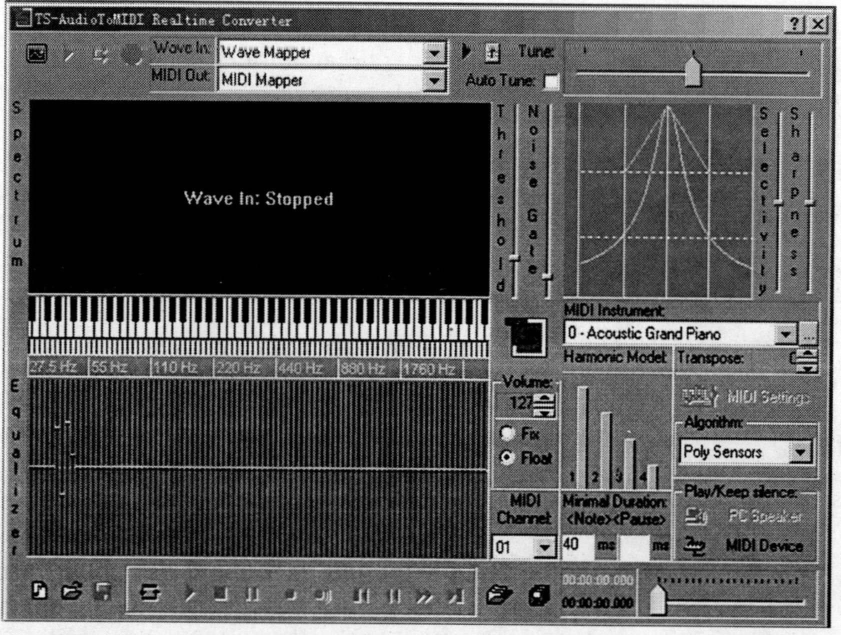


If you only need to see the notes or the score of your composition, a MIDI recording is all you need. With it, you can hear a playback of your performance through your sound card or instrument, but no actual recording of the sound occurs. In order to record the music so that others can hear it on CD, you must make an audio recording, as well. The audio recording consists of the actual analog or digital audio signal. These signals do not pass through the MIDI cable that carries MIDI data from one component to another or through the universal sound card MIDI cable that carries data from the instrument to the computer.

Some Microsoft Windows programs contain MIDI files. (Microsoft Corp.'s Microsoft Windows is a graphical user interface, or GUI. It allows users to choose icons—pictures—that represent commands and to choose commands from pull-down menus instead of having to give them manually.) According to Gideon Rosenblatt, Microsoft Corp. multimedia publishing product manager, "We use MIDI files in Microsoft Bookshelf to allow us to include the national anthems of over 160 countries."

In order to play MIDI files, you don't even need a keyboard as long as you have a sound card (an add-in circuit board that you install inside your computer's case to increase its sound capabilities) that supports MIDI. This is because sound cards contain small synthesizer chips on them.

Windows actually includes a MIDI player. So if you have your MIDI files and a sound card, you've got what you need to play MIDI files.

The keyboard may be one of the most expensive components of your home recording studio, so you'll want to give careful consideration to your purchase. If you don't own a keyboard synthesizer and aren't sure if you're ready to spend the money for one, consider purchasing a keyboard controller instead. Unlike a keyboard that has an onboard synthesizer, the keyboard controller has no internal sounds. It provides only the keyboard that you connect to your computer and play to transmit the MIDI data of the performance. Expect to pay roughly $200 for a controller as opposed to more than $500 for a keyboard that has its own internal sound synthesizer.

Advantages and disadvantages of MIDI over digital sound MIDI has several advantages over digital audio and two huge disadvantages. First, the advantages:

- MIDI files are much more compact than digital audio files, and the size of a MIDI file is completely independent of playback quality. In general, MIDI files will be 200 to 1,000 times smaller than CD-quality digital audio files. Because MIDI files are small, they don't take up as much RAM, disk space, and CPU resources.
- In some cases, MIDI files may sound better than digital audio files at the MIDI sound source you are using is of high quality.
- You can change the length of a MIDI file (by varying its tempo) without changing the pitch of the music or degrading the audio quality. MIDI data is completely editable-right down to the level of an individual note. You can manipulate the smallest detail of a MIDI composition (often with sub-millisecond accuracy) in ways that are impossible with digital audio.

**Disadvantages**

- Because MIDI does is it sound, you can be certain that playback will be accurate only if the MIDI playback device is identical to the device used for production. Even with the General MIDI standard, the sound of a MIDI instrument varies according to the electronics of the playback device and the sound generation method it uses.
- MIDI cannot easily be used to play back spoken dialog, although expensive and technically tricky digital samplers are available.

### 6.6.4 MP3

MP3 is a popular digital audio encoding and lossy compression format invented and standardised in 1991 by a team of engineers working in the framework of the ISO/IEC MPEG audio committee under the chairmanship of Professor Hans Musmann (University of Hannover - Germany). It was designed to greatly reduce the amount of data required to represent audio, yet still sound like a faithful reproduction of the original uncompressed audio to most listeners. In popular usage, MP3 also refers to files of sound or music recordings stored in the MP3 format on computers.

MP3 (MPEG Audio) — MPEG audio is a standard for high-quality audio and video files that has gained widespread use. MPEG (Motion Picture Experts Group) is a family of compression formats and audio/video storage formats developed by a cooperative effort under the joint direction of the International Standards Organization (ISO) and the International Electro-Technical Commission (IEC). There are many companies that offer free players capable of playing or creating MPEG files. It offers the advantage of high quality with a smaller file size.

CD-quality MP3 sound files can still be large, however, for use on a Web page that may be downloaded through a typical modem connection. The end user will have to have an audio player on their computer capable of handling the format. MP3 has found a receptive audience among musicians on the Net, who offer samples of their works available at sites such as the Internet Underground Music Archives. It has been used, however, to encode and transmit copyrighted music extensively by individual Internet users and the music industry has been lobbying for standards in the format that will prevent illegal copying of copyrighted works.

The name is derived from "MPEG-1 Audio Layer 3" more formally known as ISO/IEC 11172-3 Layer 3. The files recorded in this format are saved with the .mp3 filename extension. This extension is also sometimes shared by audio files encoded using the newer MPEG-2 Audio Layer 3 standard. The invention of this file extension name (.mp3) would be due to the FhG institute.

MP3 is a lossy compression format. It provides a representation of pulse-code modulation-encoded (PCM) audio data in a much smaller size by discarding portions that are considered less important to human hearing (similar to JPEG, a lossy compression for images).

A number of techniques are employed in MP3 to determine which portions of the audio can be discarded, including psychoacoustics. MP3 audio can be compressed with different bit rates, providing a range of tradeoffs between data size and sound quality.

The MP3 format uses, at its heart, a hybrid transform to transform a time domain signal into a frequency domain signal:

- 32 band polyphase quadrature filter
- 36 or 12 tap MDCT; size can be selected independent for sub-band 0...1 and 2...31
- aliasing reduction post-processing

MP3 Surround, a version of the format supporting 5.1 channels for surround sound, was introduced in December 2006. MP3 Surround is backward compatible with standard stereo MP3, and file sizes are similar.

In terms of the MPEG specifications, AAC (Advanced Audio Coding) from MPEG-4 is to be the successor of the MP3 format, although there has been a significant movement to create and popularize other audio formats. Nevertheless, any succession is not likely to happen for a significant amount of time due to MP3's overwhelming popularity (MP3 enjoys extremely wide popularity and support, not just by end-users and software but by hardware such as DVD and CD players).

#### 6.6.4.1 Quality of MP3 audio

Because MP3 is a lossy format, it is able to provide a number of different options for its "bit rate" — that is, the number of bits of encoded data that are used to represent each second of audio. Typically rates chosen are between 128 and 256 kilobit per second. By contrast, uncompressed compact disc audio has a bit rate of 1378 Kbit/s or 1411 Kbit/s.

MP3 files encoded with a lower bit rate will generally playback at a lower quality. With too low a bit rate, "compression artifacts" (i.e., sounds that were not present in the original recording) may appear in the reproduction. A good demonstration of compression artifacts is provided by the sound of applause: it is hard to compress because it is random, therefore the failings of the encoder are more obvious, and are audible as ringing.

As well as the bit rate of the encoded file, the quality of MP3 files depend on the quality of the encoder and the difficulty of the signal being encoded. For average signals with good encoders, many listeners accept the MP3 bit rate of 128 Kibit/s as near enough to compact disc quality for them, providing a compression ratio of approximately 11:1. However, listening tests show that with a bit of practice many listeners can reliably distinguish 128 Kbit/s MP3s from CD originals; in many cases reaching the point where they consider the MP3 audio to be of unacceptably low quality. Yet other listeners, and the same listeners in other environments (such as in a noisy moving vehicle or at a party) will consider the quality acceptable.

#### 6.6.4.2 Bit rate

The bit rate is variable for MP3 files. The general rule is that more information is included from the original sound file when a higher bit rate is used, and thus the higher the quality during play back. In the early days of MP3 encoding, a fixed bit rate was used for the entire file.

Bit rates available in MPEG-1 Layer 3 are 32, 40, 48, 56, 64, 80, 96, 112, 128, 160, 192, 224, 256 and 320 Kbit/s, and the available sample frequencies are 32, 46.1 and 48 KHz. 46.1 KHz is almost always used (coincides with the sampling rate of compact discs), and 128 Kbit/s has become the de facto "good enough" standard, although 192 Kbit/s is becoming increasingly popular over peer-to-peer file sharing networks. MPEG-2 and [the non-official] MPEG-2.5 includes some additional bit rates: 8, 16, 24, 32, 40, 48, 56, 64, 80, 96, 112, 128, 144, 160 Kbit/s

Variable Bit Rates (VBR) are also possible. Audio in MP3 files are divided into frames (which have their own bit rate) so it is possible to change the bit rate dynamically as the file is encoded (although not originally implemented, VBR is in extensive use today). This technique makes it possible to use more bits for parts of the sound with higher dynamics (more sound movement) and fewer bits for parts with lower dynamics, further increasing quality and decreasing storage space. This method compares to a sound activated tape recorder which reduces tape consumption by not recording silence. Some encoders utilize this technique to a great extent.

#### 6.6.4.3 Design limitations of MP3

There are several limitations inherent to the MP3 format that cannot be overcome by using a better encoder.

Newer audio compression formats such as Vorbis and AAC no longer have these limitations.

In technical terms, MP3 is limited in the following ways:

1. Bit-rate is limited to a maximum of 320 Kbit/s
2. Time resolution can be too low for highly transient signals
3. Encoder/decoder overall delay is not defined
4. No scale factor band for frequencies above 15.5/15.8 KHz
5. Joint stereo is done on a frame-to-frame basis
6. Lack of gapless playback; tracks intended to flow into another (such as in live performances) do not seamlessly flow: a short gap of silence is heard between the two tracks.

Nevertheless, a well tuned MP3 encoder can perform competitively even with these restrictions.

### 6.6.4.4 Decoding of MP3 audio

Decoding, on the other hand, is carefully defined in the standard. Most decoders are "bitstream compliant", meaning that the uncompressed output they produce from a given MP3 file will be the same (within a specified degree of rounding tolerance) as the output specified mathematically in the standard document. The MP3 file has a standard format which is a frame consisting of 576 samples and all the frames have associated header information(32 bits) and side information(17 bytes). The header and side information help the decoder to decode the associated huffman encoded data correctly.

Therefore, for the most part, comparison of decoders is almost exclusively based on how computationally efficient they are (i.e., how much memory or CPU time they use in the decoding process).

Though proponents of newer codecs such as WMA and RealAudio have asserted that their respective algorithms can achieve CD quality at 64 Kbit/s, listening tests have shown otherwise; however, the quality of these codecs at 64 Kbit/s is definitely superior to MP3 at the same bandwidth. The developers of the patent-free Ogg Vorbis codec claim that their algorithm surpasses MP3, RealAudio and WMA sound quality, and the listening tests mentioned above support that claim. Thomson claims that its mp3PRO codec achieves CD quality at 64 Kbit/s, but listeners have reported that a 64 Kbit/s mp3PRO file compares in quality to a 112 Kbit/s MP3 file and does not come reasonably close to CD quality until about 80 Kbit/s.

**The AVI Format**

The AVI (Audio Video Interleave) format was developed by Microsoft. The AVI format is supported by all computers running Windows, and by all the most popular web browsers. It is a very common format on the Internet, but not always possible to play on non-Windows computers. Videos stored in the AVI format have the extension .avi.

**The Windows Media Format**

The Windows Media format is developed by Microsoft. Windows Media is a common format on the Internet, but Windows Media movies cannot be played on non-Windows computer without an extra (free) component installed. Some later Windows Media movies cannot play at all on non-Windows computers because no player is available. Videos stored in the Windows Media format have the extension .wmv.

**The QuickTime Format**

The QuickTime format is developed by Apple. QuickTime is a common format on the Internet, but QuickTime movies cannot be played on a Windows computer without an extra (free) component installed. Videos stored in the QuickTime format have the extension .mov.

**The RealVideo Format**

The RealVideo format was developed for the Internet by Real Media. The format allows streaming of video (on-line video, Internet TV) with low bandwidths. Because of the low bandwidth priority, quality is often reduced. Videos stored in the RealVideo format have the extension .rm or .ram.

**The Shockwave (Flash) Format**

The Shockwave format was developed by Macromedia. The Shockwave format requires an extra component to play. This component comes pre-installed with the latest versions of Netscape and Internet Explorer. Videos stored in the Shockwave format have the extension .swf.

### 6.6.5 AIFF and AU

AIFF is the default audio format for the Macintosh, and AU is the default format for SUN systems. Both of these formats are supported on most other platforms and by most audio applications. Each of these formats can be compressed, but compression sometimes creates compatibility problems with other platforms.

## 6.7 STREAMING AUDIO

Streaming audio avoids many of the problems of large audio files. Instead of having to wait for the entire file to download, you can listen to the sound as the data arrives at your computer.

Streaming audio players store several seconds worth of data in a buffer before beginning playback. The buffer absorbs the bursts of data as they are delivered by the Internet and releases it at a constant rate for smooth playback.

Many digital audio formats can be streamed by wrapping them in a streaming format, such as Microsoft 's ASF (Active Streaming Format), which can be used to stream MS Audio, MP3 and other formats.

**TABLE 6.3:** Streaming Audio Systems

| Type | Primary Format | Developer |
|---|---|---|
| Windows Media Technologies | Windows Media Audio / Active Streaming Format (ASF) | Microsoft |
| Icecast (open source) | MP3 | Icecast Team |
| QuickTime | QuickTime | Apple Computer |
| RealSystem | RealAudio | RealNetworks |
| SHOUTcast | MP3 | Nullsoft |

## 6.8 WAVETABLE

A wavetable is a table of stored sound waves that are digitized samples of actual recorded sound. A wavetable is stored in read-only memory ( ROM ) on a sound card chip but it can also be supplemented with software. Originally, computer sounds (digital versions of analog waveforms) were generated through frequency modulation ( FM ). Prestoring sound waveforms in a lookup table improved quality and throughput.

Today's more advanced sound cards include wavetables with 32 "voices" or instruments (that are combined during creation and playback). Some sound cards work with software that provides additional voices. Wavetables are used as part of music or sound synthesizers that use the musical instrument digital interface ( MIDI ). MIDI lets you capture sound and play it back based on the commands in files that are essentially little "scripts" to the "orchestra" (one might think of it as a written description of what the conductor is doing and which instruments are being pointed to with the baton). A wavetable sound can be enhanced or modified using reverberation or other effects before it is saved in the table. Some wavetable chips include a special section for drum sounds to support rhythmic effects.

Many sound cards take advantage of Direct Memory Access ( DMA ). Many also include an FM synthesizer in order to playback sounds from older applications or files. A full-duplex sound card lets you record and playback at the same time or, if you're using Internet telephony, talk and hear at the same time. Wavetable sound cards use digital signal processor ( DSP ) chips.

## 6.9 COMPRESSION AND TRANSMISSION OF AUDIO ON INTERNET 

Audio compression is a companion to video compression, but the techniques are very different. First, the audio signal requires much less bandwidth than the video signal. For example, a stereo audio pair sampled at 48 KHz and using 16-bit samples requires 1.536 Mbps (compared to 124 Mbps for the video signal). It would be quite possible to send uncompressed audio. Moreover, audio compression cannot achieve the same compression ratio as video; a typical rate for the stereo audio pair is 192 Kbps, an 8:1 compression ratio.

Nevertheless, it is easy to make an economic argument for audio compression. For example, in a 40 Mbps transmission link, an additional two video channels can be carried if audio compression is used (assuming 4 Mbps video).

There are two leading contenders for audio compression for entertainment quality audio: MPEG audio compression and Dolby AC-3.

### 6.9.1 MPEG-1 Layer 2 (Musicam)

MPEG-1 Layer 2 audio compression, also known as Musicam, is specified in ISO/IEC IS 13818-3. MPEG audio compression delivers near–CD quality audio using a technique called sub-band encoding. MPEG audio compression is used mainly in Europe and is used by most direct-to-home satellite providers in the United States.

MPEG audio compression is a two-channel system, but it can encode a Dolby Pro-Logic signal, which includes two additional channels for rear and center speakers. (This is analogous to the way in which a Dolby Pro-Logic signal is carried by a BTSC [Broadcast Television System Committee] signal as part of an NTSC transmission).

### 6.9.2 Dolby AC-3

Dolby AC-3 is a more advanced system than MPEG audio compression. AC-3 was selected as the audio compression system for digital television in North America and is specified by ATSC Standard A/52. AC-3 encodes up to six discrete channels: left, right, center, left-rear, right-rear, and sub-woofer speakers. The sub-woofer channel carries only low frequencies and is commonly referred to as a 0.1 channel because it has such a limited frequency range. Thus, AC-3 5.1 gets its name from five full channels and a 0.1 channel. In addition, AC-3 has a two-channel mode that can be used to carry stereo and Dolby Pro-Logic encoded signals.

AC-3 also uses sub-band encoding but provides a number of advantages over MPEG audio compression:

In AC-3 5.1, surround-sound effects are reproduced much more faithfully than is possible with Dolby Pro-Logic because of the additional channels.

AC-3 5.1 distributes the available transmission link capacity between the 5.1 channels so that more bits are used for those channels containing more information at any particular time. This method effectively makes them statistically multiplexed discrete digital channels.

AC-3 5.1 is a consumer-grade version of the theatrical Digital Theater Sound (DTS) system, so sound tracks may be directly transferred from the theatrical release.

AC-3 has been chosen as the audio system for digital terrestrial broadcasting and for DVD in the United States. It also has been selected by OpenCable.

### 6.9.3 Other Audio Compression Algorithms

As with video, many other audio compression algorithms exist. For example, RealAudio is commonly used for sending audio over the Internet, and MP3 has caused a stir in recordable audio.

MP3 uses MPEG-1 Layer 3 audio compression, which is considerably more sophisticated than MPEG-1 Layer 2. Many audio compression algorithms have special characteristics that make them suitable for very low bit rate facilities, for software decoding on a PC, and so on. However, it is unlikely that they will pose a significant threat to Dolby AC-3 encoding for entertainment-quality audio in the near future.

The WAVE format is one of the most popular sound format on the Internet, and it is supported by all popular browsers. If you want recorded sound (music or speech) to be available to all your visitors, you should use the WAVE format. The MP3/MP4 format is the new and upcoming format for recorded music. If your website is about recorded music, the MP3 format is the choice of the future.

## 6.10 BASICS OF SOUND PROCESSING

In this book we are concerned only with manipulating sound after they are digitized into the computer, because the complexities of traditions of traditional sound processing in a recording studio are beyond the scope of this discussion.

Digitized sound, when first recorded into a computer, needs to undergo some transformation to bring it to a satisfactory level. There will be section of the sound wave that must be trimmed to keep only the sounds you find useful. There can be unwanted noises, for example, at the beginning of the recording, that you want to eliminate and to make the desired sound fade in. You may want to splice together two sound files through copying and pasting or, perhaps, you want to add another track of background music. Adding echo to a voice, making it sound as if the speaker was in an empty room or lowering the pitch of the person's voice and slowing down the overall duration of the sound are only some of the many possibilities of manipulation digital sounds.

There are two types of digital sound processing methods. On one hand, you can alter the original file in many ways and save your work with the new changes. This process is destructive because it permanently alters the original sound. Unless you saved a copy, you lose the original. in the second method certain software are used so that sound can be softer, or mixed with other sounds, but the original file remains intact. This process is non-destructive.

If you are a bit computer savvy, you have encountered file-type problems due to different computer platforms, software incompatibilities, and other computing standard difference you must learn to save your sound files in specific formats that can be read by other programs, so you can use your files in multimedia projects.

## 6.11 EMPLOYING SOUNDS IN MULTIMEDIA APPLICATIONS

There are a number of ways in which you can use sound in a multimedia project, but all sounds fall under one of two major categories-content sound and ambient sound. This is equivalent to the dialog in theater or films. As with dialog in those artistic media, content sound must be used in its proper place. In some moments dialogs add considerable interest to the story telling and in other moments silence is golden.

### (1) Content sounds

Content sound can be used in the following ways:

**Narrations**

The term refers to those sounds in which a voice describes some facts that pertain to the topic. Typically, narration follows some text explaining it further or offering some variations on the written word.

Content delivery is the most important aspect of narrations. If a presentation is made to an audience, narrations should be kept to a minimum and triggered by a button controlled by the presenter. Never introduce an unexpected narration because inevitably it plays when the presenter is talking about something else. So, narrations can become distractions that detract from a quality presentation.

Narrations also are useful when they add information about an animation that is playing onscreen, such as a manufacturing process of the function of device. Narrations are invaluable for self-directed training because they take the place of the instructor.

**Testimonials**

Whether just auditory in nature or as a video sound track the opinion of certain people can be used to reinforce a point in the presentation.

**Voice-overs**

Not to be confused with narrations, this type of content sound is used in instances where short instructions may be necessary for the user to navigate the multimedia application. Also voice-overs can be used for transitions between sections, or the explain what is ahead in the presentation.

**Music and Sounds**

These elements become content sound when they are part of the topic of a presentation, such as in music education or when the user is supposed to distinguish between certain sounds as part of a training program.

### (2) Ambient sounds

Ambient sound, as the word implies, constitute a wide array of background and sound effects that you can use for multimedia applications. They do not provide content information, yet they are used to reinforce the topics in the presentation. Some sound effects can be fun to play with but this isn't an excuse to annoy the audience. Ambient sounds because they can enhance a presentation or destroy it. Some uses of ambient sounds include the following:

**Message Reinforcing**

When discussing topics on nature, sounds of dirt waves and other ambient sound can enhance the message. Sound of people in sport activities, such as swimming pools, basketball and so on, convey a degree of realism to a presentation.

**Music Background**

Starting and ending a presentation with music sets the right mood for the audience to receive and process information. The appropriate music prompts the audience to be more open and aware of other multimedia elements such as graphics.

## 6.12 SOUND EFFECTS

A tremendous variety of sound effects exists which you can use in a multimedia presentation. A business meeting in which the audience must endure endless charts can be enlivened by adding the appropriate sound effect for entering bullets on-screen.

Sometimes, a presenter can pick up the audience's interest by providing unexpected here is to be careful. The same "fun sound" repeated many times ceases to be funny quickly. The strident noises to be adequate for Hitchock's movies can annoy an audience that otherwise would have appreciated them in the film.

## 6.13 SOUND INCORPORATION INTO A MULTIMEDIA PROJECT 

Remember to consider the following multimedia development phases:

- Concept Development
- Preproduction/Storyboarding
- Sound Production
- Post-production
- Testing and Revision
- Sound delivery

There are a number of alternative for obtaining music and sound effects to use in multimedia projects without the legal hurdles of copyright infringement or having to hire a full orchestra to record for you.

**Playback music from audio CDs**-your Authoring language is capable of controlling the computer CD-ROM to play a specific music track from an audio CD. The authoring program can also modify the music playback volume and fade in or out as necessary. The music from a CD can be played as background music, as the application component within the program (in other words as part of a music appreciation instructional module among others).

**Purchase royalty**-free music and sound effects files (clip audio)-A number of companies provide royalty-free music and sound effects files which can be incorporated into different components of your application. Read the agreement included with these products Although they are royalty-free, they may not be copyright-free. Many companies spell out in detail how you may or may not use these files.

**Compose, play, and record your own music and special sound effects**-If you or one of your multimedia development team members are musicians you can play a Musical Interface Digital Interface (MIDI) instrument, such as a keyboard, to input music digitally directly into your computer. With MIDI equipment you can play and record music, develop special effects, and perform other composition tasks. **Some MIDI equipment other composition task**. Some MIDI own sounds so that you can add the sound of a rain shower or birds singing after recording then sound yourself and saving it digitally.

**You can secure right releases from people you interview**-If you interview people or use talent to record narration, make sure you secure releases of the right to the narration.

**MPC-Level 3 Hardware requirement for sound**

One very popular standard that has been developed to ensure that a computer system has all the necessary capabilities to run multimedia software is called "MPC" standard, which stand for Multimedia PC (Tway, 1992). Only new computers that meet or exceed this standard may carry the MPC trademark. This standard, developed by Microsoft Corporation in cooperation with various hardware manufacturers, refers specifically to PCs running Multimedia under Windows. This standard also ensures that any separately sold hardware or software carrying the MPC logo will be compatible with each other and with the MPC computer system.

The audio system specified in MPC Level 3 includes:

- 8 or 16 bits per sample sampling capability
- 8, 11, 16, 22, or 44 KHz sampling rate

- A linear Pulse Code Modulation (PCM) Codec to convert the sampled analog values to digital data.
- A playback and recording of 16-bit stereo that uses no more than 13 % of CPU time for 46.1 K samples/sec.
- CD ROM drive with CD-DA outputs and volume control.
- Speakers
- One MIDI port.

The block diagram of a sound card compliant with the MPC Level 3 specifications is shown in figure 6.9.

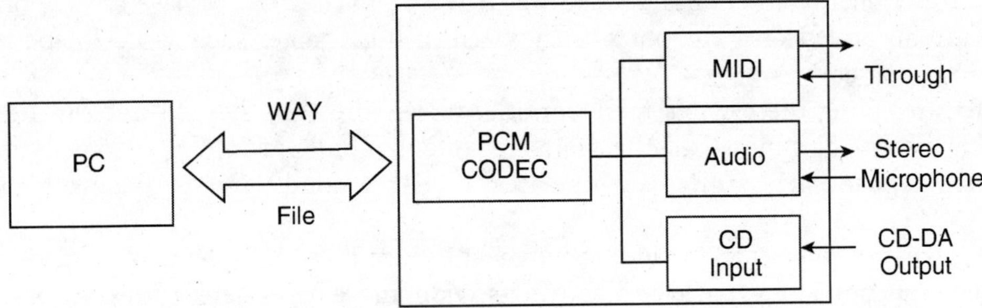


**Fig 6.9:** A block diagram of a sound card compliant with the MPC Level 3

## 6.14 EQUIPMENT NEEDED FOR SOUND PROCESSING

For sound recording in the pc platform, on computer helow the DX level should be used. The Sound Blaster card marked with an asterisk (*) may not be available from the manufacture any longer but because the price of Sound Blaster 16 card is relatively low, the cost differences between the choice listed are based on the additional equipment such as music keyboards and file storage devices. Titanium headphone may have an impressive name, but they need not be expensive. Some models cost as little as $20,00 (cost in year 2017), yet they provide the required response of 5 Hz to 20 KHz. Again, as in the previous Mac setups, A compromise was made with the inclusion of a cassette recorder for analog work. All these components can be upgraded as your budget grows.

### (1) Computer and Peripherals

In the preceding table, three choices are shown for Macintosh and PC or compatible machines. Always buy the most powerful computer your budget allows, and load it with RAM. Macintosh computers always incorporate sound circuitry, so for PCs you have to add a sound Blaster card and RAM to it. Larger monitors allow for many windows and software and software palettes to be open and available at the same time.

You not only will want to create CD-ROMs of your work, you also will want to make audio CDs of the music files. The recommended CD burner allows you (with Software such as toastpro), to create CD_ROMs, audio CDs, and other formats such as CDi and hybrid CDs in less than 25 minutes.

### (2) High-Quality Microphones

The microphones listed as the rest of the equipment shown, were tested by the author and were found to provide high-quality results. The shure Beata 87 is a condenser microphone that is excellent for both music recording and voice. It is extremely sensitive, and you would use it in a fully soundproofed environment. If air-conditioner hiss is present, its sound must be filtered electronically with the components indicated in the third column. Beware also of fluorescent lights-some can create hums. The shure Beta 87 microphone needs an external power sure to operate. This power is provided by a couple of 9-volt batteries held in a box known as phantom power.

The other microphone listed is used in radio stations to provide a deeper tone for the speakers. It originally was developed as a bass-drum microphone, so it has a great lower frequency response. Again, if you can afford a $2.000 Neumann Microphone, by all means buy it! Don't skimp on your microphone purchase because your recordings depend almost one-hundred percent on its quality.

All professional microphones are connected via XLR wires. These have a three-prong plug common to all professional equipment mentioned in this chapter such as DAT tape recorders, mixers and other devices.

When installing these wires for recording, make sure that they do not run nearby and parallel to electric current wires. The cables act antennas and pick up unwelcome human from the electromagnetic field around power wires. Run the sound wires perpendicular to power wires.

Other types of connectors for audio equipment include RCA, 1/4" phono plugs, and 1/8" mini-plugs. Phono and mini-plugs could be mono (two sections in a jack), or stereo (three sections in a jack).

### (3) DAT Tape Recorders

Unlike analog cassette recorders, DAT (Digital Audio tape) records sound digitally. The sound quality from these devices is state-of-the-art, and there is no loss in quality when copying the recordings to another digital device. The preceding table lists two kinds of DAT recorders. The 8-tracks recorder (known as ADAT) uses a-vhs tapes and as its name implies, can record up to eight tracks especially when mixing down to stereo this process takes place after all your tracks are recorded and the tape is ready for the final mix.

Usually, you connect the 8-track machine to the other Dat recorder listed which has only stereo capabilities. You do this through a mixer that controls a series of settings such as volume, panning and equalization. The procedure described is the traditional, manual one in which a technician sits at the controls and manually adjusts the many sliders and buttons in a mixer. Fortunately, for the novice the process is much easier and more accurate by using software in a computer.

### (4) Mixers

A mixer is needed for at least two basic function-recording and mixing down. When recording several sound sources at the same time, for example the instruments of a music ensemble, each instrument is channeled separately. The mixer can be set to appropriate sound level panning and equalization for each instrument. If in addition you are recording voice each could have its own channel. The advantage of this setup is the high degree of control over the entire mix.

Maxing down refers to converting the many possible tracks in a recording studio's tape and mixing all to stereo tracks so conventional home systems and computers can reproduce all those tracks in only two channels; left and right.

### (5) Synthesizers

For obtaining professional-level sound tracks in your multimedia applications, Synthesizers are mandatory. There are many models in the market some with keyboards and some in the version, without keys. The Yamaha PSR line and the Technics KN 3000 serve a dual purpose. They have a section of per-recorded rhythms and accompaniments that the most novice of non-musicians can use to sound as if a whole band backs up the player. You can select from over a 100 different rhythms at any tempo you want. You can change chords with just one finger and still sound great. The player can record a complex accompaniment into the keyboard's memory, then play it back along with the solo voice and finally record it all together into the computer. If you are musically challenged or your tempo is slow, record at half speed and playback at the correct tempo, so that you will not miss any of the notes.

The second purpose of this type of keyboards is a bank of over 100 voices. These are the many instruments from which you can choose. You can play them individually or in combination for a "fuller" sound. These keyboards have MIDI capabilities if you decide to take this route.

### (6) Amplified Speaker Systems

The sound from the mixer output has to be routed to a power amplifier which, in turn, feed the speakers. Another option is to use amplified speakers such as Yamaha MS60S. These speakers are needed to monitor the mix's sound before it is recorded. Usually, a studio has four speakers with an additional pair to imitate the likely user's system which illustrates the problem of how to mix sound for the wide array of speaker systems in the market. The selection of speakers should be done as carefully as that of microphones, because your sound quality depends greatly on their output.

### (7) Headphones

Quality headphone allows the user to hear the sound files without disturbing coworkers. You will need to repeat sound files a number of times before a satisfactory result is achieved. This constant repetition may turn your neighbors a bit edgy, so use headphones. The models recommended provide the user with a range of 5 Hz to over 20 KHz.

### (8) Sound Recorder

The Sound Recorder has a consistent interface over both Windows versions. To record, just choose File→New. Then, press the Record button (the one with a big red dot on it) and start speaking or, if you are musically inclined, playing your violin or keyboard. Once you are through, press the stop button. Now save your creation in the folder C:\Windows\Media where Windows looks for sound files. The maximum size that your audio file can be, depends upon the sound quality chosen. To change this setting you must choose Edit→Audio Properties. Choosing CD Quality in the Preferred quality drop-down list, will result in CD clear sharp audio but you can't record more than six seconds' worth. At the other end of the spectrum if you choose what's called Telephone Quality (8-bit mono at 11 KHz), you end up with 60 seconds of audio time. But the sound quality will be woefully lacking. This is a weakness of Sound Recorder itself. If you want to record several minutes of high quality digital audio then you'd be better off using a professional quality editor such as Cool Edit 96-a popular from http://www.suntrillium.com. But the Sound Recorder will do fine for creating small clips of sound to attach to Windows events.

Windows Sound Recorder can produce some fairly nifty special effects. You can add an echo effect to your way file. You can even repeat this procedure to attain a truly robotic and menacing tone of voice. You can also increase or decrease the volume of the file. Another neat touch lets you insert a second sound file into the current one or mix another sound file into your current choice. And, of course, good old copy and paste works here. Last but not the least Sound Recorder lets you reverse the sound for a truly bizarre effect.

**(9) Speakers**

Fortunately, there is little need to go in for too many specifications when it comes to buying PC speakers. You can get by, by sticking to the handful of speaker sets that are commonly available. Speakers are available in two flavours: amplified and non-amplified.

While non-amplified speakers depend upon the sound card to deliver the power needed to create sound, amplified speakers need a power source to reproduce sound. They can use batteries or a power adapter plugged into a power outlet.

While most sound cards bundles come with two similar size 'one-size-fits-all' speakers, some have three speakers; a large mid-range speaker called sub- woofers and a pair of tweeters. This trio of speakers delivers better sound reproduction than the standard two-speaker set. But these speakers are, at best, stereo speakers and cannot usually make use of the 3-D or surround sound features.

There are, however, technologies such as extended stereo which can add more punch to stereo sound. Extended stereo based products process an exciting stereo soundtrack, add spaciousness to it and make it appear as if the sound is originating from outside the two speakers. This gives a feeling of depth. This technology is found in most home theatre and hi-fi music systems. You can hook up your sound card to the system to enjoy the benefits of extended stereo. The only disadvantage of this set up is that you have to keep your home theatre or hi-fi system ON, while you are using your computer.

While buying speakers, test them by listening to any piece of music you are already familiar with. Do not buy after listening only to the sample stock of music. Ask the vendor to play something you have heard before. If you are comparing two different speaker systems, use the same settings and positioning for both of them. Feel the music by closing your eyes.

A system that overplays treble (sharp sounds) or bass (heavy beats) will soon get on your nerves. Ensure that both these effects are balanced by turning the volume all the way up and then all the way down. Look for any hissing or crackling sound. At high volume-half to two thirds of the maximum volume-listen for 'flutters', the feeling that the speakers are about to burst like a drum. The sound should crisp. Move to a distance of about ten feet from the speakers. If they still sound good, then they are worth buying.

Finally after you bring them home, place them correctly for good sound reproduction. Regardless of whether you buy stereo speakers or surround sound speakers place them symmetrically around you. Ideally, at ear level, in front of you, forming a square pattern around you.

**(10) DVD-Audio (commonly abbreviated as DVD-A)**

It is a digital format for delivering high-fidelity audio content on a DVD. DVD-Audio is not intended to be a video delivery format and is not the same as video DVDs containing concert films or music videos. The first discs entered the marketplace in 2000. DVD-Audio was in a format war with Super Audio CD (SACD), another format for delivering high-fidelity audio content. Neither has gained a strong position in the marketplace.

## 6.15 WAVE STUDIO AND SOUND FORGE

These two programs are employed in the PC platform. Wave Studio comes with the Sound Blaster cards, while Sound Forge is Macromedia's Version of SoundEdit 16 for the IBM compatibles. These two programs capabilities are similar to SoundEdit 16, using similar menus and functions. For convenience, this book will add the features of these two programs whenever SoundEdit 16 is discussed because the program's functions and logic are the same in the Macintosh or the PC platforms.

### (1) Sound Formats and Settings

When recording sounds for multimedia projects, you must balance the quality of sound desired with the storage space you have, the amount of what RAM memory available and the capability of the sound-delivery equipment to reproduce with you have recorded.

The preceding considerations determine file size and quality of the recording. Keep in mind that the sampling rate determines the frequency make-up of the recording. Recording at high-frequency content of your sound. Another aspect to determine the accuracy with which a sound can be digitized. The more bits you use in a recording the more realistic this sound playback will be.

When considering sound quality and realism, stereo recording may be your choice Stereo recordings are lifelike and realistic. Mono sounds are less realistic, flat, and note are dramatic but they are small in file size. Stereo sounds require twice the space as compared to mono recordings.

In order to help you make the decision on which format to use (mono or stereo), you can use the following formulas to determine file size in bytes:

**(a.) Monophonic Recording:**
sampling rate X duration of recording in seconds (X bit resolution / 8 ) X 1

**(b.) Stereo Recording:**
sampling rate X duration of recording in seconds X (bit resolution / 8 ) X 2

Sound formats are standard in SoundEdit 16, as well as wave Studio and sound forge. All these programs can handle mono and stereo recording and playback. Sampling rates of 22KHz and 44 KHz are the rates most often used in all programs. SoundEdit lets you know of available recording options with the little "microphone" icon next to available recording options in the pull-down menu. If you have an 8-bit system, SoundEdit will not let you record at a higher rate.

### (2) Saving sound files

Assuming that the sound file you recorded is satisfactory, you are to save it on disk. If you still need to alter the sound file in any way other than sampling or resolution, refer to the next chapter, sound processing for help on the topic.

### (3) Some of sound file saving considerations are:

Available media: Floppy disks can only store up to 1M of information, so they are limited for sound storage Archiving most of your sound files need lager media such as optical cartridges.

**File Type:** If your goal is to become a successful multimedia producer, it is important to develop products capable of playback in a multi-platform environment. There are a number of different file formats. You can classify them in two general categories—digital audio files (voice music, or sound effects converted from analog to digital) and MIDI files (music files generated by digitally controlled musical equipment). The following list describes the file formats available to store digital audio and MIDI data:

**Audio Interchange File Format (AIFF.AIF)**- This file format is used by Macintosh, IBM compatibles, Commodore Amiga and Silicon Graphic machines. A large number of sampling rates (upto 32 bits) are supported.

**Musical Instrument Digital Interface (MID,MDI,MFF)**-The internationally accepted file format is used to store MIDI data.

**Resource Interchange file format (RIFF)**-This format was developed by Microsoft and can contain a variety of types of data including digital audio and MIDI.

**Sound (SND)**- This file format was developed by Apple and is limited to a sampling rate of 8 bits.

**Roll (ROL)**- This file format was developed by AdLib, Inc. for use with their sound cards. It store MIDI-like data and Yamaha FM synthesizer information.

**Wave (WAV)**- This file format is widely supported by windows application. It was developed by Microsoft as a subset of the RIFF format. It is capable of sampling rates of 8 and 16 bits (mono and stereo).

**Sun Audio (AU)**- This file format was developed and used by Sun Microsystems workstations. Sun audio is a 16-bit compressed audio format. It is used on the Internet.

**Voice (VOC)**- This file format was developed for the sound Blaster audio card from Creative Technology. This file format can support sampling rates of 8 bit or without compression.

**Turtle SMP (SMP)**- This audio format was developed by Turtle Beach systems to be used in their audio recording and editing software.

To make your application to run on Macintoshes and PC-compatible machines, pay particular attention to two file formats- Audio Interchange File Format (AIFF) and the Musical Instrument Digital Interface (MIDI). These two formats will makes your multimedia application compatible in both platforms. This book recommends that you use MIDI files to record music and use the digital file as sound in your multimedia applications, because the control of MIDI instruments, which will play these files, through a multimedia application is limited and subjects to all kinds of instrument incompatibility. To interchange sound files between computer platforms, use the Aif extension for files stored on PC-formatted disks because the Macintosh can read these disks just as well as Mac-formatted ones. The Aiff is the choice format for Macromedia Director multimedia programs because they reside outside the application and are called when needed to play. This allows the multimedia files to be of smaller size and play faster. Sound files saved in the Aiff format also can be used as tracks for burning an audio CD.

## 6.16 MUSICAL SOUND IN PC

During later half of 1990s PC audio have advanced to such an extent that they produce quality sound that can compete with professional sound systems and in some cases, even replace them. But this was not always the case. Before the advent of Windows, sound cards were available from a score of vendors. This made choice nightmarish for both users and developers. Game developers would spend more time worrying about the compatibility of their games with each sound card rather then working on the games themselves. Today things are different. All sound card manufacturers now ensure that their card is Windows 95/98 compatible. This has, to a great extent, taken the guesswork out of software development. And even if the card is to be used under other operating systems such as DOS or Unix, manufacturers ensure that their sound card is compatible with the market leader-SoundBlaster from Creative Labs.

## 6.17 SOME MULTIMEDIA SOUND AND ANIMATION PRODUCTS

Below are some listings of multimedia sound and animation products:

- Sound Engine-Media FX adds concert hall sound to your PC. This card combination uses 16-bit stereo CD-quality sampling to add music and sound to your system. MIDI compatible with 213 preset sampled sounds. It's fairly expensive however.
- Desktop Stereo Add a stereo FM receiver to your computer. Tuning, volume, treble bass, and other functions are controlled by the software from optronics technology.
- Sound palette, sound booster record and play back sound on your PC's speaker, so you don't have to install a sound board. It includes a library of 50 sounds. Optional parallel port connector allows connection to external amplifier and speakers. Macros for adding sound to toolbook word and Excel included. From M.P Technologies. Wired for sound similar to the product above but more popular. It allows sound to be attached to any dialog box but does not record sound. It includes a talking click. From Aristosoft, Inc..
- Sound Blaster, Sound Blaster pro very popular fairly inexpensive sound boards. They contain an on-board synthesizer, microphone input digital voice input and output stereo amplifier, and MIDI interface from Creative Labs.

## Authoring Languages/Environments

Build applications containing all the elements of multimedia even if you aren't a "creative type" at using these programming or multimedia authoring products:

- Animation Works, by Gold disk inc. (310) 320-5080
- Autodesk Multimedia Explorer, by Autodesk Multimedia,
- Asymetrix Toolbook and Multimedia Resource Kit by symetrix (206) 637-1500
- Audio Tracks Libraries Contains a large library of digital sound effects and music for sound Blaster cards. Get it at HCS software at (310) 382-8441.

There are a number of alternative for obtaining music and sound effects to use in multimedia projects without the legal hurdles of copyright infringement or having to hire a full orchestra to record for you. Playback music from audio CDs- your Authoring language is capable of controlling the computer CD-ROM to play a specific music track from an audio CD. The authoring program can also modify the music playback volume and fade in or out as necessary. The music from a CD can be played as background music, as the application component within the program (in other words as part of a music appreciation instructional module among others). Purchase royalty-free music and sound effects files (clip audio)-A number of companies provide royalty-free music and sound effects files which can be incorporated into different components of your application. Read the agreement included with these products. Although they are royalty-free, they may not be copyright-free. Many companies spell out in detail how you may or may not use these files. Compose, play, and record your own music and special sound effects-If you or one of your multimedia development team members are musicians. you can play a Musical Interface Digital Interface (MIDI) instrument, such as a keyboard, to input music digitally directly into your computer. With MIDI equipment you can play and record music develop special effects, and performs other composition tasks. Some MIDI equipment other composition task. Some MIDI own sounds so that you can add the sound of a rain shower or birds singing after recording then sound yourself and saving it digitally. You can secure right releases from people you interview-If you interview people or use talent to record narration, make sure you secure releases of the right to the narration.

## 6.18 HANDLING NON-STANDARD : MIDI HARDWARE WITH MIDI MAPPER

MIDI Mapper is a control panel utility used to create or modify setting that affect windows interaction with MIDI instruments, such as synthesizers. If you don't have a MIDI-equipped sound or interface (such as the Roland MPU-401 or Sound Blaster with MIDI attachment) and a MIDI instrument or device this section won't apply to you and the icon won't show up on the control panel-so you can skip it. If you do have a MIDI setup, however and a basic working knowledge of the MIDI specification and concept Read on for a general description of what MIDI Mapper does and how to begin using it. At the least if you are using an application such as Media player that plays sound files through a MIDI port or plug-in card like the Ad Lib card you need to use MIDI Mapper to select the correct MIDI setup for the synthesizer that will be playing the file.

Because of the technical detail involved in reassigning channels, patches and key maps, the exact producers for doing so aren't covered here uses the MIDI Mapper Help system and Windows Users Guide for explicit instructions.

## 6.19 RECORDING AND PLAYING SOUND

### 6.19.1 Record Sounds

There are three different methods:

#### METHOD ONE

You can easily use Recording Wizard to customize any Sound Recorder recording actions step by step. Press Recording Wizard button (wizard_n.gif) in play&record control bar or click Recording Wizard menu item from Play&Record menu to popup Recording Wizard dialog. Summaries of recording setting are displayed in the list box when Recording Wizard dialog popups. Double click the list box item to change the recording options in Recording Wizard dialog.

**Step 1:** Customize recording source device options. Double click these list box item to popup Sound Device property page. If you have multiple sound cards, or a single card that has multiple inputs, you can choose one of them from the Recording Device drop-down list. You can also choose the follows: Channel mode-Stereo or Mono; Sample Rate; Sample Format. Any Sound Recorder is able to automatically detect the recording formats your sound card supports. The supported sample rates of the selected recording device are shown in the Sample Rate drop-down list.

**Step 2:** Customize recording sound source options. Input source (such as Microphone, Stereo Mix, CD Audio, Line In, Aux, Mono Out etc.) and input volume can be changed in Recording sound source configuration dialog. Note: you can also change these parameters from Play&Record control bar.

**Step 3:** Modify recording file output options. You can choose auto-name file options (Automatically save recording audio to file, file type format, file name rule etc.) and file output encoding options (WAV, MP3, OGG etc. encoding options).

**Step 4:** Customize Advance recording options. You can change more parameters (Time Limit, Edit Sound Recording Mode, Directly Save Sound to File Recording Mode, Silence Detection Algorithms and Actions, etc.) in Advance recording options page of options dialog.

**Step 5:** Press Record button in Recording Wizard dialog to start your recording work.

### METHOD TWO

Use Options dialog() to customize your recording work. Combine Play&Record Control Bar to preform recording work.

**Step 1:** The orations of Method One almost can be finished in Options dialog. You can directly modify those recording settings in Options dialog.

**Step 2:** Choose input source by Input Source (such as Microphone, Stereo Mix, CD Audio, Line In, Aux, Mono Out etc.) button inputsource.png on Play&Record control bar.

**Step 3:** Adjust input volume by input volume slider bar and playback volume by playback volume slider bar volume.png on Play&Record control bar.

**Step 4:** Press Record button record.png to start your recording work on Play&Record control bar.

### METHOD THREE

If you have already customized your recording options, you can directly press Record button to start recording work.

## Play Sounds

*To play a sound:*

Choose Open from the File menu. Find and select the sound you want to play. Choose the Open button. A waveform is shown in main window.

Choose the playing button play.png on the play&record control bar.

*To play part of a sound:*

Open the sound, as above. Select the part of the sound you want to play. Press the playing button on the play&record control bar.

*To play loop part of a sound:*

Open the sound, as above. Select the part of the sound you want to loop. Press `loop play button(loopplay _ n.png)` to down status. Choose the playing button on the play&record control bar. Edit Sounds Any Sound Recorder provides most useful edit tool such as special effects, cut & past, undo & redo, zoom in & out features.

## Select editing range:

**Defining a Range:** Left-click on one side of the range portion that you want to select and drag the mouse to the left or right. You can also select a range from Locate and `Select... dialog.`

**Changing Range Boundaries:** Hold down the Shift key and left-click on the range boundary that you want to move, and drag the boundary to its new location. You can also press Shift key and left arrow key or right arrow key to change range boundaries. You can also change a range boundaries from Locate and `Select... dialog.`

**Select All:** Double-click in the wave view to select all the waveform you currently see. To select entire waveform, click Edit menu and select Select All menu item. Selecting Only the Left Channel: `Click menu Edit -> Channel Select -> Left menu item` to select only the left channel. You can also right-click in waveform view to popup shortcut menu and select Select `Left Channel` menu item.

**Selecting Only the Right Channel:** `Click menu Edit -> Channel Select -> Right menu item` to select only the right channel. You can also right-click in waveform view to popup shortcut menu and select Select Right Channel menu item.

**Selecting Stereo Channel:** `Click menu Edit -> Channel Select -> Both menu item` to select only the both channel. You can also right-click in waveform view to popup shortcut menu and select Select Both Channel menu item.

**Copy & Paste & Cut & Delete & Trim & Silence Sounds:** Almost these editing commands in Any Sound Recorder operate on the currently selected part of a sound. So you must select editing range using above methods at first, and then perform these commands using edit menu or toolbar.

**Fade In & Fade Out & Invert & Reverse & Echo Effect Sounds:** You can perform these effect commands like editing commands above.

**Undo & Redo:** Undo&Redo information is stored as a temporary file on your hard drive. The undo & redo number is only limited by the amount of free hard disk space. All changes are automatically saved as one or more files in your temporary folder as long as the waveform is open in Any Sound Recorder even after it been saved to disk.

**Save Sounds to File**

Any Sound Recorder can save recording or editing sounds to WAV, MP3, OGG format file. You can customize sound encoding parameters in Save, Save As or Save Copy As file save dialog or in File output encode page of Options dialog. See help document for more information.

### 6.19.2 Record Audio with Windows Sound Recorder

Sound Recorder lets you record a sound and save it as an audio file on your computer. You can record sound from different audio devices, such as a microphone that's plugged into the sound card on your computer. The types of audio input sources you can record from depend on the audio devices you have and the input sources on your sound card.

**Notes:**

1. Make sure you have an audio input device, such as a microphone, connected to your computer.
2. To use Sound Recorder, you must have a sound card and speakers installed on your computer. If you want to record sound, you also need a microphone (or other audio input device).
3. **Installation** - If the Sound Recorder (sndrec32.exe) is not already installed on your system, you will find instructions for its installation by clicking `Start>Help`, then choosing the Index tab and typing "Sound Recorder". Display the instruction by double clicking on Installation. Also, install the Windows 95 volume control by placing a check in the volume control box when checking the Sound Recorder box during the Sound Recorder installation process.
4. **Microphone** - To record sound, any inexpensive microphone with a mini plug that fits into your sound card microphone jack on your computer will do. An inexpensive stand microphone that you can buy in a computer store is nice, since it frees your hands for keyboarding. A slightly more expensive headset/ microphone allows you to also listen in privacy without disturbing others around you.

Windows Sound Recorder is a simple audio recording utility included with all versions of the Microsoft Windows Operating System published since 1995. It hasn't changed over the years, so this tutorial should be accurate no matter what version of Windows you are running.

After installing Sound Recorder, use it to record your voice for Distance Learning courses, such as Spanish 101 and Spanish 102. You can save the recorded files and send them as e-mail attachments. To do this, your computer must have a sound card (most do) and a you'll need a headset/microphone to plug into your computer. Other features of Sound Recorder include simple editing, mixing, and adding effects to sound files with ease. Let your imagination and creativity loose to create your own sound effects.

### (1) Launching Sound Recorder

In Windows XP, navigate to `Start > All Programs > Accessories > Entertainment > Sound Recorder.`

In Windows 98 (Win98) or Win2000, navigate to Start > Programs > Accessories > Entertainment > Sound Recorder.

In Win95 or WinNT 6.0, navigate to `Start > Programs > Accessories > Multimedia > Sound Recorder.`

When the Sound Recorder pops on-screen, you'll notice that it looks a bit like a tape recorder front panel.

In the center of the window is a flat, green line. As the sound plays or records, this green line oscillates to visually represent the sound.

To the left is the Position indicator, represented in hundredths of a second.

To the right is the Length indicator, showing the total duration of the sound file.

Below these features is a Slide Bar indicator that shows where the sound file is playing, relative to its overall length. You can use the scroll bar to move through the sound file. The bar moves by either sliding it with the mouse or clicking on the right or left arrows. Finally, located below the Slide Bar, you'll see the universal symbols (from left to right) for Rewind, Fast Forward, Play, Stop, and Record. Now that you're familiar with Sound Recorder, we'll walk you through some tasks.

### (2) Playing a Sound

To play a sound, open the file and click on the `Play button.`

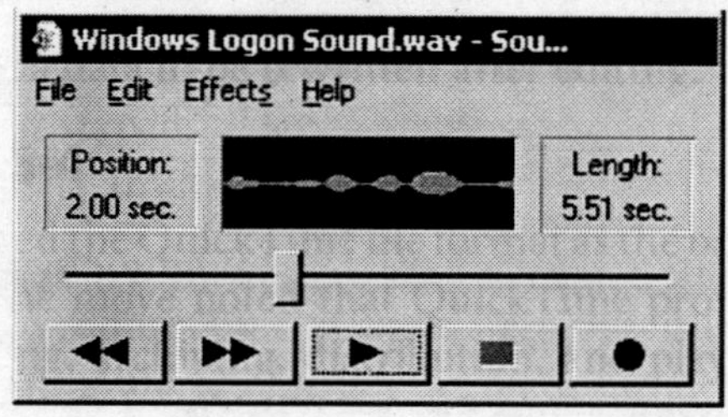

On the File menu, click `Open`. A dialog box will appear. Navigate to the folder containing the sound file you want to play, select the file and then click `Open`. Click the play button ( ▶ ) to start playing the sound. Click the stop button ( ■ ) to stop playing the sound.

### (3) Navigating a File

When working with long sound files, you'll want to move through them as quickly as possible.

To move forward or backward, use the Sound Recorder scroll bar, or the keyboard left & right arrow keys.

To move to the end of a file, click the Fast Forward button ( ▶▶ ), move the scroll bar to the right or press END on the keyboard.

To move to the beginning, click Rewind ( ◀◀ ), move the scroll bar to the left or press HOME on the keyboard.

To play part of the sound file, slide the scroll bar to any point in the file and click Play ( ▶ ).

Note that the Rewind and Fast Forward buttons work instantly; one click takes you immediately to the beginning or the end.

### (4) Setting the Recording Format

High quality recordings create large sound files. This could cause problems if you try to send those files as e-mail attachments. To avoid this, set the recording format in Windows Sound Recorder to create files that are of good quality but not so large as to choke your e-mail service.

**Step 1:** In the File menu, `click Properties`. A dialog box will appear.

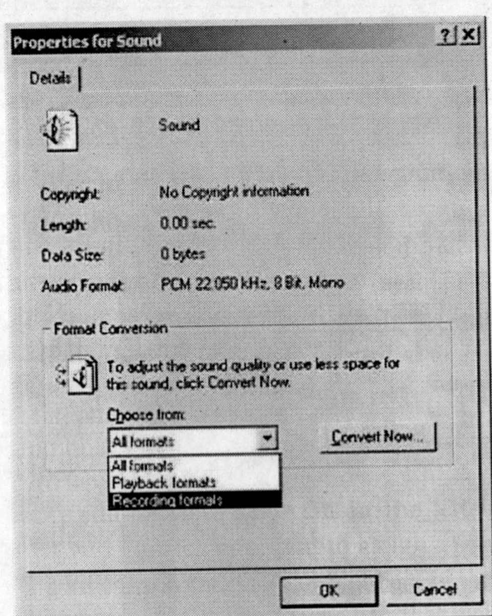


**Step 2:** Use the Choose from: pull-down menu to select Recording formats, and click `Convert Now...`

**Step 3:** In the "Sound Selection" window, use the Attributes: pull-down menu to choose 8.000 kHz, 16 Bit, Mono, 15 kb/sec. This will change the settings to create a recording that sounds comparable to a good cell phone call. A one minute sound recording should be just under 1 MB (megabyte) in size. To compare, an audio CD uses ten times as much data: 46.1 kHz/16 Bit/Stereo, for a file size of 1 minute = 10 MB.

**Step 4:** To save these settings, click the `Save As...` button. A pop-up will prompt you to "save this format as." Type in a name you'll remember, such as "Audio E-Mail," and click `OK`.

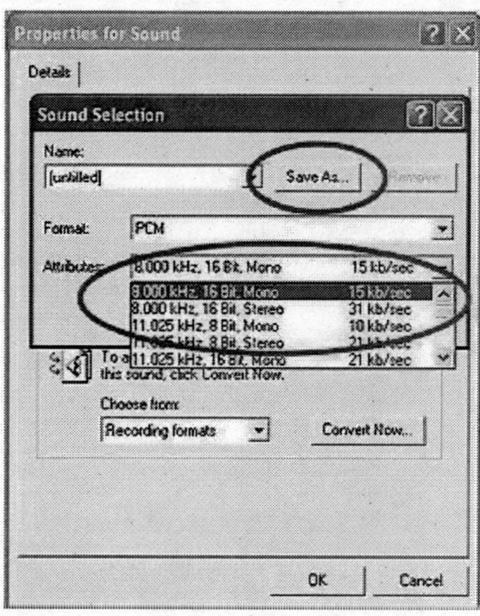


**Step 5:** You'll return to the "Properties for Sound" window. Click OK on this window, then OK on the Properties window, and your next sounds will be recorded at the 8 kHz/16 bit/Mono format.

If you've already recorded your voice at high-quality, you probably ended up with some large files. To reduce the file size of existing recordings:

Open the previously recorded sound, then click the `File menu`, and `Properties`.

Use the Choose from: pull-down menu to select Playback formats, and click `Convert Now...`

On the next dialog box, use the Name: pull-down menu to select Audio E-Mail, the name of the quality level you created above.

Click `OK` on this window, then `OK` on the Properties window, and save your file with a new name.

Compare the original file with the new file saved at lower quality. The new file size should be much smaller.

Here are 3 files created from the same recording, saved at different recording settings. Compare sound quality vs. file size.

**File Length Quality**

| (kHz/bits/channels) | File | Size |
|---|---|---|
| 8.65 seconds | CD (44/16/stereo) | 1,491 kb |
| 8.65 seconds | Radio (16/16/mono) | 271 kb |
| 8.65 seconds | Cellphone (8/16/mono) | 136 kb |

### (5) Setting the Microphone Record Level

To record and play audio, you'll need a sound card, a microphone, and speakers or headphones. If your record button can be activated, your PC is equipped to record. To record your voice, hook the microphone into the audio-in jack on your computer's sound card. Before you begin recording, check your microphone settings for a proper volume level.

After starting Sound Recorder, click on `Edit>Audio Properties.`

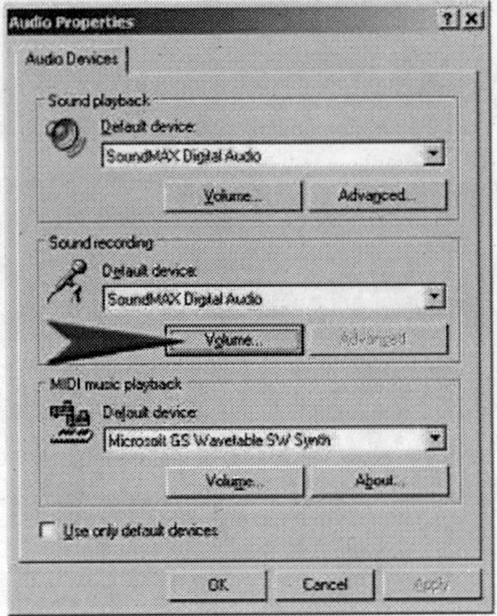


In the Audio Properties dialogue box, under the Sound recording section, check to see that your sound card is the Default device (change this if necessary). Below the Default device, click on Volume.

In the Recording Control dialogue box, be sure the microphone is the selected recording source, and turn its volume up full.

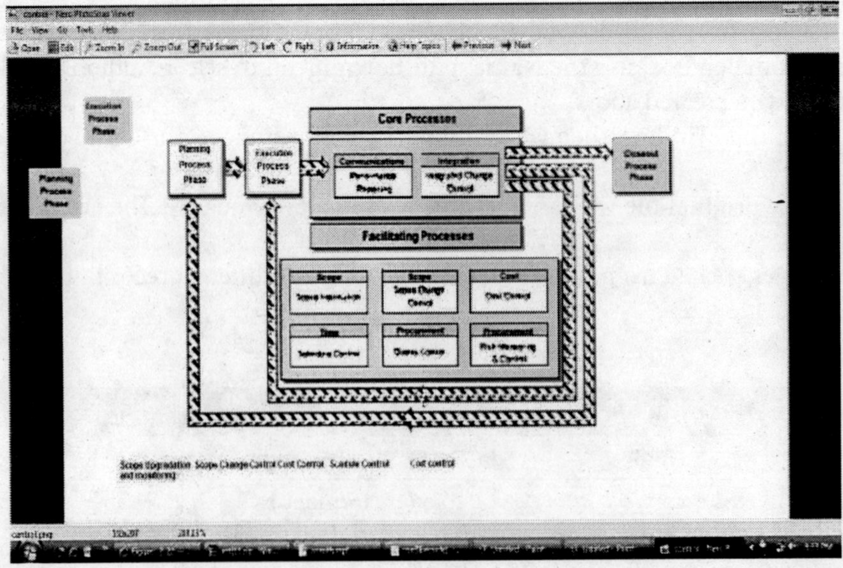


Close this dialogue box and return to the Audio Properties box. Click OK. You have successfully turned your microphone level up to record your voice at a proper volume level.

### (6) Recording a Sound

To record and play audio, you'll need a sound card, a microphone and speakers or headphones. If your record button can be activated, your PC is equipped to record. To record your voice, hook the microphone into the audio-in jack on your computer's sound card. (see above to set the microphone record level.)

Make sure you have a microphone connected to your computer.

1. On the File menu, click `New`.
2. To begin recording, click ● and speak into the microphone.
3. To stop recording, click ■.
4. To continue recording, click ● and speak into the microphone again. When finished, click ■ to stop recording.

On the File menu, click `Save As`. Type a new name for your file, select the location where it will be saved, and Click the `Save` button. You can specify the default sound quality before you record a sound (see above.)

### (7) Editing a File

The editing tools are located in Sound Recorder's Edit menu. After you edit a file, click Play to listen to your changes. If you like what you hear, save the file. (You'll probably want to change the name.) If you don't approve of the new sound, and you haven't saved the file, choose Revert from the File menu to restore the file to its previous state.

The editing options are:

Insert File

This inserts an entire sound file anywhere in the current file. An inserted file will increase the sound file's length.

To insert Ding.wav into Chord.wav, you:

Scroll to the desired location in the Chord.wav file.

Select `Insert File` from the Edit menu. The Insert File dialog box appears.

Select `Ding.wav`.

Click `OK`.

To listen, click `Play`.

Remember, if you want to save the file, change the name. (You don't want to write over the original Chord.wav file.)

### (8) Mix With File

This mixes a second file with the original file. The sounds in the files will play simultaneously.

To mix the Chord.wav file with the Chimes.wav file:

1. Scroll to the desired position in the Chord.wav file.
2. Select `Mix With File` from the Edit menu. This brings up a dialog box.
3. Select `Chimes.wav`.
4. Click `OK`.

Delete `Before Cursor Position`

This deletes information from the beginning of the file to the current position in the file.

Delete `After Current Position`

This deletes information from the current position to the end of the file.

### (9) Adding Effects

To give your file a little extra flavor, you can add special effects. These effects are available in the Effects menu and they manipulate the entire sound file. So if you only want a portion of the file to have a special effect, you'll have to copy the sound file, cut it into portions, apply the effect a portion at a time and then combine them again.

The effects in Sound Recorder are:

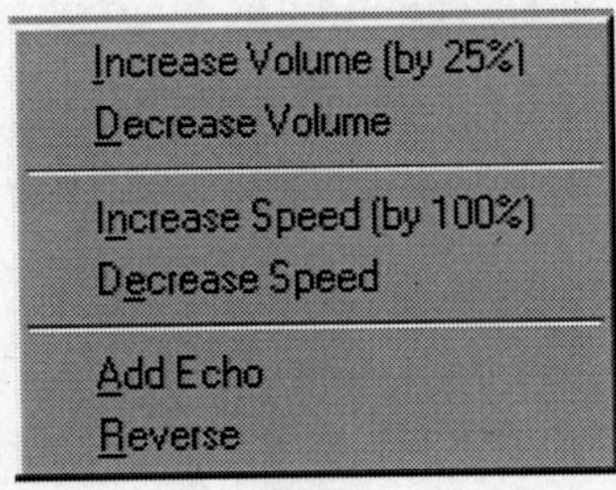


**Increase Volume**

This increases the volume by 25%. (However, you can select this option twice for a 50% increase, three times for a 75% increase, and so on.)

**Decrease Volume**

This decreases the volume by 25%.

**Increase Speed**

This doubles the rate of a sound's playback.

**Decrease Speed**

This slows the rate of a sound's playback by 50%.

**Add Echo**

This adds an audio reverb.

**Reverse**

This reverses the sound so it can be played backward.

### (10) Increasing The Maximum Recording Time

Sound Recorder included with Windows 95 and Windows 98 has a default maximum time of 60 seconds of continuous recording. If you stop recording at any point before reaching the 60 second limit, you can then continue recording and have another 60 seconds of continuous time before Sound Recorder automatically stops.

You can repeat this start-stop routine indefinitely if you need to record a long passage as one file.

Here's an alternate method to increase the maximum recording time in Sound Recorder:

Make sure your microphone is muted so it will not pick up sound.

Click `Record`, and then let Sound Recorder run for 60 seconds (recording silence).

After Sound Recorder stops recording, click `Save As` on the File menu, and name the file Blank.wav.

To increase the maximum recording time in Sound Recorder, click `Insert File` on the Edit menu, and then insert the Blank.wav file that you saved in step 3. When you do this, the maximum recording time is increased by 60 seconds. You can repeat this step once for each additional minute of recording time that you want to add. For example, for a 5-minute recording time, insert the Blank.wav file five times.

### 6.19.3 Assigning Sounds with the Control panel's Sound Utility

To assessing sound utility

1. From the control panel, choose `sound`.
2. Choose the event to assign a sound to.
3. Choose the sound you want to give it.
4. Repeat steps 2 and 3 for other events events you want to modify.
5. Click on `OK`.

The control panel's sound utility is for designating sounds so system events, such as warning dialog boxes, error messages when you click in the wrong place, and so on. Once you've installed a sound board, you can personalize your computer's beep to something more exciting than just "beep". aside from making life more interesting, having different sounds for different types of event is also more informative. You know when you've made an error as opposed to when an application is acknowledging setup you need a sound example.

To add basic sound s to you Windows setup, you need a sound card that is MPC compatible that is it must conform to the Multimedia personal Computer specification. Sounds must be stored on disk in the. WAV format to be used. The sound Records program explained later in the chapter records sounds in this format. Windows comes with a few sound files that are OK, but not great. You'll probably want to make more interesting ones yourself, but you'll need your own sounds. I have messages in my own voice such as "you made a stupid mistake you fool,"which-for a short time-seemed preferable guitar riffs and ditties off CDs.

Incidentally you can also map system events to a MIDI devices such as a synthesizer but that's covered later in this chapter in the section on the MIDI Mapper.

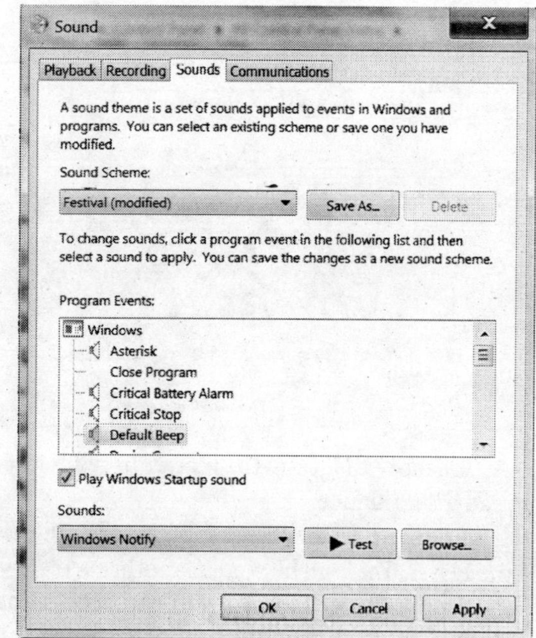


Once you're setup for sound and have some. WAV files you assign them to specific events. These events have names which you'll see in the sound dialog box. Here's what you do:

1. Open the `Control Panel` and run `sound`. The following dialog box appears:
2. Choose an event in the left list box to which you want to assign a sound. When you click on it or highlight of the sound file (.WAV file) assigned to that event will be highlighted.
3. In the right list box choose the sound file you want for that event. Click the test button if you want to hear the sound before finalizing your choice. Change the drive

and directory to choose. WAV files that are stored elsewhere by scrolling to the bottom of the files that box. Choosing <none> has the obvious effect; no sound will occur. Assigning all events to <none> will effectively silence your computer for use in a library, church , etc. You can also do this for all sounds except Windows start and Windows Exit by turning off the Enable System sounds check box. To mute the remaining two, you have to assign them manually to <nobe>.

4. Repeat the process for other events to which you want to assign or reassign sounds.
5. Click on `OK`.

Keep in mind that different applications will use event sounds differently. You'll have to do some experimenting to see when your applications use the default beep, as opposed to the Asterisk, Question, or the Exclamation.

## 6.19.4 Getting started with Windows Media Player

### Start Windows Media Player

To start Windows Media Player, click the Start button, click `All Programs`, and then click `Windows Media Player`.

**Two ways to enjoy your media: the Player Library and Now Playing mode**

Windows Media Player allows you to toggle between two modes: the Player Library, which gives you comprehensive control over the Player's many features; and Now Playing mode, which gives you a simplified view of your media ideal for playback.

From the Player Library, you can go to Now Playing mode by clicking the Switch to Now Playing button in the lower-right corner of the Player. To return to the Player Library, click the Switch to Library button in the upper-right corner of the Player. This will be seen in another screen when you have already switched the Now Playing button.

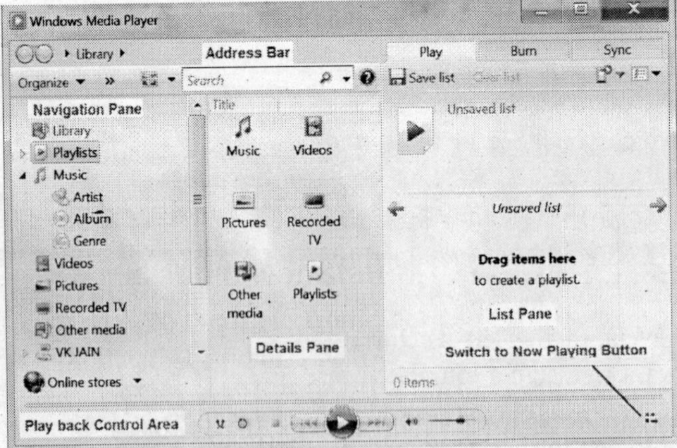


In above diagram, the matter in red is not a part of screen shot but have been putup for students/ reader's guidance.

To return to the Player Library, click the Switch to Library button in the upper-right corner of the Player. This will be seen in another screen when you have already switched the Now Playing button.

In the Player Library, you can access and organize your digital media collection. Within the navigation pane, you can choose a category, such as Music, Pictures, or Videos, to view in the details pane. For example, to see all of your music organized by genre, double-click Music, and then click Genre. Then, drag items from the details pane to the list pane to create playlists, burn CDs or DVDs, or sync to devices, such as portable music players.

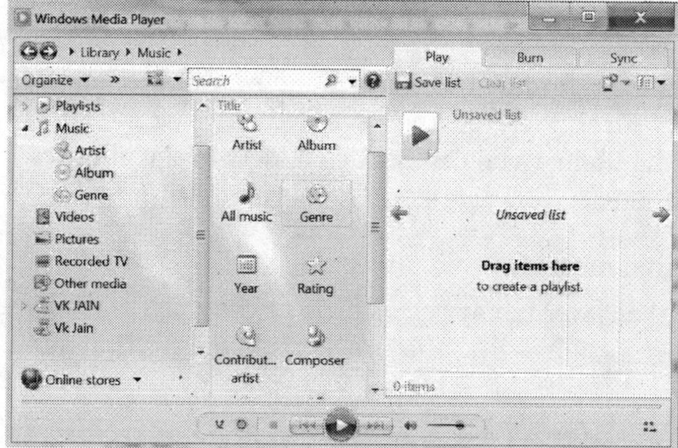


As you move between the various views in the Player Library, you can use the Back and Forward buttons in the upper-left corner of the Player to retrace your steps.

**Back and Forward buttons**

In Now Playing mode, you can view DVDs and videos or see what music is currently playing. You can decide to view only the currently playing item, or you can right-click the Player, and then click Show list to view a selection of available items.

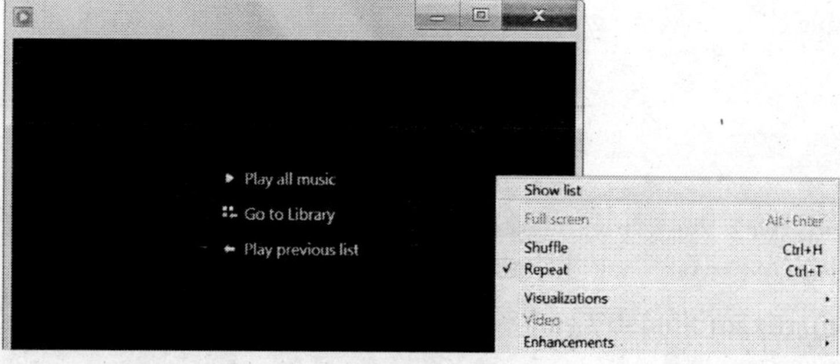


Now Playing mode

**Use Now Playing mode to do any of the following:**

- Play a CD or DVD in Windows Media Player
- Shuffle and repeat the items in Windows Media Player
- Change volume settings in Windows Media Player
- Switch between display modes in Windows Media Player

**Play from the Taskbar**

You can also control the Player when it's minimized. You can play or pause the current item, advance to the next item, and go back to the previous item using the controls in the thumbnail preview. The thumbnail preview appears when you point to the Windows Media Player icon on the taskbar.

## Build a media library

Windows Media Player looks for files in specific Windows libraries on your computer to add to the Player Library: Music, Videos, Pictures, and Recorded TV.

To build your media library, you can include folders in the libraries from other locations on your computer or external devices, such as a portable hard drive..

### Rip CDs to create digital music files

You can add music to the Player Library by using your computer's CD drive to copy CDs and store them on your computer as digital files. This process is known as ripping.

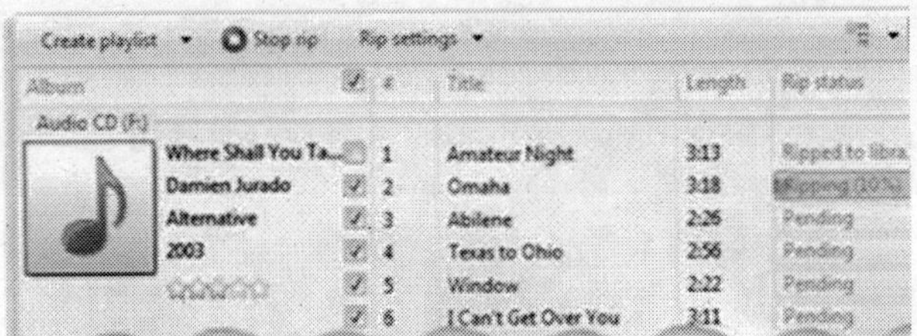


Ripping a music CD

### Use tabs to complete key tasks

The tabs at the top right of the Player open the list pane in the Player Library, making it easier for you to focus on specific tasks, such as creating playlists of your favorite songs, burning custom song lists to a recordable CD, or syncing playlists in your media library to a portable media player.

Play, Burn, and Sync tabs

To get started, click the tab that corresponds to the task you want to perform in the Player Library. To hide the list pane, click the tab that is currently open.

## Digital audio workstation (D.A.W.)

A D.A.W. is an electronic device or computer software application for recording, editing and producing audio files such as songs, musical pieces, human speech or sound effects. DAWs come in a wide variety of configurations from a single software program on a laptop, to an integrated stand-alone unit, all the way to a highly complex configuration of numerous components controlled by a central computer. Regardless of configuration, modern DAWs have a central interface that allows the user to alter and mix multiple recordings and tracks into a final produced piece.

DAWs are used for the production and recording of music, radio, television, podcasts, multimedia and nearly any other situation where complex recorded audio is needed.

The history of DAWs parallels advances in computer power with expensive-but-limited units becoming available in the 1970s, then more affordable PC-based systems in the late 1980s until the

2010s when a powerful system can be built relatively inexpensively, using open-source software and consumer audio equipment even as a market exists for professional high-end systems, essential in any 2010-era recording studio.

## Digitizing Audio

Many of today's multimedia applications include audio support. Some applications include hardware for digitizing audio, and other applications rely on third-party add-ons for audio support. Check with the application vendor to learn how audio is handled.

Like digital video, digital audio often begins from an analog source, so an analog-to-digital conversion must be made. Converting an analog signal to a digital signal involves taking a series of samples of the analog source. The aggregation of the samples yields the digital equivalent of the analog sound wave. A higher sampling rate delivers higher quality because it has more reference points to replicate the analog signal.

The sampling rate is one of three criteria that determine the quality of the digital version. The other two determining factors are the number of bits per sample and the number of channels.

Sampling rates are often quoted Hertz (Hz) or Kilohertz (KHz). Sampling rates are always measured per channel, so for stereo data recorded at 8,000 samples per second (8 KHz), there would actually be 16,000 samples per second (16 KHz). Table 6.3: Common Audio Sampling Rates lists common sampling rates.

**TABLE 6.4:** Common Audio Sampling Rates

| Samples per Second | Description |
|---|---|
| 8,000 | A telephony standard that works with μ-LAW encoding. |
| 11 K | Either 11025 (a quarter of the CD sampling rate) or half the Macintosh sampling rate (perhaps the most popular rate on Macintosh computers). |
| 16,000 | Used by the G.722 compression standard |
| 18.9 K | CD-ROM/XA standard |
| 22 K | Either 22050 (half the CD sampling rate) or the Macintosh rate, which is precisely 22254.545454545454. |
| 32,000 | Used in digital radio; Nearly Instantaneous Compoundable Audio Matrix (NICAM) (IBA/BREMA/BB), and other TV work in the U.K.; long play Digital Audio Tape (DAT); and Japanese HDTV. |
| 37.8 K | CD-ROM/XA standard for higher quality. |
| 44,056 | Used by professional audio equipment to fit an integral number of samples in a video frame. |
| 44,100 | CD sampling rate. DAT players recording digitally from CD also use this rate. |
| 48,000 | DAT sampling rate for domestic rate. |

An emerging tendency is to standardize on only a few sampling rates and encoding styles, even if the file formats differ. The emerging rates and styles are listed in Table 6.4: Sample Rates and Encoding Styles.

**TABLE 6.5:** Sample Rates and Encoding Styles

| Samples Per Second | Encoding Style |
|---|---|
| 08,000 | 8-bit μ-LAW mono |
| 22,050 | 8-bit linear unsigned mono and stereo |
| 44,100 | 16-bit linear unsigned mono and stereo |

## Audio Compression

Audio data is difficult to compress effectively. For 8-bit data, a Huffman encoding of the deltas between successive samples is relatively successful. Companies such as Sony and Phillips have developed proprietary schemes for 16-bit data. Apple Computer has an audio compression/ expansion scheme called ACE on the Apple IIGS and called MACE on the Macintosh. ACE/MACE is a lossy scheme that attempts to predict where the wave will go on the next sample. There is very little quality change on 8:4 compression, with somewhat more quality degradation at 8:3 compression. ACE/MACE guarantees exactly 50 percent or 62.5 percent compression.

Public standards for voice compression using Adaptive Delta Pulse Code Modulation (ADPCM) are as follows:

- CCIU G.721 sampling at 32 Kbps
- CCIU G.723 sampling at 24 Kbps and 40 Kbps
- GSM 06.10 is a European speech encoding standard that compresses 160 13-bit samples into 260 bits (33 bytes), or 1,650 bytes per second (at 8,000 samples per second).

When choosing a sound card, start will realistically evaluating what you will be using your multimedia computer for and what kind of speaker configuration you want. If you want the most out of your computer, consider a sound card that supports 5.1 or 7.1 surround sound. Of course then you will also need speakers that support 5.1 or 7.1 surround sound so be careful. A decent set of surround sound speakers can be quite pricey.

Still, many multimedia enthusiasts find that 2.1 speakers (two desktop speakers and one subwoofer) are enough to get the most out of multimedia computer. Remember that surround sound speakers may seem like a good idea, but you will need to mount those speakers around you to get the full effect. If you don't have the space in your computer room for surround speakers, you may want to consider investing in a very high quality set of 2.1 speakers. Something in the 150 to 250-watt range is best.

**List of hardware and software in the Multimedia Production Studios**

1. Computer A in each studio is dual bootable (Macintosh or Windows) Computer.
2. Computer B in each studio is Mac only.

**Hardware**

1. 27" standalone iMac
2. 15" monitor with multiple video inputs
3. scanner
4. DV/DVD recording deck
5. DVD/VCR recording deck
6. DV/VCR recording deck

7. DV recording deck
8. whiteboard
9. Software available in studios: As per table given below:

| Software | Description |
|---|---|
| Adobe Acrobat Pro | Protect documents and accelerate information exchange with PDF |
| Adobe Creative Suite Master Collection | Contribute, Dreamweaver, Fireworks, Flash Pro, Illustrator, InDesign, Photoshop, Premier Pro, and supporting applications |
| Facetime | Make video calls |
| Final Cut Studio Pro | Video Editing. Package includes Soundtrack Pro, Cinema Tools, and DVD Studio |
| HandBrake | Video encoder |
| iCal | Personal calendar application |
| iChart | HIPAA compliant digital medical assistant to manage patient records |
| iLife | iDVD, GarageBand, iMovie, iPhoto and iWeb |
| Image Capture | Upload pictures from digital cameras or scanners |
| iSync | Provides built-in support for a number of third-party mobile devices. |
| iTunes | Download media for Mac, PC, iPod and iPhone |
| iWork | Create documents, spreadsheets, and presentations on the MAC |
| Microsoft Office Suite | Excel, PowerPoint, Word and Access |
| PhotoBooth | Take photos and videos with an iSight camera |
| Preview | Display images and PDF documents |

**Learning Outcomes**

In this chapter we have learnt about :

1) Different Types and Characteristics of Sound
2) Sound Formats
3) Sound processing and streaming
4) Compression and Streaming audio

After reading this chapter the reader will be able to:

Incorporate different types of sound effects in Multimedia projects/presentation through different types of software

CHAPTER 7

# Video Processing

**Leaning Objectives**

In this chapter we shall learn about:

1. Difference between Analog and digital Video
2. Video Capturing and Compression
3. Video Compression standards and File Formats
4. Multimedia setup (Hardware and software) needed for Video Processing
5. MPEG, AVI and Quicktime

## 7.1 ANALOG VIDEO

Analog video is the original video recording method that stores continuous waves of *red, green* and *blue* intensities. In analog video, the number of rows is fixed. There are no real columns, and the maximum detail is determined by the frequency response of the analog system. Analog video contains the luminance (brightness) and chrominance (color) of the image, which may be carried in separate channels, as in component video (YPbPr) and S-Video, or combined in one channel, as in composite video and RF connector.

Analog video is used in both consumer and professional applications. Famous analog video formats are NTSC, VHS, composite video, S-video and component video.

### 7.1.1 Analog Video Connections

Three types of analog video connections found on Audio Visual equipment.

1. Composite,
2. S-Video and
3. Component video

Composite video (one channel) is an analog video transmission (without audio) that carries standard definition video typically at 480i or 576i resolution. Video information is encoded on one channel, unlike the higher-quality S-video (two channels) and the even higher-quality component video (three or more channels).

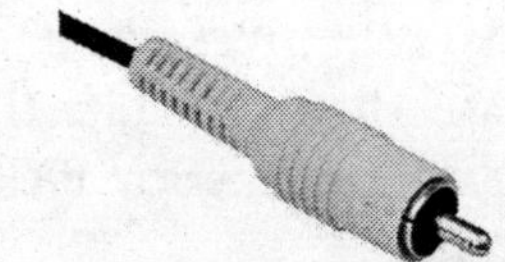

Fig. 7.1: Analog video connector: On consumer products a yellow RCA connector is typically used for composite video.

Composite video is usually in standard formats such as NTSC, PAL, and SECAM and is often designated by the CVBS initialism, for color, video, blanking and sync, or simply as video. A composite video signal combines on one wire the video information required to recreate a color picture, as well as line and frame synchronization pulses. The color video signal is a linear combination of the luminance of the picture, and a modulated subcarrier carries the chrominance or color information, a combination of hue and saturation. Details of the encoding process vary between the NTSC, PAL and SECAM systems.

## S Video Cable

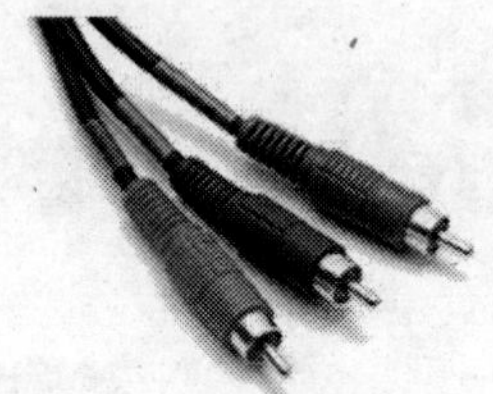

Fig. 7.2: Three cables, each with RCA plugsat both ends, are often used to carryYPbPr analog component video.

S Video cables, also called Super Video or Separate Video cables, transmit video color and luminance (brightness) information separately, minimizing interference. You can use S Video cables to connect almost any 2 S Video-capable devices, including camcorders, televisions, computers and DVD recorders. If you have the appropriate cable, you can also connect S Video-capable devices to non S-video devices;

Component video is a video signal that has been split into two or more component channels. In popular use, it refers to a type of component analog video (CAV) information that is transmitted or stored as three separate signals. Component video can be contrasted with composite video (NTSC, PAL or SECAM) in which all the video information is combined into a single line-level signal that is used in analog television. Like composite, component-video cables do not carry audio and are often paired with audio cables.

Much of today's video starts out as an analog signal, so a working knowledge of analog standards and formats is essential for understanding digital video and the digitization process. The following topics are fundamental for understanding analog video:

- Broadcast Standards
- Video Signal Standards
- Video Storage Formats
- Digitizing Video
- Digitizing Audio

## 7.2 BROADCAST STANDARDS

The principal standards for analog broadcast transmission are as follows:

- National Television Standards Committee (NTSC)-The broadcast standard in Canada, Japan, the United States, and Central America. NTSC defines 525 vertical scan lines per frame and yields 30 frames per second. The scan lines refer to the number of lines from top to bottom on the television screen. The frames per second refer to the number of complete images that are displayed per second.
- Phase Alternation Line (PAL)-The broadcast standard in Europe and in the Middle East, Africa, and South America. PAL defines 625 vertical scan lines and refreshes the screen 25 times per second.
- Système Electronique pour Couleur Avec Mémoire (SECAM)-The broadcast standard in France, Russia, and regions of Africa. SECAM is a variant of PAL but it delivers the same number of vertical scan lines as PAL and uses the same refresh rate.

To produce an image on a television screen, an electron gun scans across the television screen from left to right moving from top to bottom, as shown in Figure 7.3. Television scan gun operation.

Early television sets used a phosphor-coated tube, which meant that by the time the gun finished scanning all the lines that the broadcast standard required, the lines at the top were starting to fade. To combat fading, the NTSC adopted an interlace technique so that on the first pass from top to bottom, only every other line is scanned. With NTSC, this means that the first pass scans 262 lines. The second pass scans another 262 lines that are used to fill in the rest of the TV image.

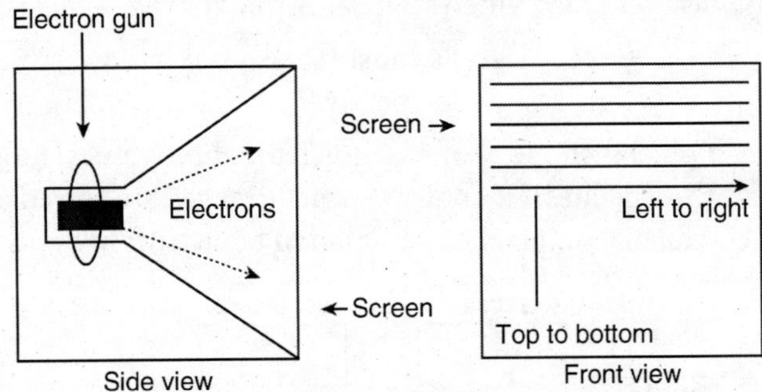


**Fig 7.3:** Television Scan Gun Operation

A frame represents the combination of the two passes, known as fields, as Figure: Interlace scan process indicates. For NTSC to deliver 30 frames per second, it must generate 60 fields per second. The rate at which fields are delivered depends on the clocking source. NTSC clocks its refresh intervals from AC power. In the United States, the AC power runs at 60 hertz or 60 oscillations per second. The 60 hertz yields 60 fields per second with every two fields yielding a frame. In Europe, AC power clocks at 50 hertz. This yields 50 fields per second or 25 frames per second.

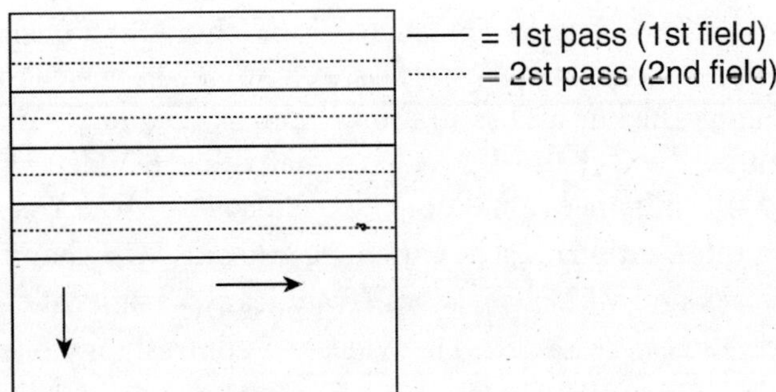


**Fig 7.4:** Interlace Scan Process

## 7.3 VIDEO SIGNAL STANDARDS

Black-and-white televisions receive one signal called luminance (also know as the Y signal). Each screen pixel is defined as some range of intensity between white (total intensity) and black (no intensity). In 1953, the NTSC was faced with the task of revising their standard to handle color. To maintain compatibility with older black-and-white sets, the NTSC set a color standard that kept the luminance signal separate and that provided the color information required for newer color television sets.

In the digital world, colors are typically expressed using red, green, and blue (RGB). The analog world has also embraced the RGB standard, at least on the acquisition side, where most cameras break the analog signal into RGB components.

Unfortunately, the NTSC could not use RGB as the color television standard because the old black- and-white sets could not decode RGB signals. Instead, they had to send a luminance signal for black-and-white sets and fill in the color information with other signals, called hue and saturation, (also known as the U and V signals). For this reason, digital color technology uses RGB and analog color technology, especially broadcast television, uses YUV (Y, U, and V signals).

RGB, however, is an inefficient analog video storage format for two reasons:

- First, to use RGB, all three color signals must have equal bandwidth in the system, which is often inefficient from a system design perspective.
- Second, because each pixel is the sum of red, green and blue values, modifying the pixel forces an adjustment of all three values. In contrast, when images are stored as luminance and color formats (that is, YUV format), a pixel can be altered by modifying only one value.

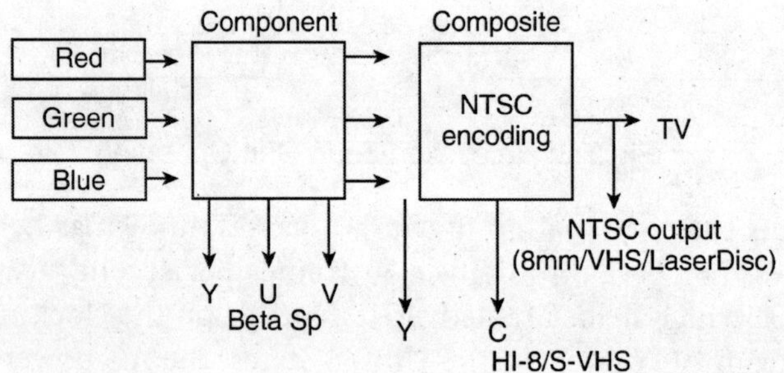


**Fig 7.5:** RGB to NTSC encoding traces an analog video signal from capture to NTSC output. On the far left is the RGB capture in which storage channels are maintained for each of the three primary colors.

Component video maintains separate channels for each color value, both in the recording device and the storage medium. Component video delivers the highest fidelity because it eliminates noise that would otherwise occur if two signals were combined in one channel.

After NTSC encoding, the hue and saturation channels (U and V signals) are combined into one chrominance channel, the C channel. A video signal, called S-Video, carries separate channels for the luminance and chrominance signals. S-Video is also known as Y/C video.

All color and other information must be combined into one YUV channel, called the composite signal, to play on old black-and-white televisions. Technically, a composite signal is any signal that contains all the information necessary to play video. In contrast, any one individual channel of component or Y/C video is not sufficient to play video.

A video signal can be transmitted as composite, S-Video, or component video. The type of video signal affects the connector that is used. The composite signal, which carries all the information in one electrical channel, uses a one-hole jack called the RCA Phono connector. The S-Video signal, composed of two electrical channels, uses a four-pin connector called the mini-DIN connector. Finally, the component signal uses three connectors.

## 7.4 WHAT ARE HDMI AND COMPONENT VIDEO?

HDMI and Component Video both are video standards which support a variety of resolutions, but which deliver the signal from the source to the display in very different ways. The principal important difference is that an HDMI cable delivers the signal in a digital format, much the same way that a file is delivered from one computer to another along a network, while Component Video is an analog format, delivering the signal not as a bitstream, but as a set of continuously varying voltages representing (albeit indirectly, as we'll get to in a moment) the red, green and blue components of the signal.

Both HDMI cable and Component Video cable deliver signals as three discrete color components, together with sync information which allows the display to determine when a new line, or a new frame, begins. The HDMI cable delivers these along three data channels in a format called T.M.D.S., which stands for "Transition Minimized Differential Signaling." Big words aside, the T.M.D.S. format basically involves a blue channel to which horizontal and vertical sync are added, and separate green and red channels (though HDMI can also be configured to use "color-difference" colorspace).

## 7.5 VIDEO STORAGE FORMATS

There are six video storage formats: 8 mm, Beta SP, HI-8, Laserdisc, Super VHS (SVHS), and VHS. The six formats use different signals to store color. The composite signal provides the lowest quality because all signals are combined, which in turn has the highest potential for noise. The S-Video signal produces less noise because the two signals are isolated in separate channels. The component signal provides the highest quality signal because all components are maintained in separate channels. The image quality that a video capture board produces can only be as good as the signal it accepts. Table: Analog Video Storage Formats lists the analog capture and storage standards for video.

**TABLE 7.1:** Analog Video Storage Formats

| | Beta SP | SVHS/HI-8 | VHS/8mm | Laserdisc |
|---|---|---|---|---|
| Color signal | Component | Y/C | Composite | Composite |
| Lines of resolution | 750 | 400 | 200 | 400 |
| Signal-to-noise ratio | 50 db | 47 db | 47 db | 47 db |

As Table: 7.1 indicates, the storage formats deliver different lines of resolution. Resolution is a measure of an image's quality. From the viewer's perspective, an image with higher resolution yields sharper picture quality than a lower resolution image.

Most consumer televisions display roughly 330 lines of horizontal resolution. Broadcast environments typically used high-end cameras to capture video. These cameras and their associated storage formats can deliver horizontal resolutions of approximately 700 lines. Each time a copy is made, the copied image loses some of its resolution. When an image is recorded in high-resolution, multiple generations of the video can be copied without a noticeable difference. When an image is recorded in a lower resolution, there is less room to manipulate the image before the viewer notices the effects.

## 7.6 DIGITAL VIDEO: VIDEO RECORDING IN DIGITAL FORM

### 7.6.1 Digitizing Video

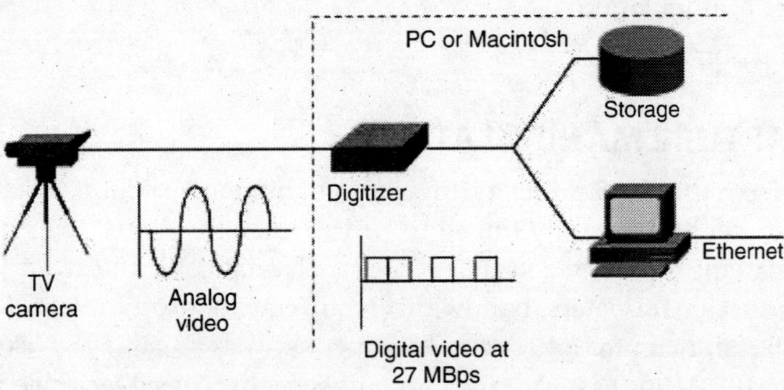


**Fig 7.6:** Analog-to-digital video conversion

Digitizing video involves taking an analog video signal and converting it to a digital video stream using a video capture board, as shown in Figure: Analog-to-digital video conversion. Today, a variety of computer platforms, including PC, Macintosh, and UNIX workstations, offer video capture capabilities. In some cases, though, the capture equipment is a third-party add-on. The analog video source can be stored in any video storage format or it can be a live video feed from a camera. The source can be connected to the video capture card using any three connectors types (component, S-Video, or composite) depending on the connector type that the card supports.

When capturing and digitizing video, the following components are critical:

- **Resolution**-The horizontal and vertical dimensions of the video session. A full-screen video session is typically 640 horizontal pixels by 480 vertical pixels. Full-screen video uses these dimensions because it yields the 4:3 aspect ratio of standard television. Of the 525 vertical scan lines in the NTSC standard, 483 lines are used to display video. The other lines are used for signaling and are referred to as the vertical blanking interval. Because the NTSC standard uses 483 vertical lines, capturing at 640 by 480 means that three lines are dropped during the digitization process.
- **Color depth**-The number of bits that are used to express color. At the high end is 24-bit color, which is capable of displaying 16.7 million colors and is the aggregate of 8 bits of red, 8 bits of green, and 8 bits of blue. The 8 bits are used to express color intensity from 0 to 255. Other common color depths are 16-bit and 8-bit, which yield roughly 65,000 and 256 colors, respectively.
- **Frame rate**-The number of frames that are displayed per second. To deliver NTSC-quality video, 30 frames per second are displayed. PAL and SECAM display 25 frames per second.

Based on these criteria, it is a simple mathematical operation to determine how much bandwidth a particular video stream requires. For example, to deliver uncompressed NTSC-quality digitized video to the network, a bandwidth of approximately 27 megabytes per second (Mbps) is needed. This number is derived from the following calculation:

$$640 \times 480 \times 3 \times 30 = 27.648 \text{ MBps (or 221.184 megabits per second [Mbps])}$$

where 640 and 480 represent the resolution in pixels, 3 represents 24-bit color (3 bytes), and 30 represents the number of frames per second.

As this calculation indicates, full-motion, full-color digital video requires considerably more bandwidth than today's typical packet-based network can support. Fortunately, two techniques reduce bandwidth consumption:

- Video Capture Manipulation
- Video Compression

## 7.7 VIDEO CAPTURE MANIPULATION

Manipulating video capture parameters involves changing resolution, color depth, and frame rate. To reduce bandwidth consumption, all three variables are often changed. For example, some multimedia applications capture video at 320 * 240 with 8-bit color and at a frame rate of 15 frames per second. With these parameters, bandwidth requirements drop to 9.216 Mbps. Although this level of bandwidth is difficult for a 10-Mbps Ethernet network to achieve, it can be provided by 16-Mbps Token Ring, 100-Mbps Fast Ethernet, and other higher-speed technologies.

## 7.8 VIDEO COMPRESSION

Video compression is a process whereby a collection of algorithms and techniques replace the original pixel-related information with more compact mathematical descriptions. Decompression is the reverse process of decoding the mathematical descriptions back to pixels for display. At its best, video compression is transparent to the end user. The true measure of a video compression scheme is how little the end user notices its presence, or how effectively it can reduce video data rates without adversely affecting video quality. An example of post-digitization video compression is shown in Figure: Post-digitization video compression.

With the increasing accessibility of technology for everyday people, things are starting to get digitalized: digital camera, digital cable, digital sound, and digital video. It is no longer the case where a video production is only possible for specialized studios. The availability of various user-friendly, inexpensive tools is pushing motion pictures into individual computer owners.

Digital video refers to the capturing, manipulation, and storage of moving images that can be displaced on computer screens (The Lycos Tech Glossary, 1999). This requires that the moving images be digitally handled by the computer. The word digital refers to a system based on discontinuous events, as opposed to analog, a continuous event.

Computers are digital systems; they do not process images the way the human eye does. Animations and digital video movies are sequences of bitmapped graphic scenes (frames), rapidly played back. But animations can also be made within the authoring system by rapidly changing the location of objects or sprites to generate an appearance of motion. Most authoring tools adopt either a frame-or object-oriented approach to animation, but rarely both. Before the Digital Era, to display analog video images on a computer monitor, the video signal had to first be converted from analog to digital form. A special video digitalizing overlay board or hardware on the motherboard had to be installed in your computer to take the video signal and convert it to digital information (Vaughan, 1998). To do this, however, required a very powerful computer to be able to read and digitalize every frame repetitively.

In order to edit video in the computer or to embed video clips into multimedia documents, a video source must originate from a digital camera or be converted to digital. Frames from analog video cameras and VCRs are converted into digital frames (bitmaps) using frame grabbers or similar devices attached to a computer. Uncompressed digital video signals require huge amounts of storage, and high- ratio real-time compression schemes, such as MPEG, are essential for handling digital video in today's computers.

Movie-making tools take advantage of QuickTime (Macintosh) and Microsoft Video for Windows (also known as AVI, or Audio Video Interleaved) technology and let you create, edit, and present digitized motion video segments, usually in a small window in your project.

To make movies from video you need special hardware to convert the analog video signal to digital data. Movie-making tools such as Premiere, VideoShop, and MediaStudio Pro let you edit and assemble video clips captured from camera, tape, other digitized movie segments, animation, scanned images, and from digitized audio or MIDI files. The completed clip, often with added transition and visual effects, can then be played back-either stand-alone or windowed within your project.

So the next step in digital video evolution was to eliminate the analog videotape. Thus, the entire procedure, including the capturing of video, is in digital form. First, a camera and a microphone capture the picture and sounds of a video session and send analog signals to a video-capture adapter board. The board only captures half of the number of frames per second that movies use in order to reduce the amount of data to be processed. Second, there is an analog-to-digital converter chip on the video-capture adapter card, and it converts the analog signals (waves) to digital patterns (0s and 1s). Third, a compression/decompression chip or software reduces the data to a minimum necessary for recreating the video signals (White, 1999). In this procedure, no analog was involved, making the process more efficient.

Famous digital video formats are DTV, HDTV and MPEG. However, digital signal formats with higher quality have been adopted, including serial digital interface (SDI), Firewire (IEEE1394), DVI and HDMI.

### 7.8.1 Advantages of digital videos

Here are three of many reasons that explain why digital videos are becoming more popular than ever.

**(1) Ease of manipulation.**

The difference between analog and digital is like comparing a typewriter with a word processor. Just like the cut and paste function is much easier and faster with a word processor, editing is easier and faster with a digital video. Also, many effects that were exclusive for specialized post production houses are now easily achieved by bringing in files from Photoshop, Flash, and Sound Edit as components in a video mix (Seecharan, 1999). In addition, the ability to separate sound from image enables editing one without affecting the other.

**(2) Preservation of data**

It is not true that DV is better simply because it is digital. Big screen films are not digital and are still highly esteemed as quality images. However, it is easier to maintain the quality of a digital video. Traditional tapes are subject to wear and tear more so than DVD or hard drive disks. Also, once done, a digital video can be copied over and over without losing its original information. Analog signals can be easily distorted and will lose much of the original data after a few transfers.

**(3) Internet**

A digital video can be sent via the Internet to countless end users without having to make a copy for every viewer. It is easy to store, retrieve, and publish.

**(4) Compression**

Digital video files can be very large. For example, one single frame from a television image with a resolution of 720 x 576 pixels and a color depth of 16 bits has a size of 1.35 MB (Fisher & Schroeder, 1999). Multiply that by 25 frame per second and then by the duration of a movie! It is not practical—sometimes impossible—to have videos of this size. Thus compression, the process of reducing file size by eliminating unnecessary data for reconstruction purposes, is a must.

There are two types of compression, "lossless" and "lossy". The lossless compression retains the original data so that the individual image sequences remain the same. It saves space by removing image areas that use the same color. The compression rate is usually no better than 3:1. The low rate makes most lossless compression less desirable. The "lossy" compression methods remove image and sound information that is unlikely to be noticed by the viewer. Some information is lost, but since it is not differentiated by the human perception, the quality perceived is still the same, while the volume is dramatically decreased.

### 7.8.2 Digital video via Internet

Due to the size of some large video files and the limited bandwidth, transmission of video and audio data via the Internet is only possible using streaming technology. The current big players in the streaming media business are Real Networks and Microsoft. But, it was big communication companies such as CNN who fist offered this technology. Now Real Network's Real Audio and Real video streaming formats are the pseudo standards (Fisher & Schroeder).

### 7.8.3 Integrating digital video into a Web Page

There are some pros and cons in putting a video on a web page. For one, it could be very compelling and could really enhance the interest level of the site, thus attract people to view the page. On the other hand, poorly designed video (or animation, for that matter), can distract viewers. If your video is too large, it will take a long time to load, and the viewer will grow impatient waiting on a blank screen and will move on to another web site. A good rule of thumb is to not let video be the only way to access information.

Offer alternatives: preview clips with lower resolution and shorter duration, a still picture with some captions, exported sound files, movies of smaller size windows (Waters, 1997). For example, if you have four videos on a page, by showing a still image of each with a sentence or two describing the video you would allow the viewer to decide which they wanted to take the time to watch and would not need to start streaming the ones in which they are not interested. Because of the limited bandwidth and the traffic load on the net, it is important to compress a digital video file as much as feasible in order to deliver good quality video. However, do not take a movie that's already compressed for CD ROM and re- compress it for the web. Compress the originally captured files with light or no compression and reedit and compress those, to ensure quality (Stern & Lettieri, 1998). Another tip is if the video you plan to use on a page uses a smaller window than the original, reduce the window before you compress it to get a smaller file. As far as color, if the compressor lets you choose the number of colors, choose the greatest number. Lowering the number of colors generally doesn't lower your final file size enough, but you might lose the quality of colors and lighting in the final product. Nevertheless, if you know that your video uses 256 colors, there is no need to go beyond that (Stern & Lettieri). To post the video on a web page, you need to make sure the server is configured for the format you are using. For example, if you use a QuickTime movie, the server needs to have a listing for QuickTime files in its configuration files. Many times this step is automated, sometimes in default format and you need not worry about it. Then, to attach the video by using HTML, include an EMBED tag in your code when and where you want the video to appear:

Code Segment

```
<HTML>
<BODY>
<EMBED SRC= "my _ video.mov" WIDTH=320 HEIGHT=256>
</BODY>
</HTML>
```

You may be using web authoring tools that enable you to skip the codes and use other mechanisms (icons, for example), to "attach" the video to your web design. This is only the beginning of posting a video to a page. There are many other features—some of them highly advanced—that can be added to a digital video online either through the HTML codes or through the video production application program , which are beyond the scope of this paper. Most video cameras still use an analogue image device which will go through a conversion stage known as sampling. The higher the sampling depth the higher the 'fidelity' of the digital signal, even cheap basic miniDv camcorders can reproduce millions of colours. Digital footage can be easily transported to a computer for editing be it through a firewire for DV format, or through a USB for dvd, hard drive and solid state cameras. Professional cameras such as XDCAM, DigiBeta, DVCPRO all sample more colours and use a 'serial digital interface. It is also easier to store digital movies on a hard drive than analogue movies on tape. MiniDV uses a spatial compression, where colour sampling takes place within an individual frame, newer formats like AVCHD, HDV, and DVD use a combination of spatial and temporal sampling where colours are sampled across many frames to save space. There is no doubt it is a digital world, although some developing countries still use analogue, I know this because my company has just sold some betacamSP format gear to a company that ships them to South Africa and Oceania. Betacam SP was the main broadcast format during the 80s and early 90s. In short digital is now cheap, easy to work with with non-linear editing (non destructive, changes can be easily redone) and everywhere. The old ways of watching telly over an analogue arial are dead, more folk are watching telly through 3G on their phone or MPEG2 terrestrial digital broadcasting or even on youtube or vimeo.

## 7.9 DIFFERENCE BETWEEN DIGITAL AND ANALOG RECORDING

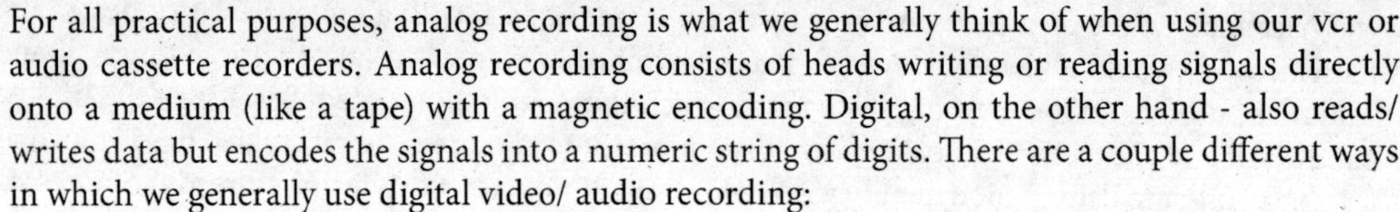

For all practical purposes, analog recording is what we generally think of when using our vcr or audio cassette recorders. Analog recording consists of heads writing or reading signals directly onto a medium (like a tape) with a magnetic encoding. Digital, on the other hand - also reads/ writes data but encodes the signals into a numeric string of digits. There are a couple different ways in which we generally use digital video/ audio recording:

1. Directly onto a computer's magnetic hard drive through a variety of compression formats- such as in PC (Windows) based systems and embedded OS / Linux based systems such as our DVR-RT4X, or;
2. Onto a magnetic tape cassette, as used with mini decks (Sony's GVD-200 and GVD-800) and new digital camcorders. The major tape formats found in new digital camcorders are Sony's 'Digital 8' or the more common 'Mini-DV'. No analog equipment will record or playback digital media, but some digital units (GVD-200/ 800) do have the ability to playback analog format(s). 8mm, Hi-8 and VHS-C are the standard tape formats for today's analog camcorders.

Mini decks and camcorders are used in limited covert and mobile uses for short-term recording, but are generally not considered part of the security / surveillance industry. Please click here to see a terrific miniature digital video recorder made for portable use.

Digital technology has become much more stable and reliable in the last 2 or 3 years and is quickly replacing analog video recording to the point of impending extinction. If you didn't rush into anything- and are still clinging to your worn out old timelapse VCR- there's no better time than **NOW** to upgrade it. Prices have finally become **AFFORDABLE** for a product which is actually both reliable **AND** user friendly.

One KEY advantage to DIGITAL is its higher resolution ability. Depending on features of individual unit, you may be able to achieve 480+ horizontal lines recording with digital recorders vs. 300 lines color (350 bw) with the highest quality analog units (such as our high band/ high density Sanyo models). Most analog recorders permit only about 280 lines for black and white and 240 lines for color.

Analog recording can still be argued to be little reliable due to the fact that a videotape (mechanical) drive system is not likely to "crash" like a computer hard drive or operating system might, risking some or all data to irretrievable loss. And many security professionals are using redundancy systems with a digital recorder as the primary system- backed up by a high density/ high resolution analog VCR.

## 7.10 ADVANTAGES AND DISADVANTAGES OF DIGITAL AND ANALOG RECORDING

In order to edit video in the computer or to embed video clips into multimedia documents, a video source must originate as digital (digital camera) or be converted to digital. Frames from analog video cameras and VCRs are converted into digital frames (bitmaps) using frame grabbers or similar devices attached to a personal computer. Uncompressed digital video signals require huge amounts of storage, and high-ratio real-time compression schemes, such as MPEG, are essential for handling digital video in today's computers.

Analogue video is in theory more accurate as the signal is infinitely variable, in practice there are very few if any analogue video cameras in production anymore, the problem comes in when editing, as you have to make analogue to analogue copies, the analogue signal doesn't hold up to repeated copying, whereas a digital signal does. It is far easier to exactly replicate a digital waveform than an analogue waveform.

Digital is certainly the way ALL video recording will be done in the future (and likely the very near future). However, it does still have some drawbacks to consider. Many systems have low frame speed ability per camera when recording multiple cameras at once. Analog recording is still generally considered a little more reliable due to the fact that a videotape (mechanical) drive system is not likely to "crash" like a computer hard drive or operating system might, risking some or all data to irretrievable loss. Most PROFESSIONAL security people will employ BOTH nowadays- generally a digital recorder connected to a (high bandwidth/ high resolution) VCR as a redundant 'backup' system.

DVRs must really be separated into 2 main categories: **PC-based** and **Linux-based** operating systems (OS). Think about it... how many times has your PC 'crashed' due to a glitch or flaw in Windows systems or programs?! Don't you want potentially life-saving evidence to be recorded into a stable and re-accessible format? We waited, watched and learned while a lot of our competition jumped right into advertising their own PC based systems. Most quickly found that they. *Even though we are highly impressed with the new Linux systems, there are great strides being currently made to bypass an operating system altogether by compressing the video through on-board hardware logic rather than any kind of software. Stay tuned but please don't let this hold you back from upgrading right now to a stable Linux-based embedded OS system.

One **KEY** advantage to **DIGITAL** is its higher resolution ability. Depending on features of individual unit, you may be able to achieve 480+ horizontal lines of color recording with digital vs. 300 lines color (350 black & white) with the highest quality analog units (such as our high band/ high density models). Little known fact- most analog VCR video recorders permit only about 280 lines BW and 240 lines of color recording- no kidding! Even for expensive consumer and security '4- head' systems. Why are there separate resolution abilities for color and black & white? Because color requires more bandwidth as it is encoding and decoding more data at one time. Audio (especially mono) requires very little bandwidth at all in comparison to video, even BW/ monochrome. Please SEE our newest 4 camera digital recorder (#DVR-RT-4X) for a really DYNAMITE unit! It has all the features of several separate and advanced units all in one.

## 7.11 FULL-MOTION VIDEO

For the first few years of its existence, the PC was a text-only device. As users' needs increased and the technology improved, graphics became commonplace on the computer screen.

Graphics are now viewed as a prerequisite for virtually all PCs, and our insatiable appetite for PCs that can do more and more has led us into the age of so-called "multimedia". Most people use PCs today that can show not just graphics but sound, animation and full-motion video as well.

The term "multimedia" is, unfortunately, one of those buzzwords that means different things depending on who says it and what they are talking about. It generally refers to the use of software that incorporates elements of sound, graphics and moving video (animation or recorded).

Many games today use video to add realism to the gaming experience. In particular, many games use video to make them more "cinematic"; these games are often a cross between a movie and a classical computer game. They are sometimes called "interactive movies" in fact.

## 7.12 VIDEO PERFORMANCE ISSUES

The idea of playing a movie or TV program on the PC is a relatively new one, and these applications make demands on the performance of a PC system that few others do. The main problem is the sheer volume of data that is involved. Let's suppose that we wanted to display a 2-hour movie in high-quality, high-resolution graphics. To keep things from getting out of hand, let's choose just 640 x 480 resolution in high color (16 bits per pixel) instead of going "all out" to say, 1024x768 in true color. Full-motion video typically means 30 frames per second. To store the data required for a full-motion, two-hour movie using these parameters, would require approximately 133 GB. (That's not a typo—133 billion bytes, and that doesn't include sound.) Also, the data to support this video stream would need to be pumped to the video card at the rate of about 150 million bits per second. In ten years these numbers won't seem like that big of a deal but of course, right now they sure are.

There is a solution to this dilemma: data compression. Due to the nature of the data, video can be easily compressed by a large factor. There are several reasons for this:

Every image that is displayed has large areas of redundancy that can be represented by a smaller amount of data using an encoding algorithm. For example, if the bottom half of the screen in a particular frame is black, that can be represented using a small number of bytes; we don't need to have 150,000 two-byte pixels all filled with zeroes.

The human eye is not sensitive to certain details in a video, which can be removed without appreciable loss to the perceived signal. If you take any two consecutive frames, the changes from one to the next are usually rather small. For example, if you have a scene centered on someone's face, the background images are probably going to remain static for hundreds or thousands of consecutive frames. There are special algorithms that can describe a frame only by the changes that it represents from the one before, which dramatically cuts down both on the amount of storage required and the time to transmit each frame of data.

## 7.13 CODECS

The basic engine that drives multimedia transmission, particularly in the videoconferencing industry, is the codec (coder-decoder), which is the video counterpart of a modem. Codecs take analog audio and video signals from video cameras and other sources, digitize them, and compress the digital values for transmission at lower bandwidth. At the receiving end codecs decompress the digitized signals, convert them back to analog, and transmit them to audio and video output devices. Current codecs operate with 384-Kbps lines, which represent a compression rate of 230:1, and some codecs also operate with 112-Kbps circuits, which means compression rates of 800:1. The highest-quality codecs offer more than 175,000 pixels-per-frame resolution, which is a measure of video quality that is so critical in multimedia video applications. This is close to top-quality-broadcast TV video quality, which ranges from 190,000 to 200,000 pixels per frame.

The quality of video images also depends on how often the screen is refreshed; the standard TV video is 30 fps frames (per minute). Codecs reduce the frame rate to 15, 10 or even 5 fps depending on the amount of motion, but most codec vendors claim a maximum potential of 30 fps. In general users cannot perceive a difference in video quality until the frame rate falls to about 18 to 16 fps. At rates typically offered over the 112-and 128-Kbps circuits, the frame rates are in the order of 10 to 15 fps, and some deterioration of video quality is noticeable when fast and continuous motion is involved. Pre and post processing of the data and motion compensation techniques further reduce the amount of data handled by codecs, and these methods are key in providing acceptable video quality in 112- and 128-Kbps facilities, which are also available at lower tariffs than those with higher bandwith.9. What can be accomplished using a photoediting program?

## 7.14 VIDEO COMPRESSION

### 7.14.1 Large amounts of Data

If we try to calculate the amount of data in the video images, we will probably be rather surprised. Images take a lot of room. The file contains 165 frames, which each take up 640 x 480 pixels. The colour depth is 24 bits and this means that every bit takes up 3 bytes.

So a single image takes up 640 x 480 x 3 bytes = 921.600 bytes, almost a whole megabyte "raw" bit map data per frame.With 165 frames, we have a total amount of data altogether of 145 MB, as seen in Figure 7.7. An image track contains a lot of data.

| Image | Amount of raw data |
|---|---|
| 165 frames, 640 × 480 pixels, 24 bits colour | 165 × 640 × 480 × 3 bytes = 145 MB |

#### Compression

So the basis material for a digital video takes up an enormous amount of space, if we are looking at "raw" uncompressed audio and image data. Just a few minutes' recording can produce enormously large files. This is why data is nearly always compressed.

The little webcam in the example encodes all the audio and image data together into a file of about 4,5 MB, which isn't so much compared with the amount of data we have just worked out. You can read in Figure 128 that video compression is carried out with Indeo Video 5. This is a video codec from the company Intel, which the camera's software uses. And the compression is effective, as shown in figure 7.8:

| Track | Amount of data |
|---|---|
| Audio, uncompressed | 190. 226 bytes |
| Images, uncompressed | 152.064.000 bytessss |
| Combined, uncompressed | 152.254.226 bytes |
| Combined, compressed AVI file | 4.695.552 bytes |

**Fig. 7.8:** A compressed file takes up a lot less space than the data it, in fact, contains.

Obviously, the *proportions of the compression* ought to be looked at. The uncompressed amount of data of 152.254.226 bytes can be divided by the file size of 4.695.552 bytes. This gives the number 32,4. So the video has been compressed in the ratio of 32: 1. This is a very heavy compression but necessary.

Encoding data to take up less storage space. Digital data is compressed by finding repeatable patterns of binary 0s and 1s. The more patterns can be found, the more the data can be compressed. Text can generally be compressed to about 40% of its original size, and graphics files from 20% to 90%. Some files compress very little. It depends entirely on the type of file and compression algorithm used. Video compression refers to reducing the quantity of data used to represent digital video images, and is a combination of spatial image compression and temporal motion compensation. Video compression is an example of the concept of source coding in Information theory. Video is basically a three-dimensional array of color pixels. Two dimensions serve as spatial (horizontal and vertical) directions of the moving pictures, and one dimension represents the time domain. A data frame is a set of all pixels that correspond to a single time moment. Basically, a frame is the same as a still picture.

Video data contains spatial and temporal redundancy. Similarities can thus be encoded by merely registering differences within a frame (spatial), and/or between frames (temporal). Spatial encoding is performed by taking advantage of the fact that the human eye is unable to distinguish small differences in color as easily as it can perceive changes in brightness, so that very similar areas of color can be "averaged out" in a similar way to jpeg images (JPEG image compression FAQ, part 1/2). With temporal compression only the changes from one frame to the next are encoded as often a large number of the pixels will be the same on a series of frames.

There are numerous compression methods in use. Two major technologies are:

1. Huffman coding and
2. Lempel-Ziv-Welch (LZW),

representing examples of the statistical and dictionary compression methods. When a compression algorithm is packaged for use for a specific platform and file format, it is called a codec (compressor/ decompressor). ADPCM, PCM and GSM are examples of codecs for sound, and Indeo, Cinepak and MPEG are examples of codecs for video. In the DOS/Windows world, PKZIP is the most widely-used compression application.

## 7.14.2 Lossy Compression Techniques

A wide range of lossy compression techniques is available for digital video. This simple rule applies to all of them: the higher the compression ratio, the higher the loss. As the loss increases, so does the number of artifacts. (An artifact is a portion of a video image for which there is little or no information.)

In addition to lossy compression techniques, video compression involves the use of two other compression techniques:

- Interframe compression-Compression between frames (also known as temporal compression because the compression is applied along the time dimension).
- Intraframe compression-Compression within individual frames (also known as spatial *compression*).

Some video compression algorithms use both interframe and intraframe compression. For example, Motion Picture Experts Group (MPEG) uses Joint Photographic Experts Group (JPEG), which is an intrafame technique, and a separate interframe algorithm. Motion-JPEG (M-JPEG) uses only intraframe compression.

### 7.14.3 Interframe Compression

Interframe compression uses a system of key and delta frames to eliminate redundant information between frames. Key frames store an entire frame, and delta frames record only changes. Some implementations compress the key frames, and others don't. Either way, the key frames serve as a reference source for delta frames. Delta frames contain only pixels that are different from the key frame or from the immediately preceding delta frame. During decompression, delta frames look back to their respective reference frames to fill in missing information.

Different compression techniques use different sequences of key and delta frames. For example, most video for Windows CODECs calculate interframe differences between sequential delta frames during compression. In this case, only the first delta frame relates to the key frame. Each subsequent delta frame relates to the immediately preceding delta frame. In other compression schemes, such as MPEG, all delta frames relate to the preceding key frame.

All interframe compression techniques derive their effectiveness from interframe redundancy. Low-motion video sequences, such as the head and shoulders of a person, have a high degree of redundancy, which limits the amount of compression required to reduce the video to the target bandwidth.

Until recently, interframe compression has addressed only pixel blocks that remained static between the delta and the key frame. Some new CODECs increase compression by tracking moving blocks of pixels from frame to frame. This technique is called motion compensation (also known as dynamic carry forwards) because the data that is carried forward from key frames is dynamic. Consider a video clip in which a person is waving an arm. If only static pixels are tracked between frames, no interframe compression occurs with respect to the moving parts of the person because those parts are not located in the same pixel blocks in both frames. If the CODEC can track the motion of the arm, the delta frame description tells the decompressor to look for particular moving parts in other pixel blocks, essentially tracking the moving part as it moves from one pixel block to another.

Although dynamic carry forwards are helpful, they cannot always be implemented. In many cases, the capture board cannot scale resolution and frame rate, digitize, and hunt for dynamic carry forwards at the same time.

Dynamic-carry forwards typically mark the dividing line between hardware and software CODECs. Hardware CODECs, as the name implies, are usually add-on boards that provide additional hardware compression and decompression operations. The benefit of hardware CODECs is that they do not place any additional burden on the host CPU in order to execute video compression and decompression.

Software CODECs rely on the host CPU and require no additional hardware. The benefit of software CODECs is that they are typically cheaper and easier to install. Because they rely on the host's CPU to perform compression and decompression, software CODECs are often limited in their capability to use techniques such as advanced tracking schemes.

### 7.14.4 Intraframe Compression

Intraframe compression is performed solely with reference to information within a particular frame. It is performed on pixels in delta frames that remain after interframe compression and on key frames. Although intraframe techniques are often given the most attention, overall CODEC performance relates more to interframe efficiency than intraframe efficiency. The following are the principal intraframe compression techniques:

- Run Length Encoding (RLE)-A simple lossless technique originally designed for data compression and later modified for facsimile. RLE compresses an image based on "runs" of pixels. Although it works well on black-and-white facsimiles, RLE is not very efficient for color video, which have few long runs of identically colored pixels.
- JPEG-A standard that has been adopted by two international standards organizations: the ITU (formerly CCITT) and the ISO. JPEG is most often used to compress still images using discrete cosine transform (DCT) analysis. First, DCT divides the image into 8¥8 blocks and then converts the colors and pixels into frequency space by describing each block in terms of the number of color shifts (frequency) and the extent of the change (amplitude). Because most natural images are relatively smooth, the changes that occur most often have low amplitude values, so the change is minor. In other words, images have many subtle shifts among similar colors but few dramatic shifts between very different colors. Next, quantization and amplitude values are categorized by frequency and averaged. This is the lossy stage because the original values are permanently discarded. However, because most of the picture is categorized in the high-frequency/low-amplitude range, most of the loss occurs among subtle shifts that are largely indistinguishable to the human eye. After quantization, the values are further compressed through RLE using a special zigzag pattern designed to optimize compression of like regions within the image. At extremely high compression ratios, more high-frequency/low-amplitude changes are averaged, which can cause an entire pixel block to adopt the same color. This causes a blockiness artifact that is characteristic of JPEG-compressed images. JPEG is used as the intraframe technique for MPEG.
- Vector quantization (VQ)-A standard that is similar to JPEG in that it divides the image into 8¥8 blocks. The difference between VQ and JPEG has to do with the quantization process. VQ is a recursive, or multistep algorithm with inherently self-correcting features. With VQ, similar blocks are categorized and a reference block is constructed for each category. The original blocks are then discarded. During decompression, the single reference block replaces all of the original blocks in the category. After the first set of reference blocks is selected, the image is decompressed. Comparing the decompressed image to the original reveals many differences. To address the differences, an additional set of reference blocks is created that fills in the gaps created during the first estimation. This is the self-correcting part of the algorithm. The process is repeated to find a third set of reference blocks to fill in the remaining gaps. These reference blocks are posted in a lookup table to be used during decompression. The final step is to use lossless techniques, such as RLE, to further compress the remaining information. VQ compression is by its nature computationally intensive. However, decompression, which simply involves pulling values from the lookup table, is simple and fast. VQ is a public-domain algorithm used as the intraframe technique for both Cinepak and Indeo.

### 7.14.5 End-User Video Compression Algorithms

The following are the most popular end-user video compression algorithms. Note that some algorithms require dedicated hardware.

1. MPEG1-A bit stream standard for compressed video and audio optimized to fit into a bandwidth of 1.5 Mbps. This rate is special because it is the data rate of uncompressed audio

CDs and DATs. Typically, MPEG1 is compressed in non-real time and decompressed in real time. MPEG1 compression is typically performed in hardware; MPEG1 decompression can be performed in software or in hardware.

2. MPEG2-A standard intended for higher quality video-on-demand applications for products such as the "set top box." MPEG2 runs at data rates between 4 and 9 Mbps. MPEG2 and variants are being considered for use by regional Bell carriers and cable companies to deliver video-on-demand to the home as well as for delivering HDTV broadcasts. MPEG2 chip sets that perform real-time encoding are available. Real-time MPEG2 decompression boards are also available. A specification for MPEG2 adaptation over ATM AAL5 has been developed.
3. MPEG4-A low-bit-rate compression algorithm intended for 64-Kbps connections. MPEG4 can be used for a wide range of applications including mobile audio, visual applications, and electronic newspaper sources.
4. M-JPEG (Motion-JPEG)-The aggregation of a series of JPEG-compressed images. M-JPEG can be implemented in software or in hardware.
5. Cell B-Part of a family of compression techniques developed by Sun Microsystems. Cell B is designed for real-time applications, such as videoconferencing, that require real-time video transmission. Cell A is a counterpart of Cell B that is intended for non-real time applications where encoding does not need to take place in real time. Both Cell A and Cell B use VQ and RLE techniques.
6. Indeo-Developed by Intel. Indeo uses VQ as its intraframe engine. Intel has released three versions of Indeo:
   a. Indeo 2.1-Focused on Intel's popular capture board, the Smart Video Recorder, using intraframe compression.
   b. Indeo 3.1-Introduced in late 1993 and incorporated interframe compression.
   c. Indeo 3.2-Requires a hardware add-on for video compression but decompression can take place in software on a high-end 486 or Pentium processor.
7. Cinepak-Developed by SuperMatch, a division of SuperMac Technologies. Cinepak was first introduced as a Macintosh CODEC and then migrated to the Windows platform in 1993. Like Indeo, Cinepak uses VQ as its intraframe engine. Of all the CODECs, Cinepak offers the widest cross-platform support, with versions for 3D0, Nintendo, and Atari platforms.
8. Apple Video-A compression technique used by applications such as Apple Computer's QuickTime Conferencing.
9. H.261-The compression standard specified under the H.320 videoconferencing standard. H.261 describes the video coding and decoding methods for the moving picture component of audio-visual services at the rate of p * 64 Kbps, where p is in the range 1 to 30. It describes the video source coder, the video multiplex coder, and the transmission coder. H.261 defines two picture formats:
   a. Common Intermediate Format (CIF)-Specifies 288 lines of luminance information (with 360 pixels per line) and 144 lines of chrominance information (with 180 pixels per line).
   b. Quarter Common Intermediate Format (QCIF)-Specifies 144 lines of luminance (with 180 pixels per line) and 72 lines of chrominance information (with 90 pixels per line). The choice between CIF and QCIF depends on available channel capacity-that is, QCIF is normally used when p is less than 3.

The actual encoding algorithm of H.261 is similar to (but incompatible with) MPEG. Also, H.261 needs substantially less CPU power for real-time encoding than MPEG. The H.261 algorithm includes a mechanism for optimizing bandwidth usage by trading picture quality against motion so that a quickly changing picture has a lower quality than a relatively static picture. When used in this way, H.261 is a constant-bit-rate encoding rather than a constant-quality, variable-bit-rate encoding.

### 7.14.6 Hardware Versus Software CODECs

In many cases, the network multimedia application dictates the video compression algorithm used. For example, Intel's ProShare videoconferencing application uses the Indeo standard or H.261, and Insoft Communique! uses Cell B compression. In some cases, such as Apple Computer's QuickTime Conferencing, the end user can specify the compression algorithm.

In general, the more CPU cycles given to video compression and decompression, the better the performance. This can be achieved either by running less expensive software CODECs on fast CPUs (Pentium, PowerPC, or RISC processors) or by investing more money in dedicated hardware add-ons such as an MPEG playback board. In some cases, the application dictates hardware or software compression and decompression. Insoft's INTV! video multicast package, for instance, uses a hardware-based compressor in the UNIX workstation, but uses a software-based decompressor for the PC workstations. The implication is that to use INTV, the PCs might need to be upgraded to deliver the requisite processing capabilities.

## 7.15 COMPRESSION RATIOS

Any of the compression standards discussed in this article are helpful in reducing the amount of bandwidth needed to transmit digital video. In fact, digital video can be compressed up to 20:1 and still deliver a VHS-quality picture. Table: 7.2 shows digital video compression ratios and the approximate quality that they yield in terms of video formats.

**TABLE 7.2:** Image Quality as a Function of Compression Ratio

| Video Compression Ratio | Analog Picture Quality Equivalent |
|---|---|
| 20:1 | VHS |
| 10:1 | SVHS/HI-8 |
| 04:1 | Broadcast quality |

As Image Quality as a Function of Compression Ratio indicates, fairly high video compression ratios can be used while still preserving high-quality video images. For example, a typical MPEG1 video stream (640 * 480, 30 frames per second) runs at 1.5 Mbps.

### 7.15.1 Lossless versus Lossy

When text and financial data are compressed, they must be decompressed back to a perfect original, bit for bit. This is known as lossless compression . However, audio and video can be compressed to as little as 5% of its original size using lossy compression. Some of the data is actually lost, but the loss is not noticeable to the human ear and eye.

### 7.15.2 Archive Files

Archives are files that contain other files. Typically the files in an archive are compressed. Archives usually have file names ending with ZIP, LZH, ARJ, or ARC, depending on how they were created. Archives make it easy to group files and make transporting and copying these files faster.

### 7.15.3 Typical Uses for Archives:

Most files available in "file areas" on bulletin boards and electronic services like CompuServe and the Internet are distributed as archives. Two benefits of using archives for electronic file distribution are that only one file transfer operation ("download") is required to obtain all related files, and file transfer time is minimized because the files in an archive are compressed. It is often useful to send a group of related files to an associate. Rather than distributing individual files it is often easier to distribute the files as an archive to benefit from the file grouping and compression.

Some files are important but not used often. To save disk space simply compress these files into an archive when they are not used, and decompress them only when needed.

### 7.15.4 Self-Extracting Zip File

A self-extracting Zip file is an executable program file (.EXE file) that includes both a Zip file and software to extract or "unzip" the contents of the Zip file. Users can extract the contents of a self-extracting Zip file by simply running it. This is convenient, because the end user does not need an unzip program (like WinZip) to extract files from these self-extracting archives. WinZip Self-Extractor Personal Edition, included with WinZip, creates native Windows self-extracting Zip files. You can also create self-extracting ARJ and LZH files.

### 7.15.5 Archive formats:

**Zip** files are the most common archive format. WinZip does not use external programs to work with Zip files.

**ARJ** files are another popular archive format. ARJ files are manipulated by the ARJ program from ARJ Software, P.O. Box 249, Norwood, Massachusetts 02062.

**LZH** files are manipulated by the LHA program from Haruyasu Yoshizaki. LHA won the October 1991 PC Magazine Editor's Choice award as the best data compression utility.

**ARC** is an older format. ARC files can be manipulated by several programs, including the original ARC, ARCE (also known as ARC-E), PKXARC, and PKUNPAK. Since almost all new archives are created in other formats and there is no single widely available program to manipulate ARC files, WinZip does not provide facilities to add to ARC files (however, all other WinZip functions are supported). *TAR, Z, GZ, TAZ, and TGZ* files are often found on Unix-based Internet sites. The relationship between these file types is less straightforward than the aforementioned file formats. The important thing to remember is that WinZip handles all these formats the same way as Zip files, so you don't need to know the details. Here is more information on these formats: TAR stands for "Tape ARchive". This is an old file format and does not provide compression; it is used only to group files. Z files are compressed with gzip or the older Unix "compress" program. GZ files are gzip files. Z and GZ files cannot contain multiple files. TAZ and TGZ files are TAR files compressed in "Z" or "GZ" format. Since almost all new archives are created in Zip format WinZip does not provide facilities to add to or create files in these formats (however, all other WinZip functions are supported). WinZip does not require external programs when working with files in these formats.

**UUencoded, XXencoded, BinHex, and MIME** files are used primarily to transfer binary files by Internet e-mail. If you encounter one of these files, you can open it and extract its contents with WinZip. You can UUencode an archive using the UUencode entry in the WinZip Actions pull-down menu. WinZip also handles many files in the Microsoft Compress format (also known as LZEXPAND format). However, there are several variations on this format, and Microsoft has not released documentation on these variations. Therefore, you are limited to decompressing files supported by your version of Windows (Windows for Workgroups supports some files not supported by Windows 3.1).

WinZip issues an appropriate message if you attempt to decompress a file not supported by your version of Windows. Microsoft Compress files usually end with a trailing underscore, for example, "commdlg.dl_". Like Z and GZ files, Microsoft Compress format files contain only one file. This format is used for many files on your Windows 3.x distribution disks and many other Microsoft products. Note that not all files ending with an underscore are Microsoft Compress format files.

## 7.16 STANDARD VIDEO COMPRESSION STANDARDS AND FILE FORMAT

Standard formats make it easier for software developers and equipment manufacturers to produce products that are less costly and more compatible with each other. The compatibility provided by standard formats helps assure consumers that their music and equipment won't become obsolete. Cassette tapes, compact discs and PCM are examples of standard audio formats that benefit both consumers and manufacturers.

Following are the three most popular video cum audio formats:

a. MPEG
b. AVI
c. Quick time

### 7.16.1 Moving Picture Experts Group (MPEG)

MPEG(pronounced em-peg) stands for Moving Picture Experts Group. The term is generally used to name the set of digital video compression standards and file formats developed by this group. MPEG uses lossy compression, and achieves a high compression rate by storing only the changes from one frame to another (the delta), and not the entire frame. There are two major standards. The most popular compressed video format is MPEG, which stands for the Motion Pictures Expert Group, the body that defined the standard. MPEG can typically compress as high as 100 to 1, bringing our 2-hour movie down to a much more manageable 1.33 GB. To use MPEG the video must be encoded using an MPEG encoder, and then viewed using an MPEG decoder. Not surprisingly, MPEG has its own problems. The chief one is that the process of encoding and decoding takes a lot of processing power, which is why dedicated MPEG encoding and decoding hardware is used for high-performance applications.

There are several ways that MPEG (or other video) files can be played on a PC. In every case, the process involves reading the file, decompressing the video data, and then feeding it to the video card for display on the monitor. Since the data is compressed to reduce storage, it must be uncompressed to restore it to a visible image. This takes a great deal of processing power. There are software programs that can be used to decode these files, allowing you to play an MPEG file on your computer. As with every other case where an application takes a lot of processing power, it is more efficient (but more costly) to let dedicated hardware do the function. This is the purpose of an MPEG Decoder. Much as is the case with 3D accelerators, it is possible to get a dedicated card for MPEG decoding, or to get a regular video card that has an MPEG decoder built into it. Dedicated MPEG decoders come with different capabilities. They often use the video feature connector on the regular video card, to supply video information directly to the card without tying up the system bus with an enormous amount of video data.

**Warning**: Beware of some video cards that advertise that they "support MPEG decoding" when all they mean is that they will work with a software MPEG decoder. Many of these cards aren't doing hardware decoding at all. They still may provide acceptable performance, but make sure you know what you are buying. The quality of MPEG decoders varies, with generally the more expensive ones providing better quality. A high-quality decoder will allow the display of full-screen, smooth video animation while leaving the system CPU free to do other tasks. A cheaper hardware decoding solution, or a software package, may have problems keeping the supply of data to the video card which can result in choppy performance or lost frames. In some cases, this is compensated for by running the video in a small window instead of full-screen, and in others by slowing the frame rate down to less than 30 frames per second. Others reduce the resolution of the screen.

(1) **MPEG-1**

MPEG-1 provides a 352 x 240 resolution at 30 frames per second. The product quality is a little below VCR videos.

(2) **MPEG-2 Compression**

MPEG-2 video compression is the de facto standard for entertainment video. MPEG-2 video compression is popular for a number of reasons:

a) It is an international standard [ISO/IEC IS 13818-2].
b) MPEG-2 places no restrictions on the video encoder implementation. This allows each encoder designer to introduce new techniques to improve compression efficiency and picture quality. Since MPEG-2 video encoders were first introduced in 1993, compression efficiency has improved by 30 to 40%, despite predictions by many that MPEG-2's fundamental theoretical limitations would prevent this.

(3) MPEG-2 fully defines the video decoder's capability at particular levels and profiles. Many MPEG-2 chip-sets are available and will work with any main level at main profile (MP@ML)–compliant MPEG-2 bit-stream from any source.

Nevertheless, quality can change significantly from one MPEG-2 video decoder to another, especially in error handling and video clip transitions.

(4) MPEG-2 video compression is part of a larger standard that includes support for transport and timing functions.

Moreover, MPEG-2 is likely to remain as the dominant standard for entertainment video because it has been so successful in establishing an inventory of standard decoders (both in existing consumer electronics products and in the chip libraries of most large semiconductor companies). Additional momentum comes from the quantity of real-time and stored content already compressed into MPEG-2 format.

Even succeeding work by the MPEG committees has been abandoned (MPEG-3) or retargeted to solve different problems (MPEG-4 and MPEG-7). MPEG-2 is a lossy video compression method based on motion vector estimation, discrete cosine transforms, quantization, and Huffman encoding. (Lossy means that data is lost, or thrown away, during compression, so quality after decoding is less than the original picture.) Taking these techniques in order:

(a) Motion vector estimation is used to capture much of the change between video frames, in the form of best approximations of each part of a frame as a translation (generally due to motion) of a similar-sized piece of another video frame. Essentially, there is a lot of temporal redundancy in video, which can be discarded. (The term temporal redundancy is applied to information that is repeated from one frame to another.)

(b) Discrete cosine transform (DCT) is used to convert spatial information into frequency information. This allows the encoder to discard information, corresponding to higher video frequencies, which are less visible to the human eye.

(c) Quantization is applied to the DCT coefficients of either original frames (in some cases) or the DCT of the residual (after motion estimation) to restrict the set of possible values transmitted by placing them into groups of values that are almost the same.

(d) Huffman encoding uses short codes to describe common values and longer codes to describe rarer values—this is a type of entropy coding.

### 7.16.2 Limitations of using MPEG-2's

Compression ratios cannot be optimized to reduce transmission cost without compromising (too much) on quality. If MPEG-2 is so perfect, why is there any need for other compression schemes? (There are a great many alternative compression algorithms, such as wavelet, pyramid, fractal, and so on.) MPEG-2 is a good solution for coding relatively high-quality video when certain transmission requirements can be met. However, MPEG-2 coding is rarely used in Internet applications because the Internet cannot generally guarantee the quality of service (QoS) parameters required for MPEG-2–coded streams.

**TABLE 7.3:** Recommended Bit Rates for various applicatoins

| Applications | Resolution | Minimum Bit Rate (CBR) |
|---|---|---|
| Movies | 360 × 240 (CIF) | 1.5 Mbps |
| Movies | 360 × 480 (half) | 2 Mbps |
| Movies | 540 × 480 (3/4) | 3 Mbps |
| Movies | 720 × 480 (full) | 4 Mbps |
| Sports (video) | 540 × 480 (3/4) | 5 Mbps |
| Sports (video) | 720 × 480 (full) | 6 Mbps |

As you can see from the table, for entertainment-quality video, MPEG-2 typically requires a reasonably high bit rate, and this bit rate must be guaranteed. Video-coding will, in general, produce a variable information rate, but MPEG-2 allows for CBR transmission facilities (for example, satellite transponders, microwave links, and fiber transmission facilities). As such, MPEG-2 encoders attempt to take advantage of every bit in the transmission link by coding extra detail during less-challenging scenes. When the going gets tough—during a car chase, for example—MPEG-2 encoders use more bits for motion and transmit less detail. Another way to think of this is that MPEG-2 encoding varies its degree of loss according to the source material. Fortunately, the human visual system tends to work in a similar way, and we pay less attention to detail when a scene contains more motion. (This is true of a car chase whether you are watching it or you are in it!)

MPEG-2 coded material is extremely sensitive to errors and lost information because of the way in which MPEG-2 puts certain vital information into a single packet. If this packet is lost or corrupted, there can be a significant impact on the decoder, causing it to drop frames or to produce very noticeable blocking artifacts. If you think of an MPEG-2 stream as a list of instructions to the decoder, you can understand why the corruption of a single instruction can play havoc with the decoded picture.

Finally, MPEG-2 is extremely sensitive to variations in transmission delay. These are not usually measurable in synchronous transmission systems (for example, satellite links) because each bit propagates through the system according to the clock rate. In packet- or cell-based networks, however, it is possible for each packet-sized group of bits to experience a different delay. MPEG-2 was designed with synchronous transmission links in mind and embeds timing information into certain packets by means of timestamps. If the timestamps experience significant jitter (or cell delay variation), it causes distortions in audio and video fidelity due to timing variations in the sample clocks—for example, color shifts due to color subcarrier phase variations.

### 7.16.3 MPEG-2 Artifacts

What are MPEG artifacts? In practice, all lossy encoders generate artifacts, or areas of unfaithful visual reproduction, all the time; if the encoder is well designed, all these artifacts will be invisible to the human eye. However, the best laid plans sometimes fail; the following are some of the more common MPEG-2 artifacts:

If the compression ratio is too high, there are sometimes simply not enough bits to encode the video signal without significant loss. The better encoders will progressively soften the picture (by discarding some picture detail); however, poorer encoders sometimes break down and overflow an internal buffer. When this happens, all kinds of visual symptoms—from bright green blocks to dropped frames—can result. After such a breakdown, the encoder will usually recover for a short period until once again the information rate gets too high to code into the available number of bits.

Another common visible artifact is sometimes visible in dark scenes or in close-ups of the face and is sometimes called contouring. As the name suggests, the image looks a little like a contour map drawn with a limited set of shades rather than a continuously varying palette. This artifact sometimes reveals the macro-block boundaries (which is sometimes called tiling). When this happens, it is usually because the encoder allocates too few quantization levels to the scene.

Macro-blocks are areas of 16-by-16 pixels that are used by MPEG for DCT and motion-estimation purposes.

High-frequency mosquito noise will sometimes be apparent in the background. Mosquito noise is often apparent in surfaces, such as wood, plaster, and wool, that contain an almost limitless amount of detail due to their natural texture. The encoder can be overtaxed by so much detail and creates a visual effect that looks as if the walls are crawling with ants.

There are many more artifacts associated with MPEG encoding and decoding; however, a well-designed system should rarely, if ever, produce annoying visible artifacts.

### 7.16.4 MPEG-2 Operating Guidelines

To avoid visible artifacts due to encoding, transmission errors, and decoding, the entire MPEG-2 system must be carefully designed to operate within certain guidelines: The compression ratio cannot be pushed too high. Just where the limit is on compression ratio for given material at a certain image resolution and frame rate is a subject of intense and interminable debate. Ultimately, the decision involves engineers and artists and will vary according to encoder performance (there is some expectation of improvements in rate with time, although also some expectation of a law of diminishing returns).

The transmission system must generate very few errors during the average viewing time of an event. For example, in a two-hour movie, the same viewers may tolerate very few significant artifacts (such as frame drop or green blocks). In practice, this means that the transmission system must employ forward error correction (FEC) techniques.

## 7.17 OTHER VIDEO COMPRESSION ALGORITHMS

There are a great many alternative video compression algorithms, such as wavelet, pyramid, fractal, and so on Many have special characteristics that make them suitable for very low bit rate facilities, for software decoding on a PC, and so on. However, it is unlikely that they will pose a significant threat to MPEG-2 encoding for entertainment video in the near future.

### 7.17.1 Compression Processing Requirements

Let's take a full-resolution video frame that contains 480 lines, each consisting of 720 pixels. The total frame, therefore, contains 345,600 pixels. Remember that a new frame arrives from the picture source every 33 milliseconds. Thus, the pixel rate is 10,368,000 per second. Imagine that the compression process requires about 100 operations per pixel. Obviously, a processor with a performance of 1,000 million instructions per second (mips) is required. In practice, custom processing blocks are often built in hardware to handle common operations, such as motion estimation and DCT used by MPEG-2 video compression.

### 7.17.2 Details of MPEG-2 Video Compression

The following sections detail some of the more practical aspects of MPEG-2 video compression:

**(1) Picture resolution**

MPEG-2 is designed to handle the multiple picture resolutions that are commonly in use for broadcast television. This section defines what is meant by picture resolution and how it affects the compression process. Compression ratio—MPEG-2 can achieve excellent compression ratios when compared to analog transmission, but there is some confusion about the definition of compression ratios. This section discusses the difference between the MPEG compression ratio and the overall compression ratio. Real-time MPEG-2 compression—Most of the programs delivered over cable systems are compressed in real-time at the time of transmission. This section discusses the special requirements for real-time MPEG-2 encoders. Non–real-time MPEG-2 compression—Stored-media content does not require a real-time encoder, and there are certain advantages to non–real-time compression systems.

**(2) Statistical multiplexing**

This section explains how statistical multiplexing works in data communications systems and what special extensions have been invented to support the statistical multiplexing of MPEG-2 program streams. Re-multiplexing–Re-multiplexing, or grooming, of compressed program streams is discussed, including a recent technique that actually allows the program stream to be dynamically reencoded to reduce its bit rate. Picture Resolution MPEG-2 compression is a family of standards that defines many different profiles and levels.

MPEG-2 compression is most commonly used in its main profile at its main level (abbreviated to MP@ML). This MPEG-2 profile and level is designed for the compression of standard definition television pictures with a resolution of 480 vertical lines. The resolution of a picture describes how many pixels are used to describe a single frame. The higher the resolution, the more pixels per frame. In many cases, the luminance information is coded with more pixels than the chrominance information.

The retina of the human eye perceives more detail with rod cells, which are sensitive only to the intensity of light—the luminance—and perceives less detail with cone cells, which are sensitive to the color of light—the chrominance. Chroma sub-sampling takes advantage of the way the human eye works by sampling the chrominance with less detail than the luminance information. In the

MPEG-2 main profile (MP), the chrominance information is subsampled at half the horizontal and vertical resolution compared to the luminance information. For example, if the luminance information is sampled at a resolution of 480 by 720, the chrominance information is sampled at a resolution of 240 by 360, requiring one-fourth the number of pixels. This arrangement is called 4:2:0 sampling. The effect of 4:2:0 sampling is to nearly halve the video bandwidth compared to sampling luminance and chrominance at the same resolution.

### (3) Compression Ratio

The compression ratio is a commonly misused term. It is used to compare the spectrum used by a compressed signal with the spectrum used by an equivalent NTSC (National Television Systems Committee) analog signal. Expressed this way, typical compression ratios achieved by MPEG-2 range from 6:1 to 14:1. Why is the term confusing?

If you take the same video signal and modulate it as an analog signal (uncompressed) and compress it using MPEG-2, you have two very different things. The analog signal is an analog waveform with certain bandwidth constraints so that it fits into 6 MHz, whereas the MPEG-2 elementary stream is just a string of bits that cannot be transmitted until further processing steps are taken. These steps include multiplexing, transport, and digital modulation, and they all affect how much bandwidth is required by the compressed signal.

To compare apples with apples, you must take the same video signal and convert it to an uncompressed digital signal (this is actually the first step in the compression process and is termed analog-to-digital conversion or simply sampling). You can now compare the uncompressed digital signal with the MPEG-2 compressed elementary stream for a true comparison of the input bit rate and the output bit rate of the compression process. A full-resolution uncompressed video signal sampled in 4:2:0 requires 124.416 Mbps. MPEG-2 can squeeze this down to about 4 Mbps with little or no loss in perceived quality; this is a true compression ratio of 124:4 or 31:1. This is very different than the commonly quoted range of 6:1 to 14:1.

To continue the math, take the 4 Mbps video elementary stream and add an audio stream at 192 Kbps to create a program stream at 4.192 Mbps. Add information to describe how the streams are synchronized and place the data into short transport packets for efficient multiplexing with other streams. You now have a payload of approximately 4.3 Mbps. Using 64-QAM modulation (see the section Broadband Transmission in this chapter), six 4.3 Mbps streams fit into its 27 Mbps payload. Thus, we could express this as a 6:1 compression ratio. This is all very confusing! In this example, a video signal with a 31:1 MPEG-2 video compression ratio is roughly equivalent to an overall compression ratio of 6:1. (If the example employs 256-QAM and statistical multiplexing, you might achieve an overall compression ratio of 12:1 although the MPEG-2 video compression ratio is still 31:1.)

### (4) Real-Time MPEG-2 Compression

Real-time compression is commonly used at satellite up-links to compress a video signal into a digital program stream as part of the transmission (or retransmission) process. Very often, the encoder runs for long periods of time without manual intervention. There must be sufficient headroom in the allocated bit rate to allow the encoder to operate correctly for all kinds of material that it is likely to encode. (Headroom refers to available, but normally unused, bits that are allocated to allow for the video compression of difficult scenes.) Each channel requires a dedicated encoder, so price is a definite issue for multichannel systems. The encoder must also be highly reliable, and in many cases automatic switching to a backup encoder is required.

**(5) Non–Real-Time MPEG-2 Compression**

Non–real-time encoders are technically similar to real-time encoders, but have very different requirements. In fact, they may encode in real-time but their application is to encode to a stored media (such as a tape or disc), and a highly-paid compressionist usually monitors the compression of each scene. (Compressionists are studio engineers who not only understand how to operate the encoding equipment but also apply their artistic judgment in selecting the best trade-off between compression ratio and picture quality.) Therefore, encoder price is less of an issue and performance is extremely important because the compressed material will be viewed over and over again. In the case of digital versatile disks (DVDs), no annoying visible artifacts, however subtle, can be tolerated, because the picture quality will be carefully evaluated by a magazine reviewer.

## 7.18 MPEG-4

MPEG-4 is a video standard defined by the Moving Picture Experts Group (MPEG). Many developers around the world contributed to MPEG-4 in the late 1990s and the format became an international standard in 2000. MPEG-4 is the global multimedia standard, delivering professional-quality audio and video streams over a wide range of bandwidths, from cell phone to broadband and beyond.

MPEG-4 was defined by the Moving Picture Experts Group (MPEG), the working group within the International Organization for Standardization (ISO) that specified the widely adopted, Emmy Award-winning standards known as MPEG-1 and MPEG-2. Hundreds of researchers around the world contributed to MPEG-4, which was finalized in 1998 and became an international standard in 2000 and included in QuickTime in 2002.

### Based on a Time-tested Technology

While audio and video are at the core of the MPEG-4 specification, MPEG-4 can also support 3D objects, sprites, text and other media types. MPEG-4 is supported by a variety of players. Apple has backed MPEG-4 strongly and MPEG-4 plays well in the Quicktime player. Microsoft was involved in the early development of MPEG-4 but is no longer actively supporting the standard, choosing instead to concentrate on the Windows Media format. MPEG-4 can only be played in Windows Media Player with a special MPEG-4 decoder pack.

### AV Objects

Whereas MPEG-1 and MPEG-2 are relatively simple video standards, MPEG-4 introduces a new level of flexibility with an object-based approach. This allows for options such as interactive video and added media components (text, graphics, etc). This is similar to the way Quicktime works with multiple media. Creating MPEG-4 Content

Many applications are available for creating MPEG-4. Because the standard is closely linked to the Quicktime architecture, applications which support Quicktime tend to support MPEG-4 (including Final Cut Pro and Adobe Premiere). An easy way to get started with MPEG-4 creation is Apple Quicktime Pro. Interoperability

MPEG-4 has suffered from imperfect interoperability between manufacturers; that is, not all products which claim to be MGEG-4 compliant are actually fully compliant with the ISO standard. In an effort to remedy this situation, the MPEG Industry Forum runs a Logo Qualification Program in which companies can verify the compliance of their products. Fully compliant products can carry the official logo.

You've been able to mix media with Apple's QuickTime technology for over a decade, storing each new type in a separate track. With this kind of extensibility, it's no surprise that the ISO chose the QuickTime file format as the foundation for the new MPEG-4 standard.

Just as QuickTime does, MPEG-4 also scales to transport media at any data rate — from media suitable for delivery over dial-up modems to high-bandwidth networks. Because of the DNA-level relationship between MPEG-4 and QuickTime, MPEG-4 inherits QuickTime's stability, extensibility and scalability.

MPEG-4 is designed to deliver DVD-quality video (MPEG-2) at lower data rates and smaller file sizes. And the same folks who created the popular .mp3 file format — a.k.a. MPEG-1 layer III — developed the new Advanced Audio Coding (AAC) codec, providing much more efficient compression than MP3 with a quality rivaling that of uncompressed CD audio.

MPEG-4 is ready to stream incredible-quality audio and video today in QuickTime. With the free QuickTime Player or browser plug-in, you can play back any compliant MPEG-4 file. Upgrade to QuickTime Pro, and you can author your own MPEG-4 content. QuickTime Streaming Server and Darwin Streaming Server are also available to stream .mp4 files. And with QuickTime Broadcaster, you can produce live events in MPEG-4, making the QuickTime workflow (Broadcaster to Server to Player) the industry's best and most cost-effective end-to-end, standards-based architecture.

But that's not all. Because hundreds of multimedia authoring applications are built upon the QuickTime architecture, QuickTime instantly adds MPEG-4 capabilities to all these tools. This allows you to immediately create MPEG-4 content in programs such as Final Cut Pro and Adobe Premiere. MPEG-4 promises to create interoperability for video delivered over the Internet and other distribution channels. MPEG-4 will play back on many different devices — from satellite television to wireless devices.

To ensure that different products that use MPEG-4 each implement the standard in the same way, Apple, together with Cisco, IBM, Kasenna, Philips and Sun Microsystems, formed the Internet Streaming Media Alliance (ISMA). Other participants include AOL Time Warner, Dolby Laboratories, Hitachi, HP, Fujitsu and 20 other companies. The ISMA defines profiles that companies implement to ensure interoperability.

That means you can rest assured that the MPEG-4 media stream you create using one company's product will run on another vendor's player.

## Gaining Momentums

In addition to being adopted by many of the premiere Internet content providers, the MPEG-4 standard is receiving tremendous support from other industries. For example, H.264 video, also known as MPEG-4 part 10, has been adopted by the ISO MPEG allowing QuickTime 7 to create ISO-complaint H.264 video in a .MP4 file. The standards for high-quality multimedia on wireless devices, 3GPP ($3^{rd}$ Generation Partnership Project) and 3GPP2 (3rd Generation Partnership Project 2), are based on the solid foundation of MPEG-4, as well.

Satellite Broadcasters like DirecTV and the DVB have adopted MPEG-4 for the delivery of digital television because of its quality at lower data rates. This means that they can offer more channels to their subscribers with the same bandwidth. Apple has developed two of its own ISO-compliant video codecs, MPEG-4 part 2 (a.k.a. MPEG-4 simple profile) and MPEG-4 part 10 (a.k.a. H.264) providing the highest quality results across a wide spectrum of data rates — from narrowband to broadband and beyond. These revolutionary codecs offer compression times and video quality that rival those of the best proprietary codecs available, yet it provides true interoperability with other MPEG-4 players and devices.

### MPEG-4 Part 2 Video

The QuickTime MPEG-4 codec leverages many advances in technology to provide superior performance. For example, the codec provides rate control—the encoder can be set to a target data rate that ensures playback at the appropriate data rate for a particular delivery mechanism. The versatile encoder can use the single-pass variable bit rate (VBR) rate controller either to maximize accuracy for the highest-quality output or to maximize speed for the fastest possible encode. In addition, the QuickTime MPEG-4 codec features rigorous color management, a high-performance quantizer and a motion estimator optimized for both precision and speed. The decoder also provides an optimized post-processing stage to remove coding artifacts. Both the encoder and decoder are heavily optimized for both the Intel Core Duo processors, as well as the 64-bit G5 and the G4 Velocity Engine

### H.264

H.264 is the next-generation video compression technology in the MPEG-4 standard, also known as MPEG-4 Part 10. H.264 can match the best possible MPEG-2 quality at up to half the data rate. H.264 also delivers excellent video quality across the entire bandwidth spectrum — from 3G to HD and everything in between (from 40 Kbps to upwards of 10 Mbps).

Windows Media 9 is proprietary, developed by a single company; H.264 has been through intense peer review by worldwide experts from a large number of industry segments and is ratified as a worldwide standard. And while video quality tests are subjective, we believe H.264 delivers superior video quality when compared with Windows Media 9.

### MPEG-7

MPEG-7 has been developed by experts representing broadcasters, electronics manufacturers, content creators and managers, publishers, intellectual property rights managers, telecommunication service providers and academia is an ISO/ IEC standard developed by MPEG (Moving Picture Experts Group), the committee that also developed the Emmy Award winning standards known as MPEG-1 and MPEG-2, and the MPEG-4 standard. MPEG-1 and MPEG-2 standards made interactive video on CD-ROM and Digital Television possible. MPEG-4 is the multimedia standard for the fixed and mobile web enabling integration of multiple paradigms.

MPEG-7, formally named "Multimedia Content Description Interface", is a standard for describing the multimedia content data that supports some degree of interpretation of the information meaning, which can be passed onto, or accessed by, a device or a computer code. MPEG-7 is not aimed at any one application in particular; rather, the elements that MPEG-7 standardizes support as broad a range of applications as possible. This document gives an overview of the MPEG-7 standard, explaining which pieces of technology it includes and what sort of applications are supported by this technology. Also the current work towards MPEG-7 version 2 is presented.

The MPEG-7 standard, formally named "Multimedia Content Description Interface", provides a rich set of standardized tools to describe multimedia content. Both human users and automatic systems that process audiovisual information are within the scope of MPEG-7.

MPEG-7 offers a comprehensive set of audiovisual Description Tools (the metadata elements and their structure and relationships, that are defined by the standard in the form of Descriptors and Description Schemes) to create descriptions (i.e., a set of instantiated Description Schemes and their corresponding Descriptors at the users will), which will form the basis for applications enabling the needed effective and efficient access (search, filtering and browsing) to multimedia content. This is a challenging task given the broad spectrum of requirements and targeted multimedia applications, and the broad number of audiovisual features of importance in such context.

MPEG-7 has been developed by experts representing broadcasters, electronics manufacturers, content creators and managers, publishers, intellectual property rights managers, telecommunication service providers and academia. MPEG-7 is a standard for describing the multimedia content data that will support these operational requirements. The requirements apply, in principle, to both real-time and non real-time as well as push and pull applications. MPEG-7 does not standardize or evaluate applications, although in the development of the MPEG-7 standard applications have been used for understanding the requirements and evaluation of technology. It must be made clear that the requirements are derived from analyzing a wide range of potential applications that could use MPEG-7 tools. MPEG-7 is not aimed at any one application in particular; rather, the elements that MPEG-7 standardizes support as broad a range of applications as possible.

## MPEG-21 FORMAT

Within the ISO/IEC 14496 MPEG-4 standard there are several parts that define file formats for the storage of time-based media (such as audio, video etc.). They are all based and derived from the ISO Base Media File Format which is a structural, media-independent definition that is also published as part of the JPEG 2000 family of standards. It has a basic box-structuring part, and a definition for timed sequences of multi-media (audio, video etc.) in such a box structured file. The MPEG-21 File Format uses the structural definition of a box-structured file as defined in the ISO Base Media File Format, but not the definitions for time-based media. It defines the storage of an MPEG-21 digital item, with some or all of its ancillary data (such as images, movies, or other non-XML data) within the same file.

### Overview

The family of the storage file formats is based on the concept of box-structured files. Box structured files are used in a number of applications, and it is possible to form 'multi-purpose' files which contain the boxes required by more than one specification. Examples include not only the MPEG-21 file format described here, but also formats using the time-structured part of the ISO Base File Format family.

As described above, the general meta-box can be used at the file level to contain a description and its associated or included data. This structure is used for MPEG-21 files. A file-level meta-box is used to hold an MPEG-21 Digital Item Declaration (DID) The meta-box also contains a list of attached resources; which may have local names, and may be located within the same file or in another file. The full structural power of the meta-box can be used to give significant flexibility in the structure of the MPEG-21 file. Items (other files) required by the digital item may be included in the same file, or in another (possibly combined together in another file). That other file could be another MPEG-21 file, another file from the family, or of another format entirely.

Items (files) included in this or other files may be fragmented, and those fragments interleaved.

Items (files) may be protected and the signaling of that protection given. Items (files) may be named, to make access of them easier.

There are URL forms defined for the items (files) defined in a meta-box, and these forms allow access to the items from within or outside the file. The general concept is that the MPEG-21 file is a 'package' of files that are 'pre-cached' at the client, and this cache obviates the need to fetch many individual files when accessing an MPEG-21 digital item.

The MPEG-21 standard, from the Moving Picture Experts Group, aims at defining an open framework for multimedia applications. MPEG-21 is ratified in the standards ISO/IEC 21000 - Multimedia framework (MPEG-21). Specifically, MPEG-21 defines a "Rights Expression Language" standard as means of sharing digital rights/permissions/restrictions for digital content from content creator to content consumer. As an XML-based standard, MPEG-21 is designed to communicate machine-readable license information and do so in a "ubiquitous, unambiguous and secure" manner.

Among the aspirations for this standard that the industry hopes will put an end to illicit file sharing is that it will constitute: "A normative open framework for multimedia delivery and consumption for use by all the players in the delivery and consumption chain. This open framework will provide content creators, producers, distributors and service providers with equal opportunities in the MPEG-21 enabled open market."

MPEG-21 is based on two essential concepts: the definition of a fundamental unit of distribution and transaction, which is the Digital Item, and the concept of users interacting with them. Digital items can be considered the kernel of the Multimedia Framework and the users can be considered as who interacts with them inside the Multimedia Framework. At its most basic level, MPEG-21 provides a framework in which one user interacts with another one, and the object of that interaction is a Digital Item. Due to that, we could say that the main objective of the MPEG-21 is to define the technology needed to support users to exchange, access, consume, trade or manipulate Digital Items in an efficient and transparent way.

## 7.19 AUDIO VIDEO INTERLACED (AVI)

AVI stands for Audio Video Interlaced. It is one of the oldest formats. It was created by Microsoft to go with Windows 3.1 and it's "Video for Windows" application. Even though it is widely used due to the number of editing systems and software that use AVI by default, this format has many restrictions, specially the compatibility with operations systems and other interface boards (Fisher & Schroeder). MOV format, created by Macintosh, is the proprietary format of the QuickTime application. It can also run on PCs. Being able to store both video and sound simultaneously, the format was once superior to AVI. The latest version of QuickTime also has streaming capabilities for internet video. However, with the new MPEG-2 format, the MOV format started to lose its popularity (Fisher & Schroeder, 1999), until it was decided that the MPEG-4 is to use the QuickTime format as the basis of its standards.

AVI is a multimedia container format introduced by Microsoft in November 1992, as part of the Video for Windows technology. AVI files contain both audio and video data in a standard container that allows simultaneous playback. Most .avi files also use the file format extensions developed by the Matrox OpenDML group in February 1996. These files are supported by Microsoft, and are known unofficially as "AVI 2.0".

Audio Video Interleaved (AVI) is Microsoft-developed software that plays full-motion interleaved video and audio sequences in Windows, without specialized hardware, at about 15 frames per second in a small window. With acceleration hardware, you can run AVI video sequences at 30 frames per second. Video data are interleaved with audio within the file that contains the motion sequence, so the audio portion of the movie remains synchronized to the video portion. Video for Windows consists of a set of tools based on the AVI file format, together with an ad-on module for Windows 3.1 and a CD-ROM. It is designed to enable developers to capture and digitise video sequences using an adapter board, edit them and use OLE to incorporate them in a wide range of applications. Users can play the same sequences back, using hardware codecs or runtime software decompression, on all versions of Windows, although the quality will depend upon the hardware. Three software codecs are included in the package: Microsoft's Video and RLE together with Indeo, Intel's video recording and playback technology based on DVI.

Like Apple's QuickTime, AVI provides the following features:

- Playback from hard disk or CD-ROM
- Playback on computers with limited memory; data is streamed from the hard disk or CD-ROM player without using great amount of memory
- Quick loading and playing, because only a fiew frames of video and a portion of audio are accessed at a time
- Video compression to boost the quality of your video sequence and reduce their size

AVI includes two tools to capture and edit video sequences and play them back: VidCap and VidEdit, respectively. AVI also includes data preparation rools (BitEdit, and WaveEdit); MCIAVI. DRV, the MCI driver for AVI; MediaPlayer; and sample video sequences.

It is a special case of the Resource Interchange File Format (RIFF), which divides the file's data up into data blocks called "chunks". Each "chunk" is identified by a FourCC tag. An .avi file takes the form of a single chunk in an RIFF formatted file, which is then subdivided into two mandatory "chunks" and one optional "chunk".

The first sub-chunk is identified by the "hdrl" tag. This chunk is the file header and contains metadata about the video such as the width, height and the number of frames. The second sub-chunk is identified by the "movi" tag. This chunk contains the actual audio/visual data that makes up the .avi movie. The third optional sub-chunk is identified by the "idxl" tag and indexes the location of the data chunks within the file.

By way of the RIFF format, the audio/visual data contained in the "movi" chunk can be encoded or decoded by a software module called a codec. The codec translates between raw data and the data format inside the chunk. An .avi file may therefore carry audio/visual data inside the chunks in almost any compression scheme, including: Full Frames (Uncompressed), Intel Real Time Video, Indeo, Cinepak, Motion JPEG, Editable MPEG, VDOWave, ClearVideo / RealVideo, QPEG, MPEG-4, XviD, DivX and others.

## 7.20 QUICKTIME

QuickTime is a multimedia technology developed by Apple Computer, capable of handling various formats of digital video, sound, text, animation, music, and immersive virtual reality panoramic images. It is currently at version 7.0.2 on the Macintosh and Windows platforms.

The QuickTime technology has three major components:

- The QuickTime file format itself openly documented and available for anyone to use royalty-free
- A media player which Apple makes available for free download on its website and bundles with each of its computers
- Software development kits available for the Macintosh and Windows platforms. These kits allow people to develop their own software to manipulate QuickTime and other media files Apple released the first version of QuickTime on December 2, 1991 as a multimedia add-on

for System 7. The first version of QuickTime laid down the basic architecture which survives essentially unchanged today, including multiple movie tracks, extensible media type support, an open-ended file format, and a full complement of editing functions. The original video codecs included:

- the Apple Video codec (also known as "Rocky Road"), suited to normal live-action video
- the Animation codec, which used simple run-length encoding and better suited cartoon-type images with large areas of flat color
- the Graphics codec, optimized for 8-bit-per-pixel images, including ones which had undergone dithering

Apple released QuickTime 1.5 for Mac OS in the latter part of 1992. This added the SuperMac-developed Cinepak vector-quantization video codec (initially known as Compact Video), which managed the unheard-of feat of playing back video at 320 x 240 resolution at 30 frames per second on a 25MHz 68040 CPU. It also added text tracks, which allowed for things like captioning, lyrics etc at very little addition to the size of a movie.

In an effort to increase the adoption of QuickTime, Apple contracted an outside company, San Francisco Canyon Company, to port QuickTime to the Windows platform. Version 1.0 of QuickTime for Windows provided only a subset of the full QuickTime API, including only movie-playback functions driven through the standard movie controller.

QuickTime 7 was released on April 29, 2005 with Mac OS X v10.4 featuring complete MPEG-4 compliance, H.264 codec, live resizing, multi-channel audio, full-screen overlay, and full support for interactive animations created with Apple's new tool Quartz Composer.

### 7.20.1 QuickTime File Format

A QuickTime file functions as a multimedia container file that contains one or more tracks, each of which store a particular type of data, such as audio, video, effects, or text (for subtitles, for example). Each track in turn contains track media, either the digitally encoded media stream (using a specific codec such as Cinepak, Sorenson codec, MP3, JPEG, DivX, or PNG) or a data reference to the media stored in another file or elsewhere on a network. It also has an "edit list" that indicates what parts of the media to use. Internally, QuickTime files maintain this format as a tree-structure of "atoms", each of which uses a 4-byte OSType identifier to determine its structure. An atom can be a parent to other atoms or it can contain data, but it cannot do both. Apple's plans for HyperCard 3.0 illustrate the versatility of QuickTime's file format.

The designers of Hypercard 3.0 originally intended to store an entire HyperCard stack (similar in structure to a complete web site, with graphics, buttons and scripts) as a QuickTime file. The ability to contain abstract data references for the media data, and the separation of the media data from the media offsets and the track edit lists means that QuickTime is particularly suited for editing, as it is capable of importing and editing in place (without data copying) other formats such as AIFF DV, MP3, MPEG-1, and AVI. Other later-developed media container formats such as Microsoft's Advanced Streaming Format or by the open source Ogg and Matroska containers lack this abstraction, and require all media data to be rewritten after editing.

### 7.20.2 QuickTime and MPEG-4

On February 11, 1998 the ISO approved the QuickTime file format as the basis of the MPEG-4 *.mp4 container standard. Supporters of the move noted that QuickTime provided a good "life-cycle" format, well suited to capture, editing, archiving, distribution, and playback (as opposed to the simple file-as-stream approach of MPEG-1 and MPEG-2, which does not mesh well with editing).

Developers added MPEG-4 compatibility to QuickTime 6 in 2002. However, Apple delayed the release of this version for months in a dispute with the MPEG-4 licensing body, claiming that proposed license fees would constrain many users and content providers. Following a compromise, Apple released QuickTime 6 on 15 July 2002.

### 7.20.3 QuickTime players

Apple releases official media player software for Mac OS and Windows for free under the brand QuickTime Player. (Earlier versions simply used the name "MoviePlayer.") The player also comes with a number of media-editing and media-creation features, but users have to unlock these by purchasing a key from Apple,turning the media player into QuickTime Pro.

### 7.20.4 Storage Media File Formats

The Yellow Book does not specify how data files are to be stored and retrieved.To access any file the computer operating system needs to know where that file is. For convenience, all files are given a unique name and are assigned to one of a number of hierarchically organised directories. Files also have associated attributes (to define read and write permissions for example). A file system facilitates the storage and retrieval of perhaps many hundreds or even thousands of files. Each computer operating system uses a different file system and therefore there are a number of CD-ROM file systems in use to suit a range of platforms including Windows, Macintosh, Unix etc. The most common file system for CD-ROM is ISO 9660 which is the international standard version of the High Sierra Group file system and is purposely designed for the PC and MSDOS. The JOLIET extensions provide long filenames. With the advent of DVD, the Micro-UDF file system has been added to the list. This is suitable for read-only and re-writable discs and allows long filenames etc.

## 7.21 VIDEO PROCESSING

The following are the essential steps in video processing

**Process the audio**. Perform the audio normalizing and equalizing mentioned above.

**Trim clips.** Make sure that your movie begins and ends with frames that make sense as still images. The first frame will appear on the user's screen while the movie is loading, and the last frame will remain on screen when the movie has finished. Take care that these images do not seem awkward and out of the context of the movie.

**Crop.** Use video editing software to crop out unwanted noise or borders from the movie image.

**Scale.** Most Web video is sized to quarter-screen (320 × 240 pixels) or smaller image quality. Reducing the image-quality setting of a movie reduces the data that is stored for each frame.

**Frame rate**. Standard NTSC video has a frame rate of 30 fps. Most Web video is set to about 10 fps.

**Codec.** Some codecs compress more efficiently than others do, though usually at the expense of image quality.

**Custom filters**. Compression software provides filters that reduce the differences between frames, permitting more efficient compression.

**Audio.** The audio track of video can be down-sampled and/or compressed to reduce the overall movie data rate.

**Delivery**

The technology of networked media consists of three main components: the server, the network, and the client machine. These three components must work in tandem to deliver good Web multimedia to the desktop. It makes no difference how high-end your video server and network are if your users are running low-end desktop machines that cannot handle the demands of playback.

The wildest of all these wild cards is bandwidth. If you purchase a high-end media server, you can expect a certain level of performance. You can predict playback performance on desktop machines. These elements are somewhat measurable. But unless you are working with a dedicated network, bandwidth will be huge variable and difficult to predict. Issues regarding bandwidth run from the basic configuration of your connection to the network to the amount of network traffic at any given time.

Given these variables, the parameters for creating and delivering Web multimedia are not easily defined. They will vary depending on the scope and content of your project. If you are creating a Web site for a corporate intranet, for example, your media can be more technologically demanding than if you send it worldwide over the Internet. The key is to be well acquainted with the configuration of your client base and prepare accordingly.

## 7.22 STREAMING

Streaming technology sends data to the desktop continuously but does not download the entire file. In the optimal scenario, the content is stored on a media server, which maintains a constant conversation with the client to determine how much data the user can support. Based on this information, the server adjusts the data stream accordingly and sends just enough data to the client.

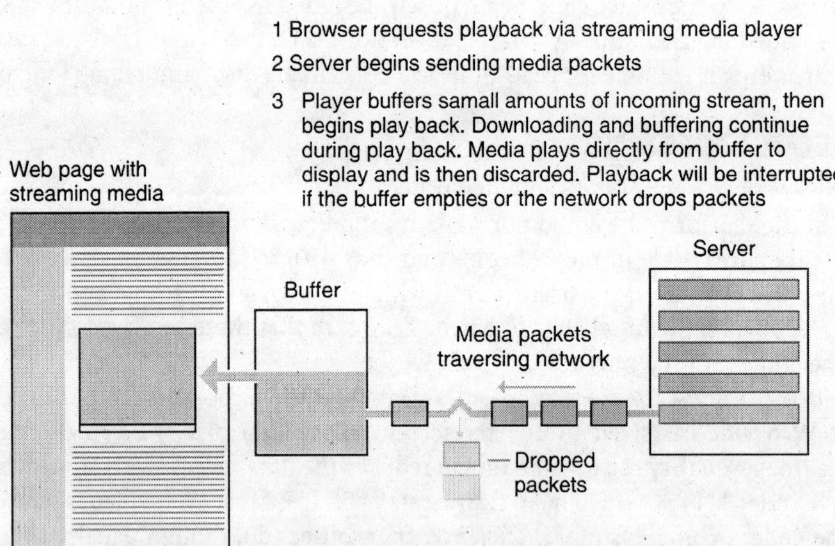


**Fig. 7.7:** Video Streaming

Streaming offers many benefits, the first of which is random access. Streaming technology permits movies to be viewed at any point in the video stream. If your reader is accessing an hour's worth of video and wishes to view only the last five minutes, he or she can use the controls to move forward to the desired starting point. Another benefit is a lower storage demand on the client machine. Streaming media plays directly to the display; it is not stored in memory or on the hard drive. The strengths of streaming are also its shortcomings. To play a movie in real time the player software needs to keep up with the incoming data sent from the server. As a result, if there are glitches in the network or if the client machine cannot handle playback, the data may simply be lost. Streaming playback requires significant processing power, so playback may be suboptimal if the processor has to drop frames to keep up with the incoming stream. Also, streaming media needs to be heavily compressed to create a file small enough to play in real time.

## 7.23 VIDEO PROCESSING OVERVIEW

### About video layers

You can use Photoshop to edit individual frames of video and image sequence files. In addition to using any Photoshop tool to edit and paint on video, you can also apply filters, masks, transformations, layers styles, and blending modes. After making edits, you can save the document as a PSD file (that can be played back in other Adobe applications such as Premiere Pro and After Effects or accessed as a static file in other applications), or you can render it as a QuickTime movie or image sequence.

*Note: You can work only with the visual images in a video file, not the audio.*

When you open a video file or image sequence in Photoshop, the frames are contained within a*video layer.* In the Layers panel, a video layer is identified with a filmstrip icon. Video layers let you paint and clone on individual frames using the brush tools and stamp tools. Like working with regular layers, you can create selections or apply masks to restrict your edits to specific areas of a frame. You navigate through the frames using the timeline mode in the Animation panel (Window > Animation).

*Note: Video layers do not work when the Animation panel is in Frame mode.*

You work with video layers just like regular layers by adjusting the blending mode, opacity, position, and layer style. You can also group video layers in the Layers panel. Adjustment layers let you apply color and tonal adjustments non-destructively to the video layers.

If you prefer to make your frame edits on a separate layer, you can create a blank video layer. Blank video layers also let you create hand-drawn animations.

*Note*: A video layer references the original file, so that edits to the video layer don't alter the original video or image sequence file. To maintain the link to the original file, ensure that it remains in the same location relative to the PSD file.

## 7.24 SUPPORTED VIDEO AND IMAGE SEQUENCE FORMATS

You can open video files and image sequences in the following formats.

### QuickTime video formats

- MPEG1 (.mpg or .mpeg)
- MPEG4 (.mp4 or .m4v)
- MOV
- AVI
- MPEG2 is supported if an MPEG2 encoder is installed on your computer.

### Image sequence formats

- BMP
- DICOM

- JPEG
- OpenEXR
- PNG
- PSD
- Targa
- TIFF
- Cineon and JPEG 2000 are supported if the plugins are installed.

### Color mode and bit depth

Video layers can contain files in the following color modes and bits per channel (bpc):

- Grayscale: 8, 16, or 32 bpc
- RGB: 8, 16, or 32 bpc
- CMYK: 8 or 16 bpc
- Lab: 8 or 16 bpc

## 7.25 ANIMATION PANEL OVERVIEW

An *animation* is a sequence of images, or *frames*, that is displayed over time. Each frame varies slightly from the preceding frame, creating the illusion of movement or other changes when the frames are viewed in quick succession.

In the standard edition of earlier versions of Photoshop, the Animation panel (Window > Animation) appears in frame mode, showing a thumbnail of each frame in your animation. Use the tools at the bottom of the panel to navigate through the frames, set looping options, add and delete frames, and preview the animation.

The Animation panel menu contains additional commands for editing frames or timeline durations, and for configuring the panel display. Click the panel menu icon to view available commands.

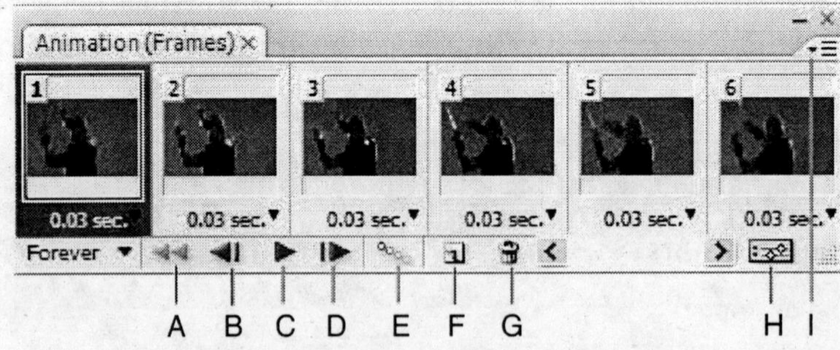


*A. Selects the first frame B. Selects the previous frame C. Plays animation D. Selects the next frame E. Tweens animation frames F. Duplicates selected frames G. Deletes selected frames H. Converts to timeline mode I. Animation panel menu*

**Fig 7.8:** Animation panel (frame mode)

You can use the Animation panel in either frame mode or timeline mode. Timeline mode shows the frame duration and animation properties for document layers. Use the tools at the bottom of the panel to navigate through frames, zoom the time display in or out, toggle onion skin mode, delete keyframes, and preview the video. You can use controls on the timeline itself to adjust frame duration for a layer, set keyframes for layer properties, and designate a section of the video as the working area.

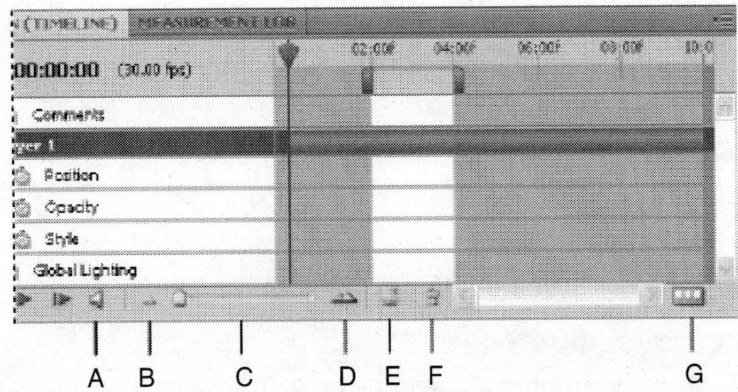


***A.** Enable audio playback **B.** Zoom out **C.** Zoom slider **D.** Zoom in **E.** Toggle onion skins*
***F.** Delete keyframes **G.** Convert to frame animation*

**Fig 7.9:** Animation panel (timeline mode)

In timeline mode, the Animation panel displays each layer in a Photoshop document (except the background layer) and is synchronized with the Layers panel. Whenever a layer is added, deleted, renamed, grouped, duplicated, or assigned a color, the changes are updated in both panels.

*Note: When animated layers are grouped as a Smart Object, the animation information from the Animation panel is stored in the Smart Object.*

**Frame mode controls**

In frame mode, the Animation panel includes the following controls:

**Looping Options**

Sets the number of times an animation plays when exported as an animated GIF file.

**Frame Delay Time**

Sets the duration of a frame during playback.

**< Tween Animation Frames>**

Adds a series of frames between two existing frames, *interpolating* (varying) the layer properties evenly between the new frames.

**Duplicate Selected Frames**

Adds a frame to the animation by duplicating the selected frame in the Animation panel.

**Convert to Timeline Animation**

Converts a frame animation to timeline animation using keyframes to animate layer properties.

**Timeline mode controls**

In timeline mode, the Animation panel includes the following features and controls:

**Cached frames indicator**

Displays a green bar to indicate the frames that are cached for playback.

**Comments track**

Choose Edit Timeline Comment from the panel menu to insert a text comment at the current time. Comments appear as icons ■ in the comments track. Move the pointer over these icons to display comments as tool tips. Double-click these icons to revise comments. To navigate from one comment to the next, click the Go To Previous ◀ or Go To Next ▶ buttons at the far left of the Comments track.

*To create an HTML table listing the time, frame number, and text of each comment, choose Export Timeline Comments from the panel menu.*

**Convert To Frame Animation**

Converts a timeline animation using keyframes to frame animation.

**Timecode Or frame number display**

Shows the timecode or frame number (depending on panel options) for the current frame.

**Current-time indicator**

Drag the current-time indicator to navigate frames or change the current time or frame.

**Global Lighting track**

Displays keyframes where you set and change the master lighting angle for layer effects such as Drop Shadow, Inner Shadow, and Bevel and Emboss.

**Keyframe navigator** ◀◇▶

Arrow buttons to the left of a track label move the current-time indicator to the previous or next keyframe from its current position. Click the center button to add or delete a keyframe at the current time.

**Layer duration bar**

Specifies a layer's place and time within a video or animation. To move the layer to another place in time, drag the bar. To trim (adjust the duration of) a layer, drag either end of the bar.

**Altered Video track**

For video layers, displays a duration bar for altered frames. To jump to altered frames, use the keyframe navigator to the left of the track label.

**Time ruler**

Measures duration (or frame count) horizontally, according to the document's duration and frame rate. (Choose Document Settings from the panel menu to change duration or frame rate.) Tick marks and numbers appear along the ruler and change in spacing with the zoom setting of the timeline.

**Time-Vary stopwatch**

Enables or disables keyframing for a layer property. Select this option to insert a keyframe and enable keyframing for a layer property. Deselect to remove all keyframes and disable keyframing for a layer property.

**Animation panel menu**

Includes functions affecting keyframes, layers, panel appearance, onion skinning, and document settings.

### Work area indicators

Drag the blue tab at either end of the topmost track to mark the specific portion of the animation or video that you want to preview or export.

### Change thumbnail size

In the Animation panel, you can change the size of the thumbnails that represent each frame or layer.

1. Choose Panel Options from the Animation panel menu.
2. Do one of the following:
   - Select a size option.
   - In timeline mode, select None to display only layer names.

### Switch timeline units

You can display the Animation panel timeline in either frame number or timecode units.

- To select units to display, choose Panel Options from the Animation panel menu and select Frame Numbers or Timecode.
- To toggle between units, Alt-click (Windows) or Option-click (Mac OS) the current-time display in the upper-left corner of the timeline.

### Show or hide layer properties in the timeline

As you add layers to a document, they appear as tracks in the timeline. Expand layer tracks to show layer properties that can be animated.

- To show or hide layer properties, click the triangle to the left of the layer name.

### Show or hide layers in the timeline

All document layers appear in the timeline by default. To show only a subset of layers, first set them as favorites.

1. In timeline mode, select one or more layers from the Animation panel, then choose Show > Set Favorite Layers in the Animation panel menu.
2. To specify which layers are displayed, choose Show from the Animation panel menu, then select All Layers or Favorite Layers.

### Navigate the timeline

With the Animation panel in timeline mode, do any of the following:

- Drag the current-time indicator.
- Click a number or location in the time ruler where you want to position the current-time indicator.
- Drag the current-time display (in the upper-left corner of the timeline).
- Double-click the current-time display and enter a frame number or time in the Set Current Time dialog box.
- Use the playback controls in the Animation panel.
- Choose Go To in the Animation panel menu, and then choose a timeline option.

### Switch animation modes

You can use the Animation panel in either frame or timeline animation mode. Frame mode shows each separate frame, letting you set unique duration and layer properties for each. Timeline mode shows frames in a continuous timeline, letting you animate properties with keyframes and play video layers.

Ideally, you should select the mode you want before starting an animation. However, it's possible to switch animation modes in an open document, converting a frame animation to a timeline animation, or vice versa.

*Note: You may lose some interpolated keyframes when converting a timeline animation to a frame animation. The animation appearance doesn't change, however.*

In the Animation panel, do any of the following:

- Click the Convert To Frame Animation icon.
- Click the Convert To Timeline Animation icon.
- From the Animation panel menu, choose either Convert To Frame Animation or Convert To Timeline.

**Specify timeline duration and frame rate**

When you are working in timeline mode, you can specify the duration and frame rate of a document containing video or animation. *Duration* is the overall time length of the video clip, from the first frame you specify to the last. *Frame rate* or frames per second (fps), is usually determined by the type of output you produce: NTSC video has a frame rate of 29.97 fps; PAL video has a frame rate of 25 fps; and motion picture film has a frame rate of 24 fps. Depending on the broadcast system, DVD video can have the same frame rate as NTSC video or PAL video, or a frame rate of 23.976. Video intended for CDROM or the web typically has a frame rate of 10 to 15 fps.

When you create a new document, the default timeline duration is 10 seconds. The frame rate depends on the chosen document preset. For non-video presets (like International Paper), the default rate is 30 fps. For video presets, the rate is 25 fps for PAL and 29.97 for NTSC.

1. From the Animation panel menu, choose Document Settings.
2. Enter or choose values for Duration and Frame Rate.

*Note: Reducing the duration of an existing video or animation has the effect of trimming frames (and any keyframes) from the end of the document.*

**Create images for video**

***About creating images for video***

Photoshop can create images of various aspect ratios so that they appear properly on devices such as video monitors. You can select a specific video option (using the New dialog box) to compensate for scaling when the final image is incorporated into video.

**Safe zones:** The Film & Video preset also creates a document with nonprinting guides that delineate the actionsafe and titlesafe areas of the image. Using the options in the Size menu, you can produce images for specific video systems—NTSC, PAL, or HDTV.

Safe zones are useful when you edit for broadcast and videotape. Most consumer TV sets use a process called overscan, which cuts off a portion of the outer edges of the picture, allowing the center of the picture to be enlarged. The amount of overscan is not consistent across TVs. To ensure that everything fits within the area that most TVs display, keep text within the titlesafe margins, and all other important elements within the actionsafe margins.

***A.** Action safe area (outer rectangle)* ***B.** Title safe area (inner rectangle)*

**Fig. 7.10:** Video preset file size guides

***Note:** If you are creating content for the web or for CD, the titlesafe and actionsafe margins do not apply to your project because the entire image is displayed in these media.*

## Preview options

To help you create images for video, Photoshop has a Pixel Aspect Ratio Correction viewing mode that displays images at the specified aspect ratio. For more accurate previews, Photoshop also has a Video Preview command that lets you immediately preview your work on a display device, such as a video monitor. To use this feature, you must have the device connected to your computer via FireWire (IEEE 1394).

## Other considerations

Both Adobe AfterEffects and Adobe Premiere Pro support PSD files created in Photoshop. However, if you're using other film and video applications, you might consider these details when you create images for use in video:

- Some video-editing programs can import individual layers from a multilayer PSD file.
- If the file has transparency, some video-editing programs preserve it.
- If the file uses a layer mask or multiple layers, you might not have to flatten the layers, but you might want to include a flattened copy of the file in PSD format to maximize backward compatibility.

## Aspect ratio

*Frame aspect ratio* describes the ratio of width to height in the dimensions of an image. For example, DV NTSC has a frame aspect ratio of 4:3 (or 4 width by 3 height) and a typical widescreen frame has a frame aspect ratio of 16:9. Some video cameras can record various frame aspect ratios. Many cameras that have a widescreen mode use the 16:9 aspect ratio. Many professional films have been shot using even wider aspect ratios.

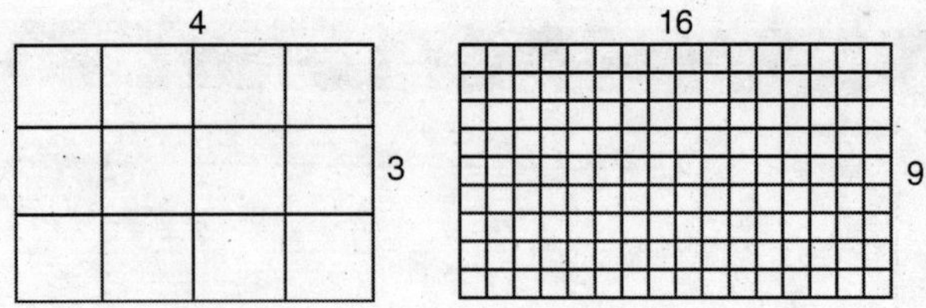


**Fig. 7.11:** 4:3 frame aspect ratio (left), and wider 16:9 frame aspect ratio (right)

*Pixel aspect ratio* describes the ratio of width to height of a single pixel in a frame. Different video standards use different pixel aspect ratios. For example, many computer video standards define a 4:3 aspect ratio frame as 640 pixels wide by 480 pixels high, which results in square pixels. The computer video pixels in this example have a pixel aspect ratio of 1:1 (square), whereas the DV NTSC pixels have a pixel aspect ratio of 0.91 (nonsquare). DV pixels, which are always rectangular, are vertically oriented in systems producing NTSC video and horizontally oriented in systems producing PAL video.

If you display rectangular pixels on a square-pixel monitor without alteration, images appear distorted; for example, circles distort into ovals. However, when displayed on a broadcast monitor, the images appear correctly proportioned because broadcast monitors use rectangular pixels.

*Note: When copying or importing images into a nonsquare pixel document, Photoshop automatically converts and scales the image to the pixel aspect ratio of the document. Images imported from Adobe Illustrator are also properly scaled.*

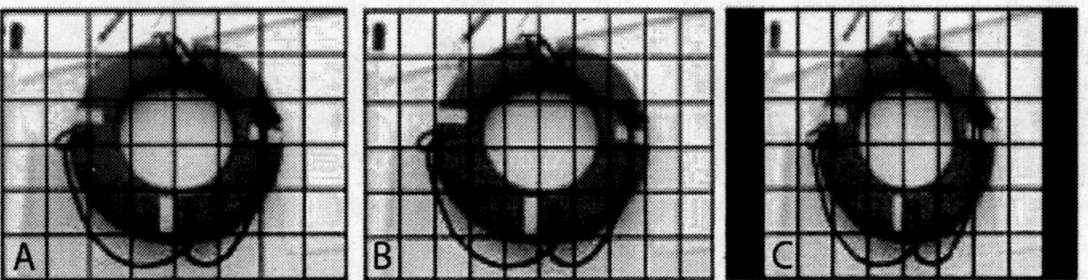


***A.** 4:3 square-pixel image displayed on 4:3 square-pixel (computer) monitor **B.** 4:3 square-pixel image interpreted correctly for display on 4:3 non-square pixel (TV) monitor **C.** 4:3 square-pixel image interpreted incorrectly for display on 4:3 non-square pixel (TV) monitor*

**Fig. 7.12:** *Pixel and frame aspect ratios*

**Create an image for use in video**

1. Create a new document.
2. From the Preset menu in the New dialog box, choose the Film & Video preset.
3. Choose the size that's appropriate for the video system on which the image will be shown.
4. Click Advanced to specify a color profile and specific pixel aspect ratio.

   *Note: By default, nonsquare pixel documents open with Pixel Aspect Ratio Correction enabled. This setting scales the image so it appears as it would on the nonsquare-pixel output device (usually a video monitor).*

5. To view the image as it would appear on a computer monitor (square pixel), choose View > Pixel Aspect Ratio Correction.

**Fig. 7.13:** Circle in NTSC DV (720 x 480 pixels) document viewed on computer (square pixel) monitor with Pixel Aspect Ratio Correction turned on (top) and Pixel Aspect Ratio Correction turned off (bottom)

You can simultaneously view an image with the Pixel Aspect Ratio Correction turned on and off. With the nonsquare pixel image open and Pixel Aspect Ratio Correction enabled, choose Window > Arrange > New Window For [name of document]. With the new window active, choose View > Pixel Aspect Ratio Correction to turn off the correction.

6. If you have a display device, such as a video monitor, connected to your computer via FireWire, you can preview the document on the device:
   - To set output options before previewing the image, choose File > Export > Video Preview.
   - To view the image without setting output options, choose File > Export > Send Video Preview To Device.

When creating images for video, you can load a set of video actions (included with Photoshop) that automate certain tasks—such as scaling images to fit video pixel dimensions and setting the pixel aspect ratio.

**Load video actions**

For video images, actions automate tasks such as constraining the luminance range and saturation levels to comply with broadcast standards, resizing and converting to nonsquare pixels for use in DVD slide shows (NTSC and PAL, standard and widescreen aspect ratios), creating an alpha channel from all currently visible layers, adjusting image areas (especially thin lines) that are likely to cause interlace flicker, and generating a titlesafe overlay.

1. Choose Window > Actions to display the Actions panel.
2. Click the triangle in the upper right corner of the panel, and choose Video Actions from the menu.

**Adjust pixel aspect ratio**

You can create a custom pixel aspect ratio in existing documents, or delete or reset pixel aspect ratios previously assigned to a document.

Assign a pixel aspect ratio value to an existing document

- With a document open, choose View > Pixel Aspect Ratio and then choose a pixel aspect ratio that's compatible with the video format that you'll be using your Photoshop file with.

**Create a custom pixel aspect ratio**

1. With a document open, choose View > Pixel Aspect Ratio > Custom Pixel Aspect Ratio.
2. In the Save Pixel Aspect Ratio dialog box, enter a value in the Factor text box, name the custom pixel aspect ratio, and click OK.

The new custom pixel aspect ratio appears in both the Pixel Aspect Ratio menu of the New dialog box and in the View > Pixel Aspect Ratio menu.

**Delete a pixel aspect ratio**

1. With the document open, choose View > Pixel Aspect Ratio > Delete Pixel Aspect Ratio.
2. In the Delete Pixel Aspect Ratio dialog box, choose the item to delete from the Pixel Aspect Ratio menu, and click Delete.

**Reset the pixel aspect ratios**

1. With the document open, choose View > Pixel Aspect Ratio > Reset Pixel Aspect Ratios.
2. In the dialog box, choose one of the following:

➢ **Append**

Replaces the current pixel aspect ratios with the default values plus any custom pixel aspect ratios. This option is useful if you deleted a default value and want to restore it to the menu but also want to retain any custom values.

➢ **OK**

Replaces the current pixel aspect ratios with the default values. Custom pixel aspect ratios are discarded.

➢ **Cancel**

Cancels the command.

**Prepare images for use in After Effects**

You can import a Photoshop (PSD) file directly into an After Effects project with the option of preserving individual layers, layer styles, transparent areas and layer masks, and adjustment layers (preserving the individual elements for animation).

***Note****: For best results, work in RGB mode, which After Effects uses. After Effects CS3 and later can convert files from CMYK to RGB. After Effects 7 and earlier cannot.*

Before you export a layered Photoshop file for use in After Effects do the following to reduce preview and rendering time and to avoid problems with importing and updating Photoshop layers:-

➢ Organize and name layers. If you change a layer name or delete a layer in a Photoshop document after you import it into After Effects, After Effects won't be able to find the renamed or deleted layer. The After Effects Project panel lists that layer as missing. (You can also group layers into Smart Objects. For example: If you used a set of layers to make a foreground object and a set of layers to make a background, you can group them as one Smart Object each, and easily animate one to fly in front of the other).

➢ Make sure that each layer has a unique name. Duplicate layer names can cause confusion.

➢ Always choose from the Maximize PSD And PSB File Compatibility menu in the File Handling Preferences dialog box.

➢ Use the appropriate pixel dimension preset for video and film in the New Document dialog box.

➢ Do any required color correction, scaling, cropping, or other edits in Photoshop so that After Effects doesn't have to do extra image-processing work. (You can also assign a color profile to the image that corresponds to the intended output type, such as Rec. 601 NTSC or Rec. 709). After Effects can read embedded color profiles and interpret the image's colors accordingly.

## 7.26 MULTIMEDIA SETUP FOR VIDEO EDITING

Here are your basic specs to look for when buying a computer for video editing:

- 8-16 GB RAM memory or as much as you can afford
- 3.0GHz Intel Core 2 Duo Processor or better
- At least 1 GB hard drive, 7200 RPM .. buy as much as you can afford, you can always add external hard drives
- Graphics card – 512-1GB nVidia Quatro or a Geforce graphics card – For Apple --- ATI Radeon HD 5670 graphics with 256-512MB memory (you only really need 512 if gaming)
- Sound card – ASUS motherboard
- Nice size screen – 19-21 inch minimum
- Windows 7, 64bit edition
- 8x SuperDrive (DVD±R DL/DVD±RW/CD-RW)
- Firewire or Thunderbolt Port

## 7.27 VIDEO ESSENTIALS CHECK LIST

Before you get started on your documentary project, there are some "must have" digital video essentials.

**Fig. 7.14:** Digital Video Camcorder

**Digital Video Camcorder** – The first and most basic item you'll need is a video camcorder. So literally, for a few hundred bucks (or FREE if you can borrow a camera), you're already in the game and ready to start shooting!

**Video Editing Computer** – A video editing computer is the same as any other computer except that it has the capacity (enough memory, processing power and hard drive space) to hold and manage video footage.

**Digital Video Editing Software** – This is where it gets fun. There are so many cool options right now, from simple video editing software, such as Apple's iMovie, to the more complex professional programs such as Premiere, Avid or Final Cut Pro. Great options exist for every skill level.

**External Hard Drive** – Unless you're only uploading a few minutes of footage to your computer, you'll need additional hard drive space to hold and manage all your video clips (13 GB holds about 1 hour of DV footage). You'll need 2 to 4 times as much space if you're working with HD (high definition) video.

**Camcorder Microphone** – Of course all camcorders come equipped with an internal microphone, however, if you want to boost the professional level of your project (Get it? *Boost the level?*), it is highly recommended that you have an external microphone such as a boom, lavaliere and/or wireless mic, depending on the project.

**Firewire Cable** – This is a simple little "must have" item, a digital video essential, that allows you to transfer high quality footage from your camcorder or video player to your computer. (Make sure your computer has a firewire port)

## 7.28 LIST OF TOP 15 BEST VIDEO EDITING SOFTWARE FOR 2016

Gone are days when creating a short film or documentary was a task of technical expertise and one should be quite a professional to deal with editing and related tasks. Now, however, after dawn of all these revolutionary technologies and their day-to-day applications, video editing too has become an easy-to-accomplish task, if you know which video editors you should use. A huge number of video editing softwares are available in industry — both paid and free — it will be probably a tough task for user to choose one editing tool from the list and then to accomplish your editing task!

In this post, however, understanding this issue, we have prepared a list of top 15 video editing tools. We shall check out note-worthy features, supported platforms and pricing of each video editing tool that is listed.

### 1. AVS Video Editor

AVS Video Editor can be the first choice of yours when you are looking for an easy to use, professional-quality-rich & quick video editor for your Windows computers. AVS Video Editor, developed by Online Media Technologies, offers a number of notable features such as a huge amount of effects, support for Blu-ray videos, multilingual support, ability to share videos directly through platforms like Facebook, Flick and MySpace and useful features such as stabilization. Considering these, AVS Video Editor is one of the best video editing software for Windows.

- Supported Platforms: Windows
- Supported Input Formats: AVI, MP4, MKV, FLV, AMV, 3GP, MPG, DAT, VCD etc.
- Supported Output Formats: AVI, MP4, WMV, SWF, FLV, MPG etc.
- Price: All software from AVS is available as a bundle for $59, but you have an unlimited trial version.
- Key Features: HD Support, Non-destructive Editing, Single Video Track, Dual Audio track.

Fig. 7.15: AVS Video Editor

### 2. Final Cut Pro

Final Cut Pro is the video editing tools that has helped filmmakers to edit some of your favourite movies including The Social Network and The Girl with the Dragon Tattoo. Being a video editing software developed by Apple Inc, Final Cut Pro has a number of noticeable features such as an impressive user interface, quite useful keyboard shortcuts & lots more. So, if you afford video editing in your Mac, Final Cut Pro is the best video editor for Mac, we assure.

- Supported Platforms: Macintosh
- Supported Input Formats: Any video format that is compatible with QuickTime
- Supported Output Formats: Any video format that is compatible with QuickTime
- Price: $299 (year 2017)
- Key Features: HD Support, Non-destructive editing, storyboard mode, up to 99 video tracks and 99 audio tracks

### 3. Sony Vegas Movie Studio

If you want to create stunning videos without consuming that much system resources, Sony Vegas Movie Studio will, most probably, be the best tool for Windows PCs. Sony Vegas Movie Studio is actually the minimized version of Sony Vegas Pro and it is meant for passionate professionals, who would find the simple interface, variety of features along with support for additional elements such as transitions, text, video stabilization, realtime effects etc. Altogether, its features make Sony Vegas Movie Studio an all-in-one solution for professionals who do not want to spend much.

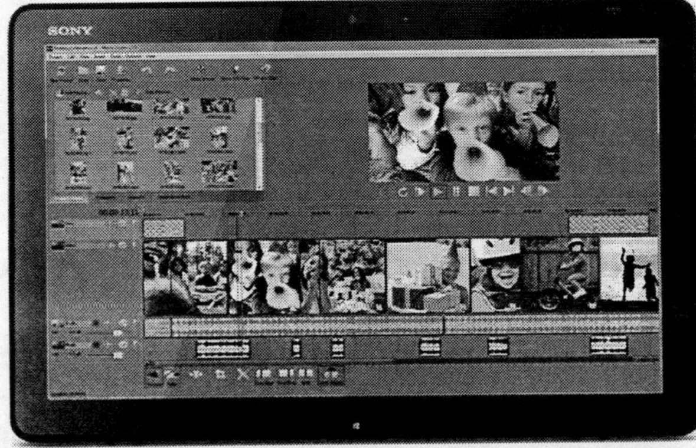


**Fig. 7.16:** Sony Vegas Movie Studio

- Supported Platform: Windows
- Supported Input Formats: MP4, AVI, WAV, WMV, QuickTime, MPEG-4 etc.
- Supported Output Formats: AVI, MP4, MPEG-4, WMV, WAV etc.
- Price: $49.95 (Trial version is available)(year 2017)

### 4. Lightworks

We've seen different video editing softwares for different platforms, but Lightworks is the only video editor that does have support for Microsoft Windows, OS X and Linux. Some un-matchable features of Lightworks include dedicated & powerful support for background I/O, dedicated keyboard to enhance video editing experience, multi-cam editing as well as an impressive set of realtime effects that will come in handy when it comes to professional video editing. The list of features also includes dedicated web export option, background export, import and rendering etc.

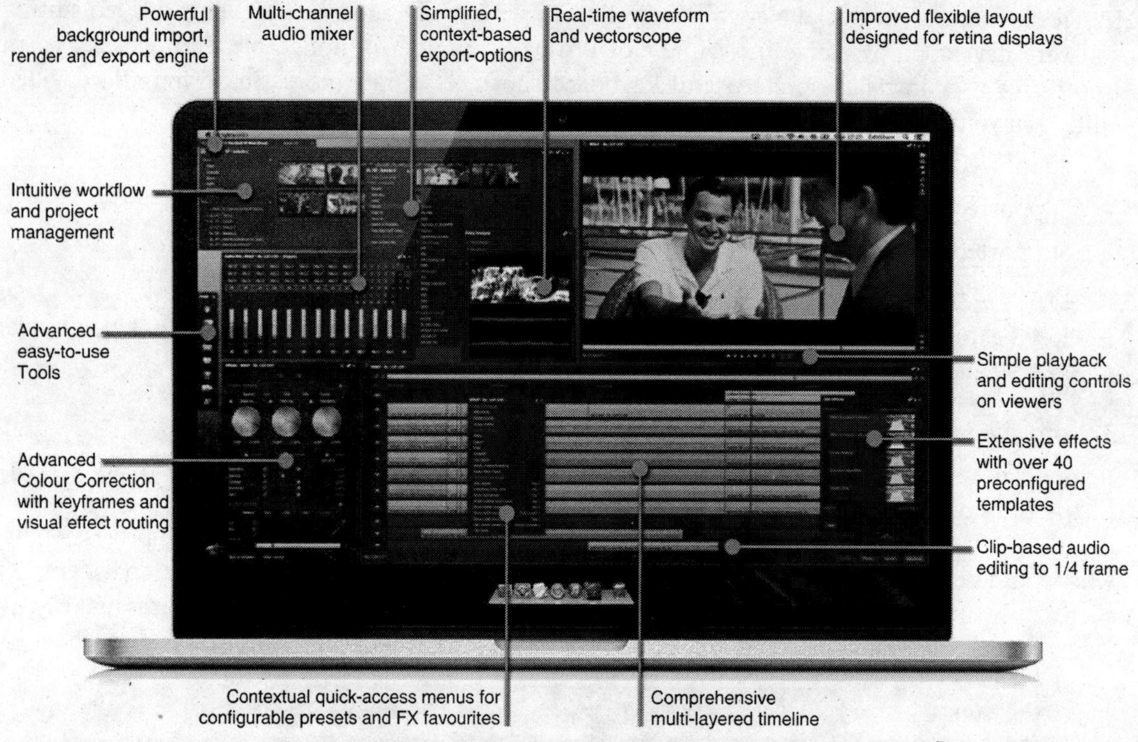


**Fig. 7.17:** The main interface of Lightworks

- Supported Platforms: Windows, Mac and Linux
- Supported Input Formats: Almost Every Video Format including High Definition ones
- Supported Output Formats: Almost Every Video Format including High Definition ones
- Price: Lightworks is free to download, but it has a Pro version as well
- Key Features: HD Support, Non-destructive editing, storyboard mode, unlimited video tracks and audio tracks, Linear timecode display

## 5. Sony Vegas Pro

Sony Vegas Pro can be called the BIG BROTHER of Sony Vegas Movie Studio, as it offers enhanced features and it will need you to pay more. Sony Vegas Pro brings a number of intuitive yet productive features such as powerful effects, support for iOS devices through corresponding application, stereoscopic 3D editing, enhanced audio control, support for 4K video, multi-track audio environment, impressive media management, DVD Layout and Design along with one option to preview what you have done. Of course, Sony Vegas Pro will be the best video editing software for those professionals who are ready to pay.

- Supported Platforms: Windows
- Supported Input Formats: AVI, MP4, WMV, WMA, OMA, OGG, AAF, AIF etc.
- Supported Output Formats: MP4, WAV, WMV, MVC, MP3 etc.

- Price: $599.95 (Trial version also available)
- Key Features: HD Support, Non-destructive editing, unlimited video & audio tracks, linear timecode display.

## 6. Cinelerra

**Fig. 7.18:** Cinelerra

Cinelerra is a video editing tool that lets Linux users edit videos in an intuitive manner that no previous experience is required. Written in C++, Cinelerra offers powerful features that are quite simplified by means of the simple UI it has. You can download Cinelerra for almost every Linux distribution and the tool will be quite useful, we bet. UI Cinelerra has three sections that help editors do their job neatly — Timeline, Viewer, Resource Window and Compositor.

- Supported Platforms: Linux
- Supported Input Formats: Almost every Video Format, including HD
- Supported Output Formats: Almost every video format, including HD
- Price: Free
- Key Features: High Definition Support, Non-destructive editing, Multi Track editing, unlimited video and audio tracks, linear time code display.

## 7. Pinnacle Studio

Pinnacle Studio is a widely used video editor available for Windows devices and it is a scaled-down version of a fully-fledged video editor from same developer. Through a number of impressive features, such as drag and drop editing of HD video, timeline-based editing up to 6 tracks, DVD authoring, title and overlay creation, free training, ability for adding sounds and music, collection of royalty-free tracks, a huge collection of transitions & effects, Pinnacle Studio has ensured top position when someone is looking for an effective video editing software for Windows.

- Supported Platforms: Windows

- Supported Input Formats: AVI, MVC, QuickTime, MKV, HDV etc.
- Supported Output Formats: DVD, MPEG-4, MP4, QuickTime, MKV and some device-based platforms
- Price: $59.95(year 2017)
- Key Features: High Definition Support, Non-destructive editing, Multi Track editing, unlimited video and audio tracks, linear timecode display.

## 8. Corel VideoStudio Pro

Corel VideoStudio comes from the same family of CorelDraw, the popular graphics suite. Powered by 64-bit power, Corel VideoStudio is something great, as the tool makes creative video editing a simple task for everyone. Also, when you purchase the ultimate version, you can get features such as variable speed in video editing, easier ways to create overlays and titles, multi-monitor support, DSLR enlarged mode, stop-motion animation etc.

- Supported Platforms: Windows
- Supported Input Formats: Almost every video format including dedicated formats for devices like iPad, DSLRs and Smartphones
- Supported Output Formats: Almost every popular video format, including ability to export files as to be quite suitable in popular devices
- Price: $79.99
- Key Features: HD Support, Non-destructive editing, storyboard mode, 6 video tracks and 4 audio tracks, linear timecode display.

### The Edit workspace

When you open Corel VideoStudio Pro, the Edit workspace appears as your default workspace. The Edit workspace and the Timeline are the heart of Corel VideoStudio Pro, where you can arrange, edit, trim, and add effects to your video clips.

**Fig. 7.19:** The editing Interface of Corel VideoStudio Pro

The Edit workspace consists of the following components:

1. **Menu bar** — provides various commands for customizing Corel VideoStudio, opening and saving movie projects, working with individual clips, and more.
2. **Preview Window** — shows the current video being played in the Player panel.
3. **Library panel** — a storage depot for everything you need to create a movie, including sample video, photo, and music clips, and your imported clips. It also includes templates, transitions, titles, graphics, filters, and paths. The Options area opens in the Library panel.
4. **Navigation area** — provides buttons for playback and for precision trimming in the Player panel.
5. **Toolbar** — lets you choose from a variety of functions related to content in the Timeline.
6. **Timeline panel** — The Timeline is where you assemble the media clips for your video project. For more information,

**Pros**

Wide selection of fun video-creation tools. Clear, simple interface. Support for 4K Ultra HD and 3D media. Motion tracking lets you add text, effects, and objects that follow a moving element. HTML5 video page creation. 64-bit performance.

**Cons**

Slightly slower rendering than best competitors. No search for effects or media. Only 20 video overlay tracks.

**Bottom Line**

Corel continues to offer one of the most feature-packed consumer video editing packages around. And this version beefs up its performance with native 64-bit support.

## 9. iMovie

Apple's iMovie has long been one of the most consumer-orientated video editors out there. It's packaged with iLife, a simple software suite that comes bundled with every Mac, and touts some serious practicability for the everyday user. The latest version of the software allows you to import and edit video clips from a variety of external devices, such as smartphones and GoPro cameras, and sports a clean interface that is attractive and easy to navigate.

Aside from video, images and audio can also be incorporated into your project by simply dragging your desired multimedia into the project area and arranging them in timeline-like fashion. The resulting video can always be previewed in real time, as well as any effects — themes, text, music, voice-overs, etc. — before exporting the file directly to YouTube or iCloud. Newer features include a basic audio editor, the option to make previews for apps you've developed, and the even ability to make your own movie trailers complete with transitions and end credits. It's not a tour de force of video editing, but it's perfectly suitable for home videos and minor projects.

iMovie can help you deal with video editing even while you are using an iOS-based device — let that be your iPhone, iPod or iPad. Although iMovie has a tremendous number of features, some of those include truly impressive collection of transitions, drag-based interface, iMovie Theatre that lets you watch movies from your Apple TV, ability to fine tune clips etc.

- Supported Platforms: Macintosh and iOS
- Supported Input Formats: QuickTime compatible with HD support

- Supported Output Formats: QuickTime compatible with HD Support
- Price: $14.99
- Key Features: NDE, HD Support, 2 video tracks and 4 audio tracks, linear timecode display and storyboard mode.

### 10. Adobe Premier Pro

Adobe Premier Pro is an immensely-popular, timeline-based video editor that is available for Windows and Mac. In a condition that you are ready to spend, Adobe Premier Pro will be an awesome video editing tool, particularly when we consider features such as Integration with After Effects and Photoshop, top-notch video masking features, superb transitions etc.

- Supported Platforms: Windows, Mac and Cloud
- Supported Formats: Almost every popular video format
- Price: Different plans (individual and combo) are available through official site of Premier Pro
- Key Features: HD Support, Multi Track editing, storyboard mode, unlimited audio and video tracks, linear timecode display and NDE.

### 11. Pitivi

Pitivi is an open-source video editing software that is available for Linux-based devices and it offers an intuitive UI in a way that Pitivi can be your favorite in a few seconds. Although Pitivi offers more than enough features for all video editors, some of notable ones are simple yet effective video editing capabilities, hundreds of transitions, filters and effects, availability in multiple languages, precision-based video editing etc.

- Supported Platforms: Linux
- Supported Formats: Almost every modern video format
- Price: Free
- Key Features: HD Support, NDE, Multi Track editing, unlimited video and audio tracks, and linear timecode display.

### 12. CyberLink PowerDirector

PowerDirector from CyberLink is a consumer-focused software for video editing, and it comes with a simple UI that is capable of allowing any user get accustomed with the tool in seconds. From Professional looking animations as well as slideshows to stunning videos, CyberLink PowerDirector has an option for you; you can keep editing even when you are away from PC because CyberLink has published Smartphone applications for this tool. Apart from a number of transitions that are built in, you can get more from DirectorZone as well.

- Supported Platforms: Windows
- Supported Input Formats: FLV, AVI, 3GP, AVI, DAT, WMV, MPEG-4, MP4 etc
- Supported Output Formats: MVC, MPEG-4, MKV, WMV, QuickTime etc.
- Price: $74.99
- Key Features: High Definition support, NDE, 100 audio and video tracks, linear timecode display and storyboard mode.

### 13. Kdenlive

Kdenlive, built on MLT Framework, is a great solution when you are looking for an open-source video editing software that makes sense. Available for Linux, FreeBSD and Mac OS X, Kdenlive offers impressive features that are impressive when it comes to preparing stunning video results. Some other features of Kdenlive include rendering that you can pause according to your need, ability to apply special transition effects, multi-track editing feature etc.

- Supported Platforms: FreeBSD, Mac and Linux
- Supported Formats: MPEG2, MP4 and other popular video formats
- Price: Free
- Key Features: HD Support, storyboard mode, 2 video tracks and 4 audio tracks, linear timecode display, NDE.

### 14. ivsEdits

If you are looking for the best free video editing software in market, for Windows PCs, ivsEdits will be one of the finer choices you can make. Through its simple User Interface, ivsEdits can impress almost every editor as far as he or she does not want to spend much on video editing solutions. Some notable features of ivsEdits are multiple live inputs, multi-camera editing, various video effects, realtime video I/O, hardware integration etc.

- Supported Platforms: Windows
- Supported Formats: Most popular video formats
- Price: Free

### 15. Windows Movie Maker

Although simple, Windows Movie Maker can come in handy if you want to create videos without using that much of system resources. Through its ultra-simple User Interface, Windows Movie Maker will help you add transitions, set up tracks and export the video into a Windows-compatible media format — things are simple enough, we hope.

- Supported Platforms: Windows
- Supported Formats: Any Windows-compatible media format
- Price: Free
- Key Features: HD Support, Storyboard Mode, 1 video track and 2 audio tracks, linear timecode display.

## Create images for video

### About creating images for video

Photoshop can create images of various aspect ratios so that they appear properly on devices such as video monitors. You can select a specific video option (using the New dialog box) to compensate for scaling when the final image is incorporated into video.

### Safe zones

The Film & Video preset also creates a document with nonprinting guides that delineate the actionsafe and titlesafe areas of the image. Using the options in the Size menu, you can produce images for specific video systems—NTSC, PAL, or HDTV.

Safe zones are useful when you edit for broadcast and videotape. Most consumer TV sets use a process called overscan, which cuts off a portion of the outer edges of the picture, allowing the center of the picture to be enlarged. The amount of overscan is not consistent across TVs. To ensure that everything fits within the area that most TVs display, keep text within the titlesafe margins, and all other important elements within the actionsafe margins.

***A.*** *Action safe area (outer rectangle)* ***B.*** *Title safe area (inner rectangle)*

**Fig. 7.20:** *Video preset file size guides*

*Note: If you are creating content for the web or for CD, the titlesafe and actionsafe margins do not apply to your project because the entire image is displayed in these media.*

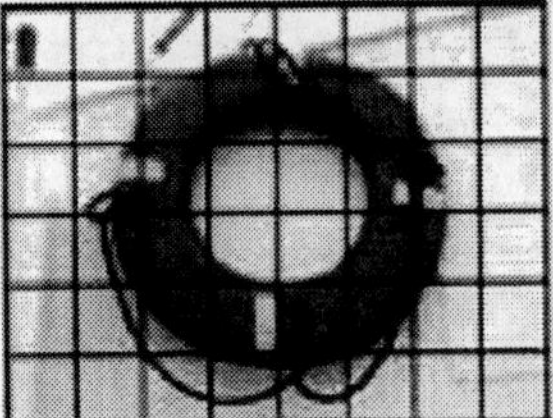

**Fig. 7.21:** Pixel and frame aspect ratios

## Preview options

To help you create images for video, Photoshop has a Pixel Aspect Ratio Correction viewing mode that displays images at the specified aspect ratio. For more accurate previews, Photoshop also has a Video Preview command that lets you immediately preview your work on a display device, such as a video monitor. To use this feature, you must have the device connected to your computer via FireWire (IEEE 1394).

## Other considerations

Both Adobe AfterEffects and Adobe Premiere Pro support PSD files created in Photoshop. However, if you're using other film and video applications, you might consider these details when you create images for use in video:

- Some video-editing programs can import individual layers from a multilayer PSD file.

- If the file has transparency, some video-editing programs preserve it.
- If the file uses a layer mask or multiple layers, you might not have to flatten the layers, but you might want to include a flattened copy of the file in PSD format to maximize backward compatibility.

## Aspect ratio

*Frame aspect ratio* describes the ratio of width to height in the dimensions of an image. For example, DV NTSC has a frame aspect ratio of 4:3 (or 4 width by 3 height) and a typical widescreen frame has a frame aspect ratio of 16:9. Some video cameras can record various frame aspect ratios. Many cameras that have a widescreen mode use the 16:9 aspect ratio. Many professional films have been shot using even wider aspect ratios.

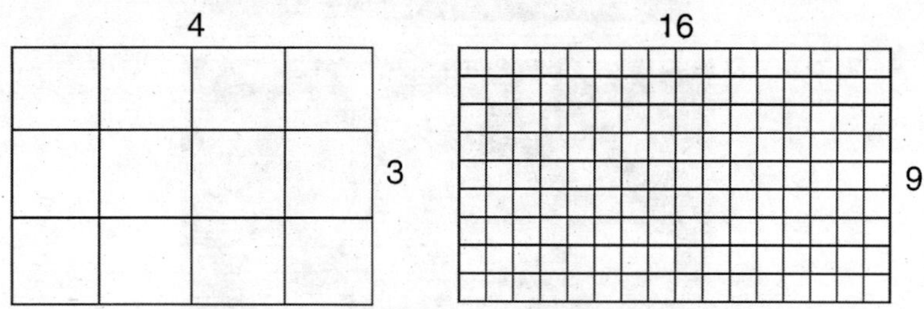


*4:3 frame aspect ratio (left), and wider 16:9 frame aspect ratio (right)*

**Fig. 7.21:** Aspect ratios 4:3 and 16:9

*Pixel aspect ratio* describes the ratio of width to height of a single pixel in a frame. Different video standards use different pixel aspect ratios. For example, many computer video standards define a 4:3 aspect ratio frame as 640 pixels wide by 480 pixels high, which results in square pixels. The computer video pixels in this example have a pixel aspect ratio of 1:1 (square), whereas the DV NTSC pixels have a pixel aspect ratio of 0.91 (nonsquare). DV pixels, which are always rectangular, are vertically oriented in systems producing NTSC video and horizontally oriented in systems producing PAL video.

If you display rectangular pixels on a square-pixel monitor without alteration, images appear distorted; for example, circles distort into ovals. However, when displayed on a broadcast monitor, the images appear correctly proportioned because broadcast monitors use rectangular pixels.

*Note: When copying or importing images into a nonsquare pixel document, Photoshop automatically converts and scales the image to the pixel aspect ratio of the document. Images imported from Adobe Illustrator are also properly scaled.*

**Create an image for use in video**

1. Create a new document.
2. From the Preset menu in the New dialog box, choose the Film & Video preset.
3. Choose the size that's appropriate for the video system on which the image will be shown.
4. Click Advanced to specify a color profile and specific pixel aspect ratio.

*Note: By default, nonsquare pixel documents open with Pixel Aspect Ratio Correction enabled. This setting scales the image so it appears as it would on the nonsquare-pixel output device (usually a video monitor).*

5. To view the image as it would appear on a computer monitor (square pixel), choose `View > Pixel Aspect Ratio Correction.`

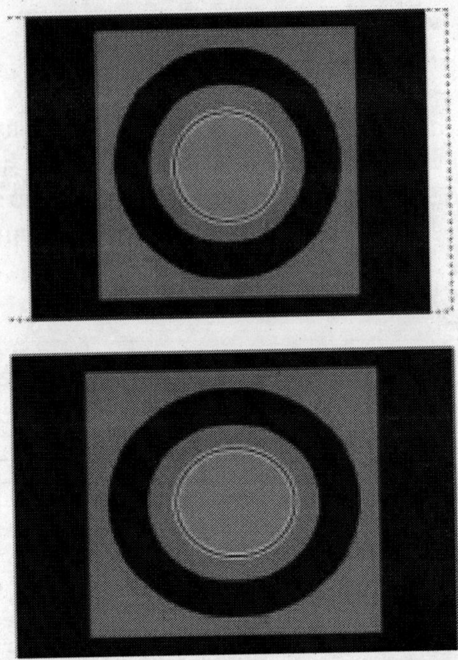

**Fig. 7.20:** Circle in NTSC DV (720 x 480 pixels) document viewed on computer (square pixel) monitor with Pixel Aspect Ratio Correction turned on (top) and Pixel Aspect Ratio Correction turned off (bottom)

You can simultaneously view an image with the Pixel Aspect Ratio Correction turned on and off. With the nonsquare pixel image open and Pixel Aspect Ratio Correction enabled, choose `Window > Arrange > New Window` For [name of document]. With the new window active, choose `View > Pixel Aspect Ratio Correction` to turn off the correction.

6. If you have a display device, such as a video monitor, connected to your computer via FireWire, you can preview the document on the device:
   - To set output options before previewing the image, choose `File > Export > Video Preview.`
   - To view the image without setting output options, choose `File > Export > Send Video Preview to Device.`

When creating images for video, you can load a set of video actions (included with Photoshop) that automate certain tasks—such as scaling images to fit video pixel dimensions and setting the pixel aspect ratio.

## Load video actions

For video images, actions automate tasks such as constraining the luminance range and saturation levels to comply with broadcast standards, resizing and converting to nonsquare pixels for use in DVD slide shows (NTSC and PAL, standard and widescreen aspect ratios), creating an alpha channel from all currently visible layers, adjusting image areas (especially thin lines) that are likely to cause interlace flicker, and generating a titlesafe overlay.

1. Choose `Window > Actions` to display the Actions panel.
2. Click the triangle in the upper right corner of the panel, and choose Video Actions from the menu.

## Adjust pixel aspect ratio

You can create a custom pixel aspect ratio in existing documents, or delete or reset pixel aspect ratios previously assigned to a document.

### Assign a pixel aspect ratio value to an existing document

➢ With a document open, choose `View > Pixel Aspect Ratio` and then choose a pixel aspect ratio that's compatible with the video format that you'll be using your Photoshop file with.

### Create a custom pixel aspect ratio

1. With a document open, choose `View > Pixel Aspect Ratio > Custom Pixel Aspect Ratio.`
2. In the Save Pixel Aspect Ratio dialog box, enter a value in the Factor text box, name the custom pixel aspect ratio, and click `OK.`

The new custom pixel aspect ratio appears in both the Pixel Aspect Ratio menu of the New dialog box and in the `View > Pixel Aspect Ratio menu.`

### Delete a pixel aspect ratio

1. With the document open, choose `View > Pixel Aspect Ratio > Delete Pixel Aspect Ratio.`
2. In the Delete Pixel Aspect Ratio dialog box, choose the item to delete from the Pixel Aspect Ratio menu, and click `Delete.`

### Reset the pixel aspect ratios

1. With the document open, choose `View > Pixel Aspect Ratio > Reset Pixel Aspect Ratios.`
2. In the dialog box, choose one of the following:

➢ **Append**

Replaces the current pixel aspect ratios with the default values plus any custom pixel aspect ratios. This option is useful if you deleted a default value and want to restore it to the menu but also want to retain any custom values.

➢ **OK**

Replaces the current pixel aspect ratios with the default values. Custom pixel aspect ratios are discarded.

➢ **Cancel**

Cancels the command.

### Prepare images for use in After Effects

You can import a Photoshop (PSD) file directly into an After Effects project with the option of preserving individual layers, layer styles, transparent areas and layer masks, and adjustment layers (preserving the individual elements for animation).

***Note**: For best results, work in RGB mode, which After Effects uses. After Effects CS3 and later can convert files from CMYK to RGB. After Effects 7 and earlier cannot.*

Before you export a layered Photoshop file for use in After Effects, do the following to reduce preview and rendering time and to avoid problems with importing and updating Photoshop layers.

- ➢ Organize and name layers. If you change a layer name or delete a layer in a Photoshop document after you import it into After Effects, After Effects won't be able to find the renamed or deleted layer. The After Effects Project panel lists that layer as missing. (You can also group layers into Smart Objects. For example: If you used a set of layers to make a foreground object and a set of layers to make a background, you can group them as one Smart Object each, and easily animate one to fly in front of the other).
- ➢ Make sure that each layer has a unique name. Duplicate layer names can cause confusion.
- ➢ Always choose from the Maximize PSD and PSB File Compatibility menu in the File Handling Preferences dialog box.
- ➢ Use the appropriate pixel dimension preset for video and film in the New Document dialog box.

Do any required color correction, scaling, cropping, or other edits in Photoshop so that After Effects doesn't have to do extra image-processing work. (You can also assign a color profile to the image that corresponds to the intended output type, such as Rec. 601 NTSC or Rec. 709. After Effects can read embedded color profiles and interpret the image's colors accordingly.

**Learning Outcomes**

In this chapter we have learnt about :

1. Analog and Digital Video
2. Video storage formats and codec and algorithm for compression
3. How to capture information and manipulate it to make video
4. Multimedia set up for making Video

After reading this chapter the reader will be able to:

Make video presentations in different formats with the help of different world famous software

CHAPTER 8

# Animation

**Leaning Objectives**

In this chapter we shall learn about:

1. Types and Principles of Animation for Multimedia
2. Digital animation techniques
3. Animation using Adobe Flash Animator CS-6 software tool
4. Flash Frames, Tools Panels, Timeline, Texts, Sounds Effects
5. Rendering, Tweening and Morphing
6. Rolling and Bouncing Ball Animation
7. Other Animation software

## 8.1 ANIMATION

To animate means "to give life to" . An animator's job is to take a static image or object and literally bring it to life by giving it movement and personality. Animation can be defined as a sequence of images which are designed to appear at about 16 fps to create the perception of movement.

This frame rate is just above the threshold of jerky motion and creates a satisfactory simulation. However, animation sequences can be developed with any specific frame rate at which objects will move across the screen for creating special effects.

Most animation objects are graphics considerably smaller than the screen although some animation sequences can be very complex. Designers exercise considerable control over animation sequences which can be arranged to reduce bandwidth requirements without affecting the quality of the presentation. With actual video this option is not available because the image itself is beyond the control of the designer and is a reflection of reality captured by a camera.

Complex high-quality animation sequences require about 20 Mbps, bandwidth and compression is normally used to reduce that requirement. Some animation forms such as those used in complex visualizations, product simulations, and virtual-reality applications require considerably more bandwith for storage and transmission.

## 8.2 PRINCIPLES OF ANIMATION

Animation is possible because of a biological phenomenon known as **persistence of vision**. An object seen by the human eye remains mapped on the eye's retina for a brief time after viewing. This makes it possible for a series of images that are changed very slightly and very rapidly, one after the other, to seemingly blend together into a visual illusion of movement. In other words, if you just change slightly the location or shape of an object rapidly enough, the eye will perceive the changes as motion.

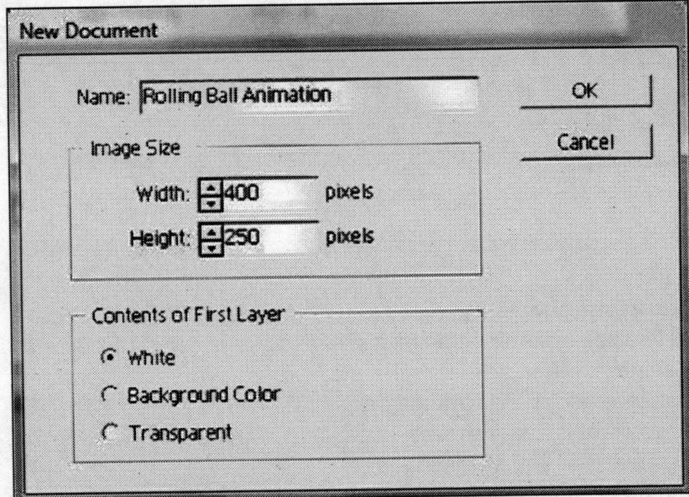


**Fig. 8.1:** Rolling Ball Animation

Television video builds 30 entire frames or pictures every second; the speed with which each frame is replaced by the next one makes the images appear to blend smoothly into movement. Movies on film are typically shot at a shutter rate of 24 frames per second, but using projection tricks (the projector's shutter flashes light through each image twice), the flicker rate is increased to 48 times per second, and the human eye thus sees a motion picture. Quickly changing the viewed image is principle of an animatic a flip-book, or a zoetrope. To make an object travel across the screen while it changes its shapes, just change the shape and also move it a few pixels for each frame. Then, when you play the frames back at a faster speed, the changes blend together and you have motion and animation. (it's the same magic as when the hand is quicker than the eye, and you don't see the pea moving in the blur of the gypsy's cups).

## 8.3 ANIMATION TECHNIQUES

**Traditional Methods:** As is evident from the history, animators have used and invented a variety of different animation techniques. Traditionally most of the animation was done by hand. All the frames in an animation had to be drawn by hand. Since each second of animation requires 24 frames (film), the amount of work required to create even the shortest of movies, can be tremendous. Some of the traditionally used methods are described below.

Key Frames In this technique a storyboard is laid out and then the artists draw the major frames of the animation. These major frames are in which a lot of changes take place. They are the key points of animation. Later a bunch of artists draw in the frames in between. This technique is, of course, very time and effort intensive.

Today, computers have taken a great deal of handwork out of the animation and rendering process, and commercial films such as Jurassic Park, Beauty and Beast, and Toy Story have utilized the power of computers.

The process of animation is of broadly three types:

1. Cel Animation
2. Particle Animation
3. Computer (CGI) Animation

### 8.3.1 Cel Animation

The animation techniques made famous by Disney use a series of progressively different graphics on each frame of movie film (which plays at 24 frames per second). A minute of animation may thus require as many as 1,440 separate frames. The term cel drives from the clear celluloid sheets that were used for drawing each frame, which have been replaced today by acetate or plastic. Cels of famous animated cartoons have become sought-after, suitable-for-framing collector's items.

Cel animation artwork begins with key-frames (the first and last frame of an action). For example, when an animated figure of a man walks across the screen, he balances the weight of his entire body on one foot and then the other in a series of falls and recoveries, with the opposite foot and leg catching up to support the body. Thus the first keyframe to portray a single step might be the man pitcthing his body weight forward off the left foot and leg, while his center of gravity shifts forward; the feet are close together and he appears to be falling. The last keyframe might be the right foot and catching the body's fall, with the center of gravity now centered between the outstretched stride, and the left and right feet positioned far apart.

The series of frames in between the keyframes are drawn in a process called ***tweening***. Tweening and action requires calculating the number of frames between keyframes and the path the action takes, and then actually sketching onto a cel with pencil the series of progressively different outlines. As tweening progresses, the action sequence is checked by flipping through the frames. The penciled frames are assembled and then actually filmed as a pencil text to check smoothness, continuity, and timing.

When the pencil frames are satisfactory, they are permanently inked, and acrylic colors are painted on. In the hands of a master, cel paint applied to the back of acetate can produce beautiful and subtle effects, with feathered edges of smudges, or simply flat and perfectly even.

**Fig. 8.2(a):** Moving Boy Animation

**Fig. 8.2(b):** Moving Boy Animation

The cells for each frame of our example of a walking man-which may consist of a text title, a background, a left arm, a right arm, legs, shoes, a body, and facial features-are carefully registered and stacked. It is this composite that becomes the final photographed frame in an animated movie.

### 8.3.2 Particle Animation

Particle systems are a special animation effect causing hundreds or thousands of points to spray from a surface, each one following specified behaviour but with randomness built in. You set up the basic parameters, such as gravity, initial direction, and velocity, and the program calculates the rest, without the need to individually animate all those points. With the correct tweaks, particle systems can simulate water, smoke, fire, and other natural phenomena as convincing 3-D graphics. Inverse Kinematics, of IK, sets up hierarchies of motion between parent and children models (models attached to parents) so that you can more easily simulate natural movement. Basically, IK lets models lower in a hierarchy affect models higher in the hierarchy. A correctly configured IK link will let you pull on a figure's foot, for example, and have the lower and upper legs follow along naturally so that you don't need to individually animate the leg components. IK is an important addition to the animator's arsenal, but isn't necessary or even desirable for convincing movement. Pixar's phenomenally successful 3-D movie, Toy Story, for instance, was created without IK.

### 8.3.3 Rotascoping

Rotascoping is a technique where images are copied from a moving video into an animation. The animator draws the motion and shape of the object by referring to the video as opposed to imagining in his head. With the help of the rotascoping one can animate some complex scenes that would be hard to visualize otherwise. The disadvantage is that one will have to hunt for the exact video that one wants to animate.

## 8.4 COMPUTER (CGI) ANIMATION

The roots of computer animation began with computer graphics pioneers in the early 1960s working at major U.S. research institutes, often with government funding Their earliest films were scientific simulations with titles like "Flow of a Viscous Fluid" and "Propagation of Shock Waves in a Solid Form" [source: Carnegie Mellon School of Computer Science].

Ed Catmull at the University of Utah was one of the first to toy with computer animation as art, beginning with a 3-D rendering of his hand opening and closing. The University of Utah was the source of the earliest important breakthroughs in 3-D computer graphics, like the hidden surface algorithm that allows a computer to conceptualize three-dimensional objects, and the Utah Teapot, a strikingly rendered 3-D teapot that signaled a turning point in the photorealistic quality of 3-D graphics .

Computer Animation programs typically employ the same logic and concepts as *cel animation, using layer, keyframe and tweening* techniques, and even borrowing from the vocabulary of classic animators. On the computer, paint is most often filled or drawn with tools using features such as gradients and anti-alissing. The work inks, in computer animation terminology, usually means special methods for computing RGB pixel values, providing edge detection, and layering so that images can blend or otherwise mix their colors to produce special transparencies, inversions, and effects.

You can usually set your own frame fates on the computer, but the rate at which changes on computer and screens are refreshed will depend on the speed and power of your display platform and hardware. Although your animations will probably never push the limits of your monitor's scan rate (about 60 to 70 frames a second), animation does put raw computing horsepower to task. If you cannot compute all your changes and display them as a new frame on your monitor within, say, 1/15 second, then the animation may appear jerky and slow.

### 8.4.1 Kinds of Computer Animation

**Computer Animation:** With time the technique of animation has become more and more computer -assisted and computer- generated. All of such techniques require a trade-off between the level of control that the animator has over the finer details of the motion and the amount of work that the computer does on its own. Broadly, the computer animation falls into three basic categories:

- keyframing,
- motion capture, and
- simulation.

**Keyframing** The significance of the term "Keyframing" can be traced back to traditional hand animation technique. Keyframing requires that the animator specify critical or key positions for the objects. The computer then automatically fills in the missing frames by smoothly interpolating between those positions. The characters for a movie called Toy Story made in 1995 were designed through key frame animation. It's believed that each character had as many as 700 controls. Keyframing requires that the animator has a well thought out plan of how the moving objects are going to behave over time as well as the talent to express that information through keyframed information. The continued popularity of keyframing is a function of the degree of control that it allows the animator to exercise over the subtle details of the motion.

**Motion Capture** Another technique is Motion Capture, in which magnetic or vision-based sensors record the actions of a human or animal object in three dimensions. A computer then uses this data to animate the object. This technology has enabled a number of famous athletes to supply the actions for characters in sports video games. Motion capture is pretty popular with the animators mainly because some of the commonplace human actions can be captured with relative ease. However, there can be serious discrepancies between the shapes or dimensions of the subject and the graphical character and this may lead to problems of exact execution.

**Simulation:** Unlike key framing and motion picture, simulation uses the laws of physics to generate motion of figures and other objects. Virtual humans are usually represented as a collection of rigid body parts. These models though physically plausible are only an approximation of the human body. With more research and complex models the simulations are becoming increasingly life like. Simulations can be easily used to produce slightly different sequences while maintaining physical realism while in other animations like key framing or motion capture a mere speeding up or slowing down the playback can spoil the naturalness of motion. Secondly real-time simulations allow a higher degree of interactivity where the real person can maneuver the actions of the simulated character. In contrast the applications based on keyframing and motion select and modify motions form a precomputed library of motions. One drawback that simulation suffers from is the expertise and time required to handcraft the appropriate controls systems. Hardware and Software Hardware and software are two of the major factors that determine the quality of computer animation that is produced. As both of these components work in conjunction with each other it is important to make the right choice for a product that is of lasting quality and accuracy.

In computer animation, animators use software to draw, model and animate objects and characters in vast digital landscapes. There are two basic kinds of computer animation:
computer-assisted and
computer-generated.

Computer or CGI animation is the art of creating moving images with the use of computers. It is a subfield of computer graphics and animation. Is a subset of both computer graphics and animation technologies. It is the creation of moving images (animation) using computer technology. Computer animation is broken down into two categories.

### 8.4.2 Computer-Assisted Animation

Computer-assisted animation is typically two-dimensional (2-D), like cartoons. The animator draws objects and characters either by hand or with a computer. Then he positions his creations in key frames, which form an outline of the most important movements. Next, the computer uses mathematical algorithms to fill in the "in-between" frames. This process is called tweening. Key framing and tweening are traditional animation techniques that can be done by hand, but are accomplished much faster with a computer.

Technology has long been a part of the animator's toolkit. Animators at Disney revolutionized the industry with innovations like the use of sound in animated short films and the multi-plane camera stand that created the parallax effect of background depth.

### 8.4.3 Computer-Generated Animation

Computer-generated animation is that where the animation is designed solely on the computer system using animation and 3D graphics software, and computer-assisted animation where traditional animations are computerized.

Increasingly it is created by means of 3D computer graphics, though 2D computer graphics are still widely used for stylistic, low bandwidth, and faster real-time rendering needs. Sometimes the target of the animation is the computer itself, but sometimes the target is another medium, such as film. It is also referred to as CGI (computer-generated imagery or computer-generated imaging), especially when used in films.

To create the illusion of movement, an image is displayed on the computer screen and repeatedly replaced by a new image that is similar to the previous image, but advanced slightly in the time domain (usually at a rate of 24 or 30 frames/second). This technique is identical to how the illusion of movement is achieved with television and motion pictures.

Computer animation is essentially a digital successor to the art of stop motion animation of 3D models and frame-by-frame animation of 2D illustrations. For 3D animations, objects (models) are built on the computer monitor (modeled) and 3D figures are rigged with a virtual skeleton. For 2D figure animations, separate objects (illustrations) and separate transparent layers are used, with or without a virtual skeleton. Then the limbs, eyes, mouth, clothes, etc. of the figure are moved by the animator on key frames. The differences in appearance between key frames are automatically calculated by the computer in a process known as tweening or morphing. Finally, the animation is rendered.

For 3D animations, all frames must be rendered after modeling is complete. For 2D vector animations, the rendering process is the key frame illustration process, while tweened frames are rendered as needed. For pre-recorded presentations, the rendered frames are transferred to a different format or medium such as film or digital video. The frames may also be rendered in real time as they are presented to the end-user audience. Low bandwidth animations transmitted via the internet (*e.g.* 2D Flash, X3D) often use software on the end-users computer to render in real time as an alternative to streaming or pre-loaded high bandwidth animations

Computer-assisted animation is typically two-dimensional (2-D), like cartoons. The animator draws objects and characters either by hand or with a computer. Then he positions his creations in key frames, which form an outline of the most important movements. Next, the computer uses mathematical algorithms to fill in the "in-between" frames. This process is called tweening. Key framing and tweening are traditional animation techniques that can be done by hand, but are accomplished much faster with a computer.

### 8.4.4 Computer-Generated 3-D Objects

Computer-generated animation is a different story. First of all, it's three-dimensional (3-D), meaning that objects and characters are modeled on a plane with an X, Y and Z axis. This can't be done with pencil and paper. Key framing and tweening are still an important function of computer-generated animation, but there are other techniques that don't relate to traditional animation. Using mathematical algorithms, animators can program objects to adhere to (or break) physical laws like gravity, mass and force. Or create tremendous herds and flocks of creatures that appear to act independently, yet collectively. With computer-generated animation, instead of animating each hair on a monster's head, the monster's fur is designed to wave gently in the wind and lie flat when wet.

Technology has long been a part of the animator's toolkit. Animators at Disney revolutionized the industry with innovations like the use of sound in animated short films and the multi-plane camera stand that created the parallax effect of background depth.

Ed Catmull at the University of Utah was one of the first to toy with computer animation as art, beginning with a 3-D rendering of his hand opening and closing. The University of Utah was the source of the earliest important breakthroughs in 3-D computer graphics, like the hidden surface algorithm that allows a computer to conceptualize three-dimensional objects, and the Utah Teapot, a strikingly rendered 3-D teapot that signaled a turning point in the photo realistic quality of 3-D graphics [source: Carnegie Mellon School of Computer Science].

In 1973, "Westworld" became the first film to contain computer-generated 2D graphics. More films in the late 1970s and early 1980s relied on computer graphics, or CG, to create primitive effects that were designed to look computer-generated. "Tron" (1982) was ideal for showcasing undeniably digital effects since the movie took place inside a computer.

"Jurassic Park" (1993) was the first feature film to integrate convincingly real, entirely computer-generated characters into a live action film, and "Toy Story" (1995) from Pixar (name of the firm) was the first full-length "cartoon" made entirely with computer-generated 3-D animation.

The increasing sophistication and realism of 3-D animation can be directly credited to an exponential growth in computer processing power. Today, a standard desktop computer runs 5,000 times faster than those used by computer graphics pioneers in the 1960s. And the cost of the basic technology for creating computer animation has gone from $500,000 to less than $2,000 [source: PBS].

**Basics of creating a 3-D computer-generated object.**

To create a 3-D computer-generated object, you'll need modeling software like Maya, 3ds Max or Blender. These programs come loaded with a large number of basic 3-D shapes, called ***primitives* or *prims,*** which are the building blocks of more complex objects. For example, you could model a car by connecting cubes, cylinders, pyramids and spheres of different shapes and sizes. Since these are 3D objects, they're modeled on the X, Y and Z axes and can be rotated and viewed from any angle.

When you first begin to model an object, it doesn't have any surface color or texture. All you see on your screen is the object's skeleton -- the lines and outlines of the individual cubes, blocks and spheres that have been used to construct it. This is called a ***wireframe***. Each shape that's formed by the lines of the wireframe is called a polygon. A pyramid, for example, is made up of four triangle-shaped polygons.

In practice, there are several ways to create a ***wireframe*** model of an object. If you don't want to be confined to constructing objects from fixed shapes like blocks and cylinders, you can use a more free-form technique called ***spline-based modeling***. Splines allow for objects with smooth, curved lines. Another method is to sculpt an object out of clay or some other physical material and use a 3-D scanner to create a wireframe copy of the object in the modeling software.

Once you have your wireframe -- through any modeling method you choose -- you can shade its surface to see what it would look like as a 3-D object. But to make the object look more realistic, you need to add ***color and surface texture***. This is done in something called the materials editor. Here you can play with an endless palette of colors or create your own by adjusting the red, green and blue values, and tinkering with hue and saturation. Common surface textures like *wood grain, rock, metal and glass* usually come with the modeling software and can be easily applied to surfaces. You can also create image files in a program like Photoshop and wrap the image around the object like wallpaper.

Lighting is perhaps the most important component for giving an object depth and realism. Modeling programs allow you to light your objects from every imaginable angle and adjust how the surface of your objects reflect or absorb light. There are three basic values that dictate how a surface responds to light:

1. **Ambient**: the color of an object's surface that's not exposed to direct light
2. **Diffuse**: the color of the surface that's directly facing the light source
3. **Specular**: the value that controls the reflectiveness or shininess of the surface.

Modeling programs are especially helpful for creating realistic looking 3D objects because they contain mathematical algorithms that replicate the natural world. For example, when you light a sphere from a certain angle, the surface reflects light in just the right way and the shadow is cast at the precise angle. These details trick the mind into thinking that this object on a two-dimensional screen actually has depth and texture.Now let's look at how animators use computers to help create vast digital landscapes and realistic animated sets.

Computers have added a whole new dimension to ***matte paintings***. Literally Digital matte painters use a combination of source photographs, 2-D Photoshop images, 3-D modeling and 3-D animation to create impressive fictional landscapes. Think of those magnificent establishing shots in the recent "Star Wars" movies, showing a sprawling intergalactic metropolis or a jungle fortress crawling with thick foliage and perched atop a raging waterfall.

For live action films, digital matte painters often get the assignment of creating a historically accurate backdrop for a scene. In "The Last Samurai," for example, the script called for Tom Cruise's character to wander out of a bar and into the streets of San Francisco, circa 1876. First, the live actors performed their scene in front of a green or blue screen. Then the digital matte painters consulted archive photos of the city to model a 3-D skyline. They took digital photos of a beautiful sunset and placed it behind their model cityscape. Then they created a computer-generated trolley that would clank down the steep street in front of the actors.

Digital matte painters use the same techniques when creating landscapes for fully animated films, like those made by Pixar. If the characters are going to interact a lot with the virtual set, then each set element is rendered in 3-D. But for large establishing shots, or an enormous backdrop that will only be seen once, the matte painters use a combination of 2D Photoshop collages and 3D models to build realistic landscapes that fit within the style of the animated film. Pixar movies, for example, have become increasingly photo realistic without losing their "cartoony" quality. So the landscapes can't look perfectly "real." They have to be built on a color and texture palette that matches the rest of the movie.

Another technology that adds impressive realism to a digital landscape is something called a particle system. Particle systems use mathematical algorithms to recreate the natural movements of animated elements like smoke, fire and flocks of birds. For digital matte paintings, the animator doesn't have to draw every flame and every wisp of smoke as the city burns. He just uses the modeling software's particle tools to program how large he wants the flames to be and how dark and billowy the smoke should be. With the same controls, he can model one CG seagull and program the software to create a flock of birds that flap their wings at different paces to take slightly different paths as they soar across the sunset.

Computer animators are artists. While their tools are high-tech, nothing replaces their creative vision. That said, over the past two decades, computers have opened up unimaginable possibilities for animators. With sophisticated modeling software and powerful computer processors, the only limit is the animator's imagination.

The applications of computer animation extend far beyond film and television.

Video games are at the forefront of interactive 2-D and 3-D animation. 3-D animators help design and model new products and industrial machines. In fields like medicine and engineering, 3-D animation can help simplify and visualize complex internal processes. And computer animators are in high demand for marketing and advertising campaigns.

## 8.5 THE COMPUTER-ANIMATION PROCESS

High-quality animated films are produced at a frame rate of 24 frames per second (fps). For a 90 minute film, that's nearly 130,000 frames of animation. At Pixar, for example, an individual animator is expected to produce 100 frames of animation a week [source: Pixar]. Pixar Animation Studios is Located in Emeryville, California, Pixar Animation Studios has created acclaimed animated feature and short films for over 25 years. Pixar is also home to the RenderMan line of software products. Half of the process of creating a computer-animated feature film has nothing to do with computers. First, the filmmakers write a treatment, which is a rough sketch of the story. When they've settled on all of the story beats — major plot points — they're ready to create a storyboard of the film. The storyboard is a 2- D, comic-book-style rendering of each scene in the movie along with some jokes and snippets of important dialogue [source: Pixar]. During the storyboarding process, the script is polished and the filmmakers can start to see how the scenes will work visually.

The next step is to have the voice actors come in and record all of their lines. Using the actors' recorded dialogue, the filmmakers assemble a video animated only with the storyboard drawings. After further editing, re-writing, and re-recording of dialogue, the real animation is ready to begin. The art department now designs all the characters, major set locations, props and color palettes for the film. The characters and props are modelled in 3-D or scanned into the computers from clay models. At Pixar, each character is equipped with hundreds of avars, little hinges that allow the animators to move specific parts of the character's body. Woody from "Toy Story," for example, had over 100 avars on his face alone.

The next step is to create all of the 3-D sets, painstakingly dressed with all of the details that bring the virtual world to life. Then the characters are placed on the set in a process called **blocking**. The director and lead animators block the key character positions and camera angles for each and every shot of the movie.

After this each of animators is assigned short snippets of scenes. They take the blocking instructions and create their own more detailed key frames. Then they begin the tweening process. The computer handles a lot of the **interpolation** — calculating the best way to tween two key frames — but the artist often has to tweak the results so they look even more lifelike. It's common for an animator to re-do a single short animated sequence several times before the director or lead animator is satisfied [source: Pixar].

The characters and props are given surface texture and color. They're dressed with clothing that wrinkles and flows naturally with body movements, hair and fur that waves in the virtual breeze, and skin that looks real enough to touch. Then it's time to light the scenes, using ambient, omni-directional and spotlights to create depth, shadows and moods.

High-quality animated films are produced at a frame rate of 24 frames per second (fps). For a 90 minute film, that's nearly 130,000 frames of animation. At Pixar, for example, an individual animator is expected to produce 100 frames of animation a week [source: Pixar].

Now the characters and props are given surface texture and color. They're dressed with clothing that wrinkles and flows naturally with body movements, hair and fur that waves in the virtual breeze, and skin that looks real enough to touch. Then it's time to light the scenes, using ambient, omnidirectional and spotlights to create depth, shadows and moods.

The final step of the process is called rendering. Using powerful computers, all of the digital information that the animators have created -- character models, key frames, tweens, textures, colors, sets, props, lighting, digital matte paintings, etcetera -- is assembled into a single frame of film. Even with the incredible computing power of a company like Pixar, it takes an average of six hours to render one frame of an animated film [source: Pixar]. That's over 88 years of rendering for a 90-minute film. Good thing they can render more than one frame at a time.

There are two main types of animations which are used in multimedia applications. The first type of animation :2D animation or linear animation, is the simple movement of objects on the screen, generally through linear translation. Multimedia development environments often provide the necessary tools to perform this simple animation procedure. The original creation of animation :3D animation, however, is very technically and artistically involved, as well as time consuming. Three dimensional objects are created using a mathematical model. Each object may be shown in various views, giving the user a realistic sense of third dimension.

### (1) 2D animation

2D animation figures are created and/or edited on the computer using 2D bitmap graphics or created and edited using 2D vector graphics. This includes automated computerized versions of traditional animation techniques such as of tweening, morphing, onion skinning and interpolated rotoscoping.

Computer animation in the 2D sense is seen often with applications like Flash. Few people know that this popular internet presentation authoring tool had it's beginnings as an animation application and that it's strong web based presence was an evolution. The movie graphics, buttons, sound and effects are all a form of 2D computer animation.

Many people use simplistic 2D computer animation with applications like Powerpoint. Video editors use applications like After Effects, Final Cut and others to create titling and animated effects for their productions.

2D Animation Two dimensional (2D) animation software adds movement and action to static images. These programs use either vector drawn or bitmapped images as objects. The motion of animation is perceived by the viewer from a series of frames. For the motion to appear smooth a minimum of 15 frames persecond (fps) is generally required. There are two types of 2D animation, path and cel.

**Cel Animation:** Cel animation is based on a series of frames or cels in which the object is redrawn in each consecutive cel to depict motion. Cel comes from the word celluloid (a transparent sheet material) which was first used to draw the images and place them on a stationary background. a set of eight cels that can be used to create an animation. Example- moving hands in two directions

**Path Animation:** Path Based animation is the simplest form of animation and the easiest to learn. It moves an object along a predetermined path on the screen. The path could be a straight line or it could include any number of curves. Often the object does not change, although it might be resized or reshaped. Path animation is used to create the illusion of a bouncing ball. This can be relatively easy process, because you need only one object (the ball), rather than several objects as in cel animation.

Besides cel and path animation, there are also other techniques in 2D animation. These include:

**Skinning:** Skinning is used in the process of creating cel animations. It allows you to see a faint outline of the previous cel so you can draw the changes for the next cel

**Tweening:** Tweening is a method where the first cel of an animation and the last cel of animation are selected and the animation program calculates all the cells in between.

## (2) 3D animation

3D animation are digitally modeled and manipulated by an animator. In order to manipulate a mesh, it is given a digital skeletal structure that can be used to control the mesh. This process is called rigging. Various other techniques can be applied, such as mathematical functions (ex. gravity, particle simulations), simulated fur or hair, effects such as fire and water and the use of Motion capture to name but a few, these techniques fall under the category of 3d dynamics. Many 3D animations are very believable and are commonly used as Visual effects for recent movies.

3D is what most people think of when referring to computer animation. Right now it is also where the "action" is with animation due to it's flexibility. The process is different to 2D in that a scene is made in 3D well before any animation starts. Then there are more than one level of animation, such as:

- ➢ Character animation
- ➢ Camera animation
- ➢ Physic and dynamics
- ➢ Composited objects

All of these combine and then the final frame by frame computer animation is generated.

## (1) Computerized character animation

Movies like Shrek and Toy Story are examples of character animation. Each character is created and motions added to make it interact with the story, lip sync to the words, etc. It's a complicated process but fortunately computers are getting better at aiding the 3D animator by automating some tasks. The movement of lips can be automated and motion of some body parts can simulate real world motions, jerks and reactions.

### (2) Camera Animation

This is the most simple form of 3D computer animation. It is simply the movement of the camera throughout the 3D scene. The motions come together just as a real world film shoot would take place and then the scene is rendered to produce the animation frames from the viewpoint of the 3D camera. This is typically what makes a 3D Walk Through Video.

### (3) Advanced effects using computer animation

Archiform 3D uses camera tracking extensively for exterior scenes. The process involves shooting real life high-definition video footage and using computers to determine the path of the real camera in 3D space. This data is then used within the 3D scene to create a duplicated motion that can be overlayed back onto the real video footage. In this case the computer animation is synced perfectly to match real life motion.

## Video and Animation Characteristics

Creating a multimedia video is like audio where it is the process of recording and storing many samples of a signal. The signal represents visual data - light intensity levels and colours. In multimedia, creating a high quality video is not as easy as it is for audio. Here are two main problems in using video in multimedia systems:

A single full screen (800 × 600) video frame in 24-bit true colour need 1.4 megabytes of storage space. A single second of video played at full speed (30 frames per second) would need over 40 megabytes of storage. Video require a fairly large amount of storage space.

The video data has to be transferred from secondary storage (*e.g.* hard disk, DVD) into RAM. It must then be processed and moved into the frame buffer without affecting the quality of the display. Video also makes big demands on the system's processing abilities.

Making compromises to overcome these problems allow a smooth full motion effect, reduction of storage space and processing power needed to play the video. Here are two most common compromises:

1. **Reduced screen size** - instead of using the entire screen area to replay the digitised video, a smaller playback area is used
2. **Reduced speed** - instead of using the VDU screen refresh rate (often 30 frames per second), a much slower playback speed of 10 or even fewer frames per second is used.

The most popular multimedia file storage formats for video images are AVI, QuickTime, and MPEG. For animations, files are stored as GIF. Multimedia animations are rarely full screen , are usually played at a reduced speed and almost always use a reduced colour palette. Resulting to only minimal problems. The best known example of multimedia animation would be the animated GIFs used on the Web, many are small icon-sized animations. Methods of animating:

## 8.6 RENDERING

The final step of the animation process is called rendering. Using powerful computers, all of the digital information that the animators have created — character models, key frames, tweens, textures, colors, sets, props, lighting, digital matte paintings, etcetera — is assembled into a single frame of film. Even with the incredible computing power of a company like Pixar, it takes an average of six hours to render one frame of an animated film [source: Pixar]. That's over 88 years of rendering for a 90-minute film. Good thing they can render more than one frame at a time.

Rendering captures a view of your 3D scene and saves it as a 2D image. An image must be rendered before you can print it or open it in an image-editing or page- layout program. Rendering is analogous to taking a photograph of your scene. The result is photorealistic because the final rendering procedure considers all of the objects in a scene simultaneously and calculates not just forms, color, and texture, but the interaction of lights and surfaces within the scene. As you move around a scene, these effects change. The rendered image that you capture of a scene from one camera viewpoint is unlike any other. CorelDREAM 3D offers a choice of renderers: the Ray Tracer or the Draft Z-Buffer.

Although you create one scene, it exists in 3D space. Therefore, you can take any number of renderings of it from different angles and with different lighting conditions. If you create an object in a 2D drawing program and want to look at it from another side, you have to redraw the object. In CorelDREAM 3D, you simply move the camera to another view and render the scene again.

A rendering is distinct from the scene from which it was taken. It is a separate file and is stored on disk in one of several standard graphic formats. You can print your renderings, open them in an image-editing program, or place them into virtually any application.

## 8.7 ADOBE FLASH ANIMATOR CS-6. SOFTWARE TOOLS

Flash is used for working with vector graphics, animation, games etc. Flash is usually used for making web banners and other types of advertising. Because you use simple images, text and vector graphics, the file size is generally small. This allows content to be uploaded, download, and played quickly and without any problems. In order for you to watch flash animations, you will need a plug-in called Flash Player, which these days, is incorporated in most, if not all, web browsers.

Adobe Flash (formerly Macromedia Flash) is a multimedia software popular for adding animation and interactivity to web pages. Originally deviced by Macromedia, Flash was introduced in 1996, and is currently developed and distributed by Adobe Systems.

Adobe Flash Professional CS6 is a flash design tool to create animations and applications. It gets integrated with other Adobe programs, such as Adobe Photoshop and Dreamweaver for design purposes and multiple SDKs for games and app development. This allows for performing complementary tasks, making the experience richer.

Flash is commonly used to create animation, advertisements, and various web page flash components, to integrate video into web pages, and more recently, to develop rich Internet applications. Flash can manipulate vector and raster graphics, and supports bidirectional streaming of audio and video. It contains a scripting language called ActionScript. Several software products, systems, and devices are able to create or display Flash content, including Adobe Flash Player, which is available free for most common web browsers, some mobile phones and for other electronic devices (using Flash Lite). The Adobe Flash Professional multimedia authoring program is used to create content for the Adobe Engagement Platform, such as web applications, games and movies, and content for mobile phones and other embedded devices.

Files in the SWF format, traditionally called "ShockWave Flash" movies, "Flash movies" or "Flash games", usually have a .swf file extension and may be an object of a web page, strictly "played" in a standalone Flash Player, or incorporated into a Projector, a self-executing Flash movie (with the .exe extension in Microsoft Windows). Flash Video files[spec 1] have a .flv file extension and are either used from within .swf files or played through a flv-aware player, such as VLC, or QuickTime and Windows Media Player with external codecs added.

- Flash is a multimedia graphics program specially for use on the Web
- Flash enables you to create interactive "movies" on the Web

- Flash uses vector graphics, which means that the graphics can be scaled to any size without losing clarity/quality
- Flash does not require programming skills and is easy to learn It provides:
  - Immersive experiences with Flash video, content and applications with full-screen mode.
  - Low-bandwidth, high-quality video with advanced compression technology.
  - High-fidelity text using the advanced text rendering engine.
  - Real-time dynamic effects with filters for Blur, DropShadow, Glow, Bevel, Gradient Glow, Gradient Bevel, Displacement Map, Convolution, and Color Matrix.
  - Innovative media compositions with 8-bit video alpha channels.
  - Blend modes, radial gradient, and stroke enhancements.
  - Additional image formats: GIF, Progressive JPEG, and PNG.

### 8.7.1 Flash vs. Animated Images and Java Applets

Animated images and Java applets are often used to create dynamic effects on Web pages.

The advantages of Flash are:

- Flash loads much faster than animated images
- Flash allows interactivity, animated images do not
- Flash does not require programming skills, java applets do

## 8.8 GENERAL FLASH WORKFLOW

To build a Flash application, you typically perform the following basic steps:

- Plan the application.
- Decide which basic tasks the application will perform : Add media elements.
- Create and import media elements, such as images, video, sound, and text : Arrange the elements.

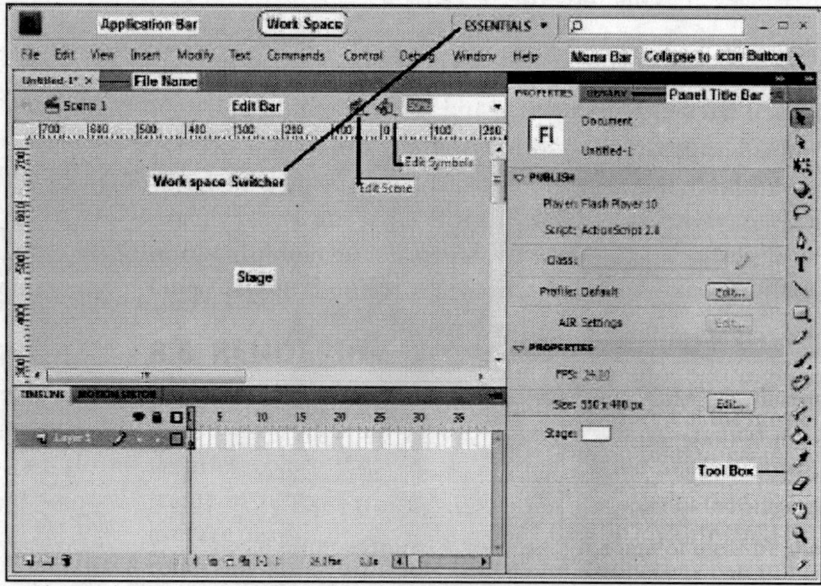


Fig. 8.3(a): The Work Space Window

- Arrange the media elements on the Stage and in the Timeline to define when and how they appear in your application : Apply special effects.
- Apply graphic filters (such as blurs, glows, and bevels), blends, and other special effects as you see fit: Use ActionScript to control behavior:Write ActionScript® code to control how the media elements behave, including how the elements respond to user interactions :Test and publish your application.
- Test to verify that your application is working as you intended and find and fix any bugs you encounter. You should test the application throughout the creation process. Publish your FLA file as a SWF file that can be displayed in a web page and played back with Flash® Player.
- Depending on your project and your working style, you might use these steps in a different order.

## 8.8.1 Get Started

To begin, open Flash CS6 Professional. The window shown here appears:
Click Flash File (ActionScript 3.0). The Workspace window appears:

The window shown is the default layout and is named Essentials. If your window has a different layout, click the down-arrow to the right of Help on the Menu bar and then select Essentials.

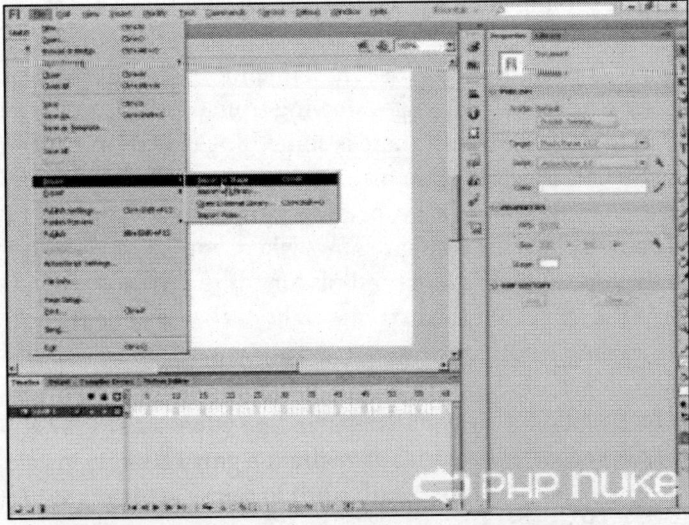


**Fig. 8.3(b):** The beginning interface of CS6 Profession

## 8.8.2 Workspace overview

You create and manipulate your documents and files using various elements, such as panels, bars, and windows. Any arrangement of these elements is called a workspace. The workspaces of the different applications in Adobe® Creative Suite® 4 share the same appearance so that you can move between the applications easily. You can also adapt each application to the way you work by selecting from several preset workspaces or by creating one of your own. `Although the default workspace layout varies in different products, you manipulate the elements much the same way in all of them. We will learn to create an animated film as shown in the figure shown below in which there is a group of buildings coverd with sky and on the road a car is moving:

You will find the flash environment very similar to a paint brush environment (say Adobe Photoshop or Image Ready), so if you are familiar with paint brush, you will very much feel at home, now on the extreme right you will find the various tool bars like Drawing tools, view tools, color tools, options tools.

On the top there is a horizontal menu bar, which is very similar to menu bar of any other software.

The Stage is in the center of the window. You create your movie on the Stage. The Property inspector and the Library panels appear to the left of the Tools panel. You use the Property inspector to set object and tool properties. You store objects in the Library. The Timeline appears in the bottom portion of the window. You use the Timeline to lay out the sequence of your movie. In timeline, you will see a bunch of rectangles starting from 0 to 570, on the left of the timeline bar you will find layers, on top of the layers1, there is something called timeline button, if you click on the timeline button you can hide the timeline, in case you want more space or room to work on with your drawings, etc. On top of the page, below the main menu you will find an edit bar, where all your scene will be on display, this edit bar shows where you are in the flash file. Besides the edit bar you will find on the top right you have symbols for editing the scenes on the stage, and also for zooming in and out of the stage. On the extreme right of the flash page, you will see some panels namely Properties and Library both by default, Color, Align & Info & Transform, Action, etc when they have been set so.You can click on the panels to make necessary changes. You can customize your panel settings by simply clicking on the windows option in the main menu, the panel will come on workspace, you can drag and drop in to the extreme right.

## 8.8.3 Tools Panel ( Tool Bar)

On extreme right you will see a vertical Tools panel (also called tool bar) which contains the tools you use to create or modify drawings and text of which further details are shown in the sketch below:

You select a tool by clicking it. If there are multiple tools in a single well, click the visible tool a second time and a popup menu appears. You can then choose the tool you want. Wells with multiple tools have a small triangle in the bottom- right corner.

Tool modifiers for the selected tool are shown at the bottom of the Tools panel. You use modifiers to set tool options. When you hover your mouse pointer over a tool or display a tool menu, you will see that each tool has a letter associated with it. You can choose a tool by pressing the letter. For example, when you hover your mouse pointer over the Selection tool , you see "Selection Tool (V)." Pressing "v" activates the Selection tool.

You will understand all the above menus better as you work on it, this is just an introduction to the flash CS6 Environment.

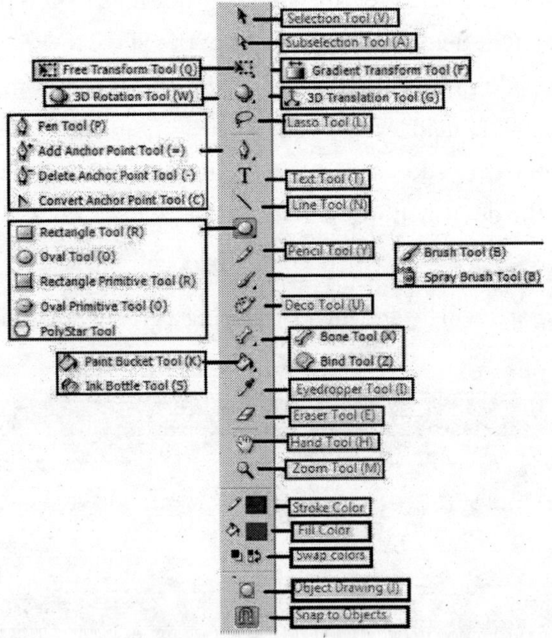


**Fig. 8.4:** The Tool Panel (Bar)

### 8.8.4 Setting Document Properties

You start creating your movie by setting the Frame Rate, Dimensions, Background colour and ruler units.

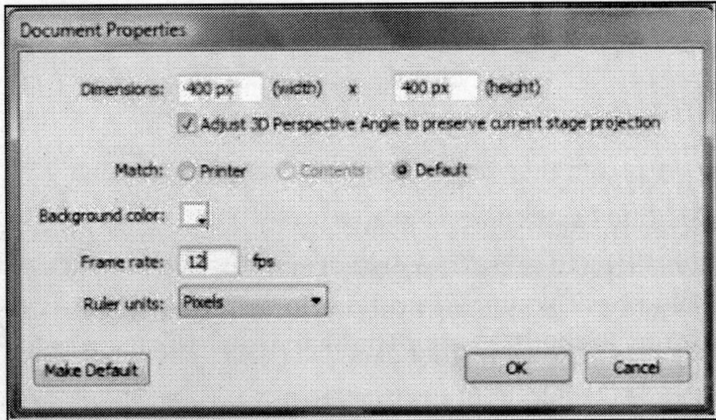


| Frame Rate | The speed of the movie. The number of frames per second. |
|---|---|
| Dimension | The size of the Stage. |
| Background Color | The color of the Stage. |
| Ruler Unite | The unit of measure shown on the rulers. To display the rulers, choose View > Rulers from the menu. |

**Fig. 8.5:** Document Properties Dialogue Box

- Choose `Modify > Document` from the menu or press `Ctrl+J`. The Document Properties dialog box appears.
- Type 400 px in the Width field to set the width of the Stage to 400 pixels.
- Type 400 px in the Height field to set the height of the Stage to 400 pixels.
- Click the Background Color box and then choose white as the background color.
- Type `12` in the Frame Rate field.
- Choose Pixels from the drop-down menu in the Ruler Units field.
- Click `OK`. Flash sets the document properties.

## 8.8.5 Displaying a Grid

In the exercises that follow, you will be drawing. Displaying a grid of horizontal and vertical lines is often helpful when drawing.

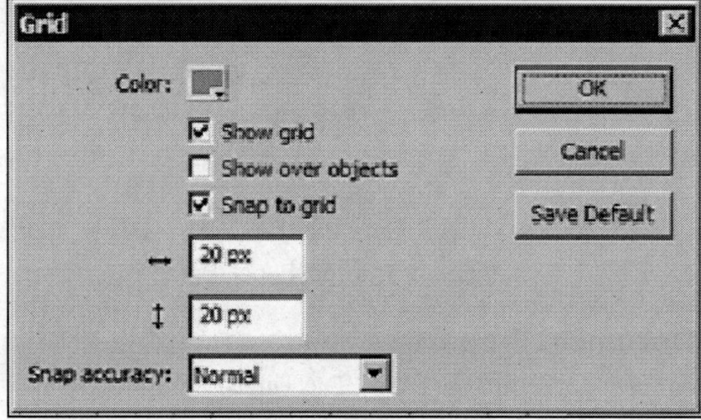


**Fig. 8.6:** Displaying a Grid

- Choose `View > Grid > Edit Grid` from the menu or press Ctrl+Alt+G. The Grid dialog box appears.
- Click the `Color box` and then choose gray to make the grid lines gray.
- Choose `Show Grid` to cause the grid to appear.
- Choose `Snap to Grid` to cause the edges of your drawing to align with the grid lines.
- Set the `Horizontal field` to 20 px to separate horizontal lines by 20 pixels.
- Set the `Vertical field` to 20 px to separate vertical lines by 20 pixels.
- Set the Snap Accuracy to Normal to tell Flash how close your drawing has to be to the gridline for Flash to use the gridline to determine where to place the drawing.
- Click `OK`. Flash creates a grid on the Stage.

## 8.8.6 Work with the Property Inspector

The Property inspector, which is located on the Properties tab, is one of the most frequently used panels in Flash. You use it to set the attributes of objects as you work. If the Property inspector is not open:

Choose `Window > Properties` from the menu. The Property inspector appears on the right side of the window.

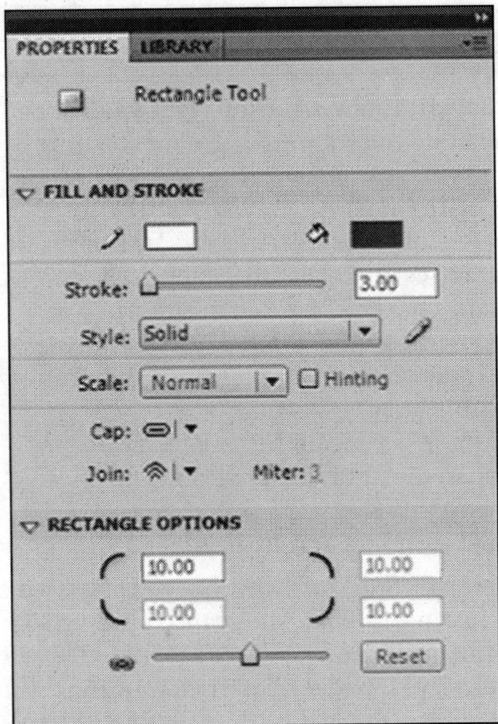


**Fig. 8.7:** Property Inspector Window

The Property inspector is one of many panels found in Flash. When you are not working in a panel, you can collapse it. To collapse a panel, click the `Collapse icon`. The Collapse icon turns into an Expand icon. To open the panel again, click the Expand icon. The Property inspector for a particular tool or object may be divided into several sections. Each section heading is preceded by a triangle. Clicking the triangle toggles the section between open and closed. When a section is open, you can set options.

## 8.9 INTRODUCTION TO FLASH AUTHORING ENVIRONMENT

Lets start by clicking on Create New – Flash File (ActionScript.2.0 or 3.0 ) You will find the flash environment very similar to a paint brush environment, so if you are familiar with paint brush, you will very much feel at home, now on the extreme right you will find the various tool bars like Drawing tools, view tools, color tools, options tools like the picture below.

On the top you will find a menu horizontal bar, which is very similar to any menu in any other program, as seen below.

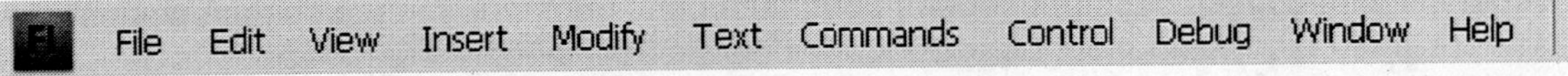


As seen in the picture below, at the bottom of the stage you will find the time line, you will see a bunch of rectangles starting from 0 to 570, on the left of the timeline bar you will find layers, on top of the layersl, there is something called timeline button, if you click on the timeline button you can hide the timeline, in case you want more space or room to work on with your drawings, etc, on top of the page, below the main menu you will find an edit bar, where all your scene will be on display, this edit bar shows where you are in the flash file.

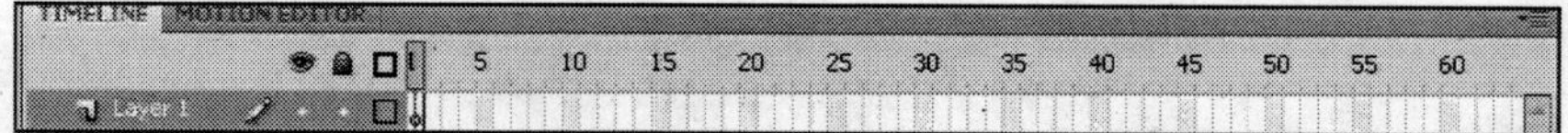


Besides the edit bar you will find on the top right you have symbols for editing the scenes on the stage, and also for zooming in and out of the stage.

On the extreme right of the flash page, you will see some panels namely Properties, Color, Align & Info & Transform, Action, Library etc, as you can see in the picture, you can click on the panels to make necessary changes. You can customize your panel settings by simply clicking on the windows option in the main menu, the panel will come on stage, you can drag and drop in to the extreme right like this picture shown.

You will understand all the above menus better as you work on it, this is just an introduction to the flash CS4 Environment.

## 8.9.1 Panels and Panel workspace in flash

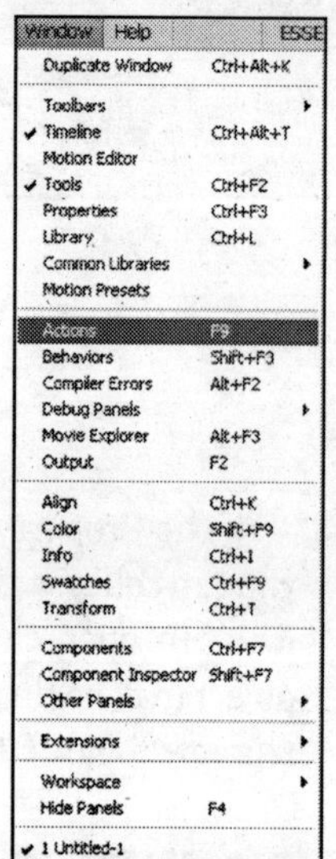


By default flash CS4 has a few panels to work with, but you may need much more panels to work with, you can customize your panels by just clicking on the window menu in the horizontal main menu bar as seen in the picture.

A list of panels are displayed under the window menu, you can simply click on each one of them to have it on your screen, sometimes it may just appear on the middle of the stage, you can simply click on the header and drag it to the right and place it in any order of your choice. At the bottom the 3rd one from the last you will find a workspace layout panel, you will find something like a save current, by clicking on it you can actually save the panel setting for that particular layout by simply naming it to layout1, etc, the next time you open the flash, you may actually have one or two panels on the right which is set as default, so instead of setting it all up again, you can go to windows menu, and click on the layout1, etc to get back all the panels you chose to work on.

## 8.10 DRAWING FIGURES

Lets learn how to draw in flash CS4, lets start by drawing a rectangle and an oval, the reason why we are starting with drawing a rectangle and an oval is because both these have a stroke and a fill. Understanding strokes and fills are important to draw in flash CS4 because they are treated as separate objects and not treated as one object. Using the oval tool on the right hand tool bar menu like this one draws an oval on the stage. You will notice that to the right bottom of this oval tool there is a small triangle, when clicked on it, you will be able to select a rectangle tool, oval tool, Polystar tool etc. As you click on the oval tool, just take a look at what happens to the options panel and the properties panel on the right of the screen.

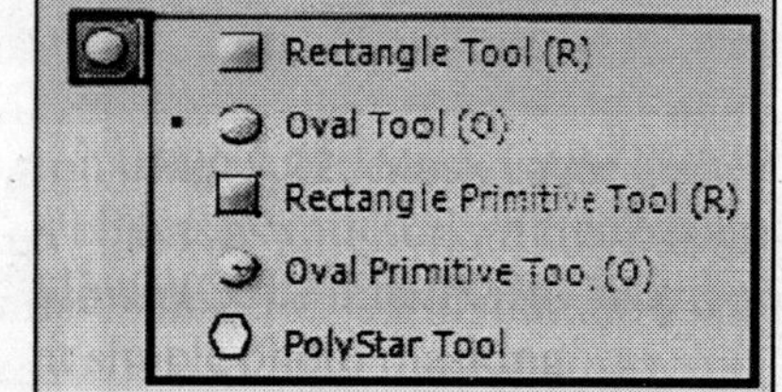


While you see the Stroke, you can either type a number in the white box, or you can simply drag the stroke button to and forth to get the size of your stroke, then you see the style, here you can select the kind of stroke whether you want a solid, dashed, dotted kind of stroke, then below is the scale, if you want normal, horizontal, vertical or none.

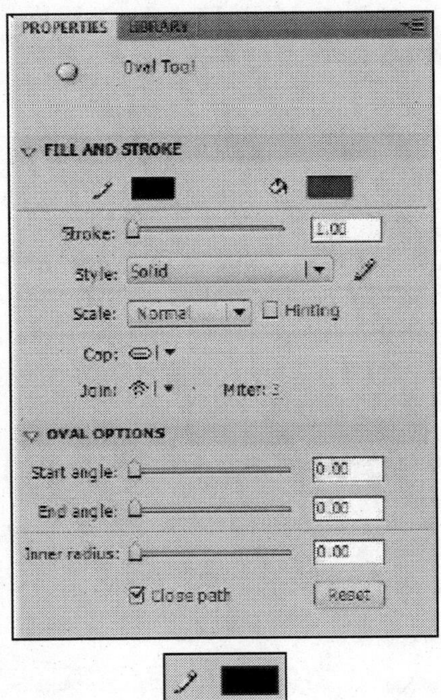


Above figure shows the details of stroke option.

This is the details of the color option. You can use the stroke option and configure the settings or simply click on the fill color and configure the settings. On the main menu we have a button which looks like a magnet. You can use this button to simply snap the objects in place. Lets draw an oval on the stage, with the oval tool selected, lets say we want to give it a red fill, easy enough we simply go to this fill color and select red here and lets have a blue stroke.

If you really want the stroke to stand out, lets make it thicker than what it is now, by simply dragging the arrow to its right or by type in a figure in the box. Lets draw an oval on to the stage, so click on the oval button and go to stage and draw an oval. When you drop and drag, you will notice that as you drag it to a circle, it will snap into place, now release the mouse button, you will find a perfect circle with the colors you chose.

You will see a blue bind box along the circle, this means that the circle has been selected on stage. You can make changes to this object, while it is selected, by simply choosing the fill color and the stroke color. If you don't want the circle to be selected on stage, simply press escape button on your keyboard, it will deselect the circle on stage. By default the snap object button is turned on, while selecting an oval tool, now you can draw a perfect circle by turning off the snap button by simply clicking on it, the background will disappear on it.

Now draw the circle by dragging the cursor on the screen and dragging it down by simply holding on to the shift key on the keyboard, You can select all objects on the stage by clicking on each, or by simply hitting Ctrl+A key in your keyboard and delete it by hitting backspace.

Now if you want to draw a circle exactly in the centre of the stage, you can draw by simply pressing the alt button on the keyboard and dragging it, it will uniformly expand in all directions.

Now lets make a rectangle on stage, you can click on the right bottom of the oval tool and you will find a rectangle, click on it and draw a rectangle on stage.

The rectangle tool works very similarly like a circle or oval tool, you can also use  the snap objects to draw a rectangle, with snap objects on, you can release the mouse button when a circle appears at the corner of the square, it becomes a perfect square.

There is another panel called rectangle options on the right panel space, if you want rounded edges to your square you can use this rectangle options and type a number in the cells provided to get the corner rounded edges. Like illustrated below:

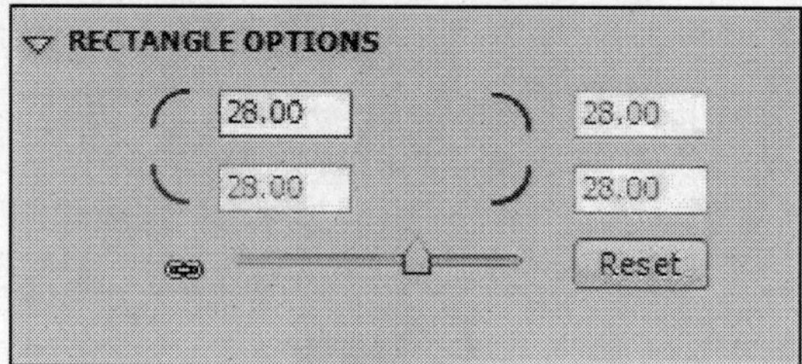


You will find something like this:

Sometimes you will not know what exactly should be the rounded edges on the rectangle or square, there is another way to do this, you can simply click on the rectangle tool bar and draw a rectangle on stage, and do not release your mouse, you can now simply use the up and down arrows to know how much of rounded edges you want to have in the rectangle, this will give you an indication what you square or rectangle will look like with rounded edges straight away.

## 8.11 OBJECT DRAWING MODE

Lets draw a circle on stage and similarly draw another circle on stage with another color chosen from the color panel box, you will find flash CS4 different from Flash Professional, in the sense both the circles are on drawing object mode and you can change the color of each the way you want, unlike flash professional, the second object drawn on stage will be considered as a grouped object and you cannot change the color, if you want to change the color you can by clicking on the grouped object, but in Flash CS4 you can change the color, use a stroke, change the color of stroke etc.,

Let's draw one circle first and draw the second one overlapping on the first circle and then moving it away from the first one, see what happens.

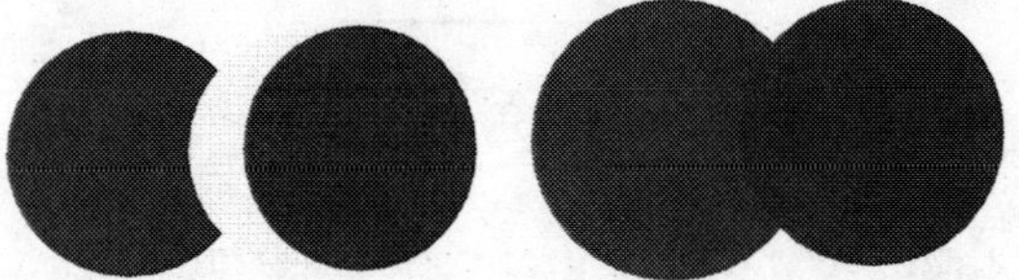

You can avoid this by selecting on each circle and clicking on the group option under the modify menu on the main menu here.

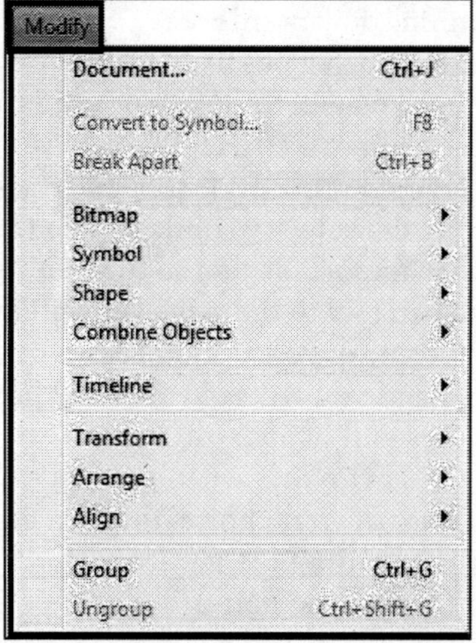


Once you group each object, you can separate them even if there are overlapped on each other by not cutting them.

You can use the object drawing mode switched on which is found on the options panel on the main menu on the extreme right bar and draw,then flash CS4 will treat circle a separate drawing.

## 8.12 LINE, PENCIL AND PEN TOOLS

It is very important to understand how the various drawing tools work in flash CS4. On the extreme right on the menu, you will find the various drawing tools The line tool is looks like this, when you click on the line tool and draw on stage, you can go any direction, but if you want to draw a square, you can draw a straight line downwards, you will see that by default the snap tool is selected and the line will snap in place, when it is perfectly straight, like wise to the right, up and left you will join the first point, you can draw a 45 degree line, and it will snap in place. This is a very important drawing tool in flash CS4. The same way you can draw with pencil tool, when clicked on the pencil tool which looks like this:

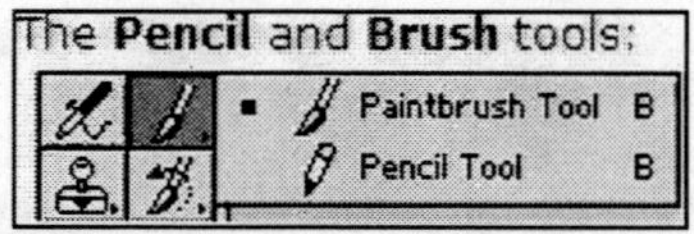


You will see that the property setting are just a stroke color, you can draw a zig zag on stage and notice that you can only select a color which is of stroke, and may not give you the option of the fill color.In the option menu box you have two options like this:

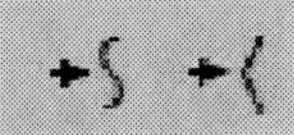

The top one is a smooth curve and the bottom one is a straight line, assuming you have drawn a zig zag on stage with a color red, selecting the drawing on stage, as you click on the smooth button the shape of the zig zag will smoothen, and the other straight button works differently than the smooth button, when selected the drawing, and clicked on the straight line, it will straighten the line to a virtual straight line running downwards.

The next tool is the brush tool, which looks like the one below,

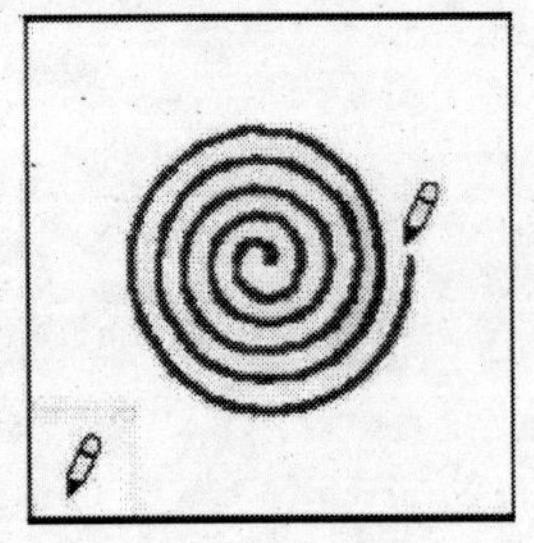

As you click on the brush tool, you will find that in your properties panel, you have only a fill color and not a stroke, this tool works very much like the pencil tool, with the smooth option tool and the straight option tool working with the brush tool very similarly like the way it works with pencil tool. Another important tool is the pen tool, this tool looks like: As you take the pen tool to the stage you will find that it make a dot with a florescent green, and once you release your mouse and make the second mark on stage, you will find a second point, and the first and second connect, this will happen till you finish all your drawings on stage and touch the start point, when pressed escape you will find the shape you drew, and accordingly fill the color of your choice, this pen tool will draw straight lines, if you want curved strokes, you can simply drag the mouse with the cursor moving either ways and then connecting the points to the starting point.

### Working with the Pencil Tool and the Paint Bucket Tool

When working in Flash, you can use the Pencil tool to draw freehand shapes and the Paint Bucket tool to fill enclosed areas with color.

## 8.13 TIMELINE

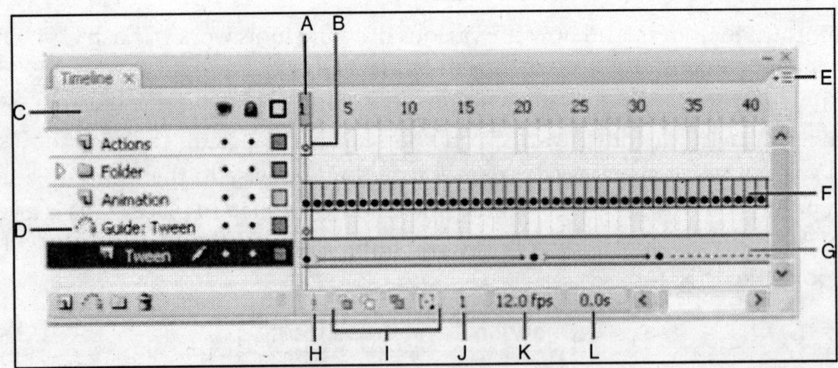


Parts of the Timeline **A.** Playhead **B.** Empty keyframe **C.** Timeline header **D.** Guide layer icon **E.** Frame View pop-up menu **F.** Frame-by-frame animation **G.** Tweened animation **H.** Center Frame button **I.** Onion-skinning buttons **J.** Current Frame indicator **K.** Frame Rate indicator **L.** Elapsed Time indicator

**Fig. 8.8:** Various elements of Time line

The timeline organizes and controls a document's content over time in layers and frames. Like films, Flash Professional documents divide lengths of time into frames. Layers are like multiple film strips stacked on top of one another, each containing a different image that appears on the Stage. The major components of the timeline are layers, frames, and the playhead. Layers in a document are listed in a column on the left side of the timeline. Frames contained in each layer appear in a row to the right of the layer name. The timeline header at the top of the timeline indicates frame numbers. The playhead indicates the current frame displayed on the Stage. As a document plays, the playhead moves from left to right through the timeline. The timeline status displayed at the bottom of the timeline indicates the selected frame number, the current frame rate, and the elapsed time to the current frame. Note: When an animation is played, the actual frame rate is displayed; this may differ from the document's frame rate setting if the computer can't calculate and display the animation quickly enough.

The timeline shows where animation occurs in a document, including frame-by-frame animation, tweened animation, and motion paths. Controls in the layers section of the timeline let you hide, show, lock, or unlock layers, as well as display layer contents as outlines. You can drag timeline frames to a new location on the same layer or to a different layer.

### 8.13.1 About Frame Rates

The frame rate, the speed the animation is played at, is measured in terms of number of frames per second (fps). A frame rate that's too slow makes the animation appear to stop and start; a frame rate that's too fast blurs the details of the animation. A frame rate of 24 fps is the default for new Flash documents and usually gives the best results on the web. The standard motion-picture rate is also 24 fps.

The complexity of the animation and the speed of the computer playing the animation affect the smoothness of the playback. To determine optimum frame rates, test your animations on a variety of computers. Because you specify only one frame rate for the entire Flash Pro document, set this rate before you begin creating animation.

### 8.13.2 Identifying animations in the Timeline

Flash Pro distinguishes tweened animation from frame-by-frame animation in the timeline by displaying different indicators in each frame that contains content. The following frame content indicators appear in the timeline:

A span of frames with a blue background indicates a motion tween.

A black dot in the first frame of the span indicates that the tween span has a target object assigned to it. Black diamonds indicate the last frame and any other property keyframes. Property keyframes are frames that contain property changes explicitly defined by you. You can choose which types of property keyframes to display by right-clicking (Windows) or Command-clicking (Macintosh) the motion tween span and choosing View Keyframes > type from the context menu. Flash displays all types of property keyframes by default. All other frames in the span contain interpolated values for the tweened properties of the target object.

A hollow dot in the first frame indicates that the target object of the motion tween has been removed. The tween span still contains its property keyframes and can have a new target object applied to it.

A span of frames with a green background indicates an inverse kinematics (IK) pose layer. Pose layers contain IK armatures and poses. Each pose appears in the timeline as a black diamond. Flash interpolates the positions of the armature in the frames in between poses.

A black dot at the beginning keyframe with a black arrow and blue background indicates a classic tween.

A dashed line indicates that the classic tween is broken or incomplete, such as when the final keyframe is missing.

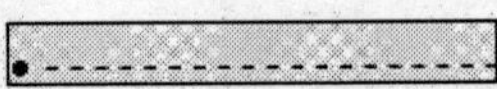

A black dot at the beginning keyframe with a black arrow and a light green background indicates a shape tween.

A black dot indicates a single keyframe. Light gray frames after a single keyframe contain the same content with no changes. These frames have a vertical black line and a hollow rectangle at the last frame of the span.

A small a indicates that the frame is assigned a frame action with the Actions panel.

A red flag indicates that the frame contains a label. A green double slash indicates that the frame contains a comment. A gold anchor indicates that the frame is a named anchor.

About layers in tweened animation

A green double slash indicates that the frame contains a comment.

A gold anchor indicates that the frame is a named anchor.

## 8.14 DISTRIBUTING OBJECTS TO LAYERS FOR TWEENED ANIMATION

### Layers

- A layer is a separate element of an image.
- When two images are seen together they appear as one image.
- Works like original cell animation for hand drawn animations

Flash Pro automatically moves an object to its own tween layer when you apply a motion tween to the object. However, you can also distribute objects to their own separate layers yourself. For example, you can choose to distribute objects yourself when you are organizing content. Manual distribution is also useful for applying animation to objects while maintaining precise control over how they move from one layer to another. When you use the Distribute To Layers command (`Modify > Timeline > Distribute To Layers`), Flash Pro distributes each selected object to a new, separate layer. Any objects that you don't select (including objects in other frames) are preserved in their original layers. You can apply the Distribute To Layers command to any element on the Stage, including graphic objects, instances, bitmaps, video clips, and broken-apart text blocks.

## 8.14.1 About new layers created with Distribute to Layers

New layers created during the Distribute To Layers operation are named according to the name of the element that each layer contains:

- A new layer containing a library asset (such as a symbol, bitmap, or video clip) receives the same name as the asset.
- A new layer containing a named instance receives the name of the instance.
- A new layer containing a character from a broken-apart text block is named with the character.
- A new layer containing a graphic object (which has no name) is named Layer1 (or Layer2, and so on), because graphic objects do not have names.

Flash Pro inserts the new layers below any selected layers. The new layers are arranged top to bottom, in the order that the selected elements were originally created. The layers in broken-apart text are arranged in the order of the characters, whether left-to-right, right-to-left, or top-to-bottom. For example, suppose you break apart the text *FLASH* and distribute it to layers. The new layers, named F, L, A, S, and H, are arranged top to bottom, with F at the top. These layers appear immediately below the layer that initially contained the text.

## 8.14.2 Distribute objects to layers

Select the objects you want to distribute to separate layers. The objects can be in a single layer, or in several layers, including non-contiguous layers.

Do one of the following:

- Select `Modify > Timeline > Distribute To Layers.`
- Right-click (Windows) or Control-click (Macintosh) one of the selected objects, and select Distribute To Layers.

## 8.14.3 Other objects in Adobe Flash Animator

Adobe Flash Animator utilizes following techniques :

### Symbols

a. Are reusable objects.
b. Examples of symbols are, Graphics, Buttons and Movie clips.
c. A copy of a symbol used in the movie is called an instance.
d. Each instance can have its own individual properties like, Colour, Size and function.

### Buttons

a. These can be used to play the animation or to alter the sequence.
b. Examples of buttons you may use, Start, Play, and scene selection.

### Frames

a. A frame is a single image within an animation.
b. Frames are played in a sequence at a specific rate, frames per second (fps). This creates an illusion of animation.
c. Key frames are special frames where and animation begins or ends.

### Controls

a. Controls are tools available to the animator within the application (tool bar).
b. They are usually contained within a toolbox on the sides of the application.

### Tweening

a. Creates movement.
b. Motion tweening.
c. Morphing.
d. The tween also has properties that can be altered such as the speed at which it is performed.

### Libraries

e. Assets such as symbols and tweens are stored in libraries within the animation software. This allows them to be reused.
f. Reusing is helpful to the animator as it saves them creating it each time it is needed, it will also allow for exact copies of the original.

## 8.15 FLASH SYMBOLS

**A symbol is a reusable object used/created in Flash**. A Symbol can be reused throughout your movie or imported and used in other movies. There are three types of symbols: Graphics, Buttons, and Movieclips. A copy of a symbol used in the movie is called an Instance, which can have its own independent properties (like color, size, function, etc.) different from the original symbol. All symbols used in a flash movie are stored in the **Library** from where you can drag-and-drop new instances of the symbols into your movie. When a symbol is edited all of its instances get updated, but changing the properties, effects or dimensions of an instance of a symbol does not affect the original symbol or other instances.

### 8.15.1 Importance of using Flash Symbols

Using flash symbols is very crucial to the file size of your Flash movie. The Flash file size depends largely on the size of all the graphics and texts used in the movie (both symbols and non-symbols) - here the major advantage of using symbols is that **a symbol's size is taken into consideration only once** even if it is used a hundred times - this is the true power of Flash. Unused symbols in your library are not counted in the size of your movie.

**Important Tip:** Get used to using symbols in flash right from the beginning and name them neatly for easy maintenance. It is a very tough job optimizing your file size if you don't use symbols from scratch!

### 8.15.2 The Three Types of Symbols

**Graphic symbols are reusable static images that are used mainly to create animations** - Any drawn vector/plain text/imported bitmap (photo), or combinations of these, can be converted into a single controllable object: as a graphic symbol. They have only one frame in their timeline.

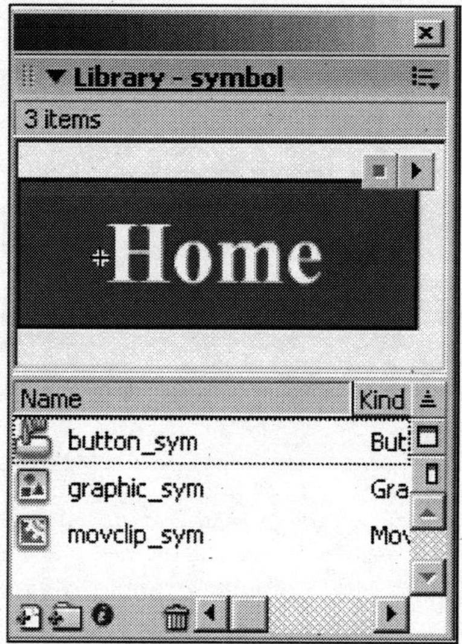


**Fig. 8.9:** Three types of symbols In Flash

**Button symbols are used for timeline navigation** - They add interactivity to the movie and respond to mouse clicks, key press or rollovers/rollout, and other actions. You define the graphics associated with various button states (Up/Over/Down/Hit), and then assign actions to the instance of a button. They have 4 frames in their timeline - one each for the up, over and down states, and one to define the hit area of the button.

**Movieclip symbols are reusable pieces of flash animation** - consisting of one or more graphic/button symbols - thus they are flash movies within your flash movie. They have their own non-restricted timeline (any number of layers and frames - just like the main timeline) that plays independent of the main movie's timeline. The best thing about using movie clips is that you can control them from actionscript - you can change their dimensions, position, color, alpha, and other properties and can even duplicate and delete them.

## 8.16 WHAT ARE GRAPHIC SYMBOLS IN FLASH?

Graphic symbols are reusable static images that are used mainly to create animations. Any drawn vector/plain text/imported bitmap (photo), or combinations of these, can be converted into a single controllable object, called a graphic symbol. Graphic Symbols have only one frame in their timeline.

### 8.16.1 How to create a graphic symbol in Flash

Please carry out the following steps in Flash to create graphic symbols.

- First create/import the object(s) to be converted into a graphic. You can import bitmaps onto the stage using **Ctrl+R**.
- Select the object(s) and then press **F8** (or **Modify** >> **Convert to Symbol**).
- Select the Graphic Behavior and name the symbol, say **'g_home'**.

- To edit it at a later point, double-click the symbol in the library (**Ctrl + L**) or any of its instances on the stage to switch to its **symbol-editing mode** as shown below. The name of the symbol will appear near the scene name ('Scene 1' by default, as shown below).
- Make the necessary changes and click **'Scene 1'** to exit from the symbol editing mode and go back to view the main movie's timeline.

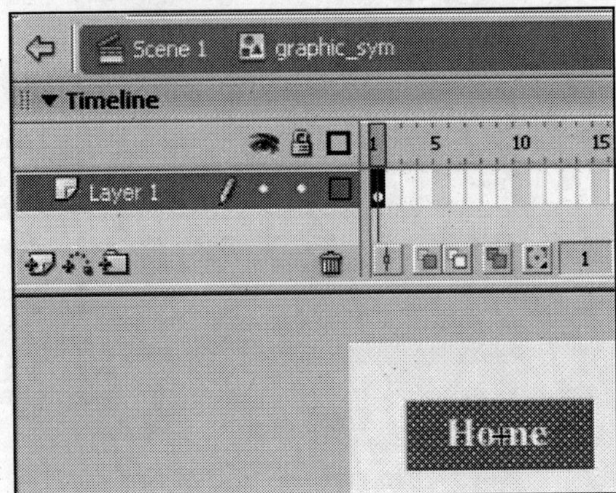


**Fig. 8.10:** Symbol-editing Mode of flash graphic 'g_home' (Flash 8 and below)

## 8.17 FLASH BUTTON SYMBOLS

Button symbols are used for timeline navigation. The button symbols add interactivity to the movie and respond to mouse clicks, key press or rollovers/rollout and other actions. You can define the graphics associated with various button states (Up/Over/Down/Hit), and then assign actions to the instance of a button. There are 4 frames in their timeline -one each for the up, over and down states, and one to define the hit area of the button.

- Please carry out the following steps in Flash to create button symbols.
- First create/import the object(s) to be converted into a button. Import bitmaps onto the stage using Ctrl+R.
- Select the object(s) and then press F8 (or `Modify >> Convert to Symbol`).
- Select the Button Behavior for the symbol and name the symbol say, 'btn_home'.
- Double-click the instance of 'btn_home' on the stage to switch to its symbol-editing mode. The timeline header changes to display four consecutive frames labeled Up, Over, Down, and Hit as shown below.

**Fig. 8.11:** Symbol-editing Mode of completed flash button 'btn_home'

- The first frame displays the drawn vector/plain text used for creating this button, now insert a Key frame (**F6**) in the frame labeled Over (Flash automatically duplicates the contents of the Up frame).
- Now change the color of the object in the Over frame to create a rollover effect in the button.
- Insert frames (**F5**) for the Down frame and the Hit frame (only defines the area of the button that responds to user action and is not visible at runtime).
- Save your work and test the Movie (**Ctrl + Enter**). That's it your simple button is ready!

## 8.18 FLASH MOVIECLIP SYMBOLS

Movieclip symbols are reusable pieces of flash animation - consisting usually of one or more graphic and button symbols - thus they are flash movies within your flash movie. They have their own non-restricted timeline (any number of layers and frames - just like the main timeline) that plays independent of the main movie's timeline.

The best thing about using movieclips is that you can control them with ease - you can change their dimensions, position, color, alpha, and other properties and can even duplicate and delete them. Thus any object that needs to be controlled using flash actionscript (no matter how simple or complex it might be) needs to be a movieclip with an instance name that is called in the actionscript code.

- Please carry out the following steps in Flash to create movieclip symbols.
- First create/import the object(s) to be converted into a movieclip. Import bitmaps onto the stage using Ctrl+R.
- Select the object(s) and then press F8 (or `Modify >> Convert to Symbol`).
- Select the Movieclip Behavior and name the symbol, say 'mc_fade').
- Double-click the instance of 'mc_fade' on the stage to switch to its symbol-editing mode.

Now create an animation sequence (you can use simple Tweened Animation or Frame-by-Frame Animation)

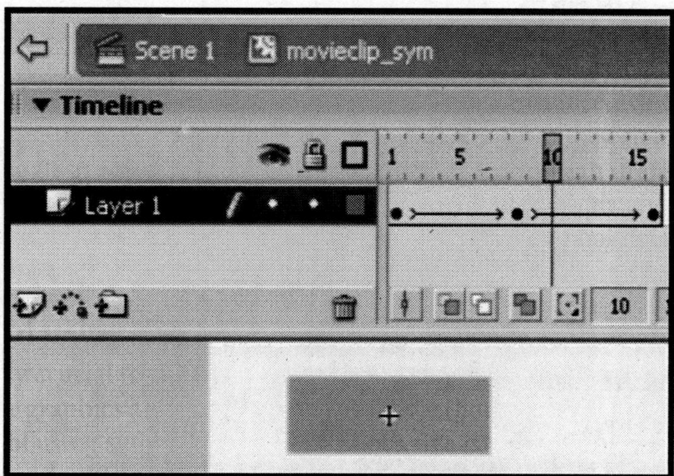


**Fig. 8.12:** Symbol-editing Mode of completed flash movieclip 'mc_fade'

- The above figure shows the Timeline of the Movieclip symbol. Click **Scene 1** to exit from the symbol editing mode.

- Save your work and test the Movie (**Ctrl + Enter**). That's it your movieclip is ready! Its that simple.

## 8.19 FLASH ACTIONSCRIPT BUTTON

Learn how to create a Flash actionscript button using actionscript controlled tweening and Movieclips in Flash. Steps to create this actionscript button effect (can be used for website links):

- Open the new flash document.
- Create a button and name this instance as **Button** then go to symbol-editing mode.
- Add new layer, draw the simple button and convert in to movie clip symbol (pressF8) then go to symbol editing mode.
- Press **F6** or (**right click >> insert key Frame**) on 10th and 20th frame and then reduce that alpha value at 1st and 20th frame.
- Select middle of the frame between 1-10 then go to property panel, select shape tween from that pop up. Do the same process between 10-20th frame.
- Add new layer above the tweening layer then press **F6** (**right click >> insert key Frame**) on 10th and 20th frame.
- Select 1st frame then go to action panel (press **F9**) stop this action, similarly do that process on 10th and 20th frame.
- Go to button editing mode, add new layer, name this layer as text, and make sure that text layer always above the movie clip layer.
- Go to scene1, and select the button then press **F9**, copy and paste the following code.

```
on (rollOver)
{
_root.Button.instance1.gotoAndPlay (2);
} on (rollOut)
{
_root.Button.instance1.gotoAndPlay (11);
}
```

- Save and test the movie Press( **Ctrl+Enter**).

## 8.20 FLASH ANIMATION

In Flash animation can be done in four basic ways:

- Motion Tween
- Shape Tween
- Frame-by-Frame Animation
- Guided Motion Tween

It is very simple and neatly explained below.

### 8.20.1 Creating Motion Tween in Flash

- Draw a vector using any of the drawing tools in Flash, say a small circle and convert it into a symbol (F8) by selecting the Graphic option and name the symbol say 'ball'.

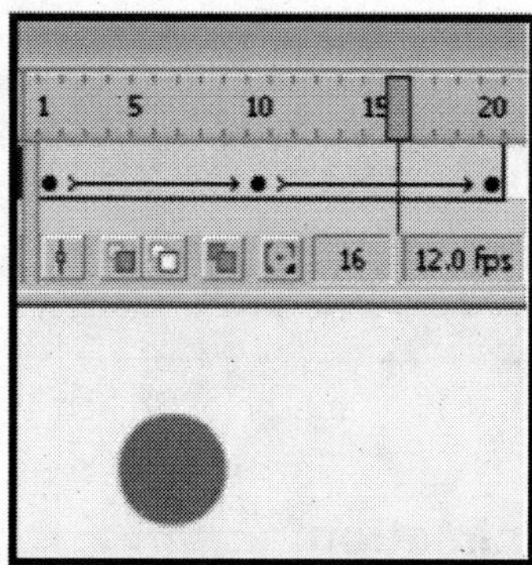


Fig. 8.13: Timeline of Motion Tween

- Click the 20th frame in the Timeline and insert a frame (F5).
- Now right-click the 20th frame in the Timeline and select Create Motion Tween (or Motion option from the Tween panel of the Properties inspector) and insert a Key Frame (F6).
- Select the 10th frame and insert a Key frame (F6) and move the ball to a different position say, above the current position to create a motion sequence (automatically tweened by Flash).
- Save your work and test the Movie (Ctrl + Enter). That's it you have created simple animation using Motion Tween.

***Note:*** *Use the Color Panel of the Properties inspector to reduce the Alpha value from 100 to 32 for the 1st and last frames to produce Simple Alpha Tweening as shown in the Example.*

## 8.20.2 Creating Shape Tween in Flash

- You can create Shape Tweened animations using Shape option from the Tween panel of the Properties inspector. Draw a vector using any of the drawing tools in Flash, say a small circle and remove its border.
- Click the 10th frame in the Timeline and insert a Key Frame (**F6**). Now draw another shape say a diamond using the rectangle tool without a border.
- Now right-click on any frame in between these two Key Frames and select Shape option from the Tween panel of the Properties inspector.
- Save your work and test the Movie (**Ctrl + Enter**). That's it you have learnt how to create Shape Tween in Flash.

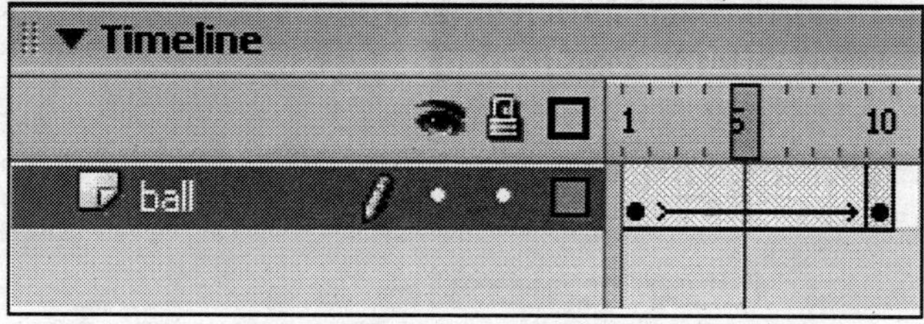


Fig. 8.14: Timeline of Shape Tween

***Note:*** *Only vectors can be Shape Tweened (Not for Symbols). Note both the Tweens have different colors along the timeline as shown above. Make sure that the line is smooth without being broken to ensure correct Tweening.*

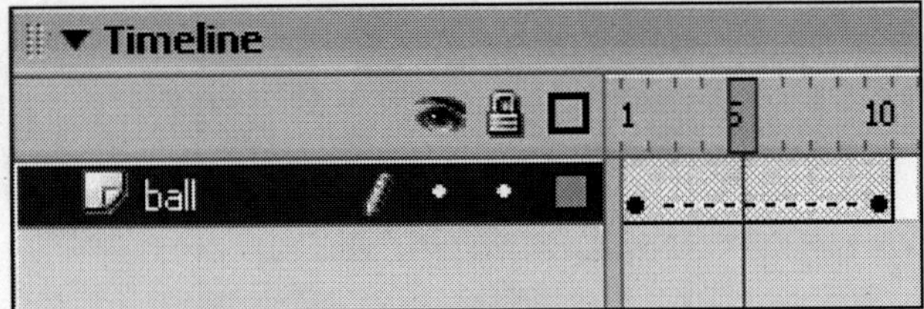


Fig. 8.15: Timeline of Broken Tween

### 8.20.3 Frame-by-Frame Animation

Create a vector/plain text using any of the drawing tools in Flash, say a text with 'Animation' typed as shown in the example and break it using Break Apart (Ctrl + B) to separate the alphabets as shown below:

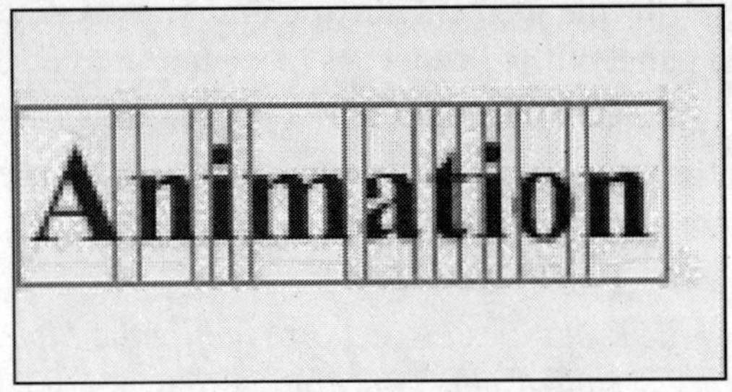


Fig. 8.16: Showing Text after Break Apart

- In Frame-by-Frame animation we create the object for each frame so as to produce an animation sequence.
- Insert Keyframe (**F6**) and move the alphabets so as to produce an animation sequence.
- Repeat the above step as far as desired to create Frame-by-Frame animation as shown in the example.
- Save your work and test the Movie (**Ctrl + Enter**). That's it you have created an animation using Frame-by-Frame animation.

Fig. 8.17: Timeline of Frame-by-Frame Animation

### 8.20.4 Creating a Guided Motion Tween in Flash

Create a vector/plain text using any of the drawing tools in Flash, say a text with 'Flash' typed and break it using Break Apart (**Ctrl + B**) as done in the previous example and put each alphabet in different layers and name the layers as shown in the picture below.

- Insert a guide layer by right-clicking the topmost layer and select '**Add Guide Layer**' (**Insert-->Timeline-->Motion Guide**), draw any path using the pencil tool in the guide layer as shown in the example.
- Now create Motion tween by selecting the object in the 1st frame and snapping its registration point to one end of the path.
- Snap the object in the last frame to the other end of the path in the guide layer.
- Repeat the same for all the objects (alphabets) by snapping their registration points to the path in the guide layer.
- Save your work and test the Movie (**Ctrl + Enter**). That's it you have learnt how to create motion along a guided path.

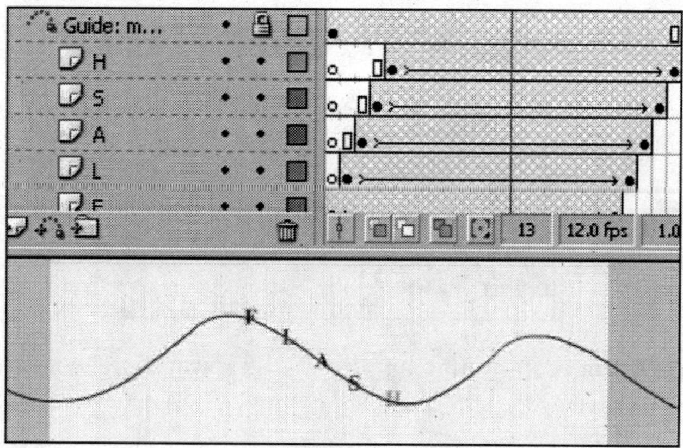


**Fig. 8.18:** Timeline of Guided Motion Tween

## 8.21 FLASH TEXT BASICS

In Flash there are 3 types of textboxes - Static, Input & Dynamic. Static texts are used for titles, labels, or other text content that appears in a flash document by default. Input text options are used for user interactivity like obtaining username or other information in a Flash form. The third type of text is Dynamic text, that are used to display text that changes dynamically at runtime.

There are 3 types of textboxes - **Static**, **Input** & **Dynamic** in Flash.

### 8.21.1 Static Text

- Drag a textbox of Fixed-width on the stage using the Text tool and select Static Text Type from the Properties window.

Static Text Box

- The Static textbox has a rectangular handle in the upper right corner, which can be used to adjust the size of the textbox.

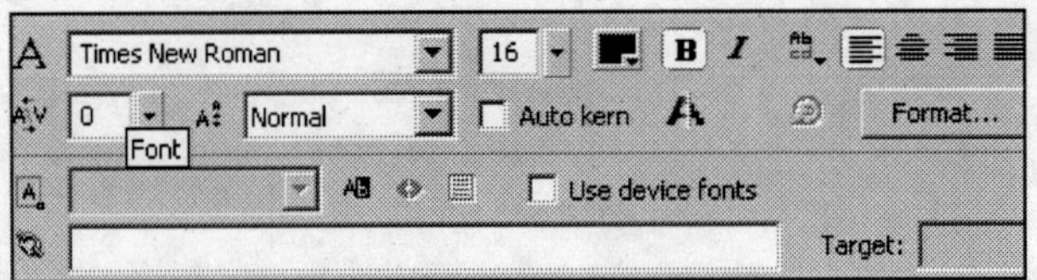


The various Text properties such as the Font, Font-size, Font-style, Font-color, Align etc. can be set using the Properties inspector as shown above.

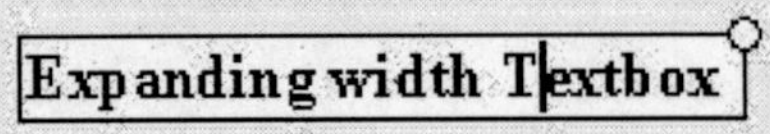


Expanding-width textboxes can be created by selecting the Text tool and clicking once on the stage without dragging it, and start typing the text in it. Note that the expanding textboxes have a round handle as shown above.

## 8.21.2 Input Text

- Drag a textbox on the stage using the Text tool and select Input Text Type from the Properties window.

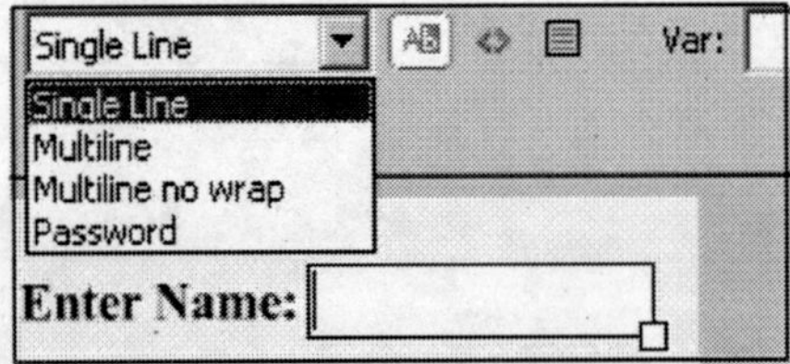


- The Input textbox has a rectangular handle in the lower right corner, which can be used to adjust the size of the textbox.
- Apart from the normal Font properties of a Static textbox, the Input textbox has more options like, Single Line to display the text as one line, Show Border Around Text to indicate the boundaries of the text field with a visible border.
- A variable name can also be given which can be used to store user input.

## 8.21.3 Dynamic Text

- Drag a textbox on the stage using the Text tool and select Dynamic Text Type from the Properties window.

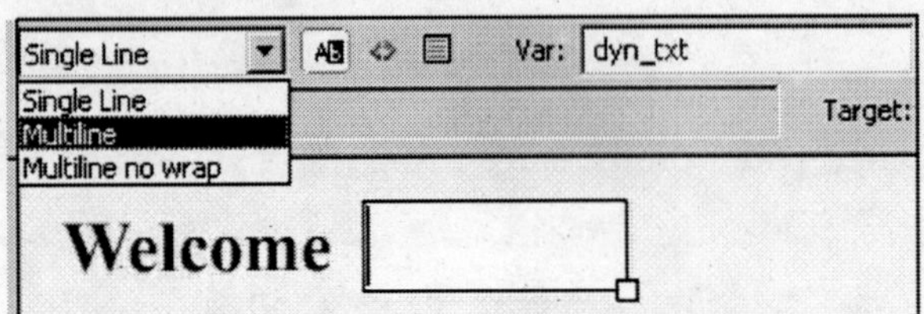


- The normal Font properties of a textbox can be set for a Dynamic textbox and it also has more options like, variable names can be given, line options can be given say, Single Line to display the text as one line, Selectable and **Render text as HTML**.

- Variable names are used to assign dynamic values at runtime or obtain values from External Sources.
  dyn_txt = "SmartWebby Visitor!"

## 8.22 FLASH SOUND BUTTON

Follow the steps given below to create a **flash button with sound**:

**Including sound files in Flash Buttons**

- Create a simple **Button** and enter into its symbol-editing mode. The timeline header changes to display four consecutive frames labeled Up, Over, Down, and Hit as shown below.

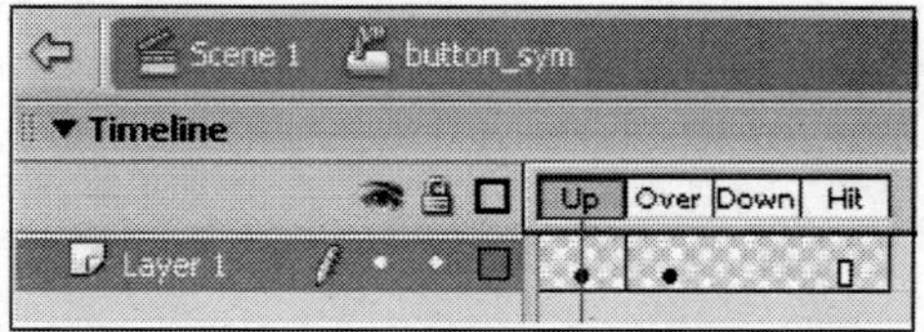


**Fig. 8.19:** Symbol-editing Mode of Button

- Insert a Keyframe (**F6**) in the Over frame to duplicate the contents of the Up frame and change the color of the object in the Over frame.
- Import the sound file (**Ctrl + R**), add a new layer for sound and select the imported sound file from the Sound Panel of the Properties window.

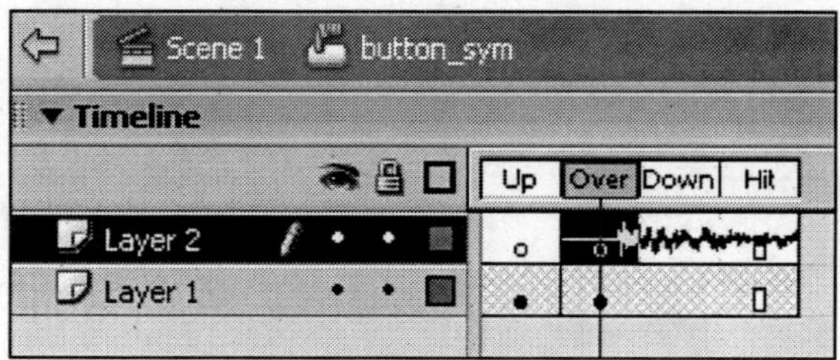


**Fig. 8.20:** Button showing sound in a Layer

- Now insert frame (**F5**) for the Down frame and the Hit frame (this frame is not visible, but only defines the area of the button that responds to mouse events).
- Save your work and test the Movie (**Ctrl + Enter**). That's it now your button can play music during mouse-overs.

## 8.23 FLASH EFFECTS

Create cool Flash effects using simple Flash techniques. Cool flash effects can be created by using simple techniques like tweening, masking, etc. As your expertise of Flash increases you will realize that all complicated animations are built up from many basic carefully created animations that work together to create a quality effect.

There are three Basic Flash Effects:

- Fade-in Fade-out Effect,
- Zooming Effect and
- Alpha Ripple Effect

### 8.23.1 Fade-in Fade-out Flash Effect

Please carry out the following steps in Flash to create the fade-in fade-out effect.

- In a new layer draw any vector object, say a circle. Convert the object into a graphic symbol (select the object and click F8) and name it, say 'g_circle'.
- Insert Keyframe (F6) in the 20th frame and create a Motion Tween from frame 1 to 20.
- Click the 10th frame on the timeline and insert a Keyframe (F6).
- Click the 'g_circle' instance displayed in the 10th frame and give it an Alpha value of 40% (for Flash MX and above, In the properties window select Alpha from the Color Panel and reduce the value from 100% to 40%).
- Save your work and test the Movie (Ctrl + Enter). That's it your, fade-in/fade-out cool effect is ready!

### 8.23.2 Flash Vector Zooming Effect

How to create a zooming effect using basic tweening in Flash

Please carry out the following steps in Flash to create the above vector zooming effect.

- In a new layer draw any vector object, say a circle. Convert this object into a graphic symbol (select the object and click F8) and name it, say 'g_circle'.
- Insert Keyframe (F6) in the 10th frame. Now go back to frame 1 and click on the circle object. Reduce its size to about 25% of its original size (use the Info panel or free transform tool).
- Now go to frame 10 and click on the circle object. Reduce its Alpha value from 100% to 20% in the Color Panel of the properties window.
- Now right click on frame 1 and select 'Create Motion Tween' (A blue arrow will be displayed in the time line between frames 1 & 10 - this shows that the motion tween was created successfully).
- Save your work and test the Movie (Ctrl + Enter). That's it, your cool zooming effect is ready!

### 8.23.3 Ripple Effect in Flash - Alpha Tweening

Follow the steps given below:

- Carry out the zooming effect steps.
- Copy frames 1 to 10 -> To do this click frame 1, press Shift key and click frame 10 (the frames will be heighlighted), now press Ctrl+Alt+C to copy the frames.
- Add a new layer, click the 4th frame on the timeline and paste the copied frames (press Ctrl+Alt+V).
- Add another new layer, click the 8th frame on the timeline and paste the copied frames (press Ctrl+Alt+V).
- Repeat the above step leaving 4 frames more than the previous layer for as many layers as desired.

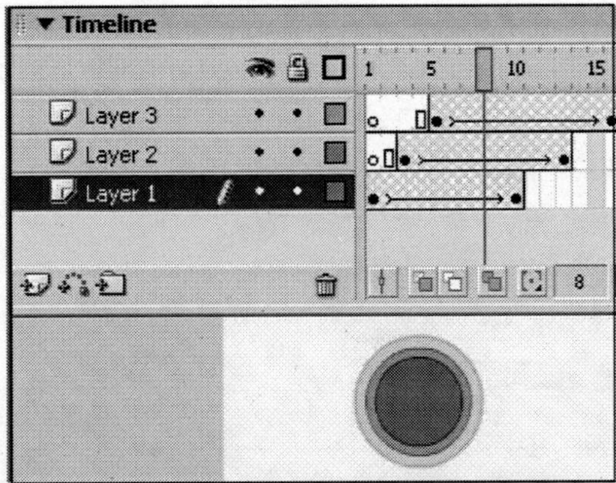


**Fig. 8.21:** Ripple Effect in Flash - Alpha Tweening

➢ Save your work and test the Movie (Ctrl + Enter). That's it, your cool ripple effect is ready!

## 8.23.4 Photo Masking Effects

### How to create simple photo masking effects with Flash

Please carry out the following steps in Flash to create the photo masking effects.

➢ Import (Ctrl + R) any color photo to be masked and its black & white version onto the stage.

➢ Now add a new Layer and move the Color picture into it. Make sure both pictures are perfectly on top of each other.

➢ Add a new Layer above the color picture layer and name it as 'Image Mask'.

➢ Draw any vector, say a rectangle with a height more than the picture height and width say 100. Convert the vector to a graphic symbol (select and press F8).

➢ Right-click the Layer named 'Image Mask' and select Mask from the pop-up menu. This command will make the current 'Image Mask' layer to mask the layer below it (containing the color photo), resulting in the color photo being shown only the area specified by the mask layer.

**Fig. 8.22:** Mask Layer

➢ Save your work and test the Movie (Ctrl + Enter). The movie will look similar to our example above. That's it you have learnt simple photo masking.

### 8.23.5 Motion Photo Masking

Advanced effects can be created by using Motion Tweened animation as a mask on an object in Flash.

- In the above example Create Motion Tween for the rectangle graphic and make the mask slide up and down, the timeline is shown below:

Fig. 8.23: Timeline of Advanced Mask

- Save your work and test the Movie (Ctrl + Enter). That's it, your cool photo masking advanced effect is ready!

## 8.24 ROLLING BALL ANIMATION

We will create two different types of Rolling ball motions:

- Vertical up and down
- Horizontal Jumping Roll over

### 8.24.1 Vertical up and down

The ball shall be rolling vertical up and down. Final Image Preview

**Step 1: New Document**

- Open Flash Animator CS6 and you will find a screen as below:

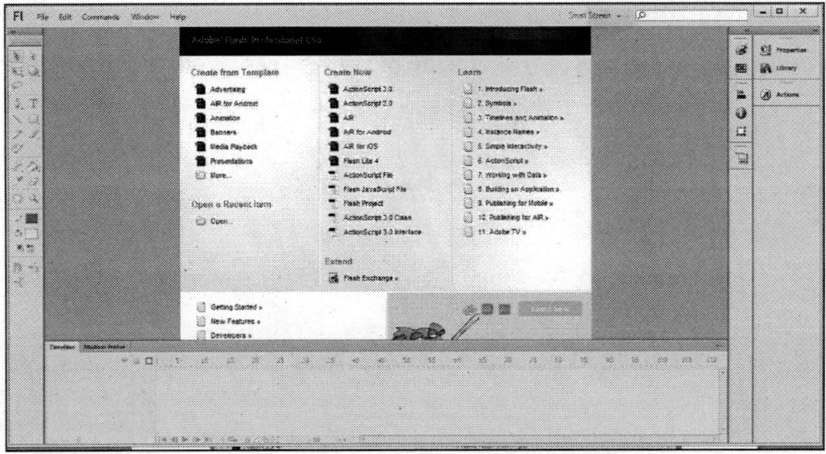

➢ In this interface see the Right of top horizontal menu line whether the word small screen is written just before the search box.Otherwise rollover and select Small screen as shown below:

➢ Let's begin by opening a new document (File > New...). In new document dialogue box choose ActionScript 2.0 document. the Actionscript version isn't relevant as we won't be using any.

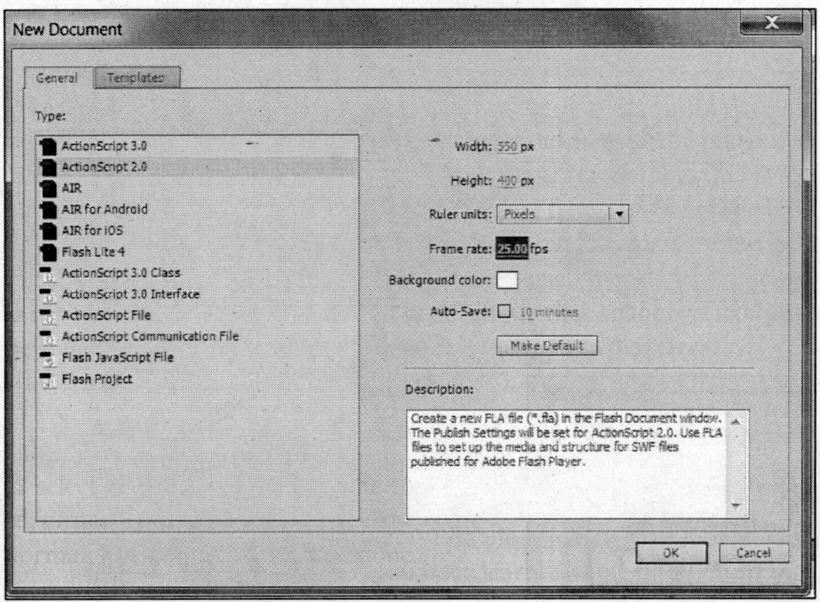

## Step 2: Document Settings

➢ Use the Properties (Inspector) at the left side of your screen to enter the Document Properties.

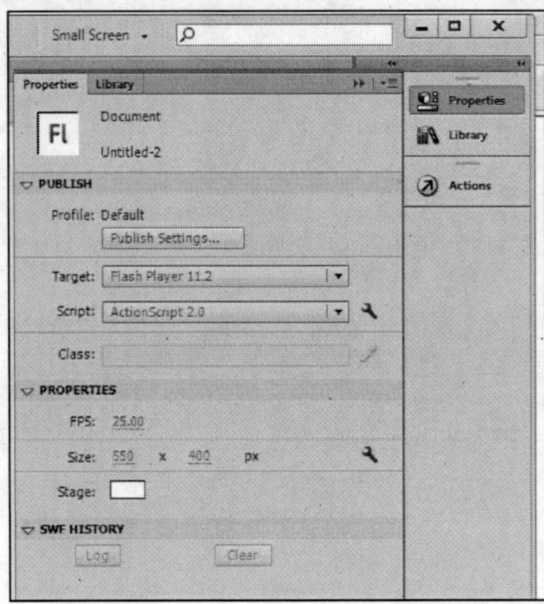


➢ Change the size (height) as 600p and width as 400px. Let the background color of stage remain white, but change the Frame Rate to 21 fps (Frames Per Second) in stead of 25. 21 fps gives a quick, smooth rate of animation.

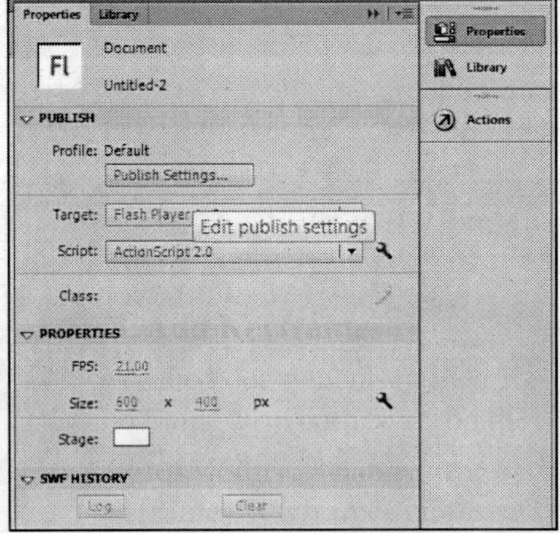

➢ Click over Public Settings as shown in above figure to get a Public Settings dialog Box as shown below in which the output file name is given as Bouncing_Ball.swf.

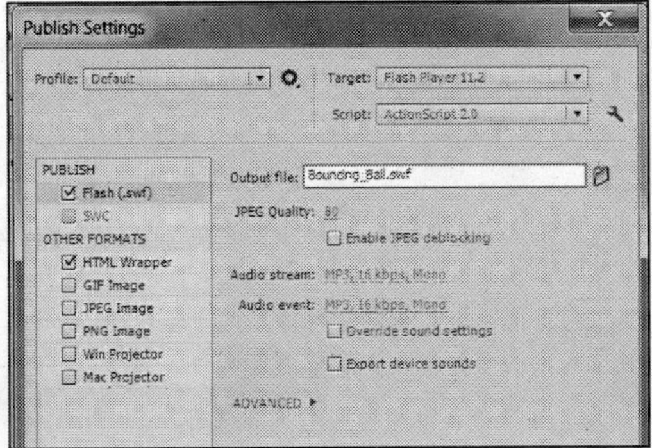


➢ Click **OK** to proceed further.

## Step 3: Layer

➢ Organization is key when working with Flash, so before we start drawing our ball, let's name the layer it's going to sit on. Double click Layer 1 in bottom left portion of Window and call it "Ball."

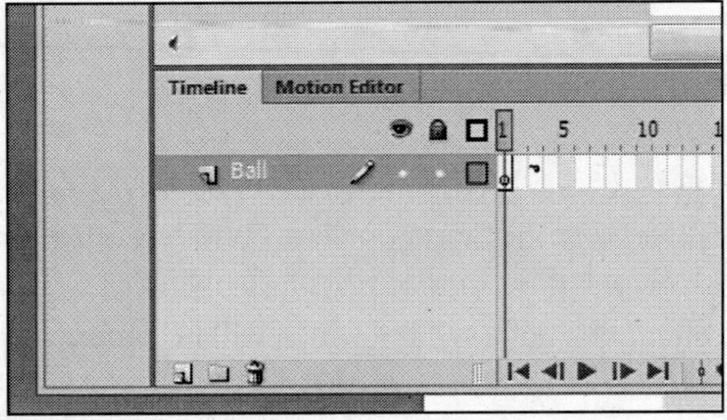


## Step 4: Ball

➢ Select the Oval Tool from tool box. For this you have click over rectangle symbol and from the pop-up select Oval Tool as shown below:

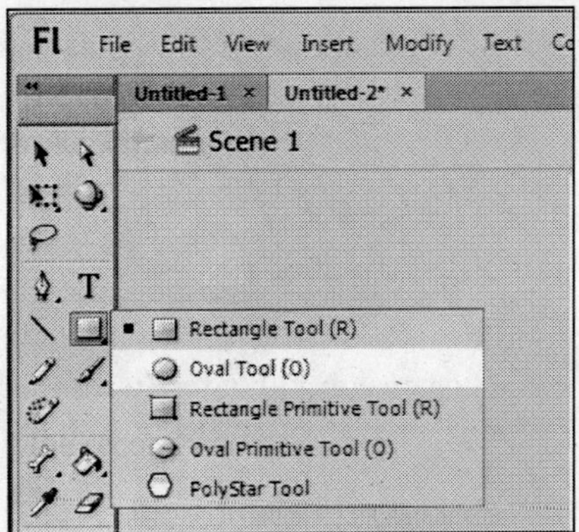

- You will see that in tool box the symbol has automatically changed to Oval shape. After selecting this symbol you have to over the mouse in workspace and create a circle i.e draw a uniform circle (by holding Shift and dragging the mouse).
- Define a stroke and a fill color, such as those shown. Next Also, use the Properties Inspector to give the Stroke a 3px weight.

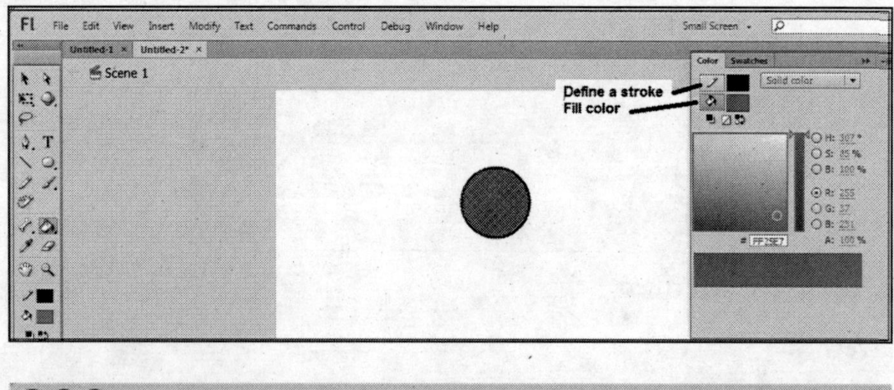


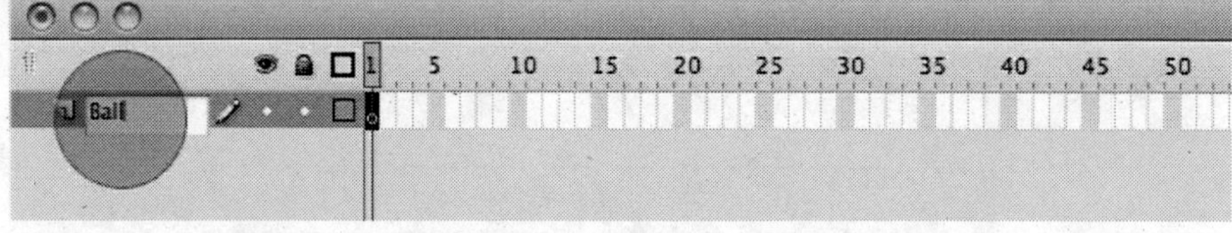


## Step 5: Symbol Creation

- By creating symbols in Flash you can use multiple instances of the same objects within one file. Symbols are all accessible from the Library palette (Window > Library). By changing a symbol, all instances of that symbol within the file will be changed.
- We're going to turn our circle into a symbol which will become our ball. Select the whole circle and press F8. Name it "mc_ball," choose to turn it into a Movie Clip symbol and click OK.

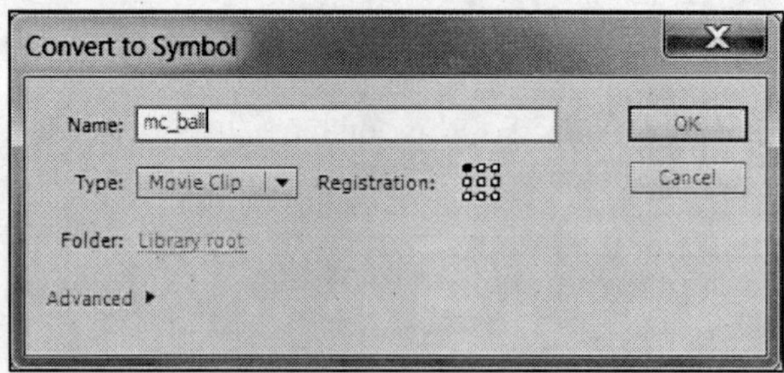


## Step 6: Shadow

- Add a second layer underneath the "Ball" layer and call it "Shadow." Within the first frame of this layer draw an ellipse to form a shadow under the ball. Remove the stroke and color it #E2E0E5. Turn it into a symbol just as you did before with the ball, then name it "mc_shadow."

## Step 7: Position

- Position the two symbols at roughly the correct height to suggest that the ball is sitting on the ground.
- In the Align palette (Window > Align) check to Stage and center the two symbols horizontally.

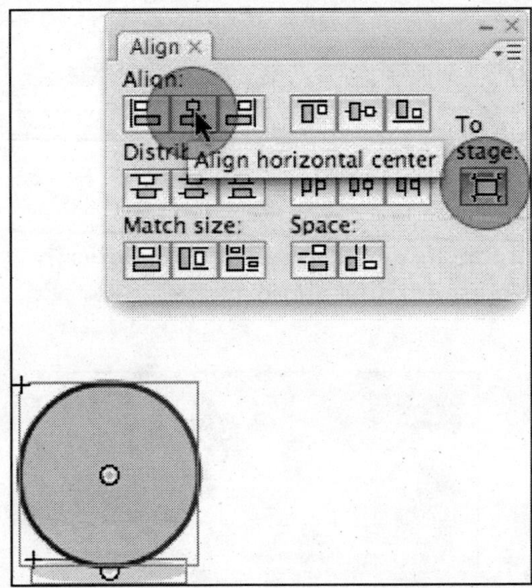


## Step 8: Add Keyframes

We've created our symbols in their most basic form, now let's begin to animate them. Hold Shift and click on frame 20 of both layers on the timeline.

- Go to Modify > Timeline > Convert to keyframes or press F6 to turn these frames into keyframes. Keyframes represent points along the timeline where something happens.
- This point on the Timeline will be the end of the animation; in other words the ball would have bounced up from the ground, reached it's apex and returned to this starting position.
- The same applies to our shadow: it would have faded as the ball rose and returned to this starting state at frame 20.

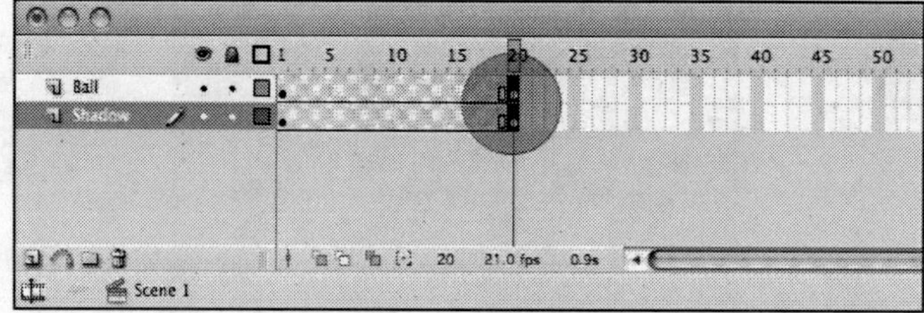


### Step 9: High Point

➢ Now let's add the point at which the ball is at it's highest. Select frame 10 on both layers and press F6 to turn them into keyframes.

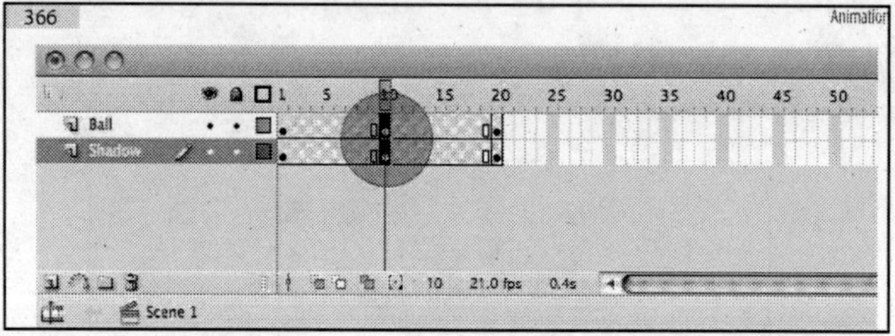


### Step 10: Move it!

➢ With the Slider still at frame 10, move the ball symbol vertically upwards to some point on the Stage. Select the Free Transform Tool and make the instance of the "shadow_main" symbol wider.

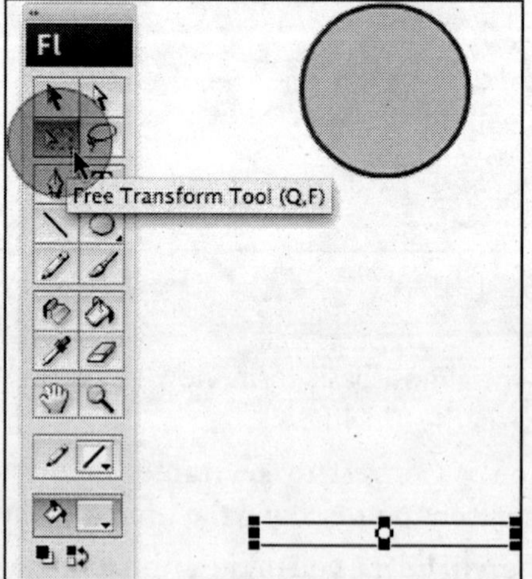

➢ Finally, with the shadow selected, go to Color on the Properties Inspector and change it to an Alpha value of 30%.

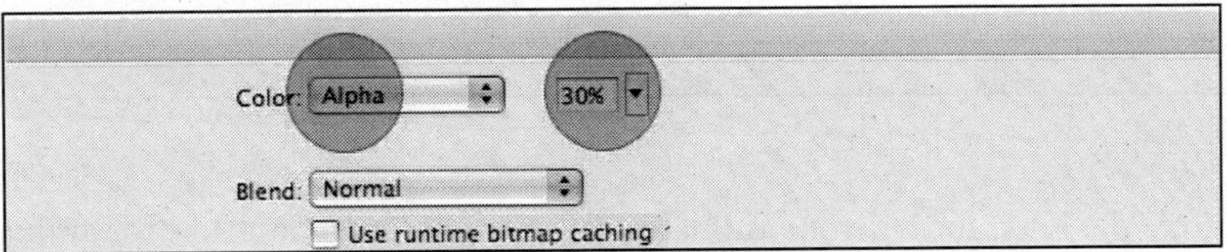


## Step 11: Tweening

Tweening is the process by which Flash automatically generates all the stages *between* an objects or shapes two states.

➢ We're going to tween the frames between our first frame and halfway along the animation at frame 10. Select any frame between 1 and 10 on both layers and refer once again to the Properties Inspector.

➢ Choose Motion from the Tween select and you'll see the resultant frames turn purple.

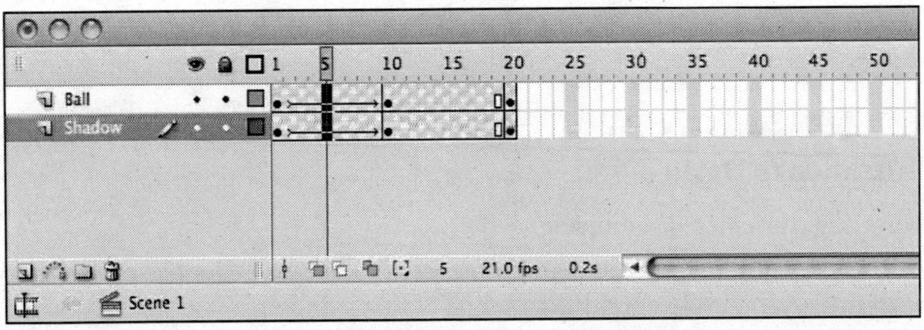


## Step 12: Easy Tiger

Move the Slider back and forth along the timeline with your mouse and you'll see the ball and shadow nicely animated. The speed of this movement is however completely uniform. We need the ball to decelerate as it reaches it's apex and we can do this with *ease*.

➢ Again, with one frame of each layer selected (within the tweened area) refer to the Properties Inspector. Change the Tweening to Ease out with a value of 100. This will slow down our climbing ball.

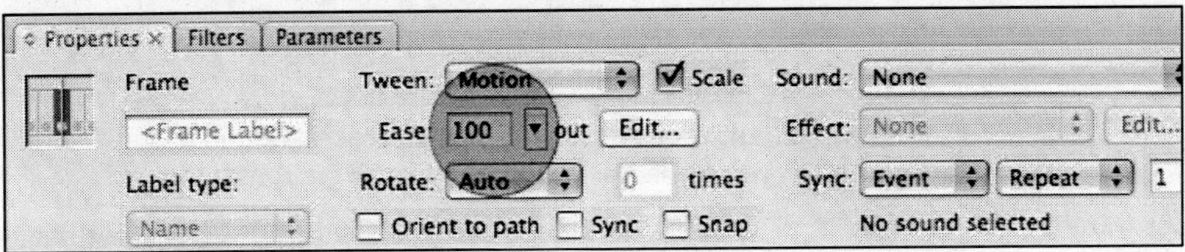


## Step 13: Back Down to Earth

Having successfully animated the rising of the ball, repeat the tweening steps for frames 11-20. This time ease the motion tween *in* -100, causing the ball to accelerate as it approaches the ground.

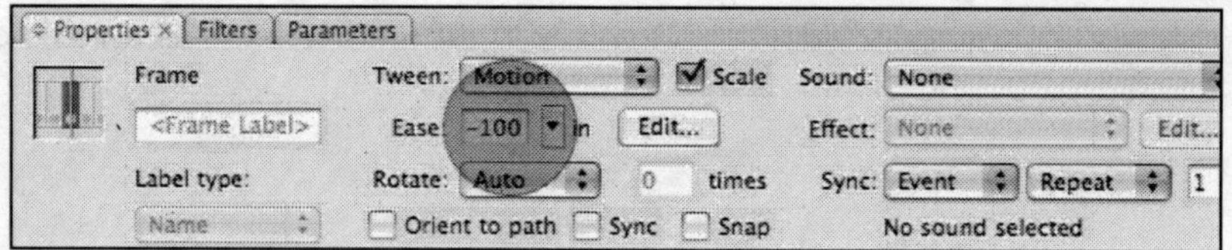


**Step 14: Check it!**

Press Command + Enter to view your animated ball so far. It should look like the animation shown below.

**Step 15: Extra Touch of Realism**

- Assuming our ball is made of something a little more flexible than diamond it's going to change form slightly upon impact with the ground. Let's add one last keyframe where the ball flattens momentarily.
- Select frame 21 on both layers and press F6 to turn them into keyframes. Then use the Free Transform Tool to *squash* the "ball" symbol from the top edge (hold Alt as you do so to keep the bottom edge where it is).

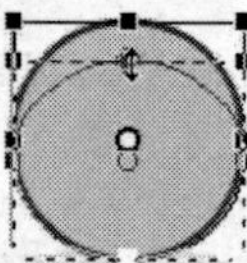

**Step 16: Attention to Detail**

- Our bouncing movement is complete.
- Now we need to add further detail and movement to our ball. Double-click the "ball" symbol on any of the keyframes to enter the timeline of that symbol.
- You'll see your current location underneath the timeline - you should be within "Scene 1, mc_ball."

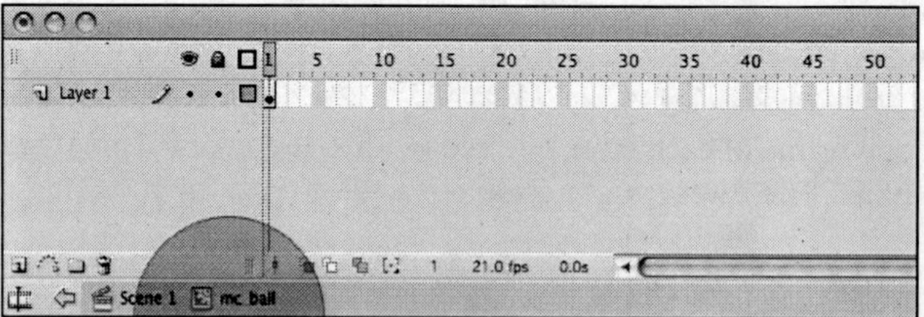


**Step 17: Layer 2**

- Click the Insert Layer icon to create a second Layer above the current one.
- Copy and Paste the circle in place from Layer 1 to Layer 2 (Command + C, Command + Shift + V).
- Now name the bottom layer "Ball Spinning" and the top one "Shade."
- Finally, lock the "Ball Spinning" layer.

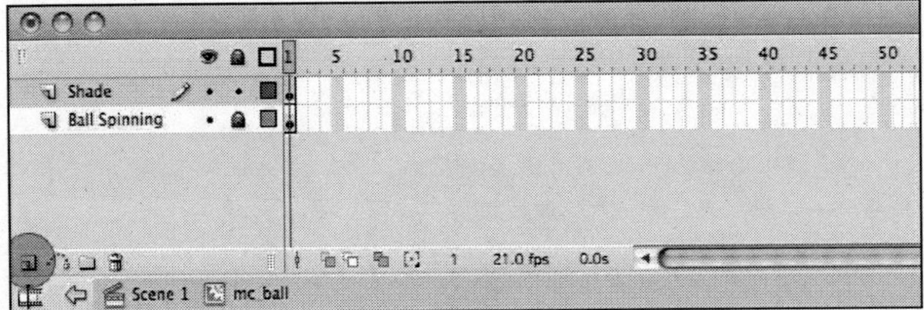


## Step 18: Chop Shop

- Draw a large circle somewhere on the stage, making sure it has a different color to the existing circle.

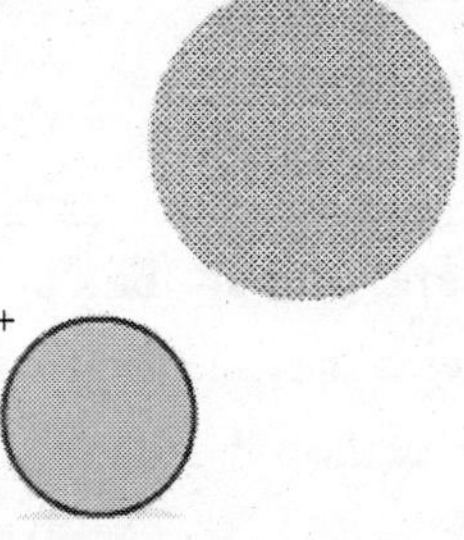

- Position the larger circle so that what can still be seen of the yellow circle is about the right shape for shading on the ball. Release all objects.

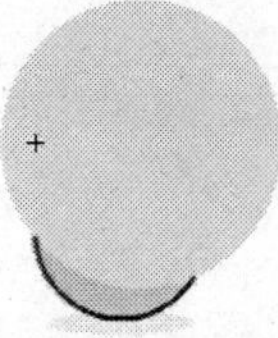

- Now select the larger circle once again and press Delete.
- By laying un-grouped or non-symbolized forms over one another you combine them in the same way that you do with pixels in paint applications.
- By now removing the larger circle you're left with just the small crescent which will become the shading on the ball. Select and remove the remaining stroke and color the crescent #E2E0E5.

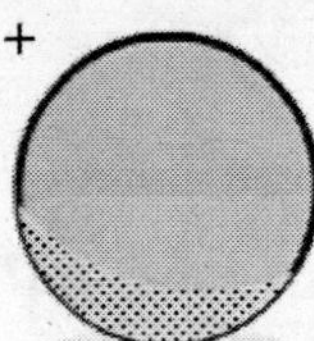

## Step 19: Shadow Opacity

- As this crescent acts as shading on our ball it would be nice to give it a Multiply Opacity.
- In order to do this we have to convert it into a Movie Clip Symbol (you should be used to this action now).

- Press F8 and name it "mc_ball_shading" (these names are getting dodgy). Refer to the Property Inspector and change it's Blend to Multiply.
- Perfect!

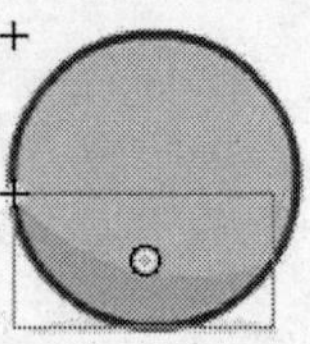

### Step 20: Check it!

- Press Command + Enter again to view your animated ball so far.
- It should look like the animation below.

### Step 21: Further Vector Manipulation

- Having dealt with the shading you can now lock the layer "Shade" (perhaps even make it invisible to make working easier) and unlock "Ball Spinning."
- We're going to add a pattern to give our circle to give it that beach ball look.
- Use the Oval Tool to draw a large oval on the stage. It needs a stroke of 1px and #FFFFFF, but no fill color.

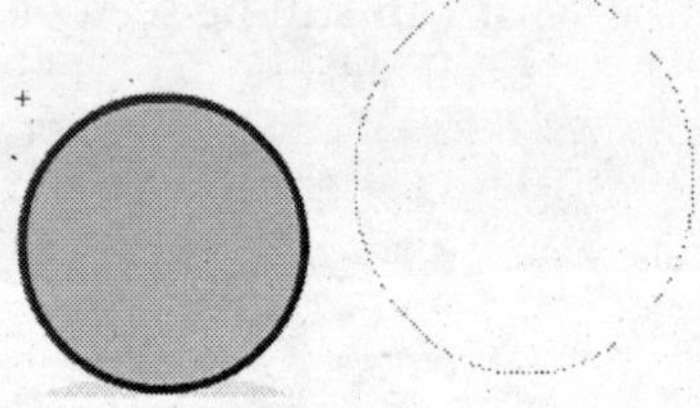

### Step 22: Remove Excess

- Place the stroke as shown in the image below and release.
- Now select the portion of the stroke which is outside the ball by simply clicking on it.
- As with making the shading crescent earlier, all the vectors on this layer have merged together, forming separate regions.
- Delete the outer portion of the stroke.

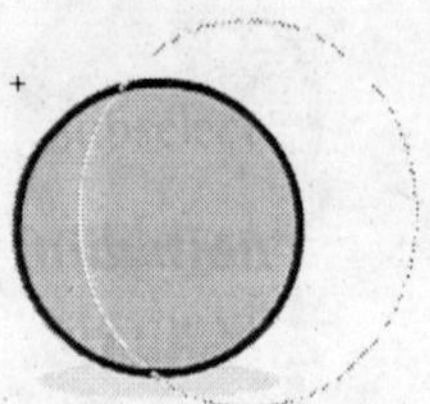

### Step 23: Rinse and Repeat

- Draw a couple of other ovals and place them on top of the circle so that they conjoin at the top somewhere.
- Then remove the excess from outside the circle.
- The ovals don't all have to be of equal size or proportions, just try to recreate something a little like the image below.
- What you will have created is a series of segments which can now be individually colored.

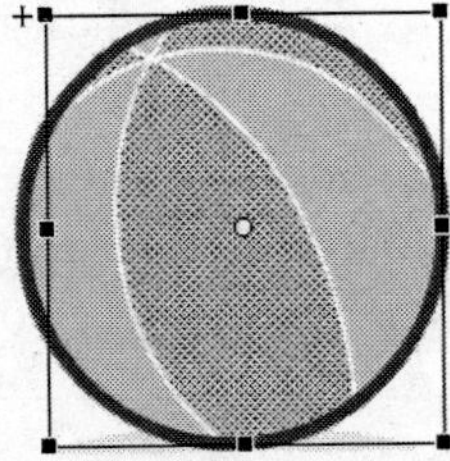

### Step 24: Check it!

- Color alternate segments with #EA512D and delete all the pieces of white stroke from the ball.
- Press Command + Enter to view what you've made so far.

### Step 25: As the Ball Turns

Let's add a final dimension of movement to the animation, we'll get the ball to slowly spin as it bounces.

- To do this we first need the ball on layer "Ball Spinning" to be converted into a symbol.
- Click on the first keyframe of the layer to ensure that everything on it is selected.
- Now press F8 and name this Movie Clip symbol "mc_ball_base."
- You'll see it's been added amongst the other symbols in the Library palette (Window > Library).

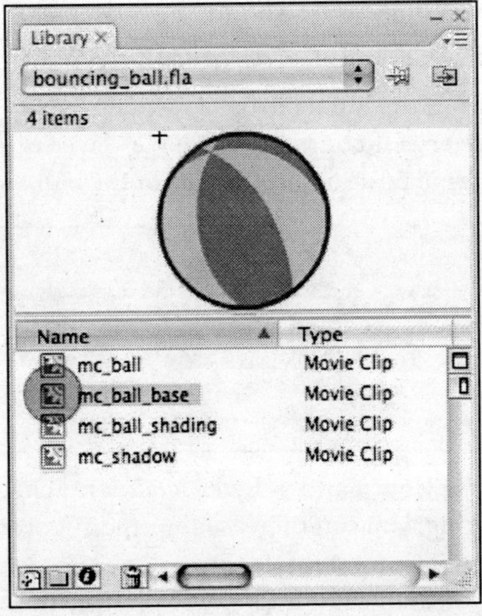

## Step 26: Add Frames

- Select frame 32 of the timeline on the layer "Spinning Ball" and press F6 to create a new Keyframe.
- Select frame 32 of the timeline on the layer above and press F5.
- This will create a new frame, but as the "Shade" symbol doesn't change state at all we don't need to make this a Keyframe.
- We just need to ensure that when the Slider reaches this point along the timeline, the "Shade" symbol is present.

Why have we chosen frame 32? Well, in doing so we are going to make our ball rotate once every 32 frames. Our ball bounces once every 20 frames and so this irregular timing will mean that the ball finds itself at continually different spin stages during the bounce. If this isn't yet clear, it soon will be..

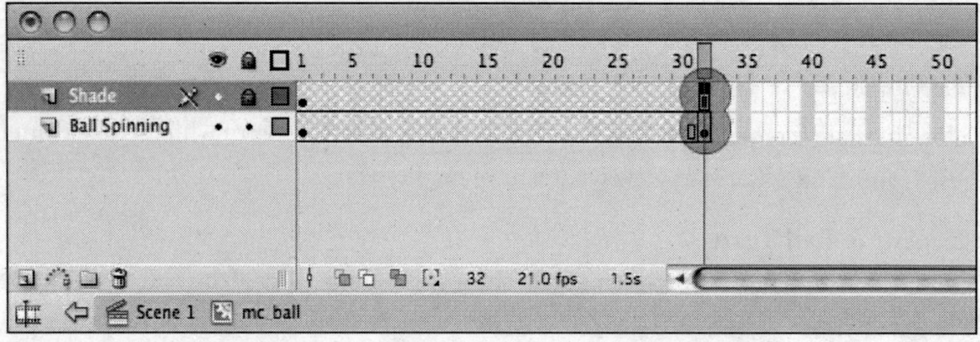


## Step 27: Rotational Tweening

- Select a frame somewhere along the timeline on layer "Ball Spinning" and refer to the Properties Inspector.
- Select Motion tween as you did with the bouncing movement.
- This time, we don't want any Ease value, we need the ball to steadily rotate at the same speed.
- Select CW (Clockwise) from the Rotate drop-down and leave *1* as the amount of times the ball will rotate during the tween. Of course, the "Shade" layer is unaffected and the shading will therefore remain in the same position on the face of the ball.

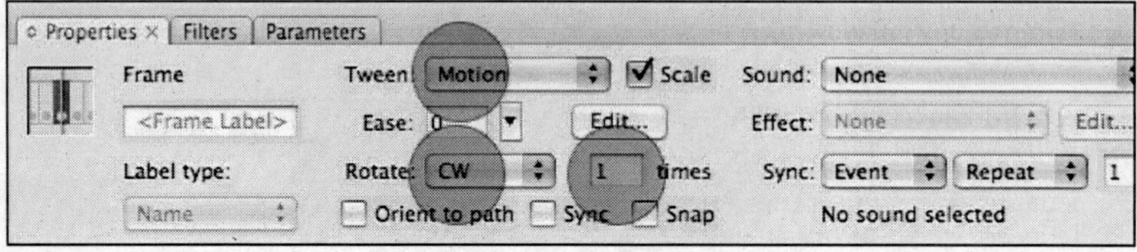


So there you have it! Press Command + Enter again and check that the movement is as you wanted. Should it need changing, you can increase the amount of frames in the tweens, change the height of the ball, the amount of times it rotates etc.

This example has given you an insight into: the Flash timeline and layers, the behavior of Flash vector drawing tools, the hierarchy of Flash symbols and objects, and motion tweening.

## 8.24.2 Bouncing Ball Horizontal Roll-over

This tutorial will go over how to animate a bouncing ball in 2D using Adobe Flash CS6. It will use the bouncing ball template pictured below as a starting point. The overall process will involve making a path of motion for reference, setting a series of keyframes on both the light and heavy ball to define their motion, and finally creating and exporting the animation from Flash.

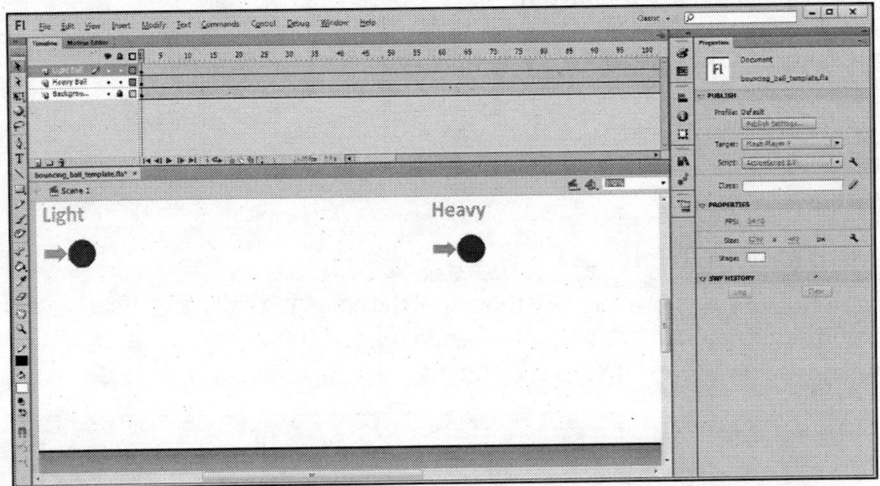


### Step-1 : Workspace Setup and Navigation

- Open Classic workspace. To activate this setup go to **Window → Workspace → Classic**. If you have used Adobe Flash before and are comfortable with another workspace that is fine, too.
- The bulk of your work will be done on the "Stage" where the light and heavy balls will be animated. To move the Stage around hold the **Spacebar**, left click and drag. To zoom in and out, hit the **'z'** key to activate the Zoom Tool. Click to zoom in and hold **Alt** and click to zoom out.
- The various tools used for animation will be covered individually as the tutorial progresses, but here's a summary of everything covered for reference:

### Step2 : Bezier Curves

- **p** - Pen Tool. Used to draw bezier curves. Click and drag to create an Anchor Point with handls, click without dragging to create an Anchor Point with no handles. Hold shift to snap handles in a horizontal, vertical, or diagonal direction. Hit the Delete key to remove a point that was just created.
- **a** - Subselection Tool. Used to move a bezier curve's Anchor Points and its handles.

### Step-3 : Animation

- **F6** - Insert a new keyframe at the current time.
- **v** - Select Tool. Used to select and move the ball.
- **q** - Free Transformation Tool for scaling and rotating the ball.
- **Ctrl+Shift+z** - Reset transformations on the selected ball.

- **Enter** - Play the animation.
- < and > - Step back or forward a frame.
- **Shift+Scroll Wheel** - Scrub the animation timeline.

**Navigation**

- **Spacebar** - Hold and click to move around the Stage.
- **z** - Zoom Tool. Click to zoom in, hold Alt and click to zoom out.

**General**

- **Ctrl+z** - Undo
- **Ctrl+y** - Redo

### Step-4 Path of Motion Reference

The next step is to plan your movement. In the case of the bouncing ball it's a bunch of arcs representing how it moves through the air. Select the *Background* layer and click the button indicated below to insert a new layer above it. Next double click the new layer and rename it to "Path".

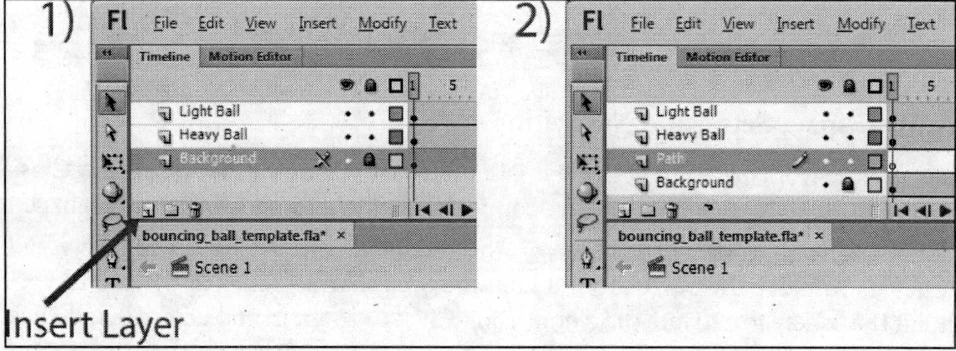


With the *Path* layer active, you can draw your path of motion using the Pen Tool.

Hit the **'p'** key to activate the Pen Tool. Before using the tool you will need to set up its line attributes. In the properties box on the right of the screen set the paint attributes to the following values.

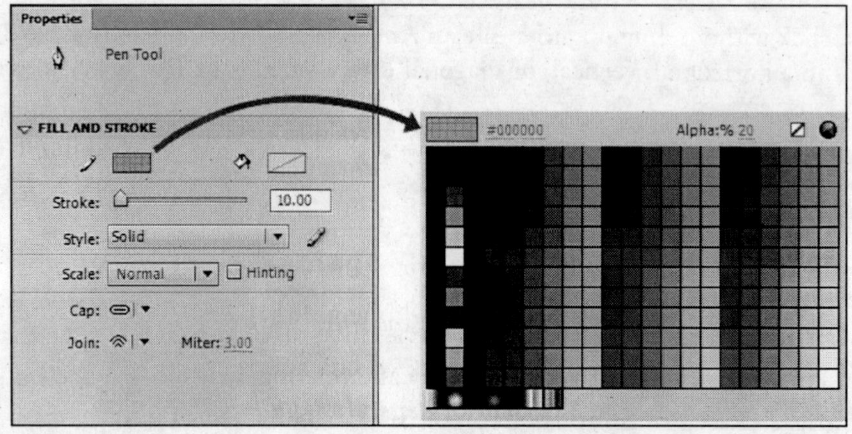

- **Color** to black (Hex value #000000)
- **Alpha** to 20%
- **Stroke** to 10
- **Style** to Solid

With the Pen Tool ready you can click around the screen to create a path. To make a smooth curve, left-click hold and drag each time you create a new path node. This will cause handles to appear that control the direction of the path. You may want to test this out a couple of times to get a feel for how it works. Repeatedly undo back using **Ctrl+z** to before you created the test paths.

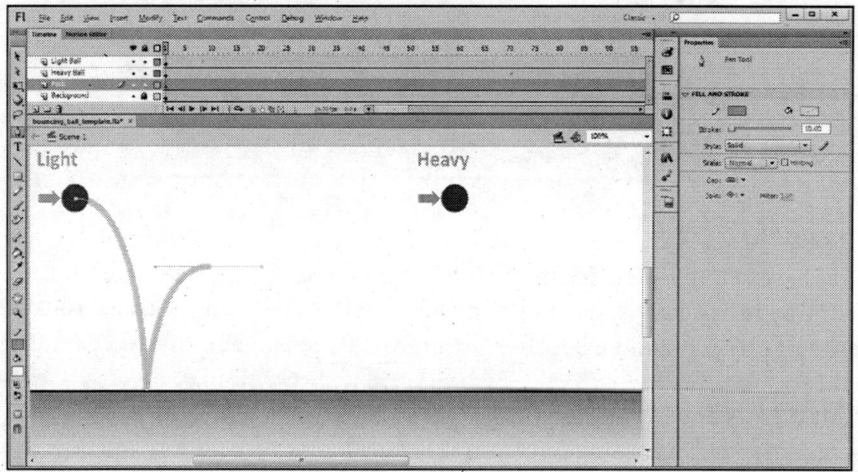


Once you've gotten the hang of the Pen Tool, it's time to start drawing the path of motion for the ball. Left-click hold at the starting position of the ball, **hold shift after moving the mouse**, then move the mouse and extend the handles out horizontally. The next node touching the ground is just a single left click. By not adding handles to the second node, the curve will end at the ground with a sharp point. For the next node, repeat the process of left-click holding, holding shift, and extending the handles horizontally. Alternate between these steps until you have a suitable path.

You can edit the nodes using the Sub-selection Tool. Hit the '**a**' key to activate it. This will allow you to select and move individual nodes along the path as well as their handles.

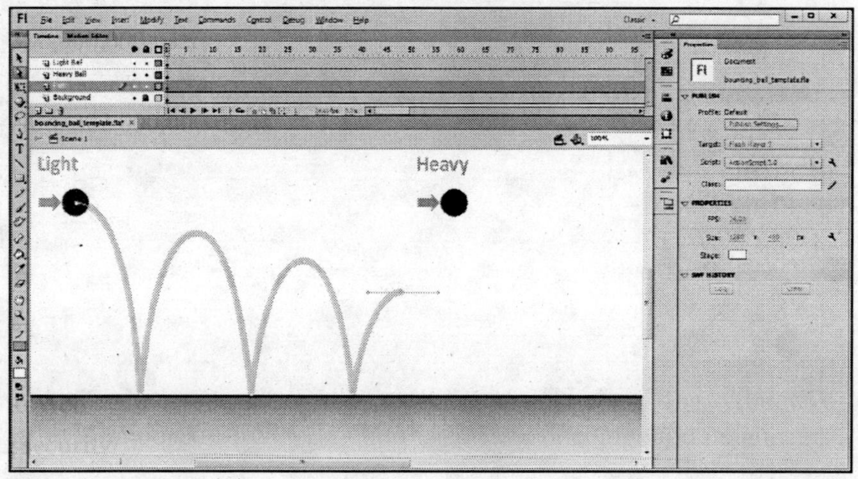

Be sure to create an additional reference path for the heavy ball on the same *Path* layer.

To finalize your reference paths, click the dot in the second column to the right of the layer name to lock the layer. This is so you won't accidentally modify it when setting keyframes on the balls.

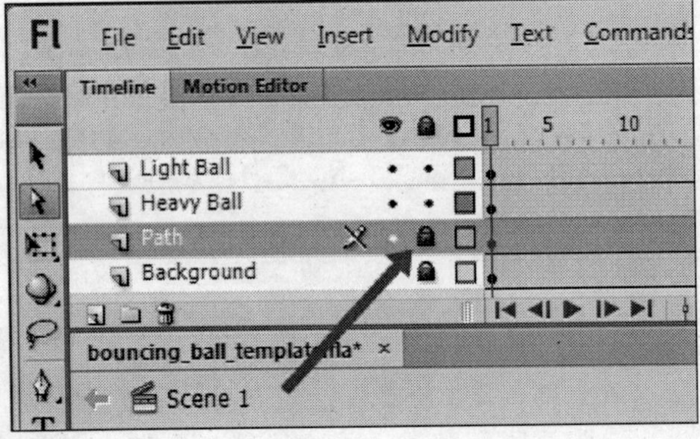


## Step-5 : Posing: Extremes

Now that you have set up the reference path it is time to define a series of keyframes on each ball layer. A keyframe is basically a "pose" defined at a particular point in time. Your animation will just be a series of these. It will be best to fully animate one ball at a time. Let's start with the light ball.

By default there is already one keyframe on each layer. The black dot on the timeline represents a keyframe, and the bar extending out from it is how long it is held for. You will be defining new keyframes within the extended bar.

Let's start by defining the extreme poses for the ball: High, low, high, low, etc. Click on frame 15 in the Light Ball layer's timeline. To create a new keyframe here press '**F6**'. Notice that a black dot appears on the timeline indicating that this is a new keyframe.

Next, activate the Selection Tool by hitting '**v**'. Now left click and drag the ball so that it is touching the ground along the path.

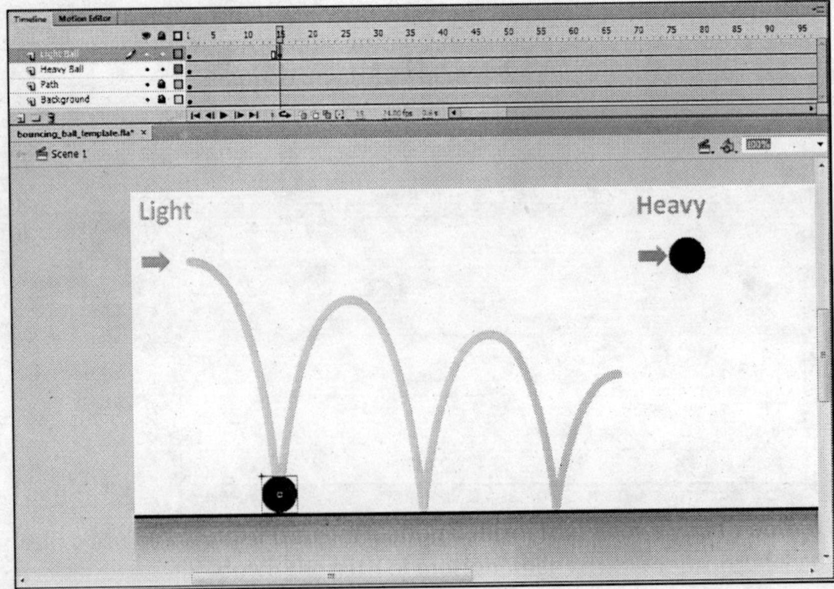

Proceed to do this for each additional high and low position. The animation will play at 24 frames per second, so keep this in mind as you insert your keyframes. Don't worry about getting the timing perfect on the first pass, right now you just want to get the frames in there.

You can hit **Enter** to preview your animation. Focus on the timing of the 'boinks', the point at which the ball hits the ground. Does it feel right for a ping pong ball? Before moving on you will want to adjust the timing so that it works.

Multiple frames can be selected by left-click dragging on the timeline. You can then move the selected frame[s] by dragging them. Note that you will want to start your selections with a keyframe at the front, because if you do not moving a section of frames will cause Flash to automatically create a keyframe there (most likely at a place where you don't want it). The first thing you will probably want to do is shift all the frames to the left, since frame 15 might be too late of a landing point.

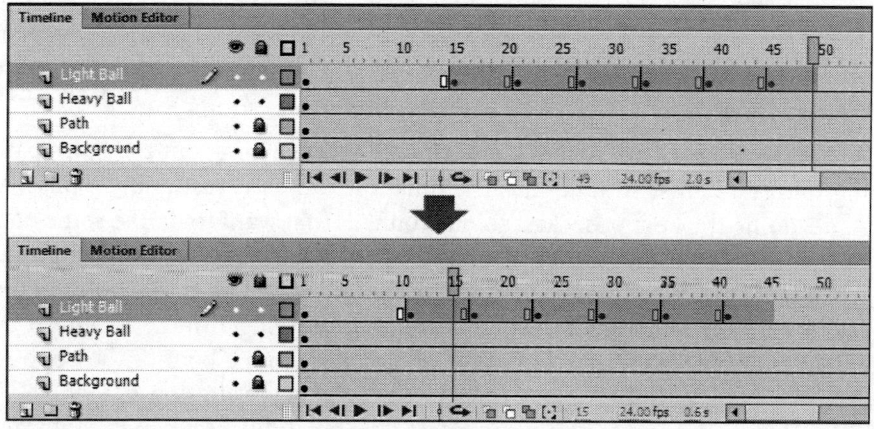


Your poses should all look something like what is pictured below. Note that all the poses are shown at once. This is via "onion skinning", which is an essential 2D animation tool that allows you to see past and future frames as you work. We will revisit this later.

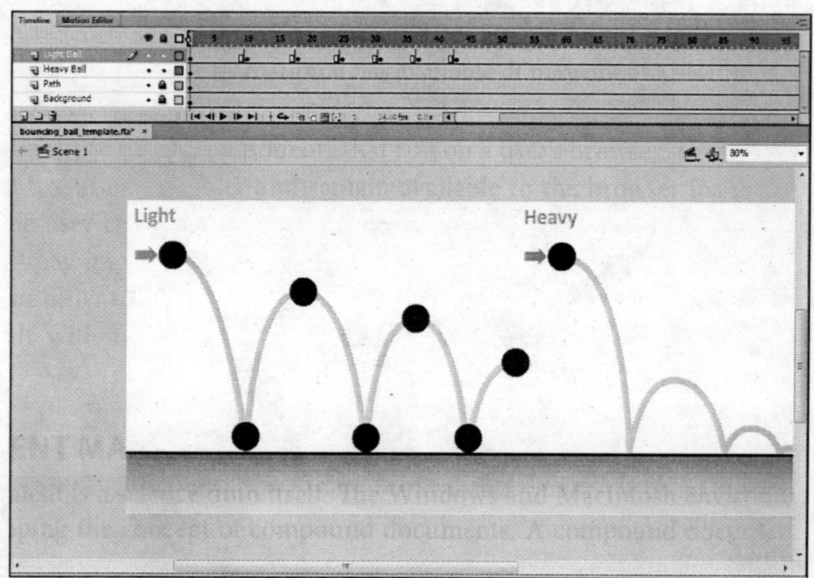

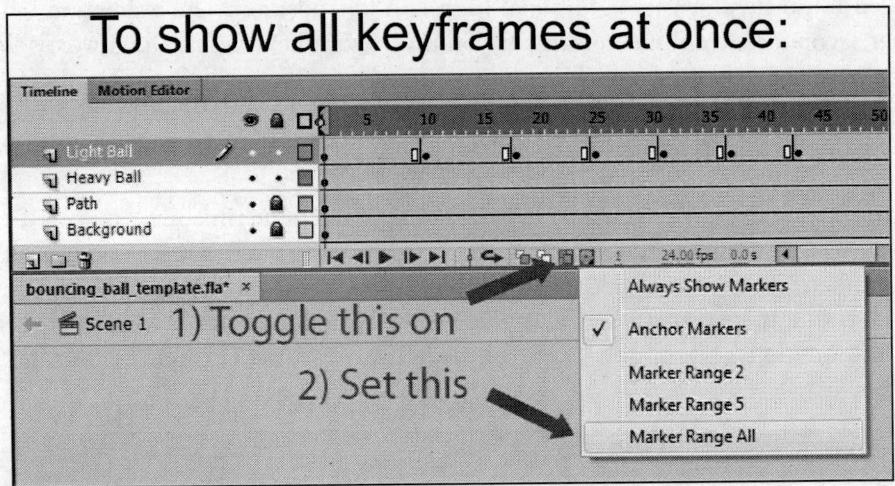


## Step 6 : Posing: Breakdowns

Now that the extreme poses are defined, it is time to start shaping out the ball's path of motion. Before going into full blown straight-ahead animation (which is just doing a pose, advancing to the next frame, doing the next pose, and so on) you will first want to define some breakdowns. In this case, they will be keyframes centered timewise between the ball's extreme high and low poses.

For each of these breakdowns, consider where the ball would be at that point in the animation. Spacing plays a critical role here. As the ball descends it will linger in the air longer before gravity takes full effect and it picks up speed. As the ball ascends from a bounce the opposite is true. Its momentum will carry it most of the way up before gravity begins to slow it down.

Check out the image below to see this in effect. The breakdowns are highlighted green. Similar to when you finished your first set of poses, you should spend some timing playing back your animation and adjusting the timing before moving on.

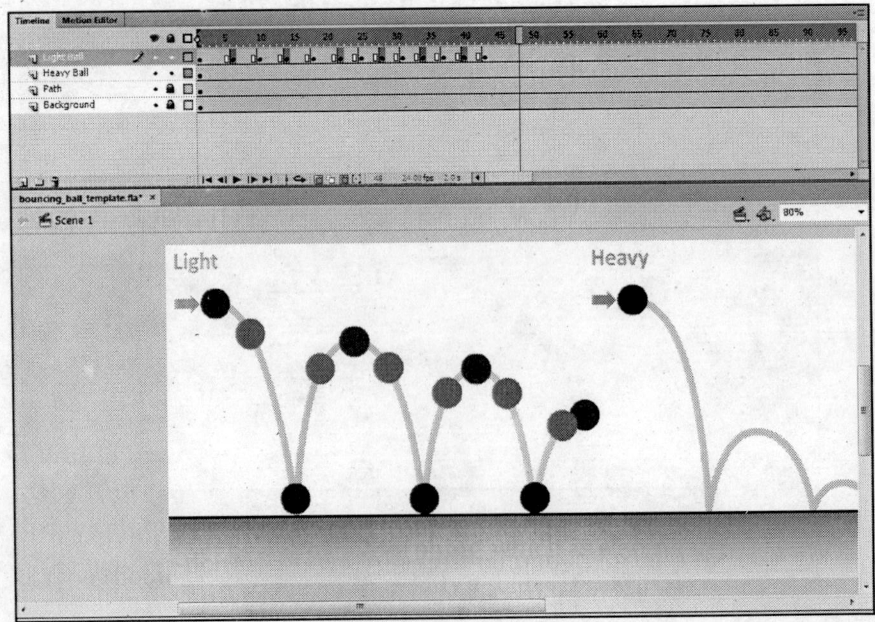

## Step 7 : Straight-ahead Animation

The next step is to fill in the rest of the frames doing some frame by frame straight-ahead animation. You will be doing this in segments, filling in each space between the ball's extreme and breakdown poses. Begin with the first two segments up until the ball hits the ground. Click on frame 2, press '**F6**', then move the ball along its path of motion. Click on frame 3, press '**F6**', move the ball, and so on.

Here are some tips that should ease the process:

- You can also press the '<' and '>' keys to step backwards and forwards between frames. So hitting '>' then '**F6**' might be a slightly less tedious way of setting a keyframe. You can also just select a span of frames and set them all as keyframes at once; however, be warned that they will all carry the same initial pose.
- Automatic snapping can be useful sometimes, but it can cause the ball to stick to other parts of the scene when you don't want it to. Go to **View → Snapping** to toggle on and off the various snapping options.
- If you want the ball to be in a very specific location it may be easier to select it and use the arrows on the keyboard for smaller, incremental movements.
- The reference path may be more helpful above the ball. Go ahead and drag the *Path* layer above the *Light Ball* layer. Now you can use the center pivot of the point as a point of reference for how to center the ball along the path.

Consider how much the ball should move from frame to frame. The same concept of spacing you used when establishing breakdowns still applies. It's just on a smaller scale. Once you have the first couple of segments complete play back your animation to make sure it looks right. Modify poses as needed, even if you need to tweak your initial extremes and breakdowns (just make sure not to change those too much).

This is where onion skinning will come in handy. It will give you a more complete view of your motion and allow you to tweak your keyframes with visible context. Follow the instructions below to enable it.

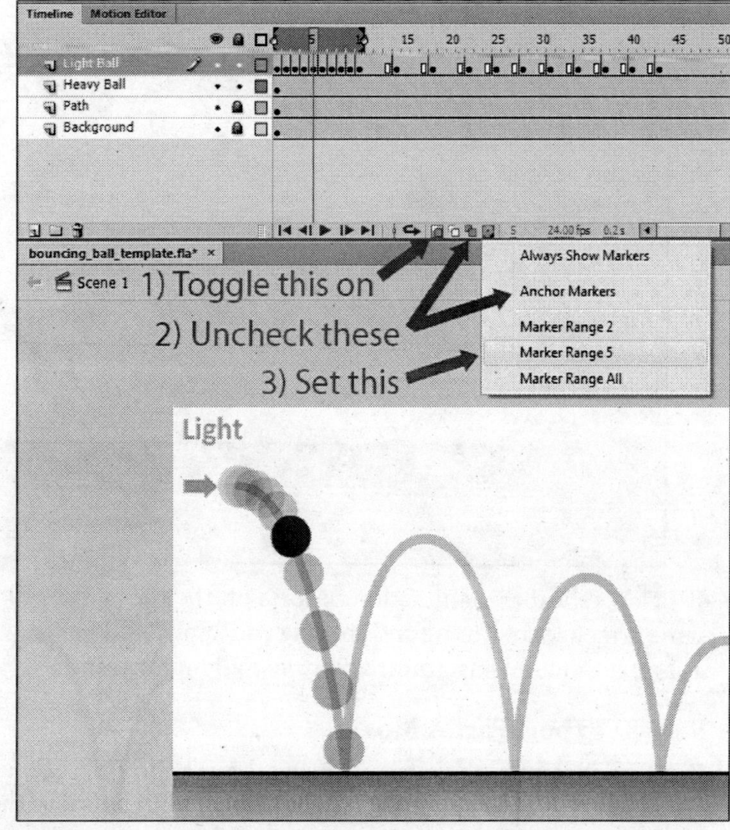

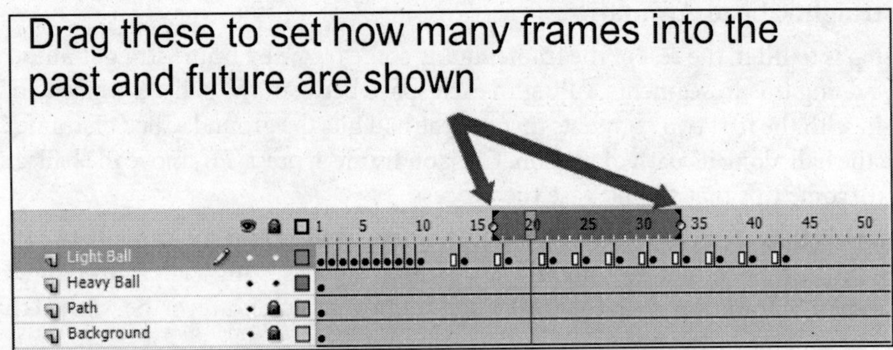


Now finish the rest of the segments. Once done, it should something like below, with most of the frames clumped at the top of its arcs and more space between the ball as it gets closer to the ground.

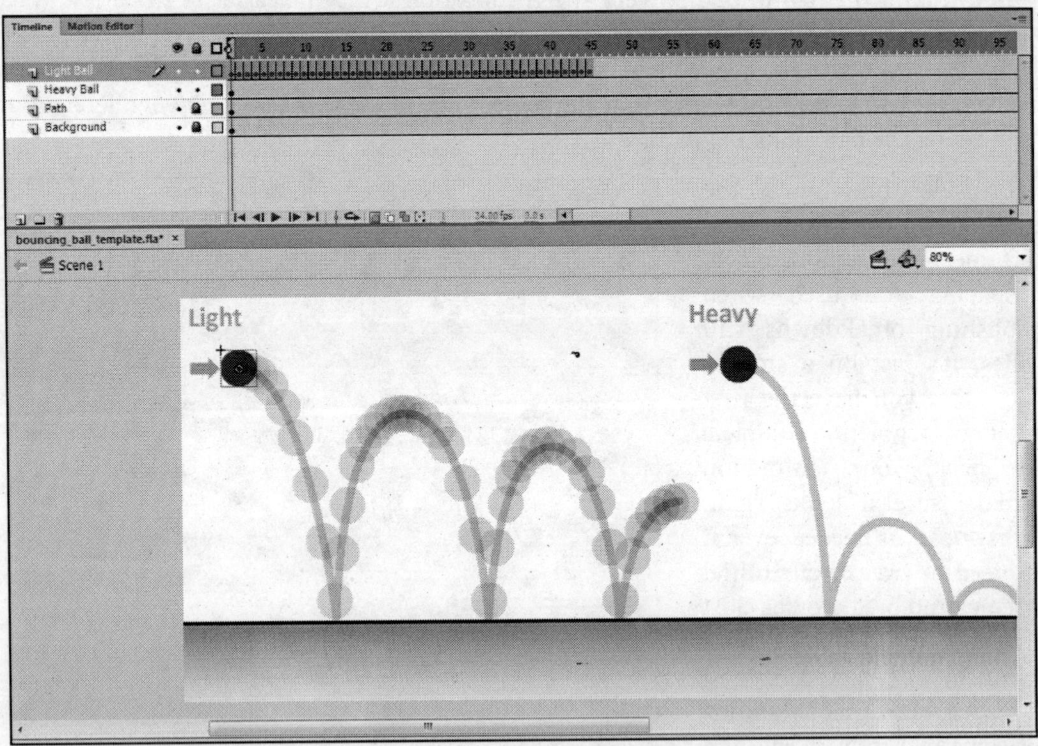


Now repeat this animation process on the heavy ball. Though it will bounce differently, the same principles of timing and spacing will apply. ***And be sure to let the heavy ball roll naturally to a stop.*** It shouldn't just immediately lose all momentum.

### Step-8 : Export Part A Movie

You are not completely finished yet, but this is a good place for a check-point. Save your Flash project file as `bb _ animation.fla`. You will be turning this and the following video into Catalyst.

Next, export your animation. Before doing so you'll need to make sure the reference paths don't show up in the final output. Right click the *Path* layer and set it to "Guide". Now it won't show up when your flash video is rendered out.

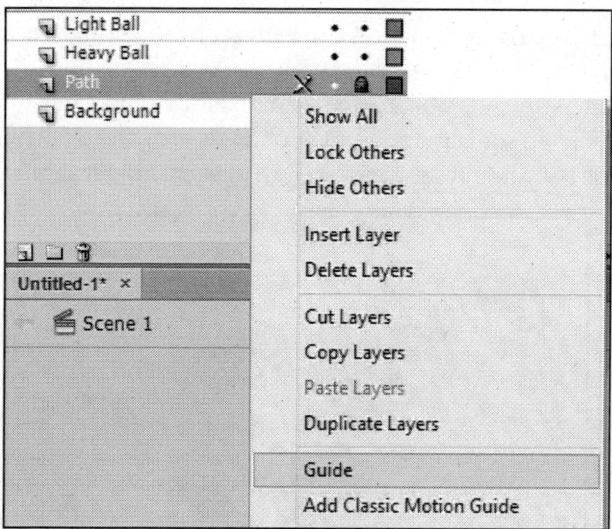


Now go to **File → Export → Export Movie...** Make sure Save As File Type is set to "QuickTime" and name your movie file `bb_animation.mov`.

When you click Save an options box will pop up. Go to Quicktime Settings on the bottom left. In the new window, uncheck Sound then under Video go to Settings. Change Compression Type to "MPEG-4 Video". Click OK on everything and then finally Export.

Before moving on, save your Flash project file again as `bb_animation_with_ss.fla`.

## Step 9 : Squash and Stretch

You've got down arcs, timing, and spacing, but now it's time to do another pass on your motion to add a bit of squash and stretch. This will not only act like motion blur, thus reducing any sort of strobing effect, but it will ultimately give your animation more life and make it more interesting to watch.

A good rule of thumb to follow here is that stretch should happen any time there is a significant gap between the ball between frames. You will most likely not have much of this in the heavy ball beyond the initial fall, but there will definitely need to be some in the light ball. Squash should happen any time there is any sudden stop in force, such as when the ball impacts the ground.

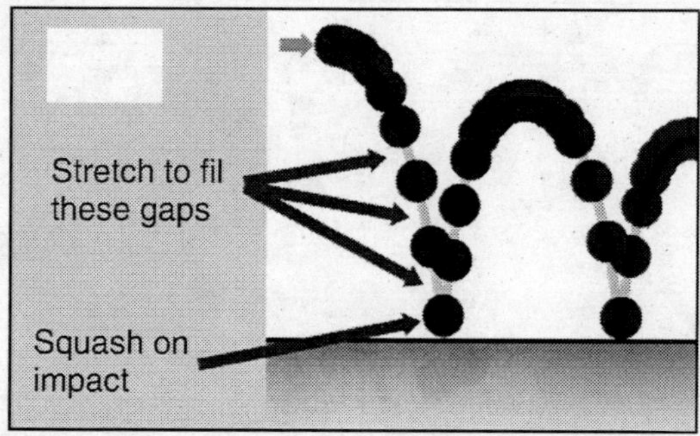


Go to the frame right before the first gap happens. You will be starting the stretch here, though on this particular frame it will only be a little bit. Select the ball shape and hit '**q**'. This will bring up a transformation control that allows you to both rotate and scale the ball. Rotate the ball to face down the path of motion, then scale it appropriately to stretch it out along the same path. If you are unhappy with the result, the transformation can be reset by selecting the shape and hitting the key combination **Ctrl+Shift+z**.

Any time squash and stretch is utilized the volume of the object must be maintained or else the resulting motion will look too squishy and like the object is growing or shrinking in size. This means that when stretching the ball should squish in and when squashing it should squish outwards.

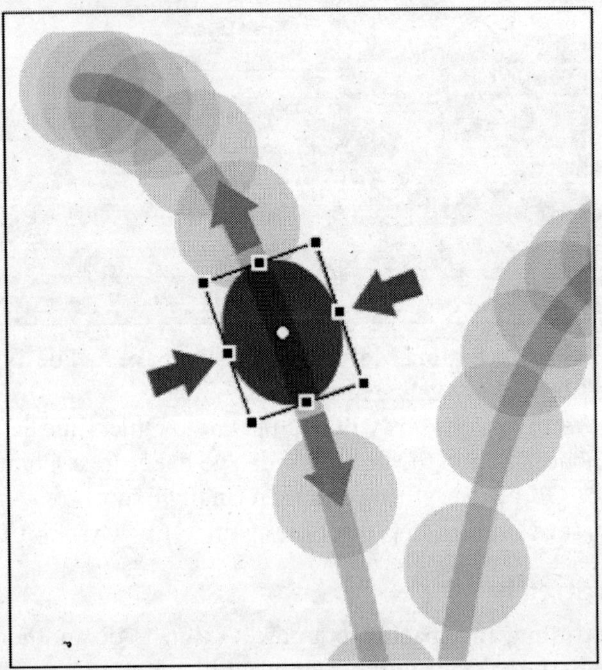

Proceed to stretch out the rest of the poses. When you get to the frame right before the ball hits, make sure the stretched ball is contacting the ground. (Also feel free to duplicate the ball's ground pose and use that as a starting point for the stretched contact pose.) This will emphasize the contrast between when the ball is stretched and when it is squashed, thus giving the impact more force. Conversely, when leaving the ground, the general convention is that the ball should *not* be contacting the ground.

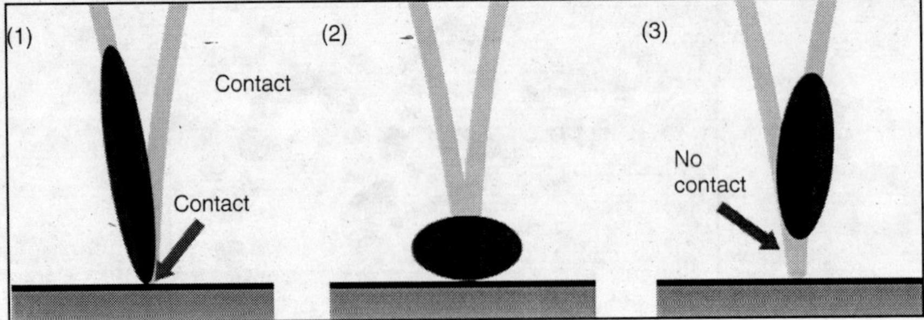


When rotating the stretched pose near the ground, you may want to drag the pivot to the point of contact to make the ball easier to aim. It's the white dot that's at the center of the ball by default. Note that the pivot will only change for that keyframe.

In the completed example below you may notice that the squash and stretch is fairly exaggerated. Yours does not necessarily have to be this way; experiment with what looks best.

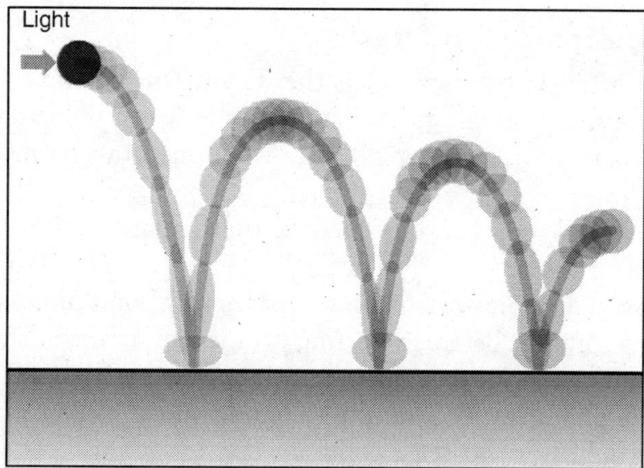


## 8.25 MORPHING

You've seen it in movies, in advertisements and on the computer. Morphing-the visual merging of one image to another-is a powerful tool that can tell a poignant visual story or earn a quick laugh. Short for metamorphosis, morphing made its Hollywood debut in the 1988 George Lucas and Ron Howard film, Willow. Morphing was around decades before Lucas and Howard used the technique to transform a goat into a woman, but until the late 1980's morphing tools were hard to use and computers were not fast enough to keep pace with technology.

The process of Morphing involves producing a special effect in motion pictures and animations that changes (or morphs) one image into another through a seamless transition.The animated transformation of one image into another by gradually distorting the first image so as to move certain chosen points to the position of corresponding points in the second image. Most often it is used to depict one person turning into another through technological means or as part of a fantasy or surreal sequence.

Morphing is a type of animation in which interpolations between specified points on two or more images are create a transitional effect. Give the illusion that the first image is changing into the last one via a series of frames. An example would be a photo kiosk in which two people would have their pictures taken and a photo would be generated by the computer that combines their images. The morphing process involves selecting sets of corresponding points on each images. Thus, in morphing the two faces shown in image above, the sets of points might include eyes, lips, ears, and outline of the head. Based on these sets of points, the morphing program rearranges the pixels to transition the original image into the second via a series of intervening images. Morphing is useful not only in showing how two images blend together, but also in showing how an image might change over time. Photo Morph, Hijact Morph, and Elastic Reality are examples of programs than can produce quite sophisticated morphing animations.

Traditionally such a depiction would be achieved through cross-fading techniques on film. Since the early 1990s, this has been replaced by computer software to create more realistic transitions.Some of the popular Morphing Software are FantaMorph, Morpheus, Photo Morpher, FaceMorpher, Fun Morph, Morph Man and Magic Morph.

Voice Morphing which is also referred to as voice transformation and voice conversion is a technique to modify a source speaker's speech utterance to sound as if it was spoken by a target speaker. There are many applications which may benefit from this sort of technology.

### (1) Choosing a Morph Source and Target

With most morphing software, the "source" is the starting image and the "target" is the ending image. Morphing is the visual merging that happens in between the two images. This transition should be so seamless that you will see several clear, whole, new images between the morph source and target photos.

You'll have to have digital copies of your start and finish images. With a scanner, you can upload regular print photos to your computer easily. The quality of the source and target images will determine if your morph is successful. Use only clear, well-lit images with good contrast. Consider touching up flaws with photo editing software before importing your images to the morphing program.

If image backgrounds are diverse or distracting, trim the background or add a border to your morph. If you stage the photos for the morph, use an identical background for each subject. For whole-body morphs, you'll want to set a common theme such as everyone wearing sunglasses or everyone saluting. However, the most intriguing whole-body morphs show bodies shifting to different positions such as legs crossed to the right shifting to legs crossed on the left. But shifting body morphs are challenging. If you are a morph beginner, stick with identical poses.

### (2) Select Morph Frames and Morph Speed

You can choose the number of morph frames to create between your photos; the more frames you have, the smoother the morph transition. We like 50 or 60 transition frames but for a quick, simple morph, you can get by with as few as five. Here are examples of each that were created in FantaMorph.

The example on the left contains 20 frames while the example on the right contains 60 frames. Some morphing software allows you to vary the speed at which the frames display. Increasing or decreasing the number of frames displayed per second will increase or decrease the time it takes to complete the morph sequence.

### (3) Mark Morph Control Points

Also called "anchors" or "control dots," control points mark the route the visual transition will take between two photos. In an eye morph, for example, you'll want to mark the visual points of the eyes-such as pupils, corners, and eyebrows. Then mark the matching points on the destination photo. During the morph, the color, detail, and location of the eye gradually takes the characteristics of the eye marks in the destination photo. Some morphing software programs let you zoom in and out of images; the more you zoom in, the more control points you can mark. Some morphing software lets you zoom in up to 800%, giving you precision morph accuracy. Placing 150 to 200 control points on each photo will give your morph a clean, smooth, convincing look. Placing so many morph control points takes some time, but the result is worth it. With practice, your skill and speed at placing control points will improve.

### (4) Save the Morph

Be certain you save your work at this point. The most common mistake people make when morphing is exporting the morph file without saving it first. Most morphing software doesn't automatically save, so you may lose some of your control points if you aren't careful. Always save the morph file before exporting it.

### (5) Review and Refine the Morph

Now it's time to check out your work. Some programs allow you to check your morph instantly. Experiment, slow it down, add new frames or add more points. With some morphing software, you can scroll through your morph frame by frame and check for inconsistencies. You can even print out a transition photo (the in-between version of your morph) to get a closer look at the merged version of your image.

## 8.26 PRINCIPLES OF ANIMATION

Animation is possible because of a biological phenomenon known as persistence of vision. An object seen by the human eye remains mapped on the eye's retina for a brief time after viewing. This makes it possible for a series of images that are changed very slightly and very rapidly, one after the other, to seemingly blend together into a visual illusion of movement. In other words, if you just change slightly the location or shape of an object rapidly enough the eye will perceive the changes as motion. The perception of motion in an animation is an illusion. The movement that we see is, like a move, made up of many still images, each in its own frame. Animation can be a set of graphic images that may be displayed quickly as a series of frames or a set of objects (or "characters") Movies on video builds 30 entire frames or pictures every second; the speed with which each frame is replaced by the next one makes the images appear to blend smoothly into movement. Computer animations can be effective at 12 to 15 fps (or more). Anything less results in a jerky motion, as the eye detects the changes from one frame to the next

### 8.26.1 Animation Special Effects

Morphing Type of animation in which interpolations between specified points on two or more images are create a transitional effect. Give the illusion that the first image is changing into the last one via a series of frames. An example would be a photo kiosk in which two people would have their pictures taken and a photo would be generated by the computer that combines their images. The morphing process involves selecting sets of corresponding points on each images. Thus, in morphing the two faces, the sets of points might include eyes, lips, ears, and outline of the head. Based on these sets of points, the morphing program rearranges the pixels to transition the original image into the second via a series of intervening images. Morphing is useful not only in showing how two images blend together, but also in showing how an image might change over time. Photo Morph, Hijact Morph, and Elastic Reality are examples of programs than can produce quite sophisticated morphing animations.

### 8.26.2 Principles of Animation

Animation is possible because of a biological phenomenon known as persistence of vision. An object seen by the human eye remains mapped on the eye's retina for a brief time after viewing. This makes it possible for a series of images that are changed very slightly and very rapidly, one after the other, to seemingly blend together into a visual illusion of movement. In other words, if you just change slightly the location or shape of an object rapidly enough, the eye will perceive the changes as motion. The following shows a few cells or frames of a rotating logo. When the images are progressively and rapidly changed, the arrow of the compass is perceived to be spinning.

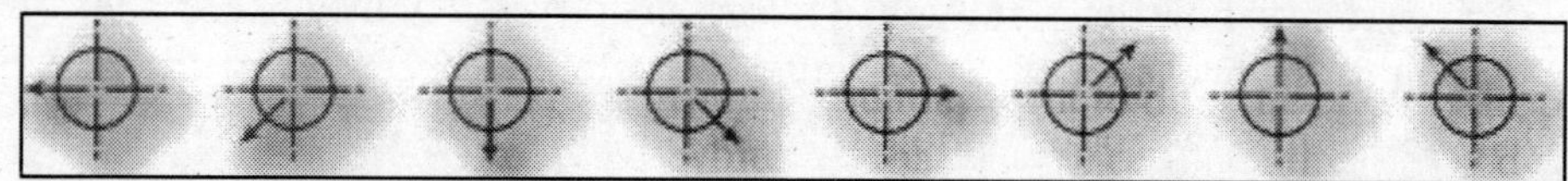

Television video builds 30 entire frames or pictures every second; the speed with which each frame is replaced by the next one makes the images appear to blend smoothly into movement. Movies on film are typically shot at a shutter rate of 24 frames per second, but using projection

tricks (the projector's shutter flashes light through each image twice), the flicker rate is increased to 48 times per second, and the human eye thus sees a motion picture.

24p (equals 24 full frames per second) should be used if you want a cinema like effect — most movies are shot at that frame rate. It is a historical thing because it is (or was) the ideal fit for conversions to international TV standards and therefore the frame rate movie directors went for.

Nowadays, with latest HD TV systems that requirement might go away. Avatar and The Hobbit were already filmed in higher frame rates, the latter in 48fps.

30p is the standard for home movies or let's say digital video outside of movies and sports. 30 frames per second capture normal paced movements quite well and in a natural way.

48p, which for example GoPro cameras offer, is well suited for faster action, but not too fast, and allows you still to slow the frames down later in editing when you aim at a 30p frame rate for your video export. A real world situation for that frame rate would be white water rafting, kayaking, etc. when you might want to slow down the motion but not to the point where you record water drops flying in slo-mo.

60p is suited for fast-paced sports where movements with 30p just don't look as smooth as they should. Again, it is already suited to slow the motion down in an editing software and the motion looks still fluent. Slowing down for 48p and 60p is meant as 'moderate'.

Quickly changing the viewed image is principle of an animatic a flip-book, or a zoetrope. To make an object travel across the screen while it changes its shapes, just change the shape and also move it a few pixels for each frame. Then, when you play the frames back at a faster speed, the changes blend together and you have motion and animation. (it's the same magic as when the hand is quicker than the eye, and you don't see the pea moving in the blur of the gypsy's cups).

The 12 principles of animation are the most crucial techniques you must master as an animator. Created by the pioneers of animation, Frank Thomas and Ollie Johnston and first introduced in The Illusion of Life: Disney Animation, these 12 principles should be your ultimate guide for creating appealing and realistic character animations.

Explore the 12 principles and start mastering them in your own work to create captivating animations. Use this as a reference if you're ever stumped on a principle or your animation needs some help.

### (1) Timing and Spacing

Timing and spacing in animation is what gives objects and characters the illusion of moving within the laws of physics. Timing refers to the number of frames between two poses. For example, if a ball travels from screen left to screen right in 24 frames that would be the timing. It takes 24 frames or one second (if you're working within the film rate of 24 frames per second) for the ball to reach the other side of the screen.

**Fig. 8.24:** Timing-and-Spacing

The spacing refers to how those individual frames are placed. For instance, in the same example the spacing would be how the ball is positioned in the other 23 frames. If the spacing is close together, the object moves slower, if the spacing is further apart the object moves faster.

### (2) Squash and Stretch

Squash and Stretch is what gives flexibility to objects. There's a lot of squash and stretch happening in real life that you may not notice; in animation this can be exaggerated. For instance, there's a lot of squash and stretch that occur in the face when someone speaks, because the face is a very flexible area.

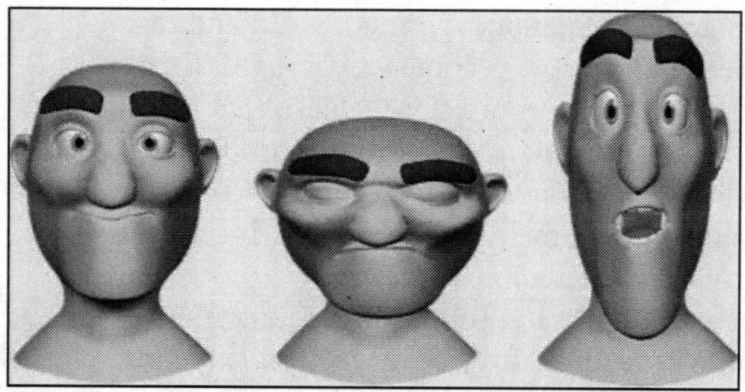

**Fig. 8.25:** Squash-and-Stratch

The easiest way to understand how squash and stretch work is to look at a bouncing ball. As the ball starts to fall and picks up speed, the ball will stretch out just before impact, and as the ball impacts the ground, it squashes, and as it takes off again it stretches.

Squash and stretch can be implemented in many different areas of animation, like the eyes during a blink or when someone gets surprised or scared, their face squashes down, and stretches. Squash and stretch is a great principle to utilize to exaggerate animations and add more appeal to a movement.

## (3) Anticipation

Anticipation is used in animation to set the audience up for an action that is about to happen. An easy way to think about this is that if a person needs to move forward, they first must move back. For example, if a character is about to walk forward, they might move back slightly, this not only gets their momentum up, but it also lets the audience know this person is about to move. Or if a character is reaching for a glass on a table, they might move their hand back, before moving it forward.

**Fig. 8.26:** Anticipation

Not only is anticipation needed to prepare the audience, but it's also required to sell believable movements. For example, before a baseball player pitches they first need to move their entire body and arm back to gain enough energy, and before a parkour enthusiast leaps of a ledge they first must bend their knees to prepare for the jump. Imagine if these actions had no anticipation – they wouldn't be believable.

### (4) Ease in Ease Out

As any object or person moves or comes to a stop there needs to be a time for acceleration and deceleration. Without ease in and ease out (or slow in slow out), movements become very unnatural and robotic. For example, as a car starts from a stop, it doesn't just reach full speed in an instant, it first must accelerate and gain speed. As it comes to a stop it doesn't go from sixty to zero in the blink of an eye, if it did, it would be extremely uncomfortable. Instead, it slowly decelerates until it reaches a complete stop.

The same must be accomplished in an animation, and the easiest way to accomplish ease in and ease out is to utilize the principle of spacing. As a character stands up from a sitting position the spacing will be closer together at the start, so they ease into the movement, and as they stand up, they will ease out of the movement. Without this acceleration and deceleration of actions everything would be very abrupt and jerky.

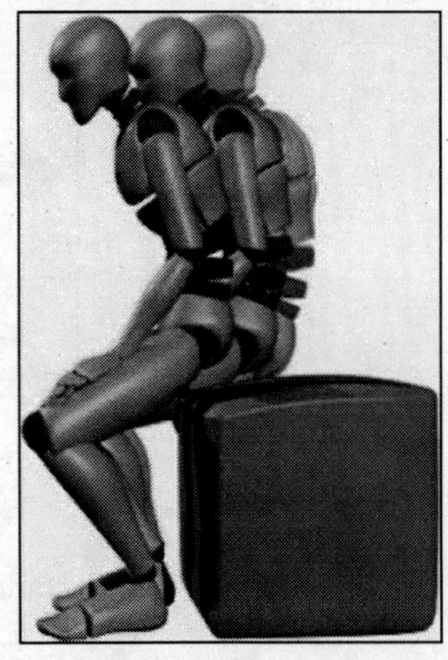

**Fig. 8.27:** Ease-in-Ease-out

### (5) Follow Through and Overlapping Action

Follow through and overlapping action can be considered two different principles, but they're still closely related.

Follow through is the idea that separate parts of the body will continue moving after the character has come to a stop. For example, as a character comes to a stop from a walk, every part of the body won't stop at the exact same time, instead, the arms may continue forward before coming to a settle. This could also be articles of clothing that continue to move as the character comes to a stop.

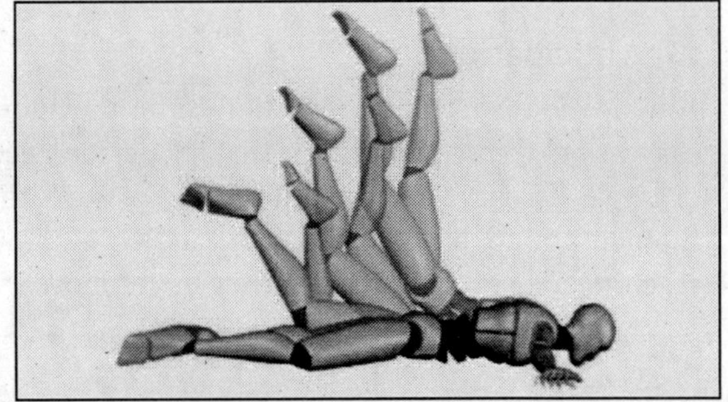

**Fig. 8.28:** Follow-Through

Overlapping action is very similar in that it means different parts of the body will move at different times. For example, if a character raises their arm up to wave, the shoulder will move first, and then the arm, and the elbow and hand may lag behind a few frames. You may have also heard this referred to as "drag" or "lead and follow" You can even see an example of overlapping action in something like a blade of grass, the base moves first, and the rest of the grass follows behind at different rates, giving you that waving motion.

In real life, everything moves at different speeds and at different moments in time, and that is why follow through and overlapping action is so important for capturing realistic and fluid movement.

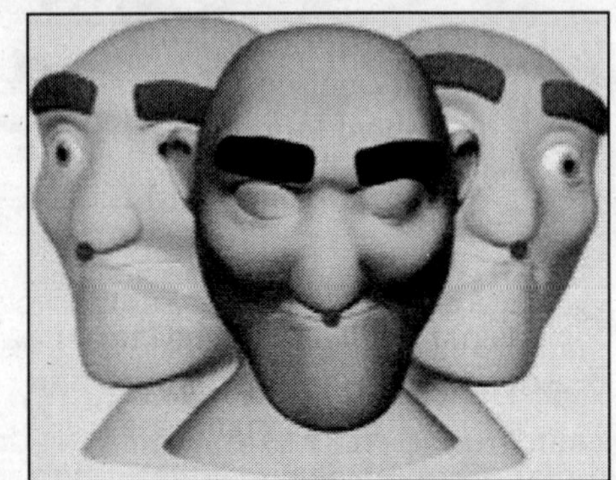

**Fig. 8.29:** Arcs

### (6) Arcs

Everything in real-life typically moves in some type of arcing motion, and in animation you should adhere to this principle of arcs to ensure your animation is smooth and moves in a realistic way. The only time something would move in a perfectly straight line is if you're trying to animate a robot, because it's unnatural for people to move in straight lines.

For example, if a character is turning their head, they will dip their head down during the turn creating an arcing motion. You also want to ensure the more subtle things move in arcs as well, for example the tips of the toes should move in rounded arcing motions as the character walks.

## (7) Exaggeration

Exaggeration is used to push movements further to add more appeal to an action. Exaggeration can be used to create extremely cartoony movements, or incorporated with a little more restrain to more realistic actions. Whether it's for a stylized animation or realistic, exaggeration should be implemented to some degree.

If you have a realistic animation you can use exaggeration to make a more readable or fun movement while staying true to reality. For example, if a character is preparing to jump off a diving board you can push them down just a little bit further before they leap off. You can also use exaggeration in the timing as well to enhance different movements or help to sell the weight of a character.

**Fig. 8.30:** Exaggeration

## (8) Solid Drawing

In 2D Animation, solid drawing is about creating an accurate drawing with volume and weight, and thinking about balance, and the anatomy in a pose. With 3D animation, animators are less likely to rely on their drawings, but the idea of solid drawing is just as important.

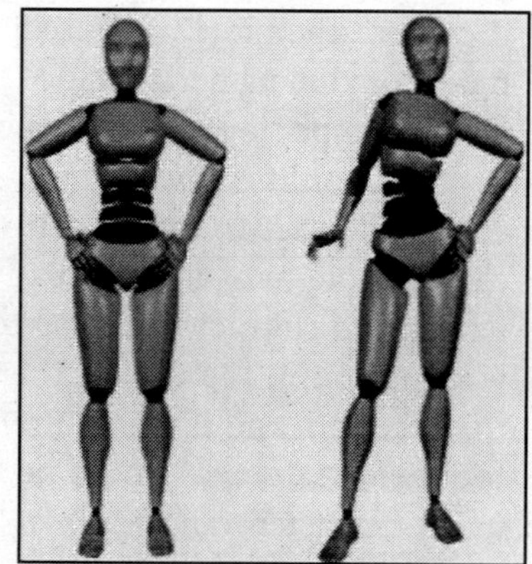

**Fig. 8.31:** Solid-Drawing

With solid drawing you need to think about how you pose out your 3D character rig, ensuring there is correct balance and weight in the pose, as well as a clear silhouette. You also want to avoid what is called "twinning," which basically means the pose you have created is mirrored across to the other side.

For example, the character may have both arms on their hips or both hands in their pockets. This creates a rather boring and unappealing pose. Making sure you implement the principle of solid drawing into your posing will ensure you avoid this issue.

## (9) Appeal

This principle can really come down to adding more appeal in many different areas of your animation, such as appeal in posing. However, the most obvious example is appeal in the character design, you want to have a character that the audience can connect to or relate to. A complicated or confusing character design can lack appeal.

You can find areas on the character to push and exaggerate to create a more unique character design that will stick out in the audience's memory. For example, simply exaggerating the jaw of the character or pushing the youthfulness in the eyes can help create more appeal.

### (10) Straight Ahead and Pose to Pose

Straight ahead and pose to pose refers to the two different techniques for how you go about animating. With straight ahead it's a very spontaneous and more of a linear approach. You'll create each pose or drawing of the animation one after the other. For example, if you're animating a character jumping in the air you would create the pose where he's standing, the next where he is beginning to kneel down, the next would be him completely crouched, and so on. You're really working through the animation as you're going.

**Fig. 8.32:** Straight-Ahead-and-Pose-to-Pose

With pose to pose it's much more methodical and planned out, with just the most important poses required to properly tell the action. For example, you could approach the exact same action with four poses, the character standing, crouched, in the air, and back on the ground. It allows you to work much simpler, and ensure the posing and timing is correct before adding more detail.

### (11) Secondary Action

Secondary action refers to creating actions that emphasize or support the main action of the animation; it can breathe more life into an animation and create a more convincing performance.

It's important to remember that the secondary action should typically be something subtle that doesn't detract from the main action happening, and can be thought of as almost a subconscious action. For example, a character talking to another character in a waiting room, the two of them talking would be the main action, and if that character began tapping their foot nervously, that would be the secondary action.

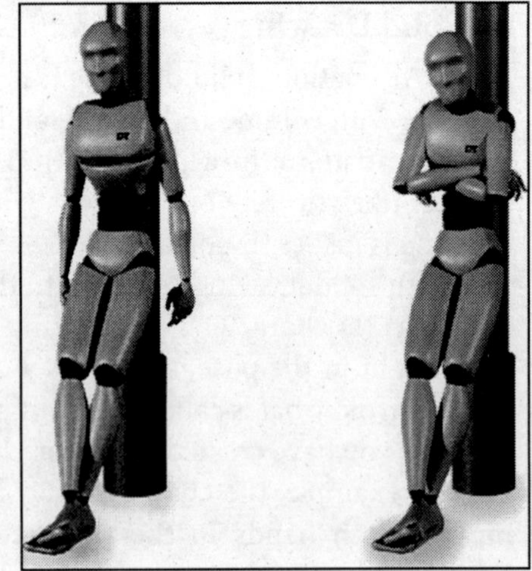
**Fig. 8.33:** Secondary-Action

A character walking down the street while whistling could be another example of secondary action or a person leaning up against a wall talking to some people at school, the main action is the character leaning against the wall and talking, and then putting in an action of them crossing their arms would be the secondary action.

### (12) Staging

Fig. 8.34: Staging

Staging is how you go about setting up your scene, from the placement of the characters to the background and foreground elements and how the camera angle is set up. The purpose of staging is to make the purpose of the animation unmistakably clear to the viewer. This could be ensuring the camera is set up in a way to communicate the characters expression clearly, or setting up two different characters so that both of them are easily viewed from the specific angle.

You want to keep focus on the purpose of the shot and what you want to communicate so the audience doesn't become confused.

Now that you know the meaning and purpose behind all of the principles of animation, be sure to implement these 12 key principles into all of your animations, and you'll be sure to create stunning work

## 8.27 ADOBE FLASH

Flash is used for working with vector graphics, animation, games etc. Flash is usually used for making web banners and other types of advertising. Because you use simple images, text and vector graphics, the file size is generally small. This allows content to be uploaded, download, and played quickly and without any problems. In order for you to watch flash animations, you will need a plug-in called Flash Player, which these days, is incorporated in most, if not all, web browsers.

Adobe flash is found almost anywhere these days, not only on PCs but also on Phones, Tablets, etc.

Flash player supports several data formats, including XML, JSON, AMF and SWF. Multimedia formats supported by the Adobe Flash Player include mp3, FLV, PNG, JPEG, GIF and RTMP, among others.

### Advantages and Limitations of Flash

**Advantages**

- It is vector based thus smaller file size.
- Vector base graphics are also resizable with zero quality lost.
- By incorporating flash into your website, you can make it more professional and trustworthy. It allows the viewers to interact within your website, watch videos and listen to audio
- Flash is a good way to advertise products, etc. By making web banners, posters, you can attract people to buy, look at your products, website, etc.
- It allows you to quickly get your point across because you can create a video introducing your website or product fast and effectively.
- A flash website viewed in mobile phone looks better than normal website.
- Loading feature made things like YouTube possible.

**Limitations**

- Designing a good Flash website takes a lot of planning.

- Programming a Flash program is quite complex.
- The readymade components are useless as they are not internet friendly.
- Flash animated website won't show in the search bar because engines cannot index them.
- Flash files don't work on Apple products such as iPads and iPhones.
- There is a content capacity on a flash file which means that if you have too much data in the file, you will have to shorten or delete work in order to save it.
- Adobe Flash is expensive to buy.
- You can only view flash if you have flash player installed into your machine or browser.

## 8.28 SHOCKWAVE PLAYER

Adobe Shockwave is a platform that allows you to implement animation and interactivity into webpages. In order to view any Shockwave objects, you must have the Shockwave Plug-in installed into your browser. Shockwave supports audio, animation, and video.It runs on Windows and Macintosh platforms.

It is also used for interactive games. For example, the BBC website has a numerous amount of small interactive games that you can play.

Shockwave Player is the web standard for powerful multimedia playback. Shockwave Player allows you to view interactive web content like games, business presentations, entertainment, and advertisements from your web browser.

Unlike Adobe Flash, Shockwave Player displays destination web content such as interactive multimedia product demos and training, e-merchandising applications, and rich-media multi-user games.

### Advantages and limitations of Shockwave

#### Advantages

- Many devices support Adobe Shockwave.
- It allows you to create interactive games, animations, audio.
- Shockwave technology allows for the creation of deep, versatile environments for internet users to interact within.

#### Limitations

- The file sizes are generally big, which means, when saving, uploading, downloading, you will find it take a fair bit of time.
- To use Shockwave you must have the plug-in installed onto your browser/PC.
- Adobe Shockwave cost a bit to purchase it.
- The main drawback of using Shockwave is that it requires the visitor to install additional software for it to function. The additional pieces of software required are referred to as 'Plug ins' and typically include Active X controls.
- Web users with Windows and Mac platforms can download the Shockwave players from the Macromedia site and use it to display and hear Shockwave files. Shockwave is especially popular for interactive games. Shockwave is more advanced and unique than other players like Flash etc.

## 8.29 QUICKTIME

QuickTime is a multimedia development, storage, and playback technology from Apple. QuickTime files combine sound, text, animation, and video in a single file. Using a QuickTime player than either comes with a Web browser or can be downloaded from Apple or the browser company, you can view and control brief multimedia sequences. QuickTime offers a lot higher quality and a fast loading time compared to RealPlayer.

Quicktime is capable of playing media on mobile devices, iPods, iPhones, TV. Quicktime allows to edit the movie and manipulate movie tracks. You can also combine two Quicktime movies into one movie and embed them into documents and presentations. If you have the internet, you can send files via e-mail, or upload them onto the web.

### Advantages and limitations of QuickTime

#### Advantages

- High quality
- Fast loading time
- Quicktime is free to download and use.
- Movie playback is high quality.
- You can edit movie, sound clips with relative ease and embed them into documents.

#### Limitations

- High memory utilizastion.
- Cannot make video play in full screen.
- Does not support many video formats.
- Quicktime files are bigger than normal which can take up time if sending via e-mail or uploading to the web.
- They don't support some file formats.
- Buffering times can be too long when watching a long movie.

## 8.30 REALPLAYER

RealPlayer is a cross-platform media player by RealNetworks that plays a number of multimedia formats including MP3, MPEG-4, QuickTime, Windows Media and multiple versions of proprietary RealAudio and RealVideo formats. Unlike other players like QuickTime or Flash, RealPlayer offers a unique ability to be able to download videos directly from web pages.

Realplayer is compatible with most Operating Systems and is also compatible with quite a few platforms. Realplayer is not pre-installed software, so you will need to download it from their website.

### Advantages and limitations of RealPlayer

#### Advantages

- Fast and free to install.
- Supports many formats and platforms. Plays RM and RMVB files flawlessly.

- Ability to download videos directly from websites.

**Limitations**

- Buffering takes a long time.
- Pesters you with free software at the start of installation.
- In order for movies to play smoothly you need a fast computer to keep up with the demand. Can lag at times.
- Requires a somewhat powerful PC

## 8.31 SILVERLIGHT

Microsoft Silverlight is Microsoft's answer to Adobe Flash, some websites require that you have Silverlight installed in order to watch embedded videos, although compared to Flash it uses larger file sizes which means slower loading time.

Silverlight is a cross-browser and cross-platform that allows you to write and run internet applications. Silverlight supports miltimedia, graphics, and animation. Silverlight can also be used for video streaming.

It competes between Adobe Flash and Quicktime player.

Silverlight supports most browsers and can also be used on most Windows Phones.

### Advantages and Limitations of Silverlight

**Advantages**

- Cheaper than most animation software.
- Integration with existing applications.
- Networking support.
- It offers a cross domain support for applications.
- It's free and easy to download.
- Offers many tools and different utilities.

**Limitations**

- Larger files, slower loading.
- Requires a plug-in to view and material online.
- Is a pain to learn how to use it. Limited image support.
- Does not support webcam usage.

## 8.32 OTHER 3D ANIMATION SOFTWARE

Animation software has gone through a major evolutionary cycle during the last ten years. Different packages have concentrated on different aspects of animation, or have looked at a particular set of applications that can benefit from their software, and so there is considerable market differentiation between different animation software.

The following is a list of 3D animation apps that are also popular.

### (1) Autodesk Maya

Maya is one of several popular software tools being used today in the motion picture and video game industries. A high end and robust tool originally developed by Alias Systems, Maya won the company an Academy Award in 2003 and was cited as making a "significant and dominant impact on the motion picture industry." Maya provides powerful tools essential to the animator, including keyframe animation, nonlinear animation, and path animation tools. Maya also provides full render controls for shading and lighting, and realistic effects tools for smoke and hair. Perhaps one of the best features to Maya is its open architecture, which allows for third-party integration and an incredible level of customization.

Maya is the **industry standard** 3D software, used in most large studios. Maya, Softimage and 3D Max all belong to Autodesk and word quite similarly. Choosing one is a matter of personal preference.

#### Supported platforms

Windows XP, Vista, 7, 8
Mac OS X
Linux

#### Autodesk can help you build a modern production pipeline for:

Fully animated features
Visual effects and post-production
Game design
Pre-visualization and virtual movie-making

### (2) Autodesk 3D animation software

With integrated workflows, streamlined data exchange, and productivity and performance enhancements, our software can help you meet even the most challenging deadlines. Use Autodesk 3D animation software for:
Sculpting and texture painting
3D modeling and animation
Simulation and effects
Realistic and stylized rendering

### (3) 3ds Max by Autodesk : 3D modeling, animation, and rendering software

3ds Max software offers integrated modeling, animation, and rendering tools for out-of-the-box productivity.

A popular and powerful modeling application from Autodesk, 3ds Max is primarily used in video game development and in TV production studios for the creation of rich, complex characters and 3D objects, as well as for design visualization. 3ds Max boasts a more user friendly interface than other packages, with a UI that makes it easier for the artist to focus on the project at hand and the creative process.

### (4) MotionBuilder 3D character animation software

MotionBuilder creates high-volume animations, pre-visualizations, and virtual movies with this 3D character animation software.

### (5) Mudbox 3D digital sculpting and texture painting software

Mudbox creates production-ready 3D assets with intuitive Mudbox 3D digital sculpting and texture painting software.

### (6) Maya LT 3D game development software

Maya LT 3D game development software offers professional indie game developers creative tools at an affordable price.

### (7) Entertainment Creation Suite 3D animation software

Entertainment Creation Suite has a collection of 3D modeling, animation, texturing, and effects tools at a significant cost savings.

### (8) Full Sail University Softimage/XSI by Softimage

A subsidiary of Avid Technology, one of the leaders of the high end video editing world, Softimage's flagship product XSI is a leading 3D graphics software used for films, video games, and advertising. XSI can be used for the creation of 3D environments, animate characters, or for 3D modeling. It offers the feature of being readily customizable through open scripting access and third-party add-ons. It can also be used for animation using the Animation Mixer feature, and its rendering system is based on the widely used Mental Ray application developed by Berlin-based Mental Images. The XSI product was released in 2000 to replace Softimage 3D and compete more effectively with products like Maya.

**Learning Outcomes**

In this chapter we have learnt about :

1. Different attributes of animation
2. Making animations with Flash Animator CS-6
3. Other Animation softrwares : Shockwave, Quickplayer, Realplayer, Silverlight

# Multimedia Authoring Tools

CHAPTER 9

**Leaning Objectives**

In this chapter we shall learn about:

1. Authoring
2. Authoring Tools for Multimedia
3. Authoring Paradigm (Metaphor)
4. Types of Authoring Tools
5. Criteria of selecting Authoring Tools
6. All in one Authoring System

## 9.1 AUTHORING

The process of making multimedia requires many different kinds of digital creations. Some are simple, such as scanned photographs or digitized music. Others are more complex, such as the actual computer instructions that are written into a software program to execute the movement and interactivity of the multimedia production. The process of laying out these instructions is called *authoring.*

In order to author multimedia, two things are necessary: a computer to develop on, and a software program that facilitates the gathering of the multimedia elements (graphics, text, sound, and so on) into a single, cohesive digital file or group of files. The software programs that allow you to make this cohesive product are extremely varied. The technology can range from a simple program containing preformatted interactivity scripts to computer languages that build every aspect of the production from the ground up. Naturally, the level of authoring has an effect on the sophistication of the project.

However, it is possible to author highly effective and compelling multimedia with simple, user-friendly authoring tools that even a layperson can quickly master. The key to the process of authoring is not so much in the tools as in the logic of the person using those tools. Many of the most important authoring decisions are made before booting a program. But which program to boot after those decisions is made is, obviously, another key decision. There are many choices of actual products, but they usually fall into one of two categories, *programming languages* or *authoring software.*

### 9.1.1 What is an Authoring System?

An Authoring System is a program which has pre-programmed elements for the development of interactive multimedia software titles. Authoring systems vary widely in orientation, capabilities, and learning curve. There is no such thing(at this time) as a completely point-and-click automated authoring system; some knowledge of heuristic thinking and algorithm design is necessary. Whether you realize it or not, authoring is actually just a speeded-up form of programming; you don't need to know the intricacies of a programming language, or worse, an API, but you do need to understand how programs work.

### 9.1.2 Need for an authoring system?

It generally takes about 1/8th the time to develop an interactive multimedia project, such as a CBT program, in an authoring system as opposed to programming it in compiled code. This means 1/8 the cost of programmer time and likely increased re-use of code (assuming that you pass this project's code to the next CBT project, and they use a similar or identical authoring system). However, the content creation (graphics, text, video, audio, animation, etc.) is not generally affected by the choice of an authoring system; any production time gains here result from accelerated prototyping, not from the choice of an authoring system over a compiled language.

## 9.2 MULTIMEDIA SOFTWARE

Multimedia software comprises a wide variety of software that allows you to combine images with text, music and sound, animation, video, and other special effects. Many kinds of multimedia software are available. Multimedia software is sometimes broadly grouped as:

1. Multimedia Authoring Tools
2. Multimedia Presentation Software
3. Multimedia Tools for the Web

Multimedia Authoring can be used to create anything from simple slide shows to full-blown games and interactive applications. A professional multimedia development program is called an authoring tool or authoring software. An authoring tool allows you to give the user interactive control over the sequence and timing of videos, graphics and animation. It also provides a scripting language, also called a macro or authoring language to control the action.

Multimedia presentation software is capable of stunning multimedia slideshows, brandishing dynamic sound, 3D Animation and cinematic quality special effects. Multimedia Presentation can be described as an intuitive book. Each page of the book can include pictures, animations, sounds and other controls. The pages can turn themselves or wait for their users to click on Next. Unlike the pages of a traditional book, they can talk to their readers too. No matter what your particular need may be, whether to e-mail an electronic photograph album to your relatives, allow users of your web page to download a multimedia catalog, show prospective clients samples of your work or make a dull subject come alive in class, multimedia presentation software can transform your ideas into a complete, professional application. In a live multimedia presentation, the slides are commonly projected onto large screens or printed on overhead transparencies.

The slides may be distributed in printed form as handouts to accompany the live presentation. Multimedia Presentation Software can build self-displaying, interactive slide shows, electronic books and brochures, clickable advertisements, distributable portfolios and all sorts of other multimedia applications. Almost everything it can accomplish requires nothing more than a few mouse clicks. It has a short learning curve. Some multimedia presentation software documents are EXE files - they can be opened on any system. They can be freely distributed on disks and CD-ROMs, and over the Internet. Multimedia Presentation Software has some great features like the ability to:

1. Build and distribute slide show style presentations.
2. Write your own clickable advertisements, to distribute alone or with other products.
3. Design training materials that include pictures, sounds and interactive elements.
4. Compile a distributable portfolio.

5. Completed presentations are frequently published in multiple formats, which may include print, the Web, or electronic files.

Multimedia Presentation Software requires a faster processor. A display adapter and screen driver capable of displaying more than 16 million colors is needed to get the best out of it.

## 9.3 MULTIMEDIA AUTHORING TOOLS : AUTHORING

Because there are many people wishing to make multimedia but who aren't computer programmers, there are applications called authoring programs. These packages essentially put a "shell" around the actual programming component, allowing the user to accomplish his or her goals through simplified means .

These means include preprogrammed "scripts" that the author can drop into the presentation, which will make things happen-black out a screen, begin an animation, move to the next screen, and so on. The idea here is to make the process of authoring more friendly and intuitive, though different programs succeed at different levels.

Authoring programs first found favor in simple "presentation" application that were used as a business communication tool. These allowed for the creation of colored slides and charts, and some of the more advanced ones eventually offered rudimentary animations for moving bar charts and the like. These eventually morphed into the basis of today's more simplified authoring packages.

Although these beginner's tools provide a good place to learn the basics, none of them is really adept for commercial multimedia production, which typically includes more elements and requires a greater degree of allowable user interactivity.

There are many types of multimedia authoring tools (software programs) which can be used for developing instructional multimedia products. However, as technology became more powerful, so did the authoring tools — permitting more complex instructional design. A multimedia authoring tool enables you to create a final application merely by linking together objects, such as a paragraph of text, an illustration,a song or animation film. Attractive and useful multimedia applications can be produced by defining the objects relationships to each other, and by sequencing them in an appropriate order. Multimedia Authoring Tool is easy and exciting for beginners, dynamic and interactive for experts. It requires less technical knowledge to master and is used exclusively for applications that present a mixture of textual, graphical, and audio data. Multimedia authoring tool can be used to create anything from simple slide shows to full-blown games and interactive applications. The splendid, yet refined, contents with multimedia materials (text, image, sound, video, animation, Flash, web document and database) with easy and convenient editing can be applied to the web as well as CDs and presentations. A multimedia authoring tool supports a wide variety of multimedia file formats including images, video, and sound. Clip-art and sound libraries are rarely bundled with a multimedia authoring tool.

## 9.4 CRITERIA FOR SELECTING MULTIMEDIA AUTHORING TOOLS

The multimedia authoring tools is the glue that holds the data together in order to inform, educate, or entertain. As with software tools, there are many variations and capabilities that depend on the needs of the end users and expertise of the developer. Authoring tools offer two basic features; first, the ability to create and edit a product; and second, a presentation scheme for delivering the product. Just as there are a number of comparable programs for word processing and graphics production, there are large number of tools available in the market for creating multimedia products. Therefore, the selection of an authoring tool based on how it works and what it does can be one of the most critical elements of multimedia product development. The criteria for selecting a tool include:

- **Function**— a complete understanding of how the product will work, especially from the user's point of view.
- **Content**— nature, volume, format, and types of data that will be incorporated into the product.
- **Hardware**— platforms expected to run a product; also unique requirements or for displaying graphics and playing audio and video.
- **Software**— unique software requirements such as operating systems of interface to other software application such as database managers.
- **Performance**— speed and efficiency expected; critical for gaming applications or fast-paced presentations. Multimedia authoring tools can be resource-intensive, using large amount of memory and disk space, that can result in multimedia products performing poorly on underpowered platforms.
- **User Interface**— screen layout, data presentation, positioning of controls, and visual and auditory cuts for the end user. The user interface depends on the ability of the end user. Therefore, it is critical that the developer understands the end user's skill level. For example, a kiosk in a shopping mall can make no assumptions about the skills (or lack thereof) of its users. Therefore, the user interface must be simple and straight forward. On the other hand, if the end users have significant computer skills or will be extensively trained on the product, then more complex functions and capabilities can be designed into the interface.
- **Database**— will the product support access to large sets of relatively structured information that need to be queried or browsed by an end user or accessed by a software application.
- **Reliability**— critical for commercial applications; reliability is essential within the product itself and how the product behaves with other products.
- **Maintenance and Update**— many multimedia products evolve over time with updates to content and functionality. It is essential that a tool be supported for the lifetime of a product to avoid having to recast into another tool.
- Other elements that play a significant role in tool selection include:
- **Personnel Skills**— many multimedia production shops have personnel skilled on a limited set of tool products. New tools require time spent on training and familiarization that may be beyond the scope of a project. Fortunately, many production houses have a reasonable array of tools at their disposal so that sound choices can be made.
- **Cost**— the cost of authoring tools range from less than $ 4500 to well over $ 450000. Presentation software sometimes requires license fees for mass distribution, which can further drive up the cost. These factors can be critical for commercial product pricing.
- **Scheduling**— the amount of time allocated to develop a project is closely related to personnel skills and cost. A short schedule requires that personnel be familiar and competent with tools, whereas a longer schedule time to train and/orient the production team.

## 9.5 AUTHORING PARADIGM (METAPHOR)

Also known as the authoring metaphor, this is the methodology by which the authoring system accomplishes its task. There are various paradigms, including:

- Scripting Language
- Iconic/Flow Control
- Frame
- Card/Scripting
- Cast/Score/Scripting
- Hierarchical Object
- Hypermedia Linkage
- Tagging

### (1) Scripting paradigm

The Scripting paradigm is the authoring method closest in form to traditional programming. The paradigm is that of a programming language, which specifies (by filename) multimedia elements, sequencing, hotspots, synchronization, etc. A powerful, object-oriented scripting language is usually the centerpiece of such a system; in-program editing of elements (still graphics, video, audio, etc.) tends to be minimal or non-existent.

Scripting languages do vary; check out how much the language is object-based or object-oriented. The scripting paradigm tends to be longer in development time (it takes longer to code an individual interaction), but generally more powerful interactivity is possible. Since most Scripting languages are interpreted, instead of compiled, the runtime speed gains over other authoring methods are minimal.

The media handling can vary widely; check out your system with your contributing package formats carefully.

### (2) Iconic/Flow Control paradigm

This tends to be the speediest (in development time) authoring style; it is best suited for rapid prototyping and short-development time projects. Many of these tools are also optimized for developing Computer-Based Training (CBT). The core of the paradigm is the Icon Palette, containing the possible functions/interactions of a program, and the Flow Line, which shows the actual links between the icons. These programs tend to be the slowest run times, because each interaction carries with it all of its possible permutations; the higher end packages, such as Authorware or IconAuthor, are extremely powerful and suffer least from runtime speed problems.

### (3) Frame paradigm

The Frame paradigm is similar to the Iconic/Flow Control paradigm in that it usually incorporates an icon palette; however, the links drawn between icons are conceptual and do not always represent the actual flow of the program. This is a very fast development system, but requires a good auto-debugging function, as it is visually un-debuggable. The best of these have bundled compiled-language scripting, such as Quest (whose scripting language is C#) or Apple Media Kit.

### (4) Card/Scripting Paradigm

The Card/Scripting paradigm provides a great deal of power (via the incorporated scripting language) but suffers from the index-card structure. It is excellently suited for Hypertext applications, and supremely suited for navigation intensive (a la Cyan's "MYST" game) applications. Such programs are easily extensible via XCMDs and DLLs; they are widely used for shareware applications. The best applications allow all objects (including individual graphic elements) to be scripted; many entertainment applications are prototyped in a card/scripting system prior to compiled-language coding.

### (5) Cast/Score/Scripting Paradigm

The Cast/Score/Scripting paradigm uses a music score as its primary authoring metaphor; the synchronous elements are shown in various horizontal "tracks" with simultaneity shown via the vertical columns. The true power of this metaphor lies in the ability to script the behavior of each of the cast members. The most popular member of this paradigm is Director, which is used in the creation of many commercial applications. These programs are best suited for animation- intensive or synchronized media applications; they are easily extensible to handle other functions (such as hypertext) via XOBJs, XCMDs, and DLLs.

### (6) Hierarchical Object Paradigm

The Hierarchical Object paradigm uses a object metaphor (like OOP) which is visually represented by embedded objects and iconic properties. Although the learning curve is non-trivial, the visual representation of objects can make very complicated constructions possible.

### (7) Hypermedia Linkage Paradigm

The Hypermedia Linkage paradigm is similar to the Frame paradigm in that it shows conceptual links between elements; however, it lacks the Frame paradigm's visual linkage metaphor.

### (8) Tagging Paradigm

The Tagging paradigm uses tags in text files (for instance, SGML/HTML and WinHelp) to link pages, provide interactivity and integrate multimedia elements. They tend to have limited tracking capability and are best suited to online reference material like dictionaries and manuals.

## 9.6 MULTIMEDIA AUTHORING TOOL FEATURES

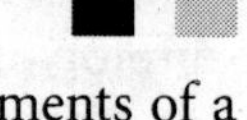

Multimedia authoring tools provide the framework for organizing and editing the elements of a multimedia project. Authoring software provides an integrated environment for combining the content and functions of a project. It enables the developer to create, edit, and import data.

In multimedia authoring systems, multimedia elements and events are often regarded as objects. Objects exist in a hierarchical order of parent and child relationships. Each object is assigned properties and modifiers. On receiving messages, objects perform tasks depending on the properties and modifiers.

Following are the common Features of authoring tools:

- Editing and organizing features.
- Programming features.
- Interactivity features.
- Performance tuning and playback features.
- Delivery, cross-platform, and Internet playability features.

Common to nearly all multimedia tool platforms is a number of features for encapsulating the current, presenting data, obtaining user input, and controlling the execution of the product. These features include:

- Page
- Controls

- Data
- Execution

In order to establish a common vocabulary for the types of tools discussed later, the following section briefly highlights these features.

## (1) Page

The page is an instant in time for a multimedia presentation. It is found in various development environments under various names such as frame, stage, template, or window. The page acts as a container for other features or objects such as text or graphic content of controls such as buttons. It is usually capable of various transitional effects such as fade in/out on the screen : The page may be the palette manager in some applications by controlling the main palette that subordinate objects such as graphic and video depend of for smooth graphics transitions.

## (2) Controls

Controls enable the user to interact with the product. Controls may be used to manage or direct sequences of events or to collect data, or to manage data objects (zooming, video controls). There are three general categories of controls:

a. **Navigation :** buttons, hot spots, hypertext. Many tools have a fixed set of objects, such as standard gray buttons, that can be modified (size, position, caption). Hot spots are used over graphic objects to allow the user to interact with the data. Hypertext is usually indicated by highlighting through changing the color of the text or underlining it. When the user selects the highlighted text, an action is initiated such as presenting a definition or related information.

b. **Input :** text, check boxes, radio buttons, combo/list boxes. These are used for collecting information from the user or controlling a sequence of the information presentation. Data collected from these may be directed to a file or other device for storage or transmission.

c. **Media Controls :** applies to managing or presentation of fonts, graphics, audio, video. Specific features for each of these include:

   - **Fonts**: select type, size, bold, italic
   - **Graphics**: zoom, scroll, mark-up/edit
   - **Audio/Video**: play, stop, pause, rewind, step, volume, zoom

## (3) Data

Depending on the authoring tool, data may be stored internally as part of the application program or as external files that are accessed during program execution. Internal storage of data usually means faster data presentation and easier transport of the application and the data. (On the other hand, external data storage means smaller executable programs and faster program startup. Another advantage of external data storage is that data can be modified to change the application without having to use the authoring tool. Data types include:

### Text

Text may be stored or accessed as ASCII, RTF, or other encoded format. Two general types of text presentation: captions, small strings for tiels, headers, or other information, and text boxes; often with scroll bars, for presenting large volumes of text.

### Graphic

A number of formats are often used; however, bitmaps are the most common to minimize decompression during program operation and provide maximum quality. Graphic file size, combined with reuse or speed requirements (an image needs to 430 Introduction to Multimedia and its applications be shown in a hurry), will usually determine whether the file is stored in the application or as an external file.

### Audio

Number of file formats are supported; may be stored internally depending on size and whether it is reused more that once in the product. Wave files are very common in formats in CD-ROM products followed by AIFF and RIFF audio formats because of the large number of these types of files on the Internet.

### Video

Various file formats and compression standards are supported; files are usually stored externally to the product because of the large file sizes. Most authoring tools support a number of digital video types and compression schemes.

### Live audio/video

Usually integrated into the product as an external function; requires specialized hardware for compatibility with the tool and product.

### Database

Large sets of "structured data" that can be queried or browsed; often stored in commercial database applications. Many authoring tools have built-in interfaces for querying and formatting data for presentation.

## 9.7 MULTIMEDIA AUTHORING TOOLS.

Also known as authorware, a program that helps you write hypertext or multimedia applications. Authoring tools usually enable you to create a final application merely by linking together objects, such as a paragraph of text, an illustration, or a song. By defining the objects' relationships to each other, and by sequencing them in an appropriate order, authors (those who use authoring tools) can produce attractive and useful graphics applications. Most authoring systems also support a scripting language for more sophisticated applications.

The distinction between authoring tools and programming tools is not clear-cut. Typically, though, authoring tools require less technical knowledge to master and are used exclusively for applications that present a mixture of textual, graphical, and audio data.

The tools that provide the capability for creating a complete multimedia presentation, including Interactive user control, are called authoring programs. An authoring tool is a software package which allow developers to write hypertext and multimedia applications by linking together objects such as a paragraph of text, an illustration, graphics or a song.

- It is an authoring system intended for use by a user who are not traditional programmer or even do not know any programming language but wish to create interactive multimedia presentations or product or computer based learning material.
- Example: Macromedia Flash, Dreamweaver, Power Point, etc.

### 9.7.1 Role of Authoring Software

1. Produce content with: Paint, text, animation tools
2. Incorporate and combine contents
3. Design screen layouts using templates
4. Create interactivity
5. Create hypertext

Products developed with authoring software .

1. Multimedia presentations
2. E- Learning
3. Computer Based Training (CBT)
4. Web pages
5. Artistic visualizations

### 9.7.2 Classifying Multimedia Authoring Tools

There are two primary ways of classifying multimedia authoring tools:

- by metaphor
- by capabilities and complexity

#### Classifying by Metaphor

All multimedia tools are based on a metaphor. The metaphor is based on three main characteristics:

1. the way the program organizes the different elements
2. the way the program sequences events that happen
3. the way the application is delivered

Most authoring programs are based on one of the following metaphors:

1. Time-based
2. Card-based or Page-based
3. Icon-based, event-driven (logic flow)
4. Theatrical-based

### 9.7.3 Time-Based Metaphors

In time-based authoring programs, the elements of the program are organized along a time line. Events may be precisely synchronized by coordinating the time, speed and display length of each one.

Examples of time-based authoring programs include:

1. Astound by Gold Disk
2. MacroMedia Flash by Macromedia
3. Cinemation from Vividus

### 9.7.4 Card/Page -Based Metaphors

In card-based and page-based authoring programs, the metaphor is one of a stack of cards or the pages of a book. Unlike the real paper item, however, the user is not limited to going through the program sequentially. It is easy to move from page to page because most programs use buttons and hot spots which allow the user to choose their own path.

A card-based program usually allows common elements, such as backgrounds and navigation bars which are common to all cards, to be placed in a background layer and elements which are different on each card to be placed on a foreground layer.

Examples of card-based programs include:

1. HyperCard by Apple Computer
2. HyperStudio by HyperStudio •Asymetrix Toolbook by Asymetrix
3. SuperCard by Allegiant

### 9.7.5 Icon-Based Metaphors

Icon-based authoring programs are designed around a visual programming approach to sequencing the events in the multimedia application. The developer drags the icons for each event, such as text, graphics, sound and video, to a flow line thus also creating a type of visual flow chart. Icons may be rearranged by dragging them to the desired position.

Examples of icon-based authoring programs include:

1. Macromedia Authorware by Macromedia
2. IconAuthor by Aimtech

### 9.7.6 Theatrical-Based Metaphors

In this type of authoring program, events are thought of as cast members and arranged in a theatre-like production or stage which combines these elements in regard to time and place.

Examples of theatrical-based authoring programs include:

- Macromedia Director by Macromedia

**Classifying By Capabilities and Complexity**

Multimedia authoring programs may also be categorized according to their capability and degree of complexity. Most authoring programs may be placed in one of these categories:

1. Multimedia-Capable Presentation Tools
2. Dedicated Media Integration Tools
3. Professional Multimedia Development Tools

### 9.7.7 Multimedia-Capable Presentation Tools

1. Slide presentation software: PowerPoint
2. Semi to non-professional applications
3. Mostly for educational or training purposes
4. Usually very efficient at integrating charts, graphs, and simple illustrations.

Examples include:

1. Microsoft PowerPoint
2. Adobe Persuasion
3. Lotus Freelance Graphics
4. WordPerfect Presentation
5. Software Publishing's Harvard Graphics

### 9.7.8 Dedicated Media Integration Tools

1. Sequence multimedia events and elements.
2. Semi to full professional use.
3. Examples: IBM's Storyboard Live.
4. Asymmetric's Media Blitz.
5. Passport Producer.

### 9.7.9 Professional MM Development Tools

- Highly interactive applications such as : games
- Full professional use
- Programming/scripting capabilities

Examples:

- Macromedia Director, Authorware, Flash
- Asymmetric's Toolbook
- Apple's HyperCard
- Aimtech's IconAuthor

Macromedia Flash allows users to create interactive movies by using the score metaphor - a timeline arranged in parallel event sequences, much like a musical score consisting of musical notes. Elements in the movie are called symbols in Flash. Symbols are added to a central repository, called a library, and can be added to the movie's timeline. Once the symbols are present at a specific time, they appear on the Stage, which represents what the movie looks like at a certain time, and can be manipulated and moved by the tools built into Flash. Finished Flash movies are commonly used to show movies or games on the web.

Macromedia Director uses a movie metaphor to create interactive presentations. This powerful program includes a built-in scripting language, Lingo, that allows creation of complex interactive movies. The "cast" of characters in Director includes bitmapped sprites, scripts, music, sounds, and palettes. It can read many bitmapped file formats. The program itself allows a good deal of interactivity, and Lingo, with its own debugger, allows more control, including control over external devices, such as VCRs and videodisc players. Director also has web authoring features available, for creation of fully interactive Shockwave movies playable over the web.

## 9.8 CATEGORIES OF AUTHORING TOOLS

For our purposes, authoring tools can be divided into four broad categories:

- Simple authoring tools such as word processors and presentation software.
- Programming tools, especially those with graphic user interface design and programming features.
- Simple interactive authoring tools that enable the developer to create applications with data and controls for basic interactivity.
- Complex interactive authoring tools that allow the developers to use programming constructs to provide a fine degree of application control.

### 9.8.1 Simple Authoring and Delivery Tools

Basic multimedia authoring starts with the premise that a product can be delivered as text on a screen using a simple word processor. Although few would seriously consider this "true" multimedia, the addition of graphics to the next starts to change this viewpoint. Graphical user interface (GUI) based word processors both text and graphics, and with embedded objects and other methods, are now able to incorporate audio and video. A number of commercial graphics programs are available offering varying levels of interactivity, graphic manipulations, and embedded audio and video capabilities.

### Word Processors

At the most basic level, these tools provide the ability to display text in a variety of font types, sizes, and color. Graphics can be created or imported and placed inline with the text. Content can be augmented with embedded objects for sound and video. Word processors can enable anyone to develop very simple multimedia presentations that are surprisingly effective. Beyond the lack of interactivity, the primary limitation of word processors, is the vertical nature of a software document presentation requiring the end user to scroll through the information. Also, embedded objects for audio and video depend on other system applications to run and may be confusing to the end user if they are unfamiliar with their use.

### Graphics Software

Graphic Software ranges from simple to very complex and includes powerful paint programs. Simple paint programs are useful for creating graphics that can be placed in other applications but are very limited for more complex multimedia presentations.

### Presentation Packages

Presentation software packages typically provide a multiple page-based medium for text and graphics with content delivered as a sequential series of slides. These slide shows often contain complex text and graphics that can be animated to glide on or off the screen. Although the presentation is linear, the end user usually controls the timing. Like the work processors, presentation packages can also contain audio and video as embedded objects.

## 9.8.2 Programming Languages for Authoring

At a fundamental level, computer programming languages form the basis for all other authoring languages. Therefore, it is conceivable that multimedia products can be developed and delivered using programming tools such as assembly languages, C, or BASIC. As with other programming tools there are advantages and disadvantages to this approach:

The advantages of implementing multimedia products using programming tools include:

- Languages such a C and assembly language tend to be very efficient and fast.
- A fine degree of control over the environment can be achieved enabling complex interation by the user or the product.
- Easier integration with other software or the operating system to access data or manage resources such as memory.
- No dependency on a third party tool developer.
- The product may be ported to similar compilers on other platforms. This is very true for C and C++.

The disadvantages of implementing multimedia products using programming tools include:

- Multimedia products are complex software programs that display data and support user integration; they are best implemented as a shell program written in the programming environment.

This allows the product of the programming effort to be reused for a number of products. However, the shell is similar in functionality to commercial multimedia authoring tools and in many cases, developers have built their own shells with many of the same features found in commercial shells.

- Programming expertise is required to create and maintain the product.
- Much more code is required making long-term maintenance difficult and correspondingly more expensive.
- The product can become platform-dependent based on the choice of language. While assembly language yields the most efficient executable code, it is not a common choice for multimedia products because of the resulting code complexity. Assembly language products are often used for high performance, special purpose functions, such as system interface programming to access special purpose devices such as disk drives or analog devices. These assembly language modules are compiled and integrated with applications written in other languages such as C or Pascal.

Third generation tools such as C and Pascal provide a higher level of coding abstraction than assembly language. However, multimedia products tend to be graphic and presentation intensive making interface programming difficult. For example, the placement of a graphic and a button on a screen would require you to know how to use the programming language. The difficulty is this approach to programming a multimedia product lies in the abstraction of the code to corresponding visual elements such as buttons or other display objects. Errors in written code, such as positioning of a button, may go undetected even through the most rigorous testing due to the interactive complexity of a multimedia product.

Fourth-generation languages with built-in graphical user programming tools have emerged with great success since the early 1990s. Fourth-generation languages, also called 4GLs, are programming environments combined with advanced tools to develop user interfaces and write software code. These tools, enable the developer to place objects such as buttons and image containers on a form using the mouse. Code for actions is directly associated with objects such as buttons based on events such as clicking or passing the mouse over the object. Most simple interactive authoring tools include the following capabilities for creating and editing products:

- A page metaphor upon which objects such as buttons or image containers are placed.
- A number of objects including buttons, hot spots, image containers, text boxes, and captions.
- Objects for audio and video including integrated controls for play, stop, frame stepping, and rewind.
- The ability to vary font type, size, color, and other characteristics.
- Importing of text and graphic files. Most tools access audio and video files directly when they are played.
- Animation of objects such as moving graphics or buttons across the screen in a predetermined path.
- Assigning event-driven actions to objects such as buttons and hot spots. For example, when clicked the presentation displays a different page or starts an action on the current page.
- Many simple interactive authoring systems generate a delivery module that contains everything a user needs to play the product. In some cases, data files may need to be included as part of the delivered product.

Simple interactive authoring tools offer many advantages. They allow you to create what-you-see-is-what-you-get (WYSIWYG) applications; that is, where you put the data or control is where it appears in the completed product. They are often easy to learn as they are build on concepts found in linear-based presentation packages. They provide a number of powerful, interactive features that satisfy most requirements for a product. Furthermore, they tend to be reasonably priced compared to many of the complex tools. The disadvantages lie in the inability to program buttons and hot spots and to integrate with other database applications.

In other words, functionality is limited to "what you see is what you get" for the tool.

### 9.8.3 Complex Interactive Authoring Tools

Complex interactive authoring tools combine features found in simple interactive tools with programming features. They also offer more complex creation and editing functions that go beyond simple page layout. Advanced tools generally fall into three categories based on how they are used for creation and editing:

- Card or Page-Based layout
- Time or Temporal-based
- Icon-based or Event Driven

Advanced authoring tools use many of the same techniques to create or edit applications. These includes:

- A page metaphor upon which objects such as buttons or image containers are placed.
- A number of objects including buttons, hot spots, image containers, text boxes, and captions.
- Objects for audio and video including integrated controls for play, stop, video stepping, and rewind.
- The ability to vary font type, size, color, and other characteristics
- Importing of text, graphic, audio, and video files for storage in the application.
- Assigning event-driven actions to objects such as buttons and hot spots. When clicked the presentation displays a different page or starts an action on the current page.

Programming, the ability to incorporate instructions into an application, is a key feature of advanced authoring tools. Typically, programming is accomplished by attaching code to objects such as buttons, graphics, or other elements of the application. Programming enables the developer to tie in system functions such as reading and writing to files or providing a series of functions when an event such as a button click occurs. For example, when a button is pressed, a text box is filled with data stored in a text file. This could be accomplished as follows:

**Code Segment**

```
On button-click
open "textfile.txt" for input
do while not end-of-file
get line-of-text
textstuff=textstuff+line-of-text
loop
close file
put textstuff into textobject
end
```

The programming language usually contains the following capabilities:

- Declaration of variables based on a variety of data types such as integers, real numbers, strings, and arrays.
- Math and data functions to set and modify variables.
- Control structure for decision support such as if/then, select; and loop structure such as for/next, do/loop, and while. Additionally, some systems will allow you to create functions and subroutines for repetitive activities.

## (1) Card or Page-Based Authoring

Card- and page-based authoring systems provide a simple and easily understood metaphor for organizing multimedia elements.
It contains media objects such as buttons, text fields, and graphic objects.
It provides a facility for linking objects to pages or cards.

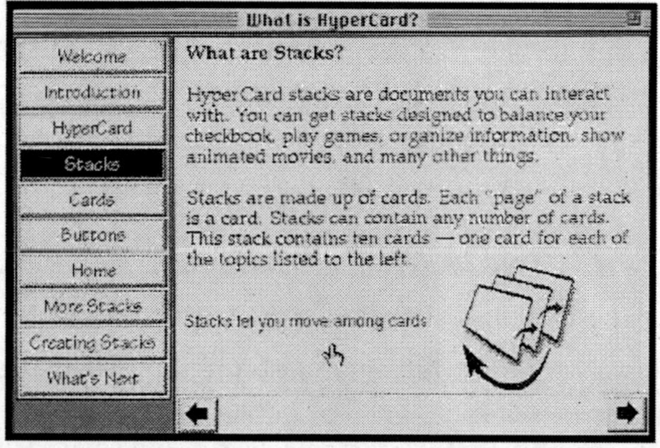


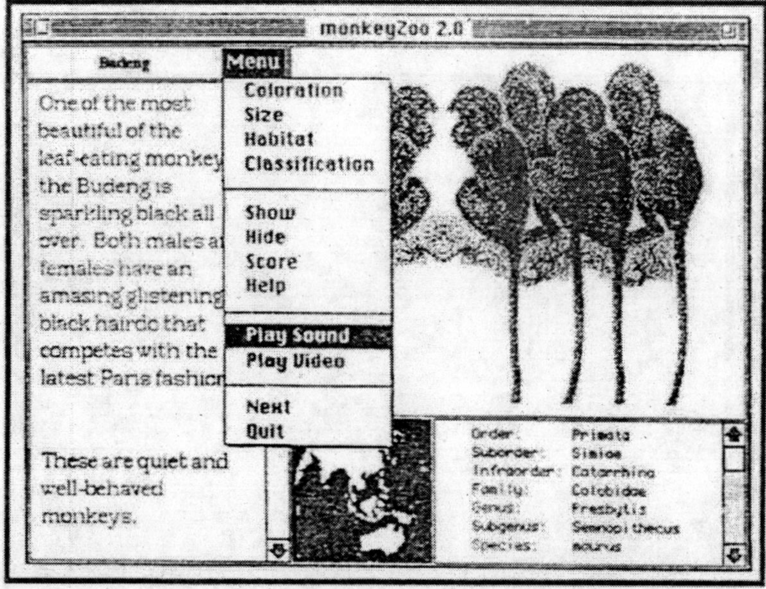


**Fig. 9.1:** Sound, animation and video can be played in card.

Page-based authoring tools are very similar to the previously mentioned simple interactive page-based tools. The major difference lies in the ability to add scripting to various objects in the environment.

Scripting, usually handles specialized functions such as graphic transitions, jumping to pages according to programmed conditions (using an IF-THEN or SELECT statement), timing, and other complex presentation metaphors.

Page-based authoring systems with programming capability are a natural transition from those tools without the programming features. In fact, if you have conventional programming experience in C, Pascal, or BASIC these tools are very easy to learn and apply.

### (2) Time or Temporal-Based Authoring

Temporal or time-based authoring systems provide the developer with the ability to develop an application that runs like a movie. Time-based tools are best suited for messages with a beginning and an end. Some time-based tools facilitate navigation and interactive control. Macro media's Director and Flash are time- based development environments.

Frames are created with objects that are sequentially played or halted to allow user input to change the flow of the program. Temporal-based systems include the following features:

- A page or display frame on which objects such as buttons, text, or audio/video data are placed. Objects may have code attached for special processes such as jumping to a different page or loading a data file.
- An array for keeping track of pages/frames including their sequence, timing, and content.
- A controller for playing, stopping, stepping, or rewinding a presentation.

The primary advantage of temporal-based tools is the ability to create complex animation and transitions. A sequence of pages of frames played in rapid succession, for example, one per 1/30 of a second, will create a movie-like effect. Unfortunately, if a single page within a sequence is flawed, for example, a picture is out of place, it can be difficult to isolate the flawed page from the larger set of good pages.

**In Macromedia Director:**

- A multimedia database, 'Cast', contains still images, sound files, text, shapes, scripts, movies, and other Director files.
- Score is a sequencer for displaying, animating, and playing Cast members.
- Lingo is an object-oriented scripting language that enables interactivity and programmed control.

**In Macromedia Flash:**

- Flash is used for delivering rich multimedia content to the Web.
- It allows the creation of simple static HTML pages with the Flash Player plug- in.

### (3) Icon-Based or Event Driven Authoring

Icon-based, event-driven tools provide a visual programming approach to organize and present multimedia. Multimedia elements and interaction cues are organized as objects in a flowchart. Flowchart can be built by dragging appropriate icons from a library, and then adding the content.

Icon-based authoring enables complex interaction and layering of multimedia products. This is accomplished by letting the author select objects, timing, and sequencing "devices" in the form of icons and placing them of a layout screen where they are interconnected as shown in Figure below:

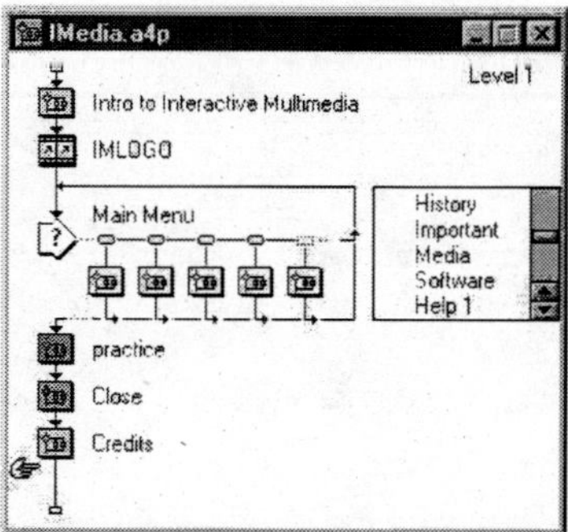


Icon based authorware provides a structural and navigational overview of entire project using icons. As icons are selected and linked, screens can be defined with text, graphic, buttons, and other objects. As with the other advanced authoring tools, code or script can be attached to objects such as buttons to facilitate user interaction or program execution. One of the major advantages of this approach is the ability to graphically design complelx interactions for repetitive applications. Templates can be constructed that are "filled in" by the developer and reused within the application or across similar applications. Templates often contain data and controls that are common to a number of pages within the application. For example, a template could contain a standard page title, background color, and positioning of recurring buttons, that can be reused over and over during development.

## 9.9 NEED OF ALL-IN-ONE AUTHORING SYSTEM

A number of all-in-one programs are available but one shouldn't take them granted. Although most packages allow you to create content using their in-built tools, these tend to be rudimentary when compared with those available in dedicated programs. For more professional output, you should use software dedicated to the creation and editing of that medium, and then import/

integrate the content into your multimedia program. Major content-development packages are likely to include:

- Paint programs for still images (photos, original digital artwork)
- Paint effects programs
- Illustration (draw) programs for still images (modeled and rendered objects)
- Modeling/Rendering programs (for 3-D objects)
- Video digitizing/editing programs
- Video effects programs
- Audio sampling/editing programs
- Word processors (script and program text)
- Database programs
- Animation programs
- Pre-Authoring programs;

**Leaning Outcomes**

In this chapter we have learnt about :

1. Selecting Proper Authoring software for Multimedia project

# Internet, Web and Social Media

CHAPTER 10

**Leaning Objectives**

In this chapter we shall learn about:

1. Internet and World Wide Web
2. Web based Multimedia
3. Types of Websites
4. Social Media and Multimedia
5. Creating Web sites
6. HTML and DHTML
7. Different Languages for Creating Web sites
8. XML, Ajax, CSS, ASP and JSP
9) Adobe Dream Weaver and other Content Development Tools

## LEARNING OBJECTIVE

### At the end of this chapter you shall be able to:

Define Web-based multimedia and list some advantages and disadvantages of using multimedia.

- Describe each of the following multimedia elements— text, images, animation, audio, and video—and tell how they differ.
- Briefly describe the basic steps and principles involved with multimedia Web site design.
- List the various tasks involved with multimedia Web site development.
- Explain how markup languages, scripting languages, and other tools are used today to create multimedia Web pages.
- Discuss the possible format of Web-based multimedia in the future

## 10.1 THE INTERNET AND WORLD WIDE WEB (WWW)

The Internet is a massive network of networks, a networking infrastructure. It connects millions of computers together globally, forming a network in which any computer can communicate with any other computer as long as they are both connected to the Internet. Information that travels over the Internet does so via a variety of languages known as protocols.

### The Web (World Wide Web)

The World Wide Web, or simply Web, is a way of accessing information over the medium of the Internet. It is an information-sharing model that is built on top of the Internet. The Web uses the HTTP protocol, only one of the languages spoken over the Internet, to transmit data. Web services, which use HTTP to allow applications to communicate in order to exchange business logic, use the the Web to share information. The Web also utilizes browsers, such as Internet Explorer or Firefox, to access Web documents called Web pages that are linked to each other via hyperlinks. Web documents also contain graphics, sounds, text and video.

### The Web is a Portion of the Internet

The Web is just one of the ways that information can be disseminated over the Internet. The Internet, not the Web, is also used for email, which relies on SMTP, Usenet news groups, instant messaging and FTP. So the Web is just a portion of the Internet, albeit a large portion, but the two terms are not synonymous and should not be confused.

Another method to differentiate between both is using the Protocol Suite – a collection of laws & regulations that govern the Internet. While internet is governed by the Internet Protocol – specifically dealing with data as whole and their transmission in packets, the World Wide Web is governed by the Hyper Text Transfer Protocol (HTTP) that deals with the linking of files, documents and other resources of the World Wide Web.

## 10.2 WHAT IS WEB-BASED MULTIMEDIA?

Web-based multimedia (also called rich media) is having Web sites containing more than one type of media : typically sound, video, or animation, in addition to text and images with following characteristics.

- Multimedia sites often contain elements that users interact with directly and control the delivery of a sound or video clip, and user is able to manipulate a 3D object or play a game, etc.
- Fast computers and broadband Internet connections are making a web-based multimedia much more feasible than in the past

## 10.3 WEB BASED MULTIMEDIA APPLICATIONS

Web Based Multimedia Applications come in a wide variety and can be found all over the Internet. A website that contains more than one type of media is considered to be multimedia. Sites that contain sound, video, animation, and/or images alongside text fall into this category. Typically, these sites use multiple applications such as these to convey certain information to the viewer of the web page. Manufacturers might use photos and PDF based user's manuals to transfer key points of interest about their products to the viewers. In other cases, multimedia can be used as a teaching tool where visitors learn through instructional videos or a news site might use podcasts and television footage to update their readers through their websites. Images and sound are also employed by many musicians when visiting their sites alongside the text-based dates of their tour. Entertainment also plays a large factor in web based multimedia applications. With the rise of Internet video streaming, people can now watch their favourite T.V. shows when they have the free time to do so, and from anywhere there is an Internet connection. Websites like Netflix and Hulu use sound, video, and often thumbnail photo icons alongside their descriptive text of the shows available. Some things to keep in mind concerning these multimedia applications are Internet connection speed and bandwidth. Most of these video streaming websites; whether news, sports, or t.v. shows, etc. require a minimum broadband connection speed of 500Kbs for standard definition viewing. The minimum speed requirement increases as the definition increases and vice versa. Bandwidth plays an important role as well since some service providers put a cap on the amount of information that can be processed. Most "smart" phone service providers set a cap of 1Gb or 2Gb a month and charge additional fees if this ceiling is ignored. Considering that a standard definition, one hour t.v. show can be close to 200Mb, it is wise to pay attention to the bandwidth being consumed as this can rapidly add up.

The pervasive use of Online Social Networks (OSN) for networking, communication and search in tandem with the ubiquitous availability of smartphones, which enables real-time multimedia capturing and sharing, have led to massive amounts of user-generated content and activities being amassed online, and made publicly available for analysis and mining. Leveraging large amounts of user-generated content creates new exciting .

First off, branding goes much deeper than simply thinking in terms of corporations and businesses. Your brand is actually who you are as an individual in society as well. Social media is one of the tools we can use to build ourselves, or our "brands" online. The way others perceive you can be controlled through social media.

A good example of how you are perceived to the world online is by simply googling your name. Try google searching your name and variations of your name. Now try searching your company name and variations of your business name. With your personal name most of the top results will be social media profiles This is why content creation and social media should be a staple for your personal and business strategies.

## 10.4 TYPES OF WEBSITES

Today we can easily identify eight different types of websites available on the Internet since the inception of the basic informational website which appeared in the early years.

(1) **Informational Websites:** Informational based websites were the first versions to hit the Internet containing photos of products, video clips, animation to convey concepts, etc. They are as they sound, sites which enable readers to find information on a particular business or topic.

(2) **Brochure/Catalogue Style Websites:** This kind of website goes further in depth than an informational site and provides general information about a store as well as the stock they carry and the prices.

(3) **E-Commerce Websites**: E-Commerce websites take brochure websites a step further by allowing you to shop directly from your computer having company profile , photos of products, technical knowhow, etc. The main difference between a brochure site and an e-commerce site is that the latter features a checkout system to enable you to order directly from the online store.

(4) **Blogs**: Blog websites (traditionally known as web logs) did not hit the mainstream until the early to mid 2000s. However since then blogging has become very popular for both business and personal use.

(5) **Personal Websites:** Personal websites are similar to that of a personal blog where an individual in all likelihood will have their own personal domain. These are created by friends and families to share their information and pictures online with each other allowing for people to keep in contact.

(6) **Social Media and Networking Websites:** More popular than ever, online forums and social networking sites like Facebook and MySpace are used on a daily basis to spread the word about businesses and keep in touch with family and friends.

(7) **Photo Sharing Websites:** Great for those in the photographic industry, these sites allow for individuals to upload and share photographs online.

(8) **Mobile Device Websites :** As technology develops, so is the variety of new websites appearing online. The latest is the creation of websites for viewing on mobile devices and mobile phones. These will be covered in detail in chapter 11 of this book on Wireless Multimedia.

(9) **Web-based training (WBT):** Delivering instruction via the Web

## 10.5 TYPES OF WEB (WEB 1, 2 AND 3)

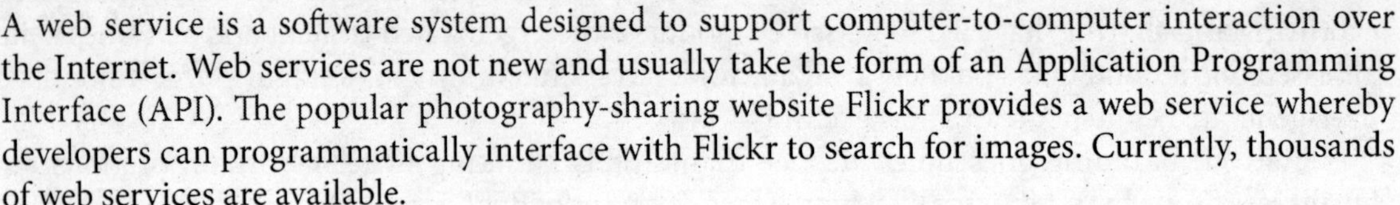

A web service is a software system designed to support computer-to-computer interaction over the Internet. Web services are not new and usually take the form of an Application Programming Interface (API). The popular photography-sharing website Flickr provides a web service whereby developers can programmatically interface with Flickr to search for images. Currently, thousands of web services are available.

### Web 1.0

In the beginning of web the information published in a static form well designed with the text and images. It is like your word document on the web with pictures and formatting done neatly. Hyper-linking the web-pages and bookmarking were two of the most important aspect of Web 1.0 world. The main features of web 1.0 are hyper-linking and bookmarking of the web pages.

Some design elements of a Web 1.0 site include:

1. Static pages instead of dynamic HTML
2. Content served from the server's filesystem instead of a RDBMS.
3. Pages built using Server Side includes or CGI instead of a web application written in a dynamic programming language such as Perl, PHP, Python or Ruby.
4. The use of HTML 3.2-era elements such as frames and tables to position and align elements on a page. These were often used in combination with spacer GIFs.
5. Proprietary HTML extensions, such as the <blink> and <marquee> tags, introduced during the first browser war.
6. Online guestbooks.
7. GIF buttons, graphics (typically 88×31 pixels in size) promoting web browsers, operating systems, text editors and various other products.
8. HTML forms sent via email. Support for server side scripting was rare on shared servers during this period. To provide a feedback mechanism for web site visitors, mailto forms were used. A user would fill in a form, and upon clicking the form's submit button, their email client would launch and attempt to send an email containing the form's details. The popularity and complications of the mailto protocol led browser developers to incorporate email clients into their browsers.

### Web2.0

The term Web 2.0 was first introduced by OReilly during the brainstorming discussion MediaLive International. The information available in this form is quite different from the past web 1.0. It began in 2002 with new ideas to exchange as well as share the content such as Wiki, Weblogs, Widgets, and Tagging etc.

**Features of web 2.0 technology**

1. Clean and simple design
2. Number of columns is few.
3. Simple navigation which is fixed in every pages of the site.
4. Central layout

**Key difference between web 1.0 and web 2.0 :**

1. In Web 1.0 it is only for read. But in web 2.0 you can express yourself by writing.

2. The former was only for corporate bodies. And the later is about you and your communities.
3. In web.20 you not only interact with site and webmaster you can also communicate with others who access that website.
4. Web 1.0 was the age of one and only language i.e. HTML web 2.0 is the field of XML.
5. **Previously was meant for website but** web 2.0 is not for site it is also about blogs.
6. In Web 1.0 there was nothing to exchange. Everything was about one way. Through the emergence of web2.0 you can exchange your thoughts with other and easily converse with them.

## The Web3.0

The Web 3.0 could be defined as semantic web, personalization like iGoogle, My Yahoo etc. However, in the context of Web 3.0, they take center stage. By combining a semantic markup and web services, the Web 3.0 promises the potential for applications that can speak to each other directly, and for broader searches for information through simpler interfaces.

The semantic web is a more developed extension of WWW. With the help of this technology the web content can be conveyed not only in form of natural language, but also be readable by software agent letting them to locate, share and assemble information more easily. The concept comes out from Sir Tim Berners-Lee the director of W3C with the vision to make the web medium for exchanging the data, information knowledge.

**Features of web 3.0**

1. It will be more portable and personal.
2. More focused on the preferences of individuals.
3. Advertising oriented.
4. Widgets with drag and drop facilities.
5. Dynamic content.
6. User behavior, user engagement etc.

Though this technology not yet capture the whole web world. It has been spreading out slowly. Some big online business houses have started to follow the standard of web 3.0 few of them are spoke.com, twine.com, wink.com. mybloglog.com, friendfeed.com etc.

## 10.6 SOCIAL MEDIA AND MULTIMEDIA

Social media is interactive media, and it's a subset of new media, since the tools that enable social media didn't exist before, and therefore are a subset of new media. Social media is by definition interactive. You can blog, podcast, crank out videos on YouTube, host Blog Talk Radio shows, etc. all by yourself and no one else has to be involved for you to be creating useful media.

Social media operate in a dialogic transmission system (many sources to many receivers). This is in contrast to traditional media that operates under a monologic transmission model (one source to many receivers). Some of the most popular social media websites are *Facebook (and its associated Facebook Messenger), WhatsApp, Tumblr, Instagram, Twitter, Baidu Tieba and Snapchat.*

**The following features are characteristic to social media**

1. Social media are Web 2.0 internet-based applications,
2. User-generated content (UGC) is the lifeblood of the social media organism,

3. Users create service-specific profiles for the site or app that are designed and maintained by the social media organization, and
4. Social media facilitate the development of online social networks by connecting a user's profile with those of other individuals and/or groups.

Web 2.0 describes World Wide Web sites that emphasize user-generated content, usability, and interoperability. A Web 2.0 site may allow users to interact and collaborate with each other in a social media dialogue as creators of user-generated content in a virtual community, in contrast to Web sites where people are limited to the passive viewing of content. Examples of Web 2.0 include social networking sites, blogs, wikis, folksonomies, video sharing sites, hosted services, Web applications, and mashups.

Social media technologies take on many different forms including blogs, business networks, enterprise social networks, forums, microblogs, photo sharing, products/services review, social bookmarking, social gaming, social networks, video sharing, and virtual worlds

Social media is the opposite – it's **media that requires the participation of others**. Twitter, for example, would never have existed without other users in the network. PodCamp as a conference would never have existed if it was only one person who showed up. Take any of the social networks, remove the people, and you have something not useful at all.

That's why **web based multi media and social media are NOT interchangeable terms.** The following list shows the names of leading social networks based on number of active user accounts as of April 2016.

1. Facebook: 1,590,000,000 users.
2. WhatsApp 1,000,000,000 users.
3. Facebook Messenger: 900,000,000 users.
4. QQ: 853,000,000 users.
5. WeChat: 697,000,000 users.
6. QZone: 640,000,000 users.
7. Tumblr: 555,000,000 users.
8. Instagram: 400,000,000 users.
9. Twitter: 320,000,000 users.
10. Baidu Tieba: 300,000,000 users.
11. Skype: 300,000,000 users.
12. Viber: 249,000,000 users.
13. Sina Weibo: 222,000,000 users.
14. Line: 215,000,000 users.
15. Snapchat: 200,000,000 users.

## 10.7 COMPONENTS OF WEB APPLICATIONS

Web application is more than creating content. It is also about

1. Document management
2. Hoisting to Web
3. Managing security

4. Maitaining the site
5. Copyright
6. Other factors.

Web page are compound documents that can hold text and individual objects like pictures, sounds, videos, Java applets, and ActiveX controls. An electronic mail message with an attachment such as a graphic is also a compound document. The original purpose of compound documents was to provide a single place where users could store all the elements related to a document and, if necessary, send the document to someone else.

It is said that a picture is worth a thousand words, and in the context of a website, it is worth a thousand more. A website hoping to make its mark in the internet and that is targeting a niche that is informal, the use of images, videos, 3D models, animations, is mandatory. Even when there is content, inclusion of an image helps pass the message in a much better way. Other multimedia additions can be included, but the constant thing has to be the content. Including a picture without having a few lines of sentence to back it up does not achieve much. A balance has to be created between the use of multimedia, and the use of content. There should not be increased use of one, at the apparent expense of the other. If the possibility of including large images does not exist, then a zooming tool can be included for the sake of the readers that want a bigger image when only a thumbnail is presented.

## 10.8 THE 5 PHASES OF WEB DESIGN

Designing a website yourself, especially if you already have a professional logo designed, is not a difficult process with the right tools. Two excellent and frequently-used programs to help in this process are Microsoft FrontPage 2000 and Macromedia's Dreamweaver 3.0 .

### Phase 1: Define the Scope

Before any work can be done on a site, you need to define the scope of the project. In most cases, this involves information gathering, background research, comparison studies, risk and budget analysis, understanding time constraints, any anticipated maintenance needs (such as updating the site with content), establishing goals and targeting audience. In order to avoid the dreaded "scope-creep" later on, the scope needs to be clearly defined and agreed upon by all parties at the on-set of the project. It is during this phase that a single contact and sign-off person on the client-side needs to be firmly agreed upon. By defining the project's scope, you're on your way to guaranteeing its success.

### Phase 2: Planning the Project

In the planning phase, all the original information gathered in Phase 1 needs to be re-evaluated and verified. The architecture of the site needs to be developed, and the framework must be built. Sitemaps and flow charts are common at this stage of the game. Content is developed and prepared to be flowed into the framework of the site. Specific features of the site (such as sound and dynamic content) are firmly defined and approved by your contact person prior to proceeding any further.

### Phase 3: Design and Testing

In most cases, the design phase starts before the architecture has been finished. Designers work to add visual representation to the thoughts and ideas presented in the first two phases. By the time the look and feel is established, the entire site is laid out and ready to enter production.

Although this phase can actually occur many times throughout the entire design and development process, it most often takes place both before and after Production and Implementation (see Phase

4). Whether testing is done with a paper prototype of a potential design, a Photoshop mockup, or a fully functional Web site, usability testing is a very important way to ensure that the final product meets both the client's expectations and the users' needs. This phase may include multiple rounds of testing, from formal focus groups or contextual interviewing, to informal audience studies. Testing can check for everything from HTML tagging bugs to typos to programming errors, or just to give feedback on the usability of an interface.

### Phase 4: Production and Implementation

The production and implementation phase encompasses the merging of content with the designed layout. All pages are coded, and graphics are produced. Testing takes place to ensure the site performs at its highest level. All of the final pieces are put into place prior to acceptance and launch.

### Phase 5: Maintenance and Updates

Once the site has been accepted and launched, it may enter into the realm of a maintenance phase -- where either the client or the developer makes any necessary changes or updates. However, because this phase could actually include all of the other phases (for instance, if the client requests a re-design or additional content), the issue of maintenance and/or changes must be addressed at the very start of the project.

Of course, every client is different; therefore every project has its own needs. This means that every project needs to follow a standard set of guidelines, or risk "project creep," or even worse "budget creep." Since you can't make up a whole new set of rules after the ninth hole, the rules have got to be set in place prior to tee-off.

## 10.9 WEB DOCUMENTS

There are three types of Web documents:

1. **Static documents** written once by the Web author and distributed to anyone that can access the URL for the document. Each document must be manually updated.
2. **Dynamic documents** created on the fly, based on information requests made by users. For example, sports scores, stock prices, or news updates are put on the page by the Web server software based on the latest information it has available. It may obtain this information from a variety of servers.
3. **Active documents** contain components that run on a user's browser. The components are downloaded to a user's browser and remain available to the browser for future use. The next time the user connects to the Web site where the components were obtained, the components may interact with the server at the site to obtain additional information or perform some other task. For example, a stock portfolio management utility automatically updates itself with information from a Web site. Java and ActiveX are part of this technology.

## 10.10 DOCUMENT MANAGEMENT

Document management is a science unto itself. The Windows and Macintosh environments were important in developing the concept of compound documents. A compound document starts as a document created in an application like Microsoft Word, i.e., it starts as a text document. The document is viewed as a container that can hold objects such as graphics, voice clips, and video clips. These objects are either

1. Embedded
2. Linked.

An embedded object such as a picture travels with the document but can still be edited using an appropriate application. A linked object may be stored in another location. The document simply contains a link to the object at that location and may display it as well. For example, a document might contain a link to a picture or to some spreadsheet data. The advantage of links is that if the linked object is edited or updated, the contents of the compound document change as well.

## 10.11 HYPERLINK DEFINITION

A *hyperlink*, commonly referred to as a *link*, is a text string (i.e., sequence of characters) or an image in an electronic document that serves as a user-activated switch that causes another, predetermined location in the same page or document or an entirely different page or document to appear on an electronic display screen in place of the original page or document. Links can also be used to initiate other activities, particularly the downloading of files from the Internet.

Hyperlinks are a fundamental component of the world wide web. But they are also used in other types of electronic documents, including PDF (portable document format) files and some word processing and spreadsheet files.

Text links can be any length, including a single letter, a word, a phrase, or an entire paragraph. They are usually indicated by a text color different from the surrounding text and/or by an underlining. The default color for an unvisited link is blue, and that for link that has recently been visited is purple; other colors can be selected by the web page designer as well as by the user by changing browser settings. Text links can also be designed so that other changes in the text occur while a mouse cursor passes (or hovers) over them, including in the color of the characters and their background color.

Both text and image links are indicated by a change in the shape of the mouse cursor when it passes over them. It typically changes from an inclined arrow (the default cursor shape) or an I-beam (the shape when it is over text) to a small image of a hand with one extended finger (perhaps representing the pushing of a switch with a single finger).

Hyperlinks are usually activated when a user places the mouse cursor over them and then clicks on a mouse button (by default the left button on a multi-button mouse). However, they can also be activated by keystrokes: first using the TAB key to select the link and then pressing the ENTER key.

To use slightly more technical terminology, each hyperlink has two ends, called anchors, and a direction. The link starts at the source anchor, usually just referred to as the link, and points to the destination anchor, also called the target. The most common target is a URL (universal resource locator), which can represent a web page (or other resource) or a location on a web page.

The term hyperlink was coined around 1965 by Theodor Nelson, an information technology pioneer. Nelson had been inspired by Vannevar Bush's classic 1945 article As We May Think, which described a microfilm-based machine in which a user could link any two pages of information into a trail of related information and then scroll among them as if they were on a single microfilm reel.

Hypertext is text which contains one or more hyperlink. The origin of the word hyperlink might have been hypertext link.

Hypertext, inclusive of its hyperlinks, is revolutionizing how information is stored, accessed and created, and it is undoubtedly one of the greatest inventions of our time. However, it will likely be many years before the full implications of this invention are known and appreciated.

## 10.12 CREATING A WEB SITE

Often a markup language is used Markup language is a coding system that uses symbols or tags to describe what a document should look like when it is displayed in a Web browser. Hypertext Markup Language (HTML) is the original markup language.

HTML or Hypertext Markup Language is mostly used to create webpages. HTML is a code made up of small pieces called tags. Tags are small pieces of the HTML code that give commands to the computer on how to format whatever it is linked to. Tags begin with a less than symbol (<), then the command is written, then closed with a greater than symbol (>). That is the beginning tag. Next the text it applies to is inserted. Then, the tag is ended with a less than symbol (<), followed by a common slash (/), then the same command code as it began with, then a greater than symbol (>). So, your basic code will look something like this: `</(insert code)> Applied Text Here </(insert code)>`.

There are so many different things you can do with HTML. You can highlight text (even in different colors), you can make text in different colors, you can (Hover Mouse Here), as well as bold face or italicize text. These are just some of the basic modifications that can be created by using HTML formatting. There are even ways to insert images as well hyperlinks. Here I have inserted A Link to Our Wikibook Homepage and even the pictures you see to the right. The possibilities are almost endless when using HTML.

The biggest problem with HTML is that most people do not want to take the time to sit down and learn all of the little codes and specifications. It is very useful when trying to organize webpages once it is mastered. HTML allows users the ability to manage where images, videos, animations, and text formatting are all located. It is a very powerful and useful design tool and something that seems to be somewhat overlooked and taken for granted.

### HTML5 source code

HTML5, was created to replace both HTML and XHTML. HTML5 is designed to be simpler and many things have changed or added to the coding for HTML5. The DOCTYPE and character encoding declarations have both changed to be simpler to code. Along with new declarations have come new elements for semantics, controls, graphics, and multimedia because more and more websites are becoming more complex with more information being packed into a website. Some of the new semantic elements include <header> and <footer>, which make it easier for a web designer to indicate where a new page will begin and end. New controls for HTML5 markup language include the date, time, and a calendar to help users be more aware. The biggest addition for HTML5 is the <audio> and <video> multimedia elements, because a multitude of users love to be able to listen or watch something that is useful on the website.

This is especially true for e-commerce websites because potential buyers would like to be able to see a product in use, which can be shown through a video. All in all, HTML5 is a newer markup language that simplifies the coding for web designers and also makes their websites more appealing to look at.

The web making process uses HTML tags to indicate where effects and elements are placed in the Web page

HTML Tags are used to:

1. Assign a title to the page
2. Identify text as headings
3. Mark end of paragraphs
4. Assign typefaces and relative size to text
5. Make text or images hyperlinks
6. Identify where elements (graphics, animations, video clips, etc.) should appear on the page
7. Specify the layout of tables and frames
8. Identify keywords and other meta tags associated with the page

| TAG | PURPOSE |
|---|---|
| <html> </html> | Marks the beginning and end of an HTML document. |
| <head> </head> | Marks the head section which contains the page title and meta tags. |
| <title> </title> | Marks the title of the Web page. |
| <body> </body> | Defines attributes of an HTML Web document, such as background color, background image, text color, margins, etc. |
| <h1> </h1> to <h6> </h6> | Formats headings larger or smaller than the regular text in the document; H1 is the largest text. |
| <img> | Indicates an image file to be inserted; includes attributes for filename, display size, alternative text, border, etc. |
| <a> </a> | Creates a hyperlink |
| <b> </b> | Bolds text. |
| <i> </i> | Italicizes text. |
| <center> </center> | Centers text. |
| <hr> | Inserts a horizontal rule. |
| <br> | Inserts a line break (new line within the same paragraph). |
| <p> | Inserts a paragraph break (starts a new paragraph). |

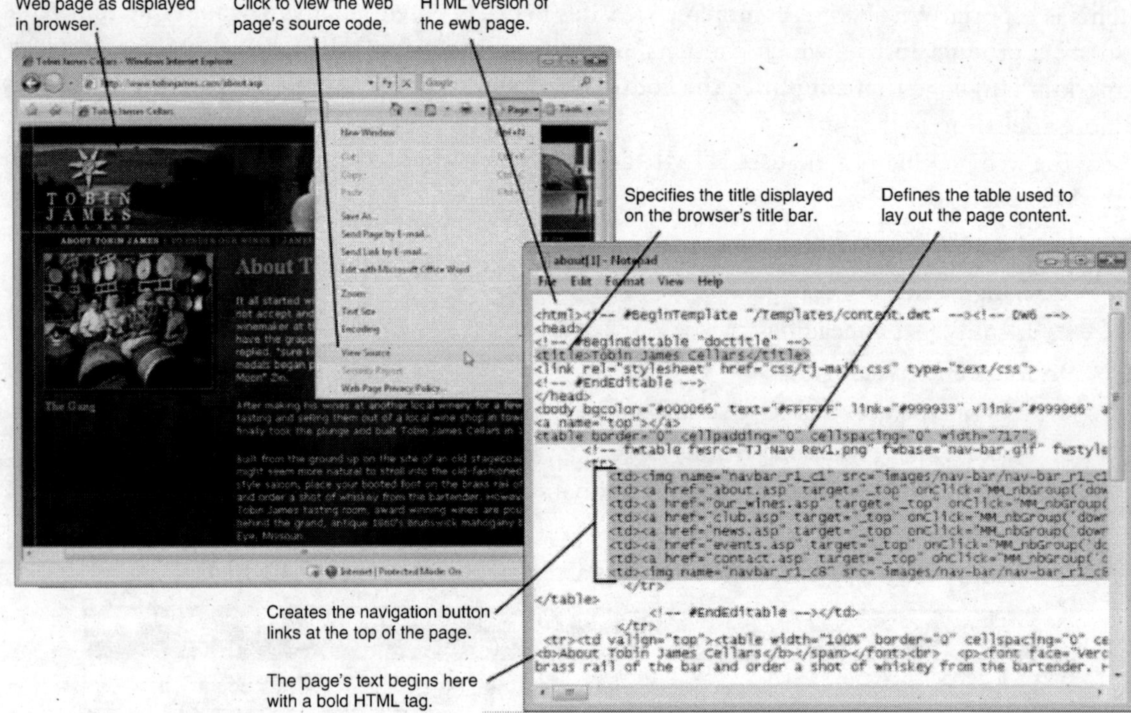


## 10.13 DYNAMIC HTML

DHTML is where the content of a website changes each time it's viewed by the audience. The webpage can change depending on where you are in the world, what time of day you access the website, security settings, previous pages viewed by the user.

DHTML is a collection of technologies that are used to create and animate websites.They use markup language, in most cases HTML, which is used for most of the pages elements, a client-side scripting, such as JavaScript, Cascading Style Sheets for the layering of the content and for the colours, fonts, etc., and the document object model, which is a heading, section, paragraph, image, list, etc.

It allows authors to create effects for their page, that would otherwise be hard to achieve. for example DHTML allows them to animate text and images, they can add a ticker, which will refresh the page after a certain time, this is used on news websites and social websites, allows roll-over buttons and drop-down menus.

### Advantages

1. DHTML is fairly fast when loading depending on your PC.
2. There is no need for plug-ins as everything needed should already be incorporated into your browser.
3. DHTML allows your webpage to look more professional, up-to-date, and interactive. By having roll-over buttons, drop-down bars, etc. People are more likely to trust you and enjoy being on your website.

**Disadvantages**

1. Although you get a great deal of different utilities and tools to use, these come with a price, and can be quite costly. A well known DHTML creator is Adobe Dreamweaver.
2. Creating and editing your website involves lots of detailed coding. If you're not familiar with coding, HTML, CSS, you will find it difficult to create a nice looking, working website.
3. When writing code, if you don't check what is compatible with different browsers, then you could get right to the end and find it won't work, which will be a waste of time. For example, if your writing code for Netscape, then that won't work in Internet Explorer.

## 10.14 MULTIMEDIA WEB SITE DESIGN

Web site design: Refers to planning what a Web site will look like and how it will work

### (1) Basic design principles

1. Users like interesting and exciting applications
2. Users have little patience with slow-to-load or hard-to-use applications
3. Plan for all needed delivery methods and devices

### (2) Careful consideration should be given to:

1. Features that require a specific browser
2. Features that require little used plug-ins
3. The size of the page content : Different devices, browser, and screen resolutions affects how Web pages display
4. High-bandwidth items
   - Watch image file size
   - Use links to audio, video, and other high band width items
   - Use streaming audio and video

### (3) Determining the intended audience and objectives

1. One of the first steps in designing a multimedia application or Web site
2. Objectives of the site affect its content
3. Intended audience affects the appearance (such as the style, graphics, fonts, and colors) of the site
4. Once the objectives and audience have been identified, you should have a good idea of the main topics to be included in the site
5. If the needed content is still unclear, rethink your audience and objectives and don't go further in the process until it becomes clear

### (4) Web Design and Development

Web site design can be extremely time consuming and costly. Successful businesses and agencies typically have both the time and the money to have intricate web sites designed. However, for a company just starting out, those things may not be available yet. Fortunately, there are many sites today that offer free website design. Some great sites that offer this are Wix.com, Weebly.com, Yola.com and Moonfruit.com. This could be a great way for a brand new company or organization to be able to get their name out on the web and begin getting some recognition. These free sites make it easy for one who may not know much about web design, as they typically offer easy to use templates and offer step by step instruction along the way to guide one through the design process. Although the web design site is free, users will first have to purchase a domain name. These are available at companies such as GoDaddy, Register.com, Domaine.com and Dyn.com. After purchasing a domain name, it is time for the user to begin filling his site with content. The user has a great deal of freedom in customizing his site to contain the elements desired. Many of the sites mentioned earlier also provide tutorials to help get the site up and running. After the design of the website is complete, the creator can now publish it and get ready for some recognition. It is important for the creator to update the website often and to market the site as much as possible. For any organization or company that may be just getting off its feet, deciding to use a free site to do its web design might be a good option, and with so many sites offering this service, it seems silly not to.

## (5) Using Flow Charts, Page Layouts, and Storyboards

When talking about website design, a flowchart is used to show how different web pages relate to each other. A flowchart is basically a map of the website. There can be links between the lines of the flowchart to take you where you want to go. When designing a website, you can make it as simple or as complicated as you want. Often times, the flowchart is designed in the early stages of the website because it provides a good building ground for the website. Page layout is used in the designing of a website. Typically people create two page layouts; one for the home page and one for all the other pages. This is when you design where you want the different logos, like the home page button, and its when you decide how visually exciting you want your website. While it's important to make it visually interesting, it is also important to keep it simple so that it does not get too confusing. Storyboards are also something commonly used in website design. Storyboards are a series of pictures that depict what is going to happen on each screen. They are typically used when creating something animated.

## How to Start a Storyboard

There are a few steps to take to make a great storyboard for a web site design. It is important to bring your ideas even if you think they are not that good. Next you need to draw them out on paper; One paper is faster and you can always toss it away if it doesn't look the way you want. Additionally it is good to use paper because on paper anyone can add to the design and you do not have to have a lot of experience making web sites. After drawing it out next is to find a focus from those drawings to make sure that each part of the website is completed. Following, take notes to see if there is anything that needs to be added. After that take the drawings that are completed and put them in a mind map to see the website more visually. Then critique the storyboard and make adjustments to the design. It is also important that other people look at it as well so you can various opinions on the storyboard. When the storyboard is all finished make sure that the navigation, site structure, and content are done well. For navigation it is important to have everything at least a click away, at the maximum it should be. For site structure check if it is too complex and that there are visuals, glossary, table of contents, and or an index. The content should be understandable, creative, and flow together.

Be sure to give users status information and controls when you are presenting multimedia materials. The QuickTime controller bar is an extremely effective interface element that provides both controls and status information. It allows users both to adjust the volume control and to play, stop, and scrub through a movie, and it provides information about the movie's download status.

If you don't include controls, users will hit your page with no way to control their viewing environment. For example, if a visitor is looking at your page at a public workstation and you have looping bird calls as a background sound without any control options, the visitor will experience an unsettling (and potentially embarrassing) moment when he or she cannot control interaction with your site. Many users in this situation will simply close the browser window to make the sound stop, which means that they never get to see the page content. When designing a media interface, let interaction with your media be entirely user-driven. Always include user controls, such as a media controller bar, and make sure that users have a way to turn it off. Avoid prescribed playback options like auto play or looping that take control from the user. With auto play, for example, media files begin playing when a Web page is loaded. If the page has other elements, such as descriptive text, the user who wants just the text will find the video distracting. Design your media interface so that files play only when the user explicitly elects to initiate playback.

**Flowcharts, page layouts, and storyboards are used to design the structure and layout of a site**

1. Flowcharts: Show how the pages in a Web site relate to one another
2. Page layouts: Show the basic layout of the pages on a Web site
3. Typically one for the home page and one for the rest of the pages on the site
4. Storyboards: Illustrate the content of an animated sequence or other multimedia component

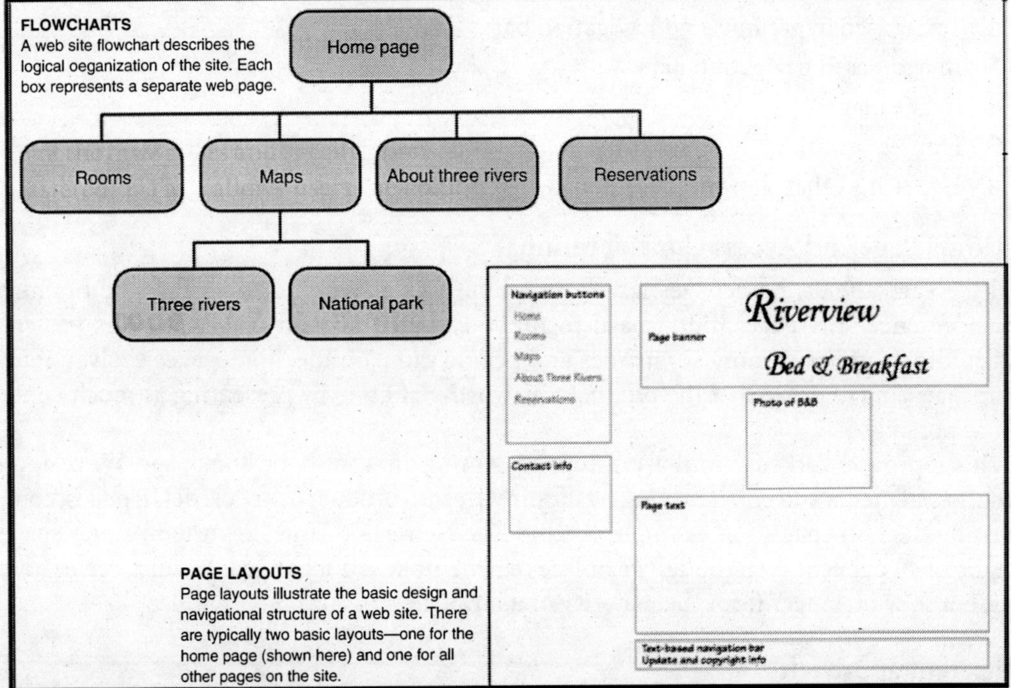


**Fig. 10.1:** A sample flowchart and page layout for a Bread and breakfast Web site

### (6) Navigational Design Considerations

While creating a Web site, it is important not to overlook small details. The structure of the site is the most significant part for easy navigation. Headlines and main menus need to be organized in a way that is understandable for users. Many experts and Internet users agree that it should only take up to three mouse clicks to return back to the main page and to search more easily. Different forms that are used in Web sites include search boxes, drop-down menus, site maps, text-based hyperlinks, navigation bars, and menu tabs. Images can also be another hyperlink to transfer to another page on the site. It is crucial that the Web site has the same links in the same location as the previous page. Things would get confusing if the user had to look over each navigation button every time they entered a new area on the site. Long Web pages should be separated into shorter, more concise pages to avoid loading and scrolling. On many Websites today users will see "Back to Top" to navigate back to the top of the page, mostly on long Web pages. Most importantly, a link to the Home Page should be listed on every Web page according to the Web site.

1. Users should be able to get to most pages on the site within three mouse clicks
2. Navigational items should be placed in the same location on every page
3. Each page should have a link to the home page of the site Long Web pages:
   a. Consider breaking into several pages
   b. Include link to view or print entire document
   c. Use table of contents and links to top of page

Navigational tools include:

1. Drop-down menus
2. Site maps
3. Search boxes
4. Text-based hyperlinks and navigation bars
5. Image-based navigation bars
6. Image maps
7. Frames
8. Hyperlinks that show more options when pointed to

### (7) Home Page and Access Considerations

Until the early 2000s, homepages largely functioned as a signal to users that the brand had an online presence. The pages didn't need to function much beyond displaying this presence and contact information. As more companies and people came online, homepages evolved into brand salesmen, trying to prove that the product was worthy of users by presenting as much content up-front as possible.

This approach worked... until users stopped coming directly to the homepage. We're now seeing search, social media and email driving traffic directly into product or article detail pages, completely bypassing the homepage. For example, in 2014 The New York Times reported its homepage visits were down 40 per cent even though its online readership was unchanged. It still receives homepage visits, but they no longer form the majority of its traffic.

### A different approach

The most important part of designing a homepage that meets your users' needs is asking the simple question: Who is currently visiting the homepage? Look at your analytics and try to understand where the user is coming from and what their internal path is after the homepage.

The New York Times found its homepage traffic was coming from power users: those who were loyal, frequent and knowledgeable about the product. It didn't need value propositions or an explanation of the brand; it needed tools and content personalised to these users' interests.

On a different type of website, these loyal users might immediately funnel into a logged-in state or purchase flow. In that case, the homepage should be designed with that flow front-and-centre, rather than making users search in the top-right corner for the correct button.

The way navigation functions is also changing. When a user comes to a site, however they may have got there, they need context. Design for a user that has zero knowledge about your brand and product. Clear navigation is crucial. Prioritise site content and embrace tiered navigation when necessary – the best navigation acts as a kind of table of contents for the site. Try not to resort to hamburger menus, which can easily end up being the equivalent of a junk drawer.

If your users are bypassing the homepage, your content pages must work extra-hard to give users all the information they might be missing – every content page should be viewed as an entry point to your brand and product.

### (8) Device Compatibility and Assistive Technology

Device Compatibility and Assistive Technology should be taken into consideration while creating a multimedia Web site. As our society grows with more ways to reach the Internet than just the computer, Web site creators need to be aware of the fact that the public is using their Web sites on Smartphones, Tablets, iPads, and much more. The layout may be different on these smaller devices than would a desktop computer. Sites are now creating multiple ways to work with any form of technology. With stricter disability laws being put into place, we have started to think about different ways to inform the physically disabled via the Internet on Web sites. Braille display and screen readers are just some of the newly advanced technology that can be used. Alternative text can be used, which is a text description for a web page image. These text descriptions of images are valuable for vision impaired users of the web site.

### (9) Creating the Multimedia Elements

Usually several different software programs are used, such as:

1. Image editing software
2. Animation software
3. Audio editing software
4. Video editing software

Each element should be saved in the appropriate size, resolution, and file format

### (10) Human Computer Interaction

Multimedia is gaining popularity on the Web with several technologies to support use of animation, video, and audio to supplement the traditional media of text and images. These new media provide more design options but also require design discipline. Unconstrained use of multimedia results in user interfaces that confuse users and make it *harder* for them to understand the information. Not every webpage needs to bombard the user with the equivalent of Times Square in impressions and movement.

The main thing about designing a website is to create a site that is interesting and will bring customers or people to look at it. Not only that, but you have to keep it interesting; people don't want to see the same things on a website at all times. It needs to be updated and changed as time passes.

Another important thing to remember is that many people aren't that tech savvy. It is important to keep the website somewhat simplistic. Confusing websites draw people away. It is important to make sure your webpages load quickly, which can be done by choosing multimedia elements carefully and to modify them as necessary, like optimizing photos to make them run as efficient as possible.

Another important thing to consider is whether or not people are going to be able to view it from other devices such as their phones, their tablets, or whatever else. It may be beneficial to also create a mobile version of the site. Its important to look at what browser people can use for this website. Some sites have certain features that can only be accessed by certain browsers, it is important to make sure to use features that work well on all common browsers. It would also be beneficial to use features that don't require plug-ins. When people visit a site they are not going to want to have to install something just to go on the site or to access something on the site. It is also important to look at the size of the page content. You want to be sure that your information can be seen on all computer screens.

### (11) Video

Video is the most challenging multimedia content to deliver via the web. Part of the reason is sheer size: one second of uncompressed, full-quality video requires approximately 27 megabytes of disk storage space. The amount of scaling and compression required to turn this quantity of data into something that can be used on a network is significant, sometimes rendering the material useless. Whenever possible, tailor your video content for the web.

1. **Shoot original video.** That way you can take steps to create video that will compress efficiently and still look good at low resolution and frame rates.
2. **Shoot close-ups**. Wide shots have too much detail to make sense at low resolution.
3. **Shoot against a simple monochromatic background** whenever possible. This will make small video images easier to understand and will increase the efficiency of compression.
4. **Use a tripod to minimize camera movement**. A camera locked in one position will minimize the differences between frames and greatly improve video compression.
5. **Avoid zooming and panning**. These can make low frame-rate movies confusing to view and interpret and can also cause them to compress poorly.
6. **When editing your video**, favor hard cuts between shots. Use the transitional effects offered by video editing software sparingly. Dissolves, elaborate wipes, or the "Ken Burns" effect of panning across still images will not compress efficiently and may not play smoothly on the web in larger display sizes.
7. If you are digitizing material that was originally recorded for video or film, choose your material carefully. Look for clips that contain minimal motion and lack essential but small details. Motion and detail are the most obvious shortcomings of low-resolution video.

A major problem with most videos on the web right now is that their production values are much too low. User studies of CD-ROM productions have found that users expect broadcast-quality production values and that users get very impatient with low-quality video.

A special consideration for video (and spoken audio) is that any narration may lead to difficulty for international users as well as for users with a hearing disability. People may be able to understand written text in a foreign language because they have time to read it at their own speed and because they can look up any unknown words in a dictionary. Spoken words are sometimes harder to understand, especially if the speaker is sloppy, has a dialect, speaks over a distracting soundtrack, or simply speaks very fast. Poor audio quality may contribute to the difficulty of understanding spoken text: it is recommended to use professional quality audio equipment and/or lavaliere microphones when recording a narrator.

Due to bandwidth constraints, use of video should currently be minimized on the web. Eventually, video will be used more widely, but for the next few years most videos will be short and will use very small viewing areas. Under these constraints, video has to serve as a supplement to text and images more often than it will provide the main content of a website.

**Currently, video is good for:**

- Promoting television shows, films, or other non-computer media that traditionally have used trailers in their advertising.
- Giving users an impression of a speaker's personality. Unfortunately, most corporate executives project a lot less personality than, say, Captain Janeway from Star Trek, so it is not necessarily a good idea to show a talking head unless the video clip truly adds to the user's experience.
- Showing things that move. For example a clip from a ballet. Product demos of physical products (*e.g.*, a coin counter) are also well suited for video, whereas software demos are often better presented as a series of full-sized screendumps where the potential customer can study the features at length.

## (12) Audio

The main benefit of audio is that it provides a channel that is separate from that of the display. Speech can be used to offer commentary or help without obscuring information on the screen. Audio can also be used to provide a sense of place or mood as done to perfection in the game *Myst*. Mood-setting audio should employ very quiet background sounds in order not to compete with the main information for the user's attention.

Music is probably the most obvious use of sound. Whenever you need to inform the user about a certain work of music, it makes much more sense to simply play it than to show the notes or to try to describe it in words. For example, if you are out to sell seats to the La Scala opera in Milan, Italy, it is an obvious ploy to allow users to hear a snippet of the opera: yes, Verdi really *could* write a good tune (AU file, 1.4 MB), so maybe I will go and hear the opera next time I am over there. In fact, the audio clip is superior to the video clip from the same opera which is too fidget to impress the user and yet takes much too long to download (QuickTime, 3.6 MB). [Both audio and video clips are now gone from the opera's website — another sad example of linkrot.]

Voice recordings can be used instead of video to provide a sense of the speaker's personality: the benefits are smaller files, easier production, and the fact that people often sound good even if they would look dull on television. Speech is also perfect for teaching users the pronunciation of words as done by the French wine site: it used to be the case that you could buy good wine cheaply by going for chateaus that were hard to pronounce (because nobody dared ask for them in shops or restaurants) -- no more in the webbed world.

Non-speech sound effects can be used as an extra dimension in the user interface to inform users about background events: for example, the arrival of new information could be signaled by the sound of a newspaper dropping on the floor and the progress of a file download could be indicated by the sound of water pouring into a glass that gradually fills up. These kinds of background sounds have to be very quiet and nonintrusive. Also, there always needs to be a user preference setting to turn them off.

Good quality sound is known to enhance the user experience substantially so it is well worth investing in professional quality sound production. The classic example is the video game study where users claimed that the graphics were better when the sound was improved, even though the exact same graphics were used for the poor-quality sound and the good-quality sound experiments. Simple examples from web user interfaces are the use of a low-key clicking sound to emphasize when users click a button and the use of opposing sounds (cheeeek chooook) when moving in different directions through a navigation space.

## (13) Animation

Moving images have an overpowering effect on the human peripheral vision. This is a survival instinct from the time when it was of supreme importance to be aware of any saber-toothed tigers before they could sneak up on you. These days, tiger-avoidance is less of an issue, but anything that moves in your peripheral vision still dominates your awareness: it is very hard to, say, concentrate on reading text in the middle of the a page if there is a spinning logo up in the corner. Never include a permanently moving animation on a web page since it will make it very hard for your users to concentrate on reading the text.

**Animation is good for:**

- **Showing continuity in transitions.** When something has two or more states, then changes between states will be much easier for users to understand if the transitions are animated instead of being instantaneous. An animated transition allows the user to track the mapping between different subparts through the perceptual system instead of having to involve the cognitive system to deduce the mappings. A great example is the winner of the first Java programming contest: proving the Pythagorean theorem by animating the movement of various squares and triangles as they move around to demonstrate that two areas are the same size (unfortunately, this otherwise good page uses animated text inappropriately: the text moves constantly and is hard to relate to the events in the main animation).
- **Indicating dimensionality in transitions.** Sometimes opposite animated transitions can be used to indicate movement back and forth along some navigational dimension. For example, paging through a series of objects can be shown by an animated sweep from the right to the left for turning the page forward (if using a language where readers start on the left). Turning back to a previous page can then be shown by the opposite animation (sweeping from the left to the right). If users move orthogonally to the sequence of pages then other animated effects can be used to visualize the transition. For example following a hypertext link to a footnote might be shown by a «down» animation and tunneling through hyperspace to a different set of objects might be shown by an "iris open" animation. One example used in several user interfaces is the use of zooming to indicate that a new object is "grown" from a previous one (*e.g.*, a detailed view or property list opened by clicking on an icon) or that an object is closed or minimized to a smaller representation. Zooming out from the small object to the enlargement is a navigational dimension and zooming in again as the enlargement is closed down is the opposite direction along that dimension.
- **Illustrating change over time.** Since an animation is a time-varying display, it provides a one-to-one mapping to phenomena that change over time. For example, deforestation of the rain forest can be illustrated by showing a map with an animation of the covered area changing over time.
- **Multiplexing the display.** Animation can be used to show multiple information objects in the same space. A typical example i client-side imagemaps with explanations that pop up as the user

moves the cursor over the various hypertext anchors. It is also possible to indicating the active areas by having them shimmer or by surrounding them with a marquee of «marching ants». As always, objects should only move when appropriate (*e.g.*, when the cursor is over the image).

- **Enriching graphical representations.** Some types of information are easier to visualize with movement than with still pictures. Consider, for example, how to visualize the tool used to remove pixels in a graphics application. The canonical icon is an eraser as shown on the left in the following figure, but in user testing I have sometimes found that people think that the icon is a tool for drawing three-dimensional boxes. Instead, one can use an animated icon as shown on the right in the figure: when the icon animates, the eraser is moved over the background and pixels are removed, clearly showing the functionality of the tool.

- **Visualizing three-dimensional structures.** Since the computer screen is two-dimensional, users can never get a full understanding of a three-dimensional structure by a single illustration, no matter how well designed. Animation can be used to emphasize the three-dimensional nature of objects and make it easier for users to visualize their spatial structure. The animation need not necessarily spin the object in a full circle: just slowly turning it back and forth a little will often be sufficient. The movement should be slow to allow the user to focus on the structure of the object. Three-dimensional objects may be moved under user control, but often it is better if the designer determines in advance how to best animate a movement that provides optimal understanding of the object: this pre-determined animation can then be activated by the user by simply placing the cursor over the object, whereas user-controlled movements require the user to understand how to manipulate the object (which is inherently difficult with a two-dimensional control device like the mouse used with most computers - to be honest, 3D is never going to make it big time in user interfaces until we get a true 3D control device).
- **Attracting attention.** Finally, there are a few cases where the ability of animation to dominate the user's visual awareness can be turned to an advantage in the interface. If the goal is to draw the user's attention to a single element out of several or to alert the user to updated information then an animated headline will do the trick. Animated text should be drawn by a one-time animation (*e.g.*, text sliding in from the right, growing from the first character, or smoothly becoming larger) and never by a continuous animation since moving text is much harder to read than static text. The user should be drawn to the new text by the initial animation and then left in peace to read the text without further distraction.

## (14) Assistive technology: Hardware and software

Designed for use by individuals with physical disabilities

1. Affects Web design because some content is not compatible with assistive devices
2. Rehabilitation Act requires federal agencies to have accessible Web pages

- Accessibility tips:

1. Use alternative text description for all images
2. Use meaningful text-based hyperlinks
3. Use alternative content for Flash, JavaScript, and other types of animated elements

4. Consider creating an alternate text-based page
5. Keep readability in mind

### Refreshable Braille Display

Refreshable Braille Displays are an electronic device, connected to a computer via a serial or USB cable, which uses small metal or plastic pins that move up and down to display braille characters so a blind person can read what is displayed visually on the computer. The "refreshable" quality means that the braille display is constantly changing as the user scrolls the mouse around the web page or document. The user can move the mouse around by through either the command keys or cursor routing keys located on the device, or through Windows and screen reader commands. Typically screen reading software, or just a screen reader, is used in conjunction with a digital braille display to give the ultimate experience for people with vision loss. A screen reader translates information on a web site into electronic text, which is sent to a speech synthesizer (so output is heard audibly) or to the refreshable braille display. The only thing that the screen reader cannot read is graphics; this is why it is important to include descriptions of pictures and "hover-over" captions when designing a web page to be sensitive to those with vision disabilities. While some may only need the speech synthesizer, most prefer to have the refreshable braille display because it provides direct access to information and thus increases efficiency in completing tasks; allows the user to check spelling, grammar, and formatting of their own input and is quiet, so it can be used anywhere without it be being disturbing to others. Refreshable Braille Displays come in 40, 70, and 80 character displays and can range from $3,500 to $15,000 (in year) depending on the character display.

### (15) Response Time

Many multimedia elements are big and take a long time to download with the horribly low bandwidth available to most users. It is recommended that the file format and size are indicated in parentheses after the link whenever you point to a file that would take more than 15 seconds to download with the bandwidth available to most of your users. If you don't know what bandwidth your users are using you should do a survey to find out since this information is important for many other page design issues. At this time, most home users have at most 28.8 Kb, meaning that files longer than 50 KB need a size warning. Business users often have higher bandwidth, but you should probably still mark files larger than about 200 KB.

The 15-second guideline in the previous paragraph was derived from the basic set of response time values that have been known since around 1968. System response needs to happen within about 10 seconds to keep the user's attention, so users should be warned before slower operations. On the web, current users have been trained to endure so much suffering that it may be acceptable to increase the limit value to 15 seconds. If we ever want the general population to start treating the web as more than a novelty, we will have to provide response times within the acceptable ranges, though.

Design of client-side multimedia effects has to consider the other two response time limits also:

- The feeling of directly manipulating objects on the screen requires **0.1 second** response times. Thus, the time from the user types a key on the keyboard or moves the mouse until the desired effect happens has to be faster than 0.1 seconds if the goal is to let the user control a screen object (*e.g.*, rotate a 3D figure or get pop-ups while moving over an image map).
- If users do not need to feel a direct physical connection between their actions and the changes on the screen, then response times of about **1.0 second** become acceptable. Any slower response and the user will start feeling that he or she is waiting for the computer instead of operating freely on the

data. So, for example, jumping to a new page or recalculating a spreadsheet should happen within a second. When response times surpass a second, users start changing their behavior to a more restricted use of the system (for example, they won't try out as many options or go to as many pages).

## 10.15 ADVANTAGES AND DISADVANTAGES OF USING WEB-BASED MULTIMEDIA

### Advantages

1) Can address a variety of learning styles
   a) Visual learners
   b) Auditory learners
   c) Kinesthetic learners
2) Material more interesting and enjoyable
3) Many ideas are easier to convey
4) **Embedded Video Footage** : Embedded video is an advantage of using multimedia in a Web design. Such videos can contain an array of footage to serve not only a website's mission but also its visitors. Multimedia of this variety is useful to site visitors who have literacy challenges and those with visual, audio or cognitive disabilities. Provide links to a narration transcript to reach the broadest audience should accessibility issues occur.
5) **Informative Images :** The advantage of using photos in a multimedia Web design goes beyond the use of images as decoration. Images in a multimedia context consist of slide shows or galleries that a website visitor can view. In situations where you use photos as multimedia objects, embed them with descriptive HTML code such as a title -- because if a browser fails to load the images, your website visitor will at least know what should be there.
6) **Animated Information :** Flash objects are multimedia elements that you can use in your Web design as well. The advantages of adding Flash animations to your design include featuring scalable, dynamic and media-rich content that stays within one container on a Web page. This content can illustrate how things work or present information in entertaining ways. Consider including an alternative animation file type that a visitor can view in the event that your Flash animation fails to load in the browser they are using.
7) **Sound** : Sound can enhance your Web design project. The sound clips you incorporate can be short or long. You may use them to deliver website visitors information in the form of recorded speech. If you incorporate multimedia of this type into your design, embed descriptions within your HTML code and consider linking to a transcript. These extra steps enable site visitors to review the contents of featured sound files in the event that an accessibility issue arises.
8) **Text instructions assisted by picture instructions :** There are many advantages that web-based multimedia can offer. One of the biggest benefits of web-based multimedia is that it can address many different types of learning styles. For example, when being taught how to make a paper airplane, someone may prefer written instructions, while someone else may prefer picture instructions. Multimedia can offer picture instructions with captions in order to meet both people's learning styles. Another advantage of web-based multimedia is that it can make information more enjoyable and interesting to a user. Text-only information can get very boring, but multimedia could be implemented in order to spice up a web-page. For example, when learning where countries

lay on a map, a simple picture might not portray the information in an enjoyable fashion. With multimedia, an interactive map could be created and used instead of a picture. An interactive map may be a more enjoyable way for a user to learn the material due to the fact that they must engage with the multimedia. Along with web-based multimedia's advantages come disadvantages. One disadvantage of web-based multimedia is that it can be very costly and time consuming. Websites that use multimedia generally take more time and skill to develop than a text-based website. Businesses often hire someone to create and arrange multimedia on their webpages.

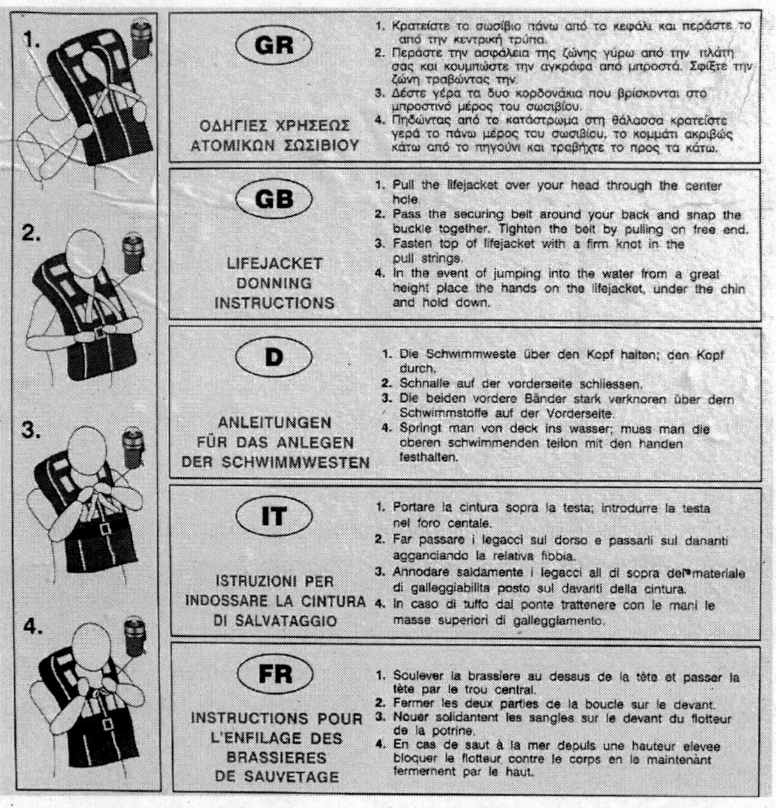


**Disadvantages:**

1. Time and cost of development
2. Compatibility and download time for Web-based multimedia

## 10.16 OVERVIEW OF LANGUAGES USED IN CREATING THE WEB SITE

Python is a programming language used in web design. Web site developers use a number of tools to create web sites. These can be divided into three large groups:

1. markup languages,
2. scripting languages, and
3. web site authoring software.

We have already learnt about Markup languages HTML and DHTML ,that are the foundation; they are coding systems that create the overall structure/appearance of the web page by the use of tags.

### 10.16.1 Scripting languages

Scripting languages allow the developer to create instructions, or scripts, that run in the code of the web page. One example of a very popular scripting language used today is **Javascript**. Scripting languages are found everywhere. For example, Ajax technology is found in the widely-used services Google Maps and Gmail. When used in combination with markup languages, scripting languages can enable developers to implement a wide-range of features and content into their web pages.

### 10.16.2 Cascading Style Sheets (CSS)

CSSs stand for Cascading Style Sheets, and they offer a way to not only specifically style a Web page but even the entire Web site to which it belongs. Before CSSs there had been individuals who created style sheets for their own purposes but thought it unnecessary to publish their developed syntax, believing that each browser should decide how best to display pages to its users. CSSs offer plenty of room for style without being needlessly complicated like some of its rival setups, such as DSSSL. The easiest way to describe what makes CSS stand out as a language is how it works to separate the content of a page from its display. CSS3 is the most popular variation of CSS right now, but number 4 is already growing in notoriety.

### 10.16.3 Asynchronous JavaScript And XML (Ajax)

Many modern websites use a technology called AJAX, for fast and effective interaction with the visitor. AJAX has become a very popular method to retrieve data from the server in the background and the Dynamic Update page. AJAX stands for "Asynchronous JavaScript And XML". Developing code to JavaScript for AJAX implementation from scratch is very time consuming and tedious process. However, many libraries JavaScript, including Query, have excellent high-level AJAX implementation as a set of methods and functions that make it easier and faster to build web sites. AJAX is a development technique for Web applications in which JavaScript code in the visitor's browser communicates with the web server asynchronously, i.e. in the background. When you click links or forms contained on Conventional Web page a request is being sent to a new URL on the web server. The server sends a completely new page of HTML, which a browser displays, replacing the original page. When using technology AJAX, JavaScript code makes a request to the URL on the server. The code may also send the data along with the request. JavaScript code then processes the response from the server, and acts accordingly. For example, the calculation can be made with the returned data is added or updated widget on the page, a message to the visitor to update the database on the server. Since AJAX request runs in the background, the code JavaScript (and a visitor) can continue to work with the page during query processing. The process is hidden from the visitor, who does not need to leave the page they are currently viewing time. This makes the page with AJAX is very pleasant to use.

### 10.16.4 Adobe Dreamweaver

Web site authoring software is used to make more complex web pages where developers can take advantage of commands that automatically generate tags and Cascading Style Sheets, which are used in the look and formatting of what was written by the markup language. This enables the developer to work in a more productive manner because animations, effects, backgrounds, etc. can be applied all at one time. For example, when menu options are selected, the appropriate JavaScript or other code used to add animation or interactivity is generated. Along with this, web site authoring programs almost always have the capability to include a variety of multimedia elements, like Shockwave and Flash animations, animated GIFs, video clips, and audio clips. Two of the most popular web site authoring programs are Adobe Dreamweaver and Microsoft Expression web. There are a few general features of web authoring applications a designer should know. This includes WYSIWYG, which stands for What You See Is What You Get, users can click and drag various website elements to a design canvas without having to code these widgets manually. Advantages of authoring software also include the ability to set up and use templates to ensure consistency between webpages and multi-media can be inserted into webpages. However, a disadvantage for using a web site authoring software is that it's not intuitive and easy to pick and use, some training or technical knowledge is needed. Web sites developed with these tools may not be coded efficiently, which leads to increased load times for users. Also, one needs a basic understanding of HTML. Furthermore, web site authoring software can be an expensive purchase.

### 10.16.5 Weebly a popular website builder

Website Builders are web-based tools that make it easy to create websites for small businesses or for personal purposes. One of the big advantages of using a website builder is that it no longer requires a very extensive knowledge of HTML. So it require minimal technical knowledge to create a website. Another advantage is that it is made to be user friendly. So making a website has been made to be an easier and less daunting task. Another big advantage, especially for businesses, is that they offer mobile web design. Now that smartphones have become the norm. Most websites have a mobile version to them. So some website builders give responsive design to websites wherein they change when viewed on a mobile device as opposed to a computer. There are also plenty of website builders. Some may be free others may not. But mostly those that require payment also end up being the ones with the most features. A disadvantage of website builders though is that they can be expensive and while they give you a domain and an address, once you want to move your website to another host, some may not be able to thanks to a custom code they use. Most website builders will include "What You see is what you get" builders that let you create it by dragging and dropping website elements into the content area. However, sometimes it is hard to differentiate between quality website builders since some products are not up to their task (costing more money or time than anticipated) but still it is a great and easy way to set up one's "virtual storefront".

## 10.17 OTHER CONTENT DEVELOPMENT TOOLS

### ActiveX

ActiveX is a component of the software in Microsoft's Windows operating system. Many of Windows' applications such as Internet Explorer, Microsoft Office, and Windows Media Player use ActiveX in order to embed their functions into other applications. Microsoft Internet Explorer replacement browser, Microsoft Edge, will not support ActiveX, marking the end of the technology.

**Learning Outcomes**

In this chapter we have learnt about :

1. Internet and World Wide Web
2. Multimedia Website Design using HTML and DHTML
3. Scripting Languages CSS, XML Ajax
4. Adobe Dream Weaver and other Content Development Tools

CHAPTER 11

# Wireless MultiMedia

**Leaning Objectives**

In this chapter we shall learn about:

1. Wireless/Mobile Multimedia
2. Mobile Social Media
3. Components of Wireless/Mobile Multimedia Video Systems
4. Architecture of Mobile Multimedia media Services
5. Interactive Interface Design for Mobile Multimedia
6. WI-fi Multimedia
7. Global Guidelines for mobile Multimedia Design

## 11.1 WIRELESS/MOBILE TECHNOLOGY

Wireless technology describes electronic devices that communicate without cords using radio frequency electromagnetic signals. Wireless technology is used in a variety of modern device to provide convenience and greater mobility, and wireless devices play an important role in voice and Internet communications.

We seem to be entering an era of enhanced digital connectivity. Computers and the Internet have become so embedded in the daily fabric of people's lives that they simply cannot live without them. We use this technology to work, to communicate, to shop, to seek out new information, and to entertain ourselves. With this ever-increasing diffusion of computers in society, *human-computer interaction* (HCI) is becoming increasingly essential in our daily lives.

The provision of IP-based multimedia services is one of the most exciting and challenging aspects of next generation wireless networks. A significant evolution has been underway for enabling such multimedia services and for ultimately migrating the Internet to the wireless world.

There is a rapid increase in the use of mobile devices such as *cell phones, tablet PCs, personal digital assistants, Web pads, and palmtop* computers by the ***younger*** generation and individuals in business, education, industry, and society.

Wireless and Mobile Multimedia has become an integral part of our lives. A vast variety of multimedia services like *voice, email, instant messaging, social networks, mobile payment and transactions, mobile video conferencing, or video and audio streaming* has already shaped the expectations towards current mobile devices, infrastructure, and services. Within the last five years, wireless and mobile multimedia has become the accepted standard, driven by developments in end-user devices, radio networks, and backend services. However, many open research questions remain, from limited battery life to heterogeneous data types, increases in quality of service, context-aware adaptation to the environment, or the ever-present security and privacy issues.

As a result, there will be more access of information and learning materials from anywhere and at anytime using these mobile devices. The trend in society today is learning and working on the go and from anywhere rather than having to be at a specific location to learn and work. Also, there is a trend toward ubiquitous computing, where computing devices are invisible to the users because of wireless connectivity of mobile devices. The challenge for designers is how to develop multimedia materials for access and display on mobile devices and how to develop user interaction strategies on these devices. Also, designers of multimedia materials for mobile devices must use strategies to reduce the user mental workload when using the devices in order to leave enough mental capacity to maximize deep processing of the information.

As per CISCO, Traffic from wireless and mobile devices will account for two-thirds of total IP traffic by 2020. By 2020, wired devices will account for 34 percent of IP traffic, and Wi-Fi and mobile devices will account for 66 percent of IP traffic. In 2015, wired devices accounted for the majority of IP traffic, at 52 percent.

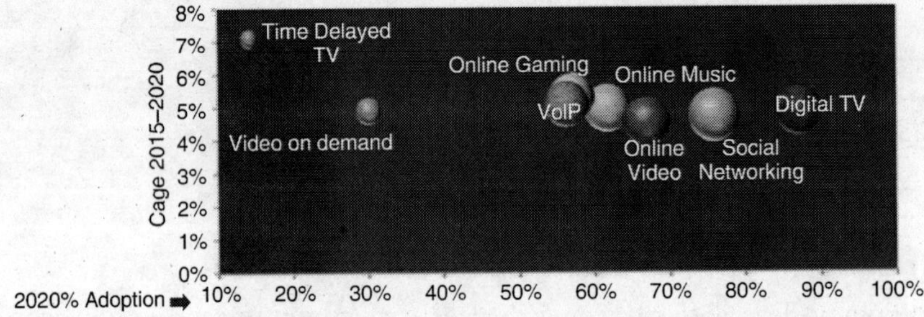


**Fig 11.1:** Global Residential Services Adoption and Growth

***Note:*** *By 2020, the global residential fixed Internet population will be 2.4 billion; the number of global TV households will be 1.8 billion.*

Globally, there will be nearly 433 million public Wi-Fi hotspots by 2020, up from 64 million hotspots in 2015, a sevenfold increase. By 2020, China will lead in total number of hotspots, followed by the United States and France. Western Europe had 45 percent of the world's Wi-Fi hotspots share in 2015.

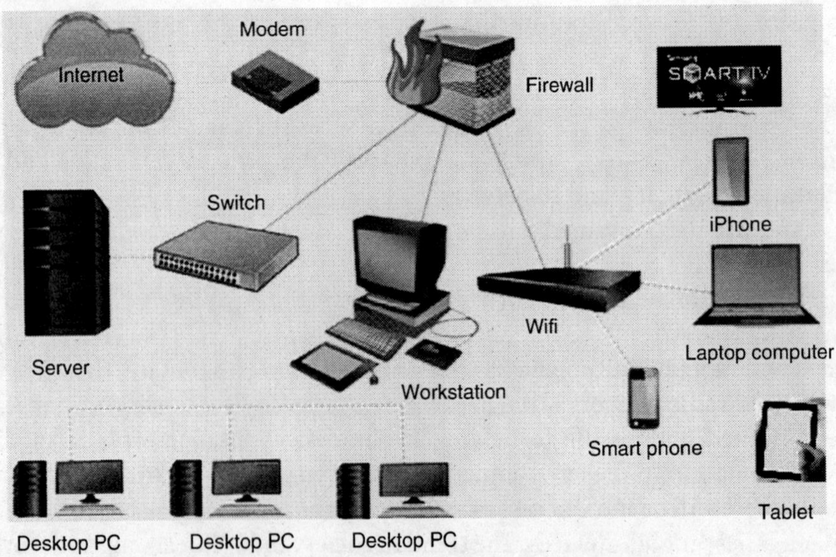


**Fig. 11.2:** Wired and Wireless Multimedia

Communication products are characterized by the fact that the benefit that results from their use is mainly dependent on the number of users of the product, the so-called installed base, and only dependent to a minor degree on the actual product characteristics. The utility of a videoconferencing system, for example, is quite small at the product launch because only a few users are present with whom adopters can communicate. Only the increase in the number of users leads to an enhancement of the utility for each user.

## 11.2 MOBILE MULTIMEDIA

**Mobile is different :** Although they are often lumped together as computing devices, smartphones and desktop computers are very different: small screen vs big screen, intermittent vs reliable connectivity, low vs high bandwidth, battery powered vs plugged in, and so on. Given this list, one might be tempted to think of mobile devices as underpowered versions of 'real' computers. But this would be a mistake.

In fact, the reverse is true: smartphones are actually more powerful than desktops in many ways. They are highly personal, always on, always with us, usually connected and directly addressable. Plus, they are crawling with powerful sensors that can detect location, movement, acceleration, orientation, proximity, environmental conditions and more.

Given the many differences between mobile and desktop computing devices, it should come as no shock that designing for mobile is very different than designing for the desktop. From my workshops, I've compiled a list of 10 principles of mobile interface design that help people familiar with desktop design and development unleash the unique power of the mobile platform.

Mobile multimedia is defined as a set of protocols and standards for multimedia information exchange over wireless networks. It enables information systems to process and transmit multimedia data to provide the end user with services from various areas, such as the mobile working place, mobile entertainment, mobile information retrieval and context based services.

Multimedia information as combined information presented by more than one media type (text [+pictures] [+graphics] [+sounds] [+animations] [+videos]) enriches the quality of the information and is a way to represent reality as adequate as possible.

Multimedia allows the user to enhance his/her understanding of the provided information and increases the potential of person to person and person to system communication.

Mobility as one of the key drivers of mobile multimedia can be decomposed into:

1. **User mobility:** The user is forced to move from one location to another location during fulfilling his activities. For him the access to information and computing resources is necessary regardless his actual position. (*e.g.* terminal services, VPNs to company-intern information systems)
2. **Device mobility:** User activities require a device to fulfill his needs regardless of the location in a mobile environment (*e.g.* PDAs, notebooks, Cell-phones,...)
3. **Service mobility**: The service itself is mobile and can be used in different systems and move seamlessly among those systems (*e.g.* mobile agents).

The special requirements coming along with the mobility of users, devices, and services and specifically the requirements of multimedia as traffic type bring the need of new paradigms in software engineering and system-development but also in nontechnical issues such as the emergence of new business models and concerns about privacy, security or digital inclusion to name a few.

### 11.2.1 Why Mobile Multimedia

The key feature of mobile multimedia is around the idea of reaching ***customers and partners*** regardless of their location and delivering multimedia content to the right place at the right time. Key drivers of this technology are on the one hand technical and on the other hand business drivers.

Evolutions in technology pushed the penetration of the mobile multimedia market and made services in this field feasible. The miniaturization of devices and the coverage of radio networks are the key technical drivers in the field of mobile multimedia.

**Miniaturization:** The first mobile phones had brick like dimensions. Their limited battery capacity and transmission range restricted the use of them in mobile environments. Actual mobile devices with multiple features fit into cases with minimal dimensions and can be (and are) carried with the user in every situation.

**Radio Networks:** Today's technology allows radio networks of every size for every application scenario. Nowadays public wireless wide area networks cover the bulk of areas especially in congested areas. They enable (most of the time) adequate quality of service.

They allow location-independent service provision and virtual private network access.

### 11.2.2 Mobile Social Media

It refers to the combination of mobile devices and social media. This is a group of mobile marketing applications that allow the creation and exchange of user-generated content. Due to the fact that mobile social media run on mobile devices, they differ from traditional social media by incorporating new factors such as the current location of the user (location-sensitivity) or the time delay between sending and receiving messages (time-sensitivity). Mobile social media applications can be differentiated among four types:

1. **Space-timers** (location and time sensitive): Exchange of messages with relevance for one specific location at one specific point in time (*e.g.* Facebook Places; Foursquare)
2. **Space-locators** (only location sensitive): Exchange of messages, with relevance for one specific location, which are tagged to a certain place and read later by others (*e.g.* Yelp; Qype)
3. **Quick-timers** (only time sensitive): Transfer of traditional social media applications to mobile devices to increase immediacy (*e.g.* posting Twitter messages or Facebook status updates)
4. **Slow-timers** (neither location, nor time sensitive): Transfer of traditional social media applications to mobile devices (*e.g.* watching a YouTube video or reading a Wikipedia entry)

### 11.2.3 Mobile social media and Business Potential

Although traditional social media offer a variety of opportunities for companies in a wide range of business sectors, economic-sector mobile social-media makes use of the location- and time-sensitive aspects of social media in order to engage in marketing research, communication, sales promotions/discounts, and relationship development/loyalty programs.

1. **Marketing research**: Mobile social media applications offer data about offline consumer movements at a level of detail heretofore limited to online companies. Any firm can know the exact time at which a customer entered one of its outlets, as well as comments made during the visit.
2. **Communication**: Mobile social media communication takes two forms: company-to-consumer (in which a company may establish a connection to a consumer based on its location and provide reviews about locations nearby) and user-generated content. For

example, McDonald's offered $5 and $10 gift-cards to 100 users randomly selected among those checking in at one of its restaurants. This promotion increased check-ins by 33% (from 2,146 to 2,865), resulted in over 50 articles and blog posts, and prompted several hundred thousand news feeds and Twitter messages.

3. **Sales promotions and discounts:** Although customers have had to use printed coupons in the past, mobile social media allows companies to tailor promotions to specific users at specific times. For example, when launching its California-Cancun service, Virgin America offered users who checked in through Loopt at one of three designated Border Grill taco trucks in San Francisco and Los Angeles between 11 a.m. and 3 p.m. on August 31, 2010, two tacos for $1 and two flights to Mexico for the price of one.
4. **Relationship development and loyalty programs**: In order to increase long-term relationships with customers, companies can construct loyalty programs that allow customers who check-in regularly at a location to earn discounts or perks. For example, American Eagle Outfitters remunerates such customers with a tiered 10%, 15%, or 20% discount on their total purchase.
5. **e-Commerce:** Mobile social media applications such as Amazon.com and Pinterest have started to influence an upward trend in the popularity and accessibility of e-commerce, or online purchases. E-commerce businesses may refer to social media as consumer-generated media (CGM). A common thread running through all definitions of social media is a blending of technology and social interaction for the co-creation of value.

People obtain information, education, news, and other data from electronic and print media. Social media are distinct from industrial or traditional media such as newspapers, television, and film as they are comparatively inexpensive and accessible. They enable anyone (even private individuals) to publish or access information. Industrial media generally require significant resources to publish information as in most cases the articles go through many revisions before being published.

One characteristic shared by both social and industrial media is the capability to reach small or large audiences; for example, either a blog post or a television show may reach no people or millions of people. Some of the properties that help describe the differences between social and industrial media are:

1. **Quality:** In industrial (traditional) publishing—mediated by a publisher—the typical range of quality is substantially narrower than in niche, unmediated markets. The main challenge posed by content in social media sites is the fact that the distribution of quality has high variance: from very high-quality items to low-quality, sometimes abusive content.
2. **Reach**: Both industrial and social media technologies provide scale and are capable of reaching a global audience. Industrial media, however, typically use a centralized framework for organization, production, and dissemination, whereas social media are by their very nature more decentralized, less hierarchical, and distinguished by multiple points of production and utility.
3. **Frequency:** The number of times an advertisement is displayed on social media platforms.
4. **Accessibility:** The means of production for industrial media are typically government and/ or corporate (privately owned); social media tools are generally available to the public at little or no cost.

5. **Usability:** Industrial media production typically requires specialized skills and training. Conversely, most social media production requires only modest reinterpretation of existing skills; in theory, anyone with access can operate the means of social media production.
6. **The time lag** between communications produced by industrial media can be long (days, weeks, or even months) compared to social media (which can be capable of virtually instantaneous responses).
7. **Permanence:** Industrial media, once created, cannot be altered (once a magazine article is printed and distributed, changes cannot be made to that same article) whereas social media can be altered almost instantaneously by comments or editing.
8. **Community media** constitute a hybrid of industrial and social media. Though community-owned, some community radio, TV, and newspapers are run by professionals and some by amateurs. They use both social and industrial media frameworks.

Social media have also been recognized for the way they have changed how public relations professionals conduct their jobs. They have provided an open arena where people are free to exchange ideas on companies, brands, and products. Social media provides an environment where *users and PR professionals* can converse, and where PR professionals can promote their brand and improve their company's image by listening and responding to what the public is saying about their product.

## 11.3 COMPONENTS OF WIRELESS VIDEO SYSTEM

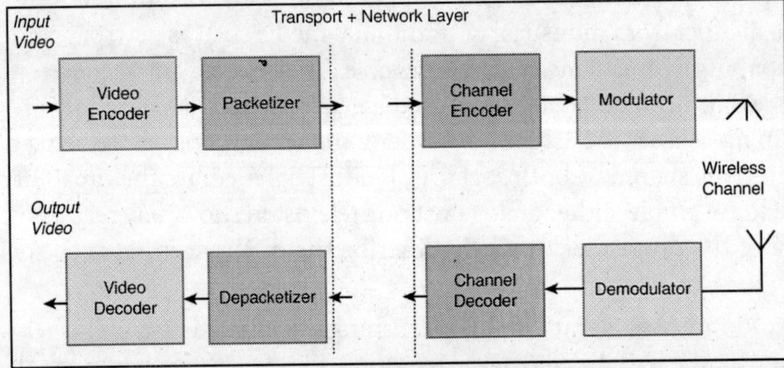


**Fig. 11.3:** Components of wireless Video System

### 11.3.1 Characteristics of a Wireless Video System

Multimedia applications are rapidly spread at an ever-increasing rate, introducing a number of challenging problems at the hands of the research community. The most significant and influential problem among them is the effective access to stored data. In spite of the popularity of the keyword-based search technique in alphanumeric databases, it is inadequate for use with multimedia data due to their unstructured nature. On the other hand, a number of content-based access techniques have been developed in the context of image and video indexing and retrieval . The basic idea of content-based retrieval is to access multimedia data by their contents, for example, using one of the visual content features.

1. The capacity of wireless channel is limited by the available bandwidth of the radio spectrum and various types of noise and interference

2. The wireless channel is the weakest link of multimedia networks – mobility causes fading and error bursts
3. Resulting transmission errors require error control techniques (such as FEC - forward error control and ARQ – automatic repeat request)
4. In emerging wireless applications, multimedia data will be streamed:
5. over various access networks (GPRS, UMTS, WLANs, etc.)
6. to a variety of devices (PCs, TVs, PDAs, cellular phones, etc.)
7. The transmission of multimedia data need to cope with unpredictable bandwidth variations:
8. due to heterogeneous access technologies of receivers (3G, 802.11a, etc.) or
9. due to dynamic changes of network conditions (interference, etc.)

## 11.4 WIRELESS MULTIMEDIA CHALLENGES

Wireless multimedia with all its resources also faces following challenges:

**Heterogeneity** - Heterogeneous wireless communication platforms require inter-operability among different networks

**Adaptive Decoding** - Optimizing rich digital media for mobile information devices with limited processing power, limited battery life and varying display sizes

**Error Resilience** - Delivering rich digital media over wireless networks that have high error rates and low and varying transmission speeds

**Network Access** - Delivering rich digital media without adversely affecting the delivery of voice and data services

**Negotiable QoS** for IP multimedia sessions as well as for individual media components

### 11.4.1 Heterogeneity and Adaptation

Next generation wireless and mobile communication systems have two important features: heterogeneity and adaptation. Heterogeneous wireless communication platforms require inter-operability among different networks such as wireless cellular networks, wireless local area networks, wireless personal area networks, internet, etc. Adaptation techniques become extremely important in such a heterogeneous environment so that quality management and provision to multimedia traffic over the unreliable wireless channels of the heterogeneous systems can satisfy the demands of various network users. With the development of multimedia compression and coding technologies, more and more real-time applications, such as video and audio can be made adaptive. Adaptation provides an alternative for resource planning, especially for bandwidth allocation/reallocation in wireless multimedia networks, where bandwidth is a scarce resource. The system may need to block incoming users if all of the bandwidth has been used up to provide the highest Quality of Service (QoS) to existing users. However, if these existing users can be degraded to a lower but acceptable QoS level, it is possible to reduce the blocking probability without degrading the QoS of existing users to an "unacceptable" level. Various approaches and algorithms adopting this idea have been proposed. It is therefore critical for wireless network designers to utilize these resources efficiently and effectively.

Future wireless networks are expected to support adaptive multimedia applications where the bandwidth of a connection can be dynamically adjusted to adapt to the highly variable wireless communication environments. Examples of adaptive multimedia traffic include the Motion Picture

Experts Group (MPEG)-4 and H.263+ coding for audiovisual contents. Advanced networks are designed to provide flexible radio resource allocation capabilities that efficiently support adaptive multimedia traffic. For example, third-generation (3G) universal mobile telecommunications services (UMTS) can reconfigure the bandwidth of ongoing calls. However, most quality-of-service (QoS) provisioning strategies proposed previously in the literature only consider nonadaptive traffic and nonadaptive networks .

## 11.5 MOBILE MULTIMEDIA SERVICES

The concept of Mobile Multimedia Services was first introduced in 1992, when the ITU realized that mobile communications was playing an increasingly important role. It began work on a project called FPLMTS (Future Public Land Mobile Telecommunications System), aiming to unite the world under a single standard. Given the fact, however, that this acronym is difficult to pronounce, it was subsequently renamed International Mobile Telecomunications—2000 (IMT-2000). IMT-2000 is a single family of compatible standards defined by a set of ITU-R Recommendations. The main objectives for IMT-2000 are :

1. High data rates, 144 Kbps/384 Kbps for high mobility users with full coverage and 2 Mbps for low mobility users with limited coverage.
2. Capability for multimedia application and all mobile applications.
3. high spectrum efficiency compared to existing systems
4. high flexibility to introduce new services
5. high degree of commonality of design worldwide
6. Use of a small pocket terminal with seamless global roaming.

The main applications will not only rely on traditional voice communications, but also on services such as e-mail, short messages, multimedia, simultaneous voice and data and the broadband integrated service digital network (B-ISDN) access . Progress has also been made in the development of other signal processing techniques and concepts for use in tomorrow's wireless systems. These include smart antennas and diversity techniques, better receivers, and hand over and power control algorithms with higher performance.

### 11.5.1 Classification of Services

Mobile multimedia services aims to combine the *Internet, telephones, and broadcast* media into a **single** device. To achieve this, IMT-2000 systems have been designed with six broad classes of service in mind. None of them are yet set in hardware but they are useful for regulators planning coverage and capacity, and perhaps for people buying terminals when they finally become available. It's likely that 3G devices will be rated according to the types of service they can access, from a simple phone to a powerful computer.

Three of the service classes are already present to some extent on 2G networks, while three more are new and involve mobile multimedia. In order of increasing data rate,

- **Voice.** Even in the age of high-speed data, this is still regarded as the "killer app" for the mobile market. 3G will offer call quality at least as good as the fixed telephone network, possibly with higher quality available at extra cost. Voicemail will also be standard and eventually integrated fully with email through computerized voice recognition and synthesis.

- **Messaging**. This is an extension of paging, combined with Internet email. Unlike the textonly messaging services built into some 2G systems, 3G will allow email attachments. It can also be used for payment and electronic ticketing.
- **Switched Data**. This includes faxing and dialup access to corporate networks or the Internet. With always-on connections available, dial-up access ought to be obsolete, so this is mainly included to support legacy equipment. In 3G terms, legacy means any product that doesn't support a fully packet-switched network.
- **Medium Multimedia.** This is likely to be the most popular 3G service. Its downstream data rate is ideal for Web surfing. Other applications include collaborative working, games, and location-based maps.
- **High Multimedia.** This can be used for very high-speed Internet access, as well as for high definition video and CD-quality audio on demand. Another possible application is online shopping for "intangible" products that can be delivered over the air; for example, music or a program for a mobile computer.
- **Interactive High Multimedia.** This can be used for fairly high-quality videoconferencing or videophones, and for telepresence, a combination of video conference and collaborative working be used as stand alone services or form the ingredients of higher level services and applications
- **Value Added Services:** Those services form the intermediate level services formed by one or more basic level services. VAS offer optimised functionality to suit the needs of diverse professional groups. Examples of such services are wireless home networking, high data rate PAN, high density networks, P2P communication collaboration, Internet/Intranet access, video conferencing, telemetry, location based services, payments, and UMS 3.

High Level Applications: Those address the specific requirements and interests of professional or consumer user groups. These are functionally stand alone and serve the full range of user needs. They are formed by supporting services. Examples can be business applications, transaction management, information applications, entertainment applications, telematics, construction, electronic healthcare, provision, e-government, e-learning, wireless home networking, etc, The above taxonomy refers to the functionality of the service and the group of users it targets. In the context of mobile multimedia, the basic level services refer to the collection, sharing and exchange of multimedia data, while the value added level refers to the provision and distribution of the multimedia information, and the high level applications are concerned about the usage and consumption of the data

## 11.6 DESIGNING FOR MOBILE SERVICES

The major problem for an average user is the combination of the overwhelming amount of multimedia content available and unsatisfactory user-interfaces for accessing it. Usability is the key success factor for such applications.

As such they want an application that enables a user to perform content-based search for AV content and play it on a mobile phone. This content includes radio and TV archive material, like documentaries or other recordings of historical, political and cultural importance, discussion programs, movies, music videos, audio books, and music. The AV content will be stored in a database containing transcribed speech from the clips as well as additional metadata, such as titles or a summary, where available. The media delivery will be based on standard web technology. This will enable people to use this service with almost any modern mobile phone. Furthermore the application addresses not only the emerging functional and cognitive needs of the users but also the objectives of the content providers.

In daily life, many people are at work or school at day time. They have no time to watch TV or listen to radio programs, as the schedule is set by the broadcasting companies. Time-delayed, played-back, and individually-delivered AV on mobile phones provide a new platform taking radio and TV into the street, car, public transport, waiting room, park, and virtually any other location. This type of application creates additional audience eager to access multimedia content during new prime times set by themselves, that is, in their commuting periods or other idle times. Also, a market survey shows that consumers are interested in using this technology and are ready to pay a realistic price for these services. The basic idea of such a system can be illustrated by the following sample usage scenarios.

### 11.6.1 Media Recommendations for Users

1. A user wants to consume some AV content but has nothing particular in mind.
2. The user asks the system for recommendations.
3. The system generates recommendations based on the user's stored preferences and on other users' recent behavior. A short description of each item is also provided.
4. The user selects an item and plays it on the mobile phone.

### 11.6.2 Media Rating by Users

1. A user listens to some AV content.
2. The user rates the clip.
3. The user rating is stored in the system and used for further recommendations.

If the user interrupts the media stream, in all scenarios it is possible to resume at the previous location at any time, even weeks later. This feature is unavailable with regular broadcasting or streaming systems. The user of this system has more exibility for consuming the AV content. This is particularly important because of the short continuous viewing or listening periods. For example, while commuting, interruptions and (possibly much) later resumptions will be the regular case. Such behavior is rather uncommon for AV consumption so far, especially for viewing video.

### 11.6.3 Iterative User-Interface Design

Usability is evaluated in small iterative steps to gain insight into whether the users' functional and cognitive requirements are met. User-interface prototypes of the system are developed and tested throughout the development process. As a result the fidelity of the prototypes increases and evolve a representative of the customer.

Developers create different paper mock-ups to collect and present ideas. A final mock-up is derived, serving as the basis for further development. The benefit of using paper mock-ups for the interaction design is that they can be designed and modified quickly. Because of that, the feedback given by the usability engineers and the users can be easily incorporated. An additional advantage is that it is easier for users to criticize simple and rough mock-ups compared to ones which look neat and perfect from the graphic design perspective. For simple interaction designs, a paper mock-up suffices as a basis for further discussions and the implementation. In more complex cases, an additional HTML mock-up is created based on the final paper mock-up.

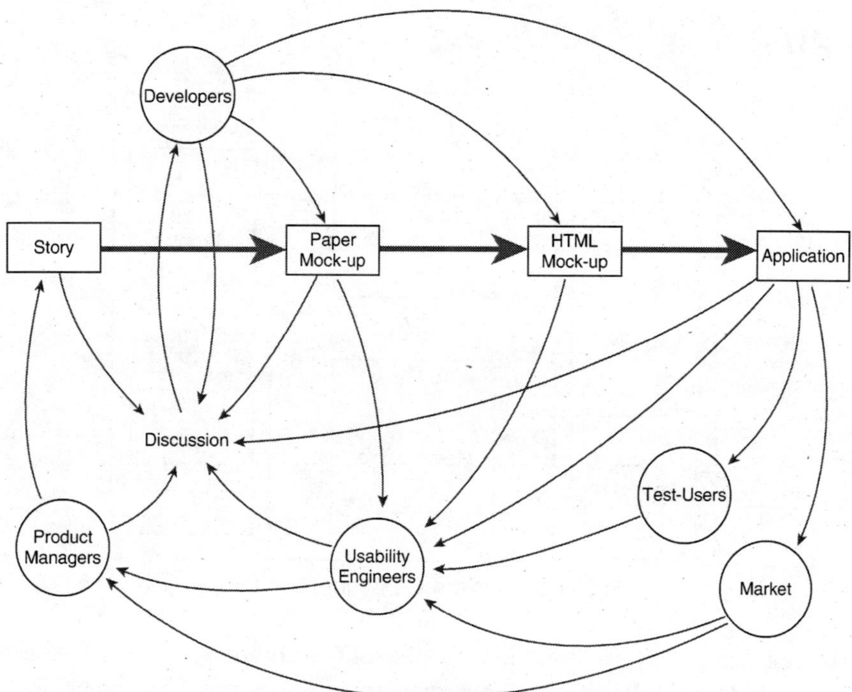


**Fig. 11.4:** Iterative User-Interface Design

The approach combines the quick feedback-and-change cycle of hand-drawn paper mock-ups with the more time-consuming process of computer-based prototypes. Paper mock-ups are used to get the basic concepts right while HTML mock-ups are used for a more detailed view. The designs are examined by usability engineers and tested by non-technical users. The feedback from the usability engineers as well as from the users is taken as input for further refinements of the design. Also, the results are incorporated into automated tests which are used as an executable specification for the actual implementation. This feedback-and-change cycle provides insights into whether the user-interface design is meeting usability criteria. For the actual user tests it is important to choose representative test users from different age groups, bearing in mind the targeted customers for the proposed service. These tests are conducted only after incorporating the feedback on the paper as well as HTML mock-up from usability engineers. Therefore, the expensive part of involving real users can be done more effectively.

### 11.6.4 User-Based Recommendations

Web-based companies already use recommendation systems with great success. Amazon, for example, has millions of customers. Seeing the benefits of recommendations, Amazon has developed its own technique called "item-to-item collaborative filtering". Their customers regularly take advantage of these recommendation facilities when making their purchases. The personalized approach of our system makes it possible to implement user-based recommendations. The unique identification of a user is necessary for accounting purposes, implying that a user profile has to be managed by the system. This profile will be augmented with additional data which is used for recommendations to the same and to other users. The data is collected by means of two information acquiring models, the interactive model and the behavior-based model.

## 11.7 ARCHITECTURE

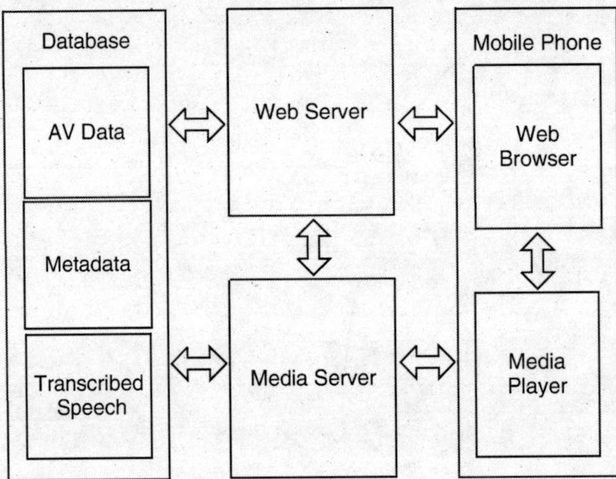


**Fig 11.5:** System Component Diagram

Figure 11.5 presents a coarse grained overview of the components of the system. The server-side system comprises a **database**, a **media server**, and a **web server**. The client side is represented by mobile phones with multimedia and web browsing capabilities.

### 11.7.1 Database

One of the essential parts of this system is the database containing the AV data, the metadata, and the transcribed speech. In the database, AV content can be stored in any standard format and codec. However, because of technical restrictions of the target platform the clips are transcoded to a compatible format (MP4 with H.264) in a preprocessing step. The metadata that is attached to the AV data enables additional search possibilities within the database. The system allows to search in metadata (*e.g.*, title, descriptive text) as well as in the transcribed speech. Furthermore, the transcription data can be used to search for speakers.

The process for generating metadata and transcription text takes an audio or video file as input. It consists of the following steps :

1. Speaker change detection to label audio input as speech or non-speech
2. Automatic speech recognition to transform audio into text
3. Speaker identification to cluster utterances of the same speaker
4. Named entity detection to identify, *e.g.*, persons, locations, or organizations
5. Topic detection to identify segments of homogeneous topic content

The indexing process produces an XML document containing the spoken text, annotated with speaker ID and time stamp. This XML document is then stored in the database.

### 11.7.2 Web Server

The web server manages client requests and hosts the user-interface for browsing and searching in the database. Because of the diversity of available mobile phones, the system is web-based and is accessed through the pre-installed web browsers of mobile phones. Therefore, the challenge of having to deal with many different client devices is alleviated.

### 11.7.3 Media Server

The media server is responsible for delivering the actual AV content to the client and supports advanced user interaction. This includes stopping, fast forwarding, skipping parts of the AV content, resuming later, and replaying a sequence. In this project, the open-source streaming server Darwin is used.

The system does not require a specific client software to be installed on the mobile phone. Instead, any state-of-the-art HTML browser and any video player capable of receiving AV streams can be used.

The provision of IP-based multimedia services is one of the most exciting and challenging aspects of next generation wireless networks. A significant evolution has been underway for enabling such multimedia services and for ultimately migrating the Internet to the wireless world

## 11.8 WI-FI MULTIMEDIA

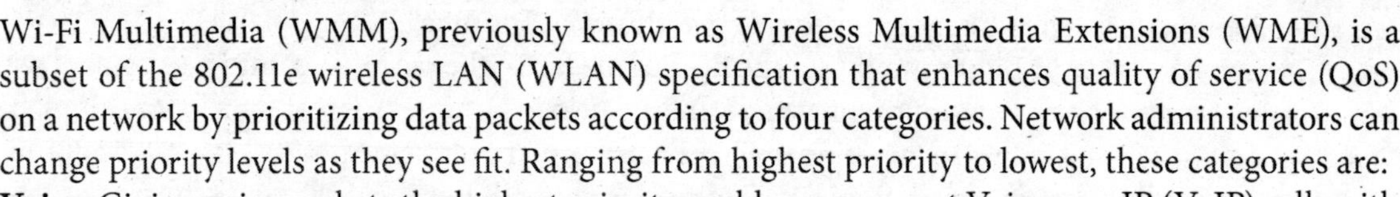

Wi-Fi Multimedia (WMM), previously known as Wireless Multimedia Extensions (WME), is a subset of the 802.11e wireless LAN (WLAN) specification that enhances quality of service (QoS) on a network by prioritizing data packets according to four categories. Network administrators can change priority levels as they see fit. Ranging from highest priority to lowest, these categories are:

**Voice:** Giving voice packets the highest priority enables concurrent Voice over IP (VoIP) calls with minimal latency and the highest quality possible.

**Video:** By placing video packets in the second tier, WMM prioritizes it over all other data traffic and enables support for three to four standard definition TV (SDTV) streams or one high definition TV (HDTV) stream on a WLAN.

**Best effort:** Best effort data packets consist of those originating from legacy devices or from applications or devices that lack QoS standards.

**Background:** Background priority encompasses file downloads, print jobs and other traffic that does not suffer from increased latency. WMM also features a Power Save certification that helps.

## 11.9 GLOBAL GUIDELINES AND DESIGN PRINCIPLES

### 11.9.1 Mobile is different

Although they are often lumped together as computing devices, smartphones and desktop computers are very different: small screen vs big screen, intermittent vs reliable connectivity, low vs high bandwidth, battery powered vs plugged in, and so on. Given this list, one might be tempted to think of mobile devices as underpowered versions of 'real' computers. But this would be a mistake.

In fact, the reverse is true: smartphones are actually more powerful than desktops in many ways. They are highly personal, always on, always with us, usually connected and directly addressable. Plus, they are crawling with powerful sensors that can detect location, movement, acceleration, orientation, proximity, environmental conditions and more.

Given the many differences between mobile and desktop computing devices, it should come as no shock that designing for mobile is very different than designing for the desktop. From my workshops, I've compiled a list of 10 principles of mobile interface design that help people familiar with desktop design and development unleash the unique power of the mobile platform.

Different apps call for different approaches, designs and techniques. That said, the inherent nature of a pocket-sized touch screen device suggests several global guidelines; i.e., the stuff that always matters.

**Responsiveness:** Responsiveness is absolutely critical. I can't stress this enough. If your user does something, your app needs to acknowledge the interaction instantly. Note that responsiveness and speed are not the same thing. It's OK if certain operations take time. Just make sure you let the user know you're working on it.

**Polish:** Polish is extremely valuable. Because of the 'constant companion' nature of our relationship to smartphones, paying a lot of attention to getting the little details perfect will be noticed and appreciated. I think of this as being like the 'fit and finish' of a car. The engine might be powerful and the body style gorgeous, but if there's a lot of road noise or rattling on the highway, the experience will begin to degrade for the commuter.

**Thumbs**: With the advent of touchscreen interfaces, everyone is always talking about 'finger this' and 'finger that'. In reality, the thumb is what we need to design for. Unless the user is interacting with her smartphone with two hands, it's almost impossible to get a finger on the screen. And even in a two handed grip, she's likely to type with two thumbs. Thumbs are the default.

**Targets**: Look at your right thumb. Not the tip, but the face – the part that comes into contact with your phone screen. Mine is the approximate size and shape of a bottle cap. Great for a lot of things, but far from precise when it comes to targeting tiny regions of my smart phone. It seems the magic number for thumb friendly UI elements is 44 pixels. Exceptions abound, but this is a good – ahem – rule of thumb. You should also be conscious of where you place your targets relative to each other. For example, putting the Backspace button directly adjacent to the Send button in an SMS app would be a bad idea.

**Content:** The revolution of touch interfaces is that they enable us to interact directly with our content. This removes abstractions (such as mouse and trackpad) and is more in line with how our brains are wired. I don't have to look far to see the significance of this: my two-year-old can operate an iPad without difficulty but a laptop is a mystery to him. Leverage the intuitive power of touch UI by minimising interface chrome (buttons, tab bars, checkboxes, sliders and so on) wherever possible and putting your content front and centre.

**Controls**: When you do have to add controls, try to put them at the bottom of the screen (in other words beneath the content). Think of an adding machine, a bathroom scale or even a computer – the controls are beneath the display. If they weren't, we wouldn't be able to see what was going on with the content while we were using them.

**Contrast** this real-world design consideration with traditional web or desktop software, where navigation and menu bars are virtually always at the top. This makes sense in a mouse context because the pointer is nearly invisible. Not so with the 'meat pointer' at the end of your arm.

**Scrolling:** Avoid scrolling. I can assure you that 'below the fold' exists for mobile. Also, having a non-scrolling screen has a more solid and dependable 'feel' than a scrolling view because it's more predictable. Of course, certain screens have to scroll, but it's good to avoid it where you can. If you think discoverability might be an issue, you can reverse animate scrollable content into its default position to give a subtle but effective indication that there is more content out of view.

### (1) Navigation Models

There are plenty of novel navigation models for mobile apps (Path's radial corner nav springs to mind) but if you're going to use one of common navigation models, be sure to pick the one that makes the most sense for your app.

***Note:*** *Single screen utility apps (eg. Weather app on iPhone) Tab bar: Three to six distinct content areas (eg. Twitter for iPhone) Drill down: List and detail content hierarchy (eg. Settings app on iPhone)*

### (2) User input

Typing stinks even on the best devices, so you should do what you can to make it easier for your users. For example:

There are about a dozen keyboard variations on popular smartphones (text, number, email, URL and so on). Consider each of your input fields and be sure to display the keyboard that will be most useful for the data entry being done.

Auto-correct can be so hilariously frustrating that there is a website devoted to it. Consider each of your input fields and decide which auto entry options should be enabled (such as auto-correct, auto-capitalisation and auto-complete).

If your app invites a lot of typing, you should ensure you support landscape orientation for fat-thumbed folks like me.

### (3) Gestures

One of the most iconic aspects of modern touch interfaces is that they support gesture-based user interaction. As cool as gestures are, there are several things you need to keep in mind:

***Invisible***: Gestures are invisible, so discovery is an issue. You have to decide how to reveal their existence to the user. The most clever approach I've seen is on the promotional iPads mounted in Apple's retail stores. When a page first loads, any scrollable areas do a quick 'reverse scroll' into their default position. This immediately invites a swipe or flick gesture from the user without having to explicitly indicate which areas are scrollable.

*Two hands:* Multi-touch gestures require two-handed operation. I find this particularly evident in the native Maps app on iOS which uses a pinch open gesture to zoom out. When I'm traveling in a foreign city with a coffee in one hand and my phone in the other, this is an annoying limitation. Android addresses this issue by including zoom in/out buttons overlaid on the map (which means you can continue enjoying your coffee while hoofing it around London).

*Nice to have:* In most cases, I consider gestures a 'nice to have' but not critical. Sort of like keyboard shortcuts – power users will love them, but most people won't even know they are there.

*No replacement:* A common vocabulary for gestures doesn't exist yet so it's too soon for most apps to skip visible controls that can be used with a single-finger.

### (4) Orientation

Portrait is by far is the most popular orientation so optimise for this case first.

If your app invites lots of typing, you should support landscape orientation so people can access the larger keyboard.

When orientation changes unexpectedly, it's, well… disorienting. If you think your app will be used for long periods of time (for example, the Kindle Reader app), consider adding an orientation lock right in the app.

### (5) Communications

**Provide feedback:** Provide instant feedback for every interaction. If you don't, the user will wonder if the app has frozen up, or if they missed the target they were trying to hit. The feedback could be tactile (like the Android 'thump' vibration), or visual (highlighting a tapped button, for instance). If the user has requested an action that is going to take a long time, display a spinner or progress bar to let them know that you received their request and are working on it.

**Modal alerts:** Modal alerts are extremely pushy and intrusive to the user's flow, so you should only use them when something is seriously wrong. Even then, try to mitigate the intensity by keeping language reassuring and friendly. Remember not to use modal alerts for 'FYI' type information.

**Confirmations:** When you have to ask a user to confirm an action, it's acceptable to display a modal confirmation dialog (such as 'Are you sure you want to delete this draft?'). Confirmations are less intrusive than alerts because they are in response to a user action and therefore in context and perhaps even expected. Be sure to make the 'safest' choice the default button in the dialog to help avoid inadvertent destructive actions.

### (6) Launching

When a user goes back into your app after having used it previously, you should resume operations right where the user left off. This will give the illusion of speed and contribute to an overall feel of responsiveness.

If possible, the launch screen you display when the app is first loading should be a 'content-less' image of your app. Anything that looks interactive (such as buttons, links, icons, content) will create frustration by inviting failed interactions.

***Note:*** *Resist the temptation to place branding materials on your launch screen. They make the user feel as if they're viewing an ad and they'll resent you for making them sit through it. Of course, a branded launch screen doesn't last any longer than an empty one, but the perception of delay exists regardless.*

### (7) First impressions

Your icon: Your icon has to compete for attention in a sea of other icons. That being the case, think of it more as the business card than an art piece. Be literal – show what your app does. Use a strong silhouette and keep text to a minimum. A polished icon suggests a polished app, so it's worth devoting serious time and money to doing it right.

First launch: First launch is a make or break situation. If a new user gets confused or frustrated while trying to acquaint themselves with your app, they'll ditch it ASAP. If your app provides complex functionality, you might want to include a 'tips and tricks' overlay, or perhaps a few panels of orientation screens. Note that this is not a substitute for a good design; if you find yourself creating a lot of help text, it could indicate that your UI needs work.

### Festival App Design Concept

The interface need not be flashy, just the basics the user often looks for.Clarity is one of the essential elements of a good UI design. It should neither confuse your users nor give them a hard time figuring out how to use your interface.

Boxes and fonts should be finger and eye-friendly.

Good user interface does not have information overload. Clicking each category leads you to more information. However, it does not give too much, just enough overview to let users know what they are. Even the information for each artist and exhibit doesn't overload on they whys and whats, just a few sentences to help your users decide whether they want to see it or not.

The sitemap tells you when and where the event is Tablets have bigger tiles than phones If you click a tile, you will get an overview of the weather for the whole week. You can favorite the location so it appears on your main screen.

## 11.10 TEN THINGS TO THINK ABOUT WHEN DESIGNING YOUR IPAD APP

### Cramming Too Many Items within the Screen

This is a friendly reminder to app designers. You are designing for a smartphone screen, not a 1366 × 768 desktop monitor. It only means that you have limited spaces to put content.

Do not try to put everything in one place. Trying to compress information within a small screen will tantamount to suicide. You need to understand how to use elements properly to your advantage

With so many mobile (Android or iPhone) apps being released in such a short period of time, designers need to really create apps that stand out. In this roundup we're sharing 50 beautiful mobile app designs with excellent UI experience in mind. Also at the end of the post you'll find some more resources to follow top mobile app design trends.

Mobile apps are even changing the way we design anything nowadays! Everybody is pushing to higher resolution with new retina displays (iPad3) and I believe whole web will get super beautiful and sleek soon enough!

### 11.10.1 Seven Tips to Keep Mobile UI Clean in Your Mobile Design

1. When in doubt, page it out. Use swipe-able pages to put all the content you want without cramming the pages.
2. Make sure elements are tappable. Reserve enough spacing for the user to interact with the element. Remember, you are dealing with non-tactile devices most of the times, so using small elements is a no-no.
3. Preserve tappable control sizes to around 44×44 points.
4. Facilitate focus by elevating important content or functions. The most important items should be placed on the upper left half (for left to right cultures) of the screen.
5. Apply balance and visual weight to make readers understand the hierarchy of element importance. Larger elements are perceived to be more important than smaller ones. You may also want to enlarge CTAs and buttons so that the users can understand that they are tappable.
6. Align elements properly. It makes your app look classy and professional.
7. Use relative sizes. Texts shouldn't be scrolled horizontally and images that are of utmost importance should be large enough so that the user won't go into troubles of zooming.
8. Be consistent. Preserve one brand of design in your app. You wouldn't want to confuse the users, right?

### 2. Using Illegible Fonts In Your Mobile Apps

Legibility of texts supersedes other concerns. If you create an app that nobody can read, it will be worthless. Typography has always been a major concern in any field of digital design. Make sure that fonts and the text can be understood properly.

### 3. Mobile App Design Readability

When we speak of 'being understood properly', we mean that the texts should always be readable.

Proper use of proper font faces, sizes, colors Use of understandable words, good grammar and superb copywriting

A lot of apps sometimes disregard texts, but mind you, they are important because they are the main delivery agents of the messages of your apps.

## 11.10.2 Seven Mobile App Design Tips to Improve Readability in Your UI Design

### (1) Text Matter

Always prioritize the content when tending to text-size adjustments. Not every text falls into the hierarchy of importance. Normally, when users select a large text size, they make the content easier to read. However, they don't want everything in the app to be larger.

1. Make sure that all fonts are legible. If you can't read it, don't use it.
2. Never use a font size lower than 11pt. Always put in mind that users may adjust the accessibility text sizes and app font-size should still be 11pt or higher even if they do.
3. Headlines and Body texts can use the same size. You can add some distinction on the font weight.
4. Use only two weights- regular or medium. Never use bold or light-font weights.
5. Use simple words. Never add fancy and highfalutin words. Follow basic app copywriting guidelines.
6. Be sure to be direct in instructions. Users don't want to read your novel, buddy.

### (2) Be Careful With Colors When Designing Your Mobile App

Colors play an important role in app design. Some app designers tend to just choose the color they want and then design the app. That is a wrong practice. Colors should always help and enhance interactivity and visual continuity in every app. When choosing the colors for your app, make sure that they jive together. Here is one article which can help you with color combinations.

Over the top colorful outfit in green purple mirrored sunglasses with reading glasses focus on color contrasts in different circumstances. Some inexperienced app designers usually make mistakes by not putting enough contrast in the navigation bar background and the bar button tiles. This makes the buttons difficult to distinguish.

Four Tips for picking good colors when designing a Mobile App :

1. Use colors with at least 50% contrast differences. Then test the results on a device under different lighting conditions such as indoors and outdoors.
2. Try looking at the app in grayscale (or desaturated) form. If you have difficulties in differentiating the interactive and the non-interactive elements, then, you need to increase the contrast between them.
3. Never use the same color in both tappable and non-tappable elements. You should always keep in mind that UI elements that need interaction should always be different from elements that don't. Make your users know where to tap.
4. Colors should always enhance the flow of information. Never use it as a distraction.

### (3) Bad Ad Placements In Mobile App Design

Now, let's talk about ads. As developers and designers, we would love ads. They make our apps earn without sending the burden to the users. But for regular users who have no idea about mobile app design and development, ads can be very irritating bugs in the UI. Some ads just pop out and shazam!, you're redirected to the App Store. Now, this is common mistake for new app creators. So, what do you do?

1. **Never use pop-out ads**. These are the advertisements that just pop over the entire page. This disturbs the proper flow of information and could distract with the user tapping on the interactive CTAs.
2. **Place ads on creative places**. Usually, ads are placed in the least important part of the screen. Normally, a small portion of the lower part of the screen is set for ads. You may want to free up a small space there.
3. Some ads, especially in games, give bonuses to the players. I guess this, too, is creative.

**(4) Making the User Wait On Your App loading**

Nobody wants to wait. But some apps need a few moments to load. But you have to be careful about this. Splash screens are risky elements to place in your app.

They are normally annoying because you are accessing the content while someone is waiting for you or the device. If you place a splash screen, make it is short as possible. While you're on it, make it creative.

**(5) Too Many Mobile App Notifications notify**

As the designer, you want your app to be noticed and used by people, right? So you might think that you should always remind them that you haven't used the app in a while? Well, if you are thinking about even doing this, don't. Notifications, unless they are essential to the users, turn the latter away from your app.

Think this as: no matter how nice you try to be, there's always this one guy who thinks you're best friends and sends you emails about his life every single hour. Do you even like that random guy? Hell no, right? Then if you don't like annoying people constantly reminding you, begging for your attention, don't put them in your apps.

## 11.10.3 Three Good Tips For App Notifications

If your app is a game, provide bonuses for users who regularly check your app out.

1. Try to design a better app. Improve your errors; make it more exciting.
2. Be nice with the ads.
3. Don't clutter the pages.

WML (Wireless Markup Language), formerly called HDML (Handheld Devices Markup Languages), is a language that allows the text portions of Web pages to be presented on cellular telephones and personal digital assistants (PDAs) via wireless access. WML is part of the Wireless Application Protocol (WAP) that is being proposed by several vendors to standards bodies. The Wireless Application Protocol works on top of standard data link protocols, such as Global System for Mobile communication, code-division multiple access, and Time Division Multiple Access, and provides a complete set of network communication programs comparable to and supportive of the Internet set of protocols.

Unfortunately, the mobile arena introduces a layer of complexity that can be difficult for developers to accommodate. Mobile development is more than cross-browser, it should be cross-platform. The vast number of mobile devices makes thorough testing a practical impossibility, leaving developers nostalgic for the days when they only had to support legacy browsers.

In addition to supporting different platforms, each device may use any number of mobile web browsers. For instance, an Android user could access your site using the native Android browser, or could have also installed Opera Mini or Firefox Mobile. It's fine as long as the smartphone uses a progressive web browser (and it's safe to say that most browsers are progressive nowadays), but it doesn't have to.

The mobile web reintroduces several issues that have been largely ignored in recent years. First, even with 4G networks, bandwidth becomes a serious issue for mobile consumers. Additionally, mobile devices have a significantly reduced screen size, which presents screen real estate issues that have not existed since the days of projection monitors. Combine these issues with cross-platform compatibility problems, and it isn't hard to see how mobile development is a lot like 'stepping backwards in time'. So let's tackle these issues one at a time and create a road map for mobile web development:

(a) How To Implement Mobile Stylesheets

(b) What To Change With Mobile Stylesheets

(c) Beyond Stylesheets

(d) Special Concerns For iPhone / iPad

(e) How To Implement Mobile Stylesheets Link

The first step to adding mobile support to a website is including a special stylesheet to adjust the CSS for mobile devices:

## SERVER-SIDE METHODS & THE UA STRING LINK

One approach to including mobile stylesheets involves detecting the user agent string with a server-side language such as PHP. With this technique, the site detects mobile devices and either serves an appropriate stylesheet or redirects the user to a mobile subdomain, for instance m.facebook.com. This server-side approach has several advantages: it guarantees the highest level of compatibility and also allows the website to serve special mark-up/content to mobile users.

While this technique is perfect for enterprise level websites, there are practical concerns that make it difficult to implement on most sites. New user agent strings come out almost daily, so keeping the UA list current is next to impossible. Additionally, this approach depends on the device to relay its true user agent. Even though, browsers have spoofed their UA string to get around this type of detection in the past. For instance, most UA strings still start with "Mozilla" to get through the Netscape checks used in the 90's, and for several years Opera pretended to be IE.

## CLIENT-SIDE METHODS & MEDIA QUERIES LINK

Alternately, the easiest approach involves detecting the mobile device on the client side. One of the earliest techniques for including mobile stylesheets involves taking advantage of the stylesheet's media type, for instance:

```
<link rel="stylesheet" href="site.css" media="screen" /> <link
rel="stylesheet" href="mobile.css" media="handheld" />
```

Here we've included two stylesheets, the first site.css targets desktops and laptops using the screen media type, while the second mobile.css targets mobile devices using handheld. While this would otherwise be an excellent approach, device support is another issue. Older mobile devices tend to support the handheld media type, however they vary in their implementation: some disable the screen stylesheets and only load handheld, whereas others load both.

Additionally, most newer devices have done away with the handheld distinction altogether, in order to serve their users fully-featured web pages as opposed to duller mobile layouts. To support newer devices, we'll need to use media queries, which allow us to target styles to the device width (you can see another practical adaptation of media queries in Ethan Marcotte's article Responsive Web Design). Since mobile devices typically have smaller screens, we can target handheld devices by detecting screens that are 480px and smaller:

```
<link rel="stylesheet" href="mobile.css" media="only screen and (max-device width:480px)"/>
```

While this targets most newer devices, many older devices don't support media queries, so we'll need a hybrid approach to get the largest market penetration.

First, define two stylesheets: screen.css with everything for normal browsers and antiscreen.css to overwrite any styles that you don't want on mobile devices. Tie these two stylesheets together in another stylesheet core.css:

```
@import url("screen.css"); @import url("antiscreen.css") handheld; @import url("antiscreen.css") only screen and (max-device-width:480px);
```

Finally, define another stylesheet handheld.css with additional styling for mobile browsers and link them on the page:

```
<link rel="stylesheet" href="core.css" media="screen"/> <link rel="stylesheet" href="handheld.css" media="handheld, only screen and (max-device-width:480px)"/>
```

While this technique reaches a large market share of mobile devices, it is by no means perfect. Some mobile devices such as iPad are more than 480 pixels wide and will not work with this method. However, these larger devices arguably don't need a condensed mobile layout. Moving forward, there will likely be more devices that don't fit into this mold. Unfortunately, it is very difficult to future-proof mobile detection, since standards are still emerging.

Besides device detection, the media query approach also presents other issues. Mainly, media queries can only style content differently and provide no control over content delivery. For instance, a media query can be used to hide a side column's content, but it cannot prevent that mark-up from being downloaded by your users. Given mobile bandwidth issues, this additional HTML should not simply be ignored.

Considering the difficulties with mobile UA detection and the pitfalls of media queries, some companies such as IKEA have opted to simply allow the user to decide whether to view the mobile version of their website. While this has the clear disadvantage of requiring more user interaction, it is arguably the most fool-proof method and also the easiest to accomplish.

The site contains a link that reads "Visit our mobile site" which transports the user to a mobile subdomain. This approach has some drawbacks. Of course, some mobile users may miss the link, and other non-mobile visitors may click it, since it is visible regardless of what device is being used. Even though, this technique has the advantage of allowing the user to make the mobile decision. Some users prefer a condensed layout that is optimized for their device, whereas other users may prefer to access the entire website, without the restrictions of a limited mobile layout.

## 1. Increase & alter screen real estate link

### CNN Standard Site vs. Mobile

The primary goal of mobile stylesheets is to alter the layout for a smaller display. First and foremost this means reducing multi-column layouts to single columns. Most mobile screens are vertical, so horizontal space becomes even more "expensive" and mobile layouts can rarely afford more than one column of content. Next, reduce clutter throughout the page by setting display: none; on any less important elements. Finally, save additional pixels by reducing margins and padding to create a tighter layout.

## 2. Reduce Bandwidth Link

Another goal of mobile stylesheets is to reduce bandwidth for slower mobile networks. First make sure to remove or replace any large background images, especially if you use a background image for the whole site. Additionally set display: none on any unnecessary content images.

If your site uses images for buttons or navigation, consider replacing these with plain-text / CSS counterparts. Finally if you'd like to force the browser to use the alternate text for any of your images, use this snippet (and use JavaScript to add the as-text class for img and make sure that alt-attributes are properly defined in your markup):

```
img.as-text { content: attr(alt); }
```

## 3. Other Changes Link

Besides addressing screen size and bandwidth concerns, there are a few additional changes that should be made in any mobile stylesheet. First, you can improve readability by increasing the font size of any small or medium-sized text. Next, clicking is generally less precise on mobile devices, so make sure to increase the clickable areas of any important buttons or links by setting display: block and adding padding to the clickable elements.

Additionally, floated elements can cause problems for mobile layouts, so consider removing any floats that aren't absolutely necessary. Remember that horizontal real estate is especially expensive on mobile, so you should always opt for adding vertical scrolling as opposed to horizontal.

Finally, mouseover states do not work with most mobile devices, so make sure to have proper definitions of :active-states. Also, sometimes it may be useful to apply definitions from the already defined :hover states to the :active states. This pseudo-class is displayed when the user clicks an item, and therefore will work on mobile devices. However this only enhances the user experience and should not be relied on for more important elements, such as drop-down navigation. In these cases it is best to show the links at all times in mobile devices.

## 4. Beyond Stylesheets Link

In addition to mobile stylesheets, we can add a number of special mobile features through mark-up.

**Clickable phone numbers link**

First, most handheld devices include a phone, so let's make our phone numbers clickable:

```
<a href="tel:15032084566" class="phone-link">(503) 208-4566</a>
```

Now mobile users can click this number to call it, however there are a few things to note. First, the number in the actual link starts with a 1 which is important since the web is international (1 is the US country code).

Second, this link is clickable whether or not the user has a mobile device. Since we're not using the server-side method described above, our best option is to simply hide the fact that the number is clickable via CSS. So use the phone-link class to disable the link styling in your screen stylesheet, and then include it again for mobile.

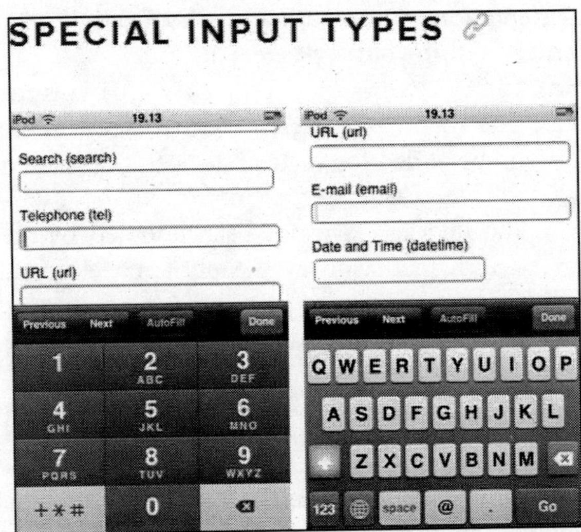


When it comes to mobile browsing, another concern is the difficulty of typing compared to a standard full-sized keyboard. But we can make it easier on our users by taking advantage of some special HTML5 input types:

```
<input type="tel" /> <input type="email" />
```

These input types allow devices such as iPhone to display a contextual keyboard that relates to the input type. In the example above type="tel" triggers a numeric keypad ideal for entering phone numbers, and type="email" triggers a keypad with @ and . buttons.

HTML5 input types also provide in-browser validation and special input menus that are useful in both mobile and non-mobile browsing. Furthermore, since non-supportive browsers naturally degrade to view these special input types as <input type="text" />, there's no loss in using HTML5 input types throughout your websites today.

See a complete list of HTML5 input types. You can find some information about the current browser support of HTML5 input attributes in the post HTML5 Input Attributes & Browser Support by Estelle Weyl.

## 5. Viewport Dimensions & Orientation Link

When modern mobile devices render a webpage, they scale the page content to fit inside their viewport, or visible area. Although the default viewport dimensions work well for most layouts, it is sometimes useful to alter the viewport. This can be accomplished using a <meta> tag that was introduced by Apple and has since been picked up by other device manufacturers. In the document's <head> include this snippet:

```
<meta name="viewport" content="width=320" />
```

In this example we've set the viewport to 320, which means that 320 pixels of the page will be visible across the width of the device.

The viewport meta tag can also be used to disable the ability to resize the page:

```
<meta name="viewport" content="width=320,user-scalable=false" />
```

However, similar to disabling the scrollbars, this technique takes control away from the user and should only be used for a good reason.

Additionally, it is possible to add certain styles based on the device orientation. This means that different styles can be applied depending on whether the user is holding their phone vertically or horizontally.

To detect the device orientation, we can use a media query similar to the client-side device detection we discussed earlier. Within your stylesheet, include:

```
@import url("portrait.css") all and (orientation:portrait); @
import url("landscape.css") all and (orientation:landscape);
```

Here portrait.css styles will be added for vertical devices and the landscape.css will be added for horizontal.

However orientation media queries have not been adopted by all devices, so this is best accomplished with the max-width media query. Simply apply different max-width queries for the different orientation widths you want to target. This is a much more robust approach, since presumably the reason to target different orientations is to style for different widths.

## 6. Special Concern For iPhone/iPad Link

### iPhone 4

With a market share of 28% and estimates of as much as 50% of mobile browsing going through iPhone, it makes sense that developers make special accommodations for the mobile giant.

### No Flash Link

Regardless of Apple's ethics, the reality is that iPhones do not play Flash unless they are jailbroken. Fortunately, there are alternatives to Flash, and iPhone's issues with this technology are often easy to get around. The main use for Flash in modern websites is Flash video, which can easily be circumvented using HTML5 video. However since older browsers don't support HTML5, make sure to include a Flash backup for non-supportive browsers (this is why the whole debate about Flash vs. HTML5 is a bit pointless, because you can actually offer both to your users and the user's device will pick up the one it can render automatically).

Beyond video, it is usually best to use JavaScript to accommodate any simple functionality. JavaScript libraries such as jQuery make it easy to build rich interactive applications without Flash. Regardless of your desire to support iPhone, these JavaScript apps typically have a number of additional advantages over Flash alternatives.

Finally, certain applications are simply too hard to recreate with HTML5 and Javascript. For these, iPhone users will have to be left out, however make sure to include appropriate alternate content. Apple Loves Adobe

## 7. Other Shortcomings Link

Besides Flash, there are a few additional caveats to supporting iPhones and iPads.

First, iPhone does not support `<input type="file" />`, since it does not have an accessible internal file structure. While most mobile devices connect to a computer as an external hard-drive, Apple has taken steps to ensure that the iPhone file structure remains obfuscated.

Next, iPhone will only cache files that are 25 kb or less, so try to keep any reused files under this restriction. This can be a bit counter-intuitive, as it often means breaking out large image sprites and concatenated JavaScripts into smaller chunks. However be careful to serve these files only to iPhone, or it will cause extra HTTP requests in all other browsers.

Finally, when it comes to @font-face font embedding, iPhone's Mobile Safari doesn't fully support it and supports the SVG file format instead. However, SVG fonts are only supported by Chrome, Opera and iPhone, so we'll need a hybrid approach to target all browsers. In addition to the SVG, we'll need an .otf or .ttf for Firefox and Safari, as well as an EOT for IE (IE has actually supported @font-face since IE4).

After obtaining the necessary files, tie them all together with the appropriate CSS: @font-face { font-family: 'Comfortaa Regular'; src: url('Comfortaa.eot'); src: local('Comfortaa Regular'), local('Comfortaa'), url('Comfortaa.ttf') format('truetype'), url('Comfortaa.svg#font') format('svg'); }

## 8. Special iPhone / iPad Enhancements Link

Despite iPhone's various shortcomings, the device offers a wonderfully rich user experience that developers can leverage in ways not possible with older mobile devices.

First, there are a variety of JavaScript libraries that can be used to access some of the more advanced functionality available in iPhone. Take a look at Sencha Touch, jQTouch and iui. These three libraries allow you to better interface with the iPhone, and also work on similar devices such as Android. Additionally, keep an eye on the much anticipated jQuery Mobile which has just been released in alpha.

Next, the App Store isn't the only way to get an icon on your users' iPhones: you can simply have them bookmark your page. Unfortunately the default bookmark icon is a condensed screen shot of the page, which doesn't usually look very good, so let's create a special iPhone icon. Also check the Icon Reference Chart by Jon Hicks for further details.

Start by saving a 57 × 57 pixel PNG somewhere on your website, then add this snippet within your <head> tag:

```
<link rel="apple-touch-icon" href="/customIcon.png"/>
```

Don't worry about rounded corners or a glossy effect, iPhone will add those by default.

**Learning Outcomes**

In this chapter we have learn about :

1. Mobile Multimedia Design
2. Designing Mobile Multimedia media Services
3. Setting up hardware of Wireless/Mobile Multimedia Video systems
4. Designing Interactive Interface Design for Mobile Multimedia

# Multimedia Projects: Multimedia Skill

CHAPTER 12

**Leaning Objectives**

In this chapter we shall learn about:

1. Multimedia Projects Design
2. Multimedia Design Process
3. Different Stages of Multimedia Projects Design
4. Conceptualisation of Multimedia Development Process
5. Planning and Costing
6. Managing Contents
7. Production
8. Testing and Delivering
9. Documentation

## 12.1 MULTIMEDIA PROJECTS

Multimedia projects are a unique type of developing innovative products and services, with a distinctive set of team members, knowledge and methods. Creativity reaches new forms, in a synergy that allows a new type of access to information, more interactive, intuitive and sometimes unexpected.

Multimedia –the combination of several media with the purpose of transmitting a message – arises thus as an attractive form of accessing and securing information and is the conceptual base of most of the apps we all use everyday. Before these innovating products are launched, they go through a development process, most of the times characterized by a creative and conceptualization initial phase, followed by the production, test and validation. This process is discussed in detail in section 12.Taking into account the amount of knowledge areas that can converge into a Multimedia Project and the amount of interdependent tasks performed by different team-members, a set of supporting methods, techniques and tools is required so that the project goals' may be reached in due time.

A multimedia project uses development technologies in the field of new digital media and is strongly characterized by the utilization of several formats, strong interaction component and interactivity promotion. These projects are distinguished from other projects in software engineering area as they assume creativity like as important as programming or specialization. The software tools used tend to be different from tools used in software area projects.

For an organization, projects are construction blocks on strategies conception and execution. They contribute to create new and better products, services and organizational processes . Weaver (2007) defines a project as a temporary effort to achieve a wished profit. The ultimate goal of a project, in short or long term, includes return on investment (ROI), profit, feature, competition and market ability.

The goal of a multimedia project is to disclose specific information to a well-defined market segment using several technological means and enabling interactivity. These projects can be seen as different from others as creativity is seen as important as technical skills. Software tools used tend to be different from software engineering projects.

Multimedia is a heterogenic mix of interactive media integration; a combination of ability variety focused on an efficient blend of artistic and computer skills and market segment vision. Multimedia is also a heterogeneous mix of manifold media with interactive nature, calling for a variety of development skills such as artistic and digital capabilities.

## Emerging Trends

- **Growth of smartphones** as the "communications hub" for social media, video consumption, tracking IoE/digitization applications (et al.), as well as traditional voice. This trend demonstrates the impact that smartphones have on how consumers and businesses users access and use the Internet and IP networks.
- **Internet gaming** is seeing a resurgence—the traffic nearly doubled in 2015 and will grow seven-fold by 2020. Gaming on demand and streaming gaming platforms have been in development for several years, with many newly released in 2014 and 2015. With traditional gaming, graphical processing is performed locally on the gamer's computer or console. With cloud gaming, game graphics are produced on a remote server and transmitted over the network to the gamer. If cloud gaming becomes popular, gaming could quickly become one of the largest Internet traffic categories.
- **Virtual reality**: With new hardware available to individuals, and a growing body of content to consume, virtual reality has experienced high growth in recent years. Traffic associated with virtual and augmented reality applications quadrupled in 2015 and is poised to grow 61-fold by 2020. This growth stems mainly from the download of large virtual reality content files and applications, but a significant wild card is the potential adoption of virtual reality streaming, which could raise our prediction of high-growth even higher.
- **Immersive video**: This emerging traffic type can cause significant new network design implications as it is a high-bandwidth consuming application. Social media platforms such as Facebook have launched support for spherical, or immersive video that integrates multiple camera angles to form a single video stream and can be watched from the viewer's preferred perspective. It can generate bit rates 3 to 10 times greater than non-immersive HD bit rates.
- **Video surveillance**: New Internet-connected video surveillanee cameras upload a constant video stream to the cloud for remote viewing. With a steady flow of video traffic from each camera, video surveillance is already having an impact on overall Internet traffic and accounts for 1.5 percent of total Internet traffic today, growing to nearly 4 percent by 2020. If such devices become mass market in the next five years, we could see video cameras generating a significantly higher volume of traffic, since Internet-enable cameras can produce up to 300 GB per camera per month for full HD-resolution monitoring of high-activity areas.

## 12.2 MULTIMEDIA DEVELOPMENT PROCESS

Multimedia development Process can be described as the use of many different communication medias, technologies and delivery platforms. A multimedia production can be expensive. Their preparation requires a team of people, each with a special skill set. Instructional designers explain how people learn and how materials should be structured. Producers coordinate the development process. Subject matter experts bring their knowledge of the subject. Interface designers are in charge of the onscreen navigational system. Writers work on scripts and any text that appears on the screen and documentation. Designers work on the program's graphics, it's overall look and feel, and interface design. Artists create graphics. Programmers put together all these elements using development software.

### (1) Multimedia Developer

The multimedia developer has communication medias such as color, text, images, graphics, music, sound, narrations, video, 2d animation, 3d animation, interactivity and light at his disposal. A multimedia developer can design, build and implement strategies that make effective use of the medias and the technology used to produce and deliver the final systems.

### (2) Multimedia Storage Cabinet

Multimedia storage solutions are available in plenty for your Compact Disc, DVD, VHS Tape and cassette collections. Holders are available in library, rack, cabinet, desktop, portable and tower styles to store from 10 to over 1500 CDs and other media. The highest quality of wood and metal are used to create the multimedia storage units. All of the pieces required for assembling the multimedia storage cabinet are provided. The time required for assembly will be 1-3 hours. For some of the larger units, two people may be necessary for assembling.

## 12.3 INTERACTIVE MULTIMEDIA PRODUCTION

The final multimedia production becomes interactive only when these distinct pieces are put together in an organized manner. Interactive multimedia does not follow a linear pattern. Research does not happen in a single step, it flows throughout the project. Deciding on a topic leads to identifying sub-topics, which in turn lead to more sub-topics. Non-linear links begin to appear between ideas in the project. These links must be researched in greater depth. The final document itself becomes non-linear. The reader does not have to start at the top and read to the bottom, they can move around within the information the author has presented. The author presents ideas and provides links for their readers to navigate. In a multimedia production classroom the number one problem is not discipline, it is running out of time.

Interactive multimedia firms derive the majority of their business from servicing Web sites and corporate businesses than home consumer, government or other institutions. Larger companies who employ greater than 100 employees appear to be performing the majority of interactive multimedia production. Productivity in smaller companies has declined slightly while it has increased in larger firms. This is because larger businesses are better able to meet the costs of doing business and have access to premier clientele. Challenges in interactive multimedia production are the lengthy decision making cycles and meeting the client's requirement on a nominal budget.

## 12.4 MULTIMEDIA SERVERS AND DATABASES

Universal servers are databases that store multimedia elements. Different fields store the text, images, sound and video files. These powerful databases can be accessed over the network and function as organizational libraries. High performance multimedia storage server software supports both streaming media data (*e.g.*, video, audio) and conventional data (*e.g.*, text, binary, images). It can be used as a next-generation file system as well as a stand alone video or audio on-demand server. Example for such a multimedia storage server is Fellini. Computers are now able to handle continuous media. Continuous media data has real-time requirements. A traditional file server cannot distinguish between continuous and non-continuous media. A multimedia storage server must be able to handle a large number of real-time requests with different rates. A multimedia storage server should support non real-time requests without violating the requirements of the real-time requests. It should support the storage and retrieval of multimedia data like: text, images, and other binary data.

### Multimedia Search

There are plenty of specialized multimedia search tools available. Some of these covers several types of multimedia content, while some focus on images and specific file types. Major search engines have the ability to search for multimedia files on the web. Many search engines index all kinds of image formats. Some are associated with general search engines; some are standalone image search engines. Some just index pictures available on the Web. Others have specialized collections of images. The image search engines are much more diverse than the general Web search engines. Copyright is one important issue to consider when searching for images.

## 12.5 TYPES OF MULTIMEDIA SYSTEMS

Multimedia Systems can be categorized based on functionality as below:

1. Multimedia Presentation Systems (for user)
2. Multimedia Development Systems (for developer)

### (1) Multimedia Presentation Systems

1. PC with high resolution screen
2. CD-ROM drive
3. Speakers and Microphone

### (2) Multimedia Development System includes the following:

1. software toolkit for development work
2. software library for support functions
3. libraries of clip art, music and video
4. Related hardware

**For Multimedia Development System**

1. Development systems has more resources and utilities.
2. Presentation systems must be checked to have the required components and resources.

## 12.6 MULTIMEDIA SKILLS

Following is the list of desirable multimedia skills :

1. Text Designing and DTP
2. Audio editing
3. Tweeting/live blogging
4. Deadline writing, multiple webhits
5. Web site Design
6. Blogging on WordPress
7. Shooting/editing photos, video
8. Storytelling through Storify
9. Interactive storytelling through sliderocket, thinglink

10. Mapping data with simple Google Fusion tables (Google Drive :Cloud computing)
11. Database journalism with Caspio, Google
12. Infographics, like those created at easel.ly, visual.ly

### 12.6.1 Multimedia skills and applications

Learner should be able to demonstrate the following outcomes:

**Professional and reflective practitioner skills**

1. An understanding of the processes involved in the development of a multimedia product from client brief through to delivery,
2. To critically consider and discuss the areas where learners have most difficulty, including scoping and evaluation, and how these can be supported by use of learning resources from e-skills .

**Practical skills**

1. To develop a simple project plan from a suitably detailed client brief,
2. To work with learners to plan and create a multimedia product that includes animation, audio and video,
3. To support learners in the evaluation process, including user testing, collecting and analysing feedback, and planning for change.

**Knowledge and understanding**

1. An understanding of the content of learning materials available from e-skills UK and how these can be used with learners to develop multimedia products,
2. An understanding of multimedia development in the business world, and how successful development is contingent on detailed client specifications, user and audience research, and design decisions taken during the planning phase.

**Cognitive skills**

1. To critically discuss how employer or client requirements are a key part of providing learners with realistic modelling of multimedia development for a purpose,
2. To discuss strategies for supporting learners in gaining confidence in the evaluation phase of multimedia product development through processes of user testing and acceptance of feedback and need for change

## 12.7 TOTAL MULTIMEDIA DEVELOPMENT PROCESS

The production of interactive multimedia applications is a complex one, involving multiple steps. This process can be divided into the following phases:

1. Conceptualisation
2. Planning and Costing
3. Preproduction (*Hardware, software and user participation*)
4. Production (Design and Development Stage)
5. Postproduction (Testing and Enhancement)

6. Documentation
7. Delivery

## 12.8 CONCEPTUALISATION

The process of making multimedia starts with an "idea" or better described as "the vision" - which is the conceptual starting point. The starting point is ironically the visualisation of the ending point - the multimedia experience that the targeted end-user will have. Conceptualisation involves identifying a relevant theme for the multimedia title. Most multimedia developer prefer choosing themes that are socially important and exciting to work on. Other criteria like availability of content, how amenable is the content to multimedia treatment and issues like copyright are also to be considered.

## 12.9 PLANNING AND COSTING

Projects are temporary structures set up with the specific aim of delivering an identifiable end-product. All projects will therefore have an identifiable life cycle, the characteristics of which will vary according to the size and complexity of the project.

Planning is done to fulfill the expectation of the audience or project masters. Steps to start a project:

1. Define the goal , objectives and scope
2. Target audience
3. Set the content
4. Estimating cost
5. Hardware
6. Software
7. Build a multimedia team

### 12.9.1 Defining project goals, objectives and scope

After a theme has been finalised for a multimedia project, specific goals, objectives and activities matrix must be laid down.

**Goals:** In multimedia production goals are general statements of anticipated project outcomes, usually more global in scope.

**Objectives:** Specific statements of anticipated project outcomes.

What is the purpose of creating the project?

- Try to achieve the objective. Define the scope or the boundary of the project.
- Consider how much time to develop the project.
- Consider the knowledge and skills needed
- Consider how to organize the project

**Activities:** These are actions, things done in order to implement an objective. Specific people are responsible for their execution, a cost is related to their implementation and there is a time frame binding their development.

### 12.9.2 Defining the Target Audience

A very important element that needs to be defined at this stage is the potential target audience of the proposed title since, this will determine how the content needs to be presented. Target audience may be applications users or information recipient.

- To whom the project is created for
- Do some background research about the target audience because this will affect the complexity of your design.
- Consider the following factors:
  1. Age
  2. Knowledge or educational background
  3. Technological background
  4. Language
  5. Gender
  6. Economical background
  7. Profession

### 12.9.3 Set the content

Content or information will determine the size of the project . Content production depend on the availability of the existing resources or the need to create new materials.

Following are the considerations before determining the content :

1. Obtaining rights to use exiting resources.
2. Digitizing pictures, audio, and video.
3. Produce materials including text, graphics, audio effects and animation
4. The amount of information available must be based on the audience expectation.

## 12.10 MANAGING CONTENT ACQUISITION

### 12.10.1 What is Content

Content is the "stuff" around which an application is developed. *It could be text, narration, graphics, colors, backgrounds, videos and animation.* In other words, content are all the elements that compose a multimedia application.

Content has a *value* and a *cost.* Cost refers to the monetary price incurred to acquire or develop content, while value refers to its merit, usefulness, importance, or significance. A balance has to be struck between the value and cost of the content against the production budget and the desired outcomes.

Content acquisition is one of the most time-consuming and budget intensive activities during the development of a multimedia application. The multimedia producer has to determine if it is feasible to incorporate the suggested content based on its cost and value; determine the alternatives; evaluate the legal implications of using proposed content; and, determine the best strategy to develop or modify the desired content.

### 12.10.2 Programme Content

Programme Content can be defined as the specific *message, data, facts or information* to be presented. The content specialist provides the programme content to the multimedia architect, who in turn prepares the narration, text, bullets, charts and tables that will be presented in the title.

The potential multimedia application users have different expectations, information needs, attention spans and learning styles. The application to have the necessary impact on its varied target audience needs to effectively and logically integrate the multimedia building blocks. The integration of a variety of multimedia elements appeals to different learning styles and helps the audience comprehend and retain the information.

## Content design deals with:

In multimedia, there are five ways to format and deliver your message. You can write it, illustrate it, wiggle it, hear it, and interact with it.

### (1) Scripting (writing)

Rules for good writing:

1. Understand your audience and correctly address them.
2. Keep your writing as simple as possible. (*e.g.*, write out the full message(s) first, then shorten it.)
3. Make sure technologies used complement each other

### (2) Graphics (illustrating)

Make use of pictures to effectively deliver your messages.

Create your own (draw, (color) scanner, PhotoCD, ...), or keep "copy files" of art works. - "Cavemen did it first."

### (3) Animation (wiggling)

### (4) Types of Animation

(a) Character Animation - humanise an object *e.g.*, a toothbrush, a car, a coke bottle, etc.

**Factors in choosing a character**

1. Emotion - Is it happy, sad, funny, sloppy, ...?
2. Movement - Is it fast, slow, bumpy, ...?
3. Visual style - Is its color/texture consistent with the rest?
4. Copyright - "Don't use Mickey before checking with Walt."
5. Adequacy - *e.g.*, Does it provide various poses (can't make a broomstick sit!)
6. Highlights and Sparkles - *e.g.*, to pop a word in/out of the screen, to sparkle a logo -> to draw attention

(b) Moving Text - *e.g.*, put up one character at a time like a typewriter *e.g.*, "pulsing" - the word grows/shrinks (or changes color) a few times

***Note:*** *Do not slowly move entire line of text, they are not readable. Instead, for example, slide the bullets in and out.*

(c) Video - live video or digitized video

1. more powerful than still images
2. often easier to obtain than graphics animation
3. takes a lot of disk space
4. sometimes needs special hardware

### (5) When to Animate

"A leaf doesn't flutter if the wind doesn't blow. Only animate when it has a specific purpose. Enhance emotional impact *e.g.*, dove softly flapping its wings. Make a point *e.g.*, show insertion of a memory chip onto the motherboard (much better than a diagram). Improve information delivery *e.g.*, "pulsing" words (in and out of screen) adds emphasis .

Indicate passage of time *e.g.*, clock/hourglass -> program still running *e.g.*, animated text -> to prompt for interaction/response

**Provide a transition to next subsection**

1. Wipes - *e.g.*, L-to-R, T-D, B-U, diagonal, iris round, center to edge, etc.
2. Dissolve - the current image distorts into an unrecognizable form before the next clear image appears, *e.g.*, boxy dissolve, cross dissolve, etc.
3. Fade - a metaphor for a complete change of scene
4. Cut - immediate change to next image, *e.g.*, for making story points using close-up ** Cuts are easy to detect in "video segmentation"

## (6) Visual Design

Following are some of the factors that should be considered in the visual design of a multimedia presentation:

### (a) Themes and Styles

A multimedia presentation should have a consistent theme/style, it should not be disjointed and cluttered with multiple themes. The choice of theme/style depends on the styles and emotions of your audience.

**Some Possible Themes:**

**Cartoon theme**: interesting / entertaining -: must be consistent with the character's personality.

**Traditional theme** – straightforward : simple, often informative but not as interesting.

**High tech theme** – contemporary computer art work (morphing, texture mapping, metal texture, explosions : attractive, easy to animate)

**Technical theme** – include blueprints, 3D models of the product, ... *e.g.*, start with a drawing, then transformed into a rendered image : shows adequate technical information and gives impression of solid design and construction.

**Color Schemes and Art Styles:**

**Natural and floral** : (outdoor scenes, *e.g.*, mountains, lakes, ...) -> getting back to nature

**Oil paints, watercolours, colored pencils, pastels:**- these art styles can be combined with *e.g.*, cartoon or high tech themes

## (7) Pace and Running length

A few guidelines:

1. Allow a block of text to be slowly read twice.
2. Transition time should be an indication of real-time.
3. dissolve - time delay, scene change
4. cut - two views of same scene at same time, or abrupt scene change

### Running length

1. self running presentation: 2-3 minutes
2. limited interaction: 5-6 minutes

3. complete analytical, hands-on demo: < 15 minutes
4. with questions, discussions: > 30 minutes
5. build in breaks for long presentations

**(8) Basic Layout**

(a) Title (b) Action area (c) Narration (d) Dialog (e) Interactive controls

Make sure that the information delivery path in the layout is smooth, not irregular/jumpy use headlines/subtitles, additional shapes, buttons, fonts, backgrounds and textures to enhance the visual appearance.

### 12.10.3 Content Identification, Selection, Development and Acquisition

Content either has to be sourced or if it is not available then it has to be created. This implies that the source must be identified, selected and the content acquired, or it must be developed. Mostly, budgetary constraints define whether content is developed, purchased or borrowed. Copyright issues are the next most important constraint that influence content generation.

The main responsibility of content development lies with the Content Specialist, Script Writer or Computer Graphic Artist. The content specialist undertakes the following tasks:

#### Content research

1. Identifying document sources
2. Identification of the building blocks like colours and graphics representative of the theme, time or period to be presented in the application
3. Identifying individuals to be interviewed
4. Location to be videotaped

The responsibilities of the Script Writer are the following:

#### Content evaluation

1. Adaptation of the content to the goals and objectives of the application
2. Development of the application script and storyboard based on the content.

The computer graphic artist is responsible for the development of the following:

1. Developing line art necessary for the application
2. Scanning and editing of photos, backgrounds, and other Graphic elements
3. Chart development
4. Maps preparation
5. Text manipulation
6. 3-D graphics and walkthrough
7. Computer animation

If content is not readily available then it needs to be developed. The creation of story, graphics, or the composition of music are examples of content development. Sometimes content needs to be adapted to meet the needs of the application. This includes editing and manipulation of existing graphics, photos, video, sound or text.

### 12.10.4 Principles for Creating Multimedia Content

One of the rules of thumb in online content creation is "Don't use only text in your course" simply because it is boring, but more importantly it does not enhance effective learning, and here is the science behind it. According to the Dual Code Theory, humans have two separate information processing channels for verbal and pictorial information. Verbal information includes on-screen text and narration. Pictorial information includes pictures and graphics. Presenting a piece of information in both channels helps learners construct connections between two forms of mental representations: verbal and non-verbal. Therefore, it is easier to learn and then recall a particular concept when explained with both text and images. When you present the information via only verbal channel, there is a lower chance that your students retain it.

Thanks to online tools available now, it is easier to integrate different types of media like images, audio, video, animation, and graphics into online courses to make them more engaging and motivating. Most of the time we create our own multimedia material such as videos produced via screen recording tools. In such cases, it gets even more important to be aware of some multimedia principles that would help us design effective content. Although putting some text, images and audio together looks straightforward, some principles need to be taken into consideration. A large amount of research suggests that multimedia elements should be combined carefully not to cause cognitive load because our cognitive capacity for processing information is in fact quite limited. Therefore, we cannot just put some random visuals, audio, and text together expecting that they would guarantee deep learning. Now here is a quick guide for creating multimedia material in online learning without causing extraneous cognitive load (Mayer, 2009).

The following 5 principles are to be adhered to :

### (1) Coherence Principle

Any kind of visuals, audio elements, or text not directly related to the content should be excluded from the presentation. Therefore, any distractive and seductive details should be removed from the online content. It also needs to be kept in mind that less is more.

### (2) Signalling Principle

It refers to the cues that you provide to highlight the important elements in your presentation. This is especially helpful when there is a lot of information to be absorbed in your content. Using visual and vocal signalling techniques such as headings, separating items and vocal emphasis on key words help your learners direct their attention to the important elements.

### (3) Redundancy Principle

This principle suggests that it is better to use graphics and audio narration instead of graphics, audio narration, and on-screen text. When you present narration and on-screen text at the same time, cognitive load is caused because learners need to work harder to process all the verbal information coming from both narration and on-screen text.

### (4) Spatial Contiguity

This refers to the spatial alignment of words and picture. Essential words need to be placed next to corresponding graphics. This helps guide your learners' cognitive processing.

### (5) Temporal Contiguity

This is helpful when you have an animation, picture, or graphic, and a narration that goes with them. Presenting the visual and auditory information simultaneously rather than successively makes it easier for learners to make the connection between the visual and auditory input.

Meaningful learning occurs when learners' essential cognitive processing is used carefully. As humans' cognitive resources are limited, Instructional Designers and content creators should design multimedia content in ways that minimize unnecessary cognitive load, and Mayer's set of principles are a great guide to achieving this.

### 12.10.5 The Multimedia Application Script

The Application Script is a written description of the proposed multimedia project. The purpose of the script is to describe the actions of all components. The script helps the development team have a clear understanding of the purpose of the programme.

#### (1) Outlining

Multimedia differs fundamentally from the conventional media like films and slide shows conventional media are linear (one event follows another in a sequence), while multimedia is a non-linear medium - it has the capacity for branching. The simplest way to define branching is to develop an outline. The major headings in the outline become the options available to the user in the main menu of the programme. When a user selects a heading, the subheadings associated with the selected major heading are displayed.

#### (2) Logic Flowchart

The logic flow chart is very important, especially if the title is interactive. It provides a road map of the proposed application for the authoring team. The flow chart illustrates the choices that the user will have in each screen. The degree of complexity of these flow charts depends on the type of application to be developed.

#### (3) Storyboard

The storyboard is a graphic representation of the proposed multimedia project. It is an extension of ideas presented in the script.The concept of storyboarding has been by animators and their like for many years.

Storyboarding is used to help plan the general organisation or content of a presentation by recording and organizing ideas on index cards, or placed on board/wall. The storyboard evolves as the media are collected and organised: new ideas and refinements to the presentation are

#### Production Script for Text, Audio and Video

The next step in the production of the interactive multimedia application is the development of specific and detailed scripts (descriptions) for text, audio (narration, music or sound effects) and video.

#### (4) Copyrights

Producers and users of multimedia programmes need to be aware of and abide by the copyright law. Multimedia productions, by definition, combine a variety of elements from varied sources. It is essential to know how the use of these materials is affected by legal constraints. It is also important to acquire copyrights for own production, after its completion.

### 12.10.6 Estimating cost

Three general elements that can vary in project estimates***: time, money and people***. If we decrease any of these elements, we may generally increase one or both of the others. People Time Money It will take longer time to develop multimedia application if developer team (people) and money is less. If there is a optimally less number of developer team, time and money (cost) to develop multimedia application could be reduced.

Cost can be saved not only if we decrease the number of developer team but by proper time management in multimedia application development.

### 12.10.7 Hardware Requirement

**This requirement is important not only for** developer side but for end-user perspective. Several types of hardware components that need to be considered:

1. Memory and storage device
2. Input devices
3. Output devices
4. Communication Device (optional)

**(1) Output device**

- The size of the monitor also should be considered because larger monitor gives the user larger view and this makes creating graphics easier.
- Projectors suitable in briefing or educational multimedia products where the information is displayed to a large number of viewers.
- Note that displaying information with projectors may not be the same as displaying on monitors because information such as text must be large enough and have contrast color so that it is easier to read.

### 12.10.8 Software requirement

Expensive software offer advance and powerful features which requires higher skill. However, there are software that can help to save time and to organize a project which are less expensive. Several types of software are available :

**Text Editing and Word Processing Tool**

- Painting and Drawing Tools
- 3D Modeling and 2D Animation Tools
- Image Editing Tools
- Sound Editing Tools

## 12.11 PREPRODUCTION

It is the process of intelligently mapping out a cohesive strategy for the entire multimedia project, including content, technical execution and marketing. Based on the goals and objectives, the three pillars of multimedia viz. *Hardware, software and user participation* are defined. At this stage the multimedia producer begins to assemble the resources and talent required for creating the multimedia application. The Production Manager undertakes the following activities.

1. Development of the budget control system
2. Hiring of all specialists involved in the multimedia application process
3. Contracting video and audio production crews and recording studios
4. Equipment rental, leasing and purchasing
5. Software acquisition and installation

6. Planning the research work of the content specialists
7. Development of the multimedia application outline, logic flow, scripts and video and audio files production scripts and schedules
8. Coordination of legal aspects of production

### 12.11.1 Project Budgeting

Once the project timeline or schedule is ready, the next step is to prepare the project budget. This is essential as time and money are not infinite resources.

Some production costs can be estimated on the following basis:

1. Scanning one picture or slide and performing minor Manipulations takes approximately 10 minutes.
2. Developing one minute of computer animation takes approximately 10 hours
3. One page of text takes approximately 15 minutes to type Into a word processing application.

If the project requires the development of video footage or audio recording, a detailed budget for these two activities needs to be developed separately, as the complexities involved in the development of these two components imply taking into consideration a number of specific costs.

### 12.11.2 Typical Budgeting Heads

- Cost of personnel (including part-timers)
- Advisors and Consultants
- Video Production
- Audio Production
- Equipment
- Equipment Rental
- Software
- Graphic and Audio Material
- Royalties
- Materials and Supplies
- Printing
- Communication Expenses
- Office Supplies
- Legal Expenses
- Travel

## 12.12 PRODUCTION (DESIGN AND DEVELOPMENT STAGE)

Once all the preproduction activities have been completed, the multimedia application enters the production phase. Activities in this phase include:

1. Content Research
2. Interface Design
3. Graphics Development
4. Selection of musical background and sound recording

5. Development of computer animation
6. Production of digital video
7. Authoring
8. Defining the Target Audience

A very important element that needs to be defined at this stage is the potential target audience of the proposed title since, this will determine how the content needs to be presented.

## 12.12.1 The Multimedia Production Team

The production of fine-quality, high-end interactive multimedia applications such as - educational applications, interactive web sites, interactive information kiosks, interactive training - is the work of a team of specialists. Typically, the team consists of:

1. Production Manager
2. Multimedia Designer
3. Content Specialist
4. Script Writer
5. Text Editor
6. Multimedia Architect (or Programme Authoring Specialist)
7. Computer Graphic Artist
8. Audio Video Specialist
9. Multimedia Programmer

### (1) Production Manager

The role of the production manager in a multimedia production is to define, coordinate and facilitate the production of the multimedia project. Capabilities of a good production manager include, knowledge of the basic principles of multimedia authoring, skillful proposal writing, good negotiating skills, conversant with relevant legal issues, good communication skills, budget management skills, experience in human resources management and overall business management.

1. The leader of a project.
2. Responsible for overall development, implementation of the project and day to day operations.
3. Strong in both technical and management aspect of the project.

### (2) Multimedia Designer

Deals with visual aspects of the project, graphic design, illustration, animation, interface design and image processing. She or He or a group maintain the flow of the information, clear and consistent navigation.

### (3) Content Specialist

The Content Specialist is the member of the production team who is responsible for performing all necessary research concerning the content of the proposed application. Programme content can be described as the specific information, data, graphics or facts to be presented through the multimedia production.

### (4 ) Script Writer

Video and film scripts present a linear sequence of events. In multimedia production, the medium has the capability of presenting events in a non-linear fashion by branching in different directions and establishing linkages between different sections or components of the programme. The scriptwriter of a multimedia production needs to visualise this almost three-dimensional environment and integration of virtual reality into the programme.

### (5) Text Editor

The content of a multimedia production, like a book or a film, needs to flow in a logical fashion and the text must be structurally and grammatically correct. Text and narration will be integrated as part of the application and the development of documentation for the application must be considered. All of the text related elements need to be revised by the text editor.

### (6) Multimedia Architect

The multimedia architect is the team member responsible for integrating all the multimedia building blocks (graphics, text, audio, music, video, photos and animation) by using an authoring programme. An authoring programme is a piece of software that allows integration of all the multimedia elements into a comprehensive presentation.

### (7) Computer Graphic Artist

The computer graphic artist is responsible for the graphic elements of the programme - such as backgrounds, buttons, photo collages - and the manipulation and editing of pictures, 3-D objects, logos, animation, renderings and the like.

### (8) Audio and Video Specialists

The audio and video specialists are needed when intensive use of narration and digitised video are integrated into a multimedia presentation. The audio specialist is responsible for recording and editing: narration; selecting, recording or editing sound effects; recording and editing music. (Music composition and performance is the responsibility of a musician). The video specialist is responsible for video capturing, editing and digitizing. The individual is responsible for taking pictures, scanning pictures or slides and editing. Duties of Audio/Video specialist is to focus on the audio and video production - shooting, capturing and editing video, digitizing and audio recording.

### (9) Multimedia Programmer

Multimedia programmer is responsible for integrating all the multimedia elements using authoring system or programming language to create a functioning and useful multimedia product.

## Delivering multimedia content through internet

Websites on internet are making CD-ROMs redundant as a medium for delivering multimedia. This is because of the economies of reach that the internet offers, coupled with the facility of day to day updation and instant worldwide reach. The pace at which technological innovation is increasing bandwidth and making instant download of real audio and real video feasible, soon internet will take over CD-ROMs for delivering multimedia content.

In the field of Humanities, especially for a country with a rich heritage like India, effective use of multimedia can go a long way in preserving the ancient culture for posterity and disseminating information to sensitise the audience.

## 12.13 TESTING AND DELIVERING MULTIMEDIA APPLICATION

### 12.13.1 The Evaluation Process

Testing of a multimedia title is essential so that the final application adheres to international quality standards and is not infested with bugs, technical snags, inaccurate information or simple grammatical or typographical errors.

The process of evaluating (testing) and revising a multimedia application project is dynamic and constant. It involves both internal and external evaluation.

Testing is unavoidable process in any multimedia projects.

- Test or review the project or Web site to ensure it is bug free, accurate, operationally and visually on target, and achieving the objective or target.
- Every feature and function must be exercised, every button or link must be clicked - will be repeated again and again with different hardware and under various conditions

### 12.13.2 Internal Evaluation

The happens within the multimedia development group, through internal discussions for evaluating the aspects of the application:

1. Application design : is it logical and facilitates learning
2. Project goals and objectives : are the established goals and Objectives being met
3. Content is the acquired content represented accurately
4. Text and narration : are the text and narration grammatically correct
5. Application graphics : are the application graphics adequate to fulfill the goals and objectives
6. Sound : is the background music, effects and other sounds well recorded
7. Application navigation : are the navigational structures and aids effective
8. Programming code : is it working as originally planned
9. Delivery : can the application be delivered via the proposed medium
10. Time and budget : is the project on-time and on-budget
11. Legal considerations: have all licenses and other copyrights been procured

The prime responsibility of this function lies with the production manager and can be most effective if the team members are open to positive criticism of their peers.

### 12.13.3 External Evaluation

The following are the components of external evaluation:

1. Alpha Testing
2. Focus Group Testing
3. Beta Testing

The terms alpha and beta are used by software developers to describe levels of product development when testing is done and feedback is sought.

**(1) Alpha Testing**

Alpha testing takes place when the project is considered a working model i.e. it is not finished but it is functional. The purpose of Alpha testing is to determine if the general direction and structure are adequate and what changes are necessary. Members of the Alpha-testing group should include a balance of friends and critiques.

Alpha releases are typically for internal circulation only, which is passed among a selected group of mock users – often just the team working on the project. Alpha testing : Alpha testing is the first phase of project testing. The alpha testing group usually consists of colleagues' friends and those who are known to the organization. The tests are conducted under all possible conditions that can be expected in the client's workplace. The bugs generated are called "Alpha Bugs" and are more serious. Alpha testing remain flexible and amenable to changes in both the design and the behavior of your project as you review the comments of your alpha testers. Alpha testing groups made up of kindly friends can provide positive criticism.

**Charcteristic features of Alpha Testing**

- Often performed only by users within the organization developing the software as a form of internal acceptance testing.
- The product is evaluated relatively in the early stage of the development phase.
- The application may be missing part of the content or functionality.
- The main interest is to review the concept, format, user interface and the layout.
- The tester may be selected users or friends, most - often the team member themselves - should be able to provide positive criticism or feedback.

The output of Alpha testing is generated as a report and the identified bugs or modifications are fixed by the programmers and fed to Beta testing.

**(2 ) Focus Group Testing**

After revising the application based on the feedback of the Alpha test, another possible strategy is to present the application to a focus group. These groups are composed of individuals who represent the expected audience of the project. Standardized forms should be used for requesting comments and suggestions from the Focus Group.

**(3) Beta Testing**

Beta" means pre-release version of the software, released for testing purposes. A beta version of a software application (*e.g.*, anti virus software) is a pre-release of the official version. Beta testing is used to test whether the software application is reliable and whether it contains any errors. Software companies usually release a number of beta versions of a software application to users to test and ask for any feedback on how the application performs.

Therefore improvements can be made before the official release of the software application.

The beta testing group should be representative of real users and should not include persons who have been involved in the project's production. Beta testers must have no preconceived ideas. Beta testers may be asked to include a detailed description of the hardware and software configuration at the time the problem occurred and a step by-step recounting of the problem, so that you can recreate it, analyze it and repair it. Beta release is sent to a wider but still select audience, which have through knowledge of software use and of finding errors and bugs.

**Charcteristic features of Beta testing**

- The product is evaluated just before the final release.
- It is a fully functioning product and should be relatively bug free.
- Main interest is to find bugs or content errors.
- The testing group should be represented by the real users and should not include the people who have been involved in the project.

- The feedbacks from these testers are very important where the errors or problems reported by the beta testers have to include the detail description of the problem.

The test report of beta test should be given equal importance as that of alpha test.

Beta test is for all computer products and done prior to commercial release. Beta testing is the last stage of testing, and normally can involve sending the product to beta test sites outside the company for real-world exposure or offering the product for a free trial download over the Internet. Beta testing is often preceded by a round of testing called alpha testing.

The software has reached "beta" stage when it is operating with most of its functionality, and is ready for user feedback.

Beta tests enable the software to be tested in customer environments, giving users the opportunity to exercise the software, find errors, and correct them before a product is released. For beta test, the software is delivered to customers' sites, along with instructions on what features to exercise in the software. The developer records, tracks, and addresses reported bugs.

The beta version or beta release usually represents the first version of a computer program that implements all required feature although additional features may be added. It is likely to be unstable but useful for internal demonstrations and previews to selected customers, but not yet ready for release. Some developers refer to this stage as a preview, as a technical preview (TP) or as an early access.

Often this stage begins when the developers announce a feature freeze on the product, indicating that no more features requirements will be accepted for this version of the product. Only software issues, or bugs and unimplemented features will be addressed.

Once the project is in a final draft form, copies should be made available to a group of potential users called a beta-testing group. Here again, standardised questionnaires should be used for collating feedback.

Quality Assurance (QA) is the formal name given to the process of beta testing. When the beta version of a multimedia application is released and the functionality testing starts, the QA process has formally begun. Beta testers check all possible paths of navigation and log all events that strike them as unusual. In addition they do things that users will not usually do like multiple mouse clicking, dragging things around and entering unneeded keystrokes. The idea is to look for things that do not work. Beta testing can be done in-house or it can be outsourced to a professional lab, depending on financial resources and product secrecy issues.

Beta testing includes:

1. Compatibility Testing
2. Functionality Testing
3. Functional Localisation Testing
4. Install Testing
5. Performance Testing
6. Stress Load Testing
7. Load Testing

Beta testing provides important input from users. A customer expects the beta testing to evaluate:

- Software functionality
- Algorithms used
- Procedures
- Solved example problems or tutorial
- Subject matter technical content
- Ease of use

- Installation instructions
- User documentation

It is required that at least one beta tester to be an actual user of the software outside EPRI. Three or more beta testers are recommended. Ideally, the EPRI project manager identifies five to ten beta testers who represent various classes or types of future end users.

The beta testers will need to check the technical accuracy of the software, and will need to use it with their own computer setups, data and workflows to make sure that the software will perform as desired in their own environments.

The beta testers will use the software and respond in writing to the assessment points. In some cases, Corporate Software Quality or the project manager may specify that certain persons or groups inside or outside EPRI be included in beta testing.

It is recommended that the names of beta testers (with their permission) are listed in the Acknowledgments section of the User Manual.

## 12.14 DOCUMENTATION

**Documentation** is any communicable material (such as text, video, audio, Advertisement etc., or a combination thereof) that is used to explain some attributes of a man-made object, system or procedure, particularly its assembly, installation, maintenance, repair and disposal. Information, however, is a much more inclusive concept and can be about not just a product (i.e., a good or service), but about any topic. When information is about a product, it can cover every aspect of it, in addition to those covered by documentation, including its historical, political, philosophical, scientific, sociological, business, economic and environmental aspects.

The characteristic features of documentation are :

- Documentation - need to provide a clear step-by- step procedure for the users to follow.
- Troubleshooting guide - potential problem that can occur and how to solve it.
- A file name README.TXT is good thing to include in the CD distribution of your project.

### 12.14.1 Developing Documentation

User documentation is a very important feature of high-end multimedia titles. This includes instructions for installing, system requirements, developing acknowledgments, copyrights, technical support and other information important for the user.

**Project Revision**

After the tests are over the production manager and the multimedia architect should discuss the merits of each of the comments and suggestions offered by the evaluating group. Based on the feedback the application should be revised, incorporating the valid changes suggested.

## 12.15 DELIVERING THE MULTIMEDIA APPLICATION

Delivering is the final stage for which the designer have to take care of following:

- Know the medium you want to use.
- Web site: can just upload to the servers and adjust some settings then it is ready.
- For more complex application where installation into the user's computer is needed. Installation should be smooth, easy and fast.

### 12.15.1 Delivering Medium CD-ROM

- It is also an optical storage and considered the most common form of packaging for multimedia products.

- It started out as a read-only technology in which user could store data once only and access it many times.
- Recent technology led to a multi-session version where user can add to the content of a CD and even fully able to write to the systems.

**Burning a CD-ROM**

Before recording a CD-ROM, it must be ensured that the application and supporting Files after they are recorded on the CD-ROM. Read and Write CD-ROM drives will allow editing in the near future. The process of burning a CD-ROM is similar to recording on any type of drive hard disc or floppy diskette.

The issue of which CD-ROM format should be used has to be considered before burning a CD-ROM. Formats to choose from include-ISO 9660 Standard, Hierarchical File System (HFS) Hybrid, Global Hybrid Mixed Mode. Of these the standard format sanctioned by the International Standards Organisation is ISO 9660. This standard has several file structure variations to accommodate the needs of different operating systems and file types.

**DVD**

- It is the latest format for optical storage up to 17GB.
- At the moment, DVD is increasingly popular for its high quality audio and video.

High-end multimedia applications that are text and graphic heavy are best delivered on a CD-ROM. The other effective way of delivery is on an internet website.

### 12.15.2 Delivery through internet website

Multimedia content is being widely disseminated through internet. Although currently bandwidth problems, requirement of a number of plug-ins to play real audio and real video, long download time and other problems exists that hamper the delivery of multimedia applications through internet, the pace of technological improvement will soon pave the way for easy and effective delivery.

One major advantage that internet will have over CD-ROMs is that are amenable to continuous updation and hance the content does not get outdated.

### 12.15.3 Integration of CD-ROM and Internet

The relationship between CD- ROM and internet is similar to the relationship between computer's hard drive and ROM. On the ROM, the information once recorded cannot be changed, while on the hard disc information can be written over and over again.

A more effective way of delivering a multimedia application is an integration of the two mediums of CD-ROM and Internet. A particular application if developed on the CD-ROM, has an embedded link to a website where regular updates are available. Vice-versa, if the application is developed as a website where information keeps accumulating, then as the archive becomes substantial it can be reproduced on a CD-ROM for convenience viewing.

**Learning Outcomes**

In this chapter we have learn about :

1. Multimedia Projects Development Process
2. Designing, Production Testing and Delivering of Multimedia projects